OFFICIAL STRATEGY GUIDE

An Introduction to World of Warcraft

World of Warcraft is a **massively multiplayer online** game in which you assume control of a character who is part of the worlds of Azeroth and Outland. These worlds are filled with magic and fantastical creatures, but you will also catch glimpses of advanced technology.

MASSIVELY MULTIPLAYER? ONLINE?

Massively multiplayer online games, or MMOs, are games played simultaneously by hundreds or thousands of players. Many of the characters you see in the game world are controlled by other players.

MMOs also do not have an offline component to the gaming experience. Where many games (such as first-person shooters or real-time strategy games) typically have a single player campaign in addition to multiplayer options, all gameplay in MMOs is done online. You must be connected to a server in order to play the game.

When you enter the game you become part of a story which is set in a time of increased friction between long-time enemies, the Alliance and Horde. The Horde consists of Blood Elves, Orcs, Goblins, Taurens, Trolls and Undead. The races of the Alliance include Draenei, Dwarves, Gnomes, Humans, Night Elves and Worgen. The recently redisocvered Pandaren may choose which side of the conflict they join.

In addition to selecting one of the races of Azeroth, you must assign a class to your character. There are eleven classes available to you, and your class selection has the greatest impact on your experience while playing the game.

Who This Is For

If you're new or are thinking about signing up, this portion of the guide is for you. If you know someone who is hesitant about signing up, this is the portion of the guide for them! If you (or someone you know) is interested in World of Warcraft but has been intimidated by the scope of the game, its large community, or the very nature of MMOs, you've come to the right place. What follows is a step-by-step navigation of signing up, selecting a realm, creating a character, and getting started with your first character.

New players should use this section of the guide to learn about the game's background, how to manage your account, and all of the game's basics. Players new to WoW and especially to online games in general will get the most from these materials.

Returning players who have been away for a year or more may also want to peruse this section. Changes are a matter of course in online games, and Blizzard has not been resting on its laurels. Even beyond the expansion itself there have been countless improvements to the general game system. If you're coming back but want a reminder or two, this is a good place to get yourself started once again.

GENERAL QUESTIONS ANSWERED

If you are new to online games, you likely have a few questions about what to expect. What follows are answers to common questions about World of Warcraft.

Q WHY SHOULD I PLAY WORLD OF WARCRAFT?

A World of Warcraft is a high-fantasy world that combines elements of storytelling, task completion, item creation, problem solving, combat, and socializing. Because the game is so vast, you can truly make it your own. Every time you play, your experience is unique.

Some people play because they're hooked on quests and item upgrades. They're looking to improve their character's weapons and armor. There is always something to do, even after you get to the "end" of the leveling process.

Others play for the people. It's amazing how many people you'll find who are involved in World of Warcraft. World of Warcraft has a large community of players, and they come from many age groups and diverse backgrounds.

Why you should play is actually a trick question (sorry!). The answer is your own, and the fact that you're reading this is all that you need to know. You suspect that there's something fun waiting for you online, and you're right. Don't be nervous. World of Warcraft introduces new players to the game at a comfortable pace, and despite online gaming's reputation you'll find that a surprising number of players are polite and helpful when someone's learning the game and needs to ask questions.

Q WHAT DOES WORLD OF WARCRAFT HAVE FOR ME?

A Major features of World of Warcraft include roleplaying, improving your characters, competing against other people in player versus player combat, upgrading gear, exploring the world, crafting items for yourself and others, and unlocking special achievements.

You're able to try anything in game with just an investment in time. Real world money is only required for the monthly subscription. You won't need to put in any cash beyond that. All equipment is available to all players, assuming that they put in the same time and effort.

Questing centers around thousands of short tasks that you are given in game. You can play these for hours on end, but someone with only 20 minutes to spare can still log on, complete a few quests, and get back to the real world. The system makes it that easy!

Roleplaying is about assuming the identity of your character. This is not a mandatory aspect of WoW, even on Roleplaying Servers (where it's encouraged). Instead, this is a game within a game that you create for yourself. You imagine a story for your character and you live through it, revealing that character's background and experiencing their development as you go.

Player versus player (PvP) competition is a big draw for some. You can limit this to consensual challenges: most servers only allow players to fight if they specifically request or accept a duel, enter a Battleground, or otherwise set themselves up for PvP combat. Other servers are called PvP servers, and they allow people from different factions to fight openly, whenever and wherever they meet. In a sense, this is consensual too because no one is forced to play on PvP servers. You choose one because it can have sudden, unexpected combat.

Achievements are given for many aspects of WoW play. Dungeons have quite a few Achievements, usually involving the defeat of certain enemies under specific conditions.

If you're looking for group activities, join a guild that has fun people. Talk to people in cities or while adventuring, and find out more about their guilds. This is how you discover a guild that's right for you; it's just like making friends in real life. In fact, you might make real life friends while playing WoW. Some guilds get so close that they plan activities together, even if they don't live in the same state (or country!).

Q WHO WILL I PLAY WITH?

A WoW enables people from all over the world to play with each other in real time. So the simple answer is that you can play with anyone you wish. You can log in and play on your own (called playing solo), you can play with your friends, or you can play with strangers. It's all up to you.

If you're just getting started, ask friends, family members, and coworkers if they play. It's entirely likely that you have experienced gamers in your circle already, even if you didn't realize that they play WoW. Ask them what server they play on, and consider joining them on that server. This ensures that you're playing in the same "world" as your friends. They'll be able to walk you through the early steps and possibly help you out with starting money, items, or joining a guild.

Coming in alone is harder, but it's still entirely doable. Read through the following pages, then start the game. Click on buttons. Play around, and remember that you cannot be destroyed in WoW. Characters can only be deleted if you choose to delete them. There is no permanent death. There are no substantial ramifications from your mistakes. WoW wants you to play around, try things, and even screw up from time to time. Come in solo if necessary. You won't get into too much trouble, even if you don't know what you're doing at first.

ADDRESSING COMMON CONCERNS

If you, or someone you know, would like to try World of Warcraft, but have some concerns about joining a massive game, the following pages address many of the questions people have about the game.

Q IS WORLD OF WARCRAFT TOO COMPLEX FOR ME?

A World of Warcraft has been designed with a gentle learning curve. You begin with basic abilities while the enemies you face initially act more like target dummies, waiting for you to initiate a fight before they respond. You gain additional abilities and options for your characters as you achieve higher levels while taking on increasingly stronger enemies. However, none of this is done in an overwhelming fashion.

The best news is that you are in control of the pace of your advancement. There are no deadlines for earning levels. You don't lose anything you've earned because you take time away from the game. People who had never gamed before have become comfortable in World of Warcraft. Despite what the Gnomes and Goblins tell you, this isn't rocket science. It's a game, and a fun one at that.

The aspect of the game that often takes the most effort to understand is the lingo used by other players. Don't worry. Gamerspeak becomes quite intuitive after you spend time in game. You pick up terms here and there, and soon they are part of your vernacular. To make this easier, a glossary with many of the terms and their definitions has been included in this guide. You do not need to memorize these. They're just here if you need them or have a question.

In the end, World of Warcraft is as complex as you wish to make it. Many players enjoy exploring the vast worlds of Azeroth and Outland on their own, performing quests as they travel. A large percentage of the players join with others to form guilds for their social aspects, to join forces for Player-versus-Player combat, or to come together to take on the challenges designed around 5, 10, or 25 characters working together.

That's the key to enjoying your time in World of Warcraft. Find what you like to do with your time and do it. Don't be afraid to dabble in other activies and test the waters, but you aren't required to do anything with your time. You control the amount of time you spend in the game, so spend it doing the things you enjoy most.

Q WILL I BECOME ADDICTED?

A Millions of people play, and most of them treat the game like any other hobby. You may have read media reports of World of Warcraft players neglecting their real-life responsibilities, with tragic consequences. However, there is nothing uniquely addictive about the World of Warcraft. It offers the same engrossing qualities of any other hobby or pastime.

Q WHAT ABOUT ALLOWING CHILDREN TO PLAY?

A World of Warcraft offers Parental Controls that enable you to restrict your child's playing schedule, even when you're not around. You can also control whether your child can use the in-game voice chat to speak to other players. There are filters to ensure that obscenities aren't shown in the chat windows, and you can avoid the vast majority of goofy or immature players by turning off general chat for your kids. These chat channels allow players communicate with a larger number of players in the game, but you can limit a child's access to random people by cutting off these channels.

With a bit of setup time, you can make it so that kids are playing with you or with people that you've checked out. There are family-oriented guilds that keep the chat clean and are out to have a good time.

PICKING THE RIGHT REALM

Millions of people can't all play in the same place at the same time. As such, World of Warcraft isn't hosted from a single computer. Instead, servers around the world host the many realms where World of Warcraft is played. Each realm is a separate copy of the game where several thousand people play.

Your first act, after you register, patch, and load the game, is to select a realm. If you have friends already playing, contact them and ask which realm to join. Otherwise, you are strongly encouraged to try out one of the realms marked for NEW PLAYERS.

TUESDAY DOWNTIME

Blizzard typically uses Tuesdays to perform server maintenance or apply the latest updates (known as patches) to World of Warcraft. The game is often unavailable from early morning until early afternoon, depending on your time zone. Downtimes are often given in Pacific Time since that is the timezone where Blizzard's offices are located.

THE REALM SELECTION SCREEN

Type
Click on this header to sort the list by type.

Your character(s)
The number of characters **you** have on a given server appears here. It lists the realms on which you have characters at the top of the list.

Realm Name
Click this header to sort the list in alphabetical order. Click on it again to switch between ascending (starting with the letter A) and descending (starting with the letter Z) order.

Population
Click on this header to sort the list by population level.

Geographic Tabs
Click on the tab that's appropriate for where you live.

TYPES OF REALMS

The list of available realms may be daunting the first time you scroll through it, so how do you know which type of realm is for you? Use the following information to help you reach a decision.

Normal	Normal realms are also known as PvE (Player-versus-Environment) realms. If you're new to the game, strongly consider a Normal server before trying any other type.
PvP	Player-versus-Player servers. In addition to all the standard aspects of the game, players from opposite factions are free to attack each other in most areas. If you don't know what PvP is, don't choose it.
RP	Roleplaying servers. Environments that encourage players to stay "in character" while playing the game. There are additional rules in place that govern player names, and behavior in public areas. There aren't any mechanical processes that force you to role play your character well (or at all), but it is encouraged in these realms.
RP-PVP	These servers combine the RP crowd with a PvP ruleset.

POPULATION

The last variable to consider is the player population of a server.

Full	New accounts are unable to create characters on Full servers.
High	A large number of players. There's always someone around who might help, but you may be waiting in a queue to log in some nights.
Medium	A robust player base but not too crowded.
Low	Sparse player base. You will always be able to do your task at-hand, but there may not be many people around to help you.
New Players	Newer servers with a lower overall population. If you are trying out World of Warcraft for the first time, choose one of these realms!
Offline	Grayed out servers are briefly unavailable, but will likely be online again soon—save for Tuesday downtimes.

TO MAKE YOUR SELECTION

Click on the realm where you want to play, then click Okay. You are now logged into that server. When joining a server with no character now, the character creation screen is automatically opened for the player.

MAKING YOUR CHARACTER
THE CHARACTER CREATION SCREENS

CHARACTER RACE AND CLASS SELECTION

The Character Creation Screen is divided into two screens. You begin with a random character (which appears in the center) that you can customize in multiple ways. The first screen lets you pick your race, class and gender.

GENDER
Choosing to play a male character or female character provides different options for the character's physical appearance.

RACE
Click on these icons to change the race of your character. Choosing a race impacts which classes are available for you to play.

CLASS
The icons for classes appear here; no race can play every class, so some of these icons will be unavailable regardless of the race you select.

MORE INFO
Clicking this button brings up two information boxes, one provides Race History, while the other is a Class Description. The information provided in these boxes updates as you click on different icons for races and classes. Each race has advantages and extra abilities which are listed at the top of the Race History box. The Class Description box displays a few brief lines that serve as an overview of the class, then provides additional details to give you a better feel for the class.

FOR MORE INFORMATION

If you are most interested in playing a specific faction or Race, turn to page 90 for Alliance races, page 134 for Horde races, or page 174 for Pandaren. If you are most interested in playing a specific Class, turn to the appropriate page number (provided on the following page).

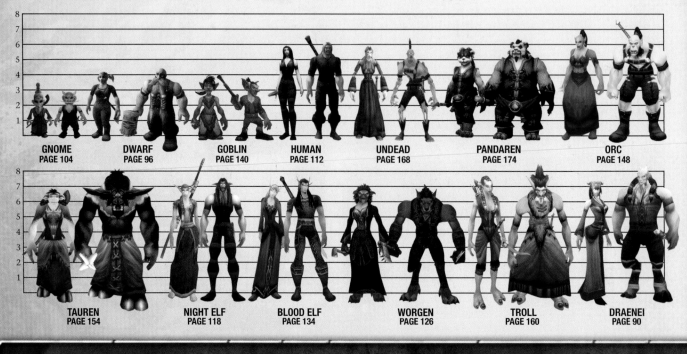

GNOME	DWARF	GOBLIN	HUMAN	UNDEAD	PANDAREN	ORC
PAGE 104	PAGE 96	PAGE 140	PAGE 112	PAGE 168	PAGE 174	PAGE 148

TAUREN	NIGHT ELF	BLOOD ELF	WORGEN	TROLL	DRAENEI
PAGE 154	PAGE 118	PAGE 134	PAGE 126	PAGE 160	PAGE 90

CHARACTER APPEARANCE AND NAME

When you are comfortable with your characters class and race, click Next to bring up the second character creation screen. This screen allows you to change your character's gender and appearance. When you click an option on the left side of the screen (under the Gender window) the available options for that category appear on the right. The number of options available vary by race.

Current Character

Each time you click on a new option for race, gender, class, or physical appearance, the character displayed here is updated. The gender and the physical appearance choices you make for your character are purely cosmetic; they have no impact on how your character performs in the game. Have fun choosing your hair color and markings. After all, this is your in-game persona; you want to like what you see! You can press Randomize to let the game show you some options.

When you're satisfied with your character's class, race, and appearance, it's time to select a name.

When choosing a name, consider that your character's name is the first impression others have of you in the game. Blizzard has a "Naming Policy" that is designed to discourage players from using character names that are inappropriate to the game. In general, you want to avoid real world names (like celebrities), offensive names, names from other fictional worlds, or trademarked names. If you really can't think of a name that you want, or if all of your good ones are taken already, try the Randomize button under the bar. It might give you a few suggestions that suit you and are available.

TAKING YOUR FIRST STEPS

With your character created, it's time to get into the real game. It seems pretty complex when you first log in to the game, with so many things up on the screen; however, you're free to take as much time as you need to get comfortable before you start adventuring. The following pages introduce you to many aspects of gameplay that you experience during your first time in World of Warcraft. Each of the topics is covered in more detail through this guide, but what you learn in this chapter will get you started in World of Warcraft.

After the opening movie ends you are given control of your character. The first things to do are skim the Beginner Tooltips that appear and take a look at the minimap located at the top right corner of your screen.

THE MINIMAP

The circle in the top right corner of your screen is the minimap. The minimap is a valuable tool that you should get to know as quickly as possible. The minimap eventually provides greater detail about the nearby area, but the basics are all you need for now.

TOOLTIPS

When a question mark appears at the bottom center of the screen, it indicates that you have encountered a new aspect of the game. Click on the question mark to bring up a box with more information. These tips are helpful to new players, so take a moment to read each one as it appears.

Your character is indicated by an arrow. It points in the same direction that your character faces. For now, look for the nearby quest-giver (marked with a yellow exclamation point). That's your first destination.

QUEST GIVER

YOUR CHARACTER

MOVE YOUR CHARACTER

There are two ways to control the movement of your character: with your keyboard, or with your mouse. If you prefer to use your keyboard to move your character then use the W, A, S, and D keys. W and S move your character forward and backward, A and D turn your character left and right. To turn, press W to move foward, then press A/S (while still holding down W). Pressing just A or S spins your character in place.

To control your character's movement with the mouse, press the left and right mouse buttons simultaneously to move forward. Your character continues to move forward so long as you hold down both mouse buttons. Slide the mouse to the left or right to turn your character in that direction.

CHAT LOG

In the bottom left corner of your screen is the chat log. Whenever the game or other players want to communicate with you, the text appears here. Two tabs are available ("General" and "Combat Log") but the General tab is all you need to focus on for now.

To say something to anyone nearby, hit enter. If screen doesn't read "Say", then hit enter and type /say. Type in the message you want to share with anyone standing nearby, then press enter.

For a private message, use /whisper to talk with a specific person. Just type in /w along with the name of the person. Type in your private message. If someone whispered you first, you can just press "r" to respond to that whisper.

Use the A, S, D and W keys to move your character.

A GAME-CONTROLLED CHARACTER'S COMMENT

ANOTHER PLAYER'S COMMENT. NOTE THAT CHARACTERS CONTROLLED BY OTHER PLAYERS ARE SET APART WITH BRACKETS AROUND THEIR NAME.

INTERACT WITH A QUEST GIVER

No matter where you start, there's a nearby character with a yellow exclamation point over his or her head. These characters have tasks for you to perform. These tasks are called Quests in World of Warcraft and they are an integral part of your gaming experience.

Right-click on the quest giver to speak with him or her. The quest giver describes a task and offers compensation in the form of money and items. In addition to the listed rewards, you earn Experience Points for completing quests.

COMPLETING QUESTS

After you accept a quest, it is tracked on the screen near the top right corner. To review the quest in greater detail, press the letter "l" on your keyboard to open your Quest Log. It lists all quests you have accepted but have not yet completed. The quest log also contains a summary of what is expected of you to complete a given quest. The Minimap is updated as well. A thick, golden arrow points in the direction you need to travel for the quest.

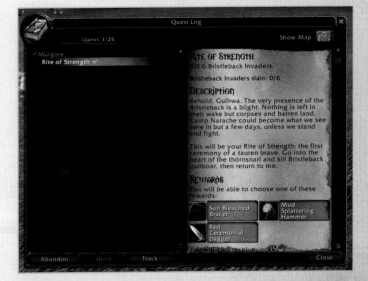

ENEMIES

Do some exploring and put your mouse cursor over the different creatures. Look near the bottom right corner of the screen for a small information box to appear. If the enemy is one you need for a quest, target it and start attacking!

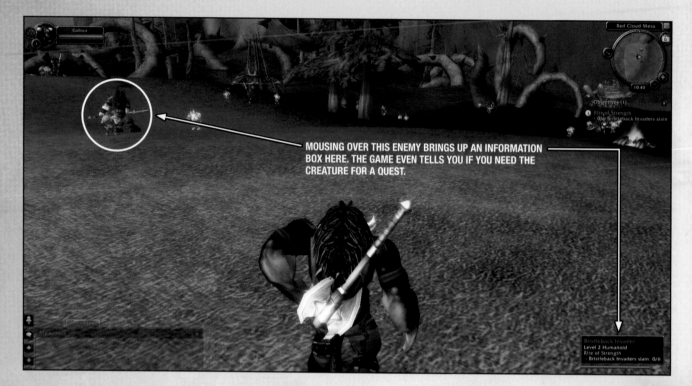

MOUSING OVER THIS ENEMY BRINGS UP AN INFORMATION BOX HERE. THE GAME EVEN TELLS YOU IF YOU NEED THE CREATURE FOR A QUEST.

COMBAT

To start fighting a creature, you must first select it by left-clicking while your mouse pointer is on it. For your first fight, move close to your target and attack it with your melee weapon by placing your pointer over it and right-click your mouse one time. Hunters are the lone exception here. They start with a ranged weapon, so they should attack from a few yards away. If you already selected the enemy with a left-click, press the letter "t" on your keyboard to start attacking. In the starting area you can defeat any enemy with this basic technique, but in future fights you should start

to use your character class abilities to make things go much faster.

If you're at close range, the first attack you make triggers what is known as your auto-attack. This means that your character will continue to strike the enemy again and again with no further action on your part. Every character can do much more than this when you're actively fighting and using abilities, but auto-attacks are good enough to bring down early enemies.

ACTION BAR

Your Action Bar appears at the bottom of the screen. At low levels, you won't have many abilities here, but that will change as you get further into the game. All characters begin with the number 1 initiating either the starting attack for your class or a simple melee attack. There are other abilities on your Action Bar, but they are different depending on which class and race you chose for your character.

LOOT

Almost all enemies offer some kind of loot. When you have loot waiting, your dead enemy sparkles. Right click to open the enemy loot box, then click on each item to put it into your inventory. If you press Shift and Right-click, at the same time, each item is sent directly to your Backpack.

Some quests also award items when you complete them. These items also go directly to your backpack. Any money you collect (just coppers at this point) are also stored in your backpack.

INVENTORY

Everything that your character owns will either be equipped, which means wearing it; or it will be stored in your Backpack. Press the letter "b" to open your backpack and to see what is inside.

As you collect items (either from killed enemies or collected on quests) they go to your backpack. Every character starts the game with a Hearthstone, which is the blue and white item in the first slot.

Now that you have taken your first steps, you are ready to handle more of what the game has to offer. Look for more quests in the game and keep playing! Keep this guide handy as there's a great deal more information inside for you. Turn the page to learn more about World of Warcraft!

WHERE TO GO NEXT

- IF YOU WANT TO LEARN MORE ABOUT THE USER INTERFACE AND CONTROLLING YOUR CHARACTER TURN TO PAGE 16.

- IF YOU WANT TO LEARN MORE ABOUT COMMUNICATING WITH OTHER PLAYERS, TURN TO PAGE 32.

- IF YOU'RE READY TO COMPLETE QUESTS, TURN TO PAGE 27.

- IF YOU WANT LEARN MORE ABOUT COMBAT AND SPECIAL ABILITIES, TURN TO PAGE 50.

- IF YOU WANT TO LEARN MORE ABOUT ENEMIES, TURN TO PAGE 56.

- IF YOU'RE LOOKING FOR MORE RESOURCES ABOUT THE GAME, INCLUDING SETTING PARENTAL CONTROLS, TURN TO PAGE 84.

- IF YOU'RE NOT SURE WHAT A GAME TERM MEANS, USE THE GLOSSARY ON PAGE 86.

The User Interface

This chapter further develops and details the concepts introduced in "Taking Your First Steps" so some of what follows may be familiar to you if you read that section already.

Using Your Mouse

The mouse pointer is your primary tool for learning about and interacting with the game world.

Take a moment to move your mouse pointer (which normally appears as a gloved hand) and hover over different people and objects. Your mouse cursor changes dynamically when you pass it over different people, monsters, and objects. Let your mouse do some of the exploration for you. Highlighting things ahead of time lets you avoid fights with monsters that are too powerful to defeat.

CURSOR SYMBOLS

SYMBOL	WHAT THIS MEANS	SYMBOL	WHAT THIS MEANS
	Acts as a basic pointer		Vendors or loot from corpses
	Characters who can give you quests		Vendors who can repair your gear
	Characters with whom you can speak		Guards who can offer directions
	Trainers who can teach you new skills		Items or objects that you can open or operate (important for quests)
	Creatures you can attack		Items which act as a Mail Box (you can send or receive in-game mail)

THE GAME INTERFACE

The game interface is everything you use to interact with the game, including your Action Bars, chat windows, and the minimap. Press Alt and Z together, then wait a second and press them again. Everything that briefly vanished from your screen is considered part of the game interface.

You can also mouse over parts of your game interface. The information you get from these tooltips is invaluable as you gain levels and learn more abilities. Because you can do so many things in the game, the game interface can appear to be complex, so it's broken down here for you.

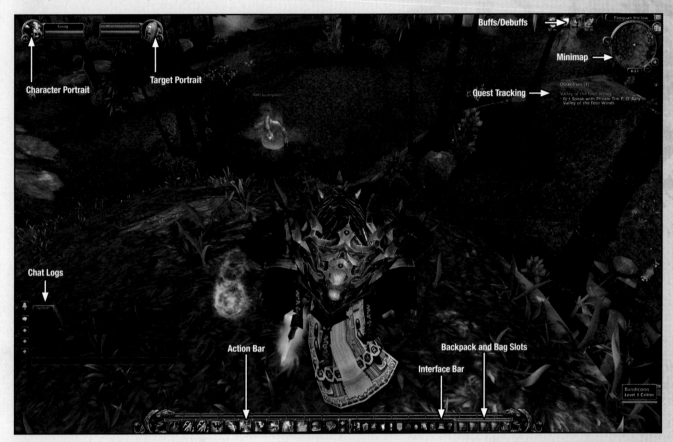

BUFFS AND DEBUFFS

Near your minimap are any positive or negative effects that are currently in place. These effects show up as icons. Buffs (the positive effects) are usually cast by your character or their group members. Debuffs (the negative ones) are usually cast by enemies you are fighting. If you mouse over a buff or debuff, you are given details about its effects and duration. When a buff or debuff is about to expire, the icon that appears here begins to blink.

The most important piece of information to learn about a debuff is what type of debuff it is (the most common are Poison, Disease, Magic, and Curse) because many classes eventually gain abilities that allow you to remove the debuff instantly.

Character Portrait

The Character Portrait shows your character's face, name, level, life bar, and a second bar which varies with the class you chose.

Life Bar

All character classes have a green health bar. If your health reaches zero, your character dies. When you're out of combat, your health gradually returns to its maximum value. Having an ally use a healing spell on you (using a healing spell on yourself works as well), or eating in-game food replenishes your character's health much faster.

Second Bar

The color of your second bar and what it represents are determined by your class. Depending on your class, there may also be an additional resource bar that appears here. The same bars are used by all characters, enemies, monsters, and animals in the game.

TARGET PORTRAIT

When you left-click on an NPC or monster, you target that character. The Target Portrait appears next to your character's portrait and shows the target's face, name, level, and life bars. There is more information about the Target Portrait on page 56.

Death Knights build a resource called Runic Power, much like a Warrior's Rage, by activating strikes and Runes to punish their enemies. The majority of their abilities are fueled by a combination of Runes and Runic Power.

Hunters and their pets have a brown focus bar that fuels special attacks. Focus regenerates over time or with the use of abilities like Steady Shot or Cobra Shot.

Mages, Priests, and Shamans all have a blue mana bar, which fuels their spells. While mana regenerates slowly over time, the quicker way to replenish your mana is to sit and drink different types of water when you're out of combat.

Paladins primarily use mana to fuel many of their spells, however they also use the Holy Power resource to bolster their abilities and trigger special actions.

Rogues have a yellow energy bar that is consumed as the Rogue uses special combat abilities. Lost Energy regenerates over time.

Warriors have a red rage bar, which increases as they take and deal damage. Warriors use accumulated rage to use their special abilities.

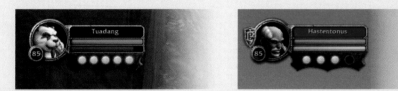

Warlocks also have the typical blue mana bar, but depending on their specialization, also develop other resources to fuel the dark powers they unleash on their enemies.

Monks use either Energy or Mana, depending on their specialization; however they also build Chi as they perform their mystical arts. Chi allows the Monk to augment special abilities as their life energy flows.

Druids start with a mana bar but use different bars as they acquire animal forms starting at level 6. In bear form, Druids use a rage bar. In cat form, Druids use an energy bar. Balance Druids have an Eclipse bar.

Minimap Buttons

Region & Town Name → **The Crossroads** ← Toggle Map

Your Character

Tracking →

← Calendar **21**

← Mail

→ Zoom In

Clock → **10:44** ← Zoom Out

TRACKING:

The smaller circle on the top left is a menu that allows you to track different things in-game. Click on the circle to get a drop down menu of all things your character can track. If you click on something specific to track, such as Food & Drink, any nearby vendors who sell Food & Drink appear on your minimap.

TOGGLE MAP:

This button opens a map of your current region. Locations you have found appear on the map; undiscovered locations remain obscured until you find them. You can also press the letter "m" to bring this up at any time.

Flight Path

Quest Location

Character →

More on Maps

One right-click on your region map opens a map of the continent. A second right-click opens the continent-wide map. A third right-click opens the map of the entire world. Left-click on parts of the map to zoom in to that area.

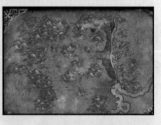

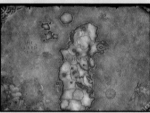

Northern Barrens is a region of the continent of Kalimdor. Kalimdor is a continent on the world of Azeroth. Azeroth is one of two planets in World of Warcraft.

UNDER ATTACK?

The game never pauses, so you can be attacked while staring at the map. If this happens, the map screen is surrounded by a red flashing border to let you know that something is chewing on your leg.

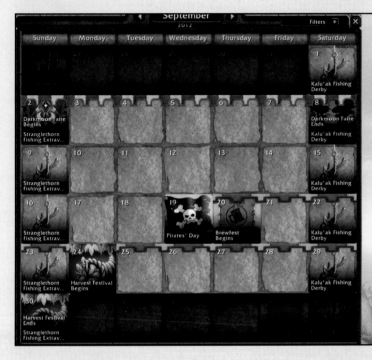

CALENDAR

The calendar shows upcoming in-game events. There are scheduled events, such as the weekly fishing contest in Stranglethorn Vale and the Darkmoon Faire, as well as seasonal feasts and holidays.

If you're in a guild, each guild has its own event tracking. The calendar also tracks battleground holidays and raid lockout resets, but those are for higher level characters. You don't need to worry about those just yet.

CHAT LOGS

If you mouse over the Chat log area, the chat tabs appear. By default, the General log is visible. This displays announcements and the General and LocalDefense channels for your region as well as Says, Whispers, Party, Guild, and Battleground chat. You'll also see Trade chat when you're in a city.

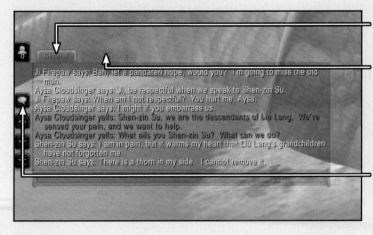

General Log Your conversations and other non-combat system messages appear under this tab.

Combat Log The Combat Log offers options for observing what happens to you, other characters nearby, and enemies during combat. You don't need to watch this log while you're fighting since your character portrait and target portrait provide an adequate summary of how any fight is going. Instead, use the combat log to review recently completed fights if you feel something didn't go the way you planned.

Chat Menu The Chat menu offers shortcuts for communicating with other players in the game. Click to open; press Esc to close. You can also type in the shortcuts listed on the right of the menu. To learn more about communicating with other players, turn to page 32.

INTERFACE BAR
OPENING AND CLOSING WINDOWS

To open a window, you can either click on the button associated with that window, or use the shortcut key. Hover over a button and look for the letter in parentheses to find out its shortcut key. Press the same button or key to close a window that was previously opened.

You can have multiple windows open at once, and if you want to close everything at the same time, just hit the Escape key.

ACTION BARS
Abilities placed in your Action Bar allow quick access to those abilities. The numbers along the top of the buttons on your Action Bar correspond to the number row on your keyboard. If you want to use the ability in the spot marked 1, you can either click on the icon with your mouse or press the number 1 (above the letter Q, not your number pad) on your keyboard. The bars have 12 slots, using keys 1-0, and then – and = as well.

REPUTATION
You have the option to track the progress of your Reputation gains with any particular faction here. To learn more about Reputations, turn to page 24.

EXPERIENCE BAR
The experience bar is a long strip of 20 bubbles at the bottom of your screen. Highlight this to find out how much experience you need before gaining the next level. This bar fills in real time, so each quest completed, enemy slain, or new area explored causes it to fill. There is a shaded region of your experience bar to represent your character's rested experience.

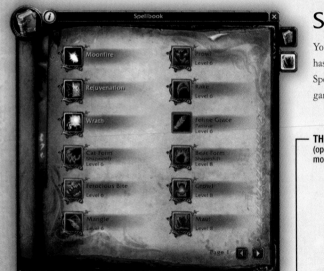

SPELLBOOK

Your Spellbook (opened with "p") lists all the spells and abilities that your character has acquired and ones that will be available as your character gains levels. The Spellbook has various tabs that organize your spells by type. When you start the game, all your character's active spells are already in your Action Bar.

THE PROFESSIONS TAB
(opened with "k") is empty until you learn a Profession. There are more details about Professions later in this guide.

RESTED

All characters start the game in a Normal state. However, if you log out your character "sleeps" and goes into a Rested State. The next time you log in, there will be a notch on your XP bar that indicates how much Rest XP you have accumulated. Logging out in an Inn or a city adds Rest XP at a much greater rate than logging out in the open. The easiest way to tell if you're in the right place is to look at your character portrait. If your name is flashing yellow, and your character level changes to "zzz", you are in the right spot.

While you are Rested you earn twice the experience you would normally gain from slaying a monster, gathering professions, and from discovering a new region on a map; the experience earned from turning in completed quests is unchanged. You become less rested as you kill monsters, gather and discover new locations. When your XP bar catches up with your Rest Marker, you feel normal.

DUNGEON FINDER
Use this window when you would like to join a group (some players call it a party, but it's the same thing) to explore a Dungeon, Raid or Scenario. This works by placing you in a queue that assembles groups based on available role compositions.

PLAYER VS. PLAYER
The Player vs. Player (often abbreviated PvP) button is the Horde insignia for Horde characters or the Alliance insignia for Alliance characters. After reaching level 10 you can queue to participate in bracket-based battle grounds against other players.

GUILD
Use the Guild Finder window to list yourself as looking to join a guild, or browse through guilds looking for potential members. After you join a guild, this pane provides detailed information about your guild's activity.

MOUNTS & PETS
This window displays the mounts and companion pets you've collected in game. Each race has specific mounts, but there are ways to acquire other types of mounts as well. You can get your first mount at Level 20. Companions, or vanity pets are fun to play with. You can summon them to wander around the world with you, or fight them against other player's pets! These are earned in a variety of ways.

DUNGEON JOURNAL
This panel details information about all the dungeon and raid encounters available in the game. It provides information about individual encounters (bosses), such as abilities they may use, or loot they may drop. This is a handy resource for a player's first time in a dungeon or raid group setting.

GAME MENU
Use the Game Menu to customize the game interface, change in-game settings, or log out of the game. Until you become more familiar with the game, you should leave the settings at their default values. There are literally hundreds of options to tweak inside this menu, so like most things in WoW it might seem daunting at first. Don't let it scare you away. Playing with the interface is a wonderful way to unlock the game's information. You tell the system how to present everything, and it is happy to oblige.

EQUIPMENT CONTAINERS
Early on, you only have a Backpack; eventually, you should acquire a bag for each of the slots in the lower right. Some enemies may drop bags, but certain players are able to create bags. There is an option to display the amount of free inventory space on your backpack icon.

CUSTOMER SUPPORT
The question mark at the end of the bottom row is your call for help. Here, you can access the Knowledge Base or contact a Game Master about problems. The Knowledge Base has searchable answers to the most common questions about game mechanics. Game Masters can only help with issues of game functions, problems with other players, or if you character is physically stuck in the game. Neither option offers tips or strategy for completing quests or defeating monsters. These are for bugs or things that just can't be helped without external intervention.

QUEST LOG
The Quest Log lists all quests you have accepted but have not yet turned in to the quest giver. There is additional information about Quests on page 27.

ACHIEVEMENTS
The Achievements window lists thousands of in-game achievements—some include rewards such as titles, or new pets, for your character. In most cases, the reward is earning the achievement itself. Click on a given achievement to learn more about how to earn it.

SPECIALIZATION & TALENTS
This button opens a panel that details your specialization and talent choices. You can also access the Glyphs window. Glyphs allow you to customize some of your character's abilities.

SPELLBOOK
See opposite page.

CHARACTER
The Character window provides all the details you need to know about your character. There's more information on page 24.

A FEW WORDS ABOUT IN-GAME MONEY:

Copper coins are indicated with 🪙 or the C abbreviation.

Silver coins are indicated with 🪙 or S.

Gold coins are indicated with 🪙 or G.

100 copper = 1 silver

100 silver = 1 gold

CHARACTER INFORMATION

The Character window has two tabs: Character and Reputation. A third tab, Currency, will become available after your character earns one of the types of currency tracked in game, such as Honor Points, Cooking Tokens, and Darkmoon Faire Prize tickets. Some classes, notably Warlocks and Hunters, have a Pets tab that provides important information about their currently active pet.

Click the yellow arrow in the bottom right corner of your character window to display detailed information about your character. It's amazing how much there is to take in at first. Luckily, you don't even need to understand all of it yet. Your character has what they need to kick monsters around. What each stat does and what you need to maximize isn't important until you earn more levels.

However, some people are curious right off the bat. If you want to understand more, here's a head's up.

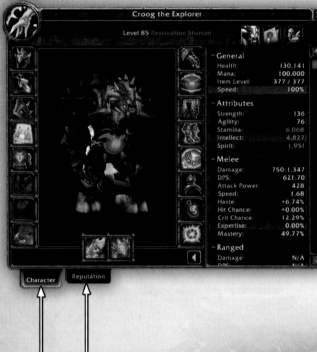

STATISTIC DEFINITIONS

CATEGORY	HOW THIS AFFECTS YOUR CHARACTER
Health	How much damage you can take before dying
Strength	Raises Attack Power (amount varies by class)
Agility	Raises Attack Power (again, the amount varies), and Critical Strike
Stamina	Increases health
Intellect	Raises mana and Spell Critical Strike (if applicable)
Spirit	Controls mana regeneration
Damage	Base damage from your weapon attacks
DPS	Damage over time of your weapon's attacks
Attack Power	Influences physical damage output
Attack Speed	How often you make auto attacks
Mastery	Improves talent bonuses
Haste	Influences Attack and Casting Speed
Hit	Improves your odds of hitting
Crit	Improves your odds of scoring criticals (extra damage attacks)
Expertise	Reduces the chance that an enemy will Dodge or Parry your attacks
Armor	Reduces physical damage (highlight to see the % mitigated)
Dodge	Chance to Dodge a physical attack, avoiding 100% damage
Parry	Chance to Parry a physical attack, avoiding 100% damage
Block	Chance to Block with a shield, mitigating additional damage (highlight to see the amount)
PVP Resilience	Provides damage reduction against all damage done by players and their pets or minions.
PVP Power	Increases damage done to players and their pets and minions, and increases healing done in PVP zones.

REPUTATION
The Reputation window indicates your character's standing with various factions. Factions are groups of associated NPCs found at various points in the game world. Many NPCs are associated with some faction. As you progress through the game, you encounter more factions, and your Reputation page will change. If your Reputation reaches higher levels with some groups, you are able to purchase special gear. If your Reputation reaches lower levels, members of that group become Hostile and eventually attack you on sight.

CHARACTER
The Character window shows all the slots for your characters clothing, armor, and weapons. It also shows all the physical and mental statistics that influence your character's performance in the game.

Controlling Your Character

In this section, you learn more about controlling your field of vision in the game and moving your character around the environment. This chapter builds on the concepts introduced in "Taking Your First Steps" so some of what follows may be familiar to you if you read that section already.

Basic Movement

There are two ways to control the movement of your character: with your keyboard, or with your mouse. By default, your character moves at a run. To switch between running speed and walking speed, press the forward slash key, which is found on the number pad.

Jump to It!

To start out, hit your space bar; it's a big target so it's a natural place to begin. The space bar causes your character to jump. Jumping is often the quickest way to avoid low obstacles, and it won't slow you down if you're running somewhere.

Keyboard Commands

If you prefer to use your keyboard to move your character then try to use the W, A, S, and D keys. The arrow keys move your character as well, but using WASD leaves your fingers closer to the number keys used to activate your character's abilities. Of course, there's nothing wrong with using the arrow keys. If you're more comfortable with those keys, then use them while you're playing.

MOUSE CONTROL

To control your character's movement with the mouse, press both mouse buttons simultaneously to move forward. Your character continues to move forward so long as you hold down both mouse buttons. Slide the mouse to the left or right to turn your character in that direction.

STRAFING

Strafing is a way to move left or right while barely changing what you see on screen. If you're not familiar with strafing, take some time now to try it out. Press the Q key to strafe to the left, and press the E key to strafe to the right. Strafing does not cancel Auto-Run.

AUTO-RUN

If you press the Num Lock key, your character starts to run and will continue to run until you cancel it. The following are the quickest ways to cancel Auto-Run:

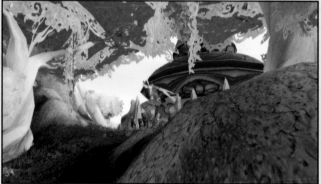

- Press Num Lock again
- Press any of the keyboard keys that cause your character to move forward or backward
- Press both mouse buttons at the same time.

You retain control of your character when Auto-Run is active. Pressing the keys to turn your character left or right still turn your character and do not cancel Auto-Run. If you want to use your mouse to turn your character, hold the right mouse button and slide the mouse left or right.

THE CAMERA

In most games, "camera" refers to your field of view of the gaming world. In World of Warcraft, the default camera view shows a small area, with your character in the middle of the screen. The smoothest way to change what you see is to press the left button on your mouse, and hold it down while you move the mouse. Your character stays in place, but what you see changes. Be careful when moving your mouse forward or back. You may end up staring at the ground or straight upward!

After you get comfortable looking around, do it while your character is in motion. It may be disorienting at first, but try to get the hang of it. It's a big help when you're on the lookout for enemies.

You can also change how far the camera is from your character. Some players like to zoom in tight on their characters; others like to zoom out for a broader view of the game.

To zoom in, press the Home key multiple times or roll your mouse wheel forward. Once you are in first person perspective (meaning you are looking through the eyes of your character) you can't zoom in anymore.

To zoom out, press the End key multiple times or roll your mouse wheel backward. There is a limit to how far you can pull back the view, and it will always center on your character.

QUESTS

Quests tell the stories of the inhabitants of World of Warcraft and sometimes reveal in-game secrets. Questing is also an efficient way to increase your character level, earn money, and acquire improved gear.

WHAT'S WITH ALL THE PUNCTUATION?

Available quest. Talk to the quest-giver now to start the quest.

Incomplete quest. You already have this quest but you have not met all the requirements to complete it yet.

Future quest. You need to gain a few levels to get this quest.

Completed quest. You have completed all the requirements of the quest and you can now speak with the quest-giver to claim your reward.

Repeatable quests. These quests can be done multiple times.

Kill a creature with a red exclamation point over its head to begin a quest.

Not a quest giver, but a flight master. Speak with these NPCs whenever you find them.

FINDING QUESTS

For most quests, you right-click on the person or item, read the quest, and (if you don't automatically accept the quest) click Accept to add the quest to your log. There are many sources of quests, so keep an eye out for any of the following characters or objects. You may get some quests simply by entering a new zone! Watch for a prompt under your minimap as you travel to new areas.

QUEST GIVERS

Quest givers are identified by the exclamation point floating over their heads. Many quest-givers offer more than one quest. Some quests even come from items!

Items as Quest Givers

The most common item that gives quests are Wanted Posters. These appear in highly populated areas, frequently offering rewards for local villains who need tracking and killing. There are also items found in the open, or in a camp of creatures that give out quests. All these items have golden exclamation points that appear over them.

Dropped items

Some enemies drop items that initiate a quest. Any item that begins a quest has a gold exclamation point integrated into its icon. Right-click the item to see the quest it offers.

TYPES OF QUESTS

Most quests are designed so you can complete them on your own and do them only once. There are other types of quests, however. Your Quest Log identifies certain quests as one of the following:

Group

A quest with a recommended number of players to complete it. Frequently, the objective is killing a high level monster.

Dungeon

Quests that must be completed inside an instanced dungeon (the earliest you'll see a dungeon is level 15). You must enter the dungeon and complete these quests as part of a group.

Raid

Quests that must be completed with a raid group. Raid groups are essentially multiple groups joined together. You won't need to worry about raid quests until you reach a much higher level.

Daily

The quests marked as "Daily" in your quest log can be completed once each day. These quests come from the quest-givers with blue exclamation points over their heads.

Class

Some quests are available only to a specific class. These quests often lead to learning a new class skill or acquiring a nice piece of gear.

Seasonal

Quests that are available during certain events during the year. Check the in-game calendar for information about events.

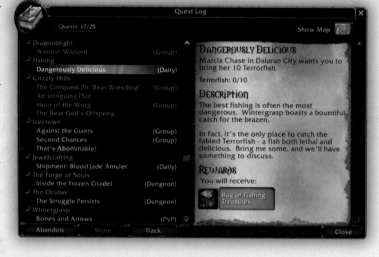

MORE QUEST TYPES

While the game doesn't categorize quests in the following ways, most quests fall into one of the following types:

Breadcrumb quests require you to speak with a character in another area, or take an item to another character. They are called breadcrumb because they are designed to lead you to a new zone or area with more quests.

There are two types of **collection quests**. The first type does not require you to fight. After accepting the quest, look for objects that sparkle. Put your mouse pointer over the object and right click on it to put it in your backpack. The second type of collection quest involves items that are carried by enemy characters. These enemies must be killed before they surrender their item. Just like the objects in the first type of collection quest, defeated enemies sparkle when they have items for you to pick up.

The objective of **kill quests** is to eliminate a number of a specific kind of enemy. These quests are simple and straightforward. Once you find the right type of enemy, it's a matter of taking them down in combat.

In an **escort quest**, you free an in-game victim and lead the character to safety. These quests are usually encountered in out-of-the-way locations while completing other quests.

A **quest chain** is a series of quests that must be completed in a certain order. Chained quests aren't marked as such in your quest log, but it's easy to tell when you're in the midst of a quest chain when you speak with the same quest giver many times. Completing a long quest chain can be one of the most satisfying and rewarding aspects of the game.

QUEST LEVELS

Your Quest Log also indicates the level of difficulty of your quest using corresponding colors. The level of difficulty is a comparison between the level of the quest and your current level. As you gain levels, the quest becomes relatively easier, so the color changes.

QUEST COLOR	DESCRIPTION
Gray	Very easy quest, but not worth much XP.
Green	Easy. Simple to complete solo.
Yellow	Normal. Likely to complete solo.
Orange	Hard. Consider finding help for the quest.
Red	Very Hard. Don't try this quest without some help.

If a quest is too difficult for you currently, leave it in your log as long as you can spare the room. The benefit to tackling red and orange quests is that the XP reward is greater; in fact, if you wait until a quest turns Gray to complete it, it's worth only 10% of the XP had you completed it as a Red quest!

? COMPLETING QUESTS

Remember to read the quest text carefully. If you complete several quests simultaneously, you can turn them in at the same point and time. When you complete a quest, the quest tracker points you to where to turn in the quest for your reward. Frequently, you return to the original quest giver, who is indicated with a gold question mark.

Not all quests require you to return to a quest giver to complete them. When you see this prompt, click on it to complete the quest and get a follow-up quest as well.

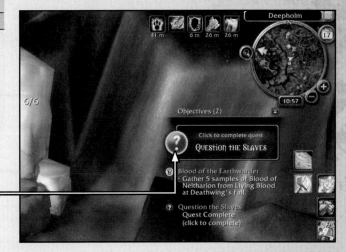

PHASING

While you are questing, or have just completed a quest, you may notice the world around your character undergoes a change. Buildings look different, NPCs might move to different areas, or monsters might be there that weren't before. This sort of change is known as phasing. If you're playing on your own, you may not even notice these changes, or you may consider them just a part of the story being told around you.

If you're in a group, however, it could cause problems. Phasing is individual to each character, meaning two people in the same group could be standing close by and not even see each other! If that happens, look next to the character portraits in the upper left portion of the screen. If you see a swirl next to a party member's portrait, that character is out of phase with you.

There are two ways to get characters back into phase. The first way is to have both players complete the same quests. The second way is to move both characters out of the phased area. Phasing isn't worldwide, so you should eventually find a spot where you can see each other again.

TRACKING YOUR QUEST PROGRESS

When you accept most quests, look for a quest tracking window to appear just under your minimap. The text here summarizes the objectives you must meet in order to complete the quests in your log. Not every quest has objectives that can be tracked, so not all quests will appear here; every active quest always appears in your quest log.

If you need more information about a specific quest, click on the text (not the numbered circle) to bring up its quest log entry. Clicking the numbered circle to the left of each quest changes which quest you are actively tracking on your map and minimap. If you want to change the order in which the quests appear (or stop tracking a certain quest), right click on the quest you want to change to bring up a menu of options.

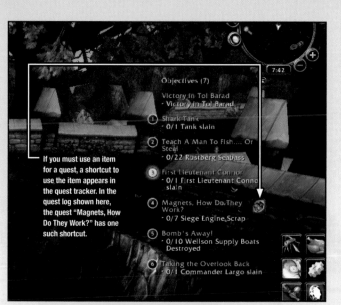

If you must use an item for a quest, a shortcut to use the item appears in the quest tracker. In the quest log shown here, the quest "Magnets, How Do They Work?" has one such shortcut.

USING THE MAP TO FIND QUEST OBJECTIVES

After accepting a quest, you often see a yellow arrow appear on your minimap. This arrow indicates the direction in which you should travel to complete the quest. The region map displays even more information, in the form of either a yellow question mark or a numbered icon. To open the region map, either press the letter "m" or click the map icon near the zone name at the top of the minimap. Click the arrow in the top right corner to expand or shrink the region map.

The numbered icons which appear on the region map are tied to the quests which are being tracked. Mousing over one of the numbered circles brings up the objectives for that quest. The yellow arrow on the minimap points you in the direction of the currently selected quest you are actively tracking. If you want to track a different quest, click on that quest's numbered circle (either on the region map or in your quest tracking list).

The smaller map above provides only the location of each quest's objective. The expanded map on the left includes a summary of the active quests in the zone as well as the full quest text for the currently selected quest below the map.

SKULLS ON THE MINIMAP

When the objective of a quest is to find a specific enemy (often referred to as a "named") that enemy appears as a regular numbered callout on the region map. However, when you are close enough, its location is marked by a skull on your minimap.

The yellow question marks are where you go to turn in already completed quests. The circle question mark indicates the turn-in for the quest which appears at the top of your quest tracking window. As you approach the indicated area the yellow question mark will appear on your minimap, providing the exact location for you to complete your quest.

Quest Rewards

Sometimes, you have a choice of the rewards you can take, but not all rewards are available to all classes. When you mouse over the available quest rewards, you get a great deal of information.

If you mouse over the item that interests you, the game compares that item with your currently equipped item, so you can see whether it's an improvement.

SOULBOUND ITEMS

Soulbound items are only usable by your current character. If you have an item that is soulbound, you can use it, sell it, or throw it away. You cannot give it to another player or even another one of your characters. Almost every quest reward is a soulbound item.

If an item is shown in red, that means your character/class can't use it. Try to find items that are ideal for your character. For instance, a Warrior can use any type of armor (cloth, leather, mail, or eventually plate). However, quest rewards that are cloth or leather are just trash to them. Don't be hasty when picking a quest reward. See if there is something awesome before you make a final decision.

When none of the rewards are an upgrade to your current gear, compare sale values. Select the most expensive quest reward if you aren't going to use it.

Faction Rewards

When you complete some quests, you receive notices in your General Chat Log, indicating that your reputation with certain factions has increased or decreased. This is a way of quantifying which groups in the game have been helped or hindered by your work in the quest.

Failed Quests

It is possible to fail to meet the goals outlined in completing a quest. The quest stays in your log and is marked as Failed. Don't despair! Just abandon the quest (right-click on it) and you can pick it up again from the quest-giver, no questions asked!

A Final Word on Quests

There are thousands of quests in World of Warcraft. You don't have to do them all! In fact, you cannot do them all. Some quests are specific to certain classes, and some are faction specific, so you can't do them without making a character that joins the other side.

You get to decide which quests you want to complete and which you don't. The game leads you through many adventures, but there's nothing stopping you from wandering on your own and finding quests just off the beaten path. You never know when you might just find a message in a bottle that leads to a new quest!

COMMUNICATING WITH OTHER PLAYERS

Like everything else in the game, you can control how much communicating and socializing you want to do with other players. This chapter tells you how to talk to other players, how to ask for help, and make in-game friends.

The most basic way to communicate in the game is to press the Enter key, which opens the Say prompt. You can just type in your comment and press Enter. This message is sent to everyone in your general vicinity.

STARTER EDITION ACCOUNTS

If you're playing the Starter Edition of the game, you have a few communication limitations:

- You cannot trade items with other players or use the Mail system

- You can only use /whisper or /tell with players that have put you on their Friends List

- You can't invite others to join a group.

- You can't speak on the local in-game channels, though you can read what others are talking about

These limitations end as soon as you pay for the account and wait for the game to register that change. A Starter Edition Account that becomes a paying one suffers no long-term penalties or problems of any sort.

WHO CAN HEAR ME?

The different speech commands are in place to let you communicate selectively. You wouldn't want to shout everything to the entire world, right?

Say:
/say goes to anyone nearby. Speak to players in your vicinity. By default, you see a speech bubble over your head. As long as people nearby are in the same faction as your character, they'll see what you type (players from the opposite faction will see what appears to be gibberish). Because this is public, avoid saying anything awkward or inappropriate.

Whisper:
/whisper (/tell works as well) is a private message for one other player. You must include the character's name after the /whisper. There is no distance limit on these messages.

Try it out for yourself! Hit Enter, then type "/whisper" followed by your character's name. When you hit space, the prompt changes, and whatever you type next becomes the message you send to yourself after you hit Enter again.

Reply:
Use /r (or just r) to reply to whomever last whispered to you.

Yell:
/yell is a broadcast message to all players in your region. This is the most awkward communication method in World of Warcraft. It's similar to /say in that it displays your text to anyone within its radius; however, the distance covered is much wider than /say.

Party Chat:
/party is a private message that lets you communicate with everyone in your current group at the same time. No one outside of your group can hear this chat even if they're standing in the middle of your party.

Guild Chat:
/guild sends a message to anyone in the same guild as you. No one else can hear you, and members will see what you're typing even if they're half a world away from you.

The Chat Menu

All these same commands are available through the Chat menu. Click on the option you want from the Chat menu (it looks like a speech bubble) and select what you want from the list.

All the messages that you send and receive appear in your General chat log. To see older messages, use the up and down arrows. To see the most recent messages, use the end arrow. If you right-click on the General tab, you can customize everything that appears in the chat log, including the background (transparent to solid black) and filters (including text color).

USING VOICE EMOTES

Voice emotes are in-game expressions that your character (not you) can say. Voice emotes have nominal benefit in group situations. You can see a list of them by clicking on the Chat menu (speech bubble) and then mousing over Voice Emote. Click one of the voice emotes to make your character speak.

USING THE CHANNELS

Each time you log into the game or enter a new region, you get a reminder in your General chat log about what channels are available to you. A list of the various common chat channels is included on this page

Channels are used to communicate with all players in the same channel. By default, you join the General Chat and LocalDefense channels; you also join the Trade channel, but that only becomes active when you enter one of the big cities found throughout World of Warcraft.

You can leave each of these channels at any time by typing /leave #, where # is the number of the channel.

GENERAL
The standard channel for your specific region or major city where your character is currently located. There's a different General channel for every region. This is a good location to ask questions about quests specific to your region.

TRADE
This channel links all the major cities in your faction. Players offer goods to be sold and seek goods to purchase. This channel is very busy (and the talk doesn't always stay on topic), so you won't want to stay on indefinitely. Your character must be inside a city to use it.

LOCALDEFENSE
This channel informs players when in-game attacks from the opposite faction are being made in your local region. This is primarily of interest to players seeking PvP (or trying to avoid it).

WORLDDEFENSE
Similar to LocalDefense, but this channel tells you about opposite faction attacks anywhere in Azeroth.

LOOKINGFORGROUP
This channel links all regions in your faction. Player must first specify what she is seeking in the Looking for Group tab (press the "i" button) in order to gain access to the LookingForGroup channel.

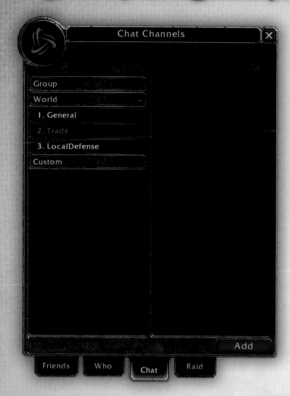

CHANNEL COMMANDS

To see which channels are available, press the letter "o" for the Social menu and click the Chat tab. In this page, you can see all the channels available in your current location. If you're on a channel, it's white; if you're not on a channel, it's gray. Click on a white channel, and the game shows you all other characters currently on the channel too.

For all the / shortcuts, you press the space bar after the command word, then you type in your message.

	COMMAND	EXAMPLE
Joining a channel	/join <fullnameofchannel>	/join General
Speaking on a channel	/# <Your question or comment goes here.>	/3 Seeking guild of mature players to run dungeons
Leaving a channel	/leave <# of channel>	/leave 3

There is absolutely no need for you to stay on any of the in-game channels. If you find them overwhelming, /leave them.

If you enjoy a quiet playing experience, leave the chat channels as soon as possible. The game becomes amazingly calm once you do this. If you like constant banter, look for a guild and/or keep yourself in as many channels as you like.

CUSTOM CHANNELS

Did you know that you can create your own chat channels? This is a powerful ability for people who are just starting on a server. Maybe you don't have a guild up yet, but you want your friends to be able to speak to you as soon as they arrive. Let them know to /join "Custom Channel Name" as soon as they come on.

Example
/join Friendschat

This puts you in the Friendschat channel, even if there wasn't one already open. Other people who type that command will be thrown in with you. It's another way to have buddies stay in touch. You can even have a guild within a guild this way, or even a group within a group, and dissolve the temporary chat system when the current task is completed.

ASKING FOR HELP

There are several ways to seek assistance. The most effective way to get a real answer to a specific question is to find another player in your current area who is doing or has done something similar to your current task. You can then use /say if you're in the same area or /whisper if they're too far away to ask a question directly.

A broader way to go about asking for help is sending your query out on the General channel. There are more people on the channel, but they may not be able or willing to help. Sometimes, the General channel is very helpful. Sometimes, it's full of chatting players being silly.

Here's the command for asking a question on the General channel:

> /# <Your question or comment goes here>

By either method, the best way to ensure you get a helpful response is to ask a specific question, and avoid being vague or demanding.

> Bad Example: "I can't find the barrow key!!!"

> Good Example: "Is anyone else looking for the barrow key?"

> Better Example: "I'm having trouble finding the barrow key. Any hints out there?"

An Internet search can be surprisingly powerful for getting a fast response as well. Odds are that if you're having a problem, someone else has bumped into the exact same thing. Searching with "WoW where is the barrow key" would likely get you answers if people in-game are just as stumped as you are.

SENDING & RECEIVING MAIL

Use the mail system to send messages, items, or money to other players. Mailboxes are found in all big cities and most towns and villages. They take on various appearances, depending upon their locale. You can track the locations of mailboxes on your minimap.

Receiving Mail

Any time you have mail waiting, the game shows you an icon near your minimap. This looks like a letter, so it's pretty clear what you're expecting.

To get your mail, right-click when you approach and target a mailbox. The first tab that opens is your Inbox. Left-click to open any messages, and click on any items to send them to your Backpack. When an attachment is removed from a piece of mail that doesn't have a message, the mail itself will be deleted.

If you read a piece of mail but leave it in your Inbox, the letter turns gray and can remain in your Inbox for 30 days. When mail expires, it is automatically deleted, including any attachments.

If someone sends you an item by mistake, you can click on Return to immediately send it back to them. You can also Reply to the sender.

BUYER BEWARE

Sometimes people would scam others through the mail system. They'd send people items through the mail (something small and trivial) but put a Cash on Delivery tag with it. Grabbing the item would cost considerable money.

World of Warcraft now has a number of systems in place to reduce or eliminate this type of scam, but it's wise to be careful of mail from strangers. In some ways, real life isn't always that different from World of Warcraft.

Should you have any issues, you can always contact Blizzard's in-game support staff, known as GMs. When other players suggest you "send in a ticket" they mean to send a message through the support system. Click on the big, red "?" to the right of your bottom action bar to get started.

Sending Mail

The second tab in the mail system is the interface to send mail. Type in the recipient's name very carefully (the game will autocomplete names from your friend list or from people in your guild), and include a subject line if you wish. You cannot send mail to yourself or to players in the opposing faction. You can, however, send mail to other characters that you control that are on the same server. The only mail you can mail directly to your characters of different factions are Bind on Account items, such as Heirloom equipment.

You decide whether to write a message, send an item, or send money. To attach an item, you can right-click on anything in your Backpack or grab and drag the item over to your letter. To send money, you type in the number of gold, silver, or copper coins you wish to send. Then press Send. The game will ask for your approval.

Each sent message costs 30 copper (plus 30 copper for each attachment), unless you use the C.O.D. option. C.O.D. is for players selling and buying items. By choosing this option, the mail system sends the item, but the transaction only completes when the recipient agrees to pay. Then, one player gets his money and another gets his gear. C.O.D. items expire after only 3 days.

Letters arrive immediately. Items and money can take one hour to arrive unless you're sending messages between members of a high level guild. One perk of these guilds is that they can send things through the mail at lightning speed.

USING THE SOCIAL WINDOW

You can use the Social Window to track new friends and find other players in your current region.

Using the Friends List

The first tab of the social window is your Friends List. If you've enjoyed chatting or questing with someone, you should add them to your Friends List so that you can find them again. To add a new name, click Add Friend, type in the name, and click Accept. That player is now added to your Friends List. Any time you open this window, you immediately see whether they are online as well as their current location. From the same window, you can send a message, invite them to a group, or remove their name.

For Private Time

World of Warcraft is a social game, but there are times when you may not want to be disturbed, such as during a tricky fight or while you're in a battleground and you need to concentrate. There are tools built into the game to cover these instances.

If you type /dnd (meaning Do Not Disturb) any player who tries to use a /whisper to contact you gets a message back saying that you're busy. Typing "/dnd" again turns off the Do Not Disturb notice and people can contact you normally.

You can't like everyone all of the time. If you want to pretend that someone doesn't exist, click the Ignore Tab on the Friends List. Click Ignore Player, type their name, and click Accept. You can always go back and remove players from this list at a later time.

When someone is on your Ignore List, they won't be able to send you messages. Their text is invisible to you, so grouping with someone in this situation is suboptimal. They could be shouting warnings to everyone while you're happily pulling away, ignorant of the trouble. If you're going to /ignore someone, please avoid them entirely!

Battle.net and Real ID

Blizzard has been expanding the things you can do between accounts. You can now try to share your Real ID with another player, giving them the ability to contact you even when you're off on another server. This is a nice feature, but you can certainly see why you wouldn't want to give this access to everyone in the game world.

To start a Real ID friend request, type in a person's account name in the friend section and wait for them to accept. Your request appears in the Pending tab of this window, and they can choose to accept or deny the request whenever they see it.

Please consider reserving this power to people that you're close with. Just because someone is in your guild doesn't mean they're your friend in real life. Real ID is certainly for people that you trust.

Real ID

This is a person you know and trust in real life. You will be able to chat with them no matter which Blizzard game you are playing. They must accept your friend invite, at which point your real name will be displayed to all of their friends.

World of Warcraft

This is a character you have enjoyed playing with on your realm. You can party and chat with this character.

REAL ID FEATURES

- Chat across game servers and even in other Battle.Net games
- Real names are shared between these friends
- See what you friends are doing, not just where they are located
- Broadcast messages to your group of buddies
- All characters from your friend's account are automatically friends of yours, so you won't have to search for each alt and sign them up

Scroll of Resurrection

Another new feature is the ability to send friends Scrolls of Resurrection. Click the scroll icon in the top-right corner of your friends list to get this process started.

Scrolls of Resurrection are used to bring a friend back to World of Warcraft. If you know someone who let their account lapse for any reason, you can use this function to give them one free week of play. Should that friend purchase additional game time, you (and they) earn some nice bonuses, like mounts, and the ability to bump a character up to level 80.

However, the inactive account must have been made before March 2012, and they can only ever accept one scroll from anyone on that account. If you have any friends who used to play, consider using a Scroll of Resurrection to tempt them to come back and help you in your World of Warcraft adventures.

INTERACTING WITH OTHER CHARACTERS

If you're in the same place as another player of your faction (meaning a character with a blue target portrait), there are several ways you can interact with them directly. Target them and then right-click on their player portrait. You get a short list of ways that you can communicate. You also see the name of the player's guild in their tooltip. Underneath their name you also see this guild identifier.

Interaction Method	Result
Add Friend	Adds the character, or the player's BattleTag, to your Friends List
Set Focus	Sets a player portrait in your interface, so that you can keep tabs on their status
Whisper	Another way to whisper to a player
Inspect	Opens the player's Character window, so you can see their armor, PvP status, Talents, and Guild
Invite	Invite the player to join a group
Compare Achievements	Used to see who has done more in-game activities
Trade	Opens the Trade window, so two players can buy, sell, trade items, enchant, or unlock items for each other
Follow	Causes your character to follow behind the other person, as long as you can keep up
Duel	Invite another player to fight to the almost-death (no permanent damage is incurred by either party)
Pet Battle Duel	If both characters have trained Pet Battles, you can challenge that character to a Pet Battle Duel.
Target Marker Icon	Set an icon for your party or raid group above this player.
Move Frame	With this option, you can move their portrait and raid frame to a position you prefer.
Report Player for	If the player has an offensive name or is violating the terms of service to cheat, you can report them to Blizzard. Check Blizzard's Harassment Policy before you use this.

TRADING WITH OTHER PLAYERS

Before initiating a trade, you and another player should agree on the item to be sold and the price to be paid. To trade with another player, you must be in close proximity. Either party can initiate the trade by right-clicking on the other player's portrait and clicking on Trade. You can also drag an item over a character to open this window.

The left window shows what you wish to trade; the right window what your comrade wishes to trade. There are three different areas for money, items, and items that you do not actually wish to trade. To make a trade, you can type in the amount of money you want to pay or you can right-click on any item in your Backpack to send it to the Trade window. When your side of the transaction is accurate, press Trade; your window turns green. When your comrade does the same, the trade completes.

The "Will not be traded" section is for items that will be modified by another player. This includes equipment that someone will enhance or locked boxes that will be opened. To complete this transaction, place your item in the bottom box, and your comrade goes to work. It is customary to tip a player that performs this service for you.

Be careful about making trades of large sums of money or valuable materials if you don't know the other person. Most players are honest, but you should always be careful about who you do business with.

MORE INFORMATION ABOUT PLAYERS

If you are chatting with someone from afar, or if you see them chatting on a channel, you can find out more about them or initiate a conversation with them by clicking on their name when you see it in the General chat log.

Click on the player name to whisper to them.

Shift+click on the player name, and the game tells you their level, race, class, guild, and current location.

If you're trying to find someone, use the /who command to search for players that match a name, level range, location, or class description. /who is quite useful in this way, but you can only search with it every few seconds. Type too quickly and the server will ignore some of your requests.

GROUPS

GROUP RULES

A group consists of two to five players, with one of them being a leader. When you're in a group, you can use the /p command to chat only with players in your group.

THESE ARE THE AUTOMATIC GROUP RULES IN THE GAME:

- Groups divide experience for kills. With enough characters in the group, there is a bonus to the total XP gained, so groups that kill quickly can make more than soloing players. However, this requires an aggressive pace.

- If multiple people are on the same collection quest, each player waits his turn to get a dropped quest item.

- If multiple people are on the same quest to kill a single enemy, all players will be able to loot the associated head, insignia, or other item the quest has requested.

- All members are awarded kill credit for targets as long as they are close enough to the fighting.

To create a group, there are two sets of commands: those you can use if you are in the same room and those you use if the player is in another location.

GROUP COMMAND SUMMARY

Command	Effect
Join	If you are asked to join a group, choose Accept or Decline
Create/Invite	If you are creating a group, type: /invite <playername>; You can also right-click on the player portrait, and click Invite. You are now the Leader. Only the Leader can Invite.
Uninvite	To remove a player from your group, type: /kick <playername>. You can also right-click on the player portrait, and click Uninvite. Only the Leader can Uninvite.
Promote to Leader	If you are the Leader, you can designate someone else the Leader. Right-click the player portrait, and click Promote to Leader.
Leave	To leave your party, right-click your own portrait, and click Leave Party.
Party Chat	/p <Anything you want to say>
F1	Target yourself
F2, F3, F4, F5	Target other party members
F-key	Assist target; this targets anything that the currently selected person is targeting.

FOCUSING FIRE

One of the most fundamental strengths of a group is their ability to kill targets quickly by focusing all attacks on a single target. Five characters attacking five monsters simultaneously are effectively soloing. What's the point? Why would that even help? A few shared buffs would be the only major difference.

However, five people that attack one monster kill it almost immediately. That takes 20% of the damage out of the fight. Always try to /assist the leaders of your group. They should let you know who to /assist. If they don't, actively state that you're going to /assist one of the damage dealers. This encourages others to do the same.

LOOTING OPTIONS

When playing in a group, there are several different options for sharing the loot you find on corpses. The default option is Group Loot, which is the most practical choice at beginning levels and for players who don't know each other. Here is the full list.

Free-For-All	Any player can loot any corpse. This is useful if one player is seeking a specific drop. However, this isn't a good option for strangers on collection quests. Friends get the most out of this because it's fast and easy.
Round Robin	Every player takes his turn in a specified order, just like a hand of cards. You know when it's your turn to loot, because the corpse "sparkles" for you.
Master Looter	The Leader takes all the loot and doles it out at the end. This is primarily used in specific guilds, where point systems are in place to figure out loot distribution.
Group Loot	Has the same rules as Round Robin, with an additional option. When an Uncommon (Green) or better item appears, the game offers an option for players to roll, as in rolling dice, for the item. This is a good default when dealing with strangers.
Need Before Greed	Similar to Group Loot except that players who cannot equip the valuable items automatically cannot roll for them. This is the automatic setting for groups created in the Dungeon Finder. While this option is engineered to be the most fair, not everyone who can equip an item needs it. And sometimes, people who can't equip an item can use it for an alt, or a disenchant. Think carefully when choosing this option.

MORE ABOUT GROUP LOOT AND NEED BEFORE GREED

Most parties tend to be in one of these two looting formats, so it's important to be able to quickly decide which is the best option to choose. When an item of high enough quality appears in the loot pool (and the loot is set to Group Loot or Need before Greed) every eligible player is prompted to roll on the item.

Need

If the item description shows that you can use the item, and it's also an upgrade for the character you're using in the group, select Need. Doing so generates a random number from 1-100. Your roll is compared against all other players who rolled Need. The item is awarded to the player with the highest roll.

However, be careful when picking Need. If you're in a group with people you don't know, it's considered proper etiquette to ask in party chat if anyone minds that you "Need" an item. By asking politely and not abusing Need to hoard items, you'll find yourself in many players' good graces.

Greed

Assuming no one selected Need, everyone who chose the Greed option generates a number between 1-100. The player with the highest result is awarded the item. If you want the item for an alt, you should choose Greed. If you plan to sell the item, you should definitely click Greed, or Pass. You will earn the goodwill of everyone in the party.

Disenchant

If your party includes an Enchanter, all players will get this option. Disenchant is considered a Greed roll. meaning if anyone clicks Need, the results of the players who chose other options are disregarded. Disenchanting causes the item to be destroyed with the resultant materials placed in the inventory of the winner. You should only choose this once you feel comfortable enough with the game that you know if loot will be more valuable to you as components than as an item.

Pass

If you simply don't want the item, or if you don't know if you have permission to roll on the item at all, choose Pass. There are many times when the benefit of stepping aside is more than the benefit of having an item. You can get another weapon, but being a polite party member could result in making new friends.

GROUP ETIQUETTE

The following is a short list of guidelines for becoming a reliable group member.

1. Be polite and communicative. Say thanks when someone helps. Apologize if you make a mistake. If someone is new and makes a mistake, be helpful. Don't forget, you were in their place at one point!

2. Confirm what role you need to play in the group: tank, damage dealer, or healer. Try to fill that role as best you can by equipping the best gear for that role and use the abilities that maximize your potential in that style of play.

3. If your class has a buff of some kind, share it with everyone in the group. Do the same with items that your class creates (such as Warlock Healthstones).

4. Share any relevant quests with party members.

5. Tell the group if you must leave at a certain time. Do this as far ahead of time as possible to avoid a sudden, unexpected departure.

6. If multiple players have the same gathering professions (Herbalism, Mining, Skinning), share the resources fairly.

7. Don't loot while others are still fighting. Wait until everyone is safe.

8. Share loot that you can't use. If you get a weapon you can't equip, consider giving it to a player who can.

9. Disband the party only after everyone has completed the quests they started together.

10. Stay close to your group members, so you don't accidentally draw the aggro of extra enemies.

11. State openly if you're going away from keyboard or taking any kind of break.

12. Don't whine if things aren't going your way. Bad groups are out there, and they happen to everyone. Leave (politely) as soon as you can if a group isn't to your liking, but don't make a scene. You never know why someone is having an off day, and hurting their feelings is unnecessary.

These guidelines go both ways. All members in your party should be cooperative and fair. If they aren't, feel free to tell them so and add them to your Ignore List. Occasionally, groups do go poorly. A good rule of thumb is to express your concern and give the group a chance to improve. If members don't cooperate, you can feel justified in leaving mid-group. When you have a great group, say thank you. You can even add your new comrades to your Friends List, or consider joining their guild. If no guild exists, consider starting one.

ADVANCED GROUP PLAY

Grouping changes the nature of World of Warcraft play considerably. Players are no longer focused on doing everything for themselves. Instead of acting as tank, healer, and damage dealer all at once, you get to focus on whatever you do best, while others in your group do the same.

Groups can carry up to five members, and that is what you need to complete most dungeon runs. This section explains more about roles in a group, and dungeon running.

WORLD DUNGEONS

World dungeons are large places designed for more intensive play than standard areas in World of Warcraft. Some world dungeons are bigger than others, but they all have instanced zones. An instance is a specific copy of the dungeon that is for your group only. In the same way that your server is a copy of World of Warcraft, your instance is a copy of a dungeon. You can only enter the same copy of the dungeon if you are in a party with your friends.

Level 15 is the minimum character level to enter the lowest level World Dungeons. You aren't required to take five characters into a dungeon. An overleveled character can solo things to farm for low-level materials. You won't be getting in anyone's way because you'll be in your own copy of the dungeon.

However, taking on any dungeon of appropriate level should be done with all five character slots filled. Everyone should also meet the level requirements of the dungeon and be geared adequately. Even if someone's gear seems a bit low, don't immediately assume they're no good for the dungeon. Give that player a chance before making a snap decision based solely on gear. Poor player skill is far more of a liability than weak gear!

WHAT TO EXPECT IN WORLD DUNGEONS

World dungeons differ from standard gameplay in many ways:

1. Dungeons are designed for groups—not solo play.

2. Completing a dungeon can be time consuming.

3. The enemies are tougher and more numerous. Expect almost all monsters to be elite.

4. Dungeons are populated with many special monsters, called bosses.

5. Dungeon quests are much harder.

6. The rewards are much richer. You find a much higher percentage of Rare or Epic gear by fighting in dungeons.

GROUP PREPARATION

When you're in a group that is considering a dungeon run, make sure that you know the answers to the following questions.

Who is the main tank? This is the person who will initiate fights, hold aggro, and protect the group. You want to ensure that their job is as easy as possible because your character's life depends on it.

Who is the main healer? Almost any group is going to need one healer, and some are going to need more than one to get through a dungeon. The main healer should be saving all resources for healing. They only try to add damage to a fight when things are going especially well.

Who is dealing damage (DPS)? Everyone who is going to focus on damage is included in the group's DPS (damage per second, but it often is just used as a way to say damage). Damage dealers should have /assist macros to ensure that they are all hitting the same targets. The most experienced DPS member should be the one that everyone assists.

Who will do the pulling? Some main tanks like to have another person bring monsters back to the group. A puller is a character who goes ahead of the group and then lures enemies back to a safer position, where they can be ambushed and killed without the danger of additional targets joining the encounter. If the main tank isn't a puller, this task often falls to a ranged character or someone with stealth.

Who is the group leader? Someone needs to lead, and the others must follow. A tradition is to have the main tank lead, but what if they don't know the dungeon well? A good leader should know an area ahead of time and be a skilled player!

Does everyone have all the dungeon quests? Look in the quest log to make sure that everyone has any pertinent quests. Share everything possible so that everyone gets the most gold and experience from their dungeon run.

How long will it take? Confirm whether anyone has to leave early. Some dungeons are much longer than others, and having someone leave in the middle is a major hassle.

What are the loot rules? Every group must decide on loot rules before starting their fights. You don't want a good item to pop up and get snatched away because you didn't decide on this ahead of time.

Has everyone shared their class buffs? Use class buffs, food, and any other bonus-producing goodies before you start a challenging quest or dungeon run.

Are hunters and warlocks managing their pets? Pets should be set to assist. For specific encounters where precision is key, people may even ask that pets be dismissed.

LEVEL REQUIREMENTS

Because the content in dungeons is difficult, each dungeon has a recommended level range that all members in your party should meet. Taking someone who is below that level requirement will be problematic, because enemies can aggro on that lower-level character from farther away. This makes it much harder to manage fights or sneak through specific areas, and even in more cautious groups it can lead to problems. Also, higher-level monsters are hard to hit; a character below the minimum isn't going to contribute much toward a group's success.

The best way to find dungeons that are appropriate for your level is to use the Dungeon Finder Tool and see what's available to you. Once you hit level 15, there will be at least one instanced dungeon available to you, although you may need to discover its entrance first.

DUNGEON PREPARATION

Here are another few things to take care of before you start a group for a dungeon run.

1. **REPAIR YOUR ARMOR.** There's no place to repair in a dungeon. Some characters can use abilities to help out with this, but you shouldn't rely on them (especially considering that most players won't have them until higher levels).

2. **EMPTY YOUR BAGS.** You often collect a great deal of loot in a dungeon, so take only essential items in your bags. Being full of crummy items is lame when you have expensive dungeon gear to snag. As a last resort, destroy low-quality loot or grey items in your bag to make room for better stuff.

3. **STOCK UP ON PROVISIONS.** Take enough food, water, potions, and reagents.

4. **BRING ANY REQUIRED QUEST ITEMS.** Double-check quest text to see if you need anything while you're in the dungeon to complete the quest.

WIPEOUTS

Wiping occurs when all members of your group die and they have no way to resurrect where they died. If this happens, you must run back from a graveyard and return to your corpse. When this happens inside a dungeon, you must go back into the dungeon's entrance before your body respawns.

Depending on the timing, all the monsters you killed may still be dead or they may have respawned, which means they've reset, and you have to fight them again. This only happens when a group takes a long time to complete a dungeon. This is sometimes a sign that things aren't going well and that people might want to try again another time.

Understandably, groups want to avoid a wipe at all costs, so it's wise to try to save a party member who can resurrect everyone else later. However, if your group does wipe, don't get too upset about it. Wipeouts happen, especially when people are learning new dungeons/encounters.

Your gear suffers a durability hit when your character dies, but the cost isn't that severe. It's easy to make money with questing, selling things on the Auction House, and by general fighting. You aren't going to end up poor because of a few lousy dungeon runs.

PICK UP GROUPS (PUGS)

In this case, PUGs aren't cute little dogs. This refers to groups that are formed by strangers, often using the dungeon finder. These are the hardest groups to win with, but that doesn't mean that they'll always be of low quality. Indeed, you might end up with several people who know a dungeon already or have impressive gear, and the dungeon will be a walk in the park because of it.

The reality of PUGs is that you won't know what to expect. Their quality has such wide variance that you might have a perfect run and follow it up with a nail-biting, hair-pulling attempt that falls flat after an hour.

To limit your time with random groups, remember to /friend people who impress you. Good players make groups a great deal more enjoyable. If you can fill two or three slots with players of known skill, you won't have nearly as much uncertainty in your dungeon delving.

Eventually, you might find a group or guild of people that adventures with you regularly. This leads to considerable advances in tactics and playstyle. It's also a great way to make friends.

TACTICS

Take a look at which abilities you use while soloing. Some of them make perfect sense when you don't have anyone watching your back. However, in a group environment, some of these become a waste of time and resources. If you're not taking aggro from monsters, why use something that raises your survivability by a substantial measure (especially if it takes away from your damage output)?

Figure out how you can best contribute within your role. If you're a tank, learn how to mitigate as much damage as possible. Use abilities that get attention from multiple monsters. Try to keep yourself from going low on health, and learn how to control monsters' positions so that the damage dealers know where to stand in each encounter.

Healers should spend a huge amount of time looking at everyone's health and saving the group from harm. Find ways to do this efficiently during long fights as well as methods to maximize your healing output and mana during tense boss fights. Consider who the most important people are to keep healed (e.g., a tank or another healer), move as necessary to keep things from pounding on you, and take enemies over to someone else if you do get attention. Being an effective healer isn't only about managing bars, it's also about good communication.

Damage dealers should lay on as much damage as possible without stealing aggro from the main tank. As long as they assist each other to stay on one target at a time, this is not terribly difficult. They'll rip down individual enemies while the tank holds onto everything else (and preferably the single target as well)!

Don't be afraid to ask questions before a fight. Ask about your role or your abilities. If you don't know a boss encounter, you should say so before the pull begins. "I've never fought this guy before. What should I do?"

Some people will be annoyed by this. The majority won't, because they know that you're trying to learn. They also know that your questions might save the group in the pull ahead. If one person didn't know what to do, maybe there were a couple more people who didn't know but were afraid to ask!

Also, use available resources to find out more about your targets. The Dungeon Journal is an in-game tool that lists all the abilities and available loot within World Dungeons.

HAVE FUN

This section might make dungeons seem awfully intimidating and tough. They can be, but they can also being very satisfying to complete. Dungeons reveal more about the Azeroth storyline, and they hold the most exotic, sometimes amusing, and powerful enemies in the game. For success, enter a dungeon, listen to your leader, and pay close attention, but also have fun!

DUNGEON FINDER TOOL

If you want to run a dungeon, whether you are a part of a full group of five players or joining on your own, the Dungeon Finder tool is a valuable resource for you. Using the Dungeon Finder to run dungeons has many advantages, but the biggest one is arguably the fact that you are transported directly to the interior of the dungeon instead of spending the time traveling to that dungeon.

WHAT ABOUT THE OTHER OPTIONS?

Raid Finder, Scenarios, and Challenges don't become available until you are at or near the maximum level for Mists of Pandaria. They are covered in a later section of this guide.

USING THE DUNGEON FINDER

The Dungeon Finder tool first becomes available at level 15. To access the Dungeon Finder tool, either click on the appropriate icon in your interface bar, or press I on your keyboard. First, you can select a specific dungeon, or set the system to assign you to a dungeon randomly. Next, select a role appropriate for your class and spec (Tank, Healer, Damage Dealer).

The Dungeon Finder places you in the queue, and the Dungeon Finder tool icon appears near your minimap. Mousing over the Dungeon Finder icon near the minimap provides the average wait time for players using the system. Tanks and Healers generally have much shorter wait times than players who choose a Damage role.

Use the drop down "Type:" menu to choose to run a random dungeon, or a specific dungeon from a listing appropriate for your party's level range. While it might be tempting to stick with dungeons you're familiar with, there are advantages to running random dungeons (more on that soon).

The Dungeon Finder always places you in dungeons appropriate to your character's level and equipment. At higher levels, you may need to meet certain requirements, such as completing a quest or discovering a dungeon's entrance, to access the dungeons through the Dungeon Finder tool.

Queuing in a Group

Groups, whether they are full or need to fill a few roster spots, can still use the Dungeon Finder. The group leader queues the entire group, but individual players must chose their role, or roles (with dual specs, most classes can select more than one role), within the group. If your group has fewer than five players, it is placed into the queue and other players already in the queue will be added to your group when a dungeon is selected.

If your group already has five characters, then you are sent to a dungeon immediately after everyone has selected a role. Keep in mind that at least one player must select Tank and another Healer in order for the Dungeon Finder to place your group.

INSIDE THE DUNGEON

After entering the dungeon, you can use the Dungeon Finder icon near your minimap to teleport out. Doing so sends you back to the spot from which you were teleported into the dungeon. Walking out of the portal at the start of the dungeon does the same thing. To find the option to return to the dungeon, right click on the Dungeon Finder icon.

RANDOM DUNGEON BONUSES

Completing a random dungeon provides extra rewards. most often the rewards are extra money, experience, and even items at lower levels. Another advantage to selecting a random dungeon is that everyone in a group with at least one random member receives a Luck of the Draw buff. Luck of the Draw increases damage done by 5%, healing done by 5%, and health by 5%. This number increases in 5% increments for each random party member included in the group, although the maximum benefit given by Luck of the Draw is 15%.

GUILDS

Guilds are player-run organizations that form to accomplish some type of goal that becomes easier to achieve through cooperative efforts. Members of a guild might be involved in PvP events, role-playing, running dungeons and endgame raiding, questing, or just about anything else you can consider. There are thousands and thousands of guilds throughout World of Warcraft, some with members that have been adventuring together for longer than World of Warcraft has been released!

Most players end up joining a guild at some point, but players join guilds for many different reasons. As long as you're playing with a full version of the game, you can join any guild that invites you. Using multiple characters, you can even be a member of different guilds!

FINDING A GUILD

It's easy to find a guild. In fact, you may be asked to join guilds by total strangers. The trick is finding an active and stable guild that suits your purposes. If you meet a player that you enjoy playing with, it's completely appropriate for you to inquire about their guild. Keep in mind that there are no rules for monitoring of guilds, so guild behavior varies widely. The following are some criteria you should consider if you're looking for a guild.

There's a Guild Finder Tool built into the game's interface as well. If you aren't currently in a guild, press "j" to open the Guild Finder Tool. Check the boxes relevant to your interests and availability and you can browse which guilds are currently recruiting and share your interests.

TYPES OF GUILDS

Questing guilds work together to explore all the lands of World of Warcraft through the completion of quests. Many guilds of this type are also thought of as leveling guilds, since the emphasis is often working with new or low-level players to increase their character level.

PvP guilds focus on player-versus-player combat in the battlegrounds or elsewhere in the world. Due to the competative nature of PvP, many PvP guilds aren't prone to accept new players without a trial period.

Dungeon and Raiding guilds are typically looking for players to fill specific roles in their 5-, 10-, or 25-man groups. Guilds running dungeons may have characters at various levels and could have a spot available for newer players. Raiding guilds are stocked with max level characters, and focus on completing endgame content and are more likely to have more specific rules on playtimes and character readiness than many other guilds.

RP guilds are together for role playing. They stay "in-character" while playing World of Warcraft.

Name	Rank	
		Player Status
Birktwo	Officer	⊙ Guild Status
Renaud	Guild M	Guild Activity (weekly)
Whimzer	Officer	Guild Activity (total)
Kibr	Veteran	Achievement Points
Telockz	Veteran	Professions
		Guild Reputation
Feloc	Veteran	6 days
Qwarra	Veteran	8 days
Montrose	Veteran	10 days
Qprie	Officer	11 days
Quinmere	Officer	13 days
Croog	Veteran	16 days
Kiberiate	Veteran	17 days
Hidova	Officer	21 days
Bensemus	Initiate	21 days

Scholars of Ydarb — View: Guild Status

✓ Show Offline Members — Members Online: 1 / 17

Guild — Roster — News — Rewards — Info

GUILD SIZE AND MEMBERSHIP

Guilds can be large or small, and neither is better than the other. Small guilds are usually more intimate and friendly, but you have fewer players to game with. A large guild can feel less personal, but there are more players on whom you can rely.

Most people feel more comfortable in a guild with members with some similar interests. If you're new to the game, you may not be comfortable in a guild of players progressing through high-level content. On the other hand, if you want to improve your combat skills, being around more experienced players may benefit you.

You can find guild members of varying age, gender, and life experiences. In addition, you should inquire about the playing hours of other guild members. That way, you'll get a sense of whether this is a place where you'll fit in.

COOPERATION

A strong guild encourages cooperation among its members. This means that players will help you complete quests—even if they don't have the same quest, and you will be expected to reciprocate. Guilds are also good opportunities for improving your Professions. Guild members are often willing to provide the raw materials for your Profession if you supply them, or the guild in general, with improved gear.

THE DOWNSIDE OF GUILDS

Really, there is only one big downside to playing with guilds. They expose you to drama. Any large group of people has its politicking and foolishness. Don't expect gaming to change that at all!

Guilds can break apart in the span of hours, even after they've been together for years. It's essential to find a guild with calm, friendly, and still firm leadership if you want to stay in one place for as long as possible. Larger isn't necessarily better for this. Age helps (both of the guild and of its player base), but that is no proof against drama either.

Instead, the actions of a guild's players speak the loudest. Observe multiple members of a guild in various circumstances. How are they in groups? Are they polite? Serious? Do they cause any trouble? How do they handle troublemakers?

For the best results, try out for a guild and let them work just as hard to impress you. Find people who like doing the same things that you enjoy. It pays for itself in the long run, even if you spend a good while on your own, looking for the right fit.

GUILD BENEFITS

The primary benefit of joining a guild is that you are never alone in the game. Being part of a guild is like being part of a club or team. Your guild mates are there when you have questions or problems in the game or when you just want to play with a group.

Playing with the same people also builds tremendous rapport. It's easier to complete dungeons and raids when you can communicate well with other people, and getting to know everyone in a guild aids that process.

Guilds have their own bank vaults to exchange materials, and they often have far more advanced crafters than people who are soloing. Because members of these Professions have multiple gatherers on their side, they raise their skills quickly and then often provide their work to others on the team at a trivial rate (or free of charge).

GUILD PERKS

Guilds are leveling creatures. The more its members gain experience, the more the guild is able to provide for them. Guild bonuses include increased experience gain for its members, faster mount speeds, and much more.

Nearly everything the members of the guild do in the game works to increase the guild's level. In addition to the experience the guild needs to reach higher levels, members of the guild must build their own standing within the guild.

GUILD ACHIEVEMENTS

Guild Achievements appear in your Achievement pane under the Guild tab. Most of these achievements mirror your standard achievements with the added stipulation of accomplishing many of them in a group made up primarily of members of your guild.

These achievements span every facet of the game. Completion of dungeons, and participation in PVP battles are examples of achievements that must be done in a guild-heavy group. Other achievements keep track of the combined efforts of the individuals in the guild. Getting at least one of every class from each possible race to maximum level is an example of such an achievement, as is having Zen Masters in every Profession.

GUILD REPUTATION AND REWARDS

Guilds can't simply add players with high level characters or maxed out Professions. Each character must achieve a certain standing with the guild in order for their accomplishments to count. This also applies to players. You can't join a guild and instantly gain access to everything the guild has unlocked. You must put in time and effort before you benefit from the work the guild as a whole has completed. Gaining Guild Reputation happens as you're accomplishing the tasks that boost your guild's level, so it's a win/win situation!

JOINING A GUILD

To join a guild, you need to get an invite from a guild officer. You might get an invitation right away, or you may have to wait until a particular member is online.

Once you accept the guild invitation, you'll be added to the guild channel, and you'll start seeing the ongoing guild chat.

LEAVING A GUILD

To leave, type /gquit.

Joining a guild is not like getting married. It is, however, like dating: you may need to join successive guilds before you find one that really suits you. If you decide to leave your guild, it's good form to tell the Guild Leader that you're leaving and why.

CREATING A GUILD

If you'd prefer to lead rather than follow, find four other people and make your own guild. This starts when you go to a major city and purchase a Guild Charter. They cost 10 silver, and you can find the Guild Master NPC that sells them with the help of the local guards.

This is the only upfront money that is needed for a guild to be put together. You use the charter to get other people to sign, and once you have all the signatures you are ready to go. Bring the charter back to the Guild Master and turn it in.

Different characters from the same account cannot log in to sign the charter once one character from that account has already signed it. Thus, you need five different players to work together when forming a guild.

People who sign your charter don't need to remain in the guild after it forms. They can leave instantly if they like, so even a single person can be in a guild (by themselves). If you pay others to help you put things together, this is quite doable. It's lonely, but some people prefer things that way.

GUILD RANKS

Guilds have the following ranks for their members: Initiate, Member, Veteran, Officer, and Leader. What the ranks actually indicate varies from guild to guild. Each guild has only one Leader, but Officers can do many guild management tasks.

GUILD TABARD

A tabard is a tunic bearing the colors and insignia of your guild. It indicates your allegiance to your guild, but there is no in-game benefit to wearing a guild tabard. Purchasing a tabard costs 1 gold. If you leave one guild and join another, you can use the same tabard; the insignia updates as you change guilds.

GUILD VAULT

Each guild can buy Guild Bank tabs at the Guild Vault. Some guilds are wealthy, and some are poor. The vault is always managed by the Guild Leader, who decides what kind of access each member gets. Vaults can hold anything, including gold, weapons, armor, recipes, and other shared items.

PLAYER VS. ENEMY COMBAT

Explore the area around your character and drag your mouse cursor over the different creatures you see. Look near the bottom right corner of the screen for a small information box to appear. Enemies appear in red text, not green like a friendly NPC or yellow like a neutral one. Some neutral targets can be attacked, but they won't fight until you go after them. Enemies are aggressive; they'll go after you if you get too close! Be ready to defend yourself.

When you chose to fight a creature, you are considered to be in combat. "In combat" means you are actively targeting, or are the target of, an enemy. It's easy to tell when you're in combat as your character portrait flashes red and your level numbers change to crossed swords. Being in combat means you are unable to perform some actions, such as eating and drinking.

A DIFFERENT WAY TO CHOOSE A TARGET

You can always left-click to select between targets, but there are other ways to find your enemies. Press the Tab key to shift between various monsters that are close to your character. Move near a group of enemies and hit Tab several times to scroll through the various available targets.

The benefits of using Tab include quick target changes with minimal loss of attention to your keyboard and that it targets any nearby enemies—even the ones you can't see. The downside to Tab targeting is that it doesn't reliably target the enemy you want to engage next nor does it always pick the closest target.

Try fighting both ways (manual selection of targets and using Tab) and find what feels more comfortable to you.

ABILITIES AND SPELLS

It's fun to watch a fight unfold, but you must pay attention to more than the action in front of you. During combat, watch for opportunities to use spells or abilities that might trigger at one time or another. Gauge your health and your resources well to know when to unload on a target, when to give up and run, and how it's all going to develop.

Each character begins with a handful of abilities that vary with the class and race you selected for that character. These initial abilities appear on your Action Bar so they are easy to access. Highlight the icons on the Action Bar (or in your spellbook) with your mouse. This brings up a tooltip that provides more information about the ability. Read that panel to find out more about any of your abilities.

Bloodthirst
Melee Range
Instant   4.5 sec cooldown
Requires Melee Weapon
Instantly attack the target, dealing 100% weapon damage plus 1,149 with your main hand weapon and restoring 1% of your health. Bloodthirst has double the normal chance to be a critical strike.

Generates 10 Rage.

PASSIVE ABILITIES

Some abilities in your spellbook are listed as Passive and don't appear on your Action Bar. These abilities are always active on your character and don't require you to perform an action for them to take effect.

You should get used to your abilities by using them, even if you're unsure of their value at first. Don't be skittish and worry about whether you're doing things perfectly. Just try out things and see how they feel and what they accomplish. The following pages will help you understand the information provided in the tooltips and what they mean to you and your character.

ABILITY TERMS

If you're not sure what an ability does or when to use it, the following terms may point you in the right direction. The same terms also apply to abilities that are used during a battle.

Common Term	Definition
Aggro/Threat	Refers to managing an enemy's attention, either increasing or reducing a monster's attention toward a character. Only applies to groups or heroes with pets
Resist/Resistance	These effects make it harder for certain spells and abilities to fully damage their target
Immune/Immunity	These effects provide full immunity to a given damage type
Fear	These abilities cause a target to run around chaotically; the effect may not break even if the victim takes damage
Daze	These abilities slow victims, making them wander aimlessly for a brief time
Stun	An ability that prevents the target from taking any action
Root/Snare	Abilities that immobilize the victim; though the target cannot move, they can still fight or use abilities
Interrupt	An ability that stops an enemy spell from completing
Area of Effect (AoE)	Something that has an effect over a wider area, influencing multiple targets within that zone of effect
Curse/Disease/Poison	Debuffs that damage a target in certain ways; these can often be Dispelled or otherwise removed
Damage over Time (DoT)	An ability that inflicts an amount of health damage over a certain number of seconds
Heal	Abilities that restore lost health
Heal over Time (HoT)	These abilities restore health every tick (duration between ticks is defined by the ability)
Aspects	Buffs that enhance players or groups for an extended period of time
Polymorph	Changes targets into helpless animals for a long time. This effect breaks if the target takes damage
Sap	Knocks out a target for a long time. This breaks if the target takes damage
Shield	The ability absorbs damage, preventing the target from losing health as quickly in a fight

MORE ABOUT DAZE

While there are abilities that daze your character, it's possible to become dazed at almost any time. If an enemy hits you from behind (if, for example, you are running away from a fight) there is a chance for you to become dazed. Being dazed is dangerous as it reduces your running speed, which allows the enemy to get in more attacks while you're trying to get away.

Knowing how abilities work can help you put together a plan of action when you face enemies. For example, if you have some sort of stun or interrupt, you can keep an enemy from hitting you with a powerful spell or healing itself.

ACTION BARS

Your Action Bar appears at the bottom of the screen. Your Action Bars are the most efficient way to access your character's spells and abilities. At low levels, you won't have many abilities here, but that will change as you get further into the game.

All players have six Action Bars. You can shuffle through your Action Bars in two ways: first, press and hold the Shift key, then press any number between 1 and 6; second, click on the up and down arrows to the right of the button marked with the equals sign (=). The number in the small circle next to the arrows tells you which Action Bar is currently active.

Be logical about the way you set up your Action Bars. It makes a huge difference in your combat effectiveness. It's a bad sign if you find that you must switch Actions Bars often in a regular fight. By the same token, you don't want to shift between numbers too dramatically. This is easier to show with an example or two.

CLICKING VERSUS TYPING

At some point, everyone must click on an ability icon with their mouse pointer. Maybe you've set up five hot bars on your screen and can't get to everything quickly. However, your goal should be to use the keyboard for all possible actions. This is often much faster and lets your character pop through abilities at lightning speed.

Demonstrate this for yourself.

Search for the ability in slot six and left click on it, even if nothing is there.

Press 6 on your keyboard. Which was faster?

Once you're used to the game, teach yourself to use abilities without even looking to see what they are. Memorize where each ability is located and watch your character transform into a killing machine. No one expects you to master this instantly, but it will make your experience in the game go much more smoothly.

People with good Action Bar set ups are much faster on the draw. They are using an ability every 1.5 seconds (that's normally the global cooldown on how quickly you can use your abilities). If your character is frequently auto-attacking while you fish around for something to do, they become inefficient.

It's also normal for a new player. Don't be upset with yourself if this takes time to learn. Instead, attempt to find a setup for yourself that makes sense. As you feel your speed improve, congratulate yourself and think about how much deadlier your character is becoming.

MORE INFORMATION ABOUT ABILITIES

Casting Time

Every spell or attack has a casting time; this tells you how much time your character needs to make the attack. Instant abilities happen as soon as you press the button with which they're associated. Timed castings can take several seconds, leaving your caster exposed for the entire process. Characters that are casting spells often cannot move to defend themselves without halting their current spell cast. They stop making any auto-attacks, and they can't use other abilities.

Some enemies (including other characters) have Interrupt abilities to stop spellcasters if used with the proper timing. In addition, damage can set a

caster back, forcing them to take more time to get their spell off.

Channeled spells take time as well, but they're a different breed. These start to take effect quickly, but the spellcaster must maintain the channel for its effects to continue. As with timed spells, these effects can be interrupted. Damage doesn't set them back; instead, it sets channeled spells forward, causing them to end prematurely.

Casters often find ways to earn time for themselves to cast spells. They slow enemies, force them to run away, or otherwise make it hard to engage in melee combat while they are busy.

Cooldowns

The Action Bar tooltips also indicate the cooldown times of your various spells and abilities. Cooldown is the amount of time you must wait to use an ability again. Once you use an ability, the Action Bar shortcut darkens that action until it's ready to be used again. This graphic representation is important because it lets you know what you can do at any given moment.

Cooldowns are represented visually on your Action Bar icons as a clockwise-moving line that moves like a stop watch. When you can't cast a spell due to a cooldown, the game tells you: "That spell isn't ready yet."

There is also a global cooldown (often abbreviated to GCD) that is triggered when most abilities are used. The global cooldown lasts 1.5 seconds (1 second if you're a Rogue, Death Knight, Windwalker Monk, or Feral Druid). When you use an ability, watch almost every other slot darken as well. Anything that isn't on the global cooldown is able to be used even when you've just finished a different action. These unlinked spells and abilities are often potent, reactive abilities that get you out of trouble without having to wait.

Some abilities have a shared cooldown beyond the global one. For example, any Shaman's Shock spell triggers the cooldowns of the others, so you can't blast someone with a different Shock every second and a half.

CATEGORIES OF ABILITIES

All character classes have numerous types of abilities that fall into different categories. It's almost impossible for you to know the exact effect of everything in the game. However, knowing the category of an ability and looking for key words in the text will give you clues as to how best to use that ability.

Schools of Magic

The schools of magic are Arcane, Fire, Frost, Holy, Nature, and Shadow. Some abilities that aren't spells can also inflict some of these types of damage. Different enemies are immune or highly resistant to different types of damage. No single school of magic is inherently more powerful than the others.

Most classes who can use spells have access to two or three schools of magic. However, until you gain access to specializations at level 10, all schools of magic are essentially equal.

BUFFS AND DEBUFFS

During combat, buffs and debuffs appear near your minimap. These are also shown underneath your character portrait if you highlight yourself.

Most classes have some sort of buff that they can cast on themselves, a weapon, or their group. You should cast those before combat begins and keep them going whenever possible. The cost of buffs is almost always trivial compared with the benefits they add to your character or others.

During combat, you can be hit with debuffs from your enemies. Most debuffs have a short lifespan, and you may need to wait them out. Other debuffs can

be countered by the right spell or item.

Many classes inflict their own debuffs on enemies. You might even be able to strip off buffs from enemies too, so these effects go both ways.

If you're buffing group members, realize that you don't need to click on individual people ahead of time. Cast the buff on one character in your party and everyone in your party should get it at the same time.

FIGHTING ADDS

An add is an additional enemy that unexpectedly joins your fight. During the course of battle, there's always a chance for adds to appear and complicate things. These additional enemies generally join battle for one of three reasons. First, some enemies try to run away when their health is nearly depleted. This is problematic because the enemy can run out of your attack range and could bring back friends. In other cases, you may be fighting too close to an enemy's patrol path. If the enemy spots you, even if you're already engaged in combat, it will join the fight, and not on your side!

There is a third, and much rarer instance, of adds joining the fight. Some powerful enemies have henchmen that may not join the fight immediately. Instead, the main enemy may wait until some portion of health is gone before calling in reinforcements. That's why it pays to always stay alert in combat!

Pull monsters away from their buddies if you're worried about adds. This is a safer way of fighting, but it takes more time. When you're confident of victory, don't bother doing this.

If you're wondering how to pull monsters, there are many ways to get the job done. For a melee character, hit the monster, step back, hit them again, and repeat. You won't miss auto-attacks by being on the run (as long as you're facing your target), and your abilities are often usable on the fly as well.

For ranged characters, this is easier to do. Cast a spell at long range to start the fight. Next, run like the wind until you're in the place where you'd like to fight them. Turn back around and resume casting.

Keep in mind that if you try to pull a monster too far, they'll "tether" back to their starting point.

RUNNING AWAY

Sometimes you see the writing on the wall, and it says that you're doomed. Perhaps another enemy joined the fight when you were already badly hurt. Maybe a monster was a tad more dangerous than you realized. Whatever the case, you know that you probably won't survive the encounter.

Go ahead and run! If you're by yourself, there is no shame in this. When you're with others, let them know that you're fleeing so that they don't die in your stead.

Some classes are much better at this than others. If you get out of melee range, the monster can't pound on your back during your flight.

Also, monsters will have a chance to daze you! Getting dazed slows your character, giving monsters even more time to attack before they tether and return home.

Thus, use anything in your repertoire to stun a target or root them in place before you start to flee. Freeze them, hamstring the suckers, use fear effects. Do something. Anything!

Once you're in motion, watch the area ahead of you (don't look back at the thing slavering behind you). Try to avoid other targets during your flight; otherwise, you're just making things worse for yourself.

Finally, avoid running through other people when you're evacuating. Pulling monsters through another person is called "training." If you die while fleeing and the monsters aren't far enough to "leash" back home, they'll attack any nearby targets. Nobody likes getting hit with a train, especially if they get killed or end up fighting creatures that aren't worth experience because you attacked them first.

EATING AND DRINKING

Between battles, you may need to replenish your health or mana. Eating food replenishes your green health bar. Drinking beverages replenishes your mana

bar, if you have one. Both health and mana regenerate naturally, but eating and drinking restores these much faster.

The regeneration rate for your mana is tied to your Spirit. At low levels, you can move between most fights with little delay.

Right-click on any food or drink that you want to use. Note that these items (and any other usable item) can be dragged onto the Action Bar at the bottom of the screen. This makes the items more convenient in the future, lowering the time you spend looking through your bags.

Well-Fed Bonus

Some food and drink provides a "Well Fed" buff if you consume them over an extended (and uninterrupted) time. Low level food that conveys the Well Fed buff lasts for fifteen minutes, while high level food buffs last for sixty minutes. Well Fed bonuses affect one or more of your character's stats, such as Stamina, Strength, or Hit. To see if a food provides a bonus, and what the benefit will be, place your mouse pointer over the food's icon until a tooltip appears.

DYING

This won't be on your list of things to do, but at some point early in your character's life, their health bar will reach zero, and they will die. It might happen because you forgot to refresh your health bar between battles; you were attacked by multiple enemies simultaneously; or you attacked an enemy who was too tough for you.

It happens. Everybody dies. Sometimes more than once. Over and over again. The only penalty to dying is that your current armor suffers a 10% durability loss. Durability is essentially the health of your gear. When you take damage, die, or resurrect at the Spirit Healer, your gear slowly loses durability.

When you die, the Release Spirit box appears over your corpse. When you click this button, your character turns into spirit form and is transported to a graveyard with a Spirit Healer.

To reunite your spirit with your body, you can run back to your corpse; or you can ask the Spirit Healer to resurrect your body at its location. If you Accept resurrection, you receive an additional 25% durability loss in your armor. At later levels, you also suffer resurrection sickness. Resurrection sickness depletes your character's stats, making it nearly impossible to do anything in the game until the sickness disappears. When the debuff icon for Resurrection sickness fades away, your stats return to normal.

Most of the time, you will simply retrieve your corpse by running back to the location where you died. A new arrow appears on your minimap that indicates the exact location of your corpse. The second arrow that appears is to guide you back to the Spirit Healer. Fortunately, ghosts run faster than living characters.

When you reach the general location of your corpse, you get the option to "Resurrect Now?" There is a generous area in which you can resurrect, so that you can avoid any enemies around you. You must retrieve your body from a safe place, because characters resurrect with only 50% of health and mana bars. Eat and drink quickly to restore your health and mana.

ENEMIES

Enemies, monsters, and mobs are all generic terms for anything that you can fight in the game. When you target an enemy, you can get helpful information about it by looking at its portrait and tooltip. The character name might indicate the class of enemy; and a blue mana bar indicates it's some kind of caster who can attack you from afar.

By mousing over the enemy, the tooltip tells you the type of enemy it is. The types of enemy include Humanoid, Beast, Undead, Demon, and Elemental. Some abilities only work against certain types of enemies and will fail if you try to use them against the wrong type of enemy.

TARGET PORTRAIT COLORS

RED

The target is hostile and will attack if you get too close. In PVP situations, players from the other faction also appear with this color.

YELLOW

The target is passive and will only fight if you attack first.

GREEN

The target is friendly.

ORANGE

The target is unfriendly. It won't attack you, but don't expect any interaction with it. There are often a series of quests that allow you to gain reputation with the target's faction in order to change its disposition.

GRAY

The target has already been attacked by another player. You can still attack this target, but killing it will not give you any experience points and you will not share in any loot. In addition, the kill will not count toward any quests you have.

BLUE

The target is a player, just like you.

LEVEL NUMBER COLORS ON TARGET PORTRAIT

The color of the target's level number provides important information to you as well.

If the numbers are gray, killing that enemy doesn't provide any benefit other than loot.

Green numbers indicate the enemy is a few levels lower than you, and should be easy for you to kill.

Yellow numbers are for enemies who are close in level to your current level and could be a challenge in a fight.

Red numbers are for enemies that are a few levels higher than you; it's best to avoid combat with them until you are more comfortable playing the game.

If you target an enemy and a skull appears in the place of its level, then that enemy is at least 10 levels higher than you. Avoid enemies like this whenever you encounter them!

SOCIAL MONSTERS

If you see a small group of enemies and aren't sure you can handle them all at the same time, observe them for a moment to see if they move apart from each other. With some patience, you can typically fight each enemy by itself.

However, some creatures are social, and will help their comrades when they are attacked even when they aren't right next to each other. There is no way of identifying which types of monsters are social except through experience.

CRITTERS

Critters are the non-combat animals you see roaming around, including rabbits, cows, snakes, and prairie dogs. If you attack them, they can't fight back; and you get no XP from killing them. Some Critters are considered wild pets and are eligible for Pet Battles.

RARE SPAWNS

Creatures with a silver dragon around their portraits are unique mobs with guaranteed drops. Some items they drop are not found on any other creature, while others are guaranteed to drop better than average loot.

If the silver dragon around the creature's portrait has wings, it is an Elite monster. These creatures have the traits of both rare spawns and elite monsters.

ELITE MONSTERS

Elite monsters are powerful enemies, usually the targets of group or dungeon quests. Elites are stronger than their level would indicate. Generally speaking, you can assume that fighting an elite will be as hard as fighting a monster three levels higher. In addition, Elite monsters often have special abilities that make fighting them even trickier.

Elites are identified by the gold dragon around their character portrait and the word Elite in their tooltip.

THEY KEEP COMING BACK

The enemies you kill don't stay gone forever. They eventually respawn, meaning an area you cleared of enemies will shortly be filled again.

LOOT

Enemies won't stand against you forever. Every target has a health bar under its name. When this green bar drops to nothing, the creature dies. Almost all enemies offer some kind of loot after they've been defeated. When you have loot waiting, your dead enemy sparkles. Look for this golden shimmering effect and rejoice. You've earned something!

Right-click to open the enemy loot box, then click on each item to put it into your inventory. If a creature drops an item related to a quest you're following, that loot will be highlighted yellow. If you press Shift and right-click at the same time, each item is sent directly to your Backpack.

You earn rewards by looting enemies and from completing quests. Quest rewards go directly to your backpack after you finish the quest. Any money you collect, from any source, goes immediately into your backpack. It can't be lost or unintentionally discarded. Also, money has no weight in World of Warcraft. You can carry half a million gold around if you like.

A loot window is opened by right-clicking on a sparkling, defeated enemy.

ADVANCING YOUR CHARACTER

For now, all of your possessions are either equipped on your character or are being carried in your backpack. Press shift plus "b" to open your backpack and see what is inside. Another way to do this is to left-click on the backpack icon on the right hand side of your action/interface bar.

MANAGING YOUR INVENTORY

Eventually, you acquire additional bags to expand your inventory. Characters can carry up to four additional containers. Some professions allow characters to craft their own bags, or sell them in the Auction House. There are in-game bag vendors, who can provide storage, but inventory space is at a premium, more slots cost more money.

Click this icon to open your backpack.

As you explore Azeroth, questing and looting defeated foes, your backpack will quickly fill with items. When your backpack is full, you won't be able to receive any more loot, and the game will tell you, "Inventory is full." To make some room, look for a vendor who will buy low quality items, other items you cannot use, or don't need. If you aren't near a vendor but still need room, you can always drop items from your backpack by left-clicking and dragging an item to pull it out of your backpack. Left click again on the desktop to drop the item. You'll get a message asking whether you want to delete the item. Click Yes.

If you get a quest reward container, or find a bag of any kind, keep it! It's far more valuable to you for storage than the money you could get from a vendor by selling it. Drag new bags into any of your Equipment Container slots, or right click them from inventory to equip them.

HEARTHSTONES

Every character starts the game with a Hearthstone. These special items teleport your character to the last place that they bound. Normally, you bind at inns. These are good locations to log out of the game because you get rested bonus (and thus free experience) by letting your character rest there when you're not playing.

Hearthstones are on a long cooldown timer; this means that you can only use them every 30 minutes, at most. It's best to save these for times when you need to cross a large distance and know where you're teleporting or for times when you're about to log out and want to get someplace safe to rest.

SELLING TO VENDORS

To complement the coppers you've collected from defeating enemies and completing quests, you can earn money by selling the unneeded items collected from slain foes. Since your bag space is limited you should return to your starting area to sell off these items. Get into the habit of selling off your unwanted loot when you turn in quests, that way you'll have bag space when you strike out into the world again. Although each vendor sells only a specific type of merchandise, they buy anything that you have. Items that aren't considered gear come in two colors: grey and white.

Grey items are often called "vendor trash" because they have no real purpose other than to be sold to vendors.

White items are useful in some way if you plan to take on a crafting Profession, but there's usually no harm in selling off the items at this point.

I DIDN'T MEAN TO SELL THAT!

If you accidentally sell something you meant to keep, don't worry. At the bottom of each vendor window is a Buyback tab. Click on that tab and purchase the item you sold by mistake.

GEAR

All new characters start out with minimal weaponry, armor, and clothing. In the starting zone, there are three sources of improved gear: looting enemies, completing quests, and armor vendors. For most starting players, the vendors aren't an option because you don't have much money. If you do have the money and you like to have your character's outfit match, then check out what the vendors have to offer.

You can tell if an item is a new piece of gear because its tooltip includes information about where you wear it (hands, back, chest, etc.). When you find a piece of gear, open your bags and mouse over the item. The color of the first line tells you about the quality of the item. At early levels, you are likely to find only gray, white, and green items.

Item Color	Quality
GRAY	POOR
WHITE	COMMON
GREEN	UNCOMMON
BLUE	RARE
PURPLE	EPIC
ORANGE	LEGENDARY

The next color to look for is red. Red text on an item tells you that you are unable to equip it. It could be that it's a weapon or type of armor you can't use, or that you are not high enough level to equip it. If you might be able to use an item after you gain levels, keep it. If you are playing with friends, see if anyone else could use the item. Otherwise, find a vendor and sell off your unusable gear.

Color-Coded Information

This tooltip for Goblet of Anger provides some basic information using colors. The name in purple means the item is Epic quality. The red text tells you why you can't use the item. In this case, the character doesn't meet the item's level requirements.

> **Goblet of Anger**
> Binds when equipped
> Held In Off-hand
> +341 Stamina
> +227 Intellect
> +137 Spirit
> Requires Level 85
> Item Level 378
> Equip: Increases your haste by 160.
> Sell Price: 5 ● 34 ● 34 ●

WEAPON SKILLS AND ARMOR PROFICIENCIES

If you're ever wondering which weapons are available to your character, press "p" to open your spellbook and look for the Weapon Skills icon. Highlight the icon to see what weapons are available for your character to use.

The Armor Proficiencies icon details the type of armor you can currently use plus whether your character can equip a shield. These limitations are determined entirely by your class. However, some classes get an armor upgrade when they reach higher levels. Warriors and Paladins start the game with only mail proficiency, but they eventually learn how to wear plate. Shaman and Hunter start out wearing leather, but can use mail armor when they hit a certain level.

COMPARING EQUIPMENT

When you mouse over a piece of equipment, you can see details about its attributes. At early levels, equipment will have an Armor stat only, so you can choose the piece with the highest level of armor protection. Later in the game, however, you will find gear that offers other stat increases as well.

Hold down the shift key while highlighting a potential upgrade. This compares your currently equipped gear with the new item. The game automatically gives you a summary of the stat changes that would occur if you switched.

At early levels, you are likely to find only Poor (gray), Common (white), and Uncommon (green) items. If you cannot use a gray item, sell it. If you find a white or green item, hopefully, you can wear it. If you cannot use a green item, you might consider selling it to another player.

After you pass through the earliest game levels, Poor and Common items stop being acceptable for use. You want to switch to Uncommon gear exclusively (i.e., all greens for your weapons, armor, and peripheral equipment).

After level 20, you start seeing more than an occasional blue item. These Rare pieces are quite nice for their time, and you should seek them out. However, it isn't until much later in your career that they become baseline equipment.

Epic gear exists before level 60, but it's not plentiful. Don't even worry about it unless you're doing something very specific. Unless you're stuck at a given level, such as being at the cap, Epic gear isn't necessary. This is equipment that rewards someone for staying a given level and doing an exceptional level of content over time. Thus, you level past the utility of Epic gear throughout most of the game.

Legendary equipment is so rare that most people will never have access to such an item. Even endgame raiders in big guilds can't count on having these items at their disposal.

HEIRLOOM ITEMS

Heirloom items are special pieces of equipment that change based on the character using them. These items are bound to accounts instead of individual characters. Generally, you must have a higher level character on your account purchase one of these items and send it through the mail to a lower level character. These items often offer experience bonuses, and improve as you level. As your character increases in levels, the items do the same.

ARMOR

When you start the game, most of your armor slots are empty. Eventually you find pieces for your head, shoulders, back, chest, waist, legs, feet, wrist, and hands. If a shield is held in the off hand the character is limited to using weapons that require only one hand to use, but shields provide an amazing amount of armor as well.

CLOTHING

Clothing pieces fill up your shirt and tabard slot. These don't often have any influence on your character's progression, but they decorate your avatar. Tabards can identify your affiliation with a guild. They can also show an association with certain in-game factions.

WEAPONS

All characters have a main hand and an off-hand inventory slot. These are taken up by a two-handed weapon, two one-handed weapons, or a weapon and an off-hand item, such as a shield. Class selection determines a great deal of what you end up equipping here.

AMULETS, RINGS AND TRINKETS

These are higher level item slots. You wear a single amulet around your neck, but get two slots each for rings and trinkets. Some of these items are active. For example, many trinkets grant abilities that you can put on your action bar to give your character a sudden boost in one aspect of play.

Don't worry too much about these until you reach higher levels.

REPAIRING YOUR EQUIPMENT

As your gear loses durability, a paperdoll of your armor appears on-screen. Yellow means damaged; red means broken. When your armor is broken, that piece no longer protects you in combat, nor applies its stat bonuses.

To repair your armor, mouse over different vendors until your mouse pointer turns into an anvil. Anvils indicate vendors who are capable of repairing your gear. When you right-click this type of vendor, two icons appear in the vendor window, showing the cost for repair. Click on Repair All Items. At low levels, you don't really need to worry about repairing your gear because you should replace it quickly. As you start gaining levels, repairing your gear becomes more important.

OTHER WAYS TO IMPROVE YOUR CHARACTER

There are other ways that you can give your character an edge. These items don't need to be equipped. Instead, they're used (often permanently) to boost your character or your character's equipment. Some effects are temporary, others are more permanent.

Some of the following suggestions discuss Professions. To learn more about Professions, turn to page 74.

POTIONS, ELIXIRS & FOOD

Characters drink potions and elixirs and consume foods to enhance their performance. Potions, elixirs, and flasks can be made by characters with the Alchemy profession. If you're lucky, potions are sometimes found in treasure chests.

Potions have short-term benefits, only working for the moment after you drink them. These restore health or mana, and they can get you through some nasty times. Potions can be taken during combat, but there is a cooldown timer for their use. You can't bring ten potions into a fight and hope to keep yourself alive indefinitely.

Elixirs buff your character for a somewhat longer period. They can enhance a number of things, including armor, health regeneration, attributes, and so forth.

There are other drinkable items called flasks. These are incredibly expensive because they demand many more reagents during creation. Flasks persist through death and are a common aspect of dungeon runs and raiding.

Food is either purchased, or created with the Cooking profession. Some food items have short-term effects and typically enhance character attributes. Regardless of the type of statistical bonus provided by food, its buff is always called Well-Fed.

ARMOR KITS

Some armor pieces can be permanently improved by adding armor kits to them. These kits are produced with the Leatherworking profession. Early armor kits mainly provide additional armor, but higher level kits offer substantial benefits.

Charscale Leg Armor
Requires Level 85
Use: Permanently attach charscale armor onto pants to increase Stamina by 145 and Agility by 55.
Can only be attached to leg armor in your inventory. Wearer must be level 85 or higher.

SPELLTHREADS

Spellthreads are made by character with the Tailoring profession. These are similar to armor kits in that they enhance armor and can provide attribute benefits, but they can only be attached to leg slot items. Applying either enhancement makes an item soulbound.

SHOULDER INSCRIPTIONS

The Inscription profession creates special Inscriptions that are applied to shoulder armor. Just like Spellthreads, these Inscriptions cause items to become soulbound. You won't see your first shoulder armor Inscription until your characters are much higher level.

ENCHANTMENTS

Another way to permanently enhance equipment is to have it enchanted. Almost every type of equipment can carry some type of enchantment. Though the temporary cost is quite high, the long-term benefits are substantial if you have most of your gear enchanted. This raises attributes, adds damage to weapons, and is fun to pursue, especially if you have some cash to spare.

GLYPHS

As you progress through the levels, Glyphs start coming more into play. Press the letter "n" to bring up the Specialization window. From there, select the tab labeled Glyphs to see which ones are open for your character.

There are two tiers of Glyphs and you unlock additional slots for Glyphs as you gain levels. Glyphs allow you to further customize the effects of some of your abilities. In some cases, especially for the Minor Tier glyphs, these effects include slight alterations to your spell's visual effects.

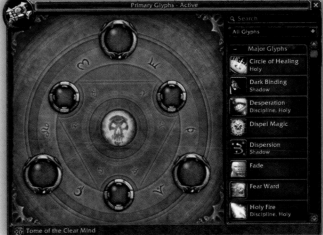

TRANSMOGRIFICATION

One last form of item improvement, though it's purely aesthetic, is Transmogrification. For a price, you can transform your equipment into a look you find more visually pleasing. There are restrictions on some equipment appearances, and the transmogrified item must be the same type item. For example, you cannot transmogrify a one-hand sword to look like a two-hand sword.

GAINING LEVELS

As you kill enemies, complete quests, gather herbs and ore, and discover new areas in the game world, you gradually earn experience points (XP), and fill the experience bar located along the top of your action bar. When the bar is full, the game congratulates you on earning a new level with a flash of light and fanfare. Completing the initial quests you find in your starting village will easily move you from Level 1 to Level 2.

TRAINING NEW ABILITIES

As you gain levels, the game lets you know when you learn new abilities. New abilities automatically (for the first few levels) go into an open slot on your Action Bar. You're free to move your newly learned skills around on your Action Bar in any way that makes sense to you.

LEVEL 5: LEARN A PROFESSION

When you hit level 5, you gain the option of learning a Profession. It isn't necessary for you to learn a Profession, but if you're interested in learning more, turn to page 74.

CHARACTER STATS

Each time your character gains a level, many of their attributes (such as health, mana, Agility, Strength, etc.) are increased. Go into the character window to find out more about these changes.

Discussion of stats is a fairly advanced topic, and stats change at each level, but here are some basics that you should know when you look in this window.

White	By default, your stats should be in white. This is a normal level.
Red	Stats in red are being affected negatively by a debuff, broken armor, or other negative effect.
Green	Stats in green are good and are likely being enhanced by a buff, enhanced armor, or potion.

LEVEL 10: THE BIG CHOICE

At level 10, your character must select a specialization to follow within his or her chosen class. Press the letter "n" to open the Specialization panel and display the options available. You're also able to look at some of the core abilities that you'll learn within each specialization.

If you're unsure about which specialization you'd like to pursue, highlight the abilities in the preview panel for each specialization to learn some details about each skill.

RESETTING YOUR SPECIALIZATION

After playing your class with your chosen specialization, you may find that it doesn't quite fit your play style. Don't worry; you can always reset your specialization by talking with one of your Class Trainers.

Changing your specialization incurs a fee that increases each time you decide to change, but it isn't so taxing that you won't be able to explore the play styles for each of your specialization choices until you find the one that best suits you.

TALENTS

Beginning at level 15 and every 15 levels after that until you reach level 90, you earn a Talent Point that you can use to purchase a talent based on your class. Press the letter "n" to open the Specialization and Talents window. Selecting the Talents tab allows you to view the talents available, and you get to choose one of the three options presented.

Typically, the choices presented either augment a spell or ability within your specialization, or provide you with a new utility ability. In some cases one of the talent choices provided grants a special ability to be used in times of dire circumstance.

Highlighting the options by using your cursor to mouse over each of the presented talents provides some detailed information about what each talent does for your character.

Talents are presented to give you a chance to add some flair to your character without impeding the other spells and abilities you use within your specialization. There is no right or wrong choice for talents, as they are presented only to enhance how you choose to play your character.

After you select your talent, click the Learn button at the bottom of the pane to add the talent to your spellbook.

RESETTING YOUR TALENTS

Over time, you may decide that one talent may offer you more benefits, according to your play style, than another. If this is the case, you can easily reset your talents by speaking with one of your Class Trainers, who will refund your Talent Points so that you may spend them again on any new talent choices you decide to make. Please bear in mind though, each time you choose to reset your talents, you are charged a fee by your trainer. This fee increases each time you decide to relearn your talents.

TRAVELING & TRANSPORTATION

At the beginning levels, your only choice is to hoof it when you want to go somewhere. Once you start getting quests that send you to new places, it helps you a great deal to know about all your transportation options.

TRAVELING BY FOOT

It's not glamorous, but everybody starts out running to get to new places. When you're going long distances, use Auto Run (defaults to the NumLock key), so you can focus on controlling your character.

It is possible to walk if you aren't in the mood to run. Though slower, this is fun for roleplaying or setting a tone; it's also good if you're escorting an NPC that is wandering around at a different pace. To walk, tap "/" once. Tap it again to resume running.

There is no sprint key, unless you're a Worgen or a Rogue, both of whom have abilities that let them put on the speed every few minutes.

BUFFS FOR RUNNING

Even on foot, some classes have skills and abilities to increase their speed. They don't start with these abilities at level 1, so keep an eye out with your class trainer to see when the following abilities become available.

DRUIDS

Druids learn a Travel Form that lets them turn into a Stag. This gives them considerable speed.

HUNTER

Hunters learn an ability called Aspect of the Cheetah, which increases speed indefinitely (they also learn Aspect of the Pack which increases the run speed of the entire group). You are immediately dazed if you take damage while using this, so it isn't useful during combat.

SHAMAN

Shamans learn how to turn into a Ghost Wolf. This form increases speed indefinitely, so it is ideal for long journeys.

SWIMMING

At times, you need to swim through bodies of water to get to your location. At other times, you need to dive to find hidden items for quests. Almost every body of water has some sort of aqualife—some of them are hostile.

Controlling your character while swimming differs from controls for running.

SWIMMING CONTROLS

Key	Effect
X	Dive deeper into the water
Spacebar	Swim to the surface
Right-click+mouse movement	Moves the direction your character is swimming
NumLock	Character continues swimming in the same direction

BUFFS FOR SWIMMING

Swimming is slower than running, unless you have some buffs or abilities. Your character can stay under water for a limited amount time before running out of air and eventually dying, unless you consume the proper potions, or have a Warlock or Shaman around to grant you underwater breathing.

Druids eventually learn how to shift into an Aquatic Form. This form allows Druids to stay underwater as long as they like. They also move faster than other classes. Shaman learn an ability called Water Walking that allows characters to cross water as if it were land. It works for mounted characters as well.

FATIGUE

Running out of breath isn't the only danger when you're out in the water. Characters get fatigued if they try to swim for too long in deep water. This prevents people from trying to cross the ocean without a ship. If you see the fatigue bar pop up, return to lighter water as fast as you can. Depth is not an issue in this, so staying at the top of the water won't help.

FLIGHT PATHS

Using flight paths is the most common means of travel in the game. Flight paths are in every city as well as in most regions. Flight Masters are identified by the winged foot icon on your region map.

To access a new flight path, you must discover the two ends of the path on foot. All characters start with access to the flight point in their home city. However, you won't be able to use that flight point until you discover another destination attached to it.

Each time you enter a new region or town, look for the flight point using the tracker in your mini-map. Right-clicking on the Flight Master with a green exclamation point gets you the flight point. Right-clicking on him again opens a map that shows you where you can fly. Click on your destination, and you're on your way immediately.

Most flight paths are specific to Alliance or Horde, and each faction flies on different types of beasts. There is a modest fee each time you fly. When you think about it, flying saves you money. The cost of the flight doesn't compare with the money you make questing and killing enemies in the time you've just saved!

Flying is one of the coolest features of the game. You can use your mouse to look around you while flying, because you can't fall off a flying mount. This isn't true once you have your own mounts, but that's a different issue.

FACTION-SPECIFIC TRAVEL METHODS

ALLIANCE SHIPS

Ships are designed for cross-continent travel. Most ship paths are for Alliance destinations, though the path betwen Booty Bay and Ratchet is available to both Horde and Alliance.

Unlike flight paths, there's no need to "discover" a ship path. Simply go to the harbor, find the right dock, and wait for the ship to arrive. Most harbors serve several ships, so you need to speak to the Harbor Master to make sure you're getting on the right one. You may have to wait a few minutes for the ship to arrive, so talk to people nearby, look at talents and achievements, practice your crafting, or just relax. There is no fee for a trip on one of these vessels. If you jump or fall off the boat, you must swim for shore.

DEEPRUN TRAM

The Deeprun Tram is a commuter trip between Stormwind and Ironforge. The trip is as fast as flying, and it's free. The tram stop in Stormwind is located in the Dwarven District. In Ironforge, it's in Tinker Town.

ZEPPELINS: HORDE REGIONS

Zeppelins are also designed for cross-continental travel. All zeppelin paths are for Horde destinations.

Unlike flight paths, there's no need to "discover" a zeppelin path. Simply go to the zeppelin tower, find the right platform, and wait for the zeppelin to arrive. Most zeppelin towers serve several ships, so you need to speak to the Zeppelin Master to make sure you're getting on the right flight. You may need to wait a few minutes for the zeppelin to arrive.

There is no fee for a zeppelin trip. If you jump off the zeppelin, your character will probably die. That said, people can jump off of the Tirisfal Glade zeppelin without dying. Usually. Just don't jump too soon.

THE SILVERMOON PORTAL

A portal connects Silvermoon City and the Undercity. The Undercity portal is located just inside the city walls. The Silvermoon portal is located in Sunfury Spire. This portal is free, but is only for players using the Burning Crusade expansion.

PERSONAL MOUNTS

At Level 20, players are eligible to purchase ground mounts. Riding a mount is 60% faster than running. To use a mount, you must purchase the mount itself and Apprentice Riding, which enables you to use the mount.

RACIAL MOUNT CHOICES

Race	Common Mount
Draenei	Elekks
Dwarves	Rams
Gnomes	Mechanostriders
Humans	Horses
Night Elves	Nightsabers
Worgen	No Mount
Pandaren	Dragon Turtle
Blood Elves	Hawkstriders
Goblins	Trike
Orcs	Wolves
Tauren	Kodos
Trolls	Raptors
Undead	Skeletal Horses

You aren't required to use the standard racial mount for your character. By exploring the world, you are likely to find other mounts. Some of these require doing repeated quests to raise your reputation with a given faction, but it's all worthwhile when you want their cool mounts.

Riding is a skill that you only need to train at each tier. Thus, you can have ten mounts and still only need to have trained Riding that first time. The only recurring expense is when you go to buy another type of mount.

There are faster mounts in the game, including epic mounts (that require more intense Riding training) and flying mounts. Flying mounts cost the most, and you won't be able to get involved with those until you're well into the game's later content.

WARLOCK AND PALADIN BONUS!

Warlocks and Paladins have special ground mounts that are class specific. Paladin mounts even change depending on your character's race. You get the first mount at level 20, and the second at level 40.

MAGE PORTALS

Mages first learn the ability to Teleport themselves to significant cities. Later, mid-level Mages are able to open Portals that teleport everyone who interacts with them to a specific major city. As Mages level, they learn how to access even more cities (with their race's capital being the first option).

WARLOCK SUMMONS

At Level 20, warlocks learn the Ritual of Summoning. The warlock and two other players can use the spell to summon another player to the warlock from anywhere in the world. This spell is frequently used to bring group members to the same location. Note that the Ritual of Summoning can only be made with everyone being in the same group or raid. This doesn't work on people outside of your group.

SUMMONING STONES

Dungeons have stones that let people call their groupmates. It only takes two people at the stone to bring everyone else in the group to the proper location. You need to be at an appropriate level for the dungeon at hand; otherwise, this feature will not work.

BANKS AND AUCTION HOUSES

This section discusses your in-game money and how to use banks and auction houses. There's also an introduction to the in-game economy and how to buy and sell items from other players. Making money is not a key focus for new players, but it will become more important to you as you advance in the game.

MONEY

You carry your money in your Backpack at all times, and there's an extremely high limit on how much personal gold you can carry. Unless you're approaching a quarter of a million gold, it's not worth worrying about.

At early levels, you won't have much money, so you may be shocked by the cost of many items and what other players are willing to pay. However, the game offers you higher rewards as you complete more difficult quests and as you pursue new ways to earn money.

HERE'S A QUICK LIST OF A FEW WAYS TO EARN MONEY:

- Loot the corpses of humanoid enemies.
- Sell off your old Soulbound items or gray items to vendors.
- Sell items directly to other players.
- Sell items through the Auction House.
- Use your profession skills to collect or create items for sale.

You can make the most money using your Professions. Other players may have access to guilds with extensive treasuries, or they might play higher-level characters that are capable of earning hundreds of gold in a single play session. Thus, they're able to pay far more than you for the same amount of work. Use that to your advantage.

BANKS

Each major city has at least one bank. Talk to a city guard for help finding one. Inside are bankers with whom you can interact (right-click). Banks really function as vaults for storing items—not money. Using a bank is a way to free up your bag space and store items that you don't need on a moment-to-moment basis.

When you right-click on a banker, you open your personal vault. The first thing most people notice is that the bank vault is quite large. You have more personal space in there than you would with just your backpack and a few tiny bags. This gets even better!

With a bit of extra money, you can purchase bag slots for your bank vault. These increase in cost dramatically after your first few slots are unlocked, but it's still a wise way to spend money if you're running out of space.

Collect spare bags for the bank vault; taking away ones from your character is foolhardy because it reduces the amount of items you can carry around. Thus, it limits your income from looting and gathering! Always invest in high-quality bags. They pay for themselves better than many alternatives. They also make your life easier.

All banks are linked by their faction. So, even though you deposit your items in one bank, you can access them from any other bank.

GUILD VAULTS

Guilds have their own bank vaults. These groups store money and items to keep them accessible to their guild members. The Guild Master sets a list of permissions that control access to the guild items. Ask members of your guild for details.

AUCTION HOUSES

Auction houses are located in all major cities. Like banks, they are linked by faction. So, you can access the same auctions from any auction house in any city. There are also several neutral auction houses that serve both Horde and Alliance, but you'll need to be around level 40 to reach them.

The Auction Houses in World of Warcraft work very much like real-life online auction sites. You set up a timed auction with a minimum starting price that sells to the highest bidder; you can also set a buyout price that enables players to purchase the item immediately. And, if you find an item you want, you can place a bid or buyout the item instantly.

Right-clicking on any Auctioneer opens the auction interface. It has three tabs: Browse, Bids, and Auctions.

BROWSING

The Browse tab enables you to search through all current auctions. Because there are thousands of available items, you need to use specific criteria to narrow your search.

For example, suppose you're looking for a nice, new piece of Mail Armor. Using the category pane on the left hand side of the Auction House window, you can open a series of menus that can help refine your search. Once you're happy with the category of search, hit the 'Search' button to return a list of everything for sale in the auction house.

There are buttons along the top of the search results screen that allow you to sort the presented list of items by Rarity, Level required to use, Time left on the auction, the Seller, and the Current Bid. Use these to help narrow down your search for the item that is perfect for you.

If you know exactly what you're looking for, you can enter its name in the 'Name' field at the top of the auction house window. Again, a list of available items will appear in the search results pane. If you use your cursor to mouse over the icon for each item, the game will return detailed information about the item, so you can confirm it's the item you want, or can use.

There are additional filters for use in the Auction House window. The 'Level Range' boxes allow you to filter the results for the level range you enter. For example, a level 12 character may enter a level range from 10 to 12, ensuring they see only items they can use, and that they haven't outgrown. Finally, the 'Useable Items' box can be checked, filtering search results to display only items that your character can use.

BIDS

To make a bid, click on the item you want, enter your bid below, and click 'Bid' button. You won't need to stay online for your bid to remain active. Auctions can last for a very long time, so it's a good idea to go off and do other things. The Auction House mails you your items if you win the bid, so the system is quite simple.

The Bids Tab enables you to keep tabs on the status of these auctions. If you are outbid while you are online, you receive a message in your General chat log. If you've been offline for a while, check the status of these sales by opening the Bids Tab. If someone else is the highest bidder, their name appears in red. This gives you an opportunity to bid again if you wish.

BUYOUT

Using the buyout option works the same way except that you must meet the buyout price. Like other online options, the benefit is that you get the item right away, but you are likely to pay more when using this option.

Because it's final, the game asks you to confirm payment. Click Accept. As soon as the transaction is complete, you receive a mail flag on your mini-map, indicating that your auction item is already in your mailbox. Retrieve it as you would regular mail.

ALWAYS SELL WITH A BUYOUT PRICE

It's rare not to have a good reason to post items and give a buyout price. Sure, the sky is the limit when people are bidding against each other, but who knows if their bidding war will ever have enough time to meet the maximum value that one of the players would have paid.

Instead, figure out the best prices for your items and go for the throat. People get quite eager for the items they want, and having instant gratification at their fingertips is worth in-game money to them.

When you're uncertain of proper pricing, use the auction house itself or research the item online to see what it's selling for elsewhere. To search locally, act as if you're shopping for the exact item that you're about to sell. Use the Auction House to search for the item, then undercut your competition by offering the item for a tiny bit less (a single gold, or maybe even a few silver). Either way puts your item above theirs when players search for it!

AUCTIONS

To create an auction of your own, use the Auctions Tab. Start by left-clicking and dragging the designated item into the Auction Item slot. By default, the game enters a common Starting Price for the item. The given starting price may or may not work for your purposes, so feel free to change it. You can also change the duration of the auction and include a Buyout price. Notice the deposit fee. This goes to the auction house, and you cannot get it back. Once you've set up the parameters, click the 'Create Auction' button.

The item appears as an auction listing for your character. Regardless of whether your item sells, you don't have to do anything more. If the item sells, you will receive confirmation and payment through the mail. If your item doesn't sell, the Auction House mails the item back to you, minus their cut.

Neutral Auction Houses take a much higher cut of your final sale price, so they're brutal for high-end sales. The nice thing about them is that they allow for one of the only means of cross-faction exchanges of items.

USING THE TRADE CHANNEL

Using the Trade channel to buy and sell is a much less structured way to conduct business. The Trade channel is designed to discuss trade; you can get feedback about the price or availability of an item, and maybe make a purchase or sale.

A word of warning, bored players often use the Trade channel to discuss just about every topic under the sun, so be prepared to endure the din of the crowd.

Use this command line to speak in the Trade channel and then Shift and left-click your item:

/Trade Want to sell <Hold down Shift and left-click the item in question>That way, players can click the link for details. Likewise, if someone posts a link in the channel, you can click it to see the item's stats. You can do this for any sort of item, including one that you are seeking for a quest.

Most players use communication shorthand for buying and selling in the Trade channel. Here are a few of the most common abbreviations:

Abbreviation	What it Means
LF	Looking For
WTB	Want To Buy
WTS	Want To Sell
LFW	Looking For Work (Someone is offering their Professional services)
PST	Please Send tell (Please whisper to them privately to get more information or to haggle)

THE BLACK MARKET AUCTION HOUSE

In the swirling mists of Pandaria, hidden at the Tavern in the Mists, in the lofty heights of The Veiled Stair, Madam Goya runs the Black Market Auction House.

The Black Market is very different than other auction houses in the game. The Black Market offers rare and exotic items, unavailable to purchase anywhere else. It offers players the opportunity to buy items that normally would come with potentially hundreds of hours of game play, or being a member of the very best of the best guilds in the game, or just being lucky.

Madam Goya caters to every whim, offering mounts, companion pets, crafting recipes, and gear that will make you the talk of the town—for a price.

Players cannot create auctions at the Black Market, and there are no Buyout options, it's a cut-throat, winner takes all style bidding that will make most players reel at the prices these items will fetch, potentially hundreds of thousands of gold.

Items will appear for sale randomly, placed on the block by notable NPCs, many of whom have a story or two tied to them, more than enough to prick the interests of those players who want to delve the depths of the game's lore. Bidding at the Black Market, can be seen as the measure of a player's success, or perhaps as their undoing, in either case, Madam Goya graciously accepts their coin.

PROFESSIONS

Professions are additional skills for your character, most of which you can learn starting at level 5. Learning Professions is completely optional, but they add additional layers of interaction (and fun!) to your time in World of Warcraft. In addition, professions give statistical bonuses that can be very useful when you're trying to optimize your character's gear.

There are two categories of Professions: primary and secondary. Each character can choose only two primary Professions. You can select as many secondary Professions as you like. There are no class or race restrictions when it comes to choosing a Profession, but some races enjoy advantages for certain Professions.

Some primary Professions involve your character going into the world and looking for specific types of loot. These are called gathering Professions. You might be hunting for metal, animal skins, or herbs. Other Professions use these materials to create items, and they are known as crafting Professions.

Crafting Professions allow characters to produce items for others to use. You might be making permanent items, such as armor or weapons, or you might be invested in short-term goodies, like potions. Crafting Professions require a higher investment in money and time than gathering Professions.

Secondary Professions are specific in what they can do. Though more limited in scope than primary Professions, these are easier to pick up, master, and play around with.

PRIMARY PROFESSIONS

There are 11 primary Professions in the game. If you're interested in a certain Profession after reading the brief introductions that follow, there is more detail about each Profession, starting on page 418.

Profession		Type	What It Does
Alchemy		Crafting	Make potions/elixirs/flasks
Blacksmithing		Crafting	Craft mail/plate armor and weapons
Enchanting		Crafting	Improve equipment
Engineering		Crafting	Create gadgets, ranged weapons, bombs and other toys
Inscription		Crafting	Make Glyphs to augment characters
Jewelcrafting		Crafting	Create rings, trinkets, and gems to improve gear
Leatherworking		Crafting	Craft leather and mail armor/armor kits
Tailoring		Crafting	Craft cloth armor and bags
Herbalism		Gathering	Gather herbs
Mining		Gathering	Gather ore
Skinning		Gathering	Gather animal skins

IMPROVING PROFESSIONS

Practicing the Gathering Professions

To increase your skill in Herbalism, Mining, or Skinning, you must simply perform those gathering tasks again and again. Performing the actual task is just like looting: you right-click on the object. Herbs are found on the ground all over the world. Mining veins are usually along ridges or tucked into valleys. They're also plentiful inside caves. Skins are taken from many normal animals or monsters.

Most times you gather an item, your skill increases as shown in your General log. Eventually a given type of object "greys out." This means that you can't get points from them anymore (you can still gather them, though). You can tell this because the tag below the object appears in grey instead of green, yellow, orange, or red.

Items shown in red are too high to use. If you try to harvest it, the game lets you know what skill level you need to achieve to harvest the item. Raise your skill in that Profession and they will eventually be accessible.

Practicing the Crafting Professions

To practice the non-gathering Professions, click on the that Profession's icon from your Spellbook or your Action Bar. This opens a window that lists all the recipes you currently know in that Profession. Clicking on the individual recipe shows you all the ingredients required.

If you have all of the required ingredients, the number of times you can use that recipe is indicated beside the name. To make an item, click on the recipe to highlight it, input the number you want, and click Create. Your character automatically cycles through all of the creations in the queue, and you get any points gained in the process.

CRAFTING PROFESSIONS

Alchemy

Alchemists use herbs and oils to create potions, elixirs, and flasks with such effects as healing, mana regeneration, invisibility, speed, underwater breathing, and increased strength. The earliest focus in this profession are potions that restore health and mana.

Blacksmithing

Blacksmithing uses metal bars to create weaponry and both mail and plate armor. Blacksmiths need a Blacksmith Hammer and access to an anvil to create items. Many merchants have crafting items, and any of these will sell your character a Blacksmith Hammer for a trivial amount of money. Anvils are found in most towns and in all cities.

Enchanting

Enchanting uses magic recipes to permanently enhance armor and weapons with improvements such as increased stats. Enchantments require magical ingredients that result from Disenchanting other items. This is a rare case where a crafting Profession is also its own gathering Profession.

Enchanting is a difficult profession for a new player to skill up easily. Guilds often offer the support a person needs to become a higher-level Enchanter without crippling themselves financially. Tailoring is a good profession to take in addition to Enchanting, as it doesn't require a Gathering profession to make its goods, and the items made can then be Disenchanted.

Engineering

Engineering uses metal and stones to create a variety of useful and fun items, such as goggles, explosives, ranged weapon scopes, and mechanical animals. Creating different items with Engineering requires a handful of tools, most of which are created by the Engineer. One exception is a Blacksmithing Hammer, which is required for the creation of many Engineering items.

Engineering is helpful for dedicated solo and PvP characters. Most Professions won't make or break you in a fight, but being able to use decent explosives is another way to stun enemies and damage them. Anything like that is a big boost when you're fighting on your own.

Inscription

Scribes create glyphs, scrolls, cards, and other paper and book items. Glyphs are class-specific recipes that enhance characters' abilities. At beginning levels, scribes need a Virtuoso Inking Set, herbs, and parchments. Scribes automatically learn Milling, which turns herbs into pigments. They are then able to combine pigments to make inks.

Jewelcrafting

Jewelcrafting is the art of creating beautiful and powerful jewelry from metals and gems. There are a number of nifty recipes that are only meant to be used when a Jewelcrafter makes the items for themselves.

At higher levels of Jewelcrafting, you create gems that are slotted into higher-tier equipment. Anything that has red, yellow, blue, or meta slots is letting you know that there are empty spaces for gems there. Jewelcrafters take gems found with metal veins or gained through Prospecting and cut them into finished items that convey various bonuses.

Leatherworking

Leatherworking uses hides and skins to create leather and mail armor, armor kits, and a few other items. Many early Leatherworking items require you to purchase materials from Trade vendors, but you won't need to worry about any required tools for making items.

Tailoring

Tailoring is the weaving and sewing of cloth into armor, shirts, bags, and other items. Cloth is available as loot drops from humanoid enemies. Almost all items require silks, which are loot drops from spiders.

GATHERING PROFESSIONS

Herbalism

Herbalism is the harvesting of herbs from plants. Herbs also occasionally drop from enemies and some enemies can be harvested once they are killed (usually ones that are affiliated with nature).

Mining

Mining is the collection of minerals and ore from natural deposits all over Azeroth. Mining is simple and inexpensive, as the only tool required is a Mining Pick (there are a few weapons that also serve as a mining pick, so read their descriptions carefully). Metal is most often found in hilly or mountainous regions.

Skinning

Skinning is the act of removing leather and hides from animal corpses. Skinning is simple, inexpensive, and requires only a Skinning Knife. Mousing over an enemy corpse indicates whether it is "skinnable." You can skin your own kills after looting them. In addition, you can skin other people's kills if they loot their targets and leave. It's good to wait a second before doing this in case the other person is also a Skinner and is planning on coming back. You don't want to steal anyone else's work!

SECONDARY PROFESSIONS

There are four secondary Professions in the game, and you can acquire as many of them as you wish. There is no reason not to take all four and to raise them whenever you have the time to spare.

Archeology

Archeology allows players to recover fragments of artifacts from various parts of the world. You turn on artifact tracking (which can be used in concert with tracking for other gathering Professions). Look for special areas within each region and use Surveying to uncover the fragments that are assembled into finished pieces.

Cooking

Cooking uses many of the ingredients you receive as loot to create food for you and your comrades. Certain recipes create food that includes temporary buffs, such as Well Fed, which increases your character's stats.

First Aid

First Aid enables you to create bandages for restoring health and antidotes to remove poison. First Aid is most valuable for classes without a healing ability, but everyone benefits from First Aid. Healers can use bandages for times when they're out of mana or are silenced. Bandages are created from cloth drops in the game.

Fishing

With Fishing, you catch fish and you may also catch other marine life, junk, or treasure. To fish, you need a Fishing Pole. Fish are found in any sufficiently deep pool of water (even inside the major cities!) and many types of fish are often found in schools.

CUSTOMIZING THE GAME INTERFACE

After playing the game for a while, you may want to adjust some of the options in the game interface to make certain functions faster or more convenient for you.

The World of Warcraft interface is highly adjustable, so this chapter doesn't try to cover every way in which you can customize the game. Instead, it lists some commonly used options that may be helpful to new players.

Using Auto Loot

Instead of manually clicking on every piece of loot to send it to your Backpack, you can auto-loot your corpses, which is much faster:

1. Press Esc to open the Game menu.
2. Click Interface, and click Controls.
3. Change the Auto Loot options as you see fit.
4. Click Okay when you're done.

In the Auto Loot options, you have several choices. If you check Auto Loot, you only need to right-click to automatically send all loot to your Backpack. The other options are better if you'd like to peruse loot more thoroughly before grabbing any of it.

Open & Close Bags Quickly

b = Open or close all bags simultaneously.

Shift + B = Open or close Backpack.

F12 = Open or close Backpack.

F8, F9, F10, F11 = Use to open or close other bags individually.

Change the Resolution of WoW

1. Press Esc to open the Game Menu.
2. Click System.
3. Select Graphics.
4. Under the Resolution pulldown, click the right one for your monitor.
5. Click Okay.

If the game isn't running quickly enough for your tastes, this is the single fastest way to improve your performance. Lower your resolution and see if that helps the situation.

There are also many other graphical options as well. Try changing these to make the game faster or more attractive. If you don't know what everything else does, play around with the bar in the middle of the Graphics window until you have speeds that suit your interests. Click the Recommended button at the bottom left of the Graphics menu to let the game choose the settings for your computer.

When in doubt, speed is better than graphical quality. Jitters, poor frame rates, and other problems with speed are insidious. They can ruin your gaming experience without it even being obvious that they are at fault.

Turn Off Beginner Tutorials

1. Press Esc to open the Game menu.
2. Click Interface, and click Help.
3. Unclick Tutorials.
4. Click Okay.

This kills the pop-ups that dominate the early experience with the game. You can turn these off if you feel comfortable with World of Warcraft.

If the pop-ups are something you want and that you'd like to see again, you can reset them here, and the game will act like you're coming back for the first time.

Access Action Bars

Shift+1 = Action bar 1

Shift+2 = Action bar 2

Shift+3 = Action bar 3

Shift+4 = Action bar 4

Shift+5 = Action bar 5

Shift+6 = Action bar 6

Once you know where your actions are located, this is much faster than switching through multiple Action Bars to get where you need. Jumping from bar one to bar five is just as easy to going from one to two! In addition, keyboard shortcuts are almost always superior to using mouse commands on the interface.

Display Action Bars

Instead of accessing other Action Bars by pressing Shift+2, Shift+3, Shift+4, Shift+5, and Shift+6, you can permanently display other Action Bars on your screen:

1. Press Esc to open the Game menu.

2. Click Interface, and click ActionBars.

3. You have the option to display as many as four additional action bars in different places on-screen.

4. Click Okay.

Right Bar corresponds to action bar 3.

Right Bar 2 corresponds to action bar action bar 4.

Bottom Right Bar corresponds to action bar 5.

Bottom Left Bar corresponds to action bar 6.

Though at first your screen seems somewhat more cluttered to have these up all the time, you soon find that it's a gift from the heavens. Having all your abilities onscreen at all times ensures that you know how all of your cooldowns are going! It's also wonderful for crafting; you can set your Profession abilities off to one side, away from your regular combat abilities, but still have access to them when you need them.

Lock Action Bars

This prevents you from accidentally dragging an icon out of an action bar:

1. Press Esc to open the Game menu.

2. Click Interface, and click ActionBars.

3. Check Lock ActionBars.

4. Click Okay.

When you want to reconfigure your Action Bars easily, uncheck Lock Action Bars. If you're truly uncomfortable with keyboard hotkeys, this is essential. It keeps you from accidentally removing your ability instead of using it!

Note that if you want to move a single ability, hold Shift while clicking on the icon you want to move. If you drop it into a spot which already has an icon, click that location but continue to hold Shift. You automatically pick up the now displaced icon and can place it elsewhere. This will be on by default, but you may need to change it or confirm that it's on.

Auto Self Cast

By selecting this, you tell the game to cast positive spells on your character unless you have another, allied character targeted first. Thus, you can heal yourself even during a fight without having to stop, select yourself, and then cast the spell or cast the spell and hit F1. This way is faster than either of those alternatives.

1. Press Esc to open the Game Menu.

2. Click Interface, and click Combat.

3. Check Auto Self Cast.

4. Click Okay.

This defaults to on, but when grouping, you may want to turn off this option to avoid mistakes. The Self Cast Key defaults to Alt, but can be changed to Ctrl or Shift.

Display Cast Bars for Targets

This option shows the channeling bars for enemy casters. Watching this may help you interrupt their timed spells (although if you see a gray shield on the cast bar, you can't interrupt the spell). It lets you see when to use your interruption abilities. Time those attacks so that the enemies waste effort on a spell only to have it countered at the last possible moment. This is toggled on by default.

1. Press Esc to open the Game Menu.

2. Click Interface, and click Combat.

3. Check Cast Bars On Targets.

4. Click Okay.

Customize Chat Logs

There are many tiny changes you can make to the way your chat system presents information. Right-click on your chat window's tabs to begin this process. You can change the size of the font. You can define which colors appear from any source of information. You can also change the background color and intensity of the window itself. This is extremely useful for people who have trouble reading the text; darken the window to make it clearer all the time instead of needing to highlight it when you want to read.

Play around with this system as much as you want. You can't really break anything. If the windows end up being too strange, simply "reset" them from the same menu and they're back where they started.

Combat Text Options

You can change the Combat Text options so that you see more on-screen text showing what's happening during combat:

1. Press Esc to open the Game Menu.
2. Click Interface, and click Floating Combat Text.
3. Check Damage to see the damage you deal, and check any other options you wish to see during combat
   - Reactive Spells & Abilities is a good reminder for players of when specific spells are ready.
   - You may need to experiment to see which features help you and which get in your way.
4. Click Okay.

Using Key Bindings

The Key Bindings option serves two purposes:

A reminder of shortcut keys already in the game.

You can map your own shortcuts keys, if you wish.

1. Press Esc to open the Game Menu.
2. Click Key Bindings. A scrollable window opens, indicating all the keys that already have shortcuts listed in white.
3. To set up a new shortcut, click the Command you want to tie to a specific key. For example, The Talent Pane has a keyboard shortcut ("n"), but the Glyphs Pane does not. Scroll down to Interface Panel Functions, and click Toggle Glyphs.
4. Choose the key you want to bind it to. If that key is already bound, like G is, a red notification appears at the bottom of the menu. You can always reset the Key Bindings to default if you need to.
5. Click Okay.

These bindings aren't limited to your keyboard! You can assign functions to your mouse or other input devices as well.

OTHER SHORTCUTS

Command	Effect
Press X	Sit or Stand
Press Z	Unsheathe or Sheathe Your Weapon(s)
Shift+P	Open Window for All Mounts and Pets
Press V	Show red nameplates and health bars directly over your target in combat and nearby creatures.
Right-click a buff	Remove any positive buff on self
Shift+I	Open Pet's Spellbook
Esc	Close an open window
Alt+Z	Turn Off Game Interface
PrintScreen	Capture Screenshot (Screenshots are automatically saved in the World of Warcraft/Screenshots directory.)

MACROS

The base game already has many options to consider, but you might want even more once you understand everything. The Macro system is in place to help you find the perfect WoW experience.

Macros let you trigger abilities in a more complex manner. You have access to any command in the game through this, and you can even chain multiple commands together. This system is found inside the Game menu. Hit the Escape key and select Macros to see what it's all about.

MAKING A MACRO

You can make character-specific Macros or you can make ones that are available to all characters on your account. There are thousands of ideas floating around for good Macros, so one of the best to find these is to hunt around class message boards and see what other people have made.

You can also fool around on your own. Click New, select an icon for your Macro and a name for it, and then type in commands. When you're done, drag the Macro onto an valid action bar slot and then you can use the Macro like any normal ability.

Standard slash commands work just fine in Macros. For example:

/say /party /dance /flirt

However, you can also use commands that you wouldn't normally type in. /cast is the most common one. This lets you trigger abilities through the Macro system!

Think of the uses for this! Imagine that you're a Rogue that is about to Sap a target. You want everyone in the group to know that you're doing this. Try the following Macro.

/cast sap

/p Sapping %t

This Macro uses Sap on the target you currently have selected. It then displays for your group that you are Sapping the monster (and the actual name of that monster will be displayed).

To avoid having to type in ability names, open your Spellbook and shift + left-click the ability while your Macro is open. This automatically fills in the /cast part of the Macro with the ability in question. It's that easy.

You might wonder, "Will this work with items too?"

Try it! Shift-click an item in your backpack or bags while the Macro system is open. The command that appears is /use, but, yes, this works just like the cast system. You can have a Macro trigger your goodies, so long as you have them in your possession when you use the Macro.

This is only the tip of the iceberg with Macros. Now that you know what to look for, you're bound to find a wealth of awesome ideas that are specific to your class or playstyle.

JUST FOR FUN

This chapter lists many of the "extras" that you can do in World of Warcraft. Some of these activities will get you in-game rewards, but most are for fun and socializing.

GET A HAIRCUT

Several major cities offer Barbershop services. All races and genders have the option for a makeover for a small fee. Features you can change include hair color, hair style, facial hair, horns, piercings, tattoos, and undead parts.

SOCIALIZE

There are always other players with whom you can chat, exchange items, inspect their gear, or check out their pets and mounts.

SEND PEOPLE GIFTS

If you want to remember a friend's birthday or send a player a thank you gift, here are some fun items you can purchase:

- Fireworks in Ironforge
- Wine & Flowers in Stormwind
- Flowers in Thunder Bluff

USE TRAINING DUMMIES

Training Dummies are mechanical NPCs that you can use for target practice. There are training dummies of different levels in all major cities.

COMPANION PETS & PET BATTLES

Companion pets, as opposed to hunter pets, are available to all classes in the game. For the most part, companion pets have no effect on gameplay, but Pet Battles have been added for Mists of Pandaria.

By going to a Battle Pet Trainer, you can learn how to pit your pets against others' pets, or face wild pets. You get Achievements as you collect more pets and as you win more battles. There are a variety of ways to collect companion pets—from purchasing them outright to gaining them as quest rewards to capturing wild pets after weakening them in a fight. Some professions are capable of creating pets, and you can find more companions by completing Achivements, or by searching for enemies that drop pets on rare occasions.

The following tables show which pets are available for purchase throughout the worlds of Azeroth and Draenor.

COMMON HORDE PETS

Pet	Location
Undercity Cockroach	Undercity
Snakes	Orgrimmar
Prairie Dog	Thunder Bluff
Dragonhawk Hatchling	Eversong Woods, Fairbreeze Village

COMMON ALLIANCE PETS

Pet	Location
Cats	Elwynn Forest, Southeast of Stormwind
Snowshoe Rabbit	Dun Morogh, Amberstill Ranch
Owls	Darnassus
Moths	The Exodar

OTHER PURCHASABLE PETS

Pet	Location
Frogs	Darkmoon Faire
Birds	The Cape of Stranglethorn, Booty Bay
Magical Creatures	Netherstorm, The Stormspire

CELEBRATE IN-GAME HOLIDAYS

The game offers numerous seasonal holidays with accompanying events, including quests, games, gifts, costumes, and holiday food. Holidays last for varying lengths of time, so check your in-game calendar regularly so you don't miss out!

AZEROTH HOLIDAY CALENDAR

Time of Year	Event
January	New Year's Day
Late Winter	Lunar Festival
February	Love Is in the Air
Spring	Noblegarden
Late Spring	Children's Week
June	Midsummer Fire Festival
September	Harvest Festival
	Pirate's Day
Fall	Brewfest
October	Hallow's End
November	Day of the Dead
	Pilgrim's Bounty
December	Feast of Winter Veil
	New Year's Eve

ATTEND IN-GAME EVENTS

The Darkmoon Faire opens monthly on its own island. The Darkmoon Faire offers unique vendors, games, and opportunities for prizes. Players can earn Darkmoon tickets by completing a quest or by bringing requested items to the carnival workers.

The Stranglethorn Fishing Extravaganza is a weekly fishing contest in the Stranglethorn region. This is predominantly a solo activity for players who have passed Level 30. When you reach Northrend around level 80, there's another fishing contest run by the Kalu'ak.

The Gurubashi Arena Booty Run is a free-for-all battle experience in Stranglethorn Vale. Go to the arena every three hours when the call goes out throughout the zone. Everyone who attends is flagged for PvP, and the winner gets a prize.

Call To Arms is a series of weekly Battleground challenges for players interested in PvP combat. The featured Battleground yields more rewards during this period, and there are usually extra players signing up, meaning that matches are buzzing all day and night.

GO FISHING

You can fish anywhere in the game, but what you catch depends on your fishing skill. Even the most unlikely bodies of water can yield fish and help increase your skill level.

Bait and lures are available from Trade Supply vendors all over Azeroth. Fishing Trainers offer lures, but they may also have better Fishing Poles that increase your skill further.

HUNT FOR ACHIEVEMENTS

Achievement hunting is incredibly addictive, especially for a certain type of player. There are people who look through the list each day, pick out a few things to try for, and make it all happen.

And why not? You don't need to wait for the level cap to do this. Sometimes it seems strange to invest time in something that doesn't improve the strength of your character, but is that really important? You can level whenever you want, and it doesn't take that long to hit the cap. Instead, the happiest people seem to be those who set their own goals and have a great time meeting them.

Try this out. You too could become an achievement hunter.

PLAYER VERSUS PLAYER BATTLES

Up to this point, PvP has been mentioned only in passing. There are two reasons for that. First, World PvP generally doesn't get extremely competitive until you're around level 20. Even on PvP servers, the zones up to level 20 are controlled by one side or the other so you're free to ignore players from the opposite faction as you see fit. Second, PvP is an advanced and incredibly deep topic that is covered later in this guide. However, that doesn't mean PvP is always serious business.

Open World PvP

Sometimes, the most fun in PvP comes from open-world PvP, which offers some of the best and most interesting fights in the game. There isn't a limit on numbers or sides. There isn't a necessity for fairness or timers. Just form a group or raid, and choose somewhere to attack. Fight, laugh, lose, regroup, and watch as more people join both sides of the engagement. These attacks can last for hours.

"What if I'm on a PvE or RP server?" you ask. That's not a big hindrance. Flag yourself for PvP combat and go into an area with players from the enemy faction. Once one of them will take the bait, they'll be flagged afterward, whether you win or lose. Encourage more of your own people to join. More of theirs will too, and soon it'll be just like a PvP server, for a while at least.

ONLINE RESOURCES

If you're looking for more help, or want to know how to restrict certain aspects of the game so your children can play, try the main website for World of Warcraft (us.battle.net/wow). From the home page, you can choose to visit its many community forums, manage your account (including setting Parental Controls), and get news updates relevant to the game in its current state and what the World of Warcraft team is working on for future patches and expansions.

COMMUNITY FORUMS

Forums are online bulletin boards where players can ask questions, brag, help other players, and read updates from Blizzard staffers. Using forums is like mining for gold: There's a plenty of valuable information in forums, but you must wade through many random topics to find it.

Some of the most helpful forums for new players are Class, Realm, Profession Discussion, and Quest Discussion. With some patience, you should find a great deal of assistance.

REMOTE AUCTION HOUSE

If you have fun "playing the Auction House," you can now access your realm's Auction House from your web browser or mobile device. Anyone can browse the Auction House for free, or subscribe to the premium service which allows you to bid on and buy out auctions with real-time results, create auctions from items in your bags, bank, or mailbox, and collect gold earned in your auctions.

PARENTAL CONTROLS

Blizzard Entertainment believes that real-world priorities such as homework, chores, and family dinner should take precedence over entertainment. Their Parental Controls provide parents and guardians with easy-to-use tools to set up rules for World of Warcraft play time and manage access to Blizzard Entertainment games in a way that fits your family's situation.

You can set Play-Time Limits, a schedule, and even have weekly reports sent to your e-mail account that provides information about the times your child was playing the game, and much more. All these options are found on the battle.net website (www.battle.net) under your account settings.

AUTHENTICATOR

If you're worried about your account being compromised, Blizzard offers another layer of protection from unauthorized access. A Blizzard Authenticator is an additional layer of security for your Battle.net account. There are multiple types of Authenticators, but they all provide the same security. The Battle.net Authenticator provides you with a unique code that is constantly changing in addition to your regular password. For more information, check the Account Security section in the Services section on World of Warcraft website.

CHARACTER SERVICES

If you want to change something about your character (and a trip to a barber in one of the major cities won't do the trick), Blizzard offers other options to you. Before you decide to use any of the following services, read the helpful FAQs on Blizzard's website for more information.

Appearance Change

Apperance Change, or Character Re-Customiation, is an option inherent in Faction and Race Changes, but if you want to change your character model or gender (remember, you can change your character's look with a visit to the barber shop!) without changing your character's race, select Appearance Change. This service lets you change your character's gender, face, hair and skin color, hairstyle, name, and other cosmetic features determined by their race and gender combination.

Character Transfer

There are two types of character transfers. If you start on one realm, but find that you have friends playing on another realm, you have the option to transfer a character to the other realm. In rare instances, usually when a realm's population grows too large, you may be able to transfer a character at no charge. The second type of character transfer involves a move between World of Warcraft accounts. There are many restrictions for this type of transfer.

Faction Change

If you want to see what life is like on the other side, you can change your character's faction from Horde to Alliance, or Alliance to Horde. As a part of the Faction Change, you must select a new race and customize your character's look.

Name Change

Changing your character's name is an option included in some of the other services, but if your character's name is the only thing you wish to change, this service is the one you should choose.

Race Change

If you want to try out a new race which is a part of your current faction, select the Race Change option. The full range of customization options offered by the Character Re-Customization service is included as well.

PAID SERVICES

Each Character Service has a cost associated with it. For more information about fees, visit us.battle.net/wow.

THE BLIZZARD STORE

The Blizzard Store offers a few items for sale that appear in World of Warcraft. Currently, you can buy a number of vanity pets, and mounts including the Celestial Steed, Winged Guardian, and Heart of the Aspects.

ARMORY

The World of Warcraft Armory is a great way to learn more about improving your character. You can look up any active characters on the Armory and see what equipment they use, how they spend their talent points, where you can find upgrades for your gear, and so on. Visit the Armory at us.battle.net/wow (you can search for characters at the top right of the page) for more information.

FIND ADDITIONAL RESOURCES

BradyGames strategy guides are a great source for information and fun ideas, but WoW is too big to put into any single book or even a group of books. There are thousands and thousands of sites with WoW information. Beyond the main forums for the game there are guild sites, fan sites, and millions of individual players to talk to.

Don't play this like it's a solo game. It isn't! There are so many knowledgeable people out there who enjoy sharing their ideas. Talk to people in game. Read the forums. Look up macros, tactics, questions, and answers as well. If you want to know what to craft or where to find a reagent, entire recipe lists are available. If you have trouble with a quest, don't drop it. Find out if other people have had trouble to. Go online and search with the exact quest name. Pretty much every single quest will pop up something, and usually there is information there that helps you get around problems.

Be eager in your quest for knowledge. None of the best players on your server got there by themselves. It's impossible to know everything about every class and situation. Even people who only play one class are bound to miss a few ideas.

GLOSSARY

The following is a list of important in-game terms and abbreviations. Not all of these are official terms used by Blizzard, but there's a good chance you'll see them used by other players fairly often. You don't need to memorize this list, but it's a handy reference in case you encounter an unfamiliar word or phrase.

A

Add
An extra monster that has joined an existing battle.

Alt
A character on your account other than your main character. A secondary character.

AoE or AE
Area of Effect. Often used to talk about abilities that damage enemies in groups.

AFK
Away From Keyboard. Used to show that the player isn't at their computer. When you see a character's name preceded by <Away>, that person is not actively playing the game.

Aggro
A monster's aggressive attention. "That Orc is aggroing on you. Look out!"

Aggro Radius
The radius around the monsters that determines their aggression. You will be attacked if you step within their aggro radius.

AGI
Agility. A character statistic that controls defensive aspects of play and damage for some classes.

AH
Auction House. A place where items are bought and sold between players.

Avatar
Your character and, thus, your representation in the game.

B

BG
Battleground. This is a place for organized PvP combat.

Buff
A beneficial spell cast on a player or monster.

C

Caster
A character or monster that uses spells, often at range.

Cheese
To exploit an imbalance in the game.

Combat Pets
A creature controlled by a player that assists during combat.

Creep
An older gaming term for a monster

Critters
Creatures that aren't a threat to a player. These include deer, bunnies, and other fauna that won't aggro on anyone.

Crowd Control (CC)
Any ability that temporarily removes an enemy from a battle. Examples are Sap, Polymorph, and Hex.

D

DD
Direct Damage. This is a spell that does all of its damage in one hit rather than spreading its damage over time.

Detaunt
Related to aggro. Abilities of this type throw aggro off of a character and force it onto someone/something else.

DMG
Short for damage.

DoT
Damage Over Time. This often refers to an effect that "ticks" every few seconds, applying damage each time there is a tick.

DPS
Damage Per Second. This is a concept that is used to universally evaluate weapons and spells of different speeds.

Debuff
A negative spell cast on a unit that makes it less powerful.

E

Elite
Monsters with a gold dragon around their icons are elite; they have more health, greater damage output, and sometimes have special abilities.

Experience (XP/EXP)
A stat that rises from exploring, killing monsters, and completing quests. Each tier of experience grants characters a higher level and, thus, more power.

F

FH
Full Health.

FM
Full Mana.

FTL
For The Lose or For The Loss. An Internet or sports term that implies that a strategy, concept, or action is weak.

FTW
For The Win. This means that something is powerful or useful.

G

Gank
To grossly overpower a target and exploit (or decimate) it. "I was fighting a monster and a level 85 Rogue ganked me."

GG
Good Game. Most often used after a battleground or arena match to thank other players for contributing or when someone is about to log off.

GM
Game Master. Someone employed by Blizzard Entertainment to assist and help players.

Griefer
A person who purposely tries to annoy or anger other players.

Grinding
To repeat any activity to achieve a conclusion through sheer investment of time. "I'll keep fighting these Boars to grind out this level." or "I'm grinding reputation with Orgrimmar."

Group
A team of up to five characters that join together to take on a dungeon or a particularly tricky quest.

H

HP
Hit Points or Health. This is a measure of a character's survivability.

I

Incoming (INC)
This means an attack is imminent.

Instancing
A copy of an area that is only shared by a specific group. The world is not instanced. Dungeons, raids, Scenarios, and battlegrounds have many copies. These are instances.

INT
Intellect. A character statistic that controls the amount of Mana and efficacy of spells.

K

Kiting
A style of combat in which a player continually stays out of the combat range of an enemy, usually by running away from it, while simultaneously causing damage to it.

KOS
Kill on Sight. Some NPCs will rush forward and attack players of a different faction the moment they see them. Example: Alliance guards toward Horde players.

KS
Kill Steal. Attempting to hit a monster and thus ensure that you or your group gets to loot it even though another person/group is about to attack the same target or is already attacking the same target.

L

LFG
Looking For a Group.

LFM
Looking For More. This implies than an existing group has open slots and wants to get more people before starting a quest/dungeon run.

Log
When you log off; disconnect from the game.

LOL
Laughing Out Loud. An Internet term expressing humor.

LOM
Low on Mana. This is a warning from casters that they don't have much healing or damage left to contribute to a fight.

LOS
Line of Sight. Often used as a warning. "Break LOS" means that you should get your character behind cover to avoid a target's attention or attacks.

Loot
To take the treasure from a monster that has been killed or from a chest. The term also refers to the treasure gained in this action.

LVL
Level. A measure of a character's power.

M

MMORPG
Massive Multiplayer Online Role-Playing Game

Mob
An old programming acronym of "Mobile Object Block." Mobs are computer-controlled characters (usually monsters) in the game.

Mount
A summoned, rideable creature. Ground mounts are available early in the game and can be ridden around many areas. Flying mounts are gained at higher level, and they allow players to soar above the world. All of these increase player speed.

MA
Main Assist. A member of a group assigned to select the target for the damage dealers in a group to attack at the same time.

MT
Main Tank. A member of a group that protects the others by holding the monster's attention (their "aggro").

N

Named
A special monster that is usually stronger than surrounding monsters, with possible special abilities and item drops.

NBG
Need Before Greed. This is a loot system. With this set, only people that need an item as an upgrade will roll dice to see who gets it.

Nerf
To downgrade, to be made softer, or make less effective.

Newbie
A new player.

Newb/Noob
Short for Newbie, but more often used as a pejorative.

Ninja
To try to loot an item without other players knowing or paying attention. Such actions are considered extremely rude.

NP
No Problem.

NPC
An in-game person that is controlled by the server, such as a quest giver.

O

OOM
Out of Mana. This marks the end of healing or damage output from a caster.

P

Pat
A patrolling monster. This may be issued as a warning that said creature is coming your way. "PAT!"

PC
Player-controlled Character.

Pet
A creature (NPC) controlled by a player such as a Wolf, Infernal, and so on. Non-combat pets, like kittens or penguins, do not affect combat but are instead summoned to add flavor to a character or used in Pet Battles.

PK
Player Kill or a Player Killer. More of a term for open-world PvP interactions.

POP/Repop   Contraction of "Repopulation." This is a warning that monsters are returning to an area after being slain.

Proc
An effect that is randomly triggered from time to time based on another action taken by a character.

PST
Please Send Tell. Indicates that the person wants to hear back regarding a certain sale or issue.

Puller
A character that pulls monsters for the party, controlling the way a battle initiates.

Pulling
The act of heading out, getting aggro from a monster, and bringing the fight back to a party.

PvE
Player vs. Environment. Combat between players and computer-controlled opponents.

PvP
Player vs. Player. Competition between players that can be as small as a duel or as large as 80 or more players.

R

Raid
A congregation of player groups that bands together for extremely challenging content or PvP situations.

Res/Rez
Short for "Resurrect." This refers to any spell or ability that can bring a character back to life. "I need a rez. I went AFK and something killed me."

Respawn
The same as "**Pop/Repop**." A monster can return to the world after being killed. The act of returning is called respawning. The creature itself may also be referred to as a respawn.

Rest
Characters accrue rested bonus while their player is out of the game. This happens when someone logs their character out while inside an inn or within the boundaries of a city. This adds bonus experience during subsequent play.

Roll
This means that you should roll a random number to determine who has the right to get an item. /roll generates a number between 1 and 100. The highest roll would win something.

Root
To trap a target in place using a spell or ability.

RP
Role Play. To interact with the game and players as though you are your character, as though you are in a theatre performance.

RPing
Role Playing. See "**RP**."

S

Shard
Disenchant an item, often while in a group. Rare quality items (which most dungeon bosses drop) are turned into shards of different types when disenchanted. Thus, instead of saying, "I'll disenchant this item," players began saying "If no one wants this item, I can shard it."

SPI
Spirit. A character statistic that influences mana regeneration.

STA
Stamina. A character statstic that determines the health (HP) of a character.

Stack
Stack has a few meanings. In your bags, some identical items can placed (stacked) in a single inventory slot to conserve space. In boss encounters, players often group up (stack) on a single spot during a special attack from a boss.

STR
Strength. A character statistic that influences damage for many melee characters.

T

Tank
A character that takes damage and holds monsters' attention to protect others.

Tap
The first point of damage a monster takes locks its future loot to the character that dealt said damage. This act is called tapping. Creatures that are tapped have their bars go grey so other people know not to mess with them.

Taunt
Related to aggro. Abilities of this type pull aggro off of a target and bring it back to a tank.

Threat
This measures how much a monster wants to kill each member of a group engaged in a fight. The person with the highest threat usually keeps the monster's aggro.

Train
Visiting your class trainer to learn new abilities.

Twink
A low-level character with the absolutely best gear, often because of guild assistance or money/gear sent down by a higher-level character played by the same person.

TY
Thank You.

U

Uber
German slang for "super." This is a common gamer term for something that is impressive.

V

Vendor Trash
An item that only a vendor/merchant would buy.

W

WoW
World of Warcraft.

WTB
Want to Buy. Shorthand for saying that someone is looking to purchase something, often listing their intentions afterward.

WTS
Want to Sell. Shorthand for saying that someone has something to sell, often listing their goods afterward.

Y

YW
You're Welcome.

Choosing Your Character's Race

There are 13 races in the game: six for the Alliance, six for the Horde and one race that can choose either side. Keep in mind that each race has limitations on available classes.

Each race has innate benefits (known as Racial Abilities) that are unique to that race. These are abilities you have in addition to what you get from choosing your class.

FACTIONS

The race you choose determines whether you will be part of the Alliance or the Horde. If you have friends in the game with whom you want to play, you need to choose the same faction if you want to work together in the game. There are no "good" or "bad" sides in this conflict. Both factions have rich storylines and compelling motives.

Horde Races

Though their ways are sometimes brutal and warlike, some of the leaders of the Horde exemplify honor and courage. The various races of the Horde have struggled to free themselves from demonic tyranny, a mindless plague, and countless wars.

Pandaren Race

The enigmatic Pandaren have long been a mystery to the other races of Azeroth. For ten thousand years, they lived in isolation in their mist-shrouded homeland, staying away from the conflicts of the world of Azeroth. Now the outside world has come to the continent of Pandaria and the Wandering Isle, giving each Pandaren the option of which faction they wish to join.

Alliance Races

The Alliance gives the appearance of being on the side of righteousness and many of its leaders are good people. However, they are also the source of hypocrisy and considerable lawlessness. The destruction left behind by the Gnomes' scientific mistakes, Dwarven civil wars, and Human misconduct have scarred much of the Eastern Kingdoms.

STARTING OUT WITH FRIENDS

Each race has its own home region, so the race you choose determines where you start in the game. If you and a friend want to start the game together, you must choose the same race so that you start at the same location.

If you and your friend can't agree on the same race, it won't take long to reach the major hubs of the game where you can join up. As a result, it's best to play the exact character you want, even if it means waiting to see your buddies a little bit longer.

THE MOST IMPORTANT FACTOR

It's not uncommon to see that one race might be better suited to the class that you've chosen compared with another, but what if that isn't the race that you had your heart set on? The best thing to do is ignore Racial Abilities if you have any strong preference for a specific race. Bonding with your character is a real thing. Choosing a race that you don't want to play is something that grates on you over time. Don't let that happen. Enjoy your time in the game. In the end, stats aren't a big deal; you won't flounder just because you picked a "weaker" race to go with your class. None of the races are especially overpowered or underpowered. Their bonuses are more of a tiny perk. They help, but they never make or break a class.

DRAENEI

The Draenei are an intelligent and spiritual race who no longer have a homeworld of their own. They fled both their home planet of Argus and then Outland as well. The Legion, a force of horrible evil, has dogged their efforts at every turn. Currently, the Draenei have crash landed on Azeroth in their capital ship (*The Exodar*). Though their ship's engines have been sabotaged, they are ready and willing to continue the battle against evil.

Draenei are dedicated to magic and Holy Light. The Draenei also have a spiritual affinity with the Naaru, energy beings who serve the Holy Light.

Draenei are 7-8 feet tall, with long tails and bipedal hooves. Females have horns of varying shapes and sizes. Males have unique cranial and facial features.

Start location: Ammen Vale in Azuremyst Isle.

RACIAL ABILITIES

GEMCUTTING

 Jewelcrafting skill (a crafting Profession) increased by 10.

GIFT OF THE NAARU

Heals the target for 20% of the caster's total health over 15 sec.

HEROIC PRESENCE

Increases your chance to hit with all spells and attacks by 1%.

SHADOW RESISTANCE

 Reduces Shadow damage taken by 1%.

Home city: The Exodar.

Elekks, the Draenei Racial Mount.

AVAILABLE CLASSES

DEATH KNIGHT DRUID HUNTER MAGE MONK PALADIN PRIEST ROGUE SHAMAN WARLOCK WARRIOR

YOUR FIRST DAY AS A
DRAENEI

Despite being a peaceful race that believes in following the Light, the Draenei had long known little else besides war and hiding when they decided to flee in *The Exodar*, hoping to find new allies to fight beside them against the Burning Legion. With the crash of the great ship, it seemed that all hope was lost. However, the Draenei emerged from the wreckage to find themselves on a remote group of islands off the western coast of Kalimdor. Claiming this mostly unpopulated land as their new home, the Draenei soon explored and established camps over Azuremyst and Bloodmyst Isles. Though you are inexperienced, it is up to you to help your people as best you can. Your path may one day take you across the world, but for now your duty begins with securing the safety of your new home.

1	Megelon
2	The Crash Site
3	Ammen Fields
4	Silverline Lake
5	Nestlewood Hills
6	Tolaan
7	Aeun

THE SACRED GROVE

CRASH SITE

AMMEN FIELDS

NESTLEWOOD THICKET

SILVERLINE LAKE

NESTLEWOOD HILLS

SHADOW RIDGE

CRASH SITE

As you come back to consciousness, Megelon is glad to see that **You Survived** the crash while so many did not. He sends you to speak with Proenitus who is waiting for you at the bottom of the hill.

With all the injured from the crash, the Draenei supply of healing crystals is quickly becoming depleted. The only local substitute is the blood of the indigenous vale moths. Proenitus needs your help with **Replenishing the Healing Crystals**. He asks you to bring him vials of this precious blood so the healing can continue. The Vale Moths are found all around the Crash Site, in almost any direction.

GIFT OF THE NAARU

All Draenei have this ability. It heals your target for 20% of your health over 15 seconds. While the Gift of the Naaru can't compare with regular healing spells, it is a great boon when you need a bit of extra healing during a fight or to get you ready for the next battle more quickly.

Once you have fulfilled these tasks, return to the Crash Site. After delivering the vials of blood, Proenitus has an **Urgent Delivery**. He needs you to take the bundle of vials to Zalduun inside the Crash Site. Though they are doing what they can for the injured inside the Crash Site, there are also injured survivors throughout Ammen Vale. Zalduun asks you to **Rescue the Survivors** by using your Gift of the Naaru ability on one of the Draenei Survivors.

Before taking care of the survivors, stop by Proentius who asks you to speak with **Botanist Taerix**. Walk around the side of the Crash Site to find her. Taerix asks you to thin out the nearby Volatile Mutations before they overrun the camp. To find the Volatile Mutations, look for the purple crystalline fragments of the power core jutting up from the ground. These weird creatures don't stray far from them. While you're out, use Gift of the Naaru on one of the Draenei Survivors. Once you are finished, return to the botanist.

She appreciated your help in thinning out the mutations, but the problem is much more wide spread. To come up with a solution she needs Lasher Samples from the mutated lashers. For now, you must do **What Must Be Done...**

Before gathering the samples, speak with Apprentice Vishael as she has some **Botanical Legwork** she would like you to do as well. She asks you to gather a few of the corrupted flowers and bring them back to her for study. Once you have finished discussing botany, head into the Crash Site and visit with Zalduun to receive your reward for rescuing the Draenei Survivor.

YOUR CLASS TRAINER

When you return to the Crash Site your trainer is waiting to speak with you. Take the time to learn the valuable skill they want to teach before moving on with your other quests.

Before heading off to complete these tasks, go out the south side of the Crash Site and speak with Technician Zhanaa and Vindicator Aldar. The technician is doing all she can to make repairs to important devices, but after the crash, the local Owlkin carried many of the devices away. She needs you to collect Emitter **Spare Parts** from them so she can complete her task.

Though you can't do anything about the Mutated Owlkin, by performing an **Inoculation** of the others you can at least keep them from becoming infected as well. Vindicator Aldar gives you a special inoculum to stave off the mutation.

After completing all these tasks, head west of the Crash Site and into the Ammen Fields. The Mutated Root Lashers that you need to eliminate are in the area. Don't forget to loot the Lasher Samples off of them. The Corrupted Flowers you need grow among the Mutated Root Lashers.

Even though you still have other tasks to perform in the south, return to Botanist Taerix and Apprentice Vishael first. Taerix has another job for you that leads you in the same direction as the spare parts you are seeking.

Botanist Taerix has developed an agent that may help in **Healing the Lake**. This substance neutralizes the power leaking from the irradiated power core. Disperse the Neutralizing Agent at the Irradiated Power Crystal to bring the energy under control.

Now you are ready to head further south. Dive into Silverline Lake and use the Neutralizing Agent near the crystal. Once you are finished you can find the Owlkin you need to inoculate on the far side of the lake. Make your way back to Nestlewood Hills, inoculating any Nestlewood Owlkin you come across on your way. Once you go through the cave passageway there are several spare parts for you to pick up. Once you've finished inoculating the Owlkin and gathered the spare parts you need, save yourself some walking and use your Hearthstone to quickly return to the Crash Site and collect your rewards.

There have been several reports of unusual activity up on Shadow Ridge and Vindicator Aldar is worried about **The Missing Scout**. He asks you to head to the other side of Silverline Lake to find his scout, Tolaan. Head southwest, around Silverline Lake until you see Tolaan crouched in the grass. Though he is still alive, you can see that he is badly injured. He was ambushed by **The Blood Elves**! Tolaan sends you to kill the Blood Elves on Shadow Ridge before they can threaten the rest of Ammen Vale.

Head up the path behind him to encounter plenty of Blood Elves. They are a little bit more difficult than the foes you've faced so far, but are not aggressive. Just pick them off one at a time until you have satisfied Tolaan's need for vengeance. When you are finished, return to Tolaan to report your success. Though you've made a good start at slaughtering them, Tolaan believes that if you slay the Blood Elves' leader, they may retreat. Travel to the top of Shadow Ridge and kill Surveyor Candress, the **Blood Elf Spy**.

Look for Surveyor Candress in her tent at the top of the ridge. Take her down as you did her minions and don't worry, the Blood Elves near her are oblivious to your attack. Loot her corpse after you finish the fight for the **Blood Elf Plans**. Right click on them and accept the quest they offer. Next, take them to Vindicator Aldar to examine. He is grateful for the job you did and decides to keep an eye out for this potential new threat. In the meantime Zhanaa has finished **The Emmitter** and wishes to speak with you.

Great news! The spare parts you recovered really came in handy. The technician was able to repair the Emitter and get in contact with another group of survivors. Zhanaa asks you to **Travel to Azure Watch** and convince them to send aid and supplies to the Crash Site. Speak with Technician Dyvuun once you arrive.

To reach Azure Watch head west across Ammen Vale. As you move towards the river crossing at Ammen Ford you notice an injured Draenei by the side of the road. Aeun was bringing **Word From Azure Watch** when a few mutated beasts jumped him and injured his leg. He asks that you report to Caregiver Chellan in his stead. Continue down the road and across the river to reach Azure Watch.

With the crash of *The Exodar* your people have no choice but to make this their home. Though the land may seem strange at first, its people fight against the same forces the Draenei have often faced. Despite the fact that the crash ended the lives of many Draenei, you have a chance at forging a new home here. Learn well, heed the teachings of Velen and lend your strength to your new allies. May the Light long prevail!

DWARF

Dwarves are a hardy people, due no doubt to living for generations in cold regions, frequently in underground fortresses. Masters of stone and ore, Dwarves are equally skilled at building cities and crafting weaponry. Dwarves are treasure seekers, explorers, and courageous fighters.

Dwarves are 4-5 feet tall, stocky, and muscular. Males prize their elaborate beards; females, their decorative hairstyles and piercings.

Start Location: Coldridge Valley in Dun Morogh

Home city: Ironforge

RACIAL ABILITIES

 FROST RESISTANCE

Reduces Frost damage taken by 1%.

 CRACK SHOT

Expertise with ranged weapons increased by 1%.

MACE SPECIALIZATION

Expertise with Maces and Two-Handed Maces increased by 1%.

 STONEFORM

Removes all poison, disease and bleed effects and reduces all damage taken by 10% for 8 sec.

 EXPLORER

You find additional fragments when looting archaelogical finds and you can survey faster than normal archaeologists.

Rams, the Dwarven Racial Mount

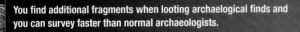

AVAILABLE CLASSES

DEATH KNIGHT | DRUID | HUNTER | MAGE | MONK | PALADIN | PRIEST | ROGUE | SHAMAN | WARLOCK | WARRIOR

YOUR FIRST DAY AS A
DWARF

The Dwarves of Dun Morogh are a hardworking, dependable people. Although they greatly enjoy a good pint or a rousing story, they are industrious and highly skilled in working with stone and metal. The great forges and intricate stone buildings of their capital city, Ironforge, attest to this innate talent. The Dwarven passion for digging in the earth has turned from gathering riches to archeological research of late and the recent earthquakes have revealed promising new treasures for study. Unfortunately, that is not all the Cataclysm has unearthed. Sheltered by the mountains of Dun Morogh, the effects of the Cataclysm are felt even here in secluded Coldridge Valley where your training begins. It is time for you to put aside simple pleasures, pick up your weapons, and join your allies in defending your world.

1	Anvilmar
2	Cask of Stormhammer Stout
3	Cask of Gnomenbrau
4	Cask of Theramore Pale Ale
5	Whitebeard's Encampment
6	Soothsayer Shi'kala
	Felix's Bucket of Bolts
7	Soothsayer Rikkari
	Felix's Chest
8	Soothsayer Mirim'koa
	Felix's Box
9	Coldridge Pass

COLDRIDGE VALLEY

While gunning down troggs, Joren Ironstock find time to explain that the big earthquake has shaken the troggs right out of the ground and made them angrier than usual. The mountaineers need help to **Hold the Line**. He asks you to head south and help out his forces by slaying some of the Rockjaw Invaders.

When you return, Joren Ironstock has another job for you. It's time to **Give 'Em What-For!** The troggs value strength above all else and bigger, stronger troggs are the closest things they have to leaders. Joren hopes that if you take out the big Rockjaw Goons the attacks might slow. Before heading out to deal with the Goons, speak with Sten Stoutarm. This all-out trogg invasion has worn down the mountaineers. Sten wants you to take his first aid kit and deliver **Aid for the Wounded**.

Head out into the field where you can see Coldridge Mountaineers doing their best to hold back the Rockjaw Invaders. Help them out by taking down the invaders and bandaging up any wounded you see. When you are finished head back up the hill to report your success.

Joren thinks you can be even more useful elsewhere. Due to the massive trogg attacks, and the earthquake earlier, all civilians have been put on **Lockdown in Anvilmar**. Joren sends you to speak with his wife, Jona Ironstock inside Anvilmar.

ANVILMAR

Jona Ironstock has things well in hand and knows just how to put you to use. She tells you that **First Things First: We're Gonna Need Some Beer**. Luckily, your fellow Dwarves put some beer in storage for just such an emergency as this. Jona gives you the important task of bringing back three casks of the stuff.

Though beer supplies are running low, they haven't yet reached emergency levels so take a moment to speak to Grundel Harkin. It seems the earthquake knocked all sorts of **Dwarven Artifacts** loose from the soil. Grundel asks you to obtain five of these archeological treasures for further study.

Head out of Anvilmar and travel around the east side of the structure to find the Cask of Gnomenbrau. Next, head back west, keeping close to the outer wall of Anvilmar to find the Cask of Stormhammer Stout. To reach the third and final cask follow the road west away from Anvilmar until you see the Cask of Theramore Pale Ale on the right. Along the way keep your eye out for small mounds in the snow. These mark the positions of the recently unearthed artifacts that Grundel Harkin asked you retrieve. After collecting the beer and the artifacts, return to Anvilmar with your prizes.

Grundel's philosophy is that you should **Make Hay While the Sun Shines**. Since you did such a good job of obtaining the Dwarven artifacts, Grundel decides to send you out on another excursion. This time he wants you to retrieve Priceless Rockjaw Artifacts from the Rockjaw Scavengers, though they are unlikely to give them up without a fight. Before doing so, check in with Jona.

Now that the most pressing need has been taken care of, Jona asks for your help in getting **All the Other Stuff**. She sends you out after Boar Haunches for eatin' and Ragged Wolf Hides for blankets.

MEETING YOUR TRAINER

Jona also delivers an Etched Rune from your Class Trainer. Before heading out on your other tasks, take the time to speak with your trainer who is in Anvilmar. Practicing as your trainer suggests will yield experience that makes your future endeavors easier to handle.

After speaking with your Class Trainer, head out of Anvilmar. Though the boars and wolves are plentiful all around the keep, travel southeast. Not only are the animals you need here but so are the Rockjaw Scavengers. Though the Scavengers seem to relish the fight, they aren't too concerned about their artifacts, often throwing them at you in an effort to do damage. After collecting what you need, return to Anvilmar.

Jona is pleased with your work, but now you are needed elsewhere. Grelin Whitebeard is having trouble with trolls. Report to his camp in Coldridge Valley. To reach the camp head southwest from Anvilmar.

WHITEBEARD'S ENCAMPMENT

Grelin is concerned about **The Troll Menace**. While Anvilmar's attention is focused on the troggs, it's more important than ever that the trolls are kept under control. Grelin tasks you with thinning out their numbers. Before you head out, check with Apprentice Soren and Felix Whindlebolt as well.

Apprentice Soren worries there is more to the trolls than just their usual aggression and wants you to go **Trolling for Information**. He tells you to listen to a soothsayer in each of the three Frostmane camps to try to find out what is going on.

Since you're heading toward the trolls anyway, Felix is hoping you can help him out with **A Refugee's Quandary**. When the earthquake happened he became turned around in all the confusion and the trolls took all of his stuff! He asks you to retrieve his Box, Chest, and Bucket of Bolts from the Frostmane Trolls.

Head southeast out of Whitebeard's camp to reach one of the Frostmane camps. Here you find Soothsayer Shi'kala and Felix's Bucket of Bolts. To eavesdrop on the Soothsayer, stand near each one. After hearing what she has to say, you are ready to pick up Felix's Bucket and move to the next camp. There are plenty of Frostmane Troll Whelps near all three camps, so thin out their numbers as you move from camp to camp.

Head west along the mountains to reach the next troll camp. Listen to Soothsayer Rikkari, grab Felix's Chest, and move on to the third camp. Here you find Soothsayer Mirim'koa and Felix's Box. When you are finished, return to Whitebeard's Encampment.

Though you came back with some good information, it doesn't change the situation much. Grelin knows that the trolls would love to kick the dwarves out of Coldridge Valley and claim it for their own. He sends you on a mission of **Ice and Fire**. Kill the Frostmane's leader, Grik'nir the Cold, Grik'nir's Servants, and the Wayward Fire Elemental.

Head back to the first camp you visited and enter the cave behind it. Make your way deeper inside, taking down the Frostmane Blades you encounter on your way. The passageway in the cavern soon splits, but either way takes you deeper into the cavern to Grik'nir. When you arrive in the large cavern, be careful not to get too close to the Wayward Fire Elemental until you are ready to fight. Unlike the other foes you have faced, the elemental is aggressive and attacks you if you get within range. Deal with the elemental, then prepare to take on Grik'nir the Cold. Though he won't attack you until you make the first move, be prepared for at least one nearby Frostmane Whelp to join the fight. Both the elemental and Grik'nir are tougher opponents than you've faced so far, but neither is anything you can't handle. If you still need to kill Grik'nir's servants, mop up a few more Frostmane Blades on your way out of the cave before returning to Whitebeard.

STONEFORM

Being a dwarf has its advantages including Stoneform. When activated this racial ability allows all dwarves to remove Poison, Disease, and Bleed effects and it also decreases your damage taken by 10%. The effect doesn't last long, but sometimes a few precious seconds are all you need to turn the tide of battle in your favor.

The appearance of the elemental tells Whitebeard that the earthquake earlier did more than just upset some troggs! He asks you to take his report to Ironforge. He sends you to speak with Hands Springsprocket in Coldridge Pass. Head east, past Anvilmar, and continue up the road to reach the pass.

COLDRIDGE PASS

Unfortunately, while you're speaking to Hands, an aftershock seals the tunnel you needed to take. Not to fear, **Follow That Gyro-Copter!** Hands sends up a distress signal to the Gnomes. Run back down the road to Anvilmar to catch a ride on Milo Geartwinge's gyrocopter.

Milo is more than happy to give you a ride but first you need to **Pack Your Bags**. Head back into Anvilmar and grab your belongings. You find your Leftover Boar Meat on a small table inside, your Coldridge Beer Flagon is right down the steps in a corner, and your Ragged Wolf-Hide Cloak is in a box upstairs near Teo Hammerstorm, the Shaman Trainer.

Take a moment to say goodbye to Jona Ironstock. She tells you **Don't Forget About Us**. Once you arrive in Kharanos, speak with Tharek Blackstone and let him know what has been happening in Coldridge. Jona is hopeful that he will send some help.

With your personal supplies gathered and your goodbyes said, you are ready to move on to Kharanos. Head back up to Coldridge Valley and let Milo know that you are ready to go.

As the gyrocopter flies, take a good look at the surrounding lands. Though you may be more comfortable sitting by the fire with a nice pint o' ale than flying over the mountains in a Gnomish contraption, you're getting an enviable view of Dwarven territory. While you may be on the inexperienced side right now, no Dwarf worth his beard has ever shirked his duty. The world outside is changing and it now falls to you to help protect your home.

GNOME

The eccentric Gnomes once thrived in Gnomeregan, a city deep in the mountains beneath Dun Morogh. When attacked by Troggs, the clever Gnomes released toxic radiation against their attackers—and the gnome citizenry as well. The surviving gnomes fled the city, still sharing their inventions and odd devices with others. They currently use Ironforge, the Dwarven capital, as a place of refuge.

Gnomish and Goblin engineers have a long-standing rivalry. It's uncertain to outsiders which side is more dangerous to their friends and enemies!

Gnomes are approximately 3 feet tall, being the shortest sentient race in Azeroth. They have petite bodies but larger facial features. Gnomes have only 4 fingers per hand. Male and female Gnomes are known for their outrageous hair colors.

Start Location: New Tinkertown in Dun Morogh.

RACIAL ABILITIES

ARCANE RESISTANCE
Reduces Arcane damage taken by 1%.

ENGINEERING SPECIALIZATION
Engineering skill (a crafting Profession) increased by 15.

ESCAPE ARTIST
Escape the effects of any immobilization or movement speed reduction effect.

EXPANSIVE MIND
Mana pool increased by 5%.

SHORTBLADE SPECIALIZATION
Expertise with Daggers and One-Handed Swords increased by 1%.

Home city: Ironforge (Tinker Town).

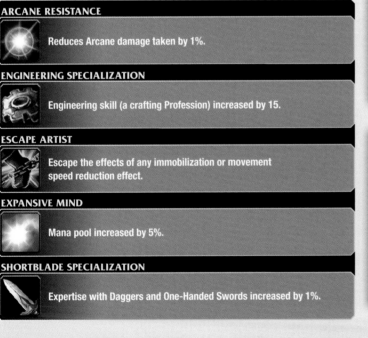

Mechanostriders, the Gnomish Racial Mount.

YOUR FIRST DAY AS A
GNOME

Though the Gnomes are grateful for the hospitality of their Dwarven allies in Ironforge, the underground Dwarven city just can't take the place of their own home. After years of exile, the time has finally come to retake Gnomeregan. High Tinker Mekkatorque and his advisors have come up with a plan—Operation: Gnomeregan. The Gnomes plan to boot out Thermaplugg and his cronies and retake their city. You are one of the lucky few to have survived the radiation in Gnomeregan with your wits intact. It's now up to you to help take back your city.

1	Gnomeregan
2	New Tinkertown
3	The Toxic Airfield
4	Jessup McCree
5	Crushcog's Arsenal
6	Brewnall Village
7	Road to Kharanos

CRUSHCOG'S ARSENAL

NEW TINKERTOWN

GNOMEREGAN

ICEFLOW LAKE

BREWNALL VILLAGE

THE TOXIC AIRFIELD

FROSTMANE HOLD

GNOMEREGAN

The first thing you see when you wake is Nevin Twistwrench, the commander of the Survivor Assistance Facilitation Expedition, or S.A.F.E. They're here to help the survivors in Gnomeregan but the irradiated Leper Gnomes are becoming too numerous to hold back and they are **Pinned Down**. Since you now look healthy enough to help out, he asks you to clear out some of the Crazed Leper Gnomes.

Head out of the Old Dormitory and into the Train Depot to see plenty of the Crazed Leper Gnomes. Attack them one at a time and they prove no match for you. You may not like taking out your former comrades, but it has to be done! When you are finished, return to Nevin in the dormitory.

After thinning the leper gnome numbers a bit, it is time to **See to the Survivors**. Nevin gives you his emergency teleport beacon so you can get those survivors out of here. Look for the traumatized survivors throughout the Train Depot. Approach them and use the Teleport Beacon to get them to safety.

Survivor

Carvo appreciates your help but now it is time to **Withdraw to the Loading Room!** Follow the ramp south out of the Train Depot and report to Gaffer Coilspring once you reach your destination. You have been down in the radiation a long time, so before you can rejoin the other gnomes on the surface you must go through **Decontamination**. Gaffer sends you to the Sanitron 500 in the next room to the east. Approach one of the hovering Sanitrons and get in. The Clean Cannons do the rest! When you emerge from the corridor you have been cleansed of radiation!

Speak with Technician Braggle who lets you know that it is time to head **To the Surface**. When you are ready, talk to Torben Zapblast nearby to arrange transport to the surface.

NEW TINKERTOWN

Nevin knows that it's Gnomes like you who will play a big part in **The Future of Gnomeregan**. He sends you to talk with your Class Trainer who oversees your training and adjustment to life back on the surface.

High Tinker Mekkatorque is the leader of all the gnomes and has made a habit of personally meeting every rescued survivor. Head to the war council beneath the tent in the center of New Tinkertown to **Meet the High Tinker**.

The High Tinker is glad to see you made it out. He asks you to watch the holo-table in front of him to learn about Operation: Gnomeregan. It seems Thermaplugg had one last trick up his sleeve and for now, only the S.A.F.E. teams dare to venture into the city. Not content with his minor victory, Thermaplugg has sent his crony, Razlo Crushcog out to harass the Gnomes on the surface. Mekkatorque knows that what the Gnomes need is **A Triumph of Gnomish Ingenuity**.

Engineer Grindspark has developed a bot that should help clean up the toxic air in the city. High Tinker Mekkatorque sends you to him to offer your help. Head northeast from the High Tinker to reach Engineer Grindspark. He's almost finished with his latest prototype but he can definitely use your help **Scrounging for Parts**. There are all kinds of spare parts just lying around New Tinkertown. Retrieve some for the engineer.

Once you have the spare parts he needs, Engineer Grindspark can finish his prototype and he's got **A Job for the Multi-Bot**. He wants you to use the GS-9x Multi-Bot to clean up Toxic Pools at the Toxic Airfield south of town. Before heading that way, stop to talk to Tock Sprysprocket northwest of Engineer Grindspark. Tock has a task for you in the Airfield as well. As strange as it sounds, he believes that the Toxic Sludges were once Gnomes and the sludge is **What's Left Behind**! He asks you to retrieve the Recovered Possessions of the Gnomes they once were from the Toxic Sludges.

Head south of town to reach the Airfield. Bring your bot close to the toxic pools and it automatically jumps right in and cleans them up. While here, take down some of the Toxic Sludges to retrieve the possessions for Tock.

YOUR CLASS TRAINER

After reporting back to Grindspark and Tock, take a moment to visit your trainer. You are now ready to practice the skill or spell you learned at level 3. Follow their instructions before moving on to your next task.

You have been instrumental in clearing up the Toxic Airfield, but there is still more to be done. Corporal Fizzwhistle needs your help in **Dealing with the Fallout**. The Living Contaminations threaten to overrun the town if they aren't thinned out. Destroy a number of them and report back to the corporal.

After accepting your reward, head to the war council in the center of town and speak with Captain Tread Sparknozzle. The Cataclysm tore open the caves beneath Frostmane Hold, flooding the troll stronghold with troggs! The troggs drove the trolls out of their home and would surely like to do the same to the Gnomes if they aren't stopped. The demolitions expert, Jessup McCree, was supposed to close the caves but the captain hasn't heard from him. He wants you to find out **What's Keeping Jessup?** Jessup can be found at his camp near Frostmane Hold.

FROSTMANE HOLD

Head south across the Toxic Airfield and you soon see the camps surrounding Frostmane Hold. Jessup has set up camp on the outskirts. He says he can still do the job, but he needs some help from you first. Jessup tells you to **Get Me Explosives Back!** The troggs stole his Powder Kegs and any of them could be carrying the explosives around. Not only did the filthy troggs steal Jessup's powder kegs, his crew is **Missing in Action**. He needs you to rescue his Captured Demolitionists from their cages.

As you move into Frostmane territory, be careful. Unlike the other foes you've faced so far, these Rockjaw Troggs are aggressive and attack you if you get too close. The troggs are scattered all around so try to clear them one at a time as you move towards the makeshift cages holding Jessup's crew. To free the prisoners all you need to do is destroy the flimsy cages. Once you are finished, return to Jessup.

With his recovered crew and powder kegs, Jessup was able to get everything ready to detonate. He now needs your help **Finishin' the Job**. Make your way to the bottom of the cave in the western part of Frostmane Hold. While you're down there, he suggests you take out the head trogg, Boss Bruggor.

To reach the bottom you must battle through a cave full of troggs, often fighting in close quarters. Try to take them one at a time and keep an eye behind you so you don't get unexpected adds! While you can do this on your own, it's a good idea to bring a friend along. When you reach the bottom clear the other troggs out before heading for Boss Bruggor. He's a bit tougher than the other troggs so be ready to use all your abilities to deal with him. With Bruggor out of the way, all you need to do is hit the detonator. Report back to Jessup when you are finished.

Jessup is moving on to other jobs, but before he goes he asks you to do **One More Thing**. Take his report to High Tinker Mekkatorque in New Tinkertown. Head back across the Toxic Airfield to reach the town and deliver the report.

Mekkatorque is happy with the news. With the troggs contained for now, he can turn his attention to other matters. In a bid to stop the Gnomes from retaking Gnomeregan, Razlo Crushcog and his flunkies have set up shop in an old arsenal to the north. The High Tinker wants you to put a stop to **Crushcog's Minions** before they can bring the old mechano-tanks online. Before heading out, check in with Hinkles Fastblast. He asks you to use his Techno-Grenade to destroy the Repaired Mechano-Tanks at the arsenal. He wants to make sure there are **No Tanks!**

Follow the road northeast to reach Crushcog's Arsenal. After thinning out his cronies and taking out the tanks, return to New Tinkertown. After receiving your reward from the High Tinker and Hinkles Fastblast, turn to Kelsey Steelspark to plan your next step, **Staging in Brewnall**.

BREWNALL VILLAGE

While High Tinker Mekkatorque and his military advisors finalize the plans to take down Razlo Crushcog, Kelsey Steelspark asks you to travel to Brewnall Village. Once there speak with Jarvi Shadowstep and offer your help. To reach Brewnall, travel southeast along the road.

When you arrive, Jarvi tells you they are almost ready to move against Crushcog, but his Sentry-Bots need to be handled first. Take the Paintinator down to the lake and use it on Crushcog's Sentry-Bots to **Paint it Black**. Head east down onto Iceflow Lake and use the Paintinator to blind them. When you are finished, return to Jarvi in Brewnall Village.

Down with Crushcog! It is now time to take on Razlo Crushcog himself! The Dwarves of Ironforge have agreed to help the Gnomes deal with this threat. Travel to the small, snow-covered island in Iceflow Lake to lend your aid. Jarvi gives you an Orbital Targeting Device to use during the battle to help guide the High Tinker's special weapons.

High Tinker Mekkatorque does most of the work against Crushcog; your job is just to help him out. When you use the device Jarvi gave you, it produces a target that you can place anywhere on the ground. Place it underneath Crushcog to aim the High Tinker's weapons. While Crushcog is too busy dealing with Mekkatorque to notice your interference, his minions are another matter. Don't get so caught up in using the device that you neglect to take out the flunkies trying to take you down.

After the battle, return to Jarvi Shadowstep. With Crushcog gone it is time for you to move on to help your Dwarven allies who have problems of their own. Follow the road east out of Brewnall Village to move **On to Kharanos**.

Gnomeregan may still lie in Thermaplugg's control, but things are certainly looking up for your people. With Crushcog vanquished and S.A.F.E. rescuing more Gnomes every day, it won't be long before Gnomeregan is under Gnome control and you can once again return to your beloved city. For now, you must leave Operation: Gnomeregan in the hands of other capable Gnomes. Your path lies outward, using the skills you've learned to aid your allies in the wake of the recent Cataclysm.

HUMAN

Humans are both proud and ambitious, seeking comfort and glory and to change the world around them. Many humans are laborers, working in the farms, mines, and lumber mills outside of Stormwind, eagerly taking all that nature offers. Humans are also courageous knights, brave on the battlefield and loyal to their comrades.

Humans are 5-6 feet tall, strong and healthy. Human physical traits vary greatly, with a wide palette of skin and hair colors.

Start location: Northshire in Elwynn Forest

RACIAL ABILITIES

DIPLOMACY
Reputation gains are increased by 10%.

EVERY MAN FOR HIMSELF
Removes all movement impairing effects and all effects which cause loss of control of your character. This effect shares a cooldown with other similar effects.

MACE SPECIALIZATION
Expertise with Maces and Two-Handed Maces increased by 1%.

SWORD SPECIALIZATION
Expertise with Swords and Two-Handed Swords increased by 1%.

THE HUMAN SPIRIT
Spirit increased by 3%.

Home city: Stormwind

Horses, the Human Racial Mount

AVAILABLE CLASSES

DEATH KNIGHT | DRUID | HUNTER | MAGE | MONK | PALADIN | PRIEST | ROGUE | SHAMAN | WARLOCK | WARRIOR

YOUR FIRST DAY AS A
HUMAN

Though they are a younger race, the Humans have carved a place for themselves among the elder races of Azeroth. With the destruction of Lordaeron, the grand city of Stormwind now stands alone as a testament to Human achievement, its forces ever at the ready to deal with any danger. Recent events have scattered the army of Stormwind far and wide to deal with Deathwing and his Twilight forces, leaving the heart of Humanity's empire at risk from lesser threats. Though you yourself are inexperienced, the King has called upon you and every other citizen to rise up to the challenge and defend your home.

1	Northshire Abbey
2	Echo Ridge Mine
3	Northshire Vineyards
4	Kurtok the Slayer
5	Falkhaan Isenstrider

NORTHSHIRE VALLEY

Northshire has long been a training ground for Humans just beginning to learn their chosen class. Deep within Elwynn Forest its sheltered location provides new recruits ample opportunity to cut their teeth on lesser threats before facing greater challenges. However, with Deathwing and his Twilight armies rampaging over Azeroth, the King has called upon all able bodied citizens to help with the defense of the realm. Speak to Marshal McBride to offer your help. Look for the Marshal standing on the front steps of the abbey.

Marshal McBride is glad to have another new recruit. The Blackrock Orcs have managed to sneak into Northshire and he can use the help **Beating Them Back!** Head into the nearby forest and kill the attacking Blackrock Worgs. Worgs appear all around the Abbey. After thinning their numbers, report back to the Marshal.

McBride knows that the Orcs won't mistake **Lions for Lambs** and are spying on you right now. Go back into the forest where you killed the Worgs and take out the Blackrock Spies who mostly skulk near the trees. When you are done, return to Marshal McBride.

MEETING YOUR TRAINER

Marshal McBride has a note for you from your Class Trainer. Read the note and take the time to speak with your class trainer before moving on. He or she wants you to learn a valuable skill or spell. Your note indicates exactly where you can find your trainer.

Once you complete the task your trainer set forth, it's time for you to **Join the Battle!** Report to Sergeant Willem at the command tent behind Northshire Abbey.

The Blackrock Orcs aren't attacking alone; **They Sent Assassins!** Willem needs a volunteer to go into the field and kill the sneaky little green monsters! Before heading out, speak with Brother Paxton nearby. The priest tells you to **Fear No Evil.** He gives you a prayer book which allows you to cast the light's healing touch on the injured. The Goblin Assassins and the Injured Stormwind Soldiers are both in the nearby woods. When you are finished, return to Brother Paxton and Sergeant Willem.

Now that you've taken care of the assassins, **The Rear is Clear.** Sergeant Willem sends you back to report to Marchall McBride. Even though the enemy has been cleared out to the north and west, there are still more of them to contend with. They've taken over the vineyard to the east and are burning the nearby forest! It is up to you to stop them. Marshal McBride wants you to thin out the numbers of the **Blackrock Invasion** and collect Blackrock Weapons as proof of their demise.

ANGER ISSUES

Unlike the non-aggressive foes faced up to this point, Blackrock Orcs attack if you get too close. Be prepared for a fight before crossing the bridge!

While Deputy Willem is concerned with the threat the Blackrock Orcs present to Elwynn Forest, Milly is more worried about what they've done to her vineyard and she longs for the days when all she had to worry about were a few Defias skulking about! Instead of just stealing produce, the Blackrock Orcs have set fire to the vineyard itself, **Extinguishing Hope.** Take Milly's fire extinguisher and put out the flames in the vineyard while you're out there dealing with the Orcs.

Head east and cross the river to reach the Northshire Vineyards. Fighting aggressive enemies is more challenging than facing their neutral counterparts and requires some caution on your part. If you aren't careful, it can be easy to end up with more enemies than you can handle at once. If your class has ranged abilities, use them to your advantage now by pulling your targets to you into an area already clear of other foes. If you are strictly melee, start with a target on the outskirts that aren't near any other enemies. To use Milly's Fire Extinguisher, face one of the vineyard fires and use the device. This puts out the fire and you can move on to the next. The fire extinguisher only works inside the vineyard, so don't bother trying to put out the flaming trees on either side of it.

After thinning the number of Blackrock Orcs and doing your part in dousing the fires, return to Milly and Deputy Willem. Be careful moving back through the vineyard. Enemies may have reappeared to block your return to the abbey.

Since you've been so successful against the Blackrock Orcs, Marchal McBride has another task to send you back towards the vineyards. . With your help there is hope of **Ending the Invasion**. This incursion of Blackrock Orcs are lead by Kurtok the Slayer, an Orc even more savage than those he leads. The deputy tasks you with ending this threat once and for all!

Follow the river north and cross it near the northern end of the burnt area. The Orc's dark hearted leader is here. Before approaching him, take out any of his nearby followers. You want to face Kurtok on his own, and not with his friends joining in unexpectedly. Kurtok is a tough foe, so be at full health before the fight begins. After taking him out, return to Deputy Willem with the good news.

Now that you've proven yourself, Marshal McBride wants you to **Report to Goldshire** to continue performing your duty of protecting Elwynn Forest. Follow the road south out of Northshire to the nearby town of Goldshire. On the way you see Falkhaan Isenstrider. He is a firm believer in getting a little **Rest and Relaxation**. His best friend runs the inn in Goldshire and can hook you up with some supplies. Speak to Innkeeper Farley at the Lion's Pride Inn in Goldshire once you arrive.

Even in the best of times, doing your duty is not always easy. Now, with Deathwing and his minions threatening the world at large and other invaders threatening your homeland, it is more important than ever that you rise to the task. Learn your lessons well, grow in your chosen field, and get ready to take your place among the heroes of Stormwind!

NIGHT ELF

Night Elves are perceived as aloof and solitary, preferring nature to conventional cities and the company of their own kind to that of other races. Rather than using nature as a resource, Night Elves seek to be in rhythm with the natural world. Night Elves blend magic and the forces of nature for their protection and strength. This belief places Night Elves in strong opposition to Blood Elves, who have consumed tremendous magic against the flow of nature and who continue to place ambition before reason.

Night Elves are approximately 7 feet tall; they are lithe and athletic. All Night Elves have prominent eyebrows and very long ears. Males have elaborate facial hair. Females have facial tattoos.

RACIAL ABILITIES

ELUSIVENESS
Reduces the chance enemies have to detect you while Shadowmelded and increases your speed while stealthed by 5%.

NATURE RESISTANCE
Reduces Nature damage taken by 1%.

QUICKNESS
Increases your chance to dodge melee and ranged attacks by 2%.

SHADOWMELD
Activate to slip into the shadows, reducing the chance for enemies to detect your presence. Lasts until cancelled or upon moving. Any threat is restored versus enemies still in combat upon cancellation of this effect.

WISP SPIRIT
Transform into a wisp upon death, increasing speed by 75%.

Start location: Shadowglen in Teldrassil

Home city: Darnassus

Nightsabers, the Night Elf Racial Mount

AVAILABLE CLASSES

DEATH KNIGHT · DRUID · HUNTER · MAGE · MONK · PALADIN · PRIEST · ROGUE · SHAMAN · WARLOCK · WARRIOR

YOUR FIRST DAY AS A
NIGHT ELF

The Night Elves, or kaldorei, are an ancient race. After the near destruction of the world tree, Nordrassil, they built the great tree, Teldrassil, where you now stand. This new homeland shelters their people as they commune with the natural world, seeking to preserve nature's balance. They are reclusive and often wary of the younger races, though many Night Elves serve the Alliance in various roles throughout

Azeroth. The recent cataclysm has once again placed the world in jeopardy and has even threatened the slowly healing Nordrassil. With many Night Elves called away to deal with the newly unleashed forces, it is more important than ever that you begin your journey along your chosen path so that you too can lend aid in this time of need.

1	Ilthalaine
2	Aldrassil
3	Melithar's Stolen Bags
4	Melithar's Stolen Bags
5	Shadowthread Cave
6	Moonwell
7	Porthannius

SHADOWGLEN

Like all young Night Elves, you begin your journey in the Shadowglen. This sheltered glade serves as a microcosm of nature's balance in the world. Ilthalaine's job is to maintain **The Balance of Nature** within Shadowglen. The Young Nightsaber population has grown too large for the environment to support. He asks you to thin their numbers so that nature's harmony is preserved. The animals you need are scattered around the immediate area. After culling the population, return to Conservator Ilthalaine.

You made a good start with thinning out the younger animal population, but unfortunately, more must be done. Since you seem to know what you're doing, Ilthalaine has another task for you regarding **Fel Moss Corruption**. Grelkin have gathered to the west. Slay them and collect Fel Moss for Ilthalaine's study. Before heading out to take care of the Grelkin, speak with Melithar Staghelm nearby. It seems that **Demonic Thieves** have stolen his bags! Search for them near the Grelkin while collecting the Fel Moss. They are found all around the Grelkin camp. Since they aren't aggressive you can just wade right in and steal back the bags. Along the way, eliminate the Grelkin to collect the Fel Moss. When you are finished, return to Melithar and Ithalaine to receive your rewards.

MEETING YOUR CLASS TRAINER

When you return to Melithar he passes on word from your trainer. Read the message your trainer left for you and take time out from your duties to speak with them in Aldrassil. You are ready to learn a valuable skill from them which helps you in your future endeavors.

After you finish the task your trainer sets forth, they request your aid in pursuing the corruption haunting Shadowglen. Seek out Dentaria Silverglade, **Priestess of the Moon.** You can find her between the two pools just north of Aldrassil.

Dentaria is tending to Iverron, who has been poisoned by Webwood Spiders. She needs your help in preparing **Iverron's Antidote.** Collect the Moonpetal Lilies growing around the nearby ponds and return to her.

Worried about the evident corruption in Teldrassil, she asks you to seek out **The Woodland Protector.** The Dryad, Tarindrella, is at the entrance to the Shadowthread Cave. Head north from the Moon Priestess to reach the foreboding entrance.

CORRUPTED SPIDERS

The spiders ar Shadowthread Cave are different from the other wildlife you have faced so far. They are violently aggressive and attack if you get too close. They can also hit you with Weak Poison, which causes damage over time. Look for Tarindrella at the cave's entrance.

The dryad has returned to deal with the lingering corruption in Teldrassil. The spiders in the Shadowthread Cave suffer more than the other nearby wildlife. She asks you to deal with the **Webwood Corruption** by slaying the affected spiders and she offers you help with this important task. Make your way deeper into the cave, eliminating the spiders you come across.

After dealing with the Webwood Spiders, Tarinella sends you to take out their broodmother, Githyiss the Vile. Her **Vile Touch** has infected the whole brood. Head to the northern end of the cave to cut out the corruption at its source. Githyiss is a tougher foe than those you've faced so far. Be sure to clear out any other spiders nearby so you can face her by herself.

Once you defeat Githyiss, Tarindrella finds that the Gnarlpine are somehow involved. These are **Signs of Things to Come.** She tells you to speak with Arthridas Bearmantly in Dolanaar if you wish to continue fighting the corruption in Teldrassil later. For now she teleports you back to Dentaria Silverglade.

Though the corruption must be dealt with, Dentaria feels that there is time for you to complete your training in Shadowglen. To learn about the recent history of **Teldrassil: Crown of Azeroth**, travel to the moonwell and retrieve a phial of its water. Head northeast to reach the sacred pool. Fill your Crystal Phial and listen to the Shade of the Kaldorei. When you are finished, return to Dentaria.

There is one last task you must perform before departing Shadowglen. Take the **Precious Waters** in the Filled Crystal Phial to Tenaron Stormgrip at the top of Aldrassil. Follow the outside ramp at the western base of the tree all the way up to the top to find him.

Though Tenaron could teach you much of your history, he has an important task for you, **Teldrassil: Passing Awareness**. Take the Partially Filled Vessel to Corithras Moonrage in Dolanaar.

SHADOWMELD

Night Elves have an innate affinity with nature. One of the ways this manifests is in the racial ability, Shadowmeld. By using this ability you can blend in with the shadows around you, becoming almost invisible. This is useful when you don't want to be noticed or when you bite off a little more than you can chew during a fight. Shadowmeld only lasts as long as you remain completely still.

Follow the road south out of Shadowglen where you encounter Porthannius who asks you to make a **Dolanaar Delivery**. He gives you a package of herbs to deliver to Innkeeper Keldamyr in Dolanaar. Keep following the road and it eventually turns west. Before you reach the town, keep an eye out for Zenn Foulhoof on your right. He also has a task for you.

The strange looking fellow asks you to bring him Nightsaber Fangs, Strigid Owl Feathers and swatches of Webwood Spider Silk. The creatures you need to slay in order to obtain these items are on both sides of the road nearby. Once you have done **Zenn's Bidding**, you are ready to finish your journey to Dolanaar.

Though the boughs of Teldrassil are an ever welcoming home, it will soon be time for you to venture out into the wider world. Your fellow Night Elves and their allies need your help to stem the tide of bloodshed and destruction the recent cataclysm unleashed. Learn well from your elders, remember your honor, and prepare to raise your weapons in defense of your world.

WORGEN

It was once thought that Worgen were evil creatures that came to Azeroth from another dimension. Time has proven this false, as newer knowledge reveals that Worgen are descendants of cursed Night Elven Druids. These Druids worshipped Goldrinn and would take on the form of the wolf. Eventually, this sect lost themselves in madness, and their curse has continued for many generations.

The Greymane Worgen are infected with this curse, but they have fought hard to retain themselves and developed a partial cure to this illness. As such, they are not driven toward uncontrolled violence. These Worgen have reached out to the Alliance, forming the sixth member race of this group.

These Worgen are both human and wolf, able to pass between the two forms. They have full control over themselves, but appear as true Worgen when in such a form, growing thick hair and possessing a canine appearance.

Start Location: Ruins of Gilneas

RACIAL ABILITIES

ABERRATION
Reduces Shadow and Nature damage taken by 1%.

DARKFLIGHT
Activates your true form, increasing current movement speed by an additional 40% for 10 sec.

FLAYER
Skinning skill increased by 15 and allows you to skin faster.

RUNNING WILD
Drop to all fours to run as fast as an animal.

VICIOUSNESS
Increases critical strike chance by 1%.

Home city: Gilneas

Worgen learn the racial ability Running Wild at level 20 in addition to the ability to use a mount.

AVAILABLE CLASSES

DEATH KNIGHT | DRUID | HUNTER | MAGE | MONK | PALADIN | PRIEST | ROGUE | SHAMAN | WARLOCK | WARRIOR

YOUR FIRST DAY AS A
WORGEN

The kingdom of Gilneas is one of the oldest human kingdoms in all of Azeroth. Proud and self sufficient, Gilneans have remained aloof from the troubles plaguing the rest of the world, safe behind the towering Greymane Wall. Though they have not shared the same dangers as the rest of Azeroth, their kingdom has its own troubles. Wall or no, Arugal's bestial creations have spread from neighboring Silverpine into Gilneas itself, causing the conflict you now see. Though the city has known many years of peace, you begin your journey during the its darkest hour. The ferocious Worgen have breached the city's defenses and are pouring into the city itself. King Genn Greymane leads the city's defenders in trying to stop the onslaught. Now it is time for you to do your duty as a loyal citizen of this great city and drive the hideous beasts from the streets!

GILNEAS

1	Prince Liam Greymane
2	Lieutenant Walden's Corpse
3	Prison Side Doors
4	Lord Darius Crowley
5	Josiah Avery's Cellar
6	Rebel Cannons

CATHEDRAL QUARTER

MERCHANT SQUARE

LIGHT'S DAWN
CATHEDRAL

GREYMANE COURT

MILITARY DISTRICT

GILNEAS

Though many citizens have been evacuated, you begin in Merchant Square. The city is under complete **Lockdown**. Prince Liam Greymane instructs you to find Lieutenant Walden at the northwestern end of the Merchant Square. He can give you further evacuation orders.

Go up the street and follow it to the northwestern corner of Merchant Square, where near the closed gate it's clear that **Something's Amiss**. At your feet you see the mauled corpse of Lieutenant Walden lying on the cobblestones. Deep claw marks gouge his flesh as if a wild beast had torn into him.

Though you hear the sounds of fighting nearby, Prince Liam no doubt needs to know what happened to the Lieutenant. Return to him to deliver the news. As you approach the Prince's position **All Hell Breaks Loose**! Though the Worgen were originally created by Archmage Arugal to fight the Scourge, it is clear that your fellow citizens are now the target of their unbridled aggression! Despite the best efforts of the Prince's men, it seems that the city is in trouble. Lend a hand by slaying a number of these Rampaging Worgen in Merchant Square. These foes aren't aggressive, so don't worry about becoming overwhelmed. Concentrate on one target at a time as you become accustomed to your chosen class.

Before thinning their numbers, return to the prince. As always, his concern is for his people, several of whom have locked themselves up in their homes, trying to remain safe. Prince Liam knows that this won't keep the Worgen at bay for long and he asks you to **Evacuate the Merchant Square** homes before the Worgen do it for you!

Before beginning the evacuation, speak to Gwen Armstead directly south of Prince Liam. Locked behind the Greymane Wall as they are, she knows that the citizens won't make it through the winter without the supplies they have stockpiled. **Salvage the Supplies** as you make your rounds evacuating people.

To evacuate the citizens, open their sparkling doors. You can't enter their homes but as soon as you open their doors they run out. While doing this you also see several supply crates from which to salvage supplies.

BE PATIENT

While nothing stops you from moving out of Merchant Square and into the rest of the city, save yourself some backtracking and wait to explore until after you have finished your tasks in Merchant Square.

After evacuating the citizens and salvaging the necessary supplies, return to Gwen Armstead to receive your payment and then report to Prince Liam. Grateful for your help, he gives you **Royal Orders** commanding you to leave Merchant Square and report to the Military District while he stays behind to guard the retreat. When you arrive report in with Gwen Armstead who has moved to the base of the steps there.

Follow the street east and then turn south. Continue along this road until you reach the stairs leading down into the Military District.

Though most of the citizens made it out of Merchant Square alive, there are Worgen on this side of the city as well. Gwen informs you that someone's looking for you. Exactly who is looking for you depends on your class. This quest leads you to your class trainer. Follow the road south to find your class specific trainer. They give you a follow up quest to learn an important skill. Learn what they have to offer before moving on to face new challenges.

After you finish your short class-specific quest, your trainer informs you that because there is **Safety in Numbers** the survivors plan to stick together and make their way to King Greymane to the south. Speak to him to see what else can be done to drive back the Worgen.

Continue following the road and you soon see the king and his royal guards conversing with Lord Godfrey. They are protecting a small group of survivors.

Though Lord Darius Crowley is considered a traitor by many, the King once called him friend. Regardless of what happened in the past, Greymane knows that with the city itself threatened, **Old Divisions** must give way. They need a man like Crowley to help them make it through this attack.

Lord Godfrey has a task for you as well. If you're going to head towards the prison anyway, **While You're At It** he wants you to take out Bloodfang Worgen on your way. Enter the side doors of Stoneward Prison and ask Captain Broderick about Crowley's whereabouts.

Head northwest to enter the prison and enter one of the side doors to the left or right. Climb the stairs to reach the walkway above. While the Bloodfang Worgen you encounter here are not aggressive and won't attack you unless you attack first, the less common Worgen Runts found at the top of the prison are very aggressive and attack when you move too close.

As you approach Lord Crowley and his men, it looks as if they are protecting an injured comrade. One of Crowley's men, Dempsey, has been hit hard and is down. So far he is surviving **By The Skin of His Teeth**, but they need a few minutes to stabilize the bleeding before attempting to move him. Help Lord Crowley defend their position against wave after wave of Worgen attacks. If you can survive the onslaught you can discuss the situation further with Crowley.

Crowley agrees with King Greymane that they must put aside their quarrel and once again become **Brothers in Arms**. He tells you to send word to Greymane that his men will join the King's forces to drive back this menace. Make your way back down out of the prison to report your success.

Once Lord Godfrey knows that you finished the task he gave you and has spoken to the king regarding Crowley, King Greymane has another job for you. Though the King is somewhat unnerved that Crowley managed to sneak such a large amount of weaponry into the city right under his nose, today **The Rebel Lord's Arsenal** might end up saving Gilnean lives. He sends you to find Josiah Avery and requisition the rebel artillery.

Follow the road west while looking for a cellar door to your right. Once you find it open the heavy doors and make your way down into the rebel arsenal. Josiah Avery is cowering in the far corner, just as you approach him he turns with a surprise attack! Luckily for you, Lorna Crowley arrives just in time!

ONCE BITTEN...

As you move along you realize that one of the Worgen got in a lucky bite. It looks minor though, surely nothing to be concerned about.

As if the run-of-the-mill Worgen weren't dangerous enough, Bloodfang Lurkers have now infiltrated the alleys of Gilneas. These creatures have the talent of hiding in the darkness and attacking **From the Shadows**. Lorna asks you to use one of her mastiffs to sniff out Worgen hiding in the nearby alleys. You need to clear the way so the defenders can move the cannon out of the cellar to where they can do some good.

Once you accept this job, a faithful mastiff follows at your heels. Head back up out of the cellar and begin moving through the nearby streets. Though they may be good at hiding, the Bloodfang Lurkers can't hide their scent from the keen nose of the trusty mastiff! When your dog spots a lurker and attacks, be sure to follow it up with attacks of your own. Once you have slain enough of the Bloodfang Lurkers return to Lorna Crowley.

When you return Lorna's dog, she asks you to deliver a **Message to Greymane**. Let King Greymane know that her father's arsenal is at his disposal. You can find the king just around the corner from the building you just left.

The news of the arsenal is most welcome, but Greymane tells you that they can't unleash Crowley's weapons just yet. There is a civilian trapped on the other side of the prison—and not just any civilian. Krennan Aranas is one of the most brilliant alchemists in the world. His knowledge is far too valuable to lose and the king sends you to **Save Krennan Aranas**. King Greymane lends you his own horse for the rescue mission.

You automatically mount the steed and it carries you to where Krennan is stuck in a tree being harried by bloodthirsty Worgen below. Use the horse's ability to rescue the alchemist when you are beneath the tree and return to Lord Godfrey near the cellar.

Lord Godfrey sends you to the king to let him know that you've managed to buy some time. Godfrey believes it is **Time to Regroup** and you must all fall back to Greymane Court.

Follow the road west as it leads into Greymane Court. After you speak with the king, Lord Darius Crowley offers to let you come along for the ride as he makes his way to Light's Dawn Cathedral, where he plans to make a final stand for Gilneas. Sometimes **Sacrifices** are necessary.

When you accept Crowley's offer, you mount up behind him on his horse and travel to the cathedral. Your goal is to round up as many Worgen as you can, getting them to chase you instead of the escaping citizens.

Throw your torch at groups of Worgen to round up as many as you can on the way to the cathedral. When you click on the torch you are given a targeting reticule. Place it on the ground anywhere where Worgen are gathered. When you reach the cathedral steps, speak to Tobias Mistmantle.

NEED MORE WORGEN?

If you don't manage to round up the required amount of Worgen while riding with Crowley, don't worry, you can remount the horse at the cathedral steps and take another turn around the courtyard.

Now that the invading worgen have gathered near the cathedral, it is time to put an end to these creatures **By Blood and Ash**. Tobias Mistmantle instructs you to take control of one of the rebel cannons and use them against the Bloodfang Stalkers gathering before the cathedral.

Aim the cannon at the worgen you see below you and fire. You should be able to amass a decent kill count quickly with such massive firepower at your command. Watch out for Stalkers that try to mount the steps. Your cannon has the ability to fire very close to itself, so keep the steps clear of enemies! Once you have done your part, return to Tobias Mistmantle.

You did a great job decimating the horde of beasts with the cannon but now ammunition is running low. Though the defenders will **Never Surrender**, **Sometimes Retreat** is necessary. Enter the cathedral and report to Lord Crowley.

Though you fought valiantly, it now comes down to this desperate **Last Stand**. Because of the narrow cathedral door the worgen are forced to filter in a few at a time. Lord Crowley tasks you with killing the Frenzied Stalkers that make it inside the cathedral.

After thinning their numbers considerably, the onslaught stops for a moment, leading Lord Crowley to believe the worst is yet to come. You can take some small comfort in knowing that you've done everything possible to defend your home against these monsters. Trapped like a rat in the cathedral, your future is uncertain. No matter what happens, next, you can be sure that your life is about to change.

BLOOD ELF

The Blood Elves are so named in honor of their High Elf ancestors who died during the Scourge invasion of their homeland, Quel'Thalas. Blood Elves seek power through arcane magic, bending it to their will to create warped, beautiful surroundings. Fiercely loyal to their race, Blood Elves will do anything to avenge their ancestors and reclaim their magic power. They are survivors hoping to regain glory once again.

Those of a weak disposition are unable to control their lust for magic and power. This burns away at their wills and turns these Elves into a pathetic, weaker version of what they once were.

Blood Elves are 5-6 feet tall, slim and wiry. Their hair and skin color reflect their affinity to fire and the sun. All Blood Elves have prominent eyebrows and long ears. Males have minimal facial hair. Females have elaborate ear jewelry.

Start location: Sunstrider Isle in Eversong Woods

Home city: Silvermoon City

RACIAL ABILITIES

ARCANE AFFINITY

Enchanting skill (an item-enhancing Profession) is increased by 10.

ARCANE TORRENT

An ability that Silences all enemies within 8 yards for 2 seconds and restores mana, Energy, Focus, Chi, or Runic Power, depending on your class. It also interrupts NPC spellcasting for 3 seconds.

ARCANE RESISTANCE

Reduces Arcane damage taken by 1%.

Hawkstriders, the Blood Elf Racial Mount

AVAILABLE CLASSES

DEATH KNIGHT | DRUID | HUNTER | MAGE | MONK | PALADIN | PRIEST | ROGUE | SHAMAN | WARLOCK | WARRIOR

YOUR FIRST DAY AS A
BLOOD ELF

For millennia the High Elves depended on the undiluted magic of the Sunwell. With it they built an enduring society, dedicated to expanding their arcane knowledge and power. This existence came to an end as the then Prince Arthas led the Scourge into Quel'thalas, poisoning the Sunwell. Many elves were lost during this war and the survivors renamed themselves Sin'dorei, or Blood Elves, in honor of their fallen kin. Now, Silvermoon City, once the shining center of elven civilization lies partially in ruins, and though the Blood Elves have retaken most of their homeland, the battle scars are still visible and remnants of the Scourge still plague the land. The effects of the Sunwell's poisoning are felt even here, on the relatively peaceful Sunstrider Isle. It is here you begin your journey.

1	The Sunspire
2	Solanian's Journal
3	Solanian's Scrying Orb
4	Solanian's Scroll of Scourge Magic
5	Shrine of Dath'Remar
6	Lanthan Perilon
7	Falthrien Academy
8	Outrunner Alarion

SUNSTRIDER ISLE

As all inexperienced Blood Elves do, you begin your training on Sunstrider Isle. The poisoning of the Sunwell has had an effect on even the wildlife on the isle and Magistrix Erona tasks you with **Reclaiming Sunstrider Isle** from these errant creatures. Though the Mana Wyrms once served the elves as guardians of the Burning Crystals, they have now become a nuisance. You must thin their numbers to bring them under control. Mana Wyrms are plentiful nearby and give you good practice with using your starting spell or skill. Once you have cleared them out a bit, return to Magistrix Erona.

The unchecked power of the Burning Crystals has corrupted more of the isle's wildlife than Erona had originally feared and has affected even the Springpaws. Nothing can restore the felines to their previous uncorrupted state and **Unfortunate Measures** must be taken. She asks you to put down the nearby Springpaw Lynxes and Springpaw Cubs and return their collars to her.

Before heading out to perform this grisly task, there are others in the Sunspire that could use your help. Enter the Sunspire and speak with Well Watcher Solanian standing on a balcony overlooking the bottom floor. He's been so busy with the recent problems at the Sunspire that he hasn't had a chance to collect some of his belongings outside. Retrieve **Solanian's Belongings** for him. They are scattered about Sunstrider Isle. The Well Watcher has another task for you as well. Solanian believes that all Blood Elves should honor the past. He tasks you with visiting **The Shrine of Dath'Remar** Sunstrider to the west. Once there, read the plaque placed there in his honor.

Head out of the Sunspire itself and across to the nearby building. Look for Arcanist Ithanas who can use your help dealing with the creatures threatening to overrun Sunstrider Isle. Bring him **A Fistful of Slivers** and he promises to reward you with a magical boon. Slay mana using creatures on the isle to collect the slivers you need. Mana Wyrms are good targets for this quest as there are plenty of them close together nearby.

After speaking with Ithanas, turn your attention to Arcanist Helion. He cautions you of the dangers of your heritage. Though your innate Arcane Powers are great, they come with a risk of the **Thirst Unending**. Helion warns you against absorbing too much power without releasing it via Arcane Torrent. Failure to expend energy this way can cause you to become one of the Wretched, addicted to arcane energy and hopelessly insane. He asks you to use your Arcane Torrent on a Mana Wyrm for practice.

ARCANE TORRENT

All Blood Elves can perform Arcane Torrent. This racial skill silences nearby enemies, keeps them from casting for a few seconds, and restores a percentage of your own resource. Be ready to use it against casters of all types once they are in range.

Once you have obtained all five quests, you are ready to head out. First, stop by the nearby Mana Wyrms and slay them to collect the Slivers you need. Take the time to use your Arcane Torrent on one to satisfy Arcanist Helion.

Next, head south from the Sunspire to collect Solanian's Journal, and take down any Springpaws in your path. From there continue south to retrieve his Scrying Orb. Now, head northwest to find his Scroll of Scourge Magic. After collecting these belongings, and taking care of any Springpaws you encountered, continue northwest to reach the Shrine of Dath'Remar. Read the plaque dedicated to this elven hero before returning to the Sunspire. If you still need to take down Springpaws, do so on your way back.

Report back to everyone who gave you a task and collect your rewards. When you are finished report to Magistrix Erona. She lets you know that you should visit your trainer but she isn't done with you yet either. Erona has decided that you can be of more use at Falthrien Academy. Follow the path west to find her assistant and **Report to Lanthan Perilon**. Before leaving be sure to finish all other business you have at the Sunspire and take the time to visit your trainer to learn new skills and spells.

FALTHRIEN ACADEMY

To reach Lanthan travel west from the Sunspire. Before he sends you on to the academy he has another task for you. The Tenders, who used to help the elves maintain Sunstrider Isle, have now grown out of control and are showing signs of **Aggression**. They have become dangerous and these walking weeds must be cleared out. Look for them west of Lanthan Perilon. You need both Tenders and the larger Feral Tenders to satisfy the assistant. As with the other creatures you've faced, these are non-aggressive so just take on one at a time to play it safe.

After helping out Lanthan with the Tender problem, he tells you about the task Magistrix Erona originally had in mind for you. Falthrien Academy is home to one of the Wretched, **Felendren the Banished**. He earned this title, and the punishment that goes with it, because he refused to learn to control his desire for more and more arcane energy. Lanthan asks you to slay Felendren's Arcane Wraiths, Tainted Arcane Wraiths and, finally, Felendren himself. Bring his head back as proof of your deed.

Follow the path southwest to reach Falthrien Academy. Once there, work your way up the ramps, eliminating your quota of Wraiths along the way. Don't worry if you don't see many Tainted Arcane Wraiths on the way up; a pair of them share the upper floor with Felendren. Once you reach the top, give the unrepentant Felendren the end he deserves. Don't forget to claim your grisly trophy before returning to Lanthan.

TAINTED ARCANE SLIVER

The Tainted Arcane Wraiths have a chance to drop a Tainted Arcane Sliver which begins a quest.

Return it to Arcanist Helion at the Sunspire to receive a reward!

With Falthrien Academy now free of Felendren's taint, Lanthan has another job for you. The messengers that keep information flowing between Silvermoon City and Sunstrider Isle are short handed and can always use help. **Aiding the Outrunners** is a task worthy of your time. Follow the road southeast from Lanthan until you reach Outrunner Alarion along the road.

DAWNING LANE

The Wretched infest the ruins of Silvermoon and attack anyone in the hopes of getting their hands on a few mana crystals. Alarion believes that one of her outrunners has been **Slain by the Wretched**. She asks you to go south into the ruins and look for the Slain Outrunner in Dawning Lane. Unlike the other foes encountered up to this point, the Wretched that haunt the land near Dawning Lane are aggressive and won't hesitate to attack if you veer from the path. If you prefer to avoid unnecessary fights stay on the road. However, if you want to earn some extra experience, take out a few of the wretched on your way. Once you find the unfortunate outrunner, a cursory examination of her body reveals that she was carrying a package belonging to Magistrix Erona. Begin the process of **Package Recovery** by returning the parcel to Outrunner Alarion.

With another slain outrunner, Alarion is short handed and **Completing the Delivery** is impossible for her to handle on her own. She asks you to deliver the package to the Inn in Falconwing Square. Follow Dawning Lane until you reach the square.

Since the poisoning of the Sunwell, life has greatly changed for your people. There are new paths and new allies that have never been considered before. Learn well from your elders and soon you will be ready to venture outside of your homeland, showing the world that, diminished or not, the power of the Blood Elves is still to be feared.

GOBLIN

Goblins are a creative race that often fails to see the forest through the trees. This might be because of their penchant for cutting down entire swaths of landscape. Many Goblins have a fascination with technology and innovative engineering.

Often found on neutral ground, many Goblins weren't interested in taking sides between the Horde and the Alliance. There isn't much profit in the choice because it closes out a huge market from the other side. However, recent developments in the world have made it impossible for the Goblin race to sit on the sidelines. As such, some have joined the Horde and are ready to lend their inventions to the cause.

Starting Location: Kezan

RACIAL ABILITIES

ROCKET JUMP
Activates a rocket belt to jump forward; the cooldown is shared with Rocket Barrage. Effects which slow the rate of falling cannot be used for 10 seconds after using this ability.

BEST DEALS ANYWHERE
Always receive the best possible gold discount regardless of faction standing.

BETTER LIVING THROUGH CHEMISTRY
Alchemy (a crafting skill) increased by 15.

PACK HOBGOBLIN
Calls in a personal servant, allowing bank access for one minute.

ROCKET BARRAGE
Launches belt rockets at an enemy, dealing fire damage.

TIME IS MONEY
Cash in on a 1% increase to attack and casting speed!

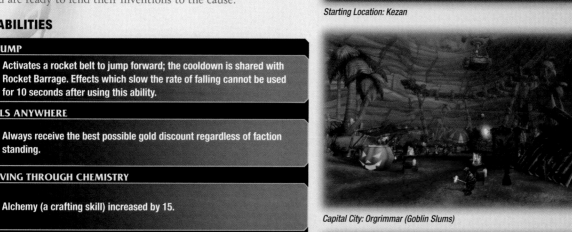

Capital City: Orgrimmar (Goblin Slums)

Motortrike, the Goblin Racial Mount.

AVAILABLE CLASSES

DEATH KNIGHT | DRUID | HUNTER | MAGE | MONK | PALADIN | PRIEST | ROGUE | SHAMAN | WARLOCK | WARRIOR

YOUR FIRST DAY AS A
GOBLIN

Under the watchful eye of Trade Prince Gallywix, the Goblins of Kezan are a busy lot. There are always deals to be brokered, goods to be moved, and, most importantly, profits to be made. The entrepreneurial spirit runs strong in every Goblin and you are no exception. As the boss at KTC Headquarters your life is good. You have the best executive assistant money can hire, the respect of your fellow citizens, and a nice stack of macaroons in the bank. There are even rumors that you might one day replace the Trade Prince himself. Yep, the best life a Goblin could ask for. As long as nothing happens to change all that…

1	KTC Headquarters
2	Kaja'Mine
3	Izzy
4	Ace
5	Kajaro Field
6	Drudgetown
7	Swindle Street
8	The First Bank of Kezan
9	Gallywix's Villa

KTC Headquarters

KTC Headquarters is the nerve center of your operation. It sits on the eastern side of Kezan, right next to the Kaja'mine that is the backbone of your business. You begin your day at headquarters by talking to Sassy Hardwrench, your Executive Assistant. There's a problem in the Kaja'mite mine and you need to be **Taking Care of Business**. Head east to find Foreman Dampwick and deliver Sassy's Incentive. Is that ticking you hear?

Head across the yard to find Foreman Dampwick at the top of the road leading down to the mine. After you deliver Sassy's "incentive" Dampwick is ready to tell you what's been going on in the mine. The foreman has a few problems eating into profits—one of them quite literally. First, he has **Trouble in the Mines**. The Tunnel Worms have come back and are eating right through the Kaja'mite. He asks you to enter the mines and exterminate them. As if the worms weren't bad enough, **Good Help is Hard to Find**. The troll slaves seem to think they can just take a break whenever they want and are in need of a serious attitude adjustment. Dampwick suggests you use your Goblin All-In-1-Der Belt to deliver the needed incentive.

Head down into the mine area and look for Defiant Trolls. The lazy good-for-nothings can be found shirking work all over the place. Give 'em a good zap with your belt to get them going again. The Tunnel Worms are found in any of the three mines. Thin them out enough so that maybe Dampwick can do his job.

Once you're done doing the foreman's jobs for him, return to receive your reward. Even though you're his boss he has the gall to ask for even more help. He's so lucky you don't fire him. He asks you to deliver the six-pack of **Kaja'Cola** to Sassy Hardwrench. When you do, she tells you that **Megs in Marketing** is looking for you. Step outside the headquarters and stop to talk with Megs Dreadshredder. She knows that image is second only to profits and suggests that you go **Riding With My Homies**. Take your new Hot Rod around and pick up your friends, Ace, Gobber, and Izzy. Use the key Megs gave you to start up your sweet ride. Drive south to reach the other side of the headquarter's pool where you find Izzy lounging. After picking her up, drive north out of KTC Headquarters and pick up Gobber just before you reach the large road running east and west. After he climbs in the car, turn left and follow the road to reach Bilgewater Port and Ace. Now that all your friends are in the Hot Rod, return to Megs. She lets you know that Coach Crosscheck, leader of the Bilgewater Buccaneers, wants you to **Report for Tryouts**. The division title is on the line and only you can bring it home. Go see him in Kajaro Field.

Before you leave, head back into the headquarters and speak with Sassy. Sometimes you have no choice but to **Do It Yourself** and Sassy has just such a job that needs your personal touch. Some deadbeats aren't paying up and you need to get down there and deliver a "collection notice," if ya know what she means. Head down into Drudgetown and deliver a beat down to Bruno Flameretardant, Frankie Gearslipper, Jack the Hammer, and Sudsy Magee.

Before leaving Headquarters either Candy Cane or Chip Endale has a task for you as well. Which quest giver you get depends on which gender of Goblin you are. Males talk with Candy Cane while Females speak to Chip Endale. Your paramour tells you that you must get some new threads before the party, which requires you to be **Off to the Bank**. Swing by the First Bank of Kezan and pick up some cash.

KAJARO FIELD

The coach tells you the Buccaneers are in a heap of trouble! His whole team's on the injured roster and the shredders have had it. The Coach needs you to help him get **The Replacements**. Gather Replacement Parts from all over the nearby area so he can get his Shredders back in the game. Look around the area of the city surrounding the field for the parts you need. Once you have them all, return to the coach.

The Buccaneers are down to their last Shredder, but the Coach gave it a few extra modifications for **Necessary Roughness**. He needs you to climb in that shredder and throw the Footbomb at the Steamwheedle Sharks. Aim at the approaching team and let the Footbombs fly until you have taken them all out. Once you are done, report back to Coach Crosscheck.

Thanks to your efforts, the game is at **Fourth and Goal**. All you have to do now is kick that goal! The coach has made another modification to the Footbomb to give you all the power you need to make a lasting impression on those Sharks. When you're finished return to the coach. Fans will be talking about the goal you kicked for a long time to come. Coach Crosscheck wants you to **Give Sassy the News**. Share your success with Sassy Hardwrench. She'll probably want to know about the dragon and Mount Kajaro too!

Now that you're done playing Footbomb it's time to get to the bank. Hop in your Hot Rod again and head west from Kajaro Field to reach the First Bank of Kezan. Don't let those long lines bother you. Important Goblins like you can go to the head of the queue. Speak with the FBoK Teller to get your Macaroons.

The Teller gives you some advice for putting together **The New You**. Buy some Shiny Bling from Gappy Silvertooth, a Hip New Outfit from Szabo, and some Cool Shades from Missa Spekkies on Swindle Street. Once you've collected your outfit you're ready to head back to headquarters.

YOUR CLASS TRAINER

Before reporting in, take a moment to speak with your trainer. You are now ready to learn an important skill or spell which helps you out in future endeavors.

After you report in to everyone who gave you a task, it's time to party. Chip or Candy wants you to put on your Awesome Party Ensemble and head on over to the party at the company pool next door to entertain your guests as the **Life of the Party**.

Your new outfit comes with some new responsibilities. You must entertain your guests, but everyone wants something different. Those that are eating could use some more Hor D'oeuvres. Guests carrying sparklers want to see some Fireworks. A few Goblins just want someone to dance with, while others need their glasses refilled with Bubbly. As is to be expected at any good party, a few guests have had a bit too much Bubbly. In these cases, handing them a Bucket is the best option. Once you've entertained your guests, return to Sassy at headquarters.

The party is a success—maybe too much of one. Southsea Pirates are crashing your party! This could be a career-ending catastrophe. Get back to the party and kill those Pirate Party Crashers before they completely ruin your celebration. Unlike the other foes faced up to this point, these pirates are aggressive and attack if you get too close. Try to avoid taking on more Pirate Party Crashers than you can handle at once. When the crashers are dealt with, head back to headquarters and talk to Sassy.

It seems that you have **An Uninvited Guest**. Trade Prince Gallywix himself is waiting for you upstairs. He has a proposition for you. It seems Mount Kajaro is exploding and he has the only way off the island. If you fork over **A Bazillion Macaroons?!** Gallywix promises to save you a spot on his private yacht. Speak with Sassy Handwrench about this proposed deal. She is right outside KTC Headquarters.

Sassy has an idea of where you can get that kind of moolah. You must perform **The Great Bank Heist**. Before heading out to the First Bank of Kezan, speak with Megs Dreadshredder. She has an idea to help collect the money as well; she thinks you should be **Robbing Hoods**. The Trade Prince has already sent hired looters out into the streets of Kezan. Take your Hot Rod and run them down, collecting their already stolen loot in the process!

Before heading out talk to Foreman Dampwick as well. He's willing to do his part to get the macaroons. The Kaja'mite deposits down by the mines are the last known deposits in the world. Use Dampwick's Kablooey Bombs for **Liberating the Kaja'mite** deposits and pick up the chunks. That stuff is priceless! Before you take off, talk to Slinky Sharpshiv. She thinks the best way to get that much money is to steal it from the trade prince himself. She gives you a disguise so you can **Waltz Right In**.

After you talk with everyone, you're ready to go. Head down into the mine first. Look for Kaja'mite deposits all around. Use the bombs to blow them apart and then pick up the chunks. Watch out for the Rebellious Trolls. Now that the Brute Enforcers are gone they are lashing out at anyone who comes near.

When you are finished in the mine, hop in your car and head down the road. The looters are running rampant all over Swindle Street and the surrounding areas. Run them down and collect their ill gotten gains! When you have finished continue on to Gallywix's Villa.

Once you are close to the villa, put on the disguise Slinky gave you. The other Mooks will never know you aren't one of them. That is, unless you get too close to Gallywix's Keensnout Potbelly Pigs. These pets can smell you a mile away so steer clear of them. Look for The Ultimate Bomb and The Goblin Lisa in small buildings near the Trade Prince's pool. Maldy's Falcon is upstairs in the villa itself.

After collecting all the priceless art you have no need for stealth anymore. Hop in your Hot Rod and head towards the bank. Once you arrive, go down the stairs to reach the bank vaults. To crack the vault you must use everything from your All-In-1-Der Belt. Once you begin, the correct tool comes up on the screen. You must quickly press this tool to successfully continue. Each time a tool appears, press the corresponding button. Once you do this enough times, the vault opens and you reclaim your personal riches! Now it's time to head back to headquarters.

After you report back to everyone, Sassy counts up your macaroons but you're still coming up short. As usual, she's got a plan. This time she's going to pull a 447. All you need to do is to collect on the insurance policy on KTC Headquarters. Go inside and Activate the Leaky Stove, Drop a Cigar on the Flammable Bed, Overload the Defective Generator, and use the Gasbot to set it all off.

Once it all goes up in flames the Claims Adjuster appears. Talk to him to turn in your claim. He doesn't have time to inspect the place and pays you the money you're owed. Check with Sassy to see if it's going to be enough. She counts up everything and your **Life Savings** should be enough to pay the Trade Prince. Now all you have to do is hand it over to him. Once you accept the quest, you both hop in the car and she drives you to Gallywix's yacht. In exchange for your Life Savings he offers you passage to Azshara—as a coal scuttling slave! Never trust the Trade Prince.

You aren't sure just what, but something goes wrong on the voyage. You wake up and look around but it sure doesn't look like Azshara to you. Oh well, you worked your way up the corporate ladder before and you can certainly do it again. This is no time to be sitting around half-drowned. Get up and prove you've got what it takes to survive not only the savage boardroom but the savage jungle as well. You've got a financial empire to rebuild. After all, time is money!

ORC

Orcs are large and terrifying to their enemies, but after numerous wars, the Orcs seek peace and a return to their shamanistic heritage. Thrall, their great Warchief, led his people to Durotar, chosen due to its desolate climate and isolated position. Due to their warring heritage, Orcs are courageous on the battlefield. They are also a hardy people, seeking a new path to glory and honor.

Orcs are approximately 6 feet tall, with muscular physiques. Males have very long and unusual facial hair. Females have eclectic hair styles and unusual piercings. All Orcs have some variation of green skin.

Start location: Valley of Trials in Durotar

Home city: Orgrimmar

Wolves, the Orc Racial Mount

RACIAL ABILITIES

AXE SPECIALIZATION

Increases Expertise with Axes and Fist Weapons by 1%. Expertise makes it harder for enemies to avoid your attacks.

BLOOD FURY

Increases attack power or spell power by an amount that increases by level. Lasts 15 seconds.

COMMAND

Damage dealt by pets is increased by 2%.

HARDINESS

Reduces the duration of Stun effects by 15%.

AVAILABLE CLASSES

DEATH KNIGHT | DRUID | HUNTER | MAGE | MONK | PALADIN | PRIEST | ROGUE | SHAMAN | WARLOCK | WARRIOR

YOUR FIRST DAY AS AN
ORC

After years of slavery and war the Orcs founded the nation of Durotar on the shores of eastern Kalimdor. Though they embrace their shamanistic heritage, they also hold the arts of war in high regard. Their capital city Orgrimmar is a city rebuilt for war, teeming with people from all factions of the Horde. Though the new Warchief, Garrosh Hellscream, has his own ideas about how to rule, the Orcs still value strength and honor above all else. The recent events of the cataclysm have made it more vital than ever that young Orcs like you rise to join the ranks of the Horde.

1	The Den
2	Hana'zua
3	Sarkoth
4	Burning Blade Coven
5	Road to Sen'jin Village

VALLEY OF TRIALS

The Valley of Trials provides a relatively safe place for young Orcs to begin their training, though it is not without its own dangers. As Kaltunk notes, you are now of age to battle in the name of the Horde! Though you may yearn for epic battles, that is not yet **Your Place in the World**. Report to Gornek for a task more suitable to one of your inexperience.

Gornek has a job designed for **Cutting Teeth** such as yours. He tells you to slaughter the Mottled Boars found on the nearby farms. When you finish, return to Gornek.

This time he has a more serious job for you. **There are Invaders in Our Home!** Despite that fact that it is in breach of a treaty, humans have infiltrated the valley. Gornek wants you to find them in the south and slay them. Before heading out to rid the valley of humans, speak with Galgar who has a tastier task for you. He wants to make **Galgar's Cactus Apple Surprise**, but he's all out of cactus apples. Collect some for him while you are out taking care of more serious business.

Head south out of the Den area and you almost immediately begin to see the Northwatch Scouts. Their clumsy attempts at stealth can't fool you! Take them down and don't forget to collect the cactus apples while you're out. When you are finished, return to Galgar and Gornek to claim your rewards.

Gornek sends you back out into the field to collect Scorpid Worker Tails. Their venom is used to make antidotes for foolish young Orcs who manage to get themselves inflicted with the **Sting of the Scorpid**.

MEETING YOUR CLASS TRAINER

Before heading out to take care of those scorpids, take a moment to read the message that Gornek gave you from your Class Trainer. Once you reach level 3, you have a new skill that you must practice.

After speaking with your trainer, stop by to talk to Foreman Thazz'ril. He has a problem with his Lazy Peons. They have a habit of napping on the job. He wants you to take his blackjack and use it on any peons you catch sleeping when they should be working!

Head north, past the farms with the Mottled Boars you slew earlier, to find Scorpid Workers. Take them out, and loot the tails from their corpses. After collecting enough tails, it's time to get those lazy peons back to work! The peons are all around the valley, mostly near the trees they are supposed to be harvesting. If you see one sleeping, walk up to him and smack him with the blackjack. Report back to the foreman when you are through.

Gornek is pleased with your progress and he has taught you all that he can. Speak to Zureetha Fargaze to continue your training. She has made a disturbing discovery. **Vile Familiars** are present in the valley. This can only mean that the Burning Blade has infiltrated the Valley of Trials and are hiding out in a cave to the north. She asks you to go there and defeat the Vile Familiars.

Before taking care of the Burning Blade, speak with Canaga Earthcaller near the Den. He is worried about his friend, **Hana'zua**. He asks you to look for him up near where the Scorpids hunt. Head northeast to find the injured troll. He is pretty bad off but his one concern is that you finish off **Sarkoth**, the large scorpid who attacked him.

Head south along the small path leading up to the plateau. Sarkoth stands out as it is larger than the Scorpid Workers and has a different coloring. When you engage the beast, watch out for its Venom Splash. It spits its venom at you, leaving a pool of it on the ground. When you see it head towards you, move quickly to avoid standing in it. Once you have obtained Sarkoth's Mangled Claw, return to Hana'zua. His injuries are such that he can't make it **Back to the Den** on his own. He wishes you to speak with Gornek to see if there is something that will help him.

BLOOD FURY

Though mostly civilized these days, when necessary Orcs can still call on their ferocious side for an edge in battle. Every Orc has the ability to use Blood Fury. This ability increases your attack power or spell power, whichever is more appropriate depending on your class. Put it to use while taking down Sarkoth.

Hana'zua has held on for this long, so he should last a bit longer. Before returning to the Den, head northwest to take care of the Vile Familiars. These vicious little demons are all around outside of the cave. Thin their numbers to lessen the Burning Blade's hold in the valley.

Return to Gornek and let him know about Hana'zua. He promises to help the injured Troll. Afterwards, report to Zureetha. You did a good job with the Familiars, but Zureetha now

sends you after something more important—an item of power. She asks you to enter the Burning Blade Coven and retrieve the **Burning Blade Medallion** and slay any Felstalkers in your way.

Before heading out, Thazz'ril has a task for you as well. Since you are entering the Burning Blade Coven anyway, you can retrieve **Thazz'ril's Pick**. He left it behind while surveying the cave and would really appreciate your bringing it back to him.

Head north to reach the Burning Blade Coven. Travel deeper into the cave to find Thazz'ril's Pick near a waterfall. It is a large tool and easy to spot. Clear out the Felstalkers you come across. They can drain your life, so finish them off as quickly as possible.

Continue deeper into the cave until you find Yarog Baneshadow. He is in possession of the Burning Blade Medallion you need. You have no choice but to relieve him of it! Baneshadow is a caster and doesn't hesitate to hit you with Fel Immolate, causing damage over time. Take him out and grab that medallion. If youe already met your quota of Felstalkers save yourself some walking and use your Hearthstone to make a quick trip back to the Den.

Your time here in the Valley of Trials is at an end, but Zureetha Fargaze needs you to take information on the Burning Blade to Sen'jin village. Once there, speak to Master Gadrin who, no doubt, has more work for you. To reach the village leave the Valley of Trials by the east road and then turn right when the road forks.

Deathwing and his minions are not the only trouble caused by the recent cataclysm. New problems have arisen around the world and now more than ever your Warchief needs strong young Orcs like you. Learn well and strive always to remember the lessons of your elders as you go forth into the world to battle for the glory of the Horde!

TAUREN

The Tauren are a spiritual and nomadic race, wandering the plains for survival and seeking the will of the Earth Mother. Though inherently peaceful, hunting skills are prized as being part of the natural order. Tribal in nature, the Tauren were united under the rule of Cairne Bloodhoof in majestic Thunder Bluff.

Tauren are 7-8 feet tall, with very large bulk and weight. Tauren have long tails, bipedal hooves, and only three fingers per hand. Both males and females have horns of varying size and shape.

Start location: Camp Narache in Mulgore

Home city: Thunder Bluff

RACIAL ABILITIES

CULTIVATION

Herbalism skill (a gathering Profession) increased by 15. Tauren also gather herb nodes faster than other races.

ENDURANCE

Base Health increased by 5%.

NATURE RESISTANCE

Reduces Nature damage taken by 1%.

WAR STOMP

Stun up to 5 enemies within 8 yards for 2 seconds.

Kodos, the Tauren Racial Mount

AVAILABLE CLASSES

DEATH KNIGHT   DRUID   HUNTER   MAGE   MONK   PALADIN   PRIEST   ROGUE   SHAMAN   WARLOCK   WARRIOR

YOUR FIRST DAY AS A
TAUREN

After centuries of war against their ancestral enemies, the centaur, the Tauren tribes banded together and made this lush land their home. All Tauren are taught to respect the Earth Mother and to honor their ancestors. Their capital city, Thunder Bluff, is a center of learning and trade and serves as a shining example of prosperity to all the Horde. Though the Tauren have managed to mostly keep the peace in Mulgore, recent incursions from the Quillboar and Grimtotem have made the area much more dangerous than it used to be. As it is with all young Tauren, it is now your turn to follow the path you have chosen and learn the skills necessary to defend your homeland.

1	Camp Narache
2	The Thornsnarl
3	Adana Thunderhorn
4	The Battleboar Pen
5	Thornmantle's Hideout
6	Fargaze Mesa

CAMP NARACHE

As a fledgling brave you begin your journey in Camp Narache. In the past the small community often happily celebrated the training of young braves but you have arrived at a time of great sorrow. Though the Tauren had managed to keep the Bristleback Quillboar under control for some time, with the recent cataclysm they have begun pouring forth from their thorny homes, expanding their territory and attacking the nearby Tauren. During one such raid, the unthinkable happened and Greatmother Hawkwind was slain. Now, the denizens of Camp Narache have but one thing on their mind—justice.

Chief Hawkwind has a simple task for you. **The First Step** is to speak to his son, Grull Hawkwind, and begin exacting vengeance on the Bristleback! Head east to find Grull. He starts you on the path to become a full fledged brave; your first challenge is the **Rite of Strength**.

To complete this task you must travel into the heart of the Thornsnarl and slay Bristleback Quillboar. New braves like yourself have been captured and it's up to you to rescue them to complete **Our Tribe Imprisoned**. After you've freed your fellow young braves return to Grull. Pleased with your work he tells you to **Go to Adana** to begin your **Rite of Courage**.

According to Adana, the Rite of Courage teaches you never to underestimate your prey. Head to the south and brave the Bristleback's wild gun fire and take back the guns they stole from Camp Narache during the battle. She also sends you to **Stop the Thorncallers** from sowing more seeds to grow their hideous vines. The Bristleback Gun Thieves don't do too much damage to you—they must not have the hang of using the stolen guns! The Thorncallers can be found towards the back of the camp raising their twisting vines. These enemies aren't aggressive so don't be concerned with accidently biting off more than you can chew.

WAR STOMP

Unlike the soft-footed races, A Tauren's hooves can serve them well in battle. Use your War Stomp to stun nearby enemies for a few precious seconds, giving you an advantage in battle. Try it out while battling the Bristleback.

When you return, Adana has other tasks for you. Though it saddens her, Adana knows that the poor, abused Armored Battleboars kept by the Bristleback can never be rehabilitated. She asks you to put a down a number of them, ending their torment. **The Battleboars** don't naturally have a taste for flesh, but the Bristleback feed them a steady diet of gore to make them hungry for the enemy. She asks you to burn this **Feed of Evil** before returning.

Head slightly southwest from Adana to find The Battleboar Pen. Because these creatures are not aggressive, you can walk right up to the feed troughs and toss in the torch by right clicking on it. It ingites the gory food trough and also any nearby battleboars, giving you easy kills at the same time as you burn the grotesque meals. After burning all three feed troughs, finish off any more Armored Battleboars you need to make Adana's quota and return to her.

Once your grisly task is completed, Adana tells you of the **Rite of Honor**. The Bristleboar you've taken down so far were just a warm up! She asks you to slay Chief Squealer Thornmantle in retribution for his killing of Greatmother Hawkwind.

Though you naturally want to seek vengeance for the Greatmother's death, before heading out speak with Rohaku Stonehoof. He gives you a note from your class trainer. Take the time to read it and return to Camp Narache. Your trainer can teach you skills that will come in handy when facing the Bristleback leader. Once you've learned what your trainer has to teach you, it is time to face the Chief.

Head southwest of Camp Narache to reach Thornmantle's Hideout. He is guarded by two Thornguards near the entrance to his small thornsnarl so be cautious when you approach. Take them out and move onto the Chief himself to extract vengeance! He is a bit tougher than the rank and file you've been cutting your teeth on, but he isn't anything you can't handle. He likes to toss his torch at you, so be ready for the additional damage this can cause.

When the enemy lies dead at your feet, return to Camp Narache and report to Chief Hawkwind that the deed is done. While nothing can return the Greatmother to your midst, it gives him some comfort to know that you dealt with her murderer. **During Last Rites, First Rites** use the Ceremonial Offering at Greatmother Hawkwind's funeral pyre near the center of Camp Narache.

Though the Greatmother can now be at rest, your journey continues. Chief Hawkwind tells you of the **Rites of the Earthmother** and instructs you to speak with Dyami Windsoar high atop Fargaze Mesa to the west of Camp Narache. Before heading there take care of any business you may still have in the camp.

You have learned all that Camp Narache has to offer and it is time for you to learn more about your chosen path and the ways of the Earth Mother. When you are ready, climb the mesa to find Dyami Windsoar. After speaking to you he begins your **Rite of the Winds**. Drink the Water of Vision he gives you to transform into a vision. This bird form delivers you safely to Bloodhoof Village where your education continues.

TROLL

The Darkspear Trolls fled Stranglethorn Vale after generations of wars with other troll tribes and invaders. The Orcs offered the Trolls a new homeland in Durotar. Sen'jin Village is named in honor of the Trolls' fallen leader. This was the temporary settling point for the Trolls, but they've now pushed out to the Echo Isles, just off the Durotar coastline.

Trolls are wild, from living in the jungle, and superstitious, due to their tribe's spiritual practices. They are 7-8 feet tall, the tallest race in Azeroth. Males frequently squat in place, but females do not. Trolls have three fingers per hand and two toes per foot. Both males and females have a variety of tusk styles and wild hair styles.

RACIAL ABILITIES

BEAST SLAYING

Damage dealt against Beasts increased by 5%.

BERSERKING

Increases your casting and attack speed by 20% for 10 seconds.

DEAD EYE

Expertise with ranged weaons increased by 1%.

DA VOODOO SHUFFLE

Reduces the duration of movement impairing effects by 15%. Trolls be flippin' out mon!

REGENERATION

Health regeneration rate increased by 10%. 10% of total health regeneration may continue during combat.

Start location: Echo Isles in Durotar

Home city: Orgrimmar (Valley of Spirits)

Raptors, the Troll Racial Mount

AVAILABLE CLASSES

DEATH KNIGHT | DRUID | HUNTER | MAGE | MONK | PALADIN | PRIEST | ROGUE | SHAMAN | WARLOCK | WARRIOR

YOUR FIRST DAY AS A
TROLL

The Darkspear Trolls have long been a race in exile. Chased from their ancestral home, they founded a settlement on the Echo Isles off the southeastern coast of Kalimdor only to be forced to abandon it to the mad witch doctor Zalazane. With the witch doctor now destroyed, the Darkspear tribe have moved back to reclaim the Echo Isles as their home. Though they remain a loyal part of the Horde, recent events have made it clear to their leader, Vol'jin, that the Darkspear Trolls must once again become a power in their own right. Though the world is facing the dangers wrought by the recent cataclysm, you have come of age at a proud time for the Darkspear. It is time for you to choose your path and learn what your elders have to teach.

1	Jin'thala
2	Darkspear Training Grounds
3	Darkspear Hold
4	Bloodtalon Shore
5	Zalazane's Fall
6	Spitescale Cove
7	Sen'jin Village

DARKSPEAR ISLE

Your training on Darkspear Isle begins with speaking to Jin'thala. The Darkspear tribe have long been victims and outcasts, fleeing their homes time and time again—but no more. Now is the time for **The Rise of the Darkspear**. It is also time for you to begin your training. He tells you to speak with your Class Trainer to begin. Head up the small hill to enter the grounds.

Who you need to speak with depends on your class, but all the trainers are inside the Darkspear Training Grounds. Though you may be eager to get out into the wide world and help your tribe, before you can move on you've got to learn **The Basics: Hitting Things**. Your trainer sends you to practice on the nearby Tiki Targets. Once you are finished, return to them.

You may be off to **A Rough Start**, but your next task gives you the chance to put your skills to a more practical use. The local Wildmane Cats are killing all the island boars. Thin their numbers and bring the pelts back to your trainer as proof of the deed. The Wildmane Cats are found all over the island. Leave the center of the training grounds to begin your hunt. Once you have collected enough pelts you are ready to return.

Now that you've displayed some promise, it's time to try something a bit more challenging. Head on over to the **Proving Pit** to face a foe who wants to kill you! When you are ready to begin, speak with the Darkspear Jailor. The Captive Spitescale Scout should be no match for a Darkspear! However, if you should fail, speak to the Jailor to try again. Once you are victorious, return to your trainer.

As your success in the Proving Pit shows, you've turned out to be **More Than Expected** and your trainer has no more to teach you. Head down to the village in the southeast and report to Vol'jin.

DARKSPEAR HOLD

Vol'jin has many concerns on his mind, but takes the time to welcome you to the Darkspear and catch you up on recent events. He lets you know that **Moraya** could use some help with the raptors. Seek her out and make yourself useful. Before heading over to Moraya speak with Tora'jin outside Vol'jin's building. He's not as young as he used to be and boar meat doesn't sit well. He asks you to go **Crab Fishin'** for Pygmy Surf Crawlers and bring him back the meat.

To find the Surf Crawlers, head north of Tora'jin and follow the path onto the beach. The tasty creatures are found all along the beach and in the water close to shore. Watch out for their Bubble Blast which can deal a decent amount of damage. After collecting the meat, return to Tora'jin.

After taking care of the old troll's need, it is time to pay Moraya a visit. She is in charge of the raptors, **A Troll's Truest Companion**. She asks you to travel to Bloodtalon Shore and speak with Kijara, one of the caretakers. Head south, across the bridge, to reach the island.

BLOODTALON SHORE

Kijara could use your help **Saving the Young**. Someone is stealing the Bloodtalon Hatchlings and she wants you to rescue them. Before heading out, talk to the other caregiver, Tegashi, as well.

Whoever stole the raptors has been corrupting them with magic. Unfortunately, there is nothing to be done but to deliver **Mercy for the Lost**. Travel to Zalazane's Fall and put down the Corrupted Bloodtalon Raptors. Though this must be done, Tegashi hates the necessity and asks you to stop the corruption at its source. He has figured out that the source of the corrupted Bloodtalons is a lone Naga, the **Consort of the Sea Witch**. He wants you to kill Naj'tess and bring back the vile orb he has been using to corrupt the poor hatchlings.

Head northwest and swim to the next island over. The Lost Bloodtalon Hatchlings you need to rescue are there. When you are near a group, blow the whistle that Kijara gave you to rescue the little guys. As you move around the island, take out the Corrupted Bloodtalons. Though they aren't aggressive and won't attack you first, they will jump in to help a fellow Bloodtalon. Be cautious in putting them down so that you don't get too many to handle at once. They have a chance of corrupting you during the fight, lowering your stats. This effect stacks and can really reduce your effectiveness. It doesn't last long so you can always wait for it to fade before starting your next fight if you need to.

Naj'tess is at the top of the hill in the center of the island. He's a bit tougher than the foes you've faced so far so wait for full health before climbing the hill. Once you are done, don't forget to grab his orb. You are now ready to return to Bloodtalon Shore.

BERSERKING

No matter how civilized a Troll might be, when battle is joined and the blood starts flowing, more primitive urges must sometimes be heeded. Berserking is an ability available to all Trolls. It significantly increases your attack power and casting speed, giving you an advantage during a tough battle. Try it out against Naj'tess!

Once you are finished helping them out, Kijara has another task for you. She wants you to take a promising raptor, one that is **Young and Vicious**, back to Moraya. Kijara needs you to use the Bloodtalon Lasso on Swiftclaw and take him back to the pens near Darkspear Hold. As his name suggests, Swiftclaw is fast and spends his time running quickly around the island. You need to be ready to use your lasso the second you see him. Once you rope hime, you mount up. He isn't stopping for anything so steer him back across the bridge until you reach the pen near the hold. Once you have delivered him safely, speak to Moraya.

After receiving your reward from Moraya, speak with Tortunga. Vol'jin has decided to launch an all out attack on the Naga on the northern part of the isle. After tasking you with **Breaking the Line**, Tortunga tells you to speak with Jornun here to get a ride to nearby Spitescale Cove. When you arrive, check in with Morrakki, Captain of the Watch.

SPITESCALE COVE

The raptor deposits you in front of Spitescale Cavern where you find the Captain of the Watch. Morakki has plenty of work for an eager young Troll like you. The Trolls will show **No More Mercy** to the atrocious Naga. He commands you to enter the cavern and kill any Spitescale Naga you see. While you are in there, Morakki also wants you to place a **Territorial Fetish** on every Naga banner you come across to let the Naga know that you mean business. Make your way into the cavern and return to Morakki when you are finished.

The Naga have long plagued the Darkspear but it seems there is a chance to settle this once and for all. The Sea Witch is an **An Ancient Enemy**, and the Trolls have been waiting a long time to get a chance at revenge. Head northeast up the hill to speak with Vol'jin. Once there offer your help in defeating Zar'jira, the Sea Witch.

During the battle, Vol'jin handles the Sea Witch but you have an important part to play. It is up to you to deal with the Manifestations of the Sea Witch. These ethereal foes keep coming throughout the fight and wiping them out deals damage to the Sea Witch herself. Once Vol'jin and Vanira have done some damage to the enemy, she unleashes freezing traps, freezing everyone but you in place. Quickly run behind her and stomp out the braziers she is using to fuel the traps. Once they are out, Vol'jin and Vanira can resume taking her down. Don't let yourself get overwhelmed by the Manifestations. They can be very challenging when not taken on one at a time. Once the witch falls, wait to speak to Vanira who transports you to Darkspear Hold where you can report to Vol'jin to receive your reward.

You've learned everything you could on Darkspear Isle. Now that you helped take down the Sea Witch, it is time for you to leave your home. Cross the shallows to the northwest to reach Sen'jin Village and report to Master Gadrin. He will be able to put a young Troll like yourself to good use.

Though it's been a long time coming, the Darkspear are once again coming into their own. The recent cataclysm has made an already dangerous world much more treacherous and your tribe needs young bloods like you more than ever. Take what you've learned here in your reclaimed homeland and use it to represent your tribe well in the coming challenges. Show your allies and enemies alike that the Darkspear are no longer fugitives, refugees, or exiles, but rather a force to be respected.

UNDEAD

A renegade group of undead broke away from the Scourge army and the rule of the Lich King. Led by Sylvanas Windrunner, this group of undead call themselves the Forsaken. Hated by the living but unwilling to return to the control of the Lich King, the Forsaken wage a continuous battle for their independent survival. They didn't choose undeath, but they see that it has its benefits.

Forsaken are 5-6 feet tall, scrawny, and gaunt. Their skin is deteriorating, and their hair is unkempt. Both males and females have a variety of decomposing features.

Start location: Deathknell in Tirisfal Glades

Home city: The Undercity

RACIAL ABILITIES

 CANNIBALIZE

When activated, regenerates 7% of your total health and mana every 2 seconds for 10 seconds. Only works on Humanoid or Undead corpses within 5 yards. Any movement, action, or damage taken while using Cannibalize will cancel the effect.

SHADOW RESISTANCE

Reduces Shadow damage taken by 1%.

TOUCH OF THE GRAVE

Your attacks and damaging spells have a chance to drain the target, dealing Shadow damage and healing you for the same amount.

 WILL OF THE FORSAKEN

Once every two minutes, an Undead can remove any Charm, Fear and Sleep Effect. This ability shares a 30 second cooldown with other similar effects.

Skeletal Horses, the Undead Racial Mount

AVAILABLE CLASSES

DEATH KNIGHT　DRUID　HUNTER　MAGE　MONK　PALADIN　PRIEST　ROGUE　SHAMAN　WARLOCK　WARRIOR

YOUR FIRST DAY AS AN
UNDEAD

Bereft of the kingdom, friends, and family that once claimed them, those undead fortunate enough to rise from the ground with their sanity intact have formed a new nation. Pledging allegiance to Lady Sylvanas Windrunner, the Banshee Queen, the Forsaken have claimed Tirisfal Glades as their home. Though the Forsaken Capital, the haunting subterranean Undercity, lies beneath the ruins of Lordaeron in central Tirisfal Glades, there are many who would challenge the Forsaken's claim to this land, seeing in them little more than monsters. Newly joined with the Alliance, the forces of Gilneas mass nearby while the zealots known as the Scarlet Crusade seek to wipe out all undead, making no distinction between the Scourge or the Forsaken. It is into this world you have risen. Take up your arms, learn well, and prepare to defend not only your new homeland, but your very right to exist.

1	The Shadow Grave
2	Deathknell
3	Night Web's Hollow
4	Rotbrain Encampment
5	Road to Calston Estate

SHADOW GRAVE

You wake to find Agatha, a val'kyn in the service of Sylvanas standing over you as she wakes you up from your dirt nap. Unlike so many **Fresh Out of the Grave** you have awoken with your sanity still intact—one of the Forsaken instead of the mindless Scourge. She tells you to talk to Undertaker Mordo to begin your new life.

No matter what you were in your former life, in this life you start out in a musty grave, working for Mordo. He sends you into **The Shadow Grave** to fetch his Thick Embalming Fluid and his Corpse-Stitching Twine. He also sends along Darnell, who knows the way. Head down into the Shadow Grave and collect the items from a table on the left. Once you have them, return to Mordo. Not everyone was as lucky as you, rising from the grave with your mid still your own. **Those That Couldn't Be Saved** must be dealt with as well. Mordo sends you to destroy the Mindless Zombies that wander the graveyard. They are pitiful foes, but must be put down. Once you are finished, return to the Undertaker.

Undertaker Mordo has no more use for you, but others might. He sends you to speak with Caretaker Caice. Not everyone who rises with their mind intact takes the news of their new circumstance well. **The Wakening** is strenuous on the dead and Caice asks you to speak with three recently risen, Marshal Redpath, Lilian Voss, and Valdred Moray. All three can be found in the graveyard. After you have spoken to them, return to Caice.

Now that he knows you are ready and willing to make yourself useful, Caretaker Caice sends you **Beyond the Grave**, along with Darnell. Follow the road into the small town of Deathknell and speak with Deathguard Saltain.

DEATHKNELL

Deathknell is a small sheltered town perfect for the freshly risen to get used to their new unlives. It has everything a fledgling Forsaken needs, such as class trainers and merchants. There are several townsfolk willing to reward you for performing tasks for them. Since you rose from the grave with little more than the tattered rags on your back, you should accept the jobs they offer you.

Deathguard Saltain has a **Recruitment** task for you. The buildings to the north and east are littered with the corpses of Scarlet Crusade members. Saltain wants you to find them and point at them so that Darnell can pick them up.

Before going out on corpse duty, go into the chapel and speak with Shadow Priest Sarvis. Though Arthas is no longer upon the Frozen Throne, his former, mindless slaves still infest the northern part of Deathknell. Sarvis asks you to deal with the **Scourge on Our Perimeter** by killing Rattlcage Skeletons and Wretched Ghouls.

These enemies aren't aggressive, so attack them one at a time and you'll have no problem taking them out. The Scarlet Crusade corpses can be found all around, inside buildings, sprawled in the street, pretty much anywhere. They are easy to spot. All you need to do is point at them to have Darnell pick them up. Don't worry—he's much stronger than he looks. Once you have gathered the corpses and thinned out the number of Scourge, return to the Forsaken held section of Deathknell to receive your rewards.

When you return to Shadow Priest Sarvis he gives you a scroll from your class trainer. Before leaving the chapel, speak with Novice Elreth, who has a task for you. As you saw when you spoke with her earlier, Lilian Voss is having trouble accepting **The Truth of the Grave**. Take Elreth's Hand Mirror to Lilian in the inn. She needs to see the truth of what she is now.

Head into the inn and look for Lilian upstairs. Speak with her to display her reflection in the mirror. Afterwards, return to Novice Elreth with news of Lilian's reaction. Though the news is disappointing, Novice Elreth can see that you, at least, are an assest to the Forsaken. She sends you to speak to **The Executor in the Field**.

CANNIBALIZE

While you may not share the Scourge's mindless aggression, you do have one thing in common with them—a taste for flesh! After a battle, use your Cannibalize skill to replenish your health by making a meal out of your fallen undead or humanoid foe.

Follow the road north out of Deathknell. When the road begins to curve, you see Executor Arren. Seeing the state of your armor he offers to help you improve it a bit with pieces of **The Damned**. Bring him Scavenger Paws and Duskbat Wings to get a useful piece of armor. You can find plenty of creatures to the north and west of Arren's location. Once you've gathered the needed items, return to Executor Arren for your reward!

The Forsaken need gold, but the nearby gold mine in **Night Web's Hollow** is overrun by spiders. Arren tasks you with clearing out both Young Night Web Spiders and the older specimens, Night Web Spiders.

MAKE SOME ROOM!

Before heading out to deal with the arachnids, visit one of the merchants in Deathknell to clear out your bag. You need as much inventory room as possible to carry any valuable loot you come across.

Head northwest of Deathknell to reach the mine. The Young Night Web Spiders you need skitter around outside of the mine while their larger counterparts make their home inside the mine. These bigger foes can inject you with a weak poison, so watch your health and don't let it get too low. You don't want to be unpleasantly surprised by the extra damage.

After exterminating your quota, return to Executor Arren who has another job for you. Since the Val'kyr arrived, more and more undead are chosing not to join the Forsaken. These troublemakers are **No Better Than the Zombies** and have gathered at a small camp nearby and plan to attack Deathknell! Head east down the road and report to Darnell.

At the request of Shadow Priest Sarvis, Darnell has been keeping an eye on the camp. It's now time for a full out **Assault on the Rotbrain Encampment**. Head southeast to the camp and kill their leader, Marshal Redpath, and 8 Rotbrain Undead. Unlike the other foes you've faced so far, these are aggressive and attack you if you get too close. If you find that you're having trouble, fight next to a Deathguard Protector for some extra help. Once you've thinned out their numbers report back to Shadow Priest Sarvis in Deathknell.

Though you were helpful in Deathknell, it's time to venture out to offer more assistance to the Forsaken. Deliver the Scarlet Crusade Documents to Sarvis's field agent at the Calston Estate, Deathguard Simmer. He will make good use of this **Vital Intelligence**. Follow the road north from Deathknell to reach the estate.

Few are lucky enough to rise from the grave at all, but you are among those rare fortunate ones to rise with your mind still intact. Though your former ties may be severed, you have now found a new home and a new purpose as a member of the Forsaken.

PANDAREN

Since breaking free of the control of the mysterious race known as the Mogu thousands of years ago, the Pandaren have lived peacefully on the continent of Pandaria, and on the Wandering Isle, which is actually Shen-zin Su, the great turtle. Pandaren are known to be tenacious and have a passion for food and imbibing spirits.

Pandaren are generally between 5 and 6 feet tall, and covered in fur from head to toe. Every Pandaren has two colors of fur; one is always white but the other color ranges from black to brown to red.

Pandaren are unique among the playable races of Azeroth in that they begin as Neutral, part of neither the Horde nor the Alliance. Pandaren who wish to see the rest of Azeroth must choose between the factions before they're allowed to depart the Wandering Isle.

Start location: Shang Xi Training Grounds on Shen-zin Su

RACIAL ABILITIES

EPICUREAN
Your love of food allows you to receive double the stats from Well Fed effects.

GOURMAND
Cooking skill increased by 15.

INNER PEACE
Your rested experience bonus lasts twice as long as normal.

BOUNCY
You take half falling damage.

QUAKING PALM
Strikes the target with lightning speed, incapacitating them for 4 seconds, and turns off your attack.

Dragon Turtle, the Pandaren Racial Mount

AVAILABLE CLASSES

DEATH KNIGHT DRUID HUNTER MAGE MONK PALADIN PRIEST ROGUE SHAMAN WARLOCK WARRIOR

YOUR FIRST DAY AS A
PANDAREN

The mysterious Pandaren have rarely been seen by the other denizens of Azeroth, and indeed, were often thought to be nothing more than a myth. Pandaria, the continent of this ancient culture, has been shrouded by the mists that kept it hidden and safe since before the Sundering.

Now, through a simple accident, they find themselves connected to the rest of Azeroth once more. They must also choose which side of the great conflict to lend their strength and wisdom.

1	Master Shang Xi
2	Shang Xi Dojo
3	Jaomin Ro
4	Fu's Pond
5	Wu-Song Village
6	Windstone
7	The Shrine of Inner-Light
8	The Singing Pools
9	Old Man Liang
10	The Pool of Reflection
11	The Dai-Lo Farmstead
12	Ki-Han Brewery
13	Gong
14	Morning Breeze Village
15	Ridge of the Laughing Winds
16	Fe-Feng Village
17	Jade Tiger Pillar
18	Ruk-ruk
19	Chamber of Whispers
20	The Wood of Staves
21	Mandori Village
22	Forlorn Hut
23	Wreck of the Skyseeker

Shang Xi Training Grounds

You begin your journey as a Pandaren at the Shang Xi Training Grounds on Shen-zin Su, the Wandering Isle. As a young Pandaren you know you have **Much to Learn**. Speak with Master Shang Xi to get started. Before he can teach you **The Lesson of the Iron Bough**, he sends you to retrieve and equip a Trainee's Weapon, appropriate to your chosen class.

Follow the path that leads down the hill to one of the Weapon Racks. Right click on it and take the Trainee's Weapon. Once you have it in your bag, right click it to equip it. Now that you are properly armed, return to Master Shang Xi.

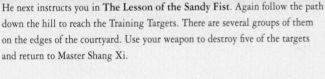

He next instructs you in **The Lesson of the Sandy Fist**. Again follow the path down the hill to reach the Training Targets. There are several groups of them on the edges of the courtyard. Use your weapon to destroy five of the targets and return to Master Shang Xi.

Though you performed well against the Training Targets, Master Shang Xi reminds you that facing a living opponent can be much more difficult. He tasks you with **The Lesson of Stifled Pride**. Head back down into the courtyard and into the dojo at the eastern edge. Inside are Tushui and Huojin Trainees. It doesn't matter which ones you choose as opponents. Approach each one individually and battle them until you are the victor. After defeating six sparring partners, return to Master Shang Xi, who has come to the dojo to watch your performance.

QUAKING PALM

Though all Pandarens aren't monks, they do all have a basic training in the Pandaren martial arts. This racial ability allows you to strike a target with lightning speed, incapacitating them for a short time. Just keep in mind that it turns off your attack. It has a fairly lengthy cooldown, so you most likely will only be able to use it once during this quest, but practicing it now is a good idea.

The master has another task for you during **The Lesson of the Burning Scroll**. When you accept the quest, Master Shang Xi asks you to "snatch" a flame from his hand. Climb the stairs all the way to the top of the temple and right click on the Edict of Temperance to burn the scroll. Once this is done, go back down the stairs to speak with Master Shang Xi.

GAINING A REPUTATION

Completing quests for Master Shang Xi and others at the Training Grounds earns you Reputation with Shang Xi's Academy.

You are now ready to face an even greater challenge. Head through the dojo, down the stairs, and across the bridge to face Jaomin Ro, one of the academy's most advanced students in **The Disciple's Challenge**. Take a moment to admire the view; your opponent will wait.

Jaomin Ro is the most challenging opponent you've faced so far. Speak to him when you are ready to initiate combat. This is a good opportunity to use Quaking Palm to give yourself a little extra time to attack while Jaomin Ro is stunned. Be wary of his favorite move, Baby Elephant Takes a Bath. When he initiates this, quickly move so that he doesn't land on you. His other special attack, Hawk Diving to Earth, does a decent amount of damage, but stuns him afterward. Take advantage of this and get in a few hits while he's defenseless. Keep up your attacks and eventually you best this star pupil. If you've taken much damage in the fight, you can always take a bite of the Small Sugarcane Stalk found in your bag. When you are ready, speak to Master Shang Xi who has moved to the center of the bridge where he had a good view of the battle.

Master Shang Xi is impressed with the progress you've made and now has a more challenging task which none of his other students have been able to perform on their own. Two of his most promising students are assigned to help you with this task. The first is **Aysa of the Tushui**. Follow the road west. You may notice the creatures populating this idyllic landscape, such as the Corsac Foxes and Amberleaf Scamps. You can engage them if you'd like but they aren't aggressive and you soon have plenty of opportunity to test your skills against them.

When you reach Fu's Pond, speak to Merchant Lorvo. It seems Aysa is in the middle of her exercises and really shouldn't be disturbed. Lorvo could use your help while you're waiting though. The good merchant ran into some trouble on the road with the Amberleaf Scamps you saw on your way here. They've taken his supplies and his cart driver ran off after the sprites. He asks you to find **The Missing Driver** and recover **Items of Utmost Importance**.

Slay the nearby Amberleaf Scamps to recover the Stolen Training Supplies. Head north from Fu's Pond to find the driver, Min Dimwind. There are also plenty of Amberleaf Scamps by the driver as well. Once you have found the driver and collected all of the Stolen Training Supplies, return to Merchant Lorvo. When you return, Aysa has finished her exercises and is waiting for you.

Aysa follows **The Way of the Tushui** and asks you to accompany her to the Cave of Meditation so she may seek the path you both must follow. Though Aysa bounds up the rocks, you must follow them around to the right to reach the nearby cave.

Inside the cave, Amberleaf Troublemakers are trying to disturb Aysa's meditation. Take them on, with the help of the Tushui Monks, so that Aysa can complete the ritual. When she is finished you must speak to Master Shang Xi outside of the cave.

Master Shang Xi now sends you to his other star pupil, **Ji of the Huojin**. Head northwest from the cave to reach Wu-Song Village where you find Ji Firepaw facing off against a hoard of Fe-Feng Hozen.

It is **The Way of the Huojin** to defend themselves against these brazen Hozen. Ji Firepaw asks you to slay the Fe-Feng attackers. These Hozen are more troublesome than the creatures you have faced so far. They are aggressive and, unlike the Amberleaf Scamps, attack you if you get too close. Be careful as you walk through the village so that you don't take on more than you can handle at once. When you're finished, return to Ji.

Ji now asks your help in **Kindling the Fire** and **Fanning the Flames**. Head south to gather Dry Dogwood Roots for kindling and to find a Living Air from which to collect a Fluttering Breeze. Look for the Roots at the base of the numerous trees to the south, but watch out for the Fe-Feng running around. When you are ready to face the Living Air, approach the Wind Stone and use the Wind Stone that Ji gave you. When the Living Air appears, you must defeat it to receive the Fluttering Breeze. Though it is most likely no match for you, it does have a nasty lightning attack, so use caution when facing it. When you have both the roots and the breeze, return to Ji Firepaw in the village.

When you have finished Ji's tasks you must once again speak with Master Shang Xi, who has traveled to meet you in Wu-Song Village. Before you can rekindle Huo, the Spirit of Fire, you must speak with Master Li Fei, **The Spirit's Guardian**. Head west out of the village and across the bridge, then veer slight to the southwest to find the cave near a waterfall.

Once you enter the cave you see a beautiful pool, but your path lies up the fire riddled path. Watch the intervals of the bursts of flame and time your passage to stay out of their fire. Speak to Master Li Fei to complete this task.

Master Li Fei knows that it would be unfair for you to face him in combat, but there is a way to level the playing field. Take the torch he gives you and light it in the brazier next to him and use it to light the other three braziers around the pool. Once you have lit the Brazier of the Blue Flame, the Red Flame, and the Violet Flame, return to Master Li Fei. These three flames illuminate not what you are, but what you have the potential to become. With their help you must defeat Master Li Fei.

As you might expect, Master Li Fei is no pushover, even with all of your future potential helping you out. Be prepared for his Feet of Fury which rain a sequence of blows on you. He also likes to teleport behind you and deliver a good kick. The good news is that he doesn't do much damage. Keep up your attacks and you should soon win the day. Upon defeating him you earn the right to proceed to **Huo, the Spirit of Fire**.

Head up the ramp behind Master Li Fei. Approach Huo and use Huo's Offerings to fan his flame! Once you have reignited Huo, speak to him. Huo is ready to follow you now and you must bring him to the Temple of the Five Dawns in the center of the island to fulfill **The Passion of Shen-zin Su**.

Exit the Shrine of Inner Light and head to the southeast. Climb the Dawning Stair to reach the Temple of the Five Dawns. Leading Huo to the temple was just the start. The other three elemental spirits must be returned as well. Master Shang Xi knows that Shen-zin Su, the great turtle on which you live, is in pain. Bringing the spirits back to the temple may give him the ability to speak with the great turtle.

Master Shang Xi tasks you to work with Aysa Cloudsinger to find the Spirit of Water in **The Singing Pools** to the east. Before leaving the temple, take advantage of the merchant, Cheng Dawnscrive, to sell any unwanted items you may have.

Leave the temple by the eastern door and follow the road to reach the Singing Pools. Before meeting up with Aysa, take a moment to speak with Jojo Ironbrow. Though he is tight lipped about the reason, he asks you to gather Hard Tearwood Reeds from the nearby pools. Once you've agreed, head over the bridge and into the water to reach Aysa. Much to your surprise, the water has transformative qualities which allow you to reach Aysa quickly.

Aysa intends to meditate on a course of action, but in the meantime collect the reeds for Jojo Ironbrow and work on **The Lesson of Dry Fur** that Aysa sets before you. While you are working on that, you may as well learn **The Lesson of the Balanced Rock**. Aysa not only expects you to balance on the poles and ring the training bell, but to also defeat the Tushui Monks practicing there as well.

All three of your quests can be handled in the same place, the nearby cursed pools. As you noticed when speaking with Aysa, the pools have transformative qualities. The other pools are inhabited by Whitefeather Cranes who don't care if the tasty morsels they snack up are really Pandarens or not. If it looks like a frog, it tastes like a frog! Be careful of these predatory birds.

Right-click to hop from pole to pole until you reach the training bell. Ring it and return to the poles. Though you've proven you can move on the balance poles you must now face the Tushui Monks. Fight them one by one until you've sent the required number down into the pool to pose as frogs. Now the cranes are their problem.

Return to Jojo Ironbrow so he can use the reeds you gathered to prove his strength, then go to Aysa who has another task for you in **Finding an Old Friend**. Her meditation has told her of Old Man Liang, who often played with Shu, the Water Spirit. Head northeast across the pools and follow the path a short way to Liang's Retreat where you find the old Pandaren looking over the pools.

Old Man Liang tells you of his friendship with Shu, the Spirit of Water, and recommends you retrieve **The Sun Pearl** to give to Shu. While you're looking for it in the pools below you can also experience **The Sting of Learning** by thinning out the Water Pincers in the pools. Their numbers have grown too great and they have become a hazard.

Head southeast toward the Sun Pearl, clearing out any Water Pincers in your path. It is a good idea to hunt as many as you need before seeking the Sun Pearl so you don't need to backtrack. Once you reach the next pool, dive under water to find the Sun Pearl. Beware the Fang-she, vicious water wyrms, who guard it. When you have the pearl, head up the bridge leading out of the northeastern side of the pool to find Old Man Liang waiting for you.

According to Old Man Lian, **Shu, the Spirit of Water**, just wants to have a friend to play with. He is sulking in the pool to the north. Cross the rocks in the pool to the east and step onto the first small whirlpool you see and the Blessing of the Water Strider gives you the power you need to reach the Pool of Reflection.

Once there head out to the center of the pool and use the Sun Pearl. Shu appears, ready to play. It looks like he found **A New Friend** in you. Show him you're ready to play by jumping into his waterspouts when they appear. Watch for Shu; when he appears on a rock run toward him. When you see him begin forming a spout, run into it! Once you've satisfied the Water Spirit speak to Aysa Cloudsinger on the southern shore of the pool.

While Aysa returns to tell Master Shang of your progress, you travel south to the farmlands to seek out Wugou, the Spirit of the Earth. You must meet up with Ji Firepaw there to investigate **The Source of Our Livelihood**. Follow the path south a short way to reach the Delivery Cart. Board the cart and ride it to the Dai-Lo Farmstead. You are welcome to walk, of course, but the cart looks like a comfortable ride.

When you reach the farmstead, speak to Ji who has been trying to rouse the sleeping Spirit of Earth. For now, Wagou refuses to wake, but there are more problems on the farmstead. Ji is going to keep trying to wake Wugou but he needs your help with some **Rascals**.

Hungry Virmen have infested the surrounding fields. Ji tasks you with thinning their numbers. Once you accept Ji's quest, Gao Summerdraft, head of the farmstead, has a task for you as well. Though killing the Virmen is a good start, Gao Summerdraft also needs you to recover some of the produce they've stolen. He has an island full of people to feed and every vegetable counts. Recover Uprooted Turnips, Stolen Carrots, and Pilfered Pumpkins while you're slaying the Virmen.

The Virmen are ravenous foes, so be careful to not get overwhelmed by too many at once. If you do find yourself in trouble, Dai-Lo Farmers are stationed throughout the fields and gladly jump in on your side if you're close enough to them.

Look for the Turnips lying near the turnip field. The Vermin evidently aren't as fond of them as of carrots and pumpkins. For the other vegetables, head into the Teeming Burrow. It has entrances in both the carrot field and pumpkin patch. Inside you find Plump Carrotcrunchers among the other Virmen. You can collect your carrots from them or find them stored inside the burrow. Enter and head down the left passage to reach Virmen Grotto, where they're storing all the pumpkins they've collected. You can also reach the grotto directly by heading east through the rows. Grab what you need and head back to the farmstead.

When you return to Ji he has decided the best course of action is to make so much noise that Wugou can't possible sleep through it. Luckily, there is a gong conveniently nearby. He asks you to retrieve the **Missing Mallet** from the nearby Ki-Han Brewery. Before you leave for the brewery, Jojo Ironbrow has a task for you as well. He is still eager to show you his prowess. He wants to you gather wood planks so he can show everyone that he is **Stronger Than Wood**.

Follow the road south out of the village as it winds to the southwest to the Ki-Han Brewery. To retrieve the Mallet, you must first deal with Raggis. (He does not drop the Mallet. It is sitting next to him.) This white Virmen is larger and more vicious than most. He can Burrow, tunneling underneath the earth only to knock you back and cause damage when he hits you. Once you've dealt with Raggis, collect the wood for Jojo and return to the farmstead. Though Plump Virmen hop around the woodpiles, they shouldn't give you too much trouble by now.

Return the wood to Jojo so he can demonstrate his prowess for you and the waiting crowd and then report back to Ji Firepaw. Now that you have the mallet, it's time for a **Raucous Rising**! Ring the Gong!

It seems that Wugou is a heavy sleeper. Oh well, Ji has another plan. Shu is playing in the small waterfall pool just north of Wugou. Maybe he will help Wake Wugou with a little water, but **Not In the Face**! Ask him and he agrees. Follow him back to Wugou and watch as he wakes the Spirit of Earth. Speak with Ji afterward.

Now that Wugou has woken it's time to see to **The Spirit and Body of Shen-zin Su**. There is a cart waiting to take you back to the Temple of Five Dawns. Hop in and enjoy the ride. Once you reach the temple grounds, climb the steps to find Master Shang Xi inside the temple itself.

With three of the four spirits returned to the temple, Master Shang Xi is well on the way to finding the answers needed to help Shen-zin Shu. The fourth and final spirit is Dafeng, the Spirit of Air. You must meet Ji Firepaw and Aysa Cloudsinger at **Morning Breeze Village** to continue your journey. There are various merchants at the temple. Once you have taken care of any buying and selling you care to do, speak with Master Shang Xi to be taken to the top of the temple. Once his winds deposit you at the top, follow Ji Firepaw across the bridge to the southwest to reach the village.

If you wish, you can go down the stairs as you cross the bridge to listen to Lorewalker Amai's stories before continuing. As you exit the bridge, you enter the Ridge of Laughing Winds. Fe-Feng infest the land on both sides of the road, so tread carefully and be ready to battle. The village is not far, and you can find Ji Firepaw on the dock, next to a hot air balloon.

While Aysa finishes her exercises, Ji has a task for you. The Fe-Fen Hozen have defiled the scrolls hanging in the grotto to the south. Since they can't be recovered it's up to you to destroy these **Rewritten Wisdoms**. Before visiting the grotto, speak with Elder Shaopai and Jojo Ironbrow. The elder tasks you with recovering the **Tools of the Enemy**. If the Hozen have no stolen brushes with which to defile the scrolls, perhaps their vandalism will stop. Not satisfied to stop with Reeds and Wood, Jojo Ironbrow now wishes to prove he is **Stronger Than Stone**. He wants you to gather some stone blocks from the Ridge of Laughing Winds.

You can accomplish all three of these tasks in the same general area. Head south into the grotto. Travel through the grotto collecting Abandoned Stone Blocks from the ground, burning the Defaced Scrolls of Wisdom, and defeating the Fe-Feng Wisemen to collect the Paint Soaked Brushes. When you are finished, return to Jojo and Elder Shaopai before finally reporting back to Ji Firepaw.

Ji has had it with the Fe-Feng Hozen! He proposes **The Direct Solution** for dealing with them and sends you to their village to take them down. While there, make sure they can **Do No Evil** by slaying their chieftain, Ruk-ruk. Also, recover the Stolen Firework Bundles so that Morning Breeze Village doesn't have to live under a **Monkey Advisory Warning**. Hozen and fireworks are not a good combination.

Head northwest to reach Fe-Fang Village. Ji Firepaw tags along, so you get some help on this one. When you enter the village, don't miss the quest from the Jade Tiger Pillar. The pillar looks amazingly strong, much stronger than reed, wood, or stone, in fact, it looks **Stronger than Bone**. You know Jojo would love to test his strength against this. Hang onto it for now and you can deliver it to him in the village when you're done with your other tasks.

Head into the village, but move forward carefully. There are many groups of Hozen, as well as some who wander the area. With Ji's help you should be able to take them out with little difficulty, as long as you use a bit of caution. Fighting Ruk-ruk isn't too much more difficult than facing his subjects, though he has a good deal more health, and likes to shoot rockets at you. When you see him Aim, move so that the rocket doesn't hit you directly. Once you're finished, speak with Ji. You must turn in all of his quests, as well as give the Jade Tiger Pillar to Jojo before continuing.

Aysa has been meditating for some time to achieve a **Balanced Perspective**. Ji wants you to climb the rope leading from the dock to reach her. They are nice, thick ropes, and if you pay close attention to where you are walking, you should be able to reach her in no time.

During her time meditating, Aysa has discovered the location of Dafeng, the Spirit of Air. He is hiding from the great Onyx Serpent who you may have seen flying through the sky. You can find Dafeng in the Chamber of Whispers, at the south side of the plateau.

Head back into the village and follow the road to the south. If any Fe-feng Hozen are foolish enough to get in your way, take them down. You soon reach the Chamber of Whispers. The Chamber is guarded by fierce winds. Wait for an opening and then cross into the next chamber. You must wait once again for an opening to reach Dafeng. You can choose to plow through the winds, but they do a great deal of damage and your survival isn't guaranteed.

After speaking with Dafeng, Aysa knows what you must do. Dafeng is frightened of the Onyx Serpent, but luckily, Ji has an idea about how to deal with it in a **Battle for the Skies**. Exit the Chamber the same way you came in, though you don't need to worry about the wind now.

When you exit the Chamber, Ji has his fireworks ready. Watch as the Onyx Serpent flies overhead. Use the various fireworks while it is directly overhead. Fire them in succession to weaken the beast. Once it takes sufficient damage, the beast lands and you can attack it with everything you have. When it rises back into the air, repeat your performance with the fireworks. Eventually it lands again where you can finish it off. While in the air the Onyx Serpent places large circles of electricity on the ground. Avoid these as they cause a great deal of damage. If you can't hit a firework because of this, move on to the next one. The Onyx Serpent is fierce beast. Face it with the caution it deserves and you win the day. When it is dead, speak with Master Shang Xi nearby.

Now that you have all four elemental spirits, Master Shang Xi has one more task. You must accompany him to the western grove to see if you are **Worthy of Passing**. Follow him to the west and up The Elders' Path where you must face the Guardian of the Elders. Once you have defeated it, you can pass into the Wood of Staves. Master Shang Xi must prepare for a ritual but he has two tasks for you. The first is **Small, But Significant**. You must collect Kun-Pai Ritual Charms from the grove. The second is slightly more challenging. Due to their **Unwelcome Nature**, you must kill the Thornbranch Scamps who infest the wood.

The charms are found hanging from trees in the wood. The Thornbranch Scamps are abundant as well. Seek them out in the wood and return to Master Shang Xi when you have completed both tasks he set before you.

Before you continue on your journey alone, stay and listen to Master Shang Xi in his effort of **Passing Wisdom** along to you. When he has finished head west and speak with Aysa Cloudsinger near Master Shang Xi's hot air balloon. It is time to see if you can alleviate **The Suffering of Shen-zin Su**.

Once you arrive at the Temple of Five Dawns, speak with Elder Shaopai. You have been **Bidden to Greatness**. You must find out more about the thorn in Shen-zin Su's side. Elder Shaopai asks you to open the gates to the Pei-Wu Forest so that you might seek a lone hermit who lives within. Exit the temple and descend the steps into Mandori Village. Head south to join Ji, Aysa, and Jojo Ironbrow in opening the village gate. Continue following the path to reach the Pei-Wu Forest gate.

Once you make it through, follow the path to reach Wei Palerage, the Hermit of the Forbidden Forest, along with some strange companions.

While Aysa and Jojo go off to find out more about the crashed ship, the hermit could use your help. Since Shen-zin Su began shaking, the creatures of the forest have become much more dangerous. He asks you to begin **Preying on the Predators** to help clear out some of these dangerous Pei-Wu Tigers. Before taking care of that, speak with the Tauren, Korga Strongmane as well. His men are malnourished, injured and exhausted, but they want to be ready to fight if the need should arise. He asks that you help in **Stocking Stalks** so that his crew can make spears out of the broken bamboo stalks.

The tigers are found throughout the forest. You should have no problem facing them one on one, but be careful of biting off more than you can chew. Look for the Broken Bamboo Stalks near growing bamboo trees. Once you've completed your tasks return to the Forlorn Hut.

To ease Shen-zin Su's suffering, you must find a way to remove the wrecked ship. To begin **Wrecking the Wreck**, you need to find Makael Bay, the engineer, in the forest. Head west to look for the engineer. Be on the lookout for Darkened Terrors and Horrors, aggressive lizard humanoids which dwell in this part of the forest.

Makael is glad to help free the ship, but he needs explosives to do it. Sift through the wreckage and bodies to the south to search for the Packed Explosive Charges. Remember to **Handle with Care**.

Now that you've made it to Makael, Ji Firepaw also has a task or you. He wants you to clear out some of the Darkened Horrors and Darkened Terrors infesting the forest. Much like the tigers you put down, these pose little risk unless you get overrun by a few at once. Explosives litter the same area of the forest. Once you collect what you need, return to Makael and Ji.

Since Makael's plan involves using the explosions, Ji wants to make sure everyone is safely away from the wreck. Head to the crash site and speak to Delora Lionheart at the Alliance camp. Though Aysa has been helping rescue the crash survivors, Delora asks you to make sure **None are Left Behind** on the ship. She also needs any **Medical Supplies** you can find. Before you head to the ship, speak with Jojo Ironbrow. He thinks things have gone **From Bad to Worse** and wants you to take out some of the nearby Deepscale Tormentors to make the area safer.

Head toward the wreck, and eliminate any Deepscale Tormentors on the way. There are Medical Supplies scattered around, as well as injured sailors. To save sailors, click on them and carry them back to camp. You have three minutes to get them there so this is plenty of time, even if you have to stop to fight.

Once you've finished and turned in the quests as well, speak with Jojo Ironbrow again. He has had word of **An Ancient Evil**. To save Aysa, you must defeat Vordraka, the Deep Sea Nightmare.

Vordraka is no pushover, so get to full health before starting the battle. If you have any health potions, it's a good idea to have one handy. When you are ready, return to the ship where Aysa Cloudsinger has already engaged the beast. Vordraka uses Deep Sea Smash, a medium range cone attack that you can see heading your way. Watch for the puffs of smoke along the ground and move before you are hit. He also uses Deep Sea Rupture, which is an attack which travels along the ground and erupts from the ground, piercing you and pulling you toward him. You can see both of these attacks heading your way, so be prepared to dodge quickly.

As if he weren't dangerous enough on his own, Vordraka also periodically summons a pair of Deepscale Aggressors to join the battle. When this happens, switch your attention to them and take them down as quickly as possible. Aysa continues to fight the boss throughout the battle, so you do have some help. Keep up the damage, stay out of Vordraka's special moves, and you soon prevail. When the beast is dead, speak to Aysa.

Next, you will be **Risking it All**. Aysa feels that Ji's plan to blow up the ship is too risky. There must be another way. Follow up into the ship to find Ji Firepaw at the top. After a discussion, Ji removes the thorn. Speak with him again after it is gone.

Now you must undertake **The Healing of Shen-zin Su**. Defeat the Deepscale Ravagers and Fleshrippers who are attacking the nearby healers. A bar appears on the screen to let you know how much healing has been done. The onslaught lasts until the bar fills up, indicating that Shen-zin Su has begun to heal. Focus on attacking the foes that are attacking the healers. Some of the healers are trapped beneath wreckage, free them so that they can heal Shen-zin Su. It is a monumental task and they need all their combined strength to accomplish it. If you're fighting by yourself, you can't get all twelve healers active. Pick a healer close to the wound and defend them. The foes keep coming as the bar rises and

you are better off keeping a few healers safe rather than running around trying to rescue them all, only to find that healers you helped out earlier are being slain by the scaly foes. Eventually the wound begins to close. When you've succeeded speak with Ji Firepaw again.

Now that the great Shen-zin Su has begun to heal, it is time to return to the Temple of the Five Dawns and decide what is to be done with these **New Allies**. Hop in the cart and return to the temple and speak to the Spirit of Master Shang Xi. It is time you selected **A New Fate** for yourself. When you are ready, speak to Master Shang Xi to leave the island with either the Alliance or the Horde. It is time for you to leave Shen-zin Su, the Wandering Isle, and continue on a bold, new path.

CHOOSING A CLASS

Of all the character-creation decisions, your class choice has the greatest impact on the type of experience you have in World of Warcraft. There are eleven available classes in the game, but not all classes are available to every race. For your first character, you have ten class choices: Druid, Hunter, Mage, Monk, Paladin, Priest, Rogue, Shaman, Warrior, and Warlock.

DEATH KNIGHT

The eleventh class is a "hero" class: the Death Knight. This class is available only to players who already have a high-level character. You must wait to create a Death Knight until your first character reaches level 55. Any race, except Pandaren, can play as a Death Knight.

A QUICK LOOK AT CLASSES

Mage 🔵, Priest ⚪, Rogue 🟡, and Warrior 🟤 are considered the four archetypal classes because they are classic role-playing and fantasy heroes from the myths and literature that inspired the creators of World of Warcraft. Warriors and Rogues are primarily melee combat classes, while Mages and Priests prefer to stay at a safe distance in combat.

Druid 🟠, Monk 🟢, Paladin 🟣, and Shaman 🔵 are "hybrid" classes because they are versatile characters, equally comfortable fighting up close or using magic spells to harm enemies or heal allies.

Hunter 🟢 and Warlock 🟣 are the "pet" classes, because both utilize a companion pet during combat. Hunters tame wild beasts, while Warlocks summon demonic creatures.

The next thing to consider is how you plan to play the game. The "how" in this case is "How many people will you be playing with?"

Going Solo

If you plan to play solo (which means you'll be playing the game alone for a majority of the time) any class is a viable choice. Because there are already a number of people who play the game alone, large portions of World of Warcraft are designed around people playing solo.

Playing in a Group

If you plan on playing with other people (even if it's just one other person), consider having someone in the group play a class with access to healing spells. If you are that person, remember that healing is just one of the roles you can assume. Every character falls into one of three categories: tank, healer, and damage dealer.

⬤ Tank

Do you enjoy shielding people from harm? Tanks are a good choice for you. They are often expected to be the leader of groups, and people respect them when they get the job done. It's not the easiest choice, but it is rewarding. Warriors, Paladins, Monks, Druids, and Death Knights may assume the role of tanks.

✚ Healer

Is it okay if someone else does the killing while you support them? Healing may be the way for you. Healers are essential to great groups. They rarely get the glory of a tank, but they are needed, and wise players are quick to thank them for being there. Priests, Shamans, Monks, Paladins, and Druids can fill this role.

⬤ Damage Dealer

Is self-reliance a big thing for you? Maybe you just want to slaughter when you get the chance. You're a damage dealer. About 60% of a given dungeon or raid group is composed of damage dealers. Some may have backup healing (or backup tanking) potential, but their primary role is to disable or kill enemies. Any class can fill this role but Rogue, Mage, Warlock, and Hunter are notable choices because they are dedicated to this task.

Tips for Choosing Your Class

Experienced players can debate all day (and they do) about which classes are the easiest to play, hardest to play, strongest, weakest, over-powered, under-powered—you get the idea. As a new player, you should make a choice based on personal preference.

When considering classes, consider the role that appeals to you and keep the following things in mind:

- Hunters, Mages, Priests, and Warlocks fight best from a safe distance. You must learn how to control the range of a fight, because you're not built for melee combat. Keep enemies away from you, and you'll be successful.

- Monks, Paladins, Rogues, Death Knights, and Warriors fight up-close and personal with their enemies. Melee combat is generally more chaotic than what ranged classes experience.

- Druids and Shaman can fight from long range or in melee combat, and it's up to you to decide which way you prefer.

WHAT'S NEXT?

Use the following pages as an introduction to the eleven classes available to you when you first play the game. If you aren't sure which class is the one for you, try a few different classes. You may not know what you like until you try it!

DEATH KNIGHT

OVERVIEW

Death Knights are a Hero class. You can't unlock these characters until you have one character reach level 55. Once there, you can create a Death Knight and have them start at level 55 themselves. There is a specific starting area just for these characters, and they have an awesome backstory that you get to experience.

Death Knights are forced to deal their damage at close range, but they wear plate and take hits well. Melee is their natural environment, and they even have abilities that pull enemies into their favored combat range. Death Knights also get combative pets, which aren't as powerful as Hunter or some Warlock pets, but they add flavor to playing as a Death Knight.

Horde Races

ORC　UNDEAD　TAUREN　TROLL　BLOOD ELF　GOBLIN

Alliance Races

HUMAN　DWARF　NIGHT ELF　GNOME　DRAENEI　WORGEN

Either Faction

PANDAREN

PROMINENT CLASS ABILITIES

Runic Power

Death Knights have six total runes, from Blood, Frost, and Unholy. Use of these builds up Runic Power, a resource that is used for specific combat abilities.

Runeforging

Death Knights get to "enchant" their own weaponry. Runeforging allows a Death Knight to tailor weapons to specific situations with greater flexibility than what is available to other classes.

Specializations

At level 55, Death Knights must choose one of the following specializations: Blood, Frost, or Unholy.

 Blood Death Knights are tanks who focus on holding the attention of enemies in combat, and surviving the resulting damage.

 Frost Death Knights combine damage from direct attacks and Frost-based spells. There are also abilities available to get out of trouble.

 Unholy Death Knights have better overall spellwork, improved damage over time, and have superior summonable pets. They even get a special Gargoyle every few minutes.

DRUID

OVERVIEW

Druids are the only class with four specializations. Druids can perform any group role. They can fight in melee combat or use powerful spells from a safe distance. At level 6, Druids begin gaining the ability to change forms. Each form gives the Druid a different appearance and different abilities. Druids even learn how to fly under their own power (other classes need mounts to fly).

There is so much Druids can do, and they have so many abilities, it's easy to become confused. However, don't be discouraged from trying out a Druid if you feel drawn to them, or if you have a background in other types of gaming and don't feel like you'll be in over your head. Remember that you do not have to perfect all four specializations at once and can progress by focusing on any single one of them.

PROMINENT CLASS ABILITIES

Shapeshifting

The versatility of Druids is highlighted by the many forms they can take. Starting at level 6, where they get cat form, Druids end up with many potential choices, and each form is designed to enhance the Druid's abilities in a certain way: bear for durability, cat for inflicting damage, and moonkin for spell damage. Druids who want to heal stay in their base caster form, but can turn into the powerful Tree of Life with the Incarnation talent.

Travel Options

In addition to their combat forms, Druids learn special forms that boost their travel speed. They can assume a travel form that boosts their land speed, an aquatic form for increased swimming speed and underwather breathing, and a flight form that allows them to take to the sky.

Specializations

At level 10, Druids must decide to follow one of the following specializations: Balance, Feral, Guardian, or Restoration.

 Balance opens the moonkin form, and causes the Druid to deal more damage with their spells.

 Feral provides a boost to the Druid's cat form, turning them into close-combat nightmares.

 Guardian enhances the tank aspects of a Druid, allowing them to act as the protector to everyone in their groups.

 Restoration is a line dedicated to healing. The ultimate expression of this line is the Druid's ability to periodically assume the form of a Tree of Life.

Horde Races

ORC UNDEAD TAUREN TROLL BLOOD ELF GOBLIN

Alliance Races

HUMAN DWARF NIGHT ELF GNOME DRAENEI WORGEN

Either Faction

PANDAREN

Hunter

OVERVIEW

If you play a Hunter, you are never alone. Hunters have a pet as a constant companion. In essence, Hunters have a tank or melee damage dealer at their beck and call, allowing them to attack from a safe range. Hunters can eventually tame a wide variety of pets, so you aren't forced to raise just one creature.

Hunters deal damage primarily with a bow, crossbow, or gun, but have other tricks at their disposal when it comes to dealing with enemies. You can even feign death to escape a difficult situation! For these reasons, many solo players choose the Hunter class.

Horde Races

ORC | UNDEAD | TAUREN | TROLL | BLOOD ELF | GOBLIN

Alliance Races

HUMAN | DWARF | NIGHT ELF | GNOME | DRAENEI | WORGEN

Either Faction

PANDAREN

PROMINENT CLASS ABILITIES

Traps

Hunters use traps on enemies during combat, and they have a variety of effects. For example, one trap damages any nearby enemies when it is set off, while another causes the first enemy that touches it to be frozen solid. Hunters learn additional types of traps as they gain levels, and can even have multiple traps set at the same time.

Aspects

Hunters use animalistic characters in the form of Aspects to encourage one type of fighting or another. One Aspect improves a Hunter's damage, while others provide additional mobility. There are even ways to improve an entire group's running speed through the use of Aspects!

Specializations

At level 10, Hunters must decide to follow one of the following specializations: Beast Mastery, Marksmanship, or Survival.

Beast Mastery puts at least half of the damage output of the Hunter/Pet team onto the pet. You get the strongest pets in the game by selecting Beast Mastery. You also get the ability to tame Exotic Pets.

Marksmanship swings the damage pendulum back onto the Hunter. This is the line for massive ranged damage. However, Marksmanship is much harder to play solo than Beast Mastery. Your pet won't hold quite as much attention from monsters, so you need to know when to switch targets when necessary, and stay more mobile.

Survival Hunters are the trickiest Hunters to play. Think of things like this: Beast Masters encourage their pet to be the hero. Marksman have their pets as sidekicks. Survival Hunters try to strike an even balance with their pets. They work together, using the best strengths of each to get the most out of the class. Survivalists bring a number of tricks to a group, but it's a challenging Hunter specialization to master. Survival enhances traps and gives some of the best crowd control abilities among Hunters.

MAGE

OVERVIEW

Mages are known for dealing large doses of direct damage from a distance, while also being capable of damaging multiple enemies at once with their numerous AoE spells. Mages are not without their share of utility, however, which includes teleportation spells (for the mage and group members), reliable crowd control and conjuring temporary items that replenish health and mana.

Depending on the situation and the talents chosen, Mages can be fragile but powerful wizards (often referred to as "glass cannons") or durable masters of snares and crowd control. Although all of a Mage's specializations are involved in dealing damage, they're vastly different in their purpose and the way they're played.

PROMINENT CLASS ABILITIES

Out of Combat Utility

Mages are excellent damage dealers, but they have an impressive list of abilities that are a huge help at other times. They gain the ability to conjure food and water to sustain adventuring parties. Mages can learn to teleport themselves to various cities available to their faction. At higher levels, they learn how to create portals that allow any one grouped with them to travel instantly to those same cities. Note that any damage caused to the caster will interrupt Teleport or Portal spells, so make sure to check for enemies before attempting to use these slow-casting spells.

Crowd Control

Polymorph is the main source of Mage crowd control. Mages can turn humanoid or beast targets into sheep (although there are objects around the world that let you pick other forms, such as pigs and penguins) and render them unable to act for some time, as long as the target doesn't take any damage. If you're in a party, it's a good idea to tell your party members if you plan to Polymorph a target; that way, they can avoid hitting it and breaking your Polymorph early (in which case, you can simply cast it again).

Horde Races

ORC UNDEAD TAUREN TROLL BLOOD ELF GOBLIN

Alliance Races

HUMAN DWARF NIGHT ELF GNOME DRAENEI WORGEN

Either Faction

PANDAREN

Specializations

At Level 10, Mages must decide to follow one the following specializations: Arcane, Fire, or Frost.

 Arcane is a good "middle of the road" specialization for Mages. They enjoy a fair number of instant spells, damage avoidance, and disabling target opportunities. They represent the balance between the damage heavy Fire Mages and the control heavy Frost Mages, and present well-rounded abilities for group or solo play.

 Fire is the most predictable Mage specialization, but that doesn't stop them from inflicting frightening amounts of damage. They have a more organized method of attack, and their sustained damage is excellent in groups. However, they aren't great at getting out of trouble.

 Frost Mages are wonderful allies or vile pests, depending on your perspective. This specialization offers a greater number of escape options than other Mages, making them hard to kill. They don't deal as much damage as Fire Mages, and may lack some of the utility of Arcane Mages but there has to be a trade-off somewhere, right?

MONK

OVERVIEW

A newcomer to Azeroth, Monk is a hybrid class able to assume any of the three group roles. Monks use Chi as the primary resource for performing many of their special abilities. Monks use leather armor and are equally adept with a variety of one-hand and two-hand weapons.

As with any hybrid, Monks come with so many tricks that they may not be an ideal choice for new players. However, once you're more familiar with the game, playing as a Monk can be incredibly fun and rewarding.

Horde Races

ORC   UNDEAD   TAUREN   TROLL   BLOOD ELF   GOBLIN

Alliance Races

HUMAN   DWARF   NIGHT ELF   GNOME   DRAENEI   WORGEN

Either Faction

PANDAREN

PROMINENT CLASS ABILITIES

Stances

Depending on their specialization, monks can adopt one of three animal-based Stances, granting them significant boosts to their abilities. There is one Stance designed for each party role (tank-ox, healer-serpent, damage dealer-tiger) Monks can assume.

Chi

Chi is a new resource introduced in Mists of Pandaria, and exclusive to Monks. Along with energy or mana, it's used as a resource to execute most of the Monk's staple abilities. Chi is generated by using certain abilities and can be then used to perform more powerful moves.

Specializations

At level 10, Monks must decide to follow one of the following specializations: Brewmaster, Mistweaver, Windwalker.

 Brewmaster Monks specialize in deflecting damage and protecting their allies. They rely on damage redirection and self-healing. Their signature battle pose, Stance of the Sturdy Ox, increases health and reduces damage taken.

 Mistweaver Monks are healers first and foremost, but retain the ability to engage enemies at melee range and dish some damage while still providing health replenishment to their allies.

 Windwalker Monks are melee damage dealers. As their name suggests, Windwalkers are mobile and versatile, having access to limited healing and tanking abilities common to all Monks.

PALADIN

OVERVIEW

Paladins are a hybrid class, making it possible to join a group as a tank, healer, or damage dealer. As a tank or damage dealer, Paladins are able to stay in the thick of battle due to their heavy armor that absorbs more damage than many other melee classes can handle.

This flexibility is extremely useful for someone who doesn't have a large guild and the ability to stick to just one role. In addition, this flexibility allows Paladins to tackle difficult tasks on their own since they are able to heal themselves in the midst of battle.

PROMINENT CLASS ABILITIES

Divine Defenses

If things ever get too hot, even for them, they have special toys to get out of trouble. Paladins have several abilities that surround them with divine power. Colloquially, this is called "bubbling," and it protects the Paladin for a brief time, allowing them to catch up on healing or get the heck out of an area.

Blessings

Paladins also aid groups by providing powerful buffs. If the target is in your party or raid, all party and raid members will be affected. Players may only have one Blessing on them per Paladin at any one time.

Specializations

At Level 10, Paladins must decide to follow one of the following specializations: Holy, Protection, or Retribution.

 Holy Paladins are dedicated healers. Their best work is done when they can focus on keeping one ally alive. They are resilient healers due to wearing plate armor and using shields.

 Protection Paladins are extraordinarily hard to kill, making them great tanks. By consecrating the ground upon which they stand, Protection Paladins do a great job of holding the attention of multiple enemies at the same time, allowing others in the group to perform their tasks unimpeded.

 Retribution Paladins use two-handed weapons to deal damage in close quarters. As a Retribution Paladin, you aren't overwhelmed with a large number of abilities, which allows you to become familiar with the class in less time than what other classes may require.

 Horde Races

 Alliance Races

 Either Faction

PRIEST

OVERVIEW

While traditionally viewed as a healing class, Priests in World of Warcraft are capable of inflicting damage as well. Wearing only cloth armor, Priests are vulnerable to attacks at early levels so you must learn to keep enemies at a safe distance, kill them quickly, or keep them occupied.

Priests are highly sought after in group situations. Though you can choose to carry a substantial burden (that of keeping the group alive), it's possible to learn the dynamic quickly, especially if you're motivated to be a good healer. It's more challenging to play a Priest that is dedicated to healing solo, but it's far from an impossible task. Priests have everything they need to kill monsters on their own.

Horde Races

ORC | UNDEAD | TAUREN | TROLL | BLOOD ELF | GOBLIN

Alliance Races

HUMAN | DWARF | NIGHT ELF | GNOME | DRAENEI | WORGEN

Either Faction

PANDAREN

PROMINENT CLASS ABILITIES

Healing Spells

Priests are in demand for groups because they have a variety of healing spells that work in different ways, but share the same function: keep allies alive. Lesser Heal and Greater Heal restore health immediately; Renew restores health to a target over time. You even learn how to encase yourself or an ally in a bubble which absorbs incoming damage!

Shadowform

For the Priests who prefer to specialize in dealing damage rather than restoring health, there is Shadowform. Shadowform literally turns the Priest into a translucent shadow. In Shadowform, Priests deal increased Shadow damage and take a reduced amount of damage. If you enjoy playing a Priest and want to play solo, Shadowform is the way to go.

Specializations

At Level 10, Priests must decide to follow one of the following specializations: Discipline, Holy, or Shadow.

 Discipline Priests balance their healing and spellcasting. This isn't a damage-dealing line, but it provides a number of effects that mitigate damage, protect Priests and their allies, or aid in casting (whether for damage or healing).

 Holy Priests are the healers' healers. Their goal is to heal well under almost any circumstance. They have almost no offensive strength, but that's the not goal for Holy Priests. Holy Priests are so dedicated to healing, they eventually learn how to continue healing after being killed!

 Shadow Priests violently diverge from the other two Priest trees. Ideal for soloing, Shadow Priests get to have fun tormenting enemies before killing them. Vampiric Embrace funnels a fraction of the health removed from enemies to restore the health of their allies, and Vampiric Touch does the same for mana.

ROGUE

OVERVIEW

Sneaky and sticky-fingered, Rogues are the dirtiest melee fighters around. Rogues use a variety of Stuns and Poisons and can even Blind enemies. Stealth and Distract help Rogues move through areas almost unnoticed, and they can pick up some extra money from enemies by picking their pockets.

If high risk and high reward intrigue you, this is a class that's worth your time and attention. Rogues strike quickly while using weapons in both hands and can often kill anything before it knows what has happened. A Rogue caught flat footed often dies quickly but with all the tricks at their disposal, even wounded Rogues are difficult to finish off before they vanish into thin air.

PROMINENT CLASS ABILITIES

Stealth

Stealth is a defining feature of the Rogue class once they reach level 5. Stealth allows Rogues to move about the world without being seen as easily. Stay a safe distance away from monsters that are slightly higher level to avoid detection.

Combo Points

Many Rogue abilities stack combo points on a target, exposing them to even nastier attacks. All abilities that use up combo points are more effective as the combo points add up. This makes Rogues especially good at finding single targets and slicing them to ribbons. It's harder for Rogues to take on several enemies at once with equal finesse.

Specializations

At Level 10, Rogues must decide to follow one of the following specializations: Assassination, Combat, or Subtlety.

 Assassination Rogues are the royalty of burst damage. They focus on using daggers, poisons, and sudden attacks. For the biggest sudden numbers, look here! Assassination Rogues gain combo points quickly, and they spend them on pure damage.

 Combat Rogues are more direct. They often use heavier weapons and stand toe to toe with the target, wailing away with an emphasis on outdamaging the enemy. "You die first" is their way of thinking. If you want to have a direct combat character and don't mind light armor, Combat Rogues are a pile of fun.

 Subtlety Rogues are, indeed, the most subtle of the bunch. They rely on more frequent use of special abilities, cooldown improvements, and damage over time abilities. It takes longer to master this talent line compared with the alternatives, but it's always been a rewarding choice for a thinking person's Rogue.

Horde Races

ORC   UNDEAD   TAUREN   TROLL   BLOOD ELF   GOBLIN

Alliance Races

HUMAN   DWARF   NIGHT ELF   GNOME   DRAENEI   WORGEN

Either Faction

PANDAREN

SHAMAN

OVERVIEW

Shamans are masters of Nature and Elemental magic. They are a hybrid class that can fill multiple roles with vastly different play styles. They can heal, deal damage with spells, or fight in close quarters.

Shamans draw their strength from the four natural elements (Air, Earth, Fire, Water). This is reflected in the totems they use to help battle enemies, and the different weapon imbues they use to enhance their weapons.

Horde Races

ORC | UNDEAD | TAUREN | TROLL | BLOOD ELF | GOBLIN

Alliance Races

HUMAN | DWARF | NIGHT ELF | GNOME | DRAENEI | WORGEN

Either Faction

PANDAREN

PROMINENT CLASS ABILITIES

Totems

Totems are small, friendly units that grant you (and your group) a buff, or inflict negative effects on hostile targets. They are very fragile and can usually be killed with one swing of an enemy's weapon. Because they are unaffected by AoE, however, enemies must manually target your totems if they wish to destroy them. There are numerous totems that offer different benefits, each utilizing facets of the four elements (Air, Earth, Fire, Water); choosing the right one for every situation is part of the fun of playing a Shaman.

Weapon Imbues

Weapon imbues are self-cast buffs that enhance a Shaman's abilities or hinder enemies. These imbues are cast on your weapon, and strike an enemy with your weapon or trigger them with spell casting. There are imbues for every situation. Some increase damage output, while one is specifically designed to improve a Shaman's healing ability.

Specializations

At Level 10, Shamans must decide to follow one of the following specializations: Elemental, Enhancement, or Restoration.

Elemental Shaman use shocks and other spells to take down enemies. They deal damage while standing at a safe distance from melee combat. Elemental Shaman have a few tricks to push away enemies who draw too close, while the Mail armor they wear allows them to stand up to punishment better than most other spell-casting damage dealers.

Enhancement Shaman thrive in the midst of battle, dealing damage to enemies with a weapon in each hand and a host of spells at their command. Where most classes focus on using either weapons or spells to deal damage, Enhancement Shaman use a balanced mix of both in combat.

Restoration Shaman offer support to the groups they join with healing spells that keep allies alive and fighting. Restoration Shamans are not designed to inflict damage, but their totems boost the abilities of others, making the overall group a more effective fighting force.

WARLOCK

OVERVIEW

Warlock is the class for anyone who wants to play something sinister. You get to curse people, summon demons, and generally have a malevolent look. Warlocks are ranged casters that employ a combative pet to supplement their already impressive damage total. Though Warlock pets aren't as powerful as Hunter pets, these demonic allies offer a bit more versatility.

Warlocks are masters of inflicting damage over time. When pushed, these casters are able to sacrifice their health to bring even more damage to an engagement. Warlocks scare their healers as much as they do their actual enemies. It's not uncommon to see a Warlock's health dwindle even when nothing is attacking them. You get used to it!

PROMINENT CLASS ABILITIES

Demonic Pets

Each Warlock pet is quite different. Imps supplement ranged damage and make the caster harder to kill. Succubi provide options to control your enemies. Felhunters are keen anti-casters. Voidwalkers act as a tank. The only downside to these pets is that you can only summon one at a time.

Dealing Damage Over Time

A Warlock's spell arsenal liberally uses damage over time (DoT) spells. These spells don't deal damage all at once. Instead, they place a debuff on an enemy target, slowly chipping away at their health. Don't be fooled by the relatively small numbers, however—DoT spells are among the most powerful damage dealing abilities in the game!

Specializations

At Level 10, Warlocks must decide to follow one of the following specializations: Affliction, Demonology, or Destruction.

 Affliction Warlocks are the damage over time specialists. They lay down damage over time spells faster than other Warlocks varieties, and they're good at moving from target to target to maximize their ability to keep damage flowing.

 Demonology Warlocks are the toughest of the bunch. They're quite hard to kill, and sometimes they even end up tanking specific events. They gain improved pets, more survivability, and can occasionally transform themselves into a Demon (it's as awesome as it sounds).

 Destruction Warlocks are the more traditional casters of the three. They improve Shadowbolts and fire spells from the Warlock's repertoire, hitting big-damage numbers and felling single targets quite well.

Horde Races

ORC   UNDEAD   TAUREN   TROLL   BLOOD ELF   GOBLIN

Alliance Races

HUMAN   DWARF   NIGHT ELF   GNOME   DRAENEI   WORGEN

Either Faction

PANDAREN

WARRIOR

OVERVIEW

Warriors are the masters of melee combat as either versatile combatants, raging berserkers, or as the stalwart defender who protects your group from the onslaught of the encounters you may face. As masters of arms, they can use nearly every weapon, and don the heaviest armor.

When you are playing a Warrior, you must be flexible and know which abilities are best suited to any situation. Carefully plan how best to spend your Rage (your primary resource), so that in the heat of battle you can fuel your abilities and devastate your foes with a staggering combination of strikes.

Horde Races

| ORC | UNDEAD | TAUREN | TROLL | BLOOD ELF | GOBLIN |

Alliance Races

| HUMAN | DWARF | NIGHT ELF | GNOME | DRAENEI | WORGEN |

Either Faction

| PANDAREN |

PROMINENT CLASS ABILITIES

Stances

Warriors eventually learn three stances: Battle Stance, Defensive Stance, and Berserker Stance. All Warriors begin with Battle Stance generating high Rage from normal attacks. Defensive Stance reduces a Warrior's Rage generation when compated to the other stances, but also reduces the amount of damage taken. Berserker Stance allows you to generate Rage from both melee attacks and damage taken.

Shouts

Warrior can use various Shouts to inspire groups, or demoralize enemies. There are several shouts; some are available only as talents, and some available only to certain specializations, but every Warrior has a few to choose from. Commanding Shout and Battle Shout are used to provide benefits for your party or raid. The remaining shouts can cause an enemy to flee, reduce the damage enemies can inflict, do AoE damage, and snare or root enemies within the Warrior's shout radius.

Specializations

At level 10, Warriors must decide to follow one of the following specialization paths: Arms, Fury, or Protection.

 Arms Warriors use a two-handed weapon to deal strong burst damage.

 Fury Warriors equip weapons in both hands which includes the option of using a two-handed weapon in one hand! Few sights instill as much fear as a plate-clad Warrior brandishing two giant weapons.

 Protection Warriors are tanks. They have options for stunning, and provoking enemies, but most of all they excel at staying alive. They gain abilities that extend their lives during tricky battles, and allow them to reduce the damage they take.

PIERCING THE MISTS
OF
PANDARIA

When you upgrade to Mists of Pandaria there are many new and exciting additions waiting for you in Azeroth. The most significant change is the addition of an entire new continent to explore! This continent was hidden from the world by the mists that protected its inhabitants, the Pandarens. Now that the Pandarens have joined in the conflict between the Horde and Alliance, they have become an available race when creating characters and have passed on their knowledge to the other races to make the new Monk class available. The good news for existing high level characters is that the level cap has been raised to 90!

NEW FEATURES

NEW RACE

Pandarens are the new playable race in this expansion. For a long time Pandarens have been shrouded in myth and folklore. One of the few Pandarens heard of in recent years is Chen Stormstout, a famous Brewmaster. His kegs of ale can still be found scattered about Azeroth. The Pandarens have been separated from the rest of the world by a mist that was created during the Sundering to protect them from the demons ravaging all of Azeroth. The long war fought by the Horde and Alliance has now come to the shores of Pandaria! As a Pandaren you choose which side to join to try and bring peace to this war torn world.

NEW CLASS

Now that the Pandarens have been revealed to the world they have shared their knowledge of the martial arts. Monks are now available as a new class for every race except Goblins and Worgen. Monks are extremely versatile and can perform every role. Whether you want to follow the Brewmaster spec and absorb incredible amounts of damage while downing massive quantities of beverages, harness your inner chi to rain devastating blows down on your enemies with the Windwalker spec, or keep your allies healed with revitalizing mists and traditional herbal medicine as a Mistweaver, the Monk can do it all!

CROSS REALM ZONES

Coming to Mists of Pandaria is a new Technology which allows low or under populated zones to be available to a select pool of Realms. This feature helps ensure that players can find groups more easily in zones that most players have outleveled or left. Now lower level zones feel much more alive and have more potential for player interaction, just like their high level counterparts!

You can form groups with anyone you meet from any other Realm as long as you are of the same faction. Don't worry about being grouped with a PvP realm if you are PvE. Realms are only linked if they are of the same type.

Another great feature is RealID Grouping. You can group with your RealID friends as long as you both are of the same faction. If you use RealID to join a friend's group who is on a different realm type than you, you will use the ruleset of the realm you are joining. So if your realm was PvE and your friend is on a PvP realm you will be automatically changed over to the PvP realm rules.

The only other restriction to Cross Realm Zones is with trading with your group members from other realms. This has the same limitation as trading with people from different realms while using the Dungeon Finder. This is to keep each realm's economy safe.

NEW ZONES

If you wish to see the Wandering Isle you must create a Pandaren and begin your journey with this new character. To reach the new high level zones available in the game you need to speak to your faction specific leader. Once that is done you travel to The Jade Forest as either Horde or Alliance via a cutscene. The quests you complete here lead you through the starting zone and begin introducing you to some new friends!

GROUNDED!

When you arrive in Pandaria you aren't able to use your flying mounts. This skill can only be obtained at level 90 in the Vale of Eternal Blossoms. There are two shrines located here and you need to visit your faction specific shrine in order to purchase the flying skill. The Horde are located at the Shrine of Two Moons and the Alliance are at Shrine of the Seven Stars.

There is greater detail about each region—such as maps, NPC locations, etc.—located later in the guide. The following paragraphs are some quick introductions to the new zones.

The Wandering Isle (Levels 1-10)

Upon creating a new Pandaren you are whisked away to an isle shrouded in myth. Shen-zin Su, the giant turtle, slowly wanders the seas and on his back is where all low level Pandaren train until they are ready to decide which faction they want to join.

Pandaria (Levels 85-90)

This is the land all Pandarens call home. Until now no one else has ever visited this continent. Your journeys here take you across lush forests, extremely fertile farmlands, and even to snow peaked mountains where Pandaren Masters practice their discipline. As your adventures take you through this mystical land, new friends require your help in maintaining order and recovering lore lost in ages past.

The Jade Forest (Levels 85-86)

The Jade Forest is the sole high level starting zone for this expansion. It is where you first meet the Pandarens and your faction's new allies. This beautiful rainforest holds many secrets as well as the first dungeon you encounter, Temple of the Jade Serpent.

Valley of the Four Winds (Levels 86-87)

The breadbasket of Pandaria is the Valley of the Four Winds. Here you encounter the Tiller faction and learn to cultivate the farmlands yourself. Even though this area is idyllic, there are many obstacles plaguing the farmers. Your assistance is required to help restore the peace. Chen Stormstout is also in the area and if you help him he may even take you to the famed Stormstout Brewery!

LEVEL PROGRESSION BY ZONE

OUTLAND

- 67-70
- 65-68
- 60-64
- 58-63
- 64-67
- 62-65
- 67-70

NORTHREND

- 77-80
- 77-80
- 76-78
- 77-80
- 74-76
- 68-72
- 71-75
- 73-75
- 68-72

KALIMDOR

- 1-10
- 10-20
- 1-10
- 10-20
- 50-55
- 45-50
- 80-82
- 10-20
- 20-25
- 25-30
- 10-20
- 1-10
- 30-35
- 1-10
- 30-35
- 35-40
- 35-40
- 40-45
- 55-60
- 50-55
- 45-50
- 83-84

PANDARIA

- 82-83
- 80-82
- 87-88
- 88-89
- 85-86
- 90
- 89-90
- 86-87
- 86-87

EASTERN KINGDOMS

- 70
- 1-10
- 10-20
- 1-10
- 35-40
- 40-45
- 10-20
- 20-25
- 30-35
- 25-30
- 20-25
- 84-85
- 1-10
- 10-20
- 47-51
- 44-48
- 49-52
- 1-10
- 15-20
- 10-15
- 20-25
- 52-54
- 55-56
- 25-30
- 54-60
- 30-35

HORDE ZONES

STARTING ZONES	6-10	10-20	20-25
Deathknell	Tirisfal Glades	Silverpine Forest	Hillsbrad Foothills
Sunstrider Isle	Eversong Woods	Ghostlands	
Valley of Trials & Echo Isles	Durotar	Azshara	
Red Cloud Mesa	Mulgore	Northern Barrens	
Isle of Kezan	The Lost Isles (5-10)		

ALLIANCE ZONES

STARTING ZONES	6-10	10-20	20-25
Coldridge Valley & Gnomeregan	Dun Morogh	Loch Modan	Wetlands
Northshire Valley	Elwynn Forest	Westfall (10-15) & Redridge Mountains (15-20)	Duskwood
Shadowglen	Teldrassil	Darkshore	
Gilneas	Gilneas City	Ruins of Gilneas	
Ammen Vale	Azuremyst Isle	Bloodmyst Isle	

NEUTRAL ZONES

STARTING ZONES	20-25	25-30	30-35	35-40	40-45	45-50	50-55	55-60
The Wandering Isle	Ashenvale	Arathi Highlands	Desolace	Dustwallow Marsh	Eastern Plaguelands	Badlands (44-48)	Searing Gorge (47-51)	Deadwind Pass (55-56)
		Northern Stranglethorn	Southern Barrens	Feralas	Thousand Needles	Tanaris	Burning Steppes (49-52)	Blasted Lands (54-60)
		Stonetalon Mountains	The Hinterlands	Western Plaguelands		Felwood	Un'Goro Crater	Winterspring
			Cape of Stranglethorn				Swamp of Sorrows (52-54)	Silithis

OUTLAND

LEVELS 58-63	LEVELS 60-64	LEVELS 62-65	LEVELS 64-67	LEVELS 65-68	LEVELS 67-70	LEVEL 70
Hellfire Peninsula	Zangarmarsh	Terokkar Forest	Nagrand	Blade's Edge Mountains	Netherstorm	Isle of Quel'Danas
					Shadowmoon Valley	

NORTHREND

LEVELS 68-72	LEVELS 71-75	LEVELS 73-75	LEVELS 74-76	LEVELS 76-78	LEVELS 77-80
Borean Tundra	Dragonblight	Grizzly Hills	Zul'Drak	Sholazar Basin	Crystalsong Forest
Howling Fjord					Icecrown
					Storm Peaks
					Wintergrasp

CATACLYSM

LEVELS 80-82	LEVELS 82-83	LEVELS 83-84	LEVELS 84-85
Mount Hyjal	Deepholm	Uldum	Twilight Highlands
Kelp'thar Forest (Vashj'ir)			
Shimmering Expanse (Vashj'ir)			
Abyssal Depths (Vashj'ir)			

MISTS OF PANDARIA

LEVELS 85-86	LEVELS 86-87	LEVELS 87-88	LEVELS 88-89	LEVEL 90
The Jade Forest	Valley of the Four Winds	Kun-Lai Summit	Townlong Steppes	Vale of Eternal Blossoms
	Krasarang Wilds		Dread Wastes	

Krasarang Wilds (Levels 86-87)

It is hard to imagine a more inhospitable place in Pandaria than the Krasarang Wilds. The Mogu, the race that once kept the Pandarens as slaves, now reside here. While they do represent a constant threat this area is filled with many ancient ruins and lost lore. Out on the waters near the coastline you can find another faction called The Anglers.

THE WANDERER'S FESTIVAL

If you check carefully along the shore in the Krasarang Wilds just east of The Incursion you will find a small beach called Turtle Beach. This is the location of a Rare Event that only happens at 9 and 11 on Sundays called the Wanderer's Festival. Not only can you earn an achievement for taking part in the festival from beginning to end but you can also earn a rare pet here!

Kun-Lai Summit (Levels 87-88)

This area of Pandaria is under heavy conflict now due to the Yaungol being forced from their homes in the Townlong Steppes and the Gurubashi Trolls who have taken over a small island on the northern coast. While the southern region is warm and inviting, the northwestern area is where some of the highest mountains in all of Azeroth exist. This area is home to the Shado-Pan Monastery which is currently plagued with the Sha due to all the negative emotions caused by the never ending battles between the Horde and Alliance. Shortly after release this will also be where you can find the raid, Mogu'shan Vaults.

Townlong Steppes (Levels 88-89)

The Pandaren in the Townlong Steppes are trying to repel a massive Mantid assault. You must help the Pandarens defeat these insects before they lay waste to the entire region. If that isn't enough, the Sha of Anger is on a rampage and Lord Taran-Zhu requests your help in tracking it. Two dungeons are in this region, The Gate of the Setting Sun and The Siege of Niuzao Temple.

Dread Wastes (Levels 89-90)

There are many swamps in the Dread Wastes. Worse still is the fact that the Sha of Fear is said to be in complete control of this area. While mantids do inhabit this landscape not all of them are enemies. There is a small settlement of the Klaxxi here that is willing to help you in your journeys. The Heart of Fear is located in this land and should only be explored by the most prepared band of Heroes.

Vale of Eternal Blossoms (Level 90)

The Vale of Eternal Blossoms is one of the most beautiful landscapes in all of Pandaria. Here you encounter the Golden Lotus faction. This area has many Daily Quests for the Golden Lotus and is also home to the Lore Walkers. There is rumored to be a giant library filled with lore. In this zone there are two shrines where the Alliance and Horde have set up camp. Each shrine has its own Auction House, Reforger and Bank. Horde and Alliance may also purchase the Flying Skill required at their respective shrine.

HIDDEN TREASURES OF PANDARIA

Treasure Chests

As you travel the world you may come across special treasure chests. While everyone can see these chests and they despawn once looted, each treasure is unique to the chest it was looted from and can't be seen again by that player once looted.

Scattered throughout Pandaria are many large scrolls that tell of Pandaria's trouble past. The Lorewalkers are eager to retrieve these scrolls and Lorewalker Cho at the Seat of Knowledge in The Vale of Eternal Blossoms can decipher the texts and show you the past events through grand storytelling and beautiful murals that come to life.

DUNGEONS & RAIDS

With a new land to explore there are also new dungeons and raids to conquer! The Mists of Pandaria expansion has nine new dungeons (including two revised classic dungeons that also include level 90 heroic versions) and four new raids available with the launch of Mists of Pandaria.

In addition to the new places to explore, Challenges and Scenarios have been added to the game, as well as a revision in the way loot is awarded while using the Looking for Raid system. There's more information about dungeons and raids later in the guide.

PLAYER VS. PLAYER COMBAT

There are quite a few changes coming for PvP in Mists of Pandaria. All PvP gear will no longer have Resilience but instead will have PvP Resilience and PvP Power. Also all PvP gear will have its item level lowered with this change, so players can no longer boost their item level to enter dungeons too early.

Two new Battlegrounds appear in this expansion, as well as one new Arena. These also include some exciting new mechanics. For example, one has players carrying and controlling artifacts to gain points while another mechanic has them controlling and protecting mine carts until they reach their destination.

CHANGES TO YOUR CHARACTERS

Not only are some stats going away but the Talent System has been completely revamped. There are also some new stats being added as well as stats like Spell and Melee Hit being normalized. Picking a specialization has never been easier as all the talents you had to pick before to be viable in a particular specialization are now just given to you when you choose that particular specialization line.

STAT CHANGES

Spell resistance is no longer in the game and any spells giving buffs to resistance have been removed. Resilience has also been removed from the game and has been converted into the previously mentioned PvP Resilience and PvP Power.

Criticals are now a base 2x damage for all spells and abilities. Hit and Spell Hit are now the same stat which negates either melee or spell miss.

Expertise now is listed as a percentage instead of having a stat. Hit and Expertise have been normalized to require the same amount of rating to grant the same percentage stat.

Block has diminishing returns like Dodge and Parry. Having more Block is still good but it takes more rating to go up effectively.

REVISIONS TO THE TALENT SYSTEM

Before Mists of Pandaria you had many talents to choose from and 41 talent points to distribute. This has all changed. Now when it is time to choose a specialization you click on the Specialization & Talents tab and pick your Primary Specialization. It shows you for which role your spec is best suited, along with a very brief description of what you are good at doing. Below this you see the Core Abilities that are granted to you for choosing this spec line. These are abilities you used to have to spend talent points to receive in the old system, but are now given automatically.

Now that you have learned your Specialization you need to click the Talents tab to select your Primary Talents. This window shows how often you get one talent point, which is every 15 levels. At every 15 levels there are three talent choices for you to choose between. So instead of 41 talents at the new max level of 90 you only have 6! Every character class has 18 unique talents to choose from that can help differentiate you from anyone else who has the same class and spec as you.

GLYPHS

The Glyph system has been altered in Mists of Pandaria. Now only six glyphs can ever be active on your character at once. Prime Glyphs have been removed, leaving only Major Glyphs and Minor Glyphs. Since Prime Glyphs were typically no brainer choices for whatever your current spec was, they have been incorporated into your specialization when applicable. Now choices you make in the glyphs help define you and make you more unique!

STORING THINGS IN THE VOID!

This special storage is not unique to Mists of Pandaria but became available after the Cataclysm expansion. When you visit the Ethereals in your capital city one of the vendors here is called a Voidkeeper. In this place you can store any gear that is soulbound to you.

To unlock the Void Storage Service you must spend 100 gold. Any items you store in Void Storage lose any modifications they currently have and become non-refundable and non-tradeable.

To deposit an item place it the Deposit area. Once you do you see a cost in the bottom left of the window and the transfer button is now active. You can deposit up to 9 items at once but you have to pay a fee for each individual item in the deposit box. The current fee is 25g per item and all items deposited must be fully repaired.

To withdraw an item from Void Storage take the item from the main Void Storage location and place it in the Withdraw area. Once you do this the transfer button becomes active and you can get your item back from storage. Also if you happen to have tons of gear stored here there is a helpful search function in the top right corner of the Void Storage window. This lights up each item that matches your search parameters so you can find items more easily!

TRANSMOGRIFYING

Even though this feature isn't new to Mists of Pandaria it is a feature that was implemented after the release of Cataclysm. The Horde and Alliance both have ethereal vendors located in their capital city that can change the appearance of an item you are wearing with another of the same type and same slot. There are some restrictions to what armor or weapon skins can be applied, but generally if it is the same weapon type or armor type and it has stats, it can have its skin placed over your current gear's skin. The cost to transmogrify an item is the vendor cost of the item you are changing.

BATTLENET ACCOUNT ACHIEVEMENTS

Some achievements are now tracked through your Battlenet Account. These achievements are easily distinguished from normal achievements by their blue banner. Once one of your characters has completed an account wide achievement all your characters immediately receive the achievement and its point value. Since this achievement is based through your Battlenet Account all other copies of World of Warcraft attached to your account also receive the achievement.

CHANGES TO PROFESSIONS

All professions now have their maximum skill level raised to Zen Master (or 600) potential skill! All professions have a large list of new recipes to learn in Mists of Pandaria and you can find a listing of them later in this guide. Secondary professions get more love in this expansion and Archaeology receives a boost in the amount of dig sites per area!

INSCRIPTION

There are quite a few changes to Inscription simply because of all the glyph changes being implemented. All of your existing glyphs have been updated and all Prime Glyphs have been removed. A lot of the glyphs have had their entire functionality reworked, so check your existing glyphs and make certain they do what you want them to. Inscription is also gaining the ability to make Inscribed Staffs and, for the offhand, Inscribed Fans.

ARCHAEOLOGY

Archaeologists rejoice! Now every site you travel to has more locations to dig in, instead of just three. There is also a ton of new lore to be discovered in Pandaria as well as items of power.

COOKING

Pandarens love their food (and their beer) so it comes as no surprise that cooking is getting a few changes for all of you master chefs. Now cooking has Specializations! Each specialization is focused on a particular stat. For the completionists out there, yes, you can train in all specializations eventually—if you spend the time and devotion to do so.

INTERFACE CHANGES

The interface has been updated to accommodate some of the new features being offered in Mists of Pandaria. One thing you notice immediately is an icon of a horse next to the Dungeon Finder icon. This is for your Mounts and Pets window. Another great addition to the interface is a more robust tracking feature for the mini-map. There is now an option for tracking critters that you can battle with the new Pet Battle system.

SPELLBOOK WINDOW

The main Spellbook window still shows what abilities you have learned as well as when you will learn new abilities. What has changed is the layout of the rest of the window. The Mounts and Companions tab has been removed and has its own main window now, which is detailed in the next section. So now you have the Spellbook tab, Professions tab and Core Abilities tab.

In the Spellbook tab all spells and abilities you know are listed in alphabetical order. The Profession tab has not changed since Cataclysm. The Core Abilities tab is new to Mists of Pandaria and shows what skills you gained automatically from choosing your current specialization.

DUNGEON FINDER

When you press the Dungeon Finder icon, (shortcut is default I) it now brings up more than just the option to queue for dungeons. Now you can queue for raids easier, as well as join groups for the newly added Scenarios! You still must meet the minimum requirements to join any of these features but forming groups or raids has never been easier.

MOUNTS & PETS

This new icon of a horse is right next to the Dungeon Finder icon at the bottom of your screen. This brings up a new window that has two tabs. One is labeled Mounts, and expectedly, includes all your mounts. The other is Pet Journal and it lists all the pets you currently own.

The Mounts tab lists all the mounts you currently own in alphabetical order on the left side of the window. On the right side of the window you get a large animated picture of the current mount you have selected. You can easily scroll to the mount you wish to ride and click the mount button on the bottom left side of this window.

The Pet Journals tab is an entirely new feature built to accommodate the new Pet Battle System. The left side of the window lists all the pets you own in alphabetical order like the mounts, but it also lists all the pets you don't have yet. If you click on the name of the pet it brings up a window to the right that shows you what abilities the pet can learn and an info panel telling you how you can acquire the pet. To the right of the pet list are three separate windows. One is unlocked immediately and you can put any pet you wish to train and already own into so it is ready for battle! The other two slots are unlocked through Pet Battle achievements.

You can sort the pets very easily with the filter that is directly above your pet names. You can do it by Collected or Not Collected or even by the Pet Family it is associated with! There is also a filter to select only the pets you have marked as your favorites. The current limit on how large your pet stable can be is 500 but you can click on a pet at any time to release it and let it run free out into the wild, freeing up another spot.

If you want to PvP with your pets just select the Find Battle button in the lower right corner of the window and the search for a worthy opponent for you and your faithful pet begins!

NEW FACTIONS & REPUTATIONS

Mists of Pandaria has many new factions to find and become friends with. This expansion no longer requires you to wear tabards for a particular faction to raise its reputation with dungeon runs. Now reputation is earned through the hundreds of new daily quests and running Scenarios. While many factions help strengthen your character for future battles, some are centered on helping you become a better farmer, historian or even Cloud Serpent Racer!

THE LOREWALKERS

The Pandaren have a rich tradition of storytelling—it's how their young are tutored and how adults kill time around the cookfires at night. The Lorewalkers travel the world discovering and sharing pandaren tales. With all these new strangers on the island, and with Pandaria coming out and rejoining the world at large, it's more important than ever to discover and catalog Pandaren history for future generations. Players can help the Lorewalkers to do so, and in the process, learn a great deal about Pandaria!

REPUTATION REWARDS

Name	Cost	Requirement	Description
Lorewalker's Map	1 Restored Artifact	The Lorewalkers – Exalted	Use: Randomizes your Archaeology digsites in Pandaria. (30 Min Cooldown)
Lorewalker's Lodestone	1 Restored Artifact	The Lorewalkers – Exalted	Use: Teleports you to a random active digsite in Pandaria. (30 Min Cooldown)
Disc of the Red Flying Cloud	600g	Level 60, Expert Riding, The Lorewalkers – Exalted	Use: Teaches you how to summon this mount. This mount changes depending on your Riding skill and location.
Lorewalkers Tabard	10g	The Lorewalkers – Exalted	Tabard

THE TILLERS

The humble Tillers are the bread-and-butter of Pandaria. That's true in a literal sense: the Valley of Four Winds is where most of the food comes from. After a disastrous campaign in Jade Forest, Chen Stormstout suggests to players that they should "Walk the earth" and win over the hearts and minds of the Pandaren from the ground level. Helping the farmers of the Four Winds will do just that! This faction allows players to befriend individual townspeople, start their own farming plot, and brush up on their cooking skill.

RELATIONSHIPS

Name	Preferred Gift	Rewards	Location
Chee Chee	Blue Feathers and Valley Stir Fry	20x Windwool Cloth & 5x Exotic Leather, Sheep for your farm.	The Heartland
Ella	Jade Cats and Shrimp Dumplings	Spring Blossom Sapling, Autumn Blossom Sapling, Winter Blossom Sapling, Cat for your farm.	The Halfhill Market & The Heartland
Fish Fellreed	Jade Cats and Twin Fish Platters	Snakeroot Seed, Magebulb Seed, Raptorleaf Seed, Songbell Seed, Windshear Cactus Seed, Pigs for your farm.	The Halfhill Market & Cattail Lake
Farmer Fung	Marsh Lillies and Wildfowl Roast	Enigma Seed, Yak for your farm.	The Halfhill Market & The Heartland
Gina Mudclaw	Marsh Lillies and Swirling Mist Soup	Red Streaks Firework, 2x Yellow Rose Firework, Red White and Blue Firework, Mailbox for the farm.	The Halfhill Market
Jogu the Drunk	Lovely Apples and Sauteed Carrots	Four Wind Soju, Plum Wine, Ginseng Tea, Jade Witch Brew, Mad Brewer's Breakfast, Free crop reading for your farm.	The Halfhill Market
Haohan Mudclaw	Ruby Shards and Charbroiled Tiger Steak	3x Songbell Seed, Mushan Beast for your farm.	The Halfhill Market & The Heartland
Old Hillpaw	Blue Feathers and Braised Turtle	Straw Hat, Chickens for your farm.	The Halfhill Market & The Heartland
Sho	Lovely Apples and Eternal Blossom Fish	Red Cricket (Pet), Orange tree for your farm.	Skyrange
Tina Mudclaw	Ruby Shards and Fire Spirit Salmon	Pearl Milk Tea, Peach Pie, New furniture for your farm.	The Halfhill Market & The Heartland

REPUTATION REWARDS

Name	Cost	Requirement	Description
Recipe: Spicy Salmon		Cooking (500), The Tillers — Exalted	Use: Teaches you how to cook Spicy Salmon.
Recipe: Spicy Vegetable Chips		Cooking (500), The Tillers — Exalted	Use: Teaches you how to prepare Spicy Vegetable Chips.
Pandaren Scarecrow	250g	The Tillers — Revered	Use: Right Click to plant your Pandaren Scarecrow. (5 Min Cooldown) "It certainly looks scary to me."
Gin-Ji Knife Set	250g	The Tillers — Exalted	Use: Chop, mince, and julienne a fresh humanoid or beast corpse. (20 Min Cooldown)
Reins of the Brown Riding Goat	500g	Level 85, Artisan Riding, The Tillers — Exalted	Use: Teaches you how to summon this mount.
Reins of the Black Riding Goat	1500g	Level 85, Artisan Riding, The Tillers — Exalted	Use: Teaches you how to summon this mount.
Reins of the White Riding Goat	3250g	Level 85, Artisan Riding, The Tillers — Exalted	Use: Teaches you how to summon this mount.
Tillers Tabard	10g	The Tillers — Exalted	Tabard ("A true greenthumb.")
Mourning Glory	125g	The Tillers — Exalted	"It is said these flowers will bloom over the graves of those who carry them."
"Jinyu Princess" Irrigation System	100g	Weeds cleared from Sunsong Ranch	"An installation kit for a sprinkler system. This can be installed at Sunsong Ranch."
"Thunder King" Pest Repellers	100g	Broken Wagon fixed at Sunsong Ranch	"An installation kit for ultrasonic pest repellers. These can be installed at Sunsong Ranch."
"Earth-Slasher" Master Plow	100g	Mossy Boulder removed from Sunsong Ranch	"An assembly kit for a large plow. This can be used to till a line of soil in Sunsong Ranch."

THE ANGLERS

Many Pandaren make their living off of the sea, and nobody is a better teller of tall tales than the typical Pandaren Angler. Much like the Tillers, the Pandaren Anglers represent the Pandaren "common man." Since the mists have parted, the Anglers are stunned to find strange sea creatures assaulting their fishing grounds. They've also discovered a plethora of treasures under the sea that have been lost since the mists closed in. Helping out the Anglers and their new fisherman friends from across the sea is a great way to build up your reputation among the Pandaren, not to mention your fishing skill!

REPUTATION REWARDS

Name	Cost	Requirement	Description
Recipe: Krasarang Fritters	5g	Cooking (525), The Anglers — Friendly	Use: Teaches you how to prepare Krasarang Fritters.
Recipe: Viseclaw Soup	5g	Cooking (525), The Anglers — Friendly	Use: Teaches you how to prepare Viseclaw Soup.
Pandaren Fishing Pole	25g	The Anglers — Honored	Two-Hand Fishing Pole: 7 – 11 Damage, Speed 3.00, Equip: Fishing skill increased by 10.
Tiny Goldfish	250g	The Anglers — Honored	Use: Teaches you how to summon this companion.
Sharpened Tuskarr Spear	1500g	The Anglers — Revered	Main Hand Weapon: 14 – 27 Damage, Speed 2.50 Use: Plant a spear in the ground, increasing Fishing skill by 15 for anyone who remains within 15 yds. Lasts 2 min. (5 Min Cooldown) "A traditional Tuskarr fishing spear; the craftsmanship is a sight to behold."
Dragon Fishing Pole	500g	Fishing (525), The Anglers — Revered	Two-Hand Fishing Pole: 42 – 63 Damage, Speed 3.00, Equip: Fishing skill increased by 30
Anglers Fishing Raft	1000g	Fishing (525), The Anglers — Revered	Use: You can raft across water. "Great for fishing, but takes on water… so don't stay out too long!"
Anglers Tabard	10g	The Anglers — Exalted	Tabard
Reins of the Aqua Water Strider	5000g	Level 90, Artisan Riding, The Anglers — Exalted	Use: Teaches you how to summon this mount. This mount can walk on water in non-battleground areas.

AUGUST CELESTIALS

Predating even the first empire, the timeless Celestials have been keeping watch over the diverse peoples of Pandaria.

Each of the animal spirits represents a different facet of the Pandaren character:

- **The Jade Serpent: Wisdom, Foresight [East Temple]**
- **The White Tiger: Strength, Focus [North Temple]**
- **The Red Crane: Hope, Confidence [South Temple]**
- **The Black Ox: Fearlessness, Steadfastness [West Temple]**

The Celestials reward all who risk their lives for the good of Pandaria.

REPUTATION REWARDS - GENERAL

Name	Cost	Requirement	Description
Celestial Offering	100g	The August Celestials – Honored	"Watched over by the celestials, they will grant you their blessing when you are near their temples."
Pattern: Royal Satchel	50g	Tailoring (600), The August Celestials – Exalted	Use: Teaches you how to craft a Royal Satchel
Formula: Enchant Bracer – Exceptional Strength	40g	Enchanting (600), The August Celestials – Revered	Use: Teaches you how to permanently enchant bracers to increase Strength by 170. Requires a level 372 or higher item.
Formula: Enchant Bracer – Greater Agility	40g	Enchanting (600), The August Celestials – Revered	Use: Teaches you how to permanently enchant bracers to increase Agility by 170. Requires a level 372 or higher item.
Formula: Enchant Bracer – Super Intellect	40g	Enchanting (600), The August Celestials – Revered	Use: Teaches you how to permanently enchant bracers to increase Intellect by 170. Requires a level 372 or higher item.
Reins of the Thundering August Cloud Serpent	10,000g	Level 90, Artisan Riding, The August Celestials – Exalted	Use: Teaches you how to summon this mount. This is a flying mount. Requires Cloud Serpent Riding from the Order of the Cloud Serpent.
Bladesong Cloak	1250 Justice Points	Level 90, The August Celestials - Honored	Back, 970 Armor, +444 Agility, +666 Stamina Equip: Increases your critical strike rating by 305, Equip: Increases your haste rating by 281
Cloak of Ancient Curses	1250 Justice Points	Level 90, The August Celestials - Honored	Back, 970 Armor, +666 Stamina, +444 Intellect Equip: Increases your hit rating by 253, Equip: Increases your haste rating by 322
Cloak of the Silent Mountain	1250 Justice Points	Level 90, The August Celestials - Honored	Back, 970 Armor, +444 Strength, +666 Stamina Equip: Increases your parry rating by 296, Equip: Increases your expertise rating by 296.
Pressed Flower Cloak	1250 Justice Points	Level 90, The August Celestials - Honored	Back, 970 Armor, +666 Stamina, +444 Intellect, +253 Spirit Equip: Increases your haste rating by 322.
Ribcracker's Cloak	1250 Justice Points	Level 90, The August Celestials - Honored	Back, 970 Armor, +444 Strength, +666 Stamina Equip: Increases your hit rating by 232, Equip: Increases your haste rating by 333.
August Celestials Tabard	10g	The August Celestials – Exalted	Tabard

REPUTATION REWARDS - LEATHER ARMOR

Name	Cost	Requirement	Description
Refurbished Zandalari Vestment	2250 Justice Points	Level 90, The August Celestials – Honored	Leather Chest, 2,470 Armor, +797 Agility, +1,195 Stamina Equip: Increases your haste rating by 555, Equip: Increases your expertise rating by 492.
Vestment of the Ascendant Tribe	2250 Justice Points	Level 90, The August Celestials – Honored	Leather Chest, 2,470 Armor, +1,195 Stamina, +797 Intellect, +599 Spirit Equip: Increases your haste rating by 416.
Tukka-Tuk's Hairy Boots	1750 Valor Points	Level 90, The August Celestials – Revered	Leather Feet, 1,951 Armor, +851 Agility, +1,277 Stamina Equip: Increases your hit rating by 601, Equip: Increases your haste rating by 512.
Boots of the High Adept	1750 Valor Points	Level 90, The August Celestials – Revered	Leather Feet, 1,951 Armor, +1,277 Stamina, +851 Intellect Equip: Increases your Critical Strike by 584, Equip: Increases your mastery rating by 539.
Ogo's Elder Gloves	1750 Valor Points	Level 90, The August Celestials – Revered	Leather Hands, 1,773 Armor, +1,277 Stamina, +851 Intellect Equip: Increases your haste rating by 568, Equip: Increases your mastery rating by 568.
Fingers of the Loneliest Monk	1750 Valor Points	Level 90, The August Celestials – Revered	Leather Hands, 1,773 Armor, +851 Agility, +1,277 Stamina Equip: Increases your expertise rating by 593, Equip: Increases your mastery rating by 526.
Quillpaw Family Bracers	1250 Valor Points	Level 90, The August Celestials – Revered	Leather Wrist, 1,241 Armor, +638 Agility, +958 Stamina Equip: Increases your hit rating by 426, Equip: Increases your Critical Strike by 426.
Clever Ashyo's Armbands	1250 Valor Points	Level 90, The August Celestials – Revered	Leather Wrist, 1,241 Armor, +958 Stamina, +638 Intellect Equip: Increases your mastery rating by 457, Equip: Increases your Critical Strike by 373.

REPUTATION REWARDS - CLOTH ARMOR

Name	Cost	Requirement	Description
Leggings of Unfinished Conquest	2250 Justice Points	Level 90 The August Celestials – Honored	Cloth Legs, 1,698 Armor, +1,195 Stamina, +797 Intellect Equip: Increases your hit rating by 479, Equip: Increases your critical strike rating by 562
Subversive Leggings	2250 Justice Points	Level 90 The August Celestials – Honored	Cloth Legs, 1,698 Armor, +1,195 Stamina, +797 Intellect, +416 Spirit Equip: Increases your mastery rating by 599.
Bracers of Inlaid Jade	1250 Valor Points	Level 90 The August Celestials – Revered	Cloth Wrist, 975 Armor, +958 Stamina, +638 Intellect, +451 Spirit Equip: Increases your critical strike rating by 384.
Gloves of Red Feathers	1750 Justice Points	Level 90 The August Celestials – Revered	Cloth Hands, 1,393 Armor, +1,277 Stamina, +851 Intellect, +498 Spirit Equip: Increases your mastery rating by 609.
Storm-Sing Sandals	1750 Valor Points	Level 90 The August Celestials – Revered	Cloth Feet, 1,533 Armor, +1,277 Stamina, +851 Intellect, +568 Spirit Equip: Increases your mastery rating by 568.
Void Flame Slippers	1750 Valor Points	Level 90 The August Celestials – Revered	Cloth Feet, 1,533 Armor, +1,277 Stamina, +851 Intellect Equip: Increases your hit rating by 553, Equip: Increases your critical strike rating by 576.
Sunspeaker's Flared Gloves	1750 Valor Points	Level 90 The August Celestials – Revered	Cloth Hands, 1,393 Armor, +1,277 Stamina, +851 Intellect Equip: Increases your hit rating by 576, Equip: Increases your critical strike rating by 553.
Minh's Beaten Bracers	1250 Justice Points	Level 90 The August Celestials – Revered	Cloth Wrist, 975 Armor, +958 Stamina, +638 Intellect Equip: Increases hit rating by 405. Increases mastery rating by 438.

REPUTATION REWARDS – MAIL ARMOR

Name	Cost	Requirement	Description
Mountain Stream Ringmail	2250 Justice Points	Level 90, The August Celestials – Honored	Mail Chest, 3,436 Armor, +1,195 Stamina, +797 Intellect, +547 Spirit Equip: Increases your haste rating by 505.
Undergrowth Stalker Chestpiece	2250 Justice Points	Level 90, The August Celestials – Honored	Mail Chest, 3,436 Armor, +797 Agility, +1,195 Stamina Equip: Increases your expertise rating by 547, Equip: Increases your mastery rating by 505.
Brewmaster Chani's Bracers	1250 Valor Points	Level 90, The August Celestials – Revered	Mail Wrist, 1,727 Armor, +958 Stamina, +638 Intellect Equip: Increases your critical strike rating by 474, Equip: Increases your haste rating by 343.
Ravenmane's Gloves	1750 Valor Points	Level 90, The August Celestials – Revered	Mail Hands, 2,467 Armor, +1,277 Stamina, +851 Intellect Equip: Increases your haste rating by 553, Equip: Increases your mastery rating by 576.
Sandals of the Elder Sage	1750 Valor Points	Level 90, The August Celestials – Revered	Mail Feet, 2,714 Armor, +1,277 Stamina, +851 Intellect, +512 Spirit Equip: Increases your critical strike rating by 601.
Sentinel Commander's Gauntlets	1750 Valor Points	Level 90, The August Celestials – Revered	Mail Hands, 2,467 Armor, +851 Agility, +1,277 Stamina Equip: Increases your hit rating by 458, Equip: Increases your mastery rating by 632.
Steps of the War Serpent	1750 Valor Points	Level 90, The August Celestials – Revered	Mail Feet, 2,714 Armor, +851 Agility, +1,277 Stamina Equip: Increases your hit rating by 526, Equip: Increases your mastery rating by 593.
Tiger-Striped Wristguards	1250 Valor Points	Level 90, The August Celestials – Revered	Mail Wrist, 1,727 Armor, +638 Agility, +958 Stamina Equip: Increases your haste rating by 323, Equip: Increases your mastery rating by 485.

REPUTATION REWARDS - PLATE ARMOR

Name	Cost	Requirement	Description
Leggings of Ponderous Advance	2250 Justice Points	Level 90, The August Celestials – Honored	Plate Legs, 4,106 Armor, +797 Strength, +1,195 Stamina Equip: Increases your critical strike rating by 562, Equip: Increases your mastery rating by 479.
Valiant's Shinguards	2250 Justice Points	Level 90, The August Celestials – Honored	Plate Legs, 4,106 Armor, +1,195 Stamina, +797 Intellect, +531 Spirit Equip: Increases your haste rating by 531.
Tankiss Warstompers	1750 Valor Points	Level 90, The August Celestials – Revered	Plate Feet, 3,707 Armor, +851 Strength, +1,277 Stamina Equip: Increases your Critical Strike by 609, Equip: Increases your expertise rating by 498.
Yu'lon Guardian Boots	1750 Valor Points	Level 90, The August Celestials – Revered	Plate Feet, 3,707 Armor, +851 Strength, +1,277 Stamina Equip: Increases your parry rating by 647, Equip: Increases your dodge by 431.
Gloves of the Overwhelming Swarm	1750 Valor Points	Level 90, The August Celestials – Revered	Plate Hands, 3,370 Armor, +851 Strength, +1,277 Stamina Equip: Increases your parry rating by 609, Equip: Increases your mastery rating by 498.
Streetfighter's Iron Knuckles	1750 Valor Points	Level 90, The August Celestials – Revered	Plate Hands, 3,370 Armor, +851 Strength, +1,277 Stamina Equip: Increases your Critical Strike by 601, Equip: Increases your haste rating by 512.
Braided Black and White Bracer	1250 Valor Points	Level 90, The August Celestials – Revered	Plate Wrist, 2,359 Armor, +638 Strength, +958 Stamina Equip: Increases your Critical Strike by 444, Equip: Increases your expertise rating by 394.
Battle Shadow Bracers	1250 Valor Points	Level 90, The August Celestials – Revered	Plate Wrist, 2,359 Armor, +485 Strength, +958 Stamina Equip: Increases your Parry by 638, Equip: Increases your hit rating by 323.

GOLDEN LOTUS

The Vale of Eternal Blossoms was sealed away after the Mogu were overthrown. The gates were sealed, and it was locked away to protect its hidden power. The Golden Lotus are the caretakers of this hidden jewel. Few in number, members are chosen in their youth by the Celestials to live their lives within the confines of the valley. This is a great honor. When the mogu return to reclaim their ancient capital, the Golden Lotus needs aid. Players petition the White Tiger to allow their factions to help. It's up to the players to prove themselves once inside!

REPUTATION REWARDS - GENERAL

Name	Cost	Requirement	Description
Pattern: Angerhide Leg Armor	25g	Leatherworking (575), Golden Lotus – Honored	Use: Teaches you how to craft Angerhide Leg Armor.
Pattern: Chestguard of Earthen Harmony	50g	Leatherworking (600), Golden Lotus – Honored	Use: Teaches you how to craft a Chestguard of Earthen Harmony.
Pattern: Gloves of Earthen Harmony	50g	Leatherworking (600), Golden Lotus – Honored	Use: Teaches you how to craft Gloves of Earthen Harmony.
Pattern: Greater Cerulean Spellthread	25g	Tailoring (575), Golden Lotus – Honored	Use: Teaches you how to craft Greater Cerulean Spellthread.
Pattern: Greater Pearlescent Spellthread	25g	Tailoring (575), Golden Lotus – Honored	Use: Teaches you how to craft Greater Pearlescent Spellthread.
Pattern: Greyshadow Chestguard	50g	Leatherworking (600), Golden Lotus – Honored	Use: Teaches you how to craft a Greyshadow Chestguard.
Pattern: Greyshadow Gloves	50g	Leatherworking (600), Golden Lotus – Honored	Use: Teaches you how to craft Greyshadow Gloves.
Pattern: Shadowleather Leg Armor	25g	Leatherworking (575), Golden Lotus – Honored	Use: Teaches you how to craft Shadowleather Leg Armor.
Pattern: Spelltwister's Gloves	50g	Tailoring (600), Golden Lotus – Honored	Use: Teaches you how to craft Spelltwister's Gloves.
Pattern: Spelltwister's Grand Robe	50g	Tailoring (600), Golden Lotus – Honored	Use: Teaches you how to craft Spelltwister's Grand Robe.
Pattern: Wildblood Gloves	50g	Leatherworking (600), Golden Lotus – Honored	Use: Teaches you how to craft Wildblood Gloves.
Pattern: Wildblood Vest	50g	Leatherworking (600), Golden Lotus – Honored	Use: Teaches you how to craft a Wildblood Vest.
Pattern: Ironscale Leg Armor	25g	Leatherworking (575), Golden Lotus – Honored	Use: Teaches you how to craft Ironscale Leg Armor.
Pattern: Robes of Creation	50g	Tailoring (600) Golden Lotus – Honored	Use: Teaches you how to craft Robes of Creation.
Pattern: Gloves of Creation	50g	Tailoring (600) Golden Lotus – Honored	Use: Teaches you how to craft Gloves of Creation.
Pattern: Lifekeeper's Gloves	50g	Leatherworking (600), Golden Lotus – Honored	Use: Teaches you how to craft Lifekeeper's Gloves.
Patten: Lifekeeper's Robe	50g	Leatherworking (600) Golden Lotus – Honored	Use: Teaches you how to craft a Lifekeeper's Robe.
Reins of the Azure Riding Crane	500g	Level 90, Artisan Riding, Golden Lotus – Exalted	Use: Teaches you how to summon this mount.
Reins of the Golden Riding Crane	2,500g	Level 90, Artisan Riding, Golden Lotus – Exalted	Use: Teaches you how to summon this mount.
Reins of the Regal Riding Crane	1,500g	Level 90, Artisan Riding, Golden Lotus – Exalted	Use: Teaches you how to summon this mount.
Golden Lotus Tabard	10g	The Golden Lotus - Exalted	Tabard

REPUTATION REWARDS - CLOTH ARMOR

Name	Cost	Requirement	Description
Bracers of Eternal Resolve	1250 Justice Points	Level 90, Golden Lotus – Honored	Cloth Wrist, 849 Armor, +666 Stamina, +444 Intellect, +333 Spirit Equip: Increases your critical strike rating by 232.
Tranquility Bindings	1250 Justice Points	Level 90, Golden Lotus – Honored	Cloth Wrist, 849 Armor, +666 Stamina, +444 Intellect Equip: Increases your critical strike rating by 326, Equip: Increases your haste rating by 246.
Robe of the Five Sisters	2250 Valor Points	Level 90, Golden Lotus – Revered	Cloth Chest, 2,229 Armor, +1,719 Stamina, +986 Intellect, +590 Spirit, Blue Socket, Yellow Socket, Socket Bonus: +120 Intellect Equip: Increases your mastery rating by 740.
Tenderheart Shoulders	1750 Valor Points	Level 90, Golden Lotus – Revered	Cloth Shoulder, 1,672 Armor, +1,277 Stamina, +771 Intellect, +544 Spirit, Yellow Socket, Socket Bonus: +60 Intellect Equip: Increases your mastery rating by 499.
Mantle of the Golden Sun	1750 Valor Points	Level 90, Golden Lotus – Revered	Cloth Shoulder, 1,672 Armor, +1,277 Stamina, +771 Intellect, Yellow Socket, Socket Bonus: +60 Intellect Equip: Increases your hit rating by 585, Equip: Increases your Critical Strike by 431.
Vestments of Thundering Skies	2250 Valor Points	Level 90, Golden Lotus – Revered	Cloth Chest, 2,229 Armor, +1,719 Stamina, +986 Intellect, Blue Socket, Yellow Socket, Socket Bonus: +120 Intellect Equip: Increases your hit rating by 718, Equip: Increases your haste rating by 646.

REPUTATION REWARDS - LEATHER ARMOR

Name	Cost	Requirement	Description
Surehand Grips	1750 Justice Points	Level 90, Golden Lotus – Honored	Leather Hands, 1,544 Armor, +592 Agility, +888 Stamina Equip: Increases your critical strike rating by 401, Equip: Increases your mastery rating by 385.
Wandering Friar's Gloves	1750 Justice Points	Level 90, Golden Lotus – Honored	Leather Hands, 1,544 Armor, +888 Stamina, +592 Intellect, +375 Spirit Equip: Increases your mastery rating by 406.
Whitepetal Shouldergarb	1750 Valor Points	Level 90, Golden Lotus – Revered	Leather Shoulders, 2,128 Armor, +1,277 Stamina, +771 Intellect, Yellow Socket, Socket Bonus: +60 Intellect Equip: Increases your Critical Strike by 561, Equip: Increases your mastery rating by 472.
Imperion Spaulders	1750 Valor Points	Level 90, Golden Lotus – Revered	Leather Shoulders, 2,128 Armor, +771 Agility, +1,277 Stamina, Yellow Socket, Socket Bonus: +60 Agility Equip: Increases your Critical Strike by 536, Equip: Increases your hit by 513.
Softfoot Silentwrap	2250 Valor Points	Level 90, Golden Lotus – Revered	Leather Chest, 2,837 Armor, +986 Agility, +1,719 Stamina, Blue Socket, Yellow Socket, Socket Bonus: +120 Agility Equip: Increases your expertise rating by 761, Equip: Increases your hit rating by 554.
Mistfall Robes	2250 Valor Points	Level 90, Golden Lotus – Revered	Leather Chest, 2,837 Armor, +1,719 Stamina, +986 Intellect, Blue Socket, Yellow Socket, Socket Bonus: +120 Intellect Equip: Increases your Critical Strike by 696, Equip: Increases your mastery rating by 665.

REPUTATION REWARDS - MAIL ARMOR

Name	Cost	Requirement	Description
Leggings of Twisted Vines	2250 Justice Points	Level 90, Golden Lotus – Honored	Mail Legs, 3,007 Armor, +797 Agility, +1,195 Stamina Equip: Increases your hit rating by 453, Equip: Increases your mastery rating by 577.
Snowpack Waders	2250 Justice Points	Level 90, Golden Lotus – Honored	Mail Legs, 3,007 Armor, +1,195 Stamina, +797 Intellect Equip: Increases your critical strike rating by 492, Equip: Increases your mastery rating by 555.
Breastplate of the Golden Pagoda	2250 Valor Points	Level 90, Golden Lotus – Revered	Mail Chest, 3,948 Armor, +986 Agility, +1,719 Stamina, Blue Socket, Yellow Socket, Socket Bonus: +120 Agility Equip: Increases your haste rating by 646, Equip: Increases your mastery rating by 718.
Mindbender Shoulders	1750 Valor Points	Level 90, Golden Lotus – Revered	Mail Shoulder, 2,961 Armor, +1,277 Stamina, +771 Intellect, Yellow Socket, Socket Bonus: +60 Intellect Equip: Increases your haste rating by 418, Equip: Increases your mastery rating by 592.
Robes of the Setting Sun	2250 Valor Points	Level 90, Golden Lotus – Revered	Mail Chest, 3,948 Armor, +1,719 Stamina, +986 Intellect, Blue Socket, Yellow Socket, Socket Bonus: +120 Intellect Equip: Increases your critical strike rating by 791, Equip: Increases your mastery rating by 500.
Windwalker Spaulders	1750 Valor Points	Level 90, Golden Lotus – Revered	Mail Shoulder, 2,961 Armor, +771 Agility, +1,277 Stamina, Yellow Socket, Socket Bonus: +60 Agility Equip: Increases your hit rating by 472, Equip: Increases your haste rating by 561.

REPUTATION REWARDS - PLATE ARMOR

Name	Cost	Requirement	Description
Bracers of Inner Light	1250 Justice Points	Level 90, Golden Lotus – Honored	Plate Wrist, 2,053 Armor, +666 Stamina, +444 Intellect Equip: Increases your haste rating by 288, Equip: Increases your mastery rating by 300.
Serrated Forearm Guards	1250 Justice Points	Level 90, Golden Lotus – Honored	Plate Wrist, 2,053 Armor, +444 Strength, +666 Stamina Equip: Increases your expertise rating by 326, Equip: Increases your mastery rating by 246.
Shoulders of Autumnlight	1750 Valor Points	Level 90, Golden Lotus – Revered	Plate Shoulder, 4,043 Armor, +529 Strength, +1,277 Stamina, Yellow Socket, Socket Bonus: +90 Stamina Equip: Increases your Dodge by 811, Equip: Increases your expertise rating by 458.
Stonetoe Spaulders	1750 Valor Points	Level 90, Golden Lotus – Revered	Plate Shoulder, 4,043 Armor, +771 Strength, +1,277 Stamina, Yellow Socket, Socket Bonus: +60 Strength Equip: Increases your hit rating by 418, Equip: Increases your Critical Strike by 592.
Dawnblade's Chestguard	2250 Valor Points	Level 90, Golden Lotus – Revered	Plate Chest, 5,391 Armor, +986 Strength, +1,719 Stamina, Blue Socket, Yellow Socket, Socket Bonus: +120 Strength Equip: Increases your hit rating by 696, Equip: Increases your expertise rating by 665.
Cuirass of the Twin Monoliths	2250 Valor Points	Level 90, Golden Lotus – Revered	Plate Chest, 5,391 Armor, +660 Strength, +1,719 Stamina, Blue Socket, Yellow Socket, Socket Bonus: +120 Strength Equip: Increases your Dodge by 1,066, Equip: Increases your expertise rating by 590.

REPUTATION REWARDS – RINGS, AMULETS & TRINKETS

Name	Cost	Requirement	Description
Mogu Rune of Paralysis	1750 Justice Points	Level 90, Golden Lotus – Honored	Trinket Equip: Increases your mastery rating by 751. Use: Place a Mogu Rune of Paralysis on the ground for 1 min, which will stun the next creature that enters it for 4 sec. (1 Min Cooldown)
Amulet of Swirling Mists	1250 Justice Points	Level 90, Golden Lotus - Honored	Neck, +444 Agility, +666 Stamina Equip: Increases your haste rating by 296, Equip: Increases your mastery rating by 296.
Gorget of Usurped Kings	1250 Justice Points	Level 90, Golden Lotus - Honored	Neck, +444 Strength, +666 Stamina Equip: Increases your dodge rating by 313, Equip: Increases your hit rating by 267.
Necklace of Jade Pearls	1250 Justice Points	Level 90, Golden Lotus - Honored	Neck, +666 Stamina, +444 Intellect Equip: Increases your hit rating by 260, Equip: Increases your critical strike rating by 317.
Pendant of Endless Inquisition	1250 Justice Points	Level 90, Golden Lotus - Honored	Neck, +666 Stamina, +444 Intellect, +305 Spirit Equip: Increases your critical strike rating by 281.
Triumphant Conqueror's Chain	1250 Justice Points	Level 90, Golden Lotus – Honored	Neck, +444 Strength, +666 Stamina Equip: Increases your hit rating by 305, Equip: Increases your critical strike rating by 281.
Alani's Inflexible Ring	1250 Valor Points	Level 90, Golden Lotus – Revered	Finger, +501 Strength, +752 Stamina Equip: Increases your Dodge by 468, Equip: Increases your Parry by 353.
Ring of the Golden Stair	1250 Valor Points	Level 90, Golden Lotus – Revered	Finger, +501 Strength, +958 Stamina Equip: Increases your expertise rating by 444, Equip: Increases your Critical Strike by 394.
Anji's Keepsake	1250 Valor Points	Level 90, Golden Lotus – Revered	Finger, +638 Agility, +958 Stamina Equip: Increases your haste rating by 485, Equip: Increases your hit rating by 323.
Leven's Circle of Hope	1250 Valor Points	Level 90, Golden Lotus – Revered	Finger, +958 Stamina, +638 Intellect, +323 Spirit Equip: Increases your Critical Strike by 485.
Simple Harmonius Ring	1250 Valor Points	Level 90, Golden Lotus – Revered	Finger, +958 Stamina, +638 Intellect Equip: Increases your hit rating by 432, Equip: Increases your haste rating by 415.

SHADO-PAN

Ten thousand years ago Shaohao, the last emperor of Pandaria, cleansed himself of all his negative energy, or "Sha." These dark emotions are a permanent part of the land. He tasked Pandaria's greatest warriors with the responsibility of keeping this negative energy locked away and controlled. They became the Shado-Pan, who maintain an eternal vigilance. After the Alliance and Horde landed on Pandaria, the sha began to overwhelm the Shado-Pan. Initially distrustful, players must earn the respect of this faction, gaining an ally in the battle to save Pandaria.

REPUTATION REWARDS

Name	Cost	Requirement	Description
Stack of Stone Blocks	47g 50s	Shadow-Pan Honored	Use: Summon a stack of stone blocks at the target location that you can break. (1 Min Cooldown)
Stack of Bamboo	23g 75s	Shado-Pan Honored	Use: Summon a stack of bamboo at the target location that you can break. (1 Min Cooldown)
Stack of Wooden Boards	9g 50s	Shado-Pan Honored	Use: Summon a stack of wooden boards at the target location that you can break. (1 Min Cooldown)
Brambleguard Leggings	2250 Justice Points	Level 90, Shado-Pan Honored	Leather Legs, 2,161 Armor, +1,195 Stamina, +797 Intellect Equip: Increases your critical strike rating by 570, Equip: Increases your haste rating by 466.
Tough Mushanhide Leggings	2250 Justice Points	Level 90, Shado-Pan Honored	Leather Legs, 2,161 Armor, +797 Agility, +1,195 Stamina Equip: Increases your hit rating by 441, Equip: Increases your mastery rating by 584.
Robe of Eternal Dynasty	2250 Justice Points	Level 90, Shado-Pan Honored	Cloth Chest, 1940 Armor, +1,195 Stamina, +797 Intellect Equip: Increases your hit rating by 531, Equip: Increases your mastery rating by 531.
Robe of Quiet Meditation	2250 Justice Points	Level 90, Shado-Pan Honored	Cloth Chest, +1,940 Armor, +1,195 Stamina, +797 Intellect Equip: Increases your haste rating by 547, Equip: Increases your mastery rating by 505.
Brushcutter's Gloves	1750 Justice Points	Level 90, Shado-Pan Honored	Mail Hands, 2,148 Armor, +592 Agility, +888 Stamina Equip: Increases your hit rating by 328, Equip: Increases your critical strike rating by 434.
Gloves of Forgotten Wisdom	1750 Justice Points	Level 90, Shado-Pan Honored	Mail Hands, 2,148 Armor, +888 Stamina, +592 Intellect Equip: Increases your critical strike rating by 450, Equip: Increases your haste rating by 300.
Gauntlets of Restraint	1750 Justice Points	Level 90, Shado-Pan Honored	Plate Hands, 2,933 Armor, +888 Stamina, +592 Intellect, +346 Spirit Equip: Increaes your critical strike rating by 423.
Wall Breaker Gauntlets	1750 Justice Points	Level 90, Shado-Pan Honored	Plate Hands, 2,933 Armor, +592 Strength, +888 Stamina Equip: Increases your haste rating by 423, Equip: Increases your expertise rating by 346.
Etched Golden Loop	1250 Justice Points	Level 90, Shado-Pan Honored	Finger, +666 Stamina, +444 Intellect Equip: Increases your hit rating by 239, Equip: Increases your mastery rating by 330.

Name	Cost	Requirement	Description
Mark of the Dancing Crane	1250 Justice Points	Level 90, Shado-Pan Honored	Finger, +444 Agility, +666 Stamina Equip: Increases your critical strike rating by 288, Equip: Increases your haste rating by 300.
Signet of the Slumbering Emperor	1250 Justice Points	Level 90, Shado-Pan Honored	Finger, +444 Strength, +666 Stamina Equip: Increases your critical strike rating by 246, Equip: Increases your haste rating by 326.
Sorcerer-King's Seal	1250 Justice Points	Level 90, Shado-Pan Honored	Finger, +666 Stamina, +444 Intellect, +296 Spirit Equip: Increases your mastery rating by 296.
Thunderstone Ring	1250 Justice Points	Level 90 Shado-Pan Honored	Finger, +444 Strength, +666 Stamina Equip: Increases your parry rating by 326, Equip: Increases your hit rating by 246.
Shado-Pan Dragon Gun	1750 Justice Points	Level 90, Shado-Pan Honored	Trinket Use: Unleash a gout of flame, dealing 10,000 fire damage to targets in a 10 yard cone in front of the caster every 0.5 sec for 4 sec. May walk while casting. (1 Min Cooldown)
Blackguard Cape	1250 Valor Points	Level 90, Shado-Pan Revered	Cloak, 1,115 Armor, +638 Agility, +958 Stamina Equip: Increases your hit rating by 444, Equip: Increases your mastery rating by 394.
Sagewhisper's Wrap	1250 Valor Points	Level 90, Shado-Pan Revered	Cloak, 1,115 Armor, +958 Stamina, +638 Intellect, +485 Spirit Equip: Increases your haste rating by 323.
Lao-Chin's Liquid Courage	1750 Valor Points	Level 90 Shado-Pan Revered	Trinket, +1,619 Stamina Use: Increases your mastery rating by 3,595 for 15 sec. (1 Min Cooldown)
Scroll of Revered Ancestors	1750 Valor Points	Level 90, Shado-Pan Revered	Trinket, +1,079 Intellect Use: Increases your Spirit by 3,595 for 15 sec. (1 Min Cooldown)
Blossom of Pure Snow	1750 Valor Points	Level 90, Shado-Pan Revered	Trinket, +1,079 Intellect Use: Increases your Critical Strike by 3,595 for 15 sec. (1 Min Cooldown)
Hawkmaster's Talon	1750 Valor Points	Level 90, Shado-Pan Revered	Trinket, +1,079 Agility Use: Increases your haste rating by 3,595 for 15 sec. (1 Min Cooldown)
Red Smoke Bandana	2250 Valor Points	Level 90, Shado-Pan Revered	Leather Head, 2,305 Armor, +906 Agility, +1,719 Stamina, Meta Socket, Blue Socket, Socket Bonus: +180 Agility Equip: Increases your hit rating by 665, Equip: Increases your mastery rating by 616.
Formula: Enchant Weapon – Dancing Steel	38g	Enchanting (600), Shado-Pan Revered	Use: Teaches you how to permanently enchant a melee weapon to sometimes increase your Strength or Agility by 1,650 when dealing melee damage. Requires a level 372 or higher item.
Formula: Enchant Weapon – Jade Spirit	38g	Enchanting (600), Shado-Pan Revered	Use: Teaches you how to permanently enchant a melee weapon to sometimes increase Intellect when healing or dealing damage with spells. Also increases Spirit if your mana is low. Requires a level 372 or higher item.
Formula: Enchant Weapon – River's Song	38g	Enchanting (600), Shado-Pan Revered	Use: Teaches you how to permanently enchant a melee weapon to sometimes increase your dodge when dealing melee damage. Requires a level 372 or higher item.
Reins of the Blue Shado-Pan Riding Tiger	475g	Level 90, Artisan Riding Shado-Pan Exalted	Use: Teaches you how to summon this mount.
Reins of the Green Shado-Pan Riding Tiger	1,425g	Level 90, Artisan Riding Shado-Pan Exalted	Use: Teaches you how to summon this mount.
Reins of the Red Shado-Pan Riding Tiger	2,375g	Level 90, Artisan Riding Shado-Pan Exalted	Use: Teaches you how to summon this mount.
Replica Shado-Pan Helmet	17g 75s 95c	Level 90, Shado-Pan Exalted	Cloth Head, 204 Armor
Shado-Pan Tabard	9g 50s	Shado-Pan Exalted	Tabard
Replica Shado-Pan Helmet	16g 85s 11c	Level 90, Shado-Pan Exalted	Leather Head, 286 Armor
Replica Shado-Pan Helmet	16g 91s 61c	Level 90, Shado-Pan Exalted	Mail Head, 435 Armor
Replica Shado-Pan Helmet	16g 97s 94c	Level 90, Shado-Pan Exalted	Plate Head, 611 Armor
Nightwatcher's Helm	2250 Valor Points	Level 90, Shado-Pan Revered	Mail Head, 3,208 Armor, +1,719 Stamina, +906 Intellect, +689 Spirit, Meta Socket, Blue Socket, Socket Bonus: +180 Intellect Equip: Increases your critical strike rating by 569.
Hawkmaster's Headguard	2250 Valor Points	Level 90, Shado-Pan Revered	Mail Head, 3,208 Armor, +906 Agility, +1,719 Stamina, Meta Socket, Blue Socket, Socket Bonus: +180 Agility Equip: Increases your hit rating by 570, Equip: Increases your critical strike rating by 680.
Cloak of Snow Blossoms	1250 Valor Points	Level 90, Shado-Pan Revered	Cloak, 1,115 Armor, +958 Stamina, +638 Intellect Equip: Increases your hit rating by 426, Equip: Increases your mastery rating by 426.
Cloak of the Dark Disciple	1250 Valor Points	Level 90, Shado-Pan Revered	Cloak, 1,115 Armor, +638 Strength, +958 Stamina Equip: Increases your Critical Strike by 363, Equip: Increases your mastery rating by 463.
Yi's Cloak of Courage	1250 Valor Points	Level 90, Shado-Pan Revered	Cloak, 1,115 Armor, +638 Strength, +958 Stamina Equip: Increases your Parry by 457, Equip: Increases your mastery rating by 373.
Iron Belly Wok	1750 Valor Points	Level 90, Shado-Pan Revered	Trinket, +1,079 Strength Use: Increases your haste rating by 3,595 for 15 sec. (1 Min Cooldown)
Six Pool's Open Helm	2250 Valor Points	Level 90, Shado-Pan Revered	Plate Head, 4,380 Armor, +1,719 Stamina, +906 Intellect, +680 Spirit, Meta Socket, Blue Socket, Socket Bonus: +180 Intellect Equip: Increase your critical strike rating by 570.
Voice Amplyifying Greathelm	2250 Valor Points	Level 90, Shado-Pan Revered	Plate Head, 4,380 Armor, +906 Agility, +1,719 Stamina, Meta Socket, Blue Socket, Socket Bonus: +180 Critical Strike Equip: Increases your Critical Strike by 741, Equip: Increases your expertise rating by 494.
Yi's Least Favorite Helmet	2250 Valor Points	Level 90, Shado-Pan Revered	Plate Head, 4,380 Armor, +906 Strength, +1,719 Stamina, Meta Socket, Blue Socket, Socket Bonus: +270 Stamina Equip: Increases your mastery rating by 570, Equip: Increases your Dodge by 680.

KLAXXI

The "Klaxxi" are an elite warrior-priesthood within the Mantid race, and the guardians of the mantid culture. They prepare new queens for birth, oversee the suicide of aging warriors, and groom/protect the sacred shrines of the Mantid. But now the main body of the Mantid are overcome by the sha, and even the queen herself is polluted. The last remaining Klaxxi wish to purge their race, to the extent of growing a new queen if the old cannot be saved. They are calling upon mantid heroes of old, the "Paragons," who have been encased in amber for as long as thousands of years. Although distrustful of outsiders, they will generously reward anyone who helps them in their cause with unique Mantid weapons, armor, and artifacts.

REPUTATION REWARDS - GENERAL

Name	Cost	Requirement	Description
Restorative Amber	10g	The Klaxxi – Honored	Use: Encase yourself in restorative amber, restoring 300,000 health and 150,000 mana over 20 sec. 1 Sec Cooldown)
Plans: Masterwork Forgewire Axe	25g	Blacksmithing (575), The Klaxxi – Honored	Use: Teaches you how to forge a Masterwork Forgewire Axe.
Plans: Breastplate of Ancient Steel	20 Kyparite	Blacksmithing (600), The Klaxxi – Honored	Use: Teaches you how to forge a Breastplate of Ancient Steel.
Plans: Gauntlets of Ancient Steel	20 Kyparite	Blacksmithing (600), The Klaxxi – Honored	Use: Teaches you how to forge Gauntlets of Ancient Steel.
Plans: Ghost Iron Shield Spike	20 Kyparite	Blacksmithing (540), The Klaxxi – Honored	Use: Teaches you how to forge a Ghost Iron Shield Spike
Plans: Living Steel Belt Buckle	20 Kyparite	Blacksmithing (600), The Klaxxi – Honored	Use: Teaches you how to forge a Living Steel Buckle.
Plans: Living Steel Breastplate	20 Kyparite	Blacksmithing (600), The Klaxxi – Honored	Use: Teaches you how to forge a Living Steel Breastplate.
Plans: Living Steel Gauntlets	20 Kyparite	Blacksmithing (600), The Klaxxi – Honored	Use: Teaches you how to forge Living Steel Gauntlets.
Plans: Living Steel Weapon Chain	20 Kyparite	Blacksmithing (540), The Klaxxi – Honored	Use: Teaches you how to forge a Living Steel Weapon Chain.
Plans: Masterwork Ghost Shard	20 Kyparite	Blacksmithing (575), The Klaxxi – Honored	Use: Teaches you how to forge a Masterwork Ghost Shard.
Plans: Masterwork Ghost-Forged Blade	20 Kyparite	Blacksmithing (575), The Klaxxi – Honored	Use: Teaches you how to forge a Masterwork Ghost-Forged Blade.
Plans: Masterwork Spiritblade Decimator	20 Kyparite	Blacksmithing (575), The Klaxxi – Honored	Use: Teaches you how to forge a Masterwork Spiritblade Decimator.
Plans: Masterwork Phantasmal Hammer	25g	Blacksmithing (575), The Klaxxi – Honored	Use: Teaches you how to forge a Masterwork Phantasmal Hammer.
Plans: Ghost Reaver's Breastplate	50g	Blacksmithing (600), The Klaxxi – Revered	Use: Teaches you how to forge a Ghost Reaver's Breastplate.
Plans: Ghost Reaver's Gauntlets	50g	Blacksmithing (600), The Klaxxi – Revered	Use: Teaches you how to forge Ghost Reaver's Gauntlets.
Reins of the Amber Scorpion	10,000g	Level 70, Artisan Riding, The Klaxxi – Exalted	Use: Teaches you how to summon this mount.
Klaxxi Tabard	10g	The Klaxxi – Exalted	Tabard

REPUTATION REWARDS - AMULETS

Name	Cost	Requirement	Description
Choker of the Klaxxi'va	1250 Valor Points	Level 90, The Klaxxi – Revered	Neck, +638 Agility, +958 Stamina Equip: Increases your hit rating by 363, Equip: Increases your Critical Strike by 463.
Links of the Lucid	1250 Valor Points	Level 90, The Klaxxi – Revered	Neck, +958 Stamina, +638 Intellect, +394 Spirit Equip: Increases your haste rating by 444.
Wire of the Wakener	1250 Valor Points	Level 90, The Klaxxi – Revered	Neck, +958 Stamina, +638 Intellect Equip: Increases your hit rating by 463, Equip: Increases your mastery rating by 363.
Bloodseeker's Solitaire	1250 Valor Points	Level 90, The Klaxxi – Revered	Neck, +638 Strength, +958 Stamina Equip: Increases your haste rating by 451, Equip: Increases your mastery rating by 384.
Paragon's Pale Pendant	1250 Valor Points	Level 90, The Klaxxi – Revered	Neck, +485 Strength, +958 Stamina Equip: Increases your Parry by 638, Equip: Increases your hit rating by 323.

REPUTATION REWARDS - CLOTH ARMOR

Name	Cost	Requirement	Description
Emperor's Riding Gloves	1750 Justice Points	Level 90, The Klaxxi – Honored	Cloth Hands, 1,213 Armor, +888 Stamina, +592 Intellect, +365 Spirit Equip: Increases your haste rating by 412.
Krompf's Fine-Tuning Gloves	1750 Justice Points	Level 90, The Klaxxi – Honored	Cloth Hands, 1,213 Armor, +888 Stamina, +592 Intellect Equip: Increases your hit rating by 429, Equip: Increases your haste rating by 337.
Klaxxi Lash of the Seeker	1750 Justice Points	Level 90, The Klaxxi – Revered	Cloth Waist, 1,254 Armor, +1,277 Stamina, +771 Intellect, +577 Spirit, Blue Socket, Socket Bonus: +60 Spirit Equip: Increases your haste rating by 444.
Poisoncrafter's Kilt	2250 Valor Points	Level 90, The Klaxxi – Revered	Cloth Legs, 1,950 Armor, +1,719 Stamina, +1,066 Intellect, +667 Spirit, Red Socket, Socket Bonus:+60 Intellect Equip: Increases your critical strike rating by 758.
Leggings of the Poisoned Soul	2250 Valor Points	Level 90, The Klaxxi – Revered	Cloth Legs, 1,950 Armor, +1,719 Stamina, +1,066 Intellect, Red Socket, Socket Bonus: +60 Intellect Equip: Increases your hit rating by 667, Equip: Increases your Critical Strike by 758.
Klaxxi Lash of the Orator	1750 Valor Points	Level 90, The Klaxxi – Revered	Cloth Waist, 1,254 Armor, +1,277 Stamina, +771 Intellect, Blue Socket, Socket Bonus: +60 Hit Equip: Increases your hit rating by 577, Equip: Increases your Critical Strike by 444.

REPUTATION REWARDS - LEATHER ARMOR

Name	Cost	Requirement	Description
Cruel Mercy Bracers	1250 Justice Points	Level 90, The Klaxxi – Honored	Leather Wrist, 1,081 Armor, +444 Agility, +666 Stamina Equip: Increases your critical strike rating by 330, Equip: Increases your mastery rating by 239.
Sudden Insight Bracers	1250 Justice Points	Level 90, The Klaxxi – Honored	Leather Wrist, 1,081 Armor, +666 Stamina, +444 Intellect Equip: Increases your critical strike rating by 305, Equip: Increases your mastery rating by 281.
Wind-Reaver Greaves	2250 Valor Points	Level 90, The Klaxxi – Revered	Leather Legs, 2,483 Armor, +1,719 Stamina, +1,066 Intellect, +736 Spirit, Red Socket, Socket Bonus: +60 Intellect Equip: Increases your mastery rating by 705.
Dreadsworn Slayer Legs	2250 Valor Points	Level 90, The Klaxxi – Revered	Leather Legs, 2,483 Armor, +1,066 Agility, +1,719 Stamina, Red Socket, Socket Bonus: +60 Agility Equip: Increases your mastery rating by 594, Equip: Increases your Critical Strike by 801.
Klaxxi Lash of the Borrower	1750 Valor Points	Level 90, The Klaxxi – Revered	Leather Waist, 1,596 Armor, +771 Agility, +1,277 Stamina, Blue Socket, Socket Bonus: +60 Critical Strike Equip: Increases your Critical Strike by 391, Equip: Increases your mastery rating by 607.
Klaxxi Lash of the Harbinger	1750 Valor Points	Level 90, The Klaxxi – Revered	Leather Waist, 1,596 Armor, +1,277 Stamina, +771 Intellect, +554 Spirit, Blue Socket, Socket Bonus: +60 Spirit Equip: Increases your Critical Strike by 499.

REPUTATION REWARDS - MAIL ARMOR

Name	Cost	Requirement	Description
Entombed Traitor's Wristguards	1250 Justice Points	Level 90, The Klaxxi – Honored	Mail Wrist, 1,503 Armor, +444 Agility, +666 Stamina Equip: Increases your critical strike rating by 317, Equip: Increases your expertise rating by 260.
Runoff Wristguards	1250 Justice Points	Level 90, The Klaxxi – Honored	Mail Wrist, 1,503 Armor, +666 Stamina, +444 Intellect, +326 Spirit Equip: Increases your critical strike rating by 246.
Klaxxi Lash of the Precursor	2250 Valor Points	Level 90, The Klaxxi – Revered	Mail Waist, 2,221 Armor, +1,277 Stamina, +771 Intellect, Blue Socket, Socket Bonus: +60 Mastery Equip: Increases your haste rating by 528, Equip: Increases your mastery rating by 528.
Klaxxi Lash of the Winnower	1750 Valor Points	Level 90, The Klaxxi – Revered	Mail Waist, 2,221 Armor, +771 Agility, +1,277 Stamina, Blue Socket, Socket Bonus: +60 Haste Equip: Increases your haste rating by 458, Equip: Increases your mastery rating by 569.
Locust Swarm Legguards	2250 Valor Points	Level 90, The Klaxxi – Revered	Mail Legs, 3,454 Armor, +1,066 Agility, +1,719 Stamina, Red Socket, Socket Bonus: +60 Agility Equip: Increases your critical strike rating by 540, Equip: Increases your mastery rating by 831.
Swarmkeeper's Leggings	2250 Valor Points	Level 90, The Klaxxi – Revered	Mail Legs, 3,454 Armor, +1,719 Stamina, +1,066 Intellect, +724 Spirit, Red Socket, Socket Bonus: +60 Intellect Equip: Increases your critical strike rating by 724.

REPUTATION REWARDS - PLATE ARMOR

Name	Cost	Requirement	Description
Chestplate of the Stone Lion	2250 Justice Points	Level 90, The Klaxxi – Honored	Plate Chest, 4,693 Armor, +797 Strength, +1,195 Stamina Equip: Increases your hit rating by 428, Equip: Increases your mastery rating by 592.
Inner Serenity Chestplate	2250 Justice Points	Level 90, The Klaxxi – Honored	Plate Chest, 4,693 Armor, +1,195 Stamina, +797 Intellect Equip: Increases your critical strike rating by 592, Equip: Increases your mastery rating by 428.
Ambersmith Legplates	2250 Valor Points	Level 90, The Klaxxi – Revered	Plate Legs, 4,717 Armor, +1,719 Stamina, +1,066 Intellect, +736 Spirit, Red Socket, Socket Bonus: +60 Intellect Equip: Increases your mastery by 705.
Klaxxi Lash of the Doubter	1750 Valor Points	Level 90, The Klaxxi – Revered	Plate Waist, 3,033 Armor, +1,277 Stamina, +771 Intellect, Blue Socket, Socket Bonus: +60 Mastery Equip: Increases your haste rating by 391, Equip: Increases your mastery by 607.
Kovok's Riven Legguards	2250 Valor Points	Level 90, The Klaxxi – Revered	Plate Legs, 4,717 Armor, +791 Strength, +1,719 Stamina, Red Socket, Socket Bonus: +60 Strength Equip: Increases your expertise rating by 540, Equip: Increases your Dodge by 1,106.
Legguards of the Unscathed	2250 Valor Points	Level 90, The Klaxxi – Revered	Plate Legs, 4,717 Armor, +1,066 Strength, +1,719 Stamina, Red Socket, Socket Bonus: +60 Strength Equip: Increases your haste by 811, Equip: Increases your mastery by 576.
Klaxxi Lash of the Rescinder	1750 Valor Points	Level 90, The Klaxxi – Revered	Plate Waist, 3,033 Armor, +771 Strength, +1,277 Stamina, Blue Socket, Socket Bonus: +60 Critical Strike Equip: Increases your Critical Strike by 528, Equip: Increases your mastery rating by 528.
Klaxxi Lash of the Consumer	1750 Valor Points	Level 90, The Klaxxi – Revered	Plate Waist, 3,033 Armor, +529 Strength, +1,277 Stamina, Blue Socket, Socket Bonus: +60 Parry Equip: Increases your Parry by 811, Equip: Increases your hit rating by 458.

REPUTATION REWARDS - WEAPONS

Name	Cost	Requirement	Description
Amber Saber of Klaxxi'vess	159g 37s 18c	Level 90, The Klaxxi – Exalted	1H Sword, 4,434 – 8,236 Damage, Speed 2.60, +578 Stamina, +385 Intellect Equip: Increases your haste rating by 279, Equip: Increases your mastery rating by 219.
Amber Sledge of Klaxxi'vess	161g 18s 62c	Level 90, The Klaxxi – Exalted	1H Mace, 4,434 – 8,236 Damage, Speed 2.60, +385 Agility, +578 Stamina Equip: Increases your Critical Strike by 219, Equip: Increases your mastery rating by 279.
Amber Slicer of Klaxxi'vess	169g 8s 72c	Level 90, The Klaxxi – Exalted	Dagger, 3,070 – 5,702 Damage, Speed 1.80, +385 Agility, +578 Stamina Equip: Increases your haste rating by 261, Equip: Increases your mastery rating by 251.
Amber Sprayer of Klaxxi'vess	120g 44s 43c	Level 90, The Klaxxi – Exalted	Gun, 6,899 – 12,813 Damage, Speed 3.00, +899 Agility, +1,349 Stamina Equip: Increases your critical strike rating by 617, Equip: Increases your mastery rating by 570.
Amber Spear of Klaxxi'vess	212g 12s 19c	Level 90, The Klaxxi – Exalted	Polearm, 9,462 – 14,193 Damage, Speed 3.60, +899 Agility, +1,349 Stamina Equip: Increases your hit rating by 617, Equip: Increases your haste rating by 570.
Amber Scythe of Klaxxi'vess	212g 88s 48c	Level 90, The Klaxxi – Exalted	Staff, 4,468 – 6,703 Damage, Speed 3.40, +1,349 Stamina, +899 Intellect Equip: Increases your haste rating by 652, Equip: Increases your mastery rating by 512, Equip: Increases Spell Power by 5,151.
Amber Spine of Klaxxi'vess	168g 47s 69c	Level 90, The Klaxxi – Exalted	Dagger, 3,070 – 5,702 Damage, Speed 1.80, +578 Stamina, +385 Intellect, +251 Spirit Equip: Increases your haste rating by 261.
Amber Espada of Klaxxi'vess	170g 90s 16c	Level 90, The Klaxxi – Exalted	1H Sword, 4,434 – 8,236 Damage, Speed 2.60, +385 Strength, +578 Stamina Equip: Increases your critical strike rating by 279, Equip: Increases your mastery rating by 219.
Amber Flammard of Klaxxi'vess	199g 97s 76c	Level 90, The Klaxxi – Exalted	2H Sword, 9,462 – 14,193 Damage, Speed 3.60, +899 Strength, +1,349 Stamina Equip: Increases your Critical Strike by 456, Equip: Increases your haste rating by 683.

ORDER OF THE CLOUD SERPENT

Twelve thousand years ago, after the Mogu were overthrown, the Zandalari invaded Pandaria. Overwhelmed by this crafty new enemy, the Pandaren needed a way to move quickly and strike at their enemies. The order of the Serpent Riders was born, and this elite air guard has been protecting Pandaria ever since. Once players hit level 90, they can prove themselves to the Serpent Riders, choosing their own serpent egg, raising it, training it, and even racing it, until it becomes their flying mount.

REPUTATION REWARDS

Name	Cost	Requirement	Description
Design: Jade Panther		Jewelcrafting (600), Order of the Cloud Serpent – Honored	Use: Teaches you how to create an Jade Panther.
Design: Sunstone Panther		Jewelcrafting (600), Order of the Cloud Serpent – Honored	Use: Teaches you how to create a Sunstone Panther.
Design: Ruby Panther		Jewelcrafting (600), Order of the Cloud Serpent – Revered	Use: Teaches you how to create a Ruby Panther.
Design: Sapphire Panther		Jewelcrafting (600), Order of the Cloud Serpent – Revered	Use: Teaches you how to create a Sapphire Panther.
Design: Jeweled Onyx Panther		Jewelcrafting (600), Order of the Cloud Serpent – Exalted	Use: Teaches you how to create a Jeweled Onyx Panther.
Floating Finish Line	95g	Order of the Cloud Serpent – Revered	Use: Summon a floating finish line at your current location for 15 Min. Can be used while mounted. (10 Min Cooldown) "Make your own race"
Finish Line	95g	Order of the Cloud Serpent – Revered	Use: Summon a finish line at the target location for 15 Min. (10 Min Cooldown) "Make your own race"
Floating Racing Flag	23g 75s	Order of the Cloud Serpent – Revered	Use: Summon a floating racing flag at your current location for 15 Min. Can be used while mounted. (30 sec Cooldown) "Make your own race"
Racing Flag	23g 75s	Order of the Cloud Serpent – Revered	Use: Summon a Racing Flag at the target location for 15 Min. (30 sec Cooldown) "Make your own race"
Cloud Ring	950g	Order of the Cloud Serpent – Revered	Use: Summon a cloud ring that your pet will jump through. Requires a flying pet. (10 Min Cooldown)
Reins of the Azure Cloud Serpent	2,850g	Level 90, Artisan Riding, Order of the Cloud Serpent – Exalted	Use: Teaches you how to summon this mount. This is a flying mount. Requires Cloud Serpent Riding from the Order of the Cloud Serpent.
Reins of the Golden Cloud Serpent	2,850g	Level 90, Artisan Riding, Order of the Cloud Serpent – Exalted	Use: Teaches you how to summon this mount. This is a flying mount. Requires Cloud Serpent Riding from the Order of the Cloud Serpent.
Reins of the Jade Cloud Serpent	2,850g	Level 90, Artisan Riding, Order of the Cloud Serpent – Exalted	Use: Teaches you how to summon this mount. This is a flying mount. Requires Cloud Serpent Riding from the Order of the Cloud Serpent.
Order of the Cloud Serpent Tabard	9g 50s	Order of the Cloud Serpent – Exalted	Tabard, "You truly belong here with us among the clouds."

LEGENDARY REPUTATION – THE BLACK PRINCE

There is a tavern located in The Veiled Stair that is just called Tavern in the Mists. Inside this tavern is the last of the black dragons, who refers to himself as Wrathion, The Black Prince. Sharing a drink with this individual sets you on the path to earning a Legendary Item. Through the course of your trials to earn this item you will be expected to kill hordes of the most powerful Mogu and Mantid foes as well as collecting Sigils of Power and Wisdom from raid locations. Once these two tasks are completed you are tasked with killing one of the dreaded Sha that is consuming the beautiful land of Pandaria. Your reward for completing this task won't be the end of your journey for your promised Legendary Item, it is just the beginning!

In order to quickly gain reputation with The Black Prince you need to kill hordes of level 90 Mantid or Mogu. The best location to gain reputation due to the sheer density of enemies is any of the scars in the Dread Wastes or Sra'vess island which is located to the west in Townlong Steppes.

PET BATTLES

Since the day it was announced as a part of Mists of Pandaria, Pet Battles has been one of the most eagerly anticipated additions to World of Warcraft. The vanity pets you've been collecting since you started playing World of Warcraft are now able to battle wild pets, pets from NPC trainers, and teams controlled by other players.

GETTING STARTED

The only requirement to get started with Pet Battles is having one character of level 5 or higher. There are Pet Battle Trainers in the towns nearest each race's starting locations. For example, look for trainers in Goldshire (Elwynn Forest) and Razor Hill (Durotar), though each faction capital (Stormwind for Alliance and Orgrimmar for Horde) has a trainer as well. Speak with any of these trainers to learn the Pet Battles ability. In addition to teaching your companions how to battle, you'll also learn how to track wild pets and return your companions to full health every 8 minutes. These trainers also sell starter pets to you, based on your character's race.

Your trainer also offers a quest called "Learning the Ropes" that sends you to your first Pet Battle. Look for wild pets in the areas outside the town where you trained. Run around the area and watch your mini-map for a green paw icon. This green paw icon indicates the locations of wild pets eligible for battle.

Before you click on a wild pet to start a battle, press Shift + "p" to open your mounts and pets window. Click on the Pets Journal tab to view the vanity pets you've collected previously. If there's a specific pet you want to use, click on the pet's icon and drag it to the top line of Pet Battle Slots. Once you click on a wild pet to start the fight, you can't switch any pets from your journal into an active slot. If you're happy with your pet choice, right click on a wild pet to start your first battle.

PETS LEARNED FROM PET BATTLE TRAINERS

The race of your character, not the race of the trainer, determines which pet a given trainer offers to you.

ALLIANCE	
RACE	**PET**
Draenei	Blue Moth
Dwarf	Snowshoe Rabbit
Gnome	Snowshoe Rabbit
Human	Orange Tabby Cat
Night Elf	Great Horned Owl
Worgen	Gilnean Raven

HORDE	
RACE	**PET**
Blood Elf	Golden Dragonhawk Hatchling
Goblin	Shore Crawler
Orc	Black Kingsnake
Tauren	Brown Prairie Dog
Troll	Black Kingsnake
Undead	Undercity Cockroach

PANDAREN	
RACE	**PET**
Pandaren	Jade Crane Chick

MORE FUN WITH THE PET JOURNAL

There are a few other commands available to you in the Pet Journal. Right click on any portrait to bring up the following options: Summon/Dismiss, Rename, Set as Favorite, and Release.

Use Rename to name your pets. Set as Favorite marks your pet and allows you to find it quickly when you choose to display only favorite pets. If you right click on a pet that's already marked as a favorite, the option becomes Remove Favorite. Release returns your pet to the wild.

There's another option available to pets that are purchased from a vendor: Put In Cage. Pets that can be put into a cage can be traded with other players or sold through the Auction House.

A BASIC PET BATTLE

In your first encounter your pet has a single ability set in its first ability slot. Pet Battles are turn-based, meaning each combatant is allowed one action each turn. Click on the icon, or press "1" on your keyboard to send your pet out to attack. After you win a battle, return to the trainer and complete your quest.

KEEPING YOUR PETS HEALTHY

Your trainer offers a follow-up quest, "On the Mend." You're tasked with locating a Stable Master (NPCs who, up to this point, had only dealt with Hunters) and getting your pets restored to full health. Speak with the indicated Stable Master, heal your pets (there's a minimal charge for the service), and turn in the completed quest with the trainer.

Stable Masters are just one way to restore your pets. Your other choice is the Revive Battle Pets ability, available once every 8 minutes. Look for the ability's icon at the top right corner of the Pet Journal page.

GETTING YOUR PET TO LEVEL 3

The next quest from the trainer is "Level Up" where you raise one pet to level 3. The only way to level up your pets is through defeating wild pets, so head back out into the wilds. While you're completing this quest, your pet learns a second ability (if it hasn't already). When your pet reaches level 2, a new ability appears in the 2 spot when you go into battle. Now you have a choice of abilities to use in each round of battle. Mouseover the ability's icon and read its description to learn more about it. Try it out a few times in battle to become more familiar with how it works.

ADDING WILD PETS TO YOUR PET JOURNAL

After turning in "Level Up" the Pet Battle trainer sends you to your faction's capital city to meet a different Pet Battle Trainer. This trainer sends you out with the quest "Got One." When your first pet reached level 3, it unlocks the ability to capture wild pets in battle. The wild pet must be at 35% health or lower before the Trap (slot 5 on your shortcut bar) becomes available for use. When the Trap is ready, click on it to try to capture the weakened wild pet. There's only a chance you will succeed in capturing the wild pet each round, so be prepared to exercise some patience when capturing wild pets.

MULTIPLE PETS AND NPC PET TRAINERS

Another quest should have popped up when your first pet reached level 3—a summons from the same trainer in your faction's capital city. This quest sends you out to take on a certain Pet Trainer (the quest is named after the Pet Trainer you're asked to challenge), but you should complete the quest "Got One" and get one pet up to level 5 before tackling the trainer. Getting a pet up to level 3 grants the achievement, Newbie, and unlocks your second battle pet slot. The third slot opens when you get a pet to level 5 (you also get the achievement, Just a Pup).

The bad news about trainer battles is that these trainers have two or three pets you must defeat instead of the single wild pets you've faced up to this point. At least one of your pets must survive the battle for you to get credited with a win and a completed achievement. The good news is that your pets get far more experience from these fights.

Defeating the first trainer leads to a battle against a second trainer in a higher level zone. This process repeats and you take on progressively tougher trainers with higher level pets. Defeating all the trainers in this chain gives the quest "A Trainer's Homecoming" that sends you back to your faction's capital city.

GOING INTO BATTLE

Regardless of the opponent you're facing, you have the same choices on each of your turns. Keep in mind that some abilities include a cooldown. When you use one of these abilities, a number appears over the icon to let you know how many rounds must pass before the ability is ready to use again. There are also certain abilities that block some of your options for a limited number of rounds. For example, many spiders use Sticky Web to keep you from switching pets for a few rounds.

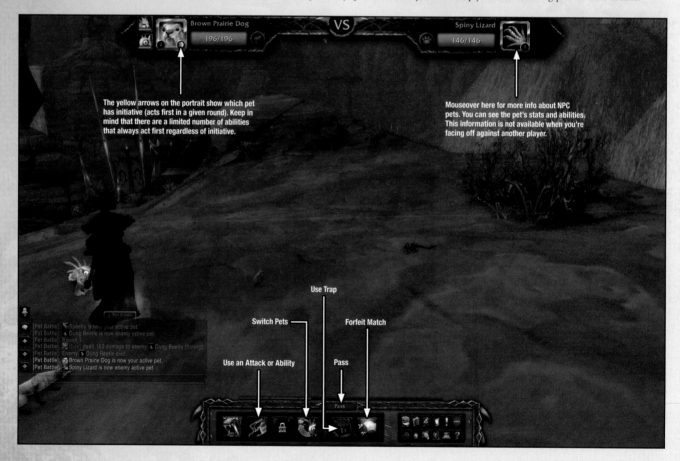

The yellow arrows on the portrait show which pet has initiative (acts first in a given round). Keep in mind that there are a limited number of abilities that always act first regardless of initiative.

Mouseover here for more info about NPC pets. You can see the pet's stats and abilities. This information is not available when you're facing off against another player.

Use Trap

Switch Pets

Forfeit Match

Use an Attack or Ability

Pass

WEATHER CONDITIONS

There are a number of abilities that change the weather conditions and impact the battle. The following list provides more information about each weather condition.

Condition	Description	Ability (Family)
Raining	During a cleansing rain, the duration of hostile damage over time effects is reduced by 1 round and Aquatic pets deal 25% more damage.	Cleansing Rain (Aquatic)
Sunny Day	Increases the maximum health of all pets by 100%. Increases healing done by 25%.	Sunlight (Elemental)
Scorched Earth	Deals Dragonkin damage to any pet who enters battle. All pets count as Burning.	Scorched Earth (Dragonkin)
Arcane Winds	During Arcane Winds, pets cannot be stunned or rooted.	Arcane Storm (Magic)
Moonlight	During Moonlight, all pets receive 25% additional healing and Magic abilities deal 25% additional damage.	Moonfire (Magic)
Blizzard	During a Blizzard, all pets are considered Chilled.	Call Blizzard (Elemental)
Darkness	During Darkness, all pets are considered Blinded and all healing received is reduced by 50%.	Call Darkness (Humanoid)
Lightning Storm	During a Lightning Storm, all pets deal bonus Mechanical damage on each attack and Mechanical abilities deal 25% additional damage.	Call Lightning (Mechanical)
Sandstorm	During a sandstorm, all pets take less damage and their accuracy is reduced by 10%.	Sandstorm (Flying)
Muddy	Muddy weather prevents any pet on the battlefield from swapping out.	Critter (Mudslide)

TYPES OF PET BATTLES

There are three types of Pet Battles:

PVP Battles are fought anonymously against other players. Use the Find Battle button on your Pet Journal window to find opponents.

Pet Duels are initiated with a click on another player's portrait. Select Pet Duel and wait for the other person to accept.

Wild Pet Battles are fought against wild pets. Locate a wild pet with the green paw icon floating over it and right click it to start the fight.

You are immune to NPC damage while engaged in a Pet Battle, but if you're flagged for PVP, you are vulnerable to other players. Be careful where you choose to battle!

PvP Pet Battles

When you click on the Find Battle button on your Pet Journal, you are randomly matched against other players. The game does not track your losses, only the number of times you've won. There are no rewards for PvP Pet Battles, other than earning Achievements and Experience for your pets.

Pet Duels

Pet Duels function basically the same as regular duels. Approach another character, right-click their portrait and invite them to a Pet Duel. Pet Duels follow the same rules as regular duels, meaning you can't duel inside a city or designated sanctuary. If your PVP flag is turned on, then Pet Duels against characters of the opposite faction are not an option. You must use an area such as the sewers under Dalaran if you want to Pet Duel when characters are flagged for PvP. There are no rewards for Pet Duels, other than earning Achievements.

Pet Battles Against NPC Trainers

There are NPC pet trainers found in many locations in every world. A line of quests sends you to battle them, and you must work your way through these trainers in order to unlock the daily quests listed in your Achievements under the Pet Battles tab.

Pet Battles Against Wild Pets

Until you're overloaded with level 25 pets, the bulk of your Pet Battles take place against wild pets. There are wild pets throughout Azeroth and Outland, with most zones having at least one that appears nowhere else. These are the battles where your pets gain most of their experience points, and the means by which you add to the population of your Pet Journal.

Pets in the wild can be any level (from 1 to 25) and they maintain the majority of their levels when you capture them. (For example, a pet caught at level 24 can be weakened to level 22 by capture.) Once they're yours, they gain experience in the same way as any other pet you own. If you want to go after higher level wild pets, you must look in increasingly higher level zones.

Picking the Best Pets to Capture

The quest "Got One" showed you how to capture pets, but how do you know which are the best ones to capture? Wild pets come in four levels of quality: Poor, Common, Uncommon, and Rare. Rare pets are the most desirable and hardest to find. Rare quality pets have the best stats (more on stats later in this section) and are sought after by every serious pet battler. You never know a pet's quality for certain until you've captured it, but comparing stats and health against other creatures of the same level should give you a good idea about which creatures are the best ones to trap. If two pets have similar health, then compare their other stats and trap the creature with higher stats.

There are also limitations to keep in mind when it comes to capturing pets. You are limited to three of the same type of pet in your Pet Journal. If you're not happy with a pet and want to capture a different one, you must have no more than two copies of that pet in your journal before you start a battle. Once the battle begins, you cannot release the pet to make room for a newer one. In any given battle, you can only capture one pet, so don't waste your trap on a creature you don't want! Once it's in the trap, you're stuck with it until the battle ends.

THE WORLD IS FULL OF BEASTS AND CRITTERS

The most common types of wild pets are Beasts and Critters. If your goal is to capture as many different pets as possible as quickly as possible, strongly consider leveling up a combination of the following: a Beast pet (Beast attacks do higher damage against Critters), a Flying pet (high resistance to Beast attacks), a Humanoid pet (high resistance to Critter attacks), and a Mechanical pet (Mechanical attacks do higher damage against Beasts).

Not all Beasts and Critters use Beast and Critter attacks at all times, but they generally include at least one ability in their repertoire.

Other Ways to Acquire Pets

Companion pets have been available in World of Warcraft since it first went live. Most of the pets you've been collecting since then are now eligible for Pet Battles. That includes the pets from:

- Vendors
- Achievements
- World Events

- Blizzard Store
- World of Warcraft Trading Card Game
- Crafted with Professions

- Quests
- World Drops
- Promotional Pets

There's a more complete listing of these pets later in this section of the guide, but use the following lists to pick up a variety of pets that require only a quick trip to a vendor.

Alliance

DARNASSUS

Vendor: Shylenai

Location: Between the Tradesmen's Terrace and Warrior's Terrace

Pet	Cost	Family
Great Horned Owl	50 silver	Flying
Hawk Owl	50 silver	Flying

DUN MOROGH

Vendor: Yarlyn Amberstill

Location: Amberstill Ranch

Pet	Cost	Family
Snowshoe Rabbit	20 silver	Critter

ELWYNN FOREST

Vendor: Donni Anthania

Location: Between Northshire Abbey and Goldshire

Pet	Cost	Family
Bombay Cat	40 silver	Beast
Cornish Rex Cat	40 silver	Beast
Orange Tabby Cat	40 silver	Beast
Silver Tabby Cat	40 silver	Beast

THE EXODAR

Vendor: Sixx

Location: The Crystal Hall

Pet	Cost	Family
Blue Moth	50 silver	Flying
White Moth	50 silver	Flying
Yellow Moth	50 silver	Flying

Horde

EVERSONG WOODS

Vendor: Jilanne

Location: Fairbreeze Village

Pet	Cost	Family
Golden Dragonhawk Hatchling	50 silver	Dragonkin
Silver Dragonhawk Hatchling	50 silver	Dragonkin
Red Dragonhawk Hatchling	50 silver	Dragonkin

ORGRIMMAR

Vendor: Xan'tish

Location: The Valley of Spirits

Pet	Cost	Family
Black Kingsnake	50 silver	Beast
Brown Snake	50 silver	Beast
Crimson Snake	50 silver	Beast

THUNDER BLUFF

Vendor: Halpa

Location: Main Rise

Pet	Cost	Family
Brown Prairie Dog	50 silver	Critter

UNDERCITY

Vendor: Jeremiah Payson

Location: Central Bank

Pet	Cost	Family
Undercity Cockroach	50 silver	Critter

Other Vendors (may require higher level characters)

CAPE OF STRANGLETHORN & BOOTY BAY

Vendor: Narkk (Booty Bay reputation)

Location: North of Booty Bay

Vendor: Harry No-Hooks (Bloodsail Buccaneers reputation)

Location: Bloodsail Ships south of Booty Bay

Pet	Cost	Family
Senegal	40 silver	Flying
Cockatiel	40 silver	Flying

DARKMOON ISLAND

Vendor: Flik

Location: Darkmoon Faire

Pet	Cost	Family
Tree Frog	1 gold	Aquatic
Wood Frog	1 gold	Aquatic

DALARAN

Vendor: Breanni

Location: Near Krassus Landing

Pet	Cost	Family
Albino Snake	50 gold	Beast
Calico Cat	50 gold	Beast
Obsidian Hatchling	50 gold	Beast

Vendor: Darahir

Location: The Underbelly

Pet	Cost	Family
Ghostly Skull	40 gold	Undead

Vendor: Jepetto Joybuzz / Clockwork Assistant

Location: Runeweaver Square

Pet	Cost	Family
Blue Clockwork Rocket Bot	50 gold	Mechanical

NETHERSTORM

Vendor: Dealer Rashaad
Location: Stormspire

Pet	Cost	Family
Blue Dragonhawk Hatchling	10 gold	Dragonkin
Brown Rabbit	10 gold	Critter
Red Moth	10 gold	Flying
Siamese Cat	60 silver	Beast
Mana Wyrmling	40 gold	Magic
Crimson Snake	50 silver	Beast
Undercity Cockroach	50 silver	Critter
Senegal	40 silver	Flying

WINTERSPRING

Vendor: Michelle De Rum
Location: Everlook

Pet	Cost	Family
Winterspring Cub	50 gold	Beast

BATTLE PETS

Everything up to this point has covered the basics of Pet Battles: obtaining pets, how to fight, who to fight, and how to keep your pets healthy. This section focuses on the pets themselves and the characteristics that make them more or less desirable to use in battle.

ABILITIES AND STATS

Open your Pet Journal (Shift + "p", then click on the Pet Journal tab) and you should see something similar to the following image.

Pet Icon and Level

Mousing over the icon tells you how to acquire the pet and provides the creature's lore. This also works with pets you haven't yet obtained.

Experience Bar

Tracks how much experience a pet has earned and how much more is needed to reach the next level.

Pet Battle Achievement Points

Total Pet Battles Achievement Points earned.

Stats

All battle pets have three stats: Health, Power, and Speed. Each stat increases as your pet gains levels.

Stat		Description
♥	Health	This is your maximum health. When a pet's health reaches zero, they're incapacitated and unable to continue fighting.
	Power	This number determines the amount of damage a pet deals in combat. The higher the number, the more damage the pet does in battle.
	Speed	Speed determines initiative, which is used to set the order in which pets act in each turn of battle.

Wild pets have an extra characteristic: Quality. Quality can be Poor (gray), Common (white), Uncommon (green), and Rare (blue). Quality never changes as pets gain levels. It's simply a way to see if you have one of the best examples of a given type of pet. While pets you purchase or earn through Achievements and the like do not have a quality stat, a select number of them are considered Rare quality.

Abilities

All pets begin with a basic attack ability. Additional abilities become available at levels 2, 4, 10, 15, and 20. Each pet has three active ability slots for battle. However, you are limited to two choices for each slot. To change between active abilities, click on the yellow notch under the ability slot and choose the ability you want to make active.

Slot #	Abilities eligible for the slot (by level earned)
1	1 or 10
2	2 or 15
3	4 or 20

Abilities are broken down into the same families as battle pets. Each family of abilities has one other family against which it is 50% more effective (noted by a green arrow) and another family against which it is 33% less effective (noted by a red arrow).

Attack Type	Deals 50% Extra Damage	Deals 33% Less Damage
Aquatic	Elemental	Magic
Beast	Critter	Flying
Critter	Undead	Humanoid
Dragonkin	Magic	Undead
Elemental	Mechanical	Critter
Flying	Aquatic	Dragonkin
Humanoid	Dragonkin	Beast
Magic	Flying	Mechanical
Mechanical	Beast	Elemental
Undead	Humanoid	Aquatic

It's important to note that there is no bonus damage from a pet using an attack of the same family as the pet. The only factors that determine how well an ability does are the attacker's Attack value, the family of the ability used, and the target's family.

Passive Family Abilities

In addition to abilities that they use in battle, each family of pets has a passive ability.

Family		Passive Ability	Description
Aquatic		Purity	Harmful damage over time effects are reduced by 25% on Aquatic pets.
Beast		Enrage	Beasts deal 25% extra damage below half health.
Critter		Elusive	Critters break out of crowd control effects more quickly.
Dragonkin		Execute	Deals 50% additional damage to targets with less than 25% health.
Elemental		Weather Immune	Elementals ignore all weather effects.
Flying		Swiftness	Flying creatures gain 50% extra speed while above 50% health.
Humanoid		Recovery	Humanoids recover 4% of their maximum health if they dealt damage this round.
Magic		Spellshield	Magic pets cannot be dealt more than 50% of their maximum health in one attack.
Mechanical		Failsafe	Mechanical pets come back to life once per battle, returning to 20% health.
Undead		Damned	Undead pets return to life immortal for one round when killed.

LISTING OF PETS

The following section lists all battle pets by family, how they are acquired, and the abilities they have in battle (assuming they're eligible for battle). The ten families of pets each have their own suite of abilities. Pets within each family may share some abilities but also have their own unique abilities.

There is a complete list of abilities immediately following the pet listings.

NON-COMBAT PETS

Not all companions are suited for battle. The following list of pets are not eligible for Pet Battles.

Pet	Acquired
Alliance Balloon	Complete quest Blown Away (Stormwind)
Argent Gruntling	Complete quest A Champion Rises (Icecrown) - Horde
Argent Squire	Complete quest A Champion Rises (Icecrown) - Alliance
Chi-ji Kite	Profession: Inscription
Darkmoon Balloon	Vendor: Lhara, Location: Darkmoon Island
Dragon Kite	Promotional pet: Trading Card Game: March of the Legion
Green Balloon	Vendor: Carl Goodup, Location: Darkmoon Island
Guild Herald	Guild Achievement: Profit Sharing. Purchase for 500 gold from a Guild Vendor
Guild Page	Guild Achievement: Horde Slayer/Alliance Slayer. Purchase for 300 gold from a Guild Vendor
Horde Balloon	Complete quest Blown Away (Orgrimmar)
Tuskar Kite	Promotional pet: Trading Card Game: Scourgewar
Yellow Balloon	Vendor: Carl Goodup, Location: Darkmoon Island
Yu'lon Kite	Profession: Inscription

AQUATIC PETS

Passive Ability	Description
Purity	Harmful damage over time effects are reduced by 25% on Aquatic pets.

NAME	ABILITY LEARNED AT LEVEL						ACQUIRED	REGION/NOTES
	1	2	4	10	15	20		
Aqua Strider	Water Jet	Healing Wave	Soothe	Poison Spit	Cleansing Rain	Pump	Drop: Nalash Verdantis	Dread Wastes
Biletoad	Water Jet	Healing Wave	Frog Kiss	Tongue Lash	Cleansing Rain	Swarm of Flies	Pet Battle	Northern Barrens, Sholazar Basin, Wailing Caverns
Chuck	Rip	Surge	Devour	Consume	Water Jet	Blood in the Water	Profession: Fishing	Shattrath (Daily Fishing Quests)
Dancing Water Skimmer	Water Jet	Healing Wave	Soothe	Poison Spit	Cleansing Rain	Pump	Pet Battle	Vale of Eternal Blossoms
Darkmoon Turtle	Bite	Shell Shield	Headbutt	Grasp	Healing Wave	Powerball	Vendor: Lhara	Darkmoon Island
Emerald Turtle	Emerald Bite	Shell Shield	Headbutt	Grasp	Healing Wave	Powerball	Pet Battle	The Jade Forest
Emperor Crab	Snap	Renewing Mists	Shell Shield	Surge	Healing Wave	Whirlpool	Pet Battle	Dread Wastes
Eternal Strider	Water Jet	Healing Wave	Soothe	Poison Spit	Cleansing Rain	Pump	Pet Battle	Vale of Eternal Blossoms
Fishy	Water Jet	Cleansing Rain	Whirlpool	Surge	Healing Wave	Pump	Quest: Let Them Burn	The Jade Forest
Frog	Water Jet	Healing Wave	Frog Kiss	Tongue Lash	Cleansing Rain	Swarm of Flies	Pet Battle	Ashenvale, The Lost Isles
Garden Frog	Water Jet	Healing Wave	Frog Kiss	Tongue Lash	Cleansing Rain	Swarm of Flies	Pet Battle	The Jade Forest
Golden Civet	Bite	Screech	Surge	Gnaw	Survival	Dive	Pet Battle	Vale of Eternal Blossoms
Golden Civet Kitten	Bite	Screech	Surge	Gnaw	Survival	Dive	Pet Battle	Vale of Eternal Blossoms
Horny Toad	Water Jet	Healing Wave	Frog Kiss	Tongue Lash	Cleansing Rain	Swarm of Flies	Pet Battle	Desolace
Huge Toad	Water Jet	Healing Wave	Frog Kiss	Tongue Lash	Cleansing Rain	Swarm of Flies	Pet Battle	Hillsbrad Foothills, Swamp of Sorrows, Twilight Highlands, Zul'Drak
Jubling	Water Jet	Healing Wave	Frog Kiss	Tongue Lash	Cleansing Rain	Swarm of Flies	World Event: Darkmoon Faire	Darkmoon Island
Jungle Darter	Water Jet	Healing Wave	Frog Kiss	Tongue Lash	Cleansing Rain	Swarm of Flies	Pet Battle	The Jade Forest
Kuitan Mongoose	Bite	Screech	Surge	Gnaw	Survival	Dive	Pet Battle	Townlong Steppes
Leopard Tree Frog	Water Jet	Healing Wave	Frog Kiss	Tongue Lash	Cleansing Rain	Swarm of Flies	Pet Battle	The Jade Forest
Mac Frog	Water Jet	Healing Wave	Frog Kiss	Tongue Lash	Cleansing Rain	Swarm of Flies	Pet Battle	Lost City of the Tol'vir, Uldum
Magical Crawdad	Snap	Renewing Mists	Whirlpool	Surge	Shell Shield	Wish	Profession: Fishing (430), (Mr. Pinchy wish granting)	Terokkar Forest (fishing nodes)
Mirror Strider	Water Jet	Healing Wave	Soothe	Poison Spit	Cleansing Rain	Pump	Pet Battle	The Jade Forest
Mojo	Water Jet	Healing Wave	Frog Kiss	Tongue Lash	Cleansing Rain	Swarm of Flies	Drop: Forest Frog	Zul'Aman (remove hex from frogs)
Mongoose	Bite	Screech	Surge	Gnaw	Survival	Dive	Pet Battle	Townlong Steppes
Mongoose Pup	Bite	Screech	Surge	Gnaw	Survival	Dive	Pet Battle	Townlong Steppes
Mr. Chilly	Peck	Frost Spit	Ice Lance	Surge	Slippery Ice	Belly Slide	Promotion: WoW/Battle.net Account Merger	Promotional Pet
Muckbreath	Rip	Surge	Devour	Consume	Water Jet	Blood in the Water	Profession: Fishing	Shattrath (Daily Fishing Quests)
Pengu	Peck	Frost Spit	Ice Lance	Surge	Slippery Ice	Belly Slide	Vendor: Sairuk / Tanaika	Dragonblight / Howling Fjord (Reputation: Kalu'ak - Exalted)
Purple Puffer	Water Jet	Spiked Skin	Whirlpool	Surge	Healing Wave	Pump	Trading Card Game: Throne of the Tides	TCG
Sea Pony	Water Jet	Surge	Whirlpool	Tidal Wave	Cleansing Rain	Pump	Profession: Fishing	Darkmoon Island
Shore Crab	Snap	Renewing Mists	Shell Shield	Surge	Healing Wave	Whirlpool	Pet Battle	Azshara, Borean Tundra, Krasarang Wilds, Howling Fjord, Twilight Highlands, Westfall
Shore Crawler	Snap	Renewing Mists	Shell Shield	Surge	Healing Wave	Whirlpool	Offered to Goblin characters by Pet Battle Trainers	Orgrimmar
Sifang Otter	Bite	Screech	Surge	Gnaw	Survival	Dive	Pet Battle	Valley of the Four Winds
Sifang Otter Pup	Bite	Screech	Surge	Gnaw	Survival	Dive	Pet Battle	Valley of the Four Winds
Small Frog	Water Jet	Healing Wave	Frog Kiss	Tongue Lash	Cleansing Rain	Swarm of Flies	Pet Battle	Arathi Highlands, Darnassus, Desolace, Dun Morogh, Elwynn Forest, Eversong Woods, Ghostlands, Gilneas, Loch Modan, Northern Barrens, Southern Barrens, Swamp of Sorrows, Teldrassil, The Lost Isles, Zangarmarsh
Snarly	Rip	Surge	Devour	Consume	Water Jet	Blood in the Water	Profession: Fishing	Shattrath (Daily Fishing Quests)
Softshell Snapling	Bite	Shell Shield	Headbutt	Grasp	Healing Wave	Powerball	Pet Battle	Valley of the Four Winds
Speedy	Bite	Shell Shield	Headbutt	Grasp	Healing Wave	Powerball	World Event: Children's Week, Quest: A Warden of the Alliance/Horde	
Spiny Terrapin	Bite	Shell Shield	Headbutt	Grasp	Healing Wave	Powerball	Pet Battle	Krasarang Wilds
Spirebound Crab	Snap	Renewing Mists	Shell Shield	Surge	Healing Wave	Whirlpool	Pet Battle	The Jade Forest

NAME	ABILITY LEARNED AT LEVEL						ACQUIRED	REGION/NOTES
	1	2	4	10	15	20		
Spotted Bell Frog	Water Jet	Healing Wave	Frog Kiss	Tongue Lash	Cleansing Rain	Swarm of Flies	Pet Battle	Un'Goro Crater
Strand Crab	Snap	Renewing Mists	Shell Shield	Surge	Healing Wave	Whirlpool	Pet Battle	Ashenvale, Dragonblight, Dun Morogh, Gilneas, Kezan, Northern Stranglethorn, Swamp of Sorrows, The Cape of Stranglethorn, The Lost Isles
Strand Crawler	Snap	Renewing Mists	Shell Shield	Surge	Healing Wave	Whirlpool	Profession: Fishing	Northrend, Stormwind, Orgrimmar, Dropped by [Bag of Fishing Treasures] Northrend daily fishing quest, [Bag of Shiny Things] Stormwind and Orgrimmar daily fishing quest
Tiny Goldfish	Water Jet	Cleansing Rain	Whirlpool	Surge	Healing Wave	Pump	Vendor: Nat Pagle	Krasarang Wilds (Reputation: The Anglers - Honored)
Toad	Water Jet	Healing Wave	Frog Kiss	Tongue Lash	Cleansing Rain	Swarm of Flies	Pet Battle	Ashenvale, Black Temple, Dun Morogh, Durotar, Dustwallow Marsh. Eversong Woods, Felwood, Ghostlands, Gilneas, Hillsbrad Foothills, Howling Fjord, Nagrand, Orgrimmar, Ruins of Gilneas, Silverpine Forest, Swamp of Sorrows, Teldrassil, Wetlands
Toothy	Rip	Surge	Devour	Consume	Water Jet	Blood in the Water	Profession: Fishing	Shattrath (Daily Fishing Quests)
Tree Frog	Water Jet	Healing Wave	Frog Kiss	Tongue Lash	Cleansing Rain	Swarm of Flies	Vendor: Flik	Darkmoon Island
Tundra Penguin	Peck	Frost Spit	Ice Lance	Surge	Slippery Ice	Belly Slide	Pet Battle	Borean Tundra, Dragonblight
Turquoise Turtle	Bite	Shell Shield	Headbutt	Grasp	Healing Wave	Powerball	Pet Battle	Azshara
Wanderer's Festival Hatchling	Bite	Shell Shield	Pump	Grasp	Perk Up	Cleansing Rain	Event: Wanderer's Festival / Pet Battle	Krasarang Wilds
Wood Frog	Water Jet	Healing Wave	Frog Kiss	Tongue Lash	Cleansing Rain	Swarm of Flies	Vendor: Flik	Darkmoon Island
Yellow-Bellied Bullfrog	Water Jet	Healing Wave	Frog Kiss	Tongue Lash	Cleansing Rain	Swarm of Flies	Pet Battle	Vale of Eternal Blossoms

BEAST PETS

Passive Ability	Description
Enrage	Beasts deal 25% extra damage below half health.

NAME	ABILITY LEARNED AT LEVEL						ACQUIRED	REGION/NOTES
	1	2	4	10	15	20		
Adder	Bite	Hiss	Burrow	Poison Fang	Counterstrike	Vicious Fang	Pet Battle	Blasted Lands, Dun Morogh, Durotar, Hellfire Peninsula, Nagrand, Northern Barrens, Northern Stranglethorn
Albino Snake	Bite	Hiss	Burrow	Poison Fang	Counterstrike	Vicious Fang	Vendor: Breanni	Crystalsong Forest (Dalaran)
Alpine Foxling	Bite	Crouch	Leap	Flurry	Howl	Dazzling Dance	Pet Battle	Kun-Lai Summit
Alpine Foxling Kit	Bite	Crouch	Leap	Flurry	Howl	Dazzling Dance	Pet Battle	Kun-Lai Summit
Amethyst Spiderling	Strike	Sticky Web	Leech Life	Poison Spit	Brittle Webbing	Spiderling Swarm	Pet Battle	Krasarang Wilds
Arctic Fox Kit	Bite	Crouch	Leap	Flurry	Howl	Dazzling Dance	Pet Battle	The Storm Peaks (Weather: Snow)
Ash Lizard	Claw	Screech	Comeback	Quick Attack	Triple Snap	Ravage	Pet Battle	Mount Hyjal, Un'Goro Crater
Ash Spiderling	Strike	Sticky Web	Leech Life	Poison Spit	Brittle Webbing	Spiderling Swarm	Pet Battle	Searing Gorge
Ash Viper	Bite	Hiss	Burrow	Poison Fang	Counterstrike	Vicious Fang	Pet Battle	Burning Steppes, Shadowmoon Valley
Baby Ape	Smash	Roar	Banana Barrage	Rake	Clobber	Barrel Toss	Pet Battle	Cape of Stranglethon (Weather: Rain)
Baby Blizzard Bear	Bite	Bash	Maul	Roar	Hibernate	Call Blizzard	Achievement: Logged in during WoW's 4th Anniversary	Achievement (Category: Feats of Strength)
Bananas	Smash	Roar	Banana Barrage	Rake	Clobber	Barrel Toss	Trading Card Game: Through the Dark Portal	TCG
Black Kingsnake	Bite	Hiss	Burrow	Poison Fang	Counterstrike	Vicious Fang	Vendor: Xan'tish	Orgrimmar
Black Tabby Cat	Claw	Rake	Devour	Pounce	Screech	Prowl	Drop: World Drop	Hillsbrad Foothills
Bombay Cat	Claw	Rake	Devour	Pounce	Screech	Prowl	Vendor: Donni Anthania	Elwynn Forest
Brown Snake	Bite	Hiss	Burrow	Poison Fang	Counterstrike	Vicious Fang	Vendor: Xan'tish	Orgrimmar
Bucktooth Flapper	Tail Slap	Screech	Woodchipper	Gnaw	Survival	Chew	Pet Battle	The Jade Forest
Calico Cat	Claw	Rake	Devour	Pounce	Screech	Prowl	Vendor: Breanni	Crystalsong Forest (Dalaran)
Cat	Claw	Rake	Devour	Pounce	Screech	Prowl	Pet Battle	Arathi Highlands, Elwynn Forest, Eversong Woods, Gilneas City, Netherstorm, Silvermoon City, The Culling of Stratholme
Cheetah Cub	Claw	Rake	Devour	Pounce	Screech	Prowl	Pet Battle	Northern Barrens
Clefthoof Runt	Smash	Survival	Horn Attack	Trample	Trumpet Strike	Stampede	Pet Battle	Nagrand
Clouded Hedgehog	Bite	Survival	Counterstrike	Poison Fang	Spiked Skin	Powerball	Pet Battle	Dread Wastes
Cobra Hatchling	Bite	Hiss	Burrow	Poison Fang	Counterstrike	Vicious Fang	Drop: Mysterious Egg	Sholazar Basin (Oracles reputation)
Coral Adder	Bite	Hiss	Burrow	Poison Fang	Counterstrike	Vicious Fang	Pet Battle	The Jade Forest
Coral Snake	Bite	Hiss	Burrow	Poison Fang	Counterstrike	Vicious Fang	Pet Battle	Stonetalon Mountains
Cornish Rex Cat	Claw	Rake	Devour	Pounce	Screech	Prowl	Vendor: Donni Anthania	Elwynn Forest
Crimson Snake	Bite	Hiss	Burrow	Poison Fang	Counterstrike	Vicious Fang	Vendor: Xan'tish / Dealer Rashaad	Orgrimmar / Netherstorm (The Stormspire)
Crunchy Scorpion	Snap	Crouch	Sting	Triple Snap	Screech	Rampage	Pet Battle	Dread Wastes
Crystal Spider	Strike	Sticky Web	Leech Life	Crystal Prison	Brittle Webbing	Spiderling Swarm	Pet Battle	Dun Morogh, The Oculus, Winterspring
Darkmoon Cub	Claw	Rake	Devour	Pounce	Screech	Prowl	Vendor: Lhara	Darkmoon Island
Darkmoon Monkey	Smash	Roar	Banana Barrage	Rake	Clobber	Barrel Toss	Vendor: Lhara	Darkmoon Island
Darkshore Cub	Bite	Hibernate	Maul	Roar	Bash	Rampage	Pet Battle	Darkshore
Darting Hatchling	Bite	Leap	Devour	Flank	Screech	Exposed Wounds	Drop: Dart's Nest	Dustwallow Marsh
Desert Spider	Strike	Sticky Web	Leech Life	Poison Spit	Brittle Webbing	Spiderling Swarm	Pet Battle	Desolace, Lost City of the Tol'Vir, Silithis, Tanaris, Uldum
Deviate Hatchling	Bite	Leap	Devour	Flank	Screech	Exposed Wounds	Drop: Deviate Guardian, Deviate Ravager	Wailing Caverns
Devouring Maggot	Chomp	Acidic Goo	Leap	Consume	Sticky Goo	Burrow	Pet Battle	Howling Fjord
Diemetradon Hatchling	Claw	Screech	Comeback	Quick Attack	Triple Snap	Ravage	Pet Battle	Un'Goro Crater
Dun Morogh Cub	Bite	Hibernate	Maul	Roar	Bash	Rampage	Vendor: Derrick Brindlebeard	Icecrown (Argent Tournament Grounds)
Durotar Scorpion	Snap	Crouch	Sting	Triple Snap	Screech	Rampage	Vendor: Freka Bloodaxe	Icecrown (Argent Tournament Grounds)
Dusk Spiderling	Strike	Sticky Web	Leech Life	Poison Spit	Brittle Webbing	Spiderling Swarm	Pet Battle	Duskwood
Emerald Boa	Bite	Hiss	Burrow	Poison Fang	Counterstrike	Vicious Fang	Pet Battle	Lost City of the Tol'Vir, Northern Barrens, Southern Barrens, Uldum, Un'Goro Crater
Feline Familiar	Onyx Bite	Stoneskin	Devour	Pounce	Call Darkness	Prowl	World Event: Hallow's End, Vendors: Chub / Dorothy	Tirisfal Glades / Stormwind City
Festering Maggot	Chomp	Acidic Goo	Leap	Consume	Sticky Goo	Burrow	Pet Battle	Eastern Plaguelands
Feverbite Hatchling	Strike	Sticky Web	Leech Life	Poison Spit	Brittle Webbing	Spiderling Swarm	Pet Battle	Krasarang Wilds
Fjord Worg Pup	Bite	Crouch	Leap	Flurry	Howl	Dazzling Dance	Pet Battle	Howling Fjord

NAME	ABILITY LEARNED AT LEVEL						ACQUIRED	REGION/NOTES
	1	2	4	10	15	20		
Forest Spiderling	Strike	Sticky Web	Leech Life	Poison Spit	Brittle Webbing	Spiderling Swarm	Pet Battle	Northern Stranglethorn, The Cape of Stranglethorn
Fox Kit	Bite	Crouch	Leap	Flurry	Howl	Dazzling Dance	Drop: Baradin Fox	Tol Barad Peninsula
Giraffe Calf	Hoof	Tranquility	Headbutt	Bleat	Stampede	Survival	Pet Battle	Soutern Barrens
Grove Viper	Bite	Hiss	Burrow	Poison Fang	Counterstrike	Vicious Fang	Pet Battle	The Jade Forest
Gundrak Hatchling	Bite	Leap	Devour	Flank	Screech	Exposed Wounds	Drop: Gundrak Raptor	Zul'Drak
Horned Lizard	Claw	Screech	Comeback	Quick Attack	Triple Snap	Ravage	Pet Battle	Badlands, Silithis
Hyjal Bear Cub	Bite	Hibernate	Maul	Roar	Bash	Rampage	Vendor: Varlan Highbough	Molten Front
Jumping Spider	Strike	Sticky Web	Leech Life	Poison Spit	Brittle Webbing	Spiderling Swarm	Pet Battle	The Jade Forest
Jungle Grub	Chomp	Acidic Goo	Leap	Consume	Sticky Goo	Burrow	Pet Battle	Krasarang Wilds
King Snake	Bite	Hiss	Burrow	Poison Fang	Counterstrike	Vicious Fang	Pet Battle	Badlands
Larva	Chomp	Acidic Goo	Leap	Consume	Sticky Goo	Burrow	Pet Battle	Ghostlands, Naxxramas
Lashtail Hatchling	Bite	Leap	Devour	Flank	Screech	Exposed Wounds	Quest: An Old Friend	Zul'Gurub
Leaping Hatchling	Bite	Leap	Devour	Flank	Screech	Exposed Wounds	Drop: Takk's Nest	The Barrens
Leopard Scorpid	Snap	Crouch	Sting	Triple Snap	Screech	Rampage	Pet Battle	Uldum
Little Black Ram	Hoof	Comeback	Headbutt	Chew	Soothe	Stampede	Pet Battle	Loch Modan
Lizard Hatchling	Claw	Screech	Comeback	Quick Attack	Triple Snap	Ravage	Pet Battle	Northern Stranglethorn, The Cape of Stranglethorn
Maggot	Chomp	Acidic Goo	Leap	Consume	Sticky Goo	Burrow	Pet Battle	Ashenvale, Dun Morogh, Ghostlands, Hillsbrad Foothills, Howling Fjord, Naxxramas, The Hinterlands, Tirisfal Glades
Moccasin	Bite	Hiss	Burrow	Poison Fang	Counterstrike	Vicious Fang	Pet Battle	Swamp of Sorrows
Molten Hatchling	Burn	Sticky Web	Magma Wave	Leech Life	Cauterize	Brittle Webbing	Pet Battle	Searing Gorge
Mr. Grubbs	Chomp	Acidic Goo	Leap	Consume	Sticky Goo	Burrow	World Drop, requires Fiona's Lucky Charm	Eastern Plaguelands
Nightsaber Cub	Claw	Rake	Devour	Pounce	Screech	Prowl	Trading Card Game: Twilight of the Dragons	TCG
Obsidian Hatchling	Bite	Leap	Devour	Flank	Screech	Exposed Wounds	Vendor: Breanni	Crystalsong Forest (Dalaran)
Orange Tabby Cat	Claw	Rake	Devour	Pounce	Screech	Prowl	Vendor: Donni Anthania (also offered to Human characters by Pet Battle Trainers)	Elwynn Forest
Panda Cub	Bite	Hibernate	Maul	Roar	Bash	Rampage	Promotion: World of Warcraft Collectors Edition	Promotional Pet
Panther Cub	Claw	Rake	Devour	Pounce	Screech	Prowl	Quest: Some Good Will Come	Northern Stranglethorn
Plains Monitor	Claw	Screech	Comeback	Quick Attack	Triple Snap	Ravage	Pet Battle	Kun-Lai Summit
Poley	Bite	Bash	Maul	Roar	Hibernate	Call Blizzard	Promotion: China iCoke promo	Promotional Pet
Rat Snake	Bite	Hiss	Burrow	Poison Fang	Counterstrike	Vicious Fang	Pet Battle	Duskwood
Rattlesnake	Bite	Hiss	Burrow	Poison Fang	Counterstrike	Vicious Fang	Pet Battle	Badlands, Tanaris, Twilight Highlands
Ravager Hatchling	Bite	Screech	Devour	Rend	Sting	Rampage	Pet Battle	Bloodmyst Isle
Ravasaur Hatchling	Bite	Leap	Devour	Flank	Screech	Exposed Wounds	Drop: Ravasaur Matriarch's Nest	Un'goro Crater
Razormaw Hatchilng	Bite	Leap	Devour	Flank	Screech	Exposed Wounds	Drop: Razormaw Matriarch's Nest	Wetlands
Razzashi Hatchling	Bite	Leap	Devour	Flank	Screech	Exposed Wounds	Drop: World Drop	Northern Stranglethorn, Cape of Stranglethorn
Rock Viper	Bite	Hiss	Burrow	Poison Fang	Counterstrike	Vicious Fang	Pet Battle	Blade's Edge Mountains, Desolace, Mount Hyjal, Silithis
Sand Kitten	Claw	Rake	Devour	Pounce	Screech	Prowl	Pet Battle	Tanaris
Scalded Basilisk Hatchling	Bite	Roar	Thrash	Crystal Prison	Feign Death	Screech	Pet Battle	Blade's Edge Mountains
Scorpid	Snap	Crouch	Sting	Triple Snap	Screech	Rampage	Pet Battle	Ahn'Qiraj, Blade's Edge Mountains, Blasted Lands, Burning Steppes, Eastern Plaguelands, Hellfire Peninsula, Orgrimmar, Ruins of Ahn'Qiraj, Shadowmoon Valley, Silithis, Thousand Needles, Twilight Highlands
Scorpling	Snap	Crouch	Sting	Triple Snap	Screech	Rampage	Pet Battle	Blasted Lands
Siamese Cat	Claw	Rake	Devour	Pounce	Screech	Prowl	Vendor: Dealer Rashaad	Netherstorm

BEAST (CONTINUED)

NAME	ABILITY LEARNED AT LEVEL						ACQUIRED	REGION/NOTES
	1	2	4	10	15	20		
Sidewinder	Bite	Hiss	Burrow	Poison Fang	Counterstrike	Vicious Fang	Pet Battle	Silithis, Uldum
Silent Hedgehog	Bite	Spiked Skin	Survival	Poison Fang	Counterstrike	Powerball	Pet Battle	Dread Wastes
Silithid Hatchling	Scratch	Hiss	Swarm	Devour	Survival	Sandstorm	Pet Battle	Tanaris (Weather: Sandstorm)
Silver Tabby Cat	Claw	Rake	Devour	Pounce	Screech	Prowl	Vendor: Donni Anthania	Elwynn Forest
Skittering Cavern Crawler	Strike	Sticky Web	Leech Life	Poison Spit	Brittle Webbing	Spiderling Swarm	Pet Battle	Blade's Edge Mountains
Smolderweb Hatchling	Strike	Sticky Web	Leech Life	Poison Spit	Brittle Webbing	Spiderling Swarm	Drop:Mother Smolderweb	Blackrock Spire
Snake	Bite	Hiss	Burrow	Poison Fang	Counterstrike	Vicious Fang	Pet Battle	Black Temple, Dun Morogh, Dustwallow Marsh, Eversong Woods, Feralas, Ghostlands, Gilneas, Gundrak, Howling Fjord, Loch Modan, Nagrand, Northern Stranglethorn, Sholazar Basin, Silverpine Forest, Sunken Temple, Terokkar Forest, The Black Morass, The Shattered Halls, Tol'Barad, Wailing Caverns, Westfall, Zangarmarsh, Zul'Drak
Snow Cub	Claw	Rake	Devour	Pounce	Screech	Prowl	Pet Battle	Dun Morogh
Spider	Strike	Sticky Web	Leech Life	Poison Spit	Brittle Webbing	Spiderling Swarm	Pet Battle	Ahn'Kahet: The Old Kingdom, Azjol-Nerub, Azshara, Black Temple, Blasted Lands, Drak'Tharon Keep, Dun Morogh, Dustwallow Marsh, Eastern Plaguelands, Elwynn Forest, Ghostlands, Gilneas, Gilneas City, Halls of Reflection, Hillsbrad Foothills, Howling Fjord, Icecrown Citadel, Karazhan, Naxxramas, Orgrimmar, Pit of Saron, Ruins of Gilneas, Stonetalon Mountains, Swamp of Sorrows, Teldrassil, The Culling of Stratholme, The Forge of Souls, The Hinterlands, The Storm Peaks, The Violet Hold, Tirisfal Glades, Utgarde Keep, Utgarde Pinnacle, Winterspring, Zul'Aman, Zul'Drak
Spiky Lizard	Claw	Screech	Comeback	Quick Attack	Triple Snap	Ravage	Pet Battle	Badlands, Silithis
Spiny Lizard	Claw	Screech	Comeback	Quick Attack	Triple Snap	Ravage	Pet Battle	Durotar, Orgrimmar
Stripe-Tailed Scorpid	Snap	Crouch	Sting	Triple Snap	Screech	Rampage	Pet Battle	Badlands,Tanaris,Terokkar Forest
Stunted Shardhorn	Smash	Trample	Trumpet Strike	Survival	Horn Attack	Stampede	Pet Battle	Sholazar Basin
Summit Kid	Hoof	Comeback	Headbutt	Chew	Soothe	Stampede	Pet Battle	Kun-Lai Summit
Temple Snake	Bite	Hiss	Burrow	Poison Fang	Counterstrike	Vicious Fang	Pet Battle	The Jade Forest
Tree Python	Bite	Hiss	Burrow	Poison Fang	Counterstrike	Vicious Fang	Pet Battle	Northern Stranglethorn, The Cape of Stranglethorn, Un'Goro Crater
Twilight Iguana	Claw	Screech	Comeback	Quick Attack	Triple Snap	Ravage	Pet Battle	Thousand Needles
Twilight Spider	Strike	Sticky Web	Leech Life	Poison Spit	Brittle Webbing	Spiderling Swarm	Pet Battle	Azshara, Deepholm, Twilight Highlands
Venomspitter Hatchling	Strike	Sticky Web	Leech Life	Poison Spit	Brittle Webbing	Spiderling Swarm	Pet Battle	Stonetalon Mountains
Warpstalker Hatchling	Claw	Screech	Ravage	Blinkstrike	Triple Snap	Comeback	Pet Battle	Terokkar Forest
Water Snake	Bite	Hiss	Burrow	Poison Fang	Counterstrike	Vicious Fang	Pet Battle	Durotar, Northern Stranglethorn, Orgrimmar, Swamp of Sorrows, Twilight Highlands, Wetlands
White Kitten	Claw	Rake	Devour	Pounce	Screech	Prowl	Vendor: Lil Timmy	Stormwind City
Widow Spiderling	Strike	Sticky Web	Leech Life	Poison Spit	Brittle Webbing	Spiderling Swarm	Pet Battle	Duskwood (Time: Night)
Wild Silkworm	Chomp	Acidic Goo	Leap	Consume	Sticky Goo	Burrow	Pet Battle	Valley of the Four Winds
Wind Rider Cub	Bite	Slicing Wind	Flock	Squawk	Adrenaline Rush	Lift-Off	Blizzard Store	Promotional Pet
Winterspring Cub	Claw	Rake	Devour	Pounce	Screech	Prowl	Vendor: Michelle De Rum	Winterspring
Worg Pup	Bite	Crouch	Leap	Flurry	Howl	Dazzling Dance	Drop: Quartermaster Zigris	Lower Blackrock Spire
Zooey Snake	Bite	Hiss	Burrow	Poison Fang	Counterstrike	Vicious Fang	Pet Battle	Kun-Lai Summit

CRITTER PETS

Passive Ability	Description
Elusive	Critters break out of crowd control effects more quickly.

NAME	ABILITY LEARNED AT LEVEL						ACQUIRED	REGION/NOTES
	1	2	4	10	15	20		
Alpine Chipmunk	Scratch	Adrenaline Rush	Nut Barrage	Woodchipper	Crouch	Stampede	Pet Battle	Mount Hyjal, Stonetalon Mountains, Winterspring
Alpine Hare	Scratch	Adrenaline Rush	Burrow	Flurry	Dodge	Stampede	Pet Battle	Dun Morogh, Winterspring
Arctic Hare	Scratch	Adrenaline Rush	Burrow	Flurry	Dodge	Stampede	Pet Battle	Borean Tundra, Dragonblight, Storm Peaks, Zul'Drak
Armadillo Pup	Scratch	Shell Shield	Infected Claw	Thrash	Roar	Powerball	Vendor: Guild Vendors	Achievement: Critter Kill Squad (Guild Achievement)
Bandicoon	Bite	Survival	Poison Fang	Tongue Lash	Counterstrike	Powerball	Pet Battle	Valley of the Four Winds
Bandicoon Kit	Bite	Survival	Poison Fang	Tongue Lash	Counterstrike	Powerball	Pet Battle	Valley of the Four Winds
Beetle	Scratch	Hiss	Swarm	Flank	Survival	Apocalypse	Pet Battle	Ahn'Qiraj, Ashenvale, Badlands, Drak'Tharon Keep, Eastern Plaguelands, Felwood, Northern Stranglethorn, Ruins of Ahn'Qiraj, Silithus, The Cape of Stranglethorn, Un'Goro Crater, Utgarde Keep, Utgarde Pinnacle
Black Lamb	Hoof	Comeback	Bleat	Chew	Soothe	Stampede	Pet Battle	Elwynn Forest
Black Rat	Scratch	Flurry	Stampede	Comeback	Poison Fang	Survival	Pet Battle	Ahn'kahet: The Old Kingdom, Badlands, Crypt of Forgotten Kings, Drak'Tharon Keep, Dun Morogh, Duskwood, Dustwallow Marsh, Eastern Plaguelands, Halls of Stone, Icecrown Citadel, Kezan, Pit of Saron, Razorfen Downs, Scholomance, Shadowfang Keep, Sunwell Plateau, The Forge of Souls, The Shattered Halls, The Violet Hold, Thousand Needles, Twilight Highlands, Utgarde Keep, Utgarde Pinnacle, Western Plaguelands, Wetlands
Blighted Squirrel	Scratch	Adrenaline Rush	Rabid Strike	Woodchipper	Crouch	Stampede	Pet Battle	Silverpine Forest
Borean Marmot	Chomp	Crouch	Leap	Comeback	Adrenaline Rush	Burrow	Pet Battle	Borean Tundra
Brown Marmot	Chomp	Crouch	Leap	Comeback	Adrenaline Rush	Burrow	Pet Battle	Blades Edge Mountains, The Hinterlands
Brown Prairie Dog	Chomp	Adrenaline Rush	Leap	Comeback	Crouch	Burrow	Vendor: Halpa / Naleen (also offered to Tauren characters by Pet Battle Trainers)	Mulgore
Brown Rabbit	Scratch	Adrenaline Rush	Burrow	Flurry	Dodge	Stampede	Vendor: Dealer Rashaad	Netherstorm (The Stormspire)
Carrion Rat	Scratch	Flurry	Stampede	Comeback	Poison Fang	Survival	Pet Battle	Mount Hyjal
Cockroach	Scratch	Hiss	Swarm	Flank	Survival	Apocalypse	Pet Battle	Burning Steppes, Eastern Plaguelands, End Time, Icecrown, The Hinterlands, Twilight Highlands, Un'Goro Crater
Creepy Crawly	Scratch	Hiss	Swarm	Flank	Survival	Apocalypse	Pet Battle	Durotar
Crystal Beetle	Scratch	Hiss	Swarm	Flank	Survival	Apocalypse	Pet Battle	Deepholm
Darkmoon Rabbit	Scratch	Vicious Streak	Burrow	Huge, Sharp Teeth	Dodge	Stampede	Drop: Darkmoon Rabbit	Darkmoon Island
Death's Head Cockroach	Scratch	Hiss	Swarm	Flank	Survival	Apocalypse	Pet Battle	Mount Hyjal
Deepholm Cockroach	Scratch	Hiss	Swarm	Flank	Survival	Apocalypse	Pet Battle	Deepholm
Dung Beetle	Scratch	Hiss	Swarm	Flank	Survival	Apocalypse	Pet Battle	Durotar, Lost City of the To'Vir, Orgrimmar, Uldum
Egbert	Bite	Shell Shield	Trample	Peck	Adrenaline Rush	Feign Death	World Event: Children's Week , Quest: A Warden of the Alliance/Horde	
Elfin Rabbit	Scratch	Adrenaline Rush	Burrow	Flurry	Dodge	Stampede	Pet Battle	Darnassus, Desolace, Mount Hyjal, Teldrassil
Elwynn Lamb	Hoof	Comeback	Bleat	Chew	Soothe	Stampede	Vendor: Corporal Arthur Flew	Icecrown (Argent Tournament Grounds)
Fawn	Hoof	Tranquility	Bleat	Stampede	Nature's Ward	Headbutt	Pet Battle	Elwynn Forest, Grizzly Hills, Teldrassil, The Culling of Stratholme
Fire Beetle	Burn	Hiss	Scorched Earth	Flank	Cauterize	Apocalypse	Pet Battle	Blasted Lands, Burning Steppes, Mount Hyjal, Searing Gorge, The Shattered Halls, Un'Goro Crater
Fire-Proof Roach	Scratch	Hiss	Swarm	Flank	Survival	Apocalypse	Pet Battle	Mount Hyjal
Fjord Rat	Scratch	Flurry	Stampede	Comeback	Poison Fang	Survival	Pet Battle	Howling Fjord
Gazelle Fawn	Hoof	Tranquility	Bleat	Stampede	Nature's Ward	Headbutt	Pet Battle	Mulgore
Giant Sewer Rat	Scratch	Flurry	Stampede	Comeback	Poison Fang	Survival	Profession: Fishing	Dalaran (Dalaran Underbelly)
Gold Beetle	Scratch	Hiss	Swarm	Flank	Survival	Apocalypse	Pet Battle	Badlands, Halls of Lightning, Halls of Stone, Tanaris
Golden Pig	Hoof	Crouch	Uncanny Luck	Diseased Bite	Buried Treasure	Headbutt	Promotion: China New Years Celebration	Promotional Pet
Grassland Hopper	Skitter	Swarm	Nature's Touch	Screech	Cocoon Strike	Inspiring Song	Pet Battle	Townlong Steppes
Grasslands Cottontail	Scratch	Adrenaline Rush	Burrow	Flurry	Dodge	Stampede	Pet Battle	Arathi Highlands
Grizzly Squirrel	Scratch	Adrenaline Rush	Nut Barrage	Woodchipper	Crouch	Stampede	Pet Battle	Grizzly Hills, Twilight Highlands
Grotto Vole	Scratch	Sting	Stampede	Flurry	Survival	Comeback	Pet Battle	Mount Hyjal
Hare	Scratch	Adrenaline Rush	Burrow	Flurry	Dodge	Stampede	Pet Battle	Arathi Highlands, Durotar, The Hinterlands
Highlands Mouse	Scratch	Flurry	Stampede	Comeback	Poison Fang	Survival	Pet Battle	Twilight Highlands
Highlands Skunk	Scratch	Rake	Stench	Flurry	Perk Up	Bleat	Pet Battle	Grizzly Hills, Stonetalon Mountains, The Storm Peaks, Wetlands, Winterspring
Irradiated Roach	Scratch	Hiss	Swarm	Flank	Survival	Apocalypse	Pet Battle	Dun Morogh

CRITTER (CONTINUED)

NAME	ABILITY LEARNED AT LEVEL						ACQUIRED	REGION/NOTES
	1	2	4	10	15	20		
Lava Beetle	Burn	Hiss	Scorched Earth	Flank	Cauterize	Apocalypse	Pet Battle	Burning Steppes
Little Fawn	Hoof	Tranquility	Bleat	Stampede	Nature's Ward	Headbutt	Achievement: Lil' Game Hunter	Achievement (Category: Pet Battles)
Locust	Scratch	Hiss	Swarm	Flank	Survival	Apocalypse	Pet Battle	Lost City of the Tol'Vir, Uldum
Long-tailed Mole	Scratch	Flurry	Stampede	Comeback	Poison Fang	Survival	Pet Battle	Dun Morogh, Northern Stranglethorn, The Cape of Stranglethorn, Un'Goro Crater
Lucky	Hoof	Crouch	Uncanny Luck	Diseased Bite	Buried Treasure	Headbutt	Promotion: Blizzard Worldwide Invitational 2007	Promotional Pet
Lucky Quilen Cub	Bite	Perk Up	Burrow	Comeback	Buried Treasure	Trample	Promotion: Mists of Pandaria Collectors Edition	Promotional Pet
Malayan Quillrat	Bite	Spiked Skin	Survival	Poison Fang	Counterstrike	Powerball	Pet Battle	Valley of the Four Winds
Malayan Quillrat Pup	Bite	Spiked Skin	Survival	Poison Fang	Counterstrike	Powerball	Pet Battle	Valley of the Four Winds
Marsh Fiddler	Skitter	Swarm	Nature's Touch	Screech	Cocoon Strike	Inspiring Song	Pet Battle	Valley of the Four Winds
Masked Tanuki	Bite	Survival	Poison Fang	Tongue Lash	Counterstrike	Powerball	Pet Battle	The Jade Forest
Masked Tanuki Pup	Bite	Survival	Poison Fang	Tongue Lash	Counterstrike	Powerball	Pet Battle	The Jade Forest
Mountain Cottontail	Scratch	Adrenaline Rush	Burrow	Flurry	Dodge	Stampede	Pet Battle	Mulgore, Redridge Mountains
Mountain Skunk	Scratch	Rake	Stench	Flurry	Perk Up	Bleat	Pet Battle	Grizzly Hills, Stonetalon Mountains, The Storm Peaks, Wetlands, Winterspring
Mouse	Scratch	Flurry	Stampede	Comeback	Poison Fang	Survival	Pet Battle	Duskwood, Dustwallow Marsh, Grizzly Hills, Mulgore, Netherstorm, Westfall, Wetlands
Mr. Wiggles	Hoof	Crouch	Uncanny Luck	Diseased Bite	Buried Treasure	Headbutt	World Event: Children's Week , Quest: A Warden of the Alliance/Horde	
Mulgore Hatchling	Bite	Shell Shield	Trample	Peck	Adrenaline Rush	Feign Death	Vendor: Doru Thunderhorn	Icecrown (Argent Tournament Grounds)
Nether Roach	Flank	Hiss	Swarm	Nether Blast	Survival	Apocalypse	Pet Battle	Netherstorm
Nuts	Scratch	Adrenaline Rush	Nut Barrage	Woodchipper	Crouch	Stampede	Achievement: Petting Zoo	Achievement (Category: Pet Battles)
Peanut	Smash	Trumpet Strike	Headbutt	Trample	Survival	Stampede	World Event: Children's Week, Quest: Back to the Orphanage	
Perky Pug	Bite	Perk Up	Burrow	Comeback	Buried Treasure	Trample	Achievement: Looking For Multitudes	Achievement (Category: Dungeons & Raids)
Pint-Sized Pink Pachyderm	Smash	Trumpet Strike	Headbutt	Trample	Survival	Stampede	World Event: Brewfest, Vendor: Belbi Quikswitch / Bliz Fixwidget	Dun Morogh / Durotar
Porcupette	Bite	Spiked Skin	Survival	Poison Fang	Counterstrike	Powerball	Drop: Sack of Pet Supplies (reward from Pet Trainer battles)	
Prairie Dog	Chomp	Leap	Burrow	Adrenaline Rush	Crouch	Comeback	Pet Battle	Arathi Highlands, Mulgore, Nagrand, Northern Barrens, Stormwind City, Westfall
Prairie Mouse	Scratch	Comeback	Stampede	Flurry	Poison Fang	Survival	Pet Battle	Kun-Lai Summit
Rabbit	Scratch	Adrenaline Rush	Burrow	Flurry	Dodge	Stampede	Pet Battle	Azshara, Azuremist Isle, Blade's Edge Mountains, Crystalsong Forest, Darkshore, Dun Morogh, Duskwood, Elwynn Forest, Eversong Woods, Feralas, Hillsbrad Foothills, Howling Fjord, Moonglade, Mount Hyjal, Mulgore, Nagrand, Redridge Mountains, Scarlet Monastery, Silvermoon City, Silverpine Forest, Stonetalon Mountains, Stormwind City, Teldrassil, The Culling of Stratholme, Tirisfal Glades, Western Plaguelands, Wetlands
Rapana Whelk	Ooze Touch	Acidic Goo	Dive	Absorb	Shell Shield	Headbutt	Pet Battle	Dread Wastes
Rat	Scratch	Flurry	Stampede	Comeback	Poison Fang	Survival	Pet Battle	Arathi Basin, Arathi Highlands, Ashenvale, Azshara, Azuremist Isle, Bloodmyst Isle, Crystalsong Forest, Darkshore, Desolace, Drak'Tharon Keep, Dun Morogh, Ghostlands, Gilneas, Gilneas City, Hillsbrad Foothills, Howling Fjord, The Deadmines, Karazhan, Loch Modan, Nagrand, Naxxramas, Ruins of Gilneas, Scarlet Monastery, Scholomance, Shattrath City, Silverpine Forest, Stonetalon Mountains, Stormwind City, Sunken Temple, Swamp of Sorrows, Terokkar Forest, The Cape of Stranglethorn, The Culling of Stratholme, The Hinterlands, The Lost Isles, The Shattered Halls, The Violet Hold, Tirisfal Glades
Red Cricket	Skitter	Swarm	Nature's Touch	Screech	Cocoon Strike	Inspiring Song	Quest from Sho	Valley of the Four Winds
Red-Tailed Chipmunk	Scratch	Adrenaline Rush	Nut Barrage	Woodchipper	Crouch	Stampede	Pet Battle	Darnassus, Desolace, Hillsbrad Foothills, Teldrassil
Redridge Rat	Scratch	Flurry	Stampede	Comeback	Poison Fang	Survival	Pet Battle	Redridge Mountains
Resilient Roach	Scratch	Hiss	Swarm	Flank	Survival	Apocalypse	Pet Battle	Dread Wastes

CRITTER (CONTINUED)

NAME	ABILITY LEARNED AT LEVEL						ACQUIRED	REGION/NOTES
	1	2	4	10	15	20		
Roach	Scratch	Hiss	Swarm	Flank	Survival	Apocalypse	Pet Battle	Ahn'Qiraj, Ahn'kahet: The Old Kingdom, Ashenvale, Azjol-Nerub, Azshara, Desolace, Dun Morogh, Duskwood, Gilneas, Gilneas City, Howling Fjord, Icecrown Citadel, Kezan, Loch Modan, Northern Stranglethorn, Razorfen Downs, Redridge Mountains, Ruins of Ahn'Qiraj, Stonetalon Mountains, The Cape of Stranglethorn, The Culling of Stratholme, Thousand Needles, Tirisfal Glades
Rusty Snail	Ooze Touch	Acidic Goo	Dive	Absorb	Shell Shield	Headbutt	Pet Battle	Ashenvale
Sand Scarab	Scratch	Hiss	Swarm	Flank	Survival	Apocalypse	Trading Card Game: Tomb of the Forgotten	TCG
Savory Beetle	Scratch	Hiss	Swarm	Flank	Survival	Apocalypse	Pet Battle	Krasarang Wilds
Scarab Hatchling	Scratch	Hiss	Swarm	Flank	Survival	Apocalypse	Pet Battle	Silithis
Scooter the Snail	Ooze Touch	Acidic Goo	Dive	Absorb	Shell Shield	Headbutt	World Event: Children's Week, Quest:A Warden of the Alliance/Horde	
Shimmershell Snail	Ooze Touch	Acidic Goo	Dive	Absorb	Shell Shield	Headbutt	Pet Battle	Darkshore
Shy Bandicoon	Bite	Survival	Poison Fang	Tongue Lash	Counterstrike	Powerball	Pet Battle	Valley of the Four Winds
Silkbead Snail	Ooze Touch	Acidic Goo	Dive	Absorb	Shell Shield	Headbutt	Pet Battle	The Jade Forest
Silver Pig	Hoof	Crouch	Uncanny Luck	Diseased Bite	Buried Treasure	Headbutt	Promotion: China New Year's Celebration	Promotional Pet
Singing Cricket	Skitter	Swarm	Nature's Touch	Screech	Cocoon Strike	Inspiring Song	Achievement: Pro Pet Mob	Achievement (Category: Pet Battles)
Skunk	Scratch	Rake	Stench	Flurry	Perk Up	Bleat	Pet Battle	Azshara, Azuremist Isle, Bloodmyst Isle, Duskwood, Gilneas, Howling Fjord, Terokkar Forest
Snowshoe Hare	Scratch	Adrenaline Rush	Burrow	Flurry	Dodge	Stampede	Pet Battle	Hillsbrad Foothills
Snowshoe Rabbit	Scratch	Adrenaline Rush	Burrow	Flurry	Dodge	Stampede	Vendor: Yarlyn Amberstill	Dun Morogh (Amberstill Ranch)
Spring Rabbit	Scratch	Adrenaline Rush	Burrow	Flurry	Dodge	Stampede	World Event: Noblegarden, Vendors: Noblegarden Vendors & Merchants (also dropped by Brightly Colored Egg)	
Squirrel	Scratch	Adrenaline Rush	Nut Barrage	Woodchipper	Crouch	Stampede	Pet Battle	Ashenvale, Azshara, Azuremist Isle, Blade's Edge Mountains, Crystalsong Forest, Darkshore, Dun Morogh, Duskwood, Dustwallow Marsh, Elwynn Forest, Feralas, Gilneas, Hillsbrad Foothills, Howling Fjord, Loch Modan, Magisters' Terrace, Moonglade, Mount Hyjal, Nagrand, Ruins of Gilneas, Sholazar Basin, Silverpine Forest, Stormwind City, Teldrassil, Terokkar Forest, Tol Barad Peninsula, Well of Eternity, Western Plaguelands, Wetlands, Zul'Aman
Stinkbug	Scratch	Hiss	Swarm	Flank	Survival	Apocalypse	Pet Battle	Tanaris
Stinker	Scratch	Rake	Stench	Flurry	Perk Up	Bleat	Achievement: Shop Smart, Shop Pet...Smart	Achievement (Category: Pet Battles)
Stone Armadillo	Scratch	Shell Shield	Infected Claw	Thrash	Roar	Powerball	Pet Battle	Desolace (Time: Night)
Stormwind Rat	Scratch	Flurry	Stampede	Comeback	Poison Fang	Survival	Pet Battle	Elwynn Forest
Stowaway Rat	Scratch	Flurry	Stampede	Comeback	Poison Fang	Survival	Pet Battle	Deepholm
Tainted Cockroach	Scratch	Hiss	Swarm	Flank	Survival	Apocalypse	Pet Battle	Felwood, Shadowmoon Valley
Tainted Rat	Scratch	Flurry	Stampede	Comeback	Poison Fang	Survival	Pet Battle	Felwood
Tol'vir Scarab	Scratch	Hiss	Swarm	Flank	Survival	Apocalypse	Pet Battle	Uldum
Tolai Hare	Scratch	Adrenaline Rush	Burrow	Flurry	Dodge	Stampede	Pet Battle	Kun-Lai Summit
Tolai Hare Pup	Scratch	Adrenaline Rush	Burrow	Flurry	Dodge	Stampede	Pet Battle	Kun-Lai Summit
Twilight Beetle	Scratch	Hiss	Swarm	Flank	Survival	Apocalypse	Pet Battle	Azshara, Deepholm, Mount Hyjal
Undercity Cockroach	Scratch	Hiss	Swarm	Flank	Survival	Apocalypse	Vendor: Jeremiah Payson / Dealer Rashaad	Tirisfal Glades (Undercity) / Netherstorm (The Stormspire)
Undercity Rat	Scratch	Flurry	Stampede	Comeback	Poison Fang	Survival	Pet Battle	Tirisfal Glades
Wharf Rat	Scratch	Flurry	Stampede	Comeback	Poison Fang	Survival	Pet Battle	The Cape of Stranglethorn, Tol Barad Peninsula
Whiskers the Rat	Scratch	Sting	Stampede	Flurry	Survival	Comeback	World Event: Children's Week, Quest reward: A Warden of the Alliance/Horde	
Winter Reindeer	Hoof	Tranquility	Bleat	Stampede	Nature's Ward	Headbutt	World Event: Feast of Winter Veil, Dropped by Gaily Wrapped Present	
Wolpertinger	Scratch	Flyby	Headbutt	Horn Attack	Sleeping Gas	Rampage	World Event: Brewfest, Quest reward: Catch the Wild Wolpertinger!	
Yakrat	Scratch	Flurry	Stampede	Comeback	Poison Fang	Survival	Pet Battle	Dread Wastes, Townlong Steppes
Yellow-Bellied Marmot	Chomp	Leap	Burrow	Adrenaline Rush	Crouch	Comeback	Pet Battle	Twilight Highlands

DRAGONKIN PETS

NAME	ABILITY LEARNED AT LEVEL						ACQUIRED	REGION/NOTES
	1	2	4	10	15	20		
Azure Whelpling	Claw	Arcane Storm	Surge of Power	Breath	Wild Magic	Ice Tomb	Drop: World Drop	Winterspring
Blue Dragonhawk Hatchling	Claw	Rake	Flame Breath	Quills	Conflagrate	Flamethrower	Vendor: Dealer Rashaad	Netherstorm (The Stormspire)
Celestial Dragon	Breath	Ancient Blessing	Moonfire	Roar	Arcane Storm	Starfall	Achievement: Littlest Pet Shop	Achievement (Category: Pet Battles)
Crimson Whelpling	Breath	Healing Flame	Lift-Off	Tail Sweep	Scorched Earth	Deep Breath	Drop: World Drop	Wetlands
Dark Whelpling	Shadowflame	Roar	Lift-Off	Tail Sweep	Call Darkness	Deep Breath	Drop: Whelplings	Wetlands, Dustwallow Marsh, Badlands, Burning Steppes
Emerald Whelpling	Breath	Moonfire	Tranquility	Emerald Bite	Emerald Presence	Emerald Dream	Drop: Noxious Whelp	Feralas
Essence of Competition	Breath	Ancient Blessing	Lift-Off	Tail Sweep	Competitive Spirit	Flamethrower	Promotion: China PVP Event	Promotional Pet
Golden Dragonhawk Hatchling	Claw	Rake	Flame Breath	Quills	Conflagrate	Flamethrower	Vendor: Jilanne (or offered to Blood Elf characters by Pet Battle Trainers)	Eversong Woods
Lil' Deathwing	Shadowflame	Call Darkness	Elementium Bolt	Tail Sweep	Roll	Cataclysm	Promotion: Cataclysm Collectors Edition	Promotional Pet
Lil' Tarecgosa	Breath	Surge of Power	Arcane Storm	Arcane Blast	Wild Magic	Arcane Explosion	Vendor: Guild Vendors	Achievement (Feat: Dragonwrath, Tarecgosa's Rest (guild achievement))
Netherwhelp	Breath	Phase Shift	Instability	Nether Blast	Accuracy	Soulrush	Promotion: Burning Crusade Collectors Edition	Promotional Pet
Onyxian Whelpling	Breath	Healing Flame	Lift-Off	Tail Sweep	Scorched Earth	Deep Breath	Achievement: WoW's 5th Anniversary	Achievement (Category: Feats of Strength)
Proto-Drake Whelp	Breath	Flamethrower	Proto-Strike	Bite	Ancient Blessing	Roar	Drop: Mysterious Egg	Sholozar Basin (Oracles)
Red Dragonhawk Hatchling	Claw	Rake	Flame Breath	Quills	Conflagrate	Flamethrower	Vendor: Jilanne	Eversong Woods
Silver Dragonhawk Hatchling	Claw	Rake	Flame Breath	Quills	Conflagrate	Flamethrower	Vendor: Jilanne	Eversong Woods
Soul of the Aspects	Claw	Sunlight	Surge of Light	Breath	Reflection	Solar Beam	Blizzard Store	Promotional Pet
Spawn of Onyxia	Breath	Healing Flame	Lift-Off	Tail Sweep	Scorched Earth	Deep Breath	Pet Battle	Dustwallow Marsh
Spirit of Competition	Breath	Ancient Blessing	Lift-Off	Tail Sweep	Competitive Spirit	Flamethrower	Event: Battleground Event	Promotional Pet
Sprite Darter Hatchling	Slicing Wind	Arcane Blast	Moonfire	Evanescence	Life Exchange	Cyclone	Drop: World Drop	Feralas
Thundering Serpent Hatchling	Breath	Call Lightning	Cyclone	Tail Sweep	Roar	Lift-Off	Vendor: Guild Vendor	Stormwind City / Orgrimmar
Tiny Green Dragon	Breath	Call Lightning	Cyclone	Tail Sweep	Roar	Lift-Off	Promotional pet: iCoke promo	Promotional Pet
Tiny Red Dragon	Breath	Call Lightning	Cyclone	Tail Sweep	Roar	Lift-Off	Promotional pet: iCoke promo	Promotional Pet
Wild Crimson Hatchling	Breath	Healing Flame	Lift-Off	Tail Sweep	Scorched Earth	Deep Breath	Pet Battle	The Jade Forest (Faction: Order of the Cloud Serpent - Exalted)
Wild Golden Hatchling	Breath	Call Lightning	Cyclone	Tail Sweep	Roar	Lift-Off	Pet Battle	The Jade Forest (Faction: Order of the Cloud Serpent - Exalted)
Wild Jade Hatchling	Breath	Call Lightning	Cyclone	Tail Sweep	Roar	Lift-Off	Pet Battle	The Jade Forest (Faction: Order of the Cloud Serpent - Exalted)

ELEMENTAL PETS

Passive Ability	Description
Weather Immune	Elementals ignore all weather effects.

NAME	ABILITY LEARNED AT LEVEL						ACQUIRED	REGION/NOTES
	1	2	4	10	15	20		
Amethyst Shale Hatchling	Burn	Sticky Web	Stone Rush	Leech Life	Poison Spit	Stoneskin	Pet Battle	Deepholm, Desolace
Ammen Vale Lashling	Lash	Soothing Mists	Stun Seed	Poison Lash	Plant	Entangling Roots	Vendor: Irisee	Icecrown (Argent Tournament Grounds)
Core Hound Pup	Scratch	Howl	Burn	Thrash	Dodge	Burrow	Promotion: Authenticator Account Link	Promotional Pet
Crimson Geode	Feedback	Crystal Overload	Stone Rush	Spark	Amplify Magic	Elementium Bolt	Pet Battle	Deepholm
Crimson Lasher	Lash	Soothing Mists	Stun Seed	Poison Lash	Plant	Entangling Roots	Vendor: Ayla Shadowstorm	Molten Front
Crimson Shale Hatchling	Burn	Sticky Web	Stone Rush	Leech Life	Poison Spit	Stoneskin	Pet Battle	Deepholm, The Stonecore
Dark Phoenix Hatchling	Burn	Darkflame	Conflagrate	Laser	Immolate	Dark Rebirth	World Vendors: Guild Vendors	Achievements (Guild Achievement: United Nations)
Elementium Geode	Feedback	Crystal Overload	Stone Rush	Spark	Amplify Magic	Elementium Bolt	Profession: Mining, Drop: Elementium Vein, Rich Elementium Vein	Deepholm, Twilight Highlands, Uldum
Emerald Shale Hatchling	Burn	Sticky Web	Stone Rush	Leech Life	Poison Spit	Stoneskin	Pet Battle	Deepholm, The Stonecore
Fel Flame	Burn	Immolate	Conflagrate	Flame Breath	Scorched Earth	Immolation	Pet Battle	Shadowmoon Valley
Frigid Frostling	Frost Shock	Frost Nova	Ice Tomb	Surge	Slippery Ice	Howling Blast	World Event: Midsummer Fire Festival, Drop: Lord Ahune	The Slave Pens
Grinder	Stone Shot	Sandstorm	Rock Barrage	Stone Rush	Rupture	Quake	Drop: Karr the Darkener	Dread Wastes
Jade Tentacle	Scratch	Poisoned Branch	Thorns	Shell Shield	Photosynthesis	Entangling Roots	Achievement: Time to Open a Pet Store	Achievements (Category: Pet Battles)
Kirin Tor Familiar	Beam	Gravity	Arcane Explosion	Arcane Blast	Arcane Storm	Dark Simulacrum	Achievement: Higher Learning	Achievement (Category: General)
Lava Crab	Burn	Shell Shield	Conflagrate	Survival	Cauterize	Magma Wave	Pet Battle	Burning Steppes, Searing Gorge
Lil' Ragnaros	Sulfuras Smash	Magma Trap	Flamethrower	Magma Wave	Conflagrate	Sons of the Flame	Blizzard Store	Promotional Pet
Lumpy	Stone Shot	Sandstorm	Rock Barrage	Stone Rush	Rupture	Quake	World Event: Feast of Winter Veil, Quest: You're a Mean One…	
Pebble	Stone Shot	Sandstorm	Rock Barrage	Stone Rush	Rupture	Quake	Achievement: Rock Lover	Achievement (Category: Quests)
Phoenix Hatchling	Burn	Cauterize	Immolation	Peck	Immolate	Conflagrate	Drop: Kael'thas Sunstrider	Magisters' Terrace
Ruby Sapling	Scratch	Thorns	Photosynthesis	Poisoned Branch	Shell Shield	Entangling Roots	Pet Battle	Eversong Woods
Sapphire Cub	Lash	Rake	Stone Rush	Pounce	Screech	Prowl	Profession: Jewelcrafting	
Searing Scorchling	Burn	Immolate	Conflagrate	Flame Breath	Scorched Earth	Immolation	Vendor: Zen'Vorka	Molten Front (random from Zen'Vorka's Cache)
Singing Sunflower	Lash	Photosynthesis	Early Advantage	Solar Beam	Inspiring Song	Sunlight	Quest: Lawn of the Dead	Hillsbrad Foothills
Sinister Squashling	Burn	Thorns	Plant	Poison Lash	Stun Seed	Leech Seed	World Event: Hallow's End	Dropped by Treat Bag (obtained via trick or treating with innkeepers), Crudely Wrapped Gift (obtained via daily Hallow's End quest), Drop: Headless Horseman - Scarlet Monastery
Spirit of Summer	Burn	Immolate	Conflagrate	Flame Breath	Scorched Earth	Immolation	World Event: Midsummer Fire Festival, Vendor: Midsummer Suppliers/ Merchants	
Teldrassil Spoutling	Scratch	Poisoned Branch	Thorns	Shell Shield	Photosynthesis	Entangling Roots	Vendor: Rook Hawkfist	Icecrown (Argent Tournament Grounds)
Terrible Turnip	Weakening Blow	Leech Seed	Sunlight	Tidal Wave	Inspiring Song	Sons of the Root	Drop: World Drop	Valley of the Four Winds
Tiny Bog Beast	Crush	Lash	Poison Lash	Clobber	Leap	Rampage	Pet Battle	Wetlands
Tiny Shale Spider	Burn	Sticky Web	Stone Rush	Leech Life	Poison Spit	Stoneskin	Drop: Jadefang	Deepholm
Tiny Snowman	Snowball	Call Blizzard	Howling Blast	Magic Hat	Frost Nova	Deep Freeze	World Event: Feast of the Winter Veil	Dropped by Gaily Wrapped Present found under Winter Veil tree
Tiny Twister	Slicing Wind	Flyby	Cyclone	Wildwinds	Bash	Sandstorm	Pet Battle	Arathi Highlands
Topaz Shale Hatchling	Burn	Sticky Web	Stone Rush	Leech Life	Poison Spit	Stoneskin	Pet Battle	Deepholm, Desolace, The Stonecore
Venus	Lash	Sunlight	Stun Seed	Poison Lash	Plant	Leech Seed	Achievement: That's a Lot of Pet Food	Achievement (Category: Pet Battles)
Water Waveling	Water Jet	Frost Nova	Geyser	Ice Lance	Frost Shock	Tidal Wave	Pet Battle	Zul'Drak
Withers	Scratch	Poisoned Branch	Thorns	Shell Shield	Photosynthesis	Entangling Roots	Vendor: Apothecary Furrows / Quest reward: Remembrance of Auberdine	Darkshore

FLYING PETS

Passive Ability	Description
Swiftness	Flying creatures gain 50% extra speed while above 50% health.

NAME	ABILITY LEARNED AT LEVEL						ACQUIRED	REGION/NOTES
	1	2	4	10	15	20		
Amber Moth	Slicing Wind	Cocoon Strike	Moth Balls	Alpha Strike	Adrenaline Rush	Moth Dust	Pet Battle	Dread Wastes, Townlong Steppes
Amorous Rooster	Peck	Squawk	Egg Barrage	Slicing Wind	Adrenaline Rush	Flock	Pet Battle	Valley of the Four Winds
Ancona Chicken	Peck	Squawk	Egg Barrage	Slicing Wind	Adrenaline Rush	Flock	Vendor: "Plucky" Johnson	Thousand Needles
Bat	Bite	Screech	Reckless Strike	Leech Life	Hawk Eye	Nocturnal Strike	Pet Battle	Eastern Plaguelands, Mount Hyjal, Tirisfal Glades
Blue Mini Jouster	Slicing Wind	Hawk Eye	Lift-Off	Thrash	Adrenaline Rush	Cyclone	Quest reward: Egg Wave	Mount Hyjal
Blue Moth	Slicing Wind	Cocoon Strike	Moth Balls	Alpha Strike	Adrenaline Rush	Moth Dust	Vendor: Sixx	The Exodar
Brilliant Kaliri	Peck	Shriek	Nocturnal Strike	Quills	Cyclone	Predatory Strike	Achievement: Menagerie	Achievement (Category: Pet Battles)
Cenarian Hatchling	Peck	Screech	Reckless Strike	Quills	Rush	Lift-Off	Blizzard Store	Promotional Pet
Chicken	Peck	Squawk	Egg Barrage	Slicing Wind	Adrenaline Rush	Flock	Pet Battle	Arathi Basin, Azuremyst Isle, Bloodmyst Isle, Duskwood, Dustwallow Marsh, Elwynn Forest, Gilneas, Hillsbrad Foothills, Howling Fjord, Northern Barrens, Redridge Mountains, Shattrath City, Tirisfal Glades, Westfall, Wetlands
Cockatiel	Slicing Wind	Hawk Eye	Lift-Off	Thrash	Adrenaline Rush	Cyclone	Vendor: Harry No-Hooks / Narkk	The Cape of Stranglethorn
Crested Owl	Peck	Shriek	Nocturnal Strike	Quills	Cyclone	Predatory Strike	Pet Battle	Teldrassil
Crimson Moth	Slicing Wind	Cocoon Strike	Moth Balls	Alpha Strike	Adrenaline Rush	Moth Dust	Pet Battle	Northern Stranglethorn, The Cape of Stranglethorn
Dragonbone Hatchling	Slicing Wind	Hawk Eye	Lift-Off	Thrash	Adrenaline Rush	Cyclone	Pet Battle	Dragonblight
Effervescent Glowfly	Scratch	Confusing Sting	Swarm	Slicing Wind	Cocoon Strike	Glowing Toxin	Pet Battle	Vale of Eternal Blossoms
Firefly	Scratch	Confusing Sting	Swarm	Slicing Wind	Cocoon Strike	Glowing Toxin	Drop: Bogflare Needler	Zangarmarsh
Fledgling Buzzard	Slicing Wind	Hawk Eye	Lift-Off	Thrash	Adrenaline Rush	Cyclone	Pet Battle	Redridge Mountains
Fledgling Nether Ray	Bite	Tail Sweep	Shadow Shock	Arcane Blast	Slicing Wind	Lash	Pet Battle	Netherstorm
Forest Moth	Slicing Wind	Cocoon Strike	Moth Balls	Alpha Strike	Adrenaline Rush	Moth Dust	Pet Battle	Ashenvale, Darnassus, Desolace, Moonglade, Mount Hyjal, Teldrassil
Fungal Moth	Slicing Wind	Cocoon Strike	Moth Balls	Alpha Strike	Adrenaline Rush	Moth Dust	Pet Battle	Deepholm
Garden Moth	Slicing Wind	Cocoon Strike	Moth Balls	Alpha Strike	Adrenaline Rush	Moth Dust	Pet Battle	The Jade Forest
Gilded Moth	Slicing Wind	Cocoon Strike	Moth Balls	Alpha Strike	Adrenaline Rush	Moth Dust	Pet Battle	Vale of Eternal Blossoms
Gilnean Raven	Peck	Darkflame	Nocturnal Strike	Alpha Strike	Call Darkness	Nevermore	Vendor: Wil Larson (also offered to Worgen characters by Pet Battle Trainers)	Lor'danel
Gold Mini Jouster	Slicing Wind	Hawk Eye	Lift-Off	Thrash	Adrenaline Rush	Cyclone	Quest: Egg Wave	Mount Hyjal
Great Horned Owl	Peck	Shriek	Nocturnal Strike	Quills	Cyclone	Predatory Strike	Vendor: Shylenai	Teldrassil (Darnassus)
Green Wing Macaw	Slicing Wind	Hawk Eye	Lift-Off	Thrash	Adrenaline Rush	Cyclone	Drop: Defias Pirate	The Deadmines
Grey Moth	Slicing Wind	Cocoon Strike	Moth Balls	Alpha Strike	Adrenaline Rush	Moth Dust	Pet Battle	Azuremyst Isle
Gryphon Hatchling	Peck	Squawk	Flock	Slicing Wind	Adrenaline Rush	Lift-Off	Blizzard Store	Promotional Pet
Guardian Cub	Slicing Wind	Roar	Reckless Strike	Onyx Bite	Wild Winds	Cyclone	Blizzard Store	Promotional Pet
Hawk Owl	Peck	Shriek	Nocturnal Strike	Quills	Cyclone	Predatory Strike	Vendor: Shylenai	Teldrassil (Darnassus)
Highlands Turkey	Peck	Squawk	Food Coma	Slicing Wind	Gobble Strike	Flock	Pet Battle	Twilight Highlands
Hippogryph Hatchling	Peck	Screech	Reckless Strike	Quills	Rush	Lift-Off	Trading Card Game: Heroes of Azeroth	TCG
Hyacinth Macaw	Slicing Wind	Hawk Eye	Lift-Off	Thrash	Adrenaline Rush	Cyclone	Drop: World Drop	Northern Stranglethorn, The Cape of Stranglethorn
Imperial Eagle Chick	Slicing Wind	Cyclone	Hawk Eye	Thrash	Adrenaline Rush	Lift-Off	Pet Battle	Grizzly Hills

NAME	ABILITY LEARNED AT LEVEL						ACQUIRED	REGION/NOTES
	1	2	4	10	15	20		
Jade Crane Chick	Slicing Wind	Hawk Eye	Cyclone	Thrash	Jadeskin	Flock	Vendor: Audrey Burnhep / Varog (or talk to Pet Battle Trainer with Pandaren character)	Stormwind City / Orgrimmar
Luyu Moth	Slicing Wind	Cocoon Strike	Moth Balls	Alpha Strike	Adrenaline Rush	Moth Dust	Pet Battle	Krasarang Wilds
Mei Li Sparkler	Scratch	Confusing Sting	Swarm	Slicing Wind	Cocoon Strike	Glowing Toxin	Pet Battle	Krasarang Wilds
Miniwing	Peck	Shriek	Nocturnal Strike	Quills	Cyclone	Predatory Strike	Quest: Skywing	Terokkar Forest
Nether Faerie Dragon	Slicing Wind	Arcane Blast	Moonfire	Evanescence	Life Exchange	Cyclone	Pet Battle	Feralas
Nether Ray Fry	Bite	Tail Sweep	Shadow Shock	Arcane Blast	Slicing Wind	Lash	Vendor: Grella	Terokkar Forest (Faction: Sha'tari Skyguard - Exalted)
Oasis Moth	Slicing Wind	Cocoon Strike	Moth Balls	Alpha Strike	Adrenaline Rush	Moth Dust	Pet Battle	Lost City of the Tol'Vir, Uldum
Parrot	Slicing Wind	Hawk Eye	Lift-Off	Thrash	Adrenaline Rush	Cyclone	Pet Battle	Northern Stranglethorn, Swamp of Sorrows, The Cape of Stranglethorn, Un'Goro Crater
Plump Turkey	Peck	Squawk	Food Coma	Slicing Wind	Gobble Strike	Flock	World Event: Pilgrim's Bounty, Achievement: Pilgrim	Achievement (Category: World Events)
Polly	Slicing Wind	Hawk Eye	Lift-Off	Thrash	Adrenaline Rush	Cyclone	Pet Battle	Northern Stranglethorn
Pterrordax Hatchling	Slicing Wind	Ancient Blessing	Lift-Off	Flyby	Apocalypse	Feign Death	Profession: Archaeology	
Red Moth	Slicing Wind	Cocoon Strike	Moth Balls	Alpha Strike	Adrenaline Rush	Moth Dust	Vendor: Dealer Rashaad	Netherstorm (The Stormspire)
Rustberg Gull	Slicing Wind	Cyclone	Hawk Eye	Thrash	Adrenaline Rush	Lift-Off	Vendor: Quartermaster Brazie / Pogg	Tol Barad Peninsula (Faction: Baradin's Wardens / Hellscream's Reach - Honored)
Sandy Petrel	Slicing Wind	Cyclone	Hawk Eye	Thrash	Adrenaline Rush	Lift-Off	Pet Battle	The Jade Forest
Sea Gull	Slicing Wind	Cyclone	Hawk Eye	Thrash	Adrenaline Rush	Lift-Off	Pet Battle	Elwynn Forest, Krasarang Wilds, Tanaris
Senegal	Slicing Wind	Hawk Eye	Lift-Off	Thrash	Adrenaline Rush	Cyclone	Vendor: Narkk & Harry No-Hooks / Dealer Rashaad	The Cape of Stranglethorn / Netherstorm (The Stormspire)
Shrine Fly	Scratch	Confusing Sting	Swarm	Slicing Wind	Cocoon Strike	Glowing Toxin	Pet Battle	The Jade Forest
Silky Moth	Slicing Wind	Cocoon Strike	Moth Balls	Alpha Strike	Adrenaline Rush	Moth Dust	Pet Battle	Moonglade, Mount Hyjal, Un'Goro Crater
Snowy Owl	Peck	Shriek	Nocturnal Strike	Quills	Cyclone	Predatory Strike	Pet Battle	Winterspring (Season: Winter)
Swamp Moth	Slicing Wind	Cocoon Strike	Moth Balls	Alpha Strike	Adrenaline Rush	Moth Dust	Pet Battle	Swamp of Sorrows
Szechuan Chicken	Peck	Squawk	Egg Barrage	Slicing Wind	Adrenaline Rush	Flock	Pet Battle	Kun-Lai Summit
Tainted Moth	Slicing Wind	Cocoon Strike	Moth Balls	Alpha Strike	Adrenaline Rush	Moth Dust	Pet Battle	Felwood
Tickbird Hatchling	Slicing Wind	Cyclone	Hawk Eye	Thrash	Adrenaline Rush	Lift-Off	Drop: Mysterious Egg	Sholozar Basin (Oracles)
Tiny Flamefly	Burn	Immolate	Swarm	Alpha Strike	Hiss	Adrenaline Rush	Quest: SEVEN! YUP! / Not Fireflies, Flameflies	Burning Steppes
Tiny Sporebat	Slicing Wind	Creeping Fungus	Spore Shrooms	Shadow Slash	Leech Seed	Confusing Sting	Vendor: Mycah	Zangarmarsh (Reputation: Sporeggar - Exalted)
Tirisfal Batling	Bite	Screech	Reckless Strike	Leech Life	Hawk Eye	Nocturnal Strike	Vendor: Eliza Killian	Icecrown (Argent Tournament Grounds)
Turkey	Peck	Squawk	Food Coma	Slicing Wind	Gobble Strike	Flock	Pet Battle	Howling Fjord
Westfall Chicken	Peck	Squawk	Egg Barrage	Slicing Wind	Adrenaline Rush	Flock	Quest: CLUCK!	Westfall
White Moth	Slicing Wind	Cocoon Strike	Moth Balls	Alpha Strike	Adrenaline Rush	Moth Dust	Vendor: Sixx	The Exodar
White Tickbird Hatchling	Slicing Wind	Cyclone	Hawk Eye	Thrash	Adrenaline Rush	Lift-Off	Drop: Mysterious Egg	Sholozar Basin (Oracles)
Wildhammer Gryphon Hatchling	Peck	Slicing Wind	Flock	Squawk	Adrenaline Rush	Lift-Off	Pet Battle	Twilight Highlands
Yellow Moth	Slicing Wind	Cocoon Strike	Moth Balls	Alpha Strike	Adrenaline Rush	Moth Dust	Vendor: Sixx	The Exodar

HUMANOID PETS

Passive Ability	Description
Recovery	Humanoids recover 4% of their maximum health if they dealt damage this round.

NAME	ABILITY LEARNED AT LEVEL						ACQUIRED	REGION/NOTES
	1	2	4	10	15	20		
Curious Oracle Hatchling	Punch	Super Sticky Goo	Backflip	Water Jet	Aged Yolk	Dreadful Breath	World Event: Children's Week	Dalaran
Curious Wolvar Pup	Punch	Snap Trap	Whirlwind	Bite	Frenzyheart Brew	Maul	World Event: Children's Week	Dalaran
Deathy	Punch	Scorched Earth	Clobber	Deep Breath	Call Darkness	Roar	Promotion: BlizzCon 2010	Promotional Pet
Father Winter's Helper	Snowball	Call Blizzard	Ice Tomb	Ice Lance	Egg Nogg	Gift of Winter's Veil	World Event: Feast of Winter Veil	Dropped by Gaily Wrapped Present found under Winter Veil tree
Feral Vermling	Crush	Sticky Goo	Backflip	Tongue Lash	Poison Lash	Dreadful Breath	Achievement: Going to Need More Leashes	Achievement (Pet Battles)
Flayer Youngling	Blitz	Focus	Kick	Triple Snap	Reflection	Rampage	Pet Battle	Hellfire Peninsula
Gregarious Grell	Punch	Immolate	Cauterize	Burn	Phase Shift	Sear Magic	Trading Card Game: Crown of the Heavens	TCG
Grunty	Gauss Rifle	Stimpack	Launch	U-238 Rounds	Shield Block	Lock-On	Promotion: BlizzCon 2009	Promotional Pet
Gurky	Punch	Acid Touch	Clobber	Flank	Lucky Dance	Stampede	Promotion: EU Fansite Promotion	Promotional Pet
Hopling	Crush	Sticky Goo	Backflip	Tongue Lash	Poison Lash	Dreadful Breath	Achievement: Ling-Ting's Herbal Journey	Achievement (Category: Dungeons & Raids)
Lurky	Punch	Acid Touch	Clobber	Flank	Lucky Dance	Stampede	Promotion: Burning Crusade Collector's Edition (EU only)	Promotional Pet
Mini Tyrael	Holy Sword	Holy Justice	Holy Charge	Omnislash	Surge of Light	Restoration	Promotion: Worldwide Invitational 2008	Promotional Pet
Moonkin Hatchling	Punch	Entangling Roots	Cyclone	Solar Beam	Clobber	Moonfire	Blizzard Store (Alliance)	Promotional Pet
Moonkin Hatchling	Punch	Entangling Roots	Cyclone	Solar Beam	Clobber	Moonfire	Blizzard Store (Horde)	Promotional Pet
Murkablo	Burn	Agony	Blast of Hatred	Bone Prison	Drain Power	Scorched Earth	Promotion: BlizzCon 2011	Promotional Pet
Murkimus the Gladiator	Punch	Shield Block	Heroic Leap	Flurry	Counterstrike	Haymaker	Promotion: Arena Tournament 2009 (Feat: Participated in 50 3v3 Arena Tournament games)	Promotional Pet
Murky	Punch	Acid Touch	Clobber	Flank	Lucky Dance	Stampede	Promotion: BlizzCon 2005	Promotional Pet
Pandaren Monk	Jab	Focus Chi	Fury of 1000 Fists	Takedown	Staggered Steps	Blackout Kick	Blizzard Store	Promotional Pet
Peddlefeet	Bow Shot	Lovestruck	Shot Through The Heart	Rapid Fire	Perfumed Arrow	Love Potion	World Event: Love is in the Air, Vendor: Lovely Merchant	
Qiraji Guardling	Crush	Hawk Eye	Reckless Strike	Whirlwind	Sandstorm	Blackout Kick	Pet Battle	Silithis (Season: Summer)
Sporeling Sprout	Jab	Creeping Fungus	Spore Shrooms	Takedown	Leech Seed	Crouch	Pet Battle	Zangarmarsh
Winter's Little Helper	Snowball	Call Blizzard	Ice Tomb	Ice Lance	Egg Nogg	Gift of Winter's Veil	World Event: Feast of Winter Veil	Dropped by Gaily Wrapped Present found under Winter Veil tree

MAGIC PETS

Passive Ability	Description
Spellshield	Magic pets cannot be dealt more than 50% of their maximum health in one attack.

NAME	ABILITY LEARNED AT LEVEL						ACQUIRED	REGION/NOTES
	1	2	4	10	15	20		
Baneling	Bite	Centrifugal Hooks	Burrow	Thrash	Adrenal Glands	Baneling Burst	Promotion StartCraft II: Heart of the Swarm Collector's Edition	Promotional Pet
Disgusting Oozeing	Ooze Touch	Corrosion	Expunge	Absorb	Creeping Ooze	Acidic Goo	Drop: World Drop	Creature: Oozes, Slimes and Worms
Enchanted Broom	Broom	Sandstorm	Clean-Up	Batter	Sweep	Wind-Up	Vendor: Trellis Morningsun	Icecrown (Argent Tournament Grounds)
Enchanted Lantern	Beam	Illuminate	Soul Ward	Burn	Flash	Light	Profession: Enchanting (525)	Formula: Enchanted Lantern
Ethereal Soul-Trader	Punch	Soul Ward	Soulrush	Beam	Inner Vision	Life Exchange	Trading Card Game: The Hunt for Illidan	TCG
Festival Lantern	Beam	Illuminate	Soul Ward	Burn	Flash	Light	World Event: Lunar Festival, Vendor: Valadar Starsong	Moonglade
Jade Oozeling	Ooze Touch	Corrosion	Expunge	Absorb	Creeping Ooze	Acidic Goo	Pet Battle	The Hinterlands
Jade Owl	Slicing Wind	Adrenaline Rush	Lift-Off	Thrash	Hawk Eye	Cyclone	Profession: Jewelcrafting	
Jade Tiger	Jade Claw	Rake	Devour	Pounce	Jadeskin	Prowl	Achievement: Jade Tiger	Achievement (Category: Feat of Strength, Feat: WoW China event)
Legs	Laser	Surge of Power	Focused Beams	Pump	Gravity	Whirlpool	World Event: Children's Week	Quest: Back to the Orphanage
Lunar Lantern	Beam	Illuminate	Soul Ward	Burn	Flash	Light	World Event: Lunar Festival, Vendor: Valadar Starsong	Moonglade
Magic Lamp	Beam	Sear Magic	Soul Ward	Arcane Blast	Gravity	Wish	Profession: Enchanting (525)	Formula: Magic Lamp
Mana Wyrmling	Feedback	Drain Power	Mana Surge	Flurry	Amplify Magic	Reflection	Vendor: Dealer Rashaad	Netherstorm (The Stormspire)
Minfernal	Crush	Immolation	Meteor Strike	Immolate	Extra Plating	Explode	Pet Battle	Felwood
Mini Diablo	Burn	Call Darkness	Weakness	Blast of Hatred	Agony	Bone Prison	Promotion: World of Warcraft Collectors Edition	Promotional Pet
Nordrassil Wisp	Beam	Flash	Soul Ward	Light	Arcane Blast	Arcane Explosion	Pet Battle	Mount Hyjal
Oily Slimling	Ooze Touch	Corrosion	Expunge	Absorb	Creeping Ooze	Acidic Goo	Pet Battle	Borean Tundra
Onyx Panther	Claw	Stoneskin	Leap	Onyx Bite	Roar	Stone Rush	Promotion: Korea World Event	Promotional Pet
Shimmering Wyrmling	Feedback	Drain Power	Mana Surge	Flurry	Amplify Magic	Reflection	Vendor: Hiren Loresong	Icecrown (Argent Crusade Tournament Grounds), Reputation: The Silver Covenant - Exalted
Spectral Tiger Cub	Claw	Evanesence	Leap	Rend	Spectral Strike	Prowl	Trading Card Game: Scourgewar	TCG
Toxic Wasteling	Ooze Touch	Corrosion	Expunge	Absorb	Creeping Ooze	Acidic Goo	World Event: Love is in the Air	Shadowfang Keep (Dropped by Apothecary Hummel)
Twilight Fiendling	Creepy Chomp	Leap	Adrenal Glands	Rake	Creeping Ooze	Siphon Life	Pet Battle	Twilight Highlands
Willy	Tongue Lash	Interrupting Gaze	Agony	Focused Beams	Eyeblast	Dark Simulacrum	World Event: Children's Week, Quest reward: Back to the Orphanage	
Zergling	Bite	Metabolic Boost	Consume	Flank	Adrenal Glands	Zergling Rush	Promotion: World of Warcraft Collectors Edition	Promotional Pet
Zipao Tiger	Onyx Bite	Rake	Devour	Pounce	Stoneskin	Prowl	Promotion: China Billing Campaign	Promotional Pet

MECHANICAL PETS

Passive Ability	Description
Failsafe	Mechanical pets come back to life once per battle, returning to 20% health.

NAME	ABILITY LEARNED AT LEVEL						ACQUIRED	REGION/NOTES
	1	2	4	10	15	20		
Blue Clockwork Rocketbot	Missile	Toxic Smoke	Sticky Grenade	Batter	Minefield	Launch Rocket	Vendor: Jepetto Joybuzz / Clockwork Assistant	Crystalsong Forest (Dalaran)
Clockwork Gnome	Metal Fist	Repair	Build Turret	Railgun	Blitz	Launch Rocket	Profession: Archaeology	
Clockwork Rocketbot	Missile	Toxic Smoke	Sticky Grenade	Batter	Minefield	Launch Rocket	World Event: Feast of the Winter Veil	
Darkmoon Tonk	Missile	Shock and Awe	Lock-On	Charge	Minefield	Ion Cannon	Vendor: Lhara	Darkmoon Island
Darkmoon Zeppelin	Missile	Flyby	Bombing Run	Thunderbolt	Decoy	Explode	Vendor: Lhara	Darkmoon Island
De-Weaponized Mechanical Companion	Metal Fist	Overtune	Demolish	Thrash	Extra Plating	Repair	Profession: Engineering	
Landro's Lil' XT	Zap	Repair	XE-321 Boombot	Thrash	Heartbroken	Tympanic Tantrum	Trading Card Game: Worldbreaker	TCG
Lifelike Toad	Water Jet	Healing Wave	Frog Kiss	Tongue Lash	Cleansing Rain	Repair	Profession: Engineering (265)	Schematic: Lifelike Mechanical Toad
Lil' Smokey	Missile	Toxic Smoke	Sticky Grenade	Batter	Minefield	Launch Rocket	Profession: Engineering (205)	Schematic: Lil' Smoky
Lil' XT	Zap	Repair	XE-321 Boombot	Thrash	Heartbroken	Tympanic Tantrum	Blizzard Store	Promotional Pet
Mechanical Chicken	Peck	Overtune	Supercharge	Batter	Rebuild	Wind-Up	Quest: An OOX of Your Own	Booty Bay
Mechanical Pandaren Dragonling	Breath	Flyby	Bombing Run	Thunderbolt	Decoy	Explode	Profession: Engineering	
Mechanical Squirrel	Metal Fist	Overtune	Wind-Up	Thrash	Extra Plating	Repair	Profession: Engineering (75)	Schematic: Mechanical Squirrel
Mechanopeep	Peck	Batter	Wind-Up	Rebuild	Overtune	Repair	Vendor: Rillie Spindlenut	Icecrown (Argent Tournament Grounds)
Mini Thor	Missile	Toxic Smoke	Sticky Grenade	Batter	Minefield	Launch Rocket	Promotion: Starcraft 2: Wings of Liberty Collectors Edition	Promotional Pet
Personal World Destroyer	Metal Fist	Repair	Screeching Gears	Thrash	Supercharge	Quake	Profession: Engineering (Goblin - 475)	Taught by Goblin Engineering Trainers
Pet Bombling	Zap	Minefield	Screeching Gears	Batter	Toxic Smoke	Explode	Profession: Engineering (205)	Schematic: Pet Bombling
Rabbot	Metal Fist	Overtune	Demolish	Thrash	Extra Plating	Repair	Pet Battle	Kezan, Winterspring
Rabid Nut Varmint 5000	Metal Fist	Overtune	Rabid Strike	Thrash	Extra Plating	Repair	Pet Battle	Azshara, Kezan, Stonetalon Mountains, Winterspring
Robo-Chick	Peck	Overtune	Supercharge	Batter	Rebuild	Wind-Up	Pet Battle	Azshara, Kezan, Orgrimmar, Winterspring
Rocket Chicken	Missile	Squawk	Extra Plating	Peck	Toxic Smoke	Launch	Trading Card Game: March of the Legion	TCG
Tiny Harvester	Metal Fist	Overtune	Demolish	Thrash	Extra Plating	Repair	Pet Battle	Westfall
Tranquil Mechanical Yeti	Metal Fist	Call Lightning	Supercharge	Thrash	Call Blizzard	Ion Cannon	Profession: Engineering (250)	Taught by Umi Rumplesnicker in Winterspring
Warbot	Missile	Toxic Smoke	Extra Plating	Batter	Minefield	Launch Rocket	Promotion: Mountain Dew Game Fuel(Summer 2009)	Promotional Pet

UNDEAD PETS

Passive Ability	Description
Damned	Undead pets return to life immortal for one round when killed.

NAME	ABILITY LEARNED AT LEVEL						ACQUIRED	REGION/NOTES
	1	2	4	10	15	20		
Blighthawk	Infected Claw	Consume Corpse	Lift-Off	Slicing Wind	Ghostly Bite	Cyclone	Pet Battle	Western Plaguelands
Crawling Claw	Shadow Slash	Ancient Blessing	Curse of Doom	Agony	Death Grip	Dark Simulacrum	Profession: Archaeology	
Creepy Crate	Creepy Chomp	Death Grip	Devour	Agony	Curse of Doom	BONESTORM	World Event: Hallow's End	
Eye of the Legion	Shadow Slash	Agony	Soul Ward	Eyeblast	Gravity	Dark Simulacrum	Trading Card Game: Timewalkers: War of the Ancients	TCG
Fetish Shaman	Shadow Slash	Immolate	Sear Magic	Flame Breath	Wild Magic	Dark Simulacrum	Promotion: Diablo 3 Collectors Edition	Promotional Pet
Fossilized Hatchling	Claw	Ancient Blessing	Bone Prison	Bone Bite	Death and Decay	BONESTORM	Profession: Archaeology	
Frosty	Diseased Bite	Call Blizzard	Ice Tomb	Frost Breath	Shriek	Blistering Cold	Promotion: Wrath of the Lich King Collectors Edition	Promotional Pet
Ghostly Skull	Shadow Slash	Siphon Life	Ghostly Bite	Death Coil	Spectral Strike	Unholy Ascension	Vendor: Darahir	Crystalsong Forest (Dalaran)
Infected Fawn	Diseased Bite	Adrenaline Rush	Siphon Life	Flurry	Consume Corpse	Death and Decay	Pet Battle	Bloodmyst Isle, Eastern Plaguelands, Silverpine Forest
Infected Squirrel	Diseased Bite	Rabid Strike	Consume	Creeping Fungus	Stampede	Corpse Explosion	Pet Battle	Bloodmyst Isle, Eastern Plaguelands, Silverpine Forest
Infested Bear Cub	Diseased Bite	Bash	Maul	Roar	Hibernate	Corpse Explosion	Pet Battle	Hillsbrad Foothills
Landro's Lichling	Shadow Slash	Siphon Life	Frost Nova	Howling Blast	Death and Decay	Curse of Doom	Trading Card Game: Worldbreaker	TCG
Lil' K.T.	Shadow Slash	Siphon Life	Frost Nova	Howling Blast	Death and Decay	Curse of Doom	Blizzard Store	Promotional Pet
Lost of Lordaeron	Shadow Slash	Siphon Life	Bone Prison	Absorb	Arcane Explosion	Curse of Doom	Pet Battle	Tirisfal Glades
Restless Shadeling	Shadow Shock	Plagued Blood	Death Coil	Arcane Blast	Death and Decay	Phase Shift	Pet Battle	Deadwind Pass (Time: Early Morning)
Scourged Whelpling	Shadowflame	Call Darkness	Plagued Blood	Tail Sweep	Death and Decay	Dreadful Breath	Pet Battle	Icecrown
Sen'jin Fetish	Shadow Slash	Immolate	Sear Magic	Flame Breath	Wild Magic	Dark Simulacrum	Vendor: Samamba	Icecrown (Argent Tournament Grounds)
Spirit Crab	Snap	Surge	Shell Shield	Amplify Magic	Whirlpool	Dark Simulacrum	Pet Battle	Ghostlands
Vampiric Batling	Bite	Leech Life	Reckless Strike	Screech	Hawk Eye	Nocturnal Strike	Drop: Prince Tenris Mirkblood	Karazhan
Voodoo Figurine	Shadow Slash	Immolate	Sear Magic	Flame Breath	Wild Magic	Dark Simulacrum	Profession: Archaeology	

Pet Abilities

Name	Family		Description
Absorb	Undead		Deals Undead damage. The user is healed for 100% of the damage dealt.
Accuracy	Flying		Increases your chance to hit by 25% for 4 rounds.
Acid Touch	Aquatic		Acid eats away at the target, dealing Aquatic damage and causing Aquatic damage each round for 4 rounds.
Acidic Goo	Critter		Spits acidic goo onto the target, dealing Critter damage each round and increasing damage taken by 25% for 3 rounds.
Adrenal Glands	Magic		Increases your critical strike chance by 50% and decreases your accuracy by 25% for 4 rounds.
Adrenaline Rush	Critter		Deals Critter damage and increases your speed by 75% for 3 rounds.
Aged Yolk	Humanoid		Removes all buffs and debuffs. 3 Round Cooldown.
Agony	Undead		Inflicts agony on the target, causing increasing Undead damage each turn for 2 turns.
Alpha Strike	Flying		Deals Flying damage. Deals additional damage if user goes first.
Amplify Magic	Magic		Increases the damage done by your team by 50% for 2 turns.
Ancient Blessing	Dragonkin		Heals the user and increases the maximum health of your team by 5 per level for 9 rounds. 3 Round Cooldown.
Apocalypse	Critter		Calls down a meteor which will fall 15 rounds from now, instantly killing all active pets. Cockroaches always survive this attack. 20 Round Cooldown.
Arcane Blast	Magic		Blasts the enemy with a surge of arcane power, dealing Magic damage. Damage increases each time it hits, up to a given maximum.
Arcane Explosion	Magic		Deals Magic damage plus half damage to the enemy's backline pets.
Arcane Storm	Magic		Deals Magic damage to all enemies and warps the weather into Arcane Winds for 9 turns. During Arcane Winds, pets cannot be stunned or rooted. 3 Round Cooldown.
Backflip	Humanoid		Performs a flip, dealing Humanoid damage. Interrupts the opponent's turn if the user goes first. 3 Round Cooldown.
Banana Barrage	Beast		Hurls bananas at the enemy, dealing Beast damage. Bananas continue to fall on the enemy team dealing Beast damage each round for 3 rounds.
Barrel Toss	Mechanical		First use: Fills a barrel. Second use: Throws the barrel, dealing Mechanical damage.
Bash	Beast		Stun the target for 1 round. 5 Round Cooldown.
Batter	Mechanical		Smacks the enemy 1-2 times, dealing Mechanical damage per hit. Attacks an additional time if the user attacks first.
Beam	Magic		Blasts the enemy with a beam of arcane power, dealing Magic damage.
Belly Slide	Flying		Deals Flying damage. This ability has a high chance to miss. This attack goes first if the weather is a Blizzard.
Bite	Beast		Bites at the enemy, dealing Beast damage.
Blackout Kick	Humanoid		Stun the target for 1 round. 5 Round Cooldown.
Blast of Hatred	Magic		Deals Magic damage. Deals extra damage if you were struck first this turn.

Name	Family		Description
Bleat	Critter		Sings an inspiring song, which restores health to all allies. 5 Round Cooldown.
Blinkstrike	Magic		Blink to the enemy, dealing Magic damage. This move always goes first.
Blistering Cold	Elemental		Chills the air around the enemy, causing them to be afflicted with Frostbite each round for 3 rounds. Frostbite's damage grows until the pet is swapped. Blistering Cold lasts for 4 rounds. Persists through pet swaps. 2 Round Cooldown.
Blitz	Humanoid		Pummels the enemy 1-2 times, dealing Humanoid damage per hit. Hits an additional time if the user attacks first.
Blood in the Water	Aquatic		Deals Aquatic damage, but has a high chance to miss. Always hits if the target is bleeding. 3 Round Cooldown.
Bombing Run	Mechanical		Deals Mechanical damage and calls in a bombing run. After 3 turns the bombs will arrive, dealing Mechanical damage to the current enemy pet. 3 Round Cooldown.
Bone Bite	Undead		Bites at the enemy, dealing Undead damage.
Bone Prison	Undead		Deals Undead damage and prevents the target from fleeing for 2 turns.
BONESTORM	Undead		Deals Undead damage, split across the enemy team but costs 15% of your total health.
Breath	Dragonkin		Overwhelms the enemy with draconic breath, dealing Dragonkin damage.
Brittle Webbing	Beast		Deals Beast damage and coats the target in brittle webbing, causing them to take Beast damage each time they attack. Lasts 3 turns.
Broom	Humanoid		Whack the enemy, dealing Humanoid damage.
Build Turret	Mechanical		Builds a turret that assaults the enemy team's front pet, dealing Mechanical damage each round. Each turret lasts 4 rounds. 1 Round Cooldown.
Buried Treasure	Critter		Digs up a bone, healing up to 25% of your health. 3 Round Cooldown.
Burn	Elemental		Burns the enemy with a blast of fire, dealing Elemental damage.
Burrow	Beast		Burrow under the ground, becoming unattackable for one round. On the next turn, you attack, dealing Beast damage. 2 Round ability. 4 Round Cooldown.
Call Blizzard	Elemental		Deals Elemental damage and causes a Blizzard. During a Blizzard, all pets are considered Chilled. 3 Round Cooldown.
Call Darkness	Humanoid		A shadow fall across the battlefield, dealing Humanoid damage and turning the weather to Darkness for 9 rounds. During Darkness, all pets are considered Blinded and all healing received is reduced by 50%. 5 Round Cooldown.
Call Lightning	Mechanical		Deals Mechanical damage and causes a Lightning Storm for 9 rounds. During a Lightning Storm, all pets deal bonus Mechanical damage on each attack and Mechanical abilities deal 25% additional damage. 3 Round Cooldown.
Cataclysm	Dragonkin		Devastates the target, dealing Dragonkin damage. This ability has a high chance to miss.
Cauterize	Elemental		Restores health plus half of the last hit taken by the user. 3 Round Cooldown.
Charge	Humanoid		Rushes to the enemy, dealing Humanoid damage. This move always goes first.
Chew	Critter		Patiently chew some grass. On the next turn, you will deal Critter damage in addition to your next attack. 1 Round Cooldown.
Chomp	Critter		Chomps on the enemy, dealing Critter damage.

Name	Family		Description
Claw	Beast		Claws at the enemy, dealing Beast damage.
Cleansing Rain	Aquatic		Restores health to your team and calls down a cleansing rain for 9 rounds. During a cleansing rain, the duration of hostile damage over time effects is reduced by 1 round and Aquatic pets deal 25% more damage. 3 Round Cooldown.
Clean-Up	Magic		Deals Magic damage and removes any objects on the battlefield. 3 Round Cooldown.
Clobber	Humanoid		Stuns the target for 1 round. 5 Round Cooldown.
Cocoon Strike	Flying		Deals Flying damage and increases your chance to block an attack by 100%. Lasts 1 round. 4 Round Cooldown.
Comeback	Critter		Deals Critter damage. Deals additional damage if the user has lower health than the target.
Competitive Spirit	Magic		Deals Magic damage and increases your damage dealt by 25% for 3 turns.
Conflagrate	Elemental		Deals Elemental damage. Deals double damage if the target is already Burning. 4 Round Cooldown.
Confusing Sting	Flying		The target is stung, dealing Flying damage every turn for 5 rounds. While stung, the target has a 10% chance to harm themselves while attacking.
Consume	Undead		Deals Undead damage. The user is healed for 100% of the damage dealt. 1 Round Cooldown.
Consume Corpse	Undead		Consume an allied corpse to restore 50% of total health. Corpses can only be used once. 5 Turn Cooldown.
Corpse Explosion	Undead		Instantly kills the user, causing 15% of their health as Undead damage to the enemy and infects the target. Infected targets receive 5% of their maximum health as Undead damage every turn for 4 turns.
Corrosion	Magic		Splashes the target with corrosive acid, causing Magic damage and increases damage taken for 2 turns.
Counterstrike	Humanoid		Deals Humanoid damage. Deals additional damage if you were struck this turn.
Creeping Fungus	Undead		A creeping fungus infects the target, causing Undead damage each round for 4 rounds. Deals additional damage in Moonlight.
Creeping Ooze	Magic		Covers the target in a growing ooze, which deals Magic damage plus additional damage each turn. Lasts 4 turns.
Creepy Chomp	Undead		Chomps on the enemy, dealing Undead damage.
Crouch	Critter		The user lowers its body close to the ground, reducing all damage taken by 50% for 2 turns. 4 Round Cooldown.
Crush	Humanoid		Crush the enemy, dealing Humanoid damage.
Crystal Overload	Elemental		Your next attack deals double damage, but deals Elemental damage to you. 1 Round Cooldown.
Crystal Prison	Beast		Seals the target in crystal, stunning them for 1 round. 5 Round Cooldown.
Curse of Doom	Undead		Deals Undead damage after 5 turns.
Cyclone	Flying		Creates a cyclone which has a 25% chance to deal Flying damage to the enemy team each round. Lasts 5 rounds. 5 Round Cooldown.
Dark Rebirth	Elemental		If killed on the next turn, you are reborn with full health, but lose 20% health each round. 5 Round Cooldown.
Dazzling Dance	Critter		Increases your team's speed by 50% for 9 rounds.

Name	Family		Description
Death and Decay	Undead		Deals Undead damage to the enemy's active pet every round for 9 rounds. Persists through pet swaps.
Death Coil	Undead		Deals Undead damage and heals the user for 100% of the damage dealt. 1 Turn Cooldown.
Death Grip	Undead		Deals Undead damage and forces the opponent's lowest health pet to swap into battle. 3 Round Cooldown.
Decoy	Mechanical		Creates a wooden decoy that protects your team from 2 attacks. 5 Turn Cooldown.
Deep Breath	Dragonkin		Takes one round to breathe in deeply. The next turn the user unleashes a devastating breath attack, dealing Dragonkin damage. 2 Round Ability.
Deep Freeze	Elemental		Deals Elemental damage and has a 25% chance to stun the target 1 round. The chance to stun becomes 100% if the target is Chilled. 3 Round Cooldown.
Demolish	Mechanical		Rams the target, dealing Mechanical damage. This ability has a high chance to miss.
Devour	Beast		Deals Beast damage. If the user kills an enemy with Devour, they restore some health. Devour continues for 2 rounds. 1 Round Cooldown.
Diseased Bite	Undead		Infects the enemy, dealing Undead damage.
Dive	Aquatic		Submerges, becoming unattackable for one turn. On the next turn, you attack, dealing Aquatic damage. 2 Round Ability. 4 Round Cooldown.
Dodge	Humanoid		Increases your chance to dodge an attack by 100%. Lasts 1 turn. 4 Round Cooldown.
Drain Power	Magic		Deals Magic damage, reduces the target's damage by 25% for 2 rounds and increases the user's damage by 25% for 2 turns. 4 Round Cooldown.
Dreadful Breath	Humanoid		Channels a dreadful toxic breath which deals Humanoid damage to the enemy team. Deals additional damage if the weather is rainy. Your pet continues performing this attack for 3 rounds.
Early Advantage	Elemental		Deals Elemental damage. Deals double damage if the user has lower health. 4 Round Cooldown.
Elementium Bolt	Dragonkin		Launches an elementium bolt at the enemy team. After 3 turns, the bolt strikes, causing the current enemy pet to take Dragonkin damage and become stunned for 1 round. 5 Round Cooldown.
Emerald Bite	Magic		Bites the enemy with Emerald teeth, dealing Magic damage.
Emerald Dream	Dragonkin		Fall asleep, restoring health on the first turn, health on the second, then health on the third. While in the Emerald Dream, you cannot swap pets. 5 Round Cooldown.
Emerald Presence	Dragonkin		Reduces damage taken from each attack against you. Lasts 5 turns.
Entangling Roots	Elemental		Causes a thick nest of vines to begin growing around the enemy team. Next turn, the opponent's pet will take Elemental damage and be rooted for 2 rounds. 3 Round Cooldown.
Evanescence	Magic		Fade into a cloud of mist, increasing your chance to dodge by 100%. Lasts 1 turn. 4 Round Cooldown.
Explode	Mechanical		Instantly kills the caster, dealing damage equal to a percentage of the user's total health to the current enemy. Using explode will prevent the caster from activating Failsafe mechanisms.
Exposed Wounds	Beast		Adds damage to every attack against the target. Lasts 5 turns.
Expunge	Magic		Deals Magic damage to the target. Has a moderate chance to miss. 3 Round Cooldown.
Extra Plating	Mechanical		The user equips additional plating, reducing all damage taken by 50% for 2 turns. 4 Round Cooldown.
Eyeblast	Magic		Deals Magic damage and reduces the target's speed for 4 turns.

Name	Family		Description
Feedback	Magic		Launches a surge of mana at the enemy, dealing Magic damage.
Feign Death	Beast		The user feigns death, avoiding the opponent's attack. The user then swaps automatically with your highest health pet. 5 Round Cooldown.
Flame Breath	Dragonkin		Deals Dragonkin damage instantly. Deals additional Dragonkin damage per turn for 4 turns.
Flamethrower	Elemental		Turns the battlefield into a raging inferno, dealing Elemental damage. Fire continues to burn the enemy team dealing Elemental damage each turn for 2 turns. 3 Round Cooldown.
Flank	Critter		Flanks the enemy 1-2 times, dealing Critter damage per hit. Hits an additional time if the user attacks first.
Flash	Magic		A brilliant flash deals Magic damage and blinds the target, reducing their accuracy by 100% for 2 rounds. 3 Round Cooldown.
Flock	Flying		Flocks the target, causing Flying damage every turn. Lasts 3 rounds. Opponents struck by the flock take double damage for 2 rounds. 3 Round Ability.
Flurry	Critter		Rapidly strikes at the enemy 1-2 times, dealing Critter damage per hit. Attacks an additional time if the user attacks first.
Flyby	Flying		Deals Flying damage and increase the target's damage taken by 25% for 4 turns.
Focus	Humanoid		Focuses intensely, increasing your chance to hit by 100% for 3 rounds.
Focus Chi	Humanoid		Increases the damage of your next attack by 100%. 1 Round Cooldown.
Focused Beams	Magic		Blasts the enemy with a beam of arcane power, dealing Magic damage. Damage increases each time it hits, up to a maximum.
Food Coma	Critter		Puts the target to sleep for 2 rounds. 5 Round Cooldown.
Frenzyheart Brew	Humanoid		A fierce brew enrages the user, causing them to attack, dealing Humanoid damage and increasing the damage they deal by 25% for 3 rounds.
Frog Kiss	Aquatic		Deals Aquatic damage and has a 25% chance to turn the target into a frog for 1 round. Damage increases each time it hits, up to a maximum.
Frost Breath	Dragonkin		Freezes the target, dealing Dragonkin damage.
Frost Nova	Elemental		Deals Elemental damage and prevents the target from fleeing for 2 turns. While rooted the target is Chilled. 3 Round Cooldown.
Frost Shock	Elemental		Chills the target, dealing Elemental damage and reducing their speed by 25% for 4 turns.
Frost Spit	Elemental		Spits a blast of ice at the target, dealing Elemental damage.
Fury of 1000 Fists	Humanoid		Deals Humanoid damage and has a 25% chance to stun the target for 1 turn. The chance to stun becomes 100% if the target is Blinded. 3 Round Cooldown.
Gauss Rifle	Humanoid		Take a shot, dealing Humanoid damage.
Geyser	Elemental		Causes a water geyser to form under the enemy team. After 3 turns, the geyser erupts, causing the current enemy pet to take Elemental damage and be stunned for 1 round. 5 Round Cooldown.
Ghostly Bite	Undead		Deals Undead damage and stuns the user for 1 round. 3 Round Cooldown.
Gift of Winter's Veil	Magic		Deals Magic damage to the enemy. 5 Round Cooldown.
Glowing Toxin	Flying		Deals a percentage of the target's max health as damage every turn. Lasts 4 rounds.
Gnaw	Beast		Deals Beast damage plus additional damage if the user goes first.

Name	Family		Description
Gobble Strike	Critter		Deals Critter damage and increases your speed by 50% for 4 turns.
Grasp	Aquatic		Grabs the target, dealing Aquatic damage. The target cannot swap for 2 rounds.
Gravity	Magic		Slams the target into the ground, dealing Magic damage. If used again on the same target, they are levitated and unable to flee for 2 turns. 1 Round Cooldown.
Hawk Eye	Flying		Increases your critical strike chance by 25% for 4 turns.
Headbutt	Beast		Deals Beast damage and has a 25% chance to stun the target. 3 Round Cooldown.
Healing Flame	Dragonkin		Restores health plus half of the last hit taken by the user. 3 Round Cooldown.
Healing Wave	Aquatic		Restores health to the user. 3 Round Cooldown.
Heartbroken	Mechanical		Next turn you take 50% additional damage. If hurt, you will deal 100% additional damage for 1 round. 2 Round Cooldown.
Hibernate	Beast		Fall asleep, restoring health on the first turn, health on the second, then health on the third. While Hibernating you cannot swap pets. 5 Round Cooldown.
Hiss	Beast		Deals Beast damage and reduces the target's speed by 25% for 4 turns.
Hoof	Critter		Stomps the enemy, dealing Critter damage.
Horn Attack	Beast		Deals Beast damage. If the user is faster than the target, they have a 50% chance to be trampled and lose their turn. 1 Round Cooldown.
Howl	Beast		A distant howl frightens the target, increasing the damage they take by 100% for 1 round. 2 Round Cooldown.
Howling Blast	Elemental		Deals Elemental damage to the enemy. Deals additional damage to the enemy team if the target is Chilled. 3 Round Cooldown.
Ice Lance	Elemental		Splashes the enemy with freezing damage, dealing Elemental damage. Deals additional damage if the target is Chilled.
Ice Tomb	Elemental		Launches an orb of freezing energy at the target. After 3 turns, the ice hits, causing the current enemy pet to take Elemental damage and be stunned for 1 turn. 5 Round Cooldown.
Illuminate	Magic		Deals Magic damage and transforms the weather into a Sunny Day for 9 rounds. During a Sunny Day, the maximum health of all pets is increased and healing done is increased by 25%. 5 Round Cooldown.
Immolate	Elemental		Deals Elemental damage instantly. Deals additional Elemental damage per round for 4 rounds.
Immolation	Elemental		Ignites the caster, causing them to deal Element damage to the current enemy pet every round. Lasts 9 rounds.
Infected Claw	Undead		Tears at the enemy with plagued claws, dealing Undead damage.
Inner Vision	Magic		Increases the damage of your next attack by 100%. 1 Round Cooldown.
Inspiring Song	Elemental		Sings an inspiring song, which restores health to all allies. 3 Round Cooldown.
Instability	Dragonkin		Deals Dragonkin damage. This attack has a high change to miss. 1 Round Cooldown.
Interrupting Gaze	Humanoid		Deals Humanoid damage and interrupts multi-turn attacks. 3 Round Cooldown.
Ion Cannon	Mechanical		Instantly deals Mechanical damage. The user must recharge for two rounds afterwards. While recharging, you cannot perform any other actions. 3 Round Ability. 5 Round Cooldown.
Jab	Humanoid		Jabs at the enemy, dealing Humanoid damage.

Name	Family		Description
Jade Claw	Magic		Rakes the enemy with jade claws, dealing Magic damage.
Jadeskin	Magic		Reduces damage from each attack against you. Lasts 5 turns.
Laser	Magic		Blasts the enemy with a laser of arcane power, dealing Magic damage. Laser has a 100% hit chance.
Lash	Elemental		Lashes the enemy 1-2 times, dealing Elemental damage per lash. Attacks an additional time if the user attacks first.
Launch	Mechanical		Launch up high, becoming unattackable for one turn. On the next turn, you attack, dealing Mechanical damage. 2 Round Ability. 4 Round Cooldown.
Launch Rocket	Mechanical		First use: Creates a rocket. Second use: Launches the rocket, dealing Mechanical damage.
Leap	Beast		Instantly deals Beast damage and increases your speed by 100% for 1 round.
Leech Life	Undead		Deals Undead damage. The user restores some health. Double if the target is webbed. 1 Round Cooldown.
Life Exchange	Magic		Equalizes the health between the user and his enemy. 5 Round Cooldown.
Lift-Off	Flying		Fly up high, becoming unattackable for one round. On your next turn, you attack, dealing Flying damage. 2 Round Ability. 4 Round Cooldown.
Light	Magic		Covers the enemy in brilliant light, dealing Magic damage. Deals double damage if the target is Blinded. 3 Round Cooldown.
Lock-On	Mechanical		First use: Locks onto the target. Second use: Blasts the target, dealing Mechanical damage.
Magic Hat	Magic		Throws his hat at the enemy, dealing Magic damage.
Magma Wave	Elemental		Deals Elemental damage to the enemy's pets. Destroys objects created by both teams.
Mana Surge	Magic		Deals Magic damage. Damage increased during an Arcane Storm. 3 Round Ability. Mana Surge continues for 3 rounds. You cannot swap or perform any other actions until the surge has finished. 3 Round Cooldown.
Maul	Beast		Savagely mauls the enemy, dealing Beast damage. Deals double damage if the target is Bleeding. 3 Round Cooldown.
Metabolic Boost	Magic		Instantly deals Magic damage and increases your speed by 100% for 1 round.
Metal Fist	Mechanical		Punches the target, dealing Mechanical damage.
Meteor Strike	Magic		Launch up high, becoming unattackable for one turn. On the next turn, you impact, dealing Magic damage. 2 Round Ability. 4 Round Cooldown.
Minefield	Mechanical		Lays down a field of mines behind the opponent. The next pet to swap into the battle will receive Mechanical damage.
Missile	Mechanical		Launches a rocket at the target, dealing Mechanical damage.
Moonfire	Magic		Deals Magic damage and turns the weather into Moonlight for 9 turns. During Moonlight, all pets receive 25% additional healing and Magic abilities deal 10% additional damage. 3 Round Cooldown.
Moth Balls	Flying		Launches a barrage of smelly pheromones at the target, each dealing Flying damage and reducing the target's speed by 25% for 3 rounds. This ability has a high chance to miss. 1 Round Cooldown.
Moth Dust	Flying		Deals Flying damage and has a 25% chance to put the target to sleep for 1 round. This ability has a moderate chance to miss. 3 Round Cooldown.
Nature's Touch	Critter		Restores health to the user. 3 Round Cooldown.
Nature's Ward	Elemental		Restores health every round for 5 rounds. While healing, your pet is transformed into Elemental.

Name	Family		Description
Nether Blast	Magic		Blasts the enemy with a surge of arcane power, dealing Magic damage. Damage increases each time it hits, up to a maximum.
Nocturnal Strike	Flying		Deals Flying damage. This ability has a high chance to miss. Always hits if the target is blinded. 3 Round Cooldown.
Nut Barrage	Critter		Hurls nuts at the enemy dealing Critter damage. Nuts continue to fall on the enemy team dealing Critter damage each round for 4 rounds. 3 Round Cooldown.
Onyx Bite	Magic		Bites the enemy with Onyx teeth, dealing Magic damage.
Ooze Touch	Magic		Oozes onto the enemy, dealing Magic damage.
Overtune	Mechanical		Overtunes the user's central power core, dealing Mechanical damage and increasing the user's speed by 100% for 2 turns.
Peck	Flying		Pokes at the enemy with a sharp beak, dealing Flying damage.
Perk Up	Critter		Restores health and increases the maximum health of your team by 5 per level for 9 rounds. 3 Round Cooldown.
Photosynthesis	Elemental		Restores health every turn. Lasts 5 turns. Twice as effective in sunny weather. 5 Round Cooldown.
Plant	Elemental		Activate: Plant your roots into the ground, absorbing nutrients. While planted your pet cannot swap. Deactivate: For every round spent planted, you gain health.
Poison Fang	Beast		Instantly deals Beast damage and deals additional Elemental damage per round for 5 rounds.
Poison Lash	Elemental		Instantly deals Elemental damage and deals additional Elemental damage per round for 4 rounds.
Poison Spit	Beast		Instantly deals Beast damage and deals additional Elemental damage per round for 4 rounds.
Poisoned Branch	Elemental		Instantly deals Elemental damage and deals additional Elemental damage per round for 5 rounds.
Pounce	Beast		Pounces the enemy, dealing Beast damage plus additional Beast damage if the user strikes first.
Powerball	Critter		Roll at the enemy, dealing Critter damage and increasing your speed by 20%. Your speed continues to increase each time you use Powerball.
Predatory Strike	Flying		Deals Flying damage. If the target is below 25% health, they are instantly killed. 4 Round Cooldown.
Proto-Strike	Dragonkin		2 Round Ability. Fly up high, becoming unattackable for one turn. On the next turn, you attack, dealing Dragonking damage. 4 Round Cooldown.
Prowl	Beast		Reduces your speed by 30% and increases the damage of your next attack by 150%.
Pump	Aquatic		First use: Increases your damage dealt by 10%. Second use: Blasts the target with a surge of water, dealing Aquatic damage.
Punch	Humanoid		Bashes the enemy with your fists, dealing Humanoid damage.
Quake	Mechanical		3 Round Ability. Pounds the ground, dealing Mechanical damage to the enemy and half that damage to their backline pet. Quake continues for 3 rounds and can effect enemies underground. 3 Round Cooldown.
Quick Attack	Critter		Deals Critter damage. This ability always goes first.
Quills	Flying		Flings 1-2 Quills at the enemy, dealing Flying damage per hit. Hits an additional time if the user attacks first.
Rabid Strike	Undead		Deals Undead damage and turns the target rabid for 3 rounds. While rabid, the target deals 25% additional damage and receives 50% additional damage.
Railgun	Elemental		Burns the enemy with a blast of fire, dealing Elemental damage.

Name	Family	Description
Rake	Beast	Deals Beast damage and reduces the target's next attack by 50%.
Rampage	Beast	3 Round Ability. Goes on rampage, dealing Beast damage. Rampage continues for 3 rounds. 3 Round Cooldown.
Ravage	Beast	2 Round Ability. Deals Beast damage. If the user kills an enemy with Ravage, they restore health. Ravage continues for 2 rounds. 1 Round Cooldown.
Rebuild	Elemental	Rebuilds itself and any mechanical allies, restoring health. 3 Round Cooldown.
Reckless Strike	Flying	Deals Flying damage, but increases the damage you take for 1 turn by 25%.
Reflection	Humanoid	Your opponent's next ability misses you and you perform the attack instead.
Renewing Mists	Aquatic	Fills the area with a healing mist, causing your front pet to restore health every round. Lasts 5 rounds. Persists through pet swaps.
Repair	Mechanical	Enters repair mode, performing no actions for two turns, then repairing heavily. 3 Round Ability. 5 Round Cooldown.
Rip	Beast	Deals Beast damage and deals Beast damage per round for 4 rounds.
Roar	Beast	A fierce roar deals Beast damage and enrages the user, increasing the damage they deal by 25% for 3 rounds.
Rock Barrage	Elemental	Hurls rocks at the enemy, dealing Elemental damage. Rocks continue to fall on the enemy team dealing Elemental damage each round for 3 rounds.
Rush	Beast	Rushes the enemy, dealing Beast damage and causes the user to go first next turn.
Sandstorm	Flying	Deals Flying damage and turns the weather into a sandstorm. During a sandstorm all pets take less damage and their accuracy is reduced by 10%. 3 Round Cooldown.
Scorched Earth	Dragonkin	Scorches the ground, dealing Dragonkin damage to all active pets each round for 9 rounds. During Scorched Earth, all pets count as Burning. 3 Round Cooldown.
Scratch	Critter	Scratches the enemy, dealing Critter Damage.
Screech	Beast	Frightens the target, dealing Beast damage and reducing their speed by 25% for 4 rounds.
Shadow Shock	Undead	Shocks the target with dark energy, dealing Undead damage.
Shadow Slash	Undead	Slashes at the target with dark energy, dealing Undead damage.
Shadowflame	Dragonkin	Overwhelms the enemy with draconic breath, dealing Dragonkin damage.
Shell Shield	Beast	Reduces damage from each attack against you. Lasts 5 rounds.
Shock and Awe	Mechanical	Deals Mechanical damage and has a 25% chance to stun the target for 1 turn. 3 Round Cooldown.
Shriek	Dragonkin	Lets out a loud shriek, dealing Dragonkin damage and reducing the damage the target deals by 25% for 3 rounds.
Siphon Life	Undead	Deals Undead damage per round for 5 rounds. The user is healed for 100% of the damage dealt.
Skitter	Critter	Pokes the enemy, dealing Critter damage.
Sleeping Gas	Dragonkin	Deals Dragonkin damage and has a 25% chance to put the target to sleep for 1 round. Damage increases each time it hits.
Slicing Wind	Flying	Attacks the enemy with 1-3 blades of wind, dealing Flying damage per attack.

Name	Family	Description
Slippery Ice	Elemental	Shoots a jet of rapidly chilling ice, dealing Elemental damage and coats the ground near the enemy with ice. Frozen ground increases the chance they will slip and miss by 20%. Lasts 4 rounds. Persists through pet swaps.
Smash	Beast	Smash the enemy, dealing Beast damage.
Snap	Beast	Snaps at the enemy, dealing Beast damage.
Snap Trap	Mechanical	Places a snap trap onto the ground. Opponents have a chance to trigger the trap each time they attack. When the opponent triggers the trap, they will take Mechanical damage and be unable to attack for 1 round. 5 Round Cooldown.
Snowball	Elemental	Hits the enemy with a ball of snow, dealing Elemental damage.
Sons of the Flame	Elemental	Submerge, becoming unattackable for 2 rounds. During this time, the Sons of the Living Flame attack the opponent, dealing Elemental damage each turn. 8 Round Cooldown.
Soothe	Critter	Sings to the target, causing them to become drowsy. Drowsy targets will fall asleep at the end of next round unless hit. 4 Round Cooldown.
Soothing Mists	Elemental	Restores health to your active pet every round for 5 rounds. Persists through pet swaps.
Spark	Elemental	Fires a spark 1-2 times, dealing Elemental damage per hit. Attacks an additional time if the user attacks first.
Spectral Strike	Magic	Strikes at the enemy with the power of a spirit beast, causing Magic damage. This ability has a high chance to miss, but always hits if the target is blinded. 3 Round Cooldown.
Spiderling Swarm	Beast	Swarms the enemy with spiderlings, dealing Beast damage. Deals double damage if the target is Webbed. 2 Round Cooldown.
Spiked Skin	Dragonkin	Reduces damage from each attack against you and deals Dragonkin damage each time you are struck. Lasts 5 rounds.
Squawk	Flying	Lets out a loud squawk, dealing Flying damage and reducing the damage the target deals by 25% for 3 rounds. 2 Round Cooldown.
Staggered Steps	Humanoid	The user shrugs off attacks, reducing all damage taken by 50% for 2 turns. 4 Round Cooldown.
Stampede	Critter	Starts a stampede, causing Critter damage. Opponents struck by the stampede take double damage for 2 rounds. Stampede continues for 3 rounds. 3 Round Ability.
Starfall	Dragonkin	Deals Dragonkin damage to all enemy pets, restores health to all allies and turns the weather into Moonlight for 9 turns. During Moonlight, all pets receive 25% additional healing and Magic abilities deal 25% additional damage. 5 Round Cooldown.
Stench	Critter	Reduces the enemy team's accuracy by 25% for 3 turns. 5 Round Cooldown.
Sticky Goo	Elemental	Flings a sticky goo at the target, dealing Elemental damage and making it impossible to flee for 5 turns.
Sticky Grenade	Mechanical	Throws a sticky grenade at the target. After 3 turns, the grenade detonates, dealing Mechanical damage.
Sticky Web	Beast	Flings a sticky web at the target, dealing Beast damage and making it impossible to flee for 2 turns.
Sting	Beast	Deals Beast damage every round for 5 rounds.
Stone Rush	Elemental	Slams into the enemy, dealing Elemental damage and dealing Elemental damage to themselves.
Stoneskin	Magic	Reduces damage from each attack against you. Lasts 5 rounds.
Strike	Beast	Strikes at the enemy, dealing Beast damage.
Stun Seed	Elemental	Plants a seed in the enemy. After 3 rounds, the seed blooms, causing the enemy to take Elemental damage and be stunned for 1 round. 5 Round Cooldown.

Name	Family		Description
Sunlight	Elemental		A Solar Beam strikes all enemies, dealing Elemental damage and transforms the weather into a sunny day for 9 rounds. During a sunny day, the maximum health of all pets is increased and healing done is increased by 25%. 5 Round Cooldown.
Super Sticky Goo	Elemental		Flings a sticky goo at the target, dealing Elemental damage and making it impossible to flee for 2 turns.
Supercharge	Mechanical		Increases the damage of your next attack by 150%. 3 Round Cooldown.
Surge	Aquatic		Rushes to the enemy on a stream of water, dealing Aquatic damage. This move always goes first.
Surge of Power	Magic		Instantly deals Magic damage. The user must recharge for two turns afterwards. While recharging, you cannot perform any other actions. 3 Round Ability. 5 Round Cooldown.
Survival	Critter		You endure the next attack, preventing your health from being reduced below 1 health. 3 Round Cooldown.
Swarm	Critter		Starts a swarm, causing Critter damage. Opponents struck by the swarm take double damage for 2 rounds. Swarm continues for 3 rounds. 3 Round Ability.
Swarm of Flies	Critter		A swarm of flies attacks the enemy team, dealing Critter damage every round for 5 rounds. Persists through pet swaps.
Sweep	Magic		Sweeps the enemy off the battlefield. Ejected enemies cannot return for 2 rounds. 5 Round Cooldown.
Tail Slap	Aquatic		Slaps the enemy with its tail, dealing Aquatic damage. Has an above average chance to miss.
Tail Sweep	Dragonkin		Deals Dragonkin damage. Deals additional damage if the user goes last.
Takedown	Humanoid		Takes down an enemy, dealing Humanoid damage. Deals double damage if the target is Stunned. 3 Round Cooldown.
Thorns	Elemental		Deals Elemental damage each time you are struck. Lasts 5 rounds.
Thrash	Beast		Wildly flails at the enemy 1-2 times, dealing Beast damage per hit. Attacks an additional time if the user attacks first.
Tidal Wave	Aquatic		Deals Aquatic damage to the enemy's pets. Destroys objects created by both teams.
Tongue Lash	Critter		Licks the enemy 1-2 times, dealing Critter damage per hit. Hits an additional time if the user attacks first.
Toxic Smoke	Mechanical		Covers the enemy team in toxic smoke, dealing Mechanical damage every turn for 4 turns. Persists through pet swaps.
Trample	Beast		Tramples the target, dealing Beast damage plus an additional 10% of the target's health.
Tranquility	Critter		Fills the area with peace, causing your active pet to restore health every turn. Lasts 4 rounds. Persists through pet swaps.
Triple Snap	Beast		Wildly flails at the enemy 1-3 times, dealing Beast damage per hit.
Trumpet Strike	Beast		Enrages the user, causing them to attack, dealing Beast damage and increasing the damage they deal by 25% for 3 rounds.
Tympanic Tantrum	Mechanical		3 Round Ability. Pounds the ground, dealing Mechanical damage to the enemy and half that damage to their backline pets. Tantrum continues for 3 rounds and can affect enemies underground. 3 Round Cooldown.
Uncanny Luck	Critter		Increases your team's accuracy by 50% and critical strike chance by 25% for 4 rounds. Persists through pet swaps.
Unholy Ascension	Undead		Sacrifices your remaining life to haunt the enemy team, increasing all damage they take by 50% for 9 turns.
Vicious Fang	Beast		Deals Beast damage. Damage increases each time it hits until it reaches a maximum damage. If the target is poisoned, it always deals maximum damage.

Name	Family		Description
Water Jet	Aquatic		Blasts the enemy with a spray of water, dealing Aquatic damage.
Weakening Blow	Elemental		Unleashes a restrained attack, dealing Elemental damage. This attack cannot reduce the opponent's health below 1.
Weakness	Magic		Deals Magic damage and reduces the target's speed by 50% and damage done by 50% for 1 round. 1 Round Cooldown.
Whirlpool	Aquatic		Causes a whirlpool to form under the enemy team. In two turns, the opponent's pet will take Aquatic damage and be rooted for 2 turns. 3 Round Cooldown.
Whirlwind	Humanoid		Whirls around wildly, dealing Humanoid damage to the enemy team. 3 Round Cooldown.
Wild Magic	Magic		Adds damage to every attack against the target. Lasts 5 turns.
Wild Winds	Flying		A sharp wind gust deals Flying damage and the enemy team takes Flying damage every turn for 4 rounds. Persists through pet swaps.
Wind-Up	Mechanical		First use: Increases your damage dealt by 10%. Second use: Unleashes a flurry of attacks, dealing Mechanical damage.
Wish	Magic		Next turn, your active pet will be healed by 50%. 5 Round Cooldown.
Woodchipper	Beast		Instantly deals Beast damage and deals additional damage per round for 5 rounds.
XE-321 Boombot	Mechanical		Creates a Boombot who detonates after 3 turns, dealing Mechanical damage.
Zap	Mechanical		Launches an electrical bolt at the target, dealing Mechanical damage.
Zergling Rush	Magic		3 Round Ability. Starts a Zergling Rush, causing Magic damage. Opponents struck by the rush take double damage for 2 rounds. Zergling Rush continues for 3 rounds.

WORLD DUNGEONS

With a new land to explore there are also new dungeons to conquer! The Mists of Pandaria expansion has six new dungeons and two classic dungeons revisited and made into level 90 heroic versions. Many dungeons can now be visited in quest lines for solo adventurers and are on a 1 to 1 scale when you step into the instance from the outside world, making them an even more integral part of your journey.

DUNGEON JOURNAL

The Dungeon Journal holds a wealth of information about the bosses found in every dungeon in World of Warcraft, and raid bosses post-Cataclysm. To open the Dungeon Journal, either click on the icon in the interface bar or press Shift and the letter "j" (clicking on a boss icon on a dungeon's map also opens the Dungeon Journal).

Click on the icon for the dungeon or raid you want to learn about to bring up a bit of lore and a list of bosses. Click on a boss to see a listing of abilities or loot. Clicking on an ability brings up additional information about it, and the icons listed on the ability provide additional information.

ICONS IN THE DUNGEON JOURNAL

	Heroic Ability Only
	Enrage
	Deadly
	Important
	Magic Effect
	Poison Debuff
	Curse Debuff
	Disease Debuff
	Damage Dealer Alert
	Healer Alert
	Tank Alert
	Interruptable Ability

DUNGEON FINDER TOOL

The Dungeon Finder has undergone changes since it was first introduced. When you click the Dungeon Finder icon (or press the letter "i"), it brings up more than just the option to queue for dungeons. Now all the Dungeons, Raids, and Scenarios appropriate to your current level in the game are at your fingertips. Use the tabs on the left to select from Dungeons, Scenarios, and Raids.

First, select the role or roles (Tank, Healer, Damage) you're comfortable playing when part of a group. If you pick more than one, note which role you're assigned to when you enter the dungeon as you may be required to change your spec. Additionally, you can check the fourth box, the green flag, to indicate that you are experienced with the dungeon or dungeons you're preparing to venture into. Don't select this unless you're able to offer sound advice and battle plans.

The drop down menu 'Type:' allows you to choose whether you want to run a specific dungeon or if you prefer a random dungeon. If you have a specific dungeon in mind, check the one you want from the full list. If you prefer random dungeons, select which category of dungeons you want and click Find Group. The Dungeon Finder offers only the dungeons where you meet the minimum requirements (whether that's appropriate level, equipment, or prerequisites), so don't worry about stumbling into a dungeon too powerful for you.

While it might be tempting to run only the dungeons you're familiar with or which you want loot from, there are many advantages in choosing a random dungeon. After picking a random category, the tool displays the additional rewards heaped upon players who take the plunge and allow the server to choose. Rewards are level dependent and include bonus items, gold, experience points, Valor Points, or Justice Points. The other benefit from choosing a random dungeon with less than a full party is that you're likely to find a group much quicker.

One of the best features of the Dungeon Finder is that you don't need to travel to and from the dungeons, a definite benefit for The Stockades and Ragefire Chasm! When you use the Dungeon Finder, your group is teleported to the dungeon's entrance. When you decide to leave the dungeon you are returned to where you were when you jumped to the dungeon, unless you use your Hearthstone or a Mage's portal, or accept a Warlock's summon.

New Dungeons for Mists of Pandaria

TEMPLE OF THE JADE SERPENT (LEVELS 85-90)

The Temple of the Jade Serpent has been corrupted by the Sha of Doubt. The guardians of this temple are being controlled by the Sha and must be defeated before they cause any more harm. It is up to the players to find the source of this corruption and stop it at any cost.

STORMSTOUT BREWERY (LEVELS 85-90)

Chen Stormstout is trying to reclaim his family's home but the Hozen are having one crazy party inside! Clear the Virmen and Hozen from Chen's family home and discover what has caused the ale to become a new form of elemental. Succeed or the entire land will be without beer for the foreseeable future!

MOGU'SHAN PALACE (LEVELS 87-90)

Players encounter three great clans of Mogu here and have to face the Saurok underneath the palace proper. It is said that Xin the Weaponmaster is here for those brave enough, or foolish enough, to face him in his throne room. If he is not defeated it could spell doom for all of Pandaria.

SHADO-PAN MONASTERY (LEVELS 87-90)

Because of the war between the Horde and Alliance, the Sha of Anger, Hatred, and Violence have escaped their prisons within the once serene Shado-Pan Monastery. Even though the Sha of Anger fled, the other two Sha are devastating the Shado-Pan ranks and corrupting the monks inside. Help the Masters of this Monastery restore order before it is too late.

SIEGE OF NIUZAO TEMPLE (LEVEL 90 - HEROIC ONLY)

The Mantids have seized one of the two islands fortified by the Pandarens and are sending massive waves of troops into the Temple grounds. Travel through the root system the Mantids grew and bring relief to the few remaining Pandaren guardians trying to hold back the tide!

GATE OF THE SETTING SUN (LEVEL 90 - HEROIC ONLY)

The Serpent's Spine is a massive wall built to hold back the Mantid and keep the rest of Pandaria safe from the warlike insects. While the Mantid always attacked in fairly predictable cycles, this time they attacked early and the Pandarens need your help to keep them from completely overwhelming the defenders and destroying the Serpent's Spine's gates.

Revised Dungeons for Mists of Pandaria

RAGEFIRE CHASM (LEVELS 15-21)

Ragefire Chasm has undergone a change, but it did not get a heroic upgrade. Rumors of a Dark Shaman trying to harness the power of the elementals found under Orgrimmar have prompted calls for an investigation.

SCARLET HALLS & SCARLET MONASTERY (HEROIC: LEVEL 90)

The Scarlet Crusade is building an army to lay waste to the unliving inside the Scarlet Halls, while their fanatical leaders plot inside the Scarlet Cathedral to destroy any who seek to stop them. Put an end to their "righteous cause" before their hatred inflicts any more suffering. In these two re-envisioned dungeons, Scarlet Halls now consists of the former Library and Armory, and the Scarlet Monastery is made up of the former Graveyard and Cathedral.

SCHOLOMANCE (HEROIC: LEVEL 90)

Beneath the crypts of Caer Darrow, Darkmaster Gandling has mastered even more of the dark arts of Necromancy. Many changes have come over the new students as well as the old Instructors. The abominations that await you within are not for the faint of heart!

RAIDS

A few new features have also been added to raids, like a panel for loot rolls and a new way of receiving loot in Looking For Raid. No more scrolling through your chat window to see what everyone rolled for gear!

RAID FINDER

The Raid Finder functions much the same way as the Dungeon Finder. It automatically matches you with other players looking to take on a specific or random raid. The main differences here are the same as the differences between dungeons and raids. Raids are bigger, have more players and more rewards. The random raid rewards are quite a bit meatier than the dungeon rewards for this reason. Another update for raids is that the Loot system is now significantly changed.

Personal Loot System

Another exciting new feature is the Personal Loot System, which is only available while Looking For Raid. When a boss is killed in a raid you have joined through LFR, the game rolls for everyone. If you get a piece of loot from this boss' loot table roll, it will be class and spec appropriate for your character. No more useless loot!

For example, three Paladins are in a raid and each of them wants an awesome helm that drops from a certain boss. Each Paladin has an equal chance of getting the item. The raid kills the boss and the game rolls for everyone separately. Each roll is independent so it is possible for all Paladins to receive the helm or another piece of class and spec specific loot. Each Paladin (and everyone else in the raid of course) has the same chance to get a piece of loot, regardless of what other players in the raid do or do not win.

This system helps alleviate the problems associated with LFR. Now everyone can simply down bosses and have a good shot of receiving loot after each kill. If you don't get loot from that certain boss, it will just be from the randomness of the rolls and not an issue with someone leading a pick-up group being less than fair. Last, but not least by any means, there are Bonus Tokens you can acquire that allow you to add a bonus to rolls on loot if you must have an item from a specific boss. When it is time to loot, a window pops up asking if you want to use your Bonus Tokens. If you do so, it increases your chances to get an item but does not guarantee it.

Raids

The new raids consist of battling spirits of long dead Mogu, the Mantid Empress, and even the Sha of Fear! The continent of Pandaria also includes new world encounters.

MOGU'SHAN VAULTS

Battle your way through ancient guardians and enormous vaults to help Lorewalker Cho uncover lost lore of the old Mogu'shan Emperors. Be wary, as ghosts and ancient guardians aren't all you face here. The Zandalari Trolls also wish to uncover the hidden relics within the Mogu'shan Vaults and will stop at nothing to destroy you before you get too far inside. Do you dare face the horrors that lie in wait in the deepest reaches of these sacred vaults?

HEART OF FEAR

The Grand Empress of the Mantid has been corrupted by the Sha of Fear. The Klaxxi, whose sole purpose is to preserve the Mantid culture, has been driven to desperation and seek outside help to purge the Sha of Fear from their beloved Empress by any means necessary. Players must overcome all the great Mantid Lords as they battle their way through the Mantid palace to the throne room of the Grand Empress herself!

TERRACE OF ENDLESS SPRING

This sacred terrace has been a refuge for all who sought peace and understanding throughout Pandaria. Its fountains are said to heal any who drink from its waters. That all changed when the Sha of Fear attacked and turned its guardians against each other or drove them mad with despair. You must overcome all the Sha's protectors before you face the Sha of Fear itself, which is trying to devour the pure light radiating from the center of the Terrace of Endless Spring!

SCENARIOS

Scenarios are a new form of adventuring that can be done much more quickly than a dungeon. In order to enter a Scenario, look under the Dungeon Finder tab and queue as you normally would for a dungeon.

Instead of selecting roles and settling down for a long dungeon with a full party, scenarios allow 2-3 players to engage in an instanced, short adventure. These scenarios are shorter and easier than dungeons, but longer and more difficult than a quest. For this reason, you don't need to select a role. Just be yourself and seek your rewards.

With better rewards and no waiting for monsters to reappear like in the normal world, Scenarios offer a chance for fast, rewarding fun.

CHALLENGE MODE

Another new feature introduced in Mists of Pandaria is Challenges. You can queue for Challenge Mode in the Dungeon Finder tab. These challenges allow a party to test their mettle in dungeons they believe they've mastered. Every player's gear is standardized, making these dungeons harder than Heroics! Players are required to run through the instance as quickly as they can to earn either a bronze, silver, or gold medal. Your group's skill is the only thing that matters here, so only the best have a chance at the gold! No loot is dropped from any enemies you fight in Challenge Mode.

At the end of a challenge, your party's time determines the medal awarded and the amount of bonus points awarded for this feat. Hustle and battle for not only better rewards, but also for the feeling that comes with showing everyone in your guild your record-breaking time.

Challenge Mode is available for most heroic dungeons. Once everyone is inside the dungeon and ready, you start the timer and begin. The game tracks your best times as well as your guild's best times. These Challenge Dungeons reward you with prestige, cosmetic rewards, and Valor Points!

The rewards you earn from Challenge Mode are special titles, mounts, and specially designed gear. This gear has a unique look, but no stats, and can be transmogrified to your existing gear. This armor is the highest tier reward and shows everyone that sees you that you have mastered all the dungeons.

Legend

- ● Alliance Area
- ● Horde Area
- ● Neutral Area
- ☠ World Dungeon Entrance

ISLE OF RECKONING

20 ZOUCHIN VILLAGE

19

PEAK OF SERENITY

SHADO-PAN MONASTERY

28

18

MOGU'SHAN TERRACE

27 16 15 17

25 TEMPLE OF THE WHITE TIGER

WINTER'S BLOSSOM

23

24

12 10 9

THE YAUNGOL ADVANCE

11 7

13 8

KOTA BASECAMP

14

5 WESTWIND REST

22 2

TOWNLONG STEPPES

3 4 BINAN VILLAGE 6

29

21

26 1

SHADO-PAN FALLBACK

THE CONTINENT OF
PANDARIA

The following pages include the maps for the regions of Pandaria in alphabetical order. Each region includes

DREAD WASTES

The east border of Dread Wastes is blocked from the rest of Pandaria unless you fly over the wall or swim around it, the north connects to Townlong Steppes, and the rest is surrounded by water. The Heart of Fear raid is located west of the central hub of Klaxxi'vess. Complete daily quests for the Klaxxi to improve your reputation with them.

REPUTATION INFORMATION
The Anglers, The Klaxxi

RESOURCE LEGEND

FISHING

FISH - FRESHWATER
Flying Tiger Gourami (rare)
Redbelly Mandarin

FISH - OCEAN
Giant Mantis Shrimp
Mimic Octopus (rare)
Reef Octopus

FISH - SHA-TOUCHED WATER
Spinefish
Spinefish Alpha (rare)

MINING

METAL	MIN SKILL
Ghost Iron Deposit	500
Rich Ghost Iron Deposit	550
Kyparite Deposit	550
Rich Kyparite Deposit	575
Trillium Vein	600
Rich Trillium Vein	600

HERBALISM

HERB	MIN SKILL
Green Tea Leaf	500
Golden Lotus	550
Sha-Touched Herb	575
Fool's Cap	600

QUESTING IN DREAD WASTES

After defeating the Sha of Hatred, Taoshi gives you a quest to meet up with Bowmistress Li at Serpent's Spine. Fly up to the wall to find her and she gives you a couple quests that take you down into Terrace of Gurthan. You can enter from Townlong Steppes and start questing at The Sunset Brewgarden

DREAD WASTES LEGEND

(1) TERRACE OF GURTHAN
Kil'ruk the Wind-Reaver (Quest Giver)
Klaxxi'va Tik (Quest Giver)
Marksman Lann (Quest Giver)

(2) KLAXXI'VESS
Ambersmith Zikk (Quest Giver) <Klaxxi Quartermaster>
Handler Kla'vik <Stable Master>
Hisek the Swarmkeeper (Quest Giver) (Daily Quest Giver)
Iyyokuk the Lucid
Ka'roz the Locust
Kaz'tik the Manipulator (Daily Quest Giver)
Kik'tik <Flight Master>
Kil'ruk the Wind-Reaver (Quest Giver) (Daily Quest Giver)
Klaxxi'va Ik
Klaxxi'va Kek
Klaxxi'va Krik
Klaxxi'va Set
Klaxxi'va Sra
Klaxxi'va Vor
Klaxxi'va Zan
Kor'ik (Quest Giver)
Korven the Prime (Daily Quest Giver)
Malik the Unscathed (Quest Giver)
Poisoncrafter Kil'zit <Alchemy Trainer>
Rik'kal the Dissector (Daily Quest Giver)
Skeer the Bloodseeker
Xaril the Poisoned Mind
Zer'ik
Zit'tix <Innkeeper>

(3) THE CLUTCHES OF SHEK'ZEER
Sha-Haunted Crystal (Quest Giver)

(4) AMBERGLOW HOLLOW
Kor'ik (Quest Giver)
Zer'ik (Quest Giver)

(5) THE BRINY MUCK
Infiltrator Ik'thal <Flight Master>
Kaz'tik the Manipulator (Quest Giver)

(6) SOGGY'S GAMBLE
Captain "Soggy" Su-Dao (Quest Giver)
Deck Boss Arie (Quest Giver)
Master Angler Ju Lien
Min the Breeze Rider <Flight Master>
Rough-rider Kim <Stable Master>
San the Sea Calmer <Innkeeper>

(7) LAKE OF STARS
Korven the Prime (Quest Giver)

(8) KYPARI ZAR
Korven the Prime (Quest Giver)

(9) THE SUNSET BREWGARDEN
Big Dan Stormstout
Chen Stormstout (Quest Giver)
Cook Jun <Food & Drink>
Defender Azzo (Quest Giver)
Han Stormstout
Jin the Flying Keg <Flight Master>
Lien the Maintainer <Supplies>
Lya of Ten Songs (Quest Giver)
Olon (Quest Giver)
Sapmaster Vu (Quest Giver)
Thirsty Missho (Quest Giver)

(10) THE AMBER VAULT
Scroll of Auspice (Quest Giver)

(11) THE HORRID MARCH
Chen Stormstout (Quest Giver)

(12) RIKKITUN VILLAGE
Boggeo (Quest Giver)
Chief Rikkitun (Quest Giver)
Lya of Ten Songs (Quest Giver)
Olon (Quest Giver)
Sapmaster Vu (Quest Giver)

(13) VENOMOUS LEDGE
Xaril the Poisoned Mind (Quest Giver)

(14) MURKSCALE GROTTO
Skeer the Bloodseeker (Quest Giver)

(15) AMBER QUARRY
Rik'kal the Dissector (Daily Quest Giver) (Quest Giver)

THE JADE FOREST (ALLIANCE)

The Jade Forest is your introduction to the Pandarian island. It is connected to Valley of the Four Winds, Vale of Eternal Blossoms, Krasarang Wilds, and Kun-Lai Summit on the west and otherwise surrounded by water. As the name suggests, it is mostly made up of thick forest. The first Pandaren dungeon, Temple of the Jade Serpent, can be found on the east coast. Horde begin their questing at the far north at The Wreck of the Sky Shark and Alliance begin at Wayward Landing to the far south.

REPUTATION INFORMATION
Order of the Cloud Serpent, Pearlfin Jinyu, The Anglers

RESOURCE LEGEND

FISHING

FISH - FRESHWATER

Emperor Salmon
Flying Tiger Gourami (rare)
Jade Lungfish
Krasarang Paddlefish
Redbelly Mandarin
Golden Carp

FISH - OCEAN

Giant Mantis Shrimp
Mimic Octopus (rare)
Reef Octopus
Golden Carp

MINING

METAL	MIN SKILL
Ghost Iron Deposit	500
Rich Ghost Iron Deposit	550

HERBALISM

HERB	MIN SKILL
Green Tea Leaf	500
Rain Poppy	525
Golden Lotus	550

QUESTING IN THE JADE FOREST

As an Alliance character, visit Stormwind Keep and talk to Rell Nightwind to start "The Mission." Meet Admiral Rogers on The Skyfire and tell her you are ready to head for Pandaria.

As a Horde character, speak to General Nazgrim in Orgrimmar and then meet him on Hellscream's Fist above Bladefist Bay. Talking to him again takes you to The Jade Forest.

THE JADE FOREST LEGEND (ALLIANCE)

1 THE SKYFIRE
Captain Day
Captain Kerwin
Corporal Rasmussen
Mishka <SI:7>
Sky Admiral Rogers (Quest Giver)
Sky Mage Harlan

2 GARROSH'AR POINT
Alliance Battlemage
Rell Nightwind (Quest Giver) <SI:7>
Sully "The Pickle" McLeary (Quest Giver) <SI:7>
Taran Zhu <Lord of the Shado-Pan>

3 PAW'DON VILLAGE
Brewmaid Qi
Bucci
Burma Risingblossom
Cheung <Stable Master>
Chut Sri Nu
Craftsman Hui <Trader>
Cui Applebloom <Mistress of Cider>
Elder Daelo
Elder Yoon Su
Hao of the Stag's Horns <Skinning Trainer>
Jaan Yu
Jadori Ironeye <Toolsmith>
Jiayi Applebloom <Innkeeper>
Jor Jor
Ju Applebloom
Kheila Fallingwater
Lieutenant Daniel
Lieutenant Stanton

Matthew Owens <Alliance Mage>
Mishka (Quest Giver) <SI:7>
Nimm Codejack <SI:7>
Orchard Keeper Li Mei <Herbalism Trainer>
Rell Nightwind (Quest Giver) <SI:7>
Rockseeker Guo <Mining Trainer>
Scrollkeeper Mushu
Seer Yong (Quest Giver)
Serenity <Brews>
Sikki
Sky Admiral Rogers (Quest Giver)
Soraka
Sunke Khang (Quest Giver) <Mayor>
Taran Zhu <Lord of the Shado-Pan>
Tender Long
Teng Applebloom (Quest Giver) <Brewer>
Toud Duskgale
Trader Jina <General Goods>
Watcher Jo Lin
Wing Kyo <Flight Master>

4 PAW'DON GLADE
Lin Applebloom (Quest Giver) <Brewer>
Teng Applebloom <Brewer>

5 TWINSPIRE KEEP
Rell Nightwind (Quest Giver) <SI:7>
Sully "The Pickle" McLeary (Quest Giver <SI:7>
Taran Zhu <Lord of the Shado-Pan>

6 WRECK OF THE VANGUARD
Nodd Codejack (Quest Giver) <SI:7>

7 SLINGTAIL PITS

Admiral Taylor
Bold Karasshi (Quest Giver)

8 PEARLFIN VILLAGE
Admiral Taylor (Quest Giver)
Amber Kearnen (Quest Giver) <SI:7>
Beastslayer Insshu
Bold Karasshi (Quest Giver)
Bubblemaker Ashji <Pet Vendor>
Cheerful Jessu <Innkeeper>
Eel-Charmer Shaoshu <Food Vendor>
Elder Lusshan (Quest Giver) <Waterspeaker>
Instructor Sharpfin
Little Lu (Quest Giver)
Lorewalker Cho (Quest Giver)
Metalworker Sashi <Trade Goods>
Mishka (Quest Giver) <SI:7>
Ot-Temmdo <Watersmith>
Pearldiver Su-Su <Rare Gems>
Pearlkeeper Fujin (Quest Giver)
Rell Nightwind (Quest Giver) <SI:7>
Silkweaver Rui <Adventuring Supplies>
Steepmaster Puoba <Drink>
Sully "The Pickle" McLeary (Quest Giver) <SI:7>
Ut-Nam <Kite Master>

9 DREAMER'S PAVILLION
Lorewalker Cho (Quest Giver)

10 DEN OF SORROW
Anduin Wrynn (Quest Giver) <Prince of Stormwind>
Lina Whitepaw (Quest Giver)
Ren Whitepaw (Quest Giver)

THE JADE FOREST (HORDE/NEUTRAL)

REPUTATION INFORMATION
Forest Hozen, Order of the Cloud Serpent, The Anglers

THE JADE FOREST LEGEND (HORDE/NEUTRAL)

11 HELLSCREAM'S FIST
General Nazgrim (Quest Giver)
Kor'kron Dubs
Kor'kron Jo'mag
Kor'kron Spisak
Rivett Clutchpop (Quest Giver)
Sergeant Gorrok
Shikyo
Sky Marshal Schwind
Sky Master Corpora
Warbringer Ho'Gan

12 HONEYDEW GLADE
Ellie Honeypaw
General Nazgrim (Quest Giver)
Gi-Oh (Quest Giver)
Kai-Lin Honeydew (Quest Giver)
Sue-Ji the Tender (Quest Giver)

13 THUNDER HOLD
General Nazgrim (Quest Giver)
Taran Zhu (Quest Giver)

14 HONEYDEW VILLAGE
Aimee Morningbreeze
Brewmother Kiki <Innkeeper>
Cook Tsu (Quest Giver)
Elder Honeypaw <Trade Goods>
Elder Muur
Ellie Honeypaw
Ethan Graveborn <Horde Mage>
Fieldwatcher Mao
Grower Miao <Herbalism Trainer>
Herim Woo <General Goods>
Kan the Spiritful
Kofa the Swift <Repair> <Fletcher>
Lo Don
Lu Jon Sun

Mayor Honeydew
Mitsua
Pio
Puya
Sergeant Gorrok (Quest Giver)
Siat Honeydew
Sona Morningbreeze
Stonebreaker Ruian <Mining Trainer>
Su Mi <Stable Master>
Taran Zhu <Lord of the Shado-Pan>
Tau Be
Trapper Ri <Skinning Trainer>
Wing Hya <Flight Master>

15 ASCENT OF SWIRLING WINDS
Ancient Statue (Quest Giver)
Zin'Jun (Quest Giver)

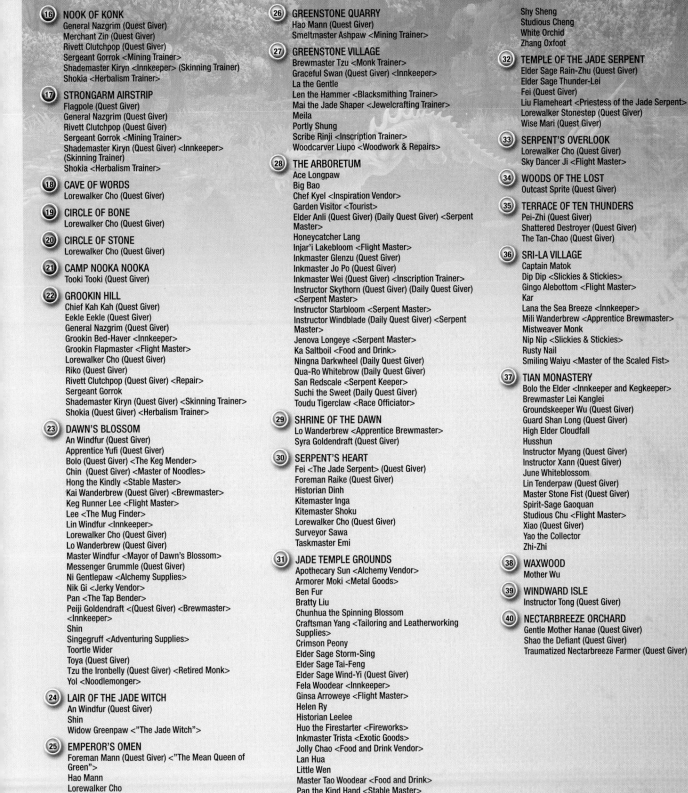

(16) NOOK OF KONK
General Nazgrim (Quest Giver)
Merchant Zin (Quest Giver)
Rivett Clutchpop (Quest Giver)
Sergeant Gorrok <Mining Trainer>
Shademaster Kiryn <Innkeeper> (Skinning Trainer)
Shokia <Herbalism Trainer>

(17) STRONGARM AIRSTRIP
Flagpole (Quest Giver)
General Nazgrim (Quest Giver)
Rivett Clutchpop (Quest Giver)
Sergeant Gorrok <Mining Trainer>
Shademaster Kiryn (Quest Giver) <Innkeeper>
(Skinning Trainer)
Shokia <Herbalism Trainer>

(18) CAVE OF WORDS
Lorewalker Cho (Quest Giver)

(19) CIRCLE OF BONE
Lorewalker Cho (Quest Giver)

(20) CIRCLE OF STONE
Lorewalker Cho (Quest Giver)

(21) CAMP NOOKA NOOKA
Tooki Tooki (Quest Giver)

(22) GROOKIN HILL
Chief Kah Kah (Quest Giver)
Eekle Eekle (Quest Giver)
General Nazgrim (Quest Giver)
Grookin Bed-Haver <Innkeeper>
Grookin Flapmaster <Flight Master>
Lorewalker Cho (Quest Giver)
Riko (Quest Giver)
Rivett Clutchpop (Quest Giver) <Repair>
Sergeant Gorrok
Shademaster Kiryn (Quest Giver) <Skinning Trainer>
Shokia (Quest Giver) <Herbalism Trainer>

(23) DAWN'S BLOSSOM
An Windfur (Quest Giver)
Apprentice Yufi (Quest Giver)
Bolo (Quest Giver) <The Keg Mender>
Chin (Quest Giver) <Master of Noodles>
Hong the Kindly <Stable Master>
Kai Wanderbrew (Quest Giver) <Brewmaster>
Keg Runner Lee <Flight Master>
Lee <The Mug Finder>
Lin Windfur <Innkeeper>
Lorewalker Cho (Quest Giver)
Lo Wanderbrew (Quest Giver)
Master Windfur <Mayor of Dawn's Blossom>
Messenger Grumble (Quest Giver)
Ni Gentlepaw <Alchemy Supplies>
Nik Gi <Jerky Vendor>
Pan <The Tap Bender>
Peiji Goldendraft <(Quest Giver) <Brewmaster>
<Innkeeper>
Shin
Singegruff <Adventuring Supplies>
Toortle Wider
Toya (Quest Giver)
Tzu the Ironbelly (Quest Giver) <Retired Monk>
Yol <Noodlemonger>

(24) LAIR OF THE JADE WITCH
An Windfur (Quest Giver)
Shin
Widow Greenpaw <"The Jade Witch">

(25) EMPEROR'S OMEN
Foreman Mann (Quest Giver) <"The Mean Queen of Green">
Hao Mann
Lorewalker Cho
Supplier Towsa <Flight Master>

(26) GREENSTONE QUARRY
Hao Mann (Quest Giver)
Smeltmaster Ashpaw <Mining Trainer>

(27) GREENSTONE VILLAGE
Brewmaster Tzu <Monk Trainer>
Graceful Swan (Quest Giver) <Innkeeper>
La the Gentle
Len the Hammer <Blacksmithing Trainer>
Mai the Jade Shaper <Jewelcrafting Trainer>
Meila
Portly Shung
Scribe Rinji <Inscription Trainer>
Woodcarver Liupo <Woodwork & Repairs>

(28) THE ARBORETUM
Ace Longpaw
Big Bao
Chef Kyel <Inspiration Vendor>
Garden Visitor <Tourist>
Elder Anli (Quest Giver) (Daily Quest Giver) <Serpent Master>
Honeycatcher Lang
Injar'i Lakebloom <Flight Master>
Inkmaster Glenzu (Quest Giver)
Inkmaster Jo Po (Quest Giver)
Inkmaster Wei (Quest Giver) <Inscription Trainer>
Instructor Skythorn (Quest Giver) (Daily Quest Giver) <Serpent Master>
Instructor Starbloom <Serpent Master>
Instructor Windblade (Daily Quest Giver) <Serpent Master>
Jenova Longeye <Serpent Master>
Ka Saltboil <Food and Drink>
Ningna Darkwheel (Daily Quest Giver)
Qua-Ro Whitebrow (Daily Quest Giver)
San Redscale <Serpent Keeper>
Suchi the Sweet (Daily Quest Giver)
Toudu Tigerclaw <Race Officiator>

(29) SHRINE OF THE DAWN
Lo Wanderbrew <Apprentice Brewmaster>
Syra Goldendraft (Quest Giver)

(30) SERPENT'S HEART
Fei <The Jade Serpent> (Quest Giver)
Foreman Raike (Quest Giver)
Historian Dinh
Kitemaster Inga
Kitemaster Shoku
Lorewalker Cho (Quest Giver)
Surveyor Sawa
Taskmaster Emi

(31) JADE TEMPLE GROUNDS
Apothecary Sun <Alchemy Vendor>
Armorer Moki <Metal Goods>
Ben Fur
Bratty Liu
Chunhua the Spinning Blossom
Craftsman Yang <Tailoring and Leatherworking Supplies>
Crimson Peony
Elder Sage Storm-Sing
Elder Sage Tai-Feng
Elder Sage Wind-Yi (Quest Giver)
Fela Woodear <Innkeeper>
Ginsa Arroweye <Flight Master>
Helen Ry
Historian Leelee
Huo the Firestarter <Fireworks>
Inkmaster Trista <Exotic Goods>
Jolly Chao <Food and Drink Vendor>
Lan Hua
Little Wen
Master Tao Woodear <Food and Drink>
Pan the Kind Hand <Stable Master>

Shy Sheng
Studious Cheng
White Orchid
Zhang Oxfoot

(32) TEMPLE OF THE JADE SERPENT
Elder Sage Rain-Zhu (Quest Giver)
Elder Sage Thunder-Lei
Fei (Quest Giver)
Liu Flameheart <Priestess of the Jade Serpent>
Lorewalker Stonestep (Quest Giver)
Wise Mari (Quest Giver)

(33) SERPENT'S OVERLOOK
Lorewalker Cho (Quest Giver)
Sky Dancer Ji <Flight Master>

(34) WOODS OF THE LOST
Outcast Sprite (Quest Giver)

(35) TERRACE OF TEN THUNDERS
Pei-Zhi (Quest Giver)
Shattered Destroyer (Quest Giver)
The Tan-Chao (Quest Giver)

(36) SRI-LA VILLAGE
Captain Matok
Dip Dip <Slickies & Stickies>
Gingo Alebottom <Flight Master>
Kar
Lana the Sea Breeze <Innkeeper>
Mili Wanderbrew <Apprentice Brewmaster>
Mistweaver Monk
Nip Nip <Slickies & Stickies>
Rusty Nail
Smiling Waiyu <Master of the Scaled Fist>

(37) TIAN MONASTERY
Bolo the Elder <Innkeeper and Kegkeeper>
Brewmaster Lei Kanglei
Groundskeeper Wu (Quest Giver)
Guard Shan Long (Quest Giver)
High Elder Cloudfall
Husshun
Instructor Myang (Quest Giver)
Instructor Xann (Quest Giver)
June Whiteblossom
Lin Tenderpaw (Quest Giver)
Master Stone Fist (Quest Giver)
Spirit-Sage Gaoquan
Studious Chu <Flight Master>
Xiao (Quest Giver)
Yao the Collector
Zhi-Zhi

(38) WAXWOOD
Mother Wu

(39) WINDWARD ISLE
Instructor Tong (Quest Giver)

(40) NECTARBREEZE ORCHARD
Gentle Mother Hanae (Quest Giver)
Shao the Defiant (Quest Giver)
Traumatized Nectarbreeze Farmer (Quest Giver)

KRASARANG WILDS

Located south of Valley of the Four Winds, Krasarang Wilds is made up of a dense jungle surrounded by water to the south and east. Rivers runs through the middle—giving you some good fishing opportunities. You can enter the area near Nesingwary's Safari in the west or across the Thunderfoot Fields bridge to the east; otherwise it is a big drop off the cliff from the farmland above. This drop can be navigated easily with an appropriate skill or by using a rappelling rope located south of Silken Fields. Anglers Wharf on the far south side gives you some nice daily quests if you are into the Fishing profession.

REPUTATION INFORMATION
The Anglers

RESOURCE LEGEND

FISHING

FISH - FRESHWATER
Emperor Salmon
Flying Tiger Gourami (rare)
Jade Lungfish
Jewel Danio
Krasarang Paddlefish
Redbelly Mandarin
Tiger Gourami
Golden Carp

FISH - OCEAN
Giant Mantis Shrimp
Mimic Octopus (rare)
Reef Octopus
Golden Carp

MINING

METAL	MIN SKILL
Ghost Iron Deposit	500
Rich Ghost Iron Deposit	550

HERBALISM

HERB	MIN SKILL
Green Tea Leaf	500
Rain Poppy	525
Silkweed	545
Golden Lotus	550

QUESTING IN KRASARANG WILDS

Two quests from Valley of the Four Winds send you into Krasarang Wilds. Ken-Ken sends you to Zhu's Watch and Kang Bramblestaff wants to meet you at Thunder Cleft (Horde) or The Incursion (Alliance).

KRASARANG WILDS LEGEND

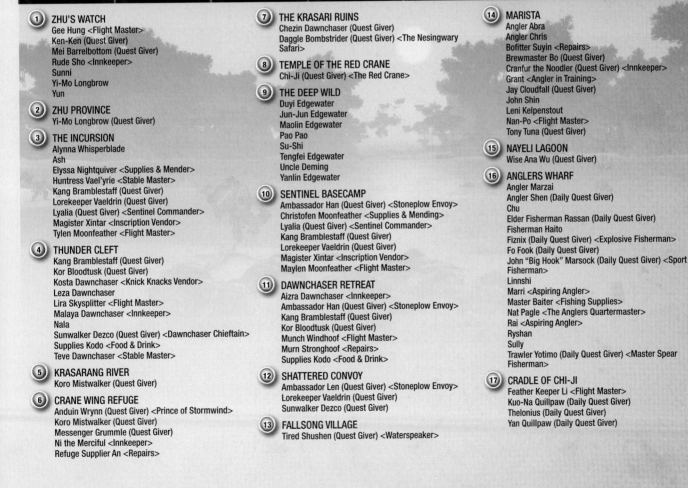

1 ZHU'S WATCH
Gee Hung <Flight Master>
Ken-Ken (Quest Giver)
Mei Barrelbottom (Quest Giver)
Rude Sho <Innkeeper>
Sunni
Yi-Mo Longbrow
Yun

2 ZHU PROVINCE
Yi-Mo Longbrow (Quest Giver)

3 THE INCURSION
Alynna Whisperblade
Ash
Elyssa Nightquiver <Supplies & Mender>
Huntress Vael'yrie <Stable Master>
Kang Bramblestaff (Quest Giver)
Lorekeeper Vaeldrin (Quest Giver)
Lyalia (Quest Giver) <Sentinel Commander>
Magister Xintar <Inscription Vendor>
Tylen Moonfeather <Flight Master>

4 THUNDER CLEFT
Kang Bramblestaff (Quest Giver)
Kor Bloodtusk (Quest Giver)
Kosta Dawnchaser <Knick Knacks Vendor>
Leza Dawnchaser
Lira Skysplitter <Flight Master>
Malaya Dawnchaser <Innkeeper>
Nala
Sunwalker Dezco (Quest Giver) <Dawnchaser Chieftain>
Supplies Kodo <Food & Drink>
Teve Dawnchaser <Stable Master>

5 KRASARANG RIVER
Koro Mistwalker (Quest Giver)

6 CRANE WING REFUGE
Anduin Wrynn (Quest Giver) <Prince of Stormwind>
Koro Mistwalker (Quest Giver)
Messenger Grummle (Quest Giver)
Ni the Merciful <Innkeeper>
Refuge Supplier An <Repairs>

7 THE KRASARI RUINS
Chezin Dawnchaser (Quest Giver)
Daggle Bombstrider (Quest Giver) <The Nesingwary Safari>

8 TEMPLE OF THE RED CRANE
Chi-Ji (Quest Giver) <The Red Crane>

9 THE DEEP WILD
Duyi Edgewater
Jun-Jun Edgewater
Maolin Edgewater
Pao Pao
Su-Shi
Tengfei Edgewater
Uncle Deming
Yanlin Edgewater

10 SENTINEL BASECAMP
Ambassador Han (Quest Giver) <Stoneplow Envoy>
Christofen Moonfeather <Supplies & Mending>
Lyalia (Quest Giver) <Sentinel Commander>
Kang Bramblestaff (Quest Giver)
Lorekeeper Vaeldrin (Quest Giver)
Magister Xintar <Inscription Vendor>
Maylen Moonfeather <Flight Master>

11 DAWNCHASER RETREAT
Aizra Dawnchaser <Innkeeper>
Ambassador Han (Quest Giver) <Stoneplow Envoy>
Kang Bramblestaff (Quest Giver)
Kor Bloodtusk (Quest Giver)
Munch Windhoof <Flight Master>
Murn Stronghoof <Repairs>
Supplies Kodo <Food & Drink>

12 SHATTERED CONVOY
Ambassador Len (Quest Giver) <Stoneplow Envoy>
Lorekeeper Vaeldrin (Quest Giver)
Sunwalker Dezco (Quest Giver)

13 FALLSONG VILLAGE
Tired Shushen (Quest Giver) <Waterspeaker>

14 MARISTA
Angler Abra
Angler Chris
Bofitter Suyin <Repairs>
Brewmaster Bo (Quest Giver)
Cranfur the Noodler (Quest Giver) <Innkeeper>
Grant <Angler in Training>
Jay Cloudfall (Quest Giver)
John Shin
Leni Kelpenstout
Nan-Po <Flight Master>
Tony Tuna (Quest Giver)

15 NAYELI LAGOON
Wise Ana Wu (Quest Giver)

16 ANGLERS WHARF
Angler Marzai
Angler Shen (Daily Quest Giver)
Chu
Elder Fisherman Rassan (Daily Quest Giver)
Fisherman Haito
Fiznix (Daily Quest Giver) <Explosive Fisherman>
Fo Fook (Daily Quest Giver)
John "Big Hook" Marsock (Daily Quest Giver) <Sport Fisherman>
Linnshi
Marri <Aspiring Angler>
Master Baiter <Fishing Supplies>
Nat Pagle <The Anglers Quartermaster>
Rai <Aspiring Angler>
Ryshan
Sully
Trawler Yotimo (Daily Quest Giver) <Master Spear Fisherman>

17 CRADLE OF CHI-JI
Feather Keeper Li <Flight Master>
Kuo-Na Quillpaw (Daily Quest Giver)
Thelonius (Daily Quest Giver)
Yan Quillpaw (Daily Quest Giver)

KUN-LAI SUMMIT

Your adventures in Kun-Lai Summit start in the far southeast at Binan Village which is accessed through the Ancient Passage of The Veiled Stair. Make your way across the barren land into the mountains of Kun-Lai. On the far-east side is The Temple of the White Tiger where Xuen gives you three tests to prove your worthiness and Gurgthock challenges you to the Arena of Annihilation scenario. On the side of the mountains overlooking Zouchin Village, Mogu'shan Vaults presents a six-boss raid and high in the peaks on the far northwest side lies the dungeon, Shado-Pan Monastery. Fly up to the Peak of Serenity if you are in need of a Monk trainer.

QUESTING IN KUN-LAI SUMMIT

In The Road to Kun-Lai quest, Lorewalker Cho sends you a message to travel to Binan Village. In the Veiled Stair, talk to Brewmaster Boof and hop into the boat. This takes you to the Binan Village dock. Quests are found around this town.

REPUTATION INFORMATION
The Lorewalkers

RESOURCE LEGEND

FISHING

FISH - FRESHWATER

Flying Tiger Gourami (rare)

Jade Lungfish

Redbelly Mandarin

Tiger Gourami

FISH - OCEAN

Giant Mantis Shrimp

Mimic Octopus (rare)

Reef Octopus

FISH - SHA-TOUCHED WATER

Spinefish

Spinefish Alpha

MINING

METAL	MIN SKILL
Ghost Iron Deposit	500
Rich Ghost Iron Deposit	550
Trillium Vein	600

HERBALISM

HERB	MIN SKILL
Green Tea Leaf	500
Golden Lotus	550
Sha-Touched Herb	575
Snow Lily	575

KUN-LAI SUMMIT LEGEND

1 BINAN VILLAGE
Admiral Taylor (Quest Giver)
Apothecary Cheng (Quest Giver) <First Aid Trainer>
Brewmaster Boof (Quest Giver)
Commander Hsieh (Quest Giver)
Egg Shell
General Nazgrim (Quest Giver)
Jo the Wind Watcher <Flight Master>
Little Elsa <Cook>
Mayor Bramblestaff (Quest Giver)
The Metal Paw <Adventuring Supplies>
Mishka <SI:7>
Puli the Even Handed <Innkeeper>
Rivett Clutchpop
Shademaster Kiryn
Sully "The Pickle" McLeary <SI:7>
Wanderer Chu (Quest Giver)

2 EASTWIND REST
Armorer Gang <Repairs>
Elder Shiao (Quest Giver)
Farmhand Ko (Quest Giver)
General Nazgrim (Quest Giver)
Mai the Sleepy <Innkeeper>
Rivett Clutchpop (Quest Giver)
Shademaster Kiryn (Quest Giver)
Soaring Paw <Flight Master>

3 WESTWIND REST
Admiral Taylor (Quest Giver)
Elder Tsulan (Quest Giver)
Farmhand Bo (Quest Giver)
Kai the Restless <Innkeeper>
Mishka <SI:7> (Quest Giver)
Steelbender Jin <Repairs>
Sully "The Pickle" McLeary (Quest Giver) <SI:7>
Tabo the Flyer <Flight Master>

4 CHOW FARMSTEAD
Farmer Chow (Quest Giver)
Uyen Chow (Quest Giver)

5 MOGUJIA
Bao Jian (Quest Giver)
Farmhand Bo

6 INKGILL MERE
Merchant Shi (Quest Giver)
Swordmistress Mei (Quest Giver)
Waterspeaker Gorai (Quest Giver)
Wu-Peng (Quest Giver)

7 LAO & SON'S YAKWASH
Lao Muskpaw (Quest Giver) <Yak Herder>
Muskpaw Jr. (Quest Giver) <Yak Herder>

8 PRANKSTERS' HOLLOW
Floof
Muskpaw Jr. (Quest Giver)
Tuffi

9 THE GRUMMLE BAZAAR
Brewmaster Chani <Drinks>
Clean Pelt <Leatherworking Trainer>
Clovercatcher <Burlap Trail Organizer>
Cousin Slowhands <Travelling Trader>
Herder Muskfree <Stable Master>
Li Goldendraft <Innkeeper>

Lucky Eightcoins (Quest Giver) <Caravan Master>
Madam Lani
Merchant Qiu
Mystic Birdhat <Arcane Reforger>
Slimy Inkstain (Quest Giver) <Reagent Vendor>
Smokey Sootassle (Quest Giver) <Burlap Trail Supplies>
Uncle Bigpocket <Used Yak Salesgrummle>
Whetstone <Repair Vendor>
Wishbone <Grummlecakes & Luckydos>

10 ONE KEG
Alchemist Yuan <Purveyor of Trade Goods>
Big Sal (Quest Giver) <General Goods Vendor>
Brother Brokendice
Brother Furtrim
Brother Lintpocket (Quest Giver) <Burlap Trail Organizer>
Chiyo Mistpaw <Innkeeper>
Ironshaper Shou <Blacksmith>
Ji-Lu the Lucky (Quest Giver)
Little Cleankite <Flight Master>
Lorewalker Cho (Quest Giver)
Lucky Bluestring
Nephew Bentnail <Junior Mountain Guide>
Uncle Cloverleaf (Quest Giver)
Yoona
Zaiyu
Zengi

11 THE BURLAP WAYSTATION
Brother Rabbitsfoot (Quest Giver)
Brother Trailscenter (Quest Giver) <Burlap Trail Organizer>
Brother Yakshoe

12 KNUCKLETHUMB HOLE
Brother Yakshoe <Quest Giver>

13 KOTA BASECAMP
Brother Oilyak <Burlap Trail Organizar>
Clover Keeper <Innkeeper>
Cousin Copperfinder <Grummlecakes & Luckydos>
Cousin Gootfur (Quest Giver) <Keenbean Kafa Co.>
Cousin Mountainmusk <Stable Master>
Cousin Tealeaf <Grummlegrogs>
Kota Kon <The Terror of Kota Peak>
Nephew Burrberry (Quest Giver) (Daily Quest Giver) <Keenbean Kafa Co.>
Uncle Eastwind <Flight Master>
Uncle Keenbean (Quest Giver) <Keenbean Kafa Co.>

14 KOTA PEAK
Nephew Burrberry (Quest Giver) <Keenbean Kafa Co.>

15 NEVEREST BASECAMP
Lucky Bluestring (Quest Giver)

16 SEEKER'S POINT
Lorewalker Cho (Quest Giver)

17 VALLEY OF EMPERORS
Curious Text (Quest Giver)
Image of Lorewalker Cho (Quest Giver)

18 WHISPERCLOUD RISE
Lin Whispercloud
Shin Whispercloud <Flight Master>

19 ZOUCHIN VILLAGE
Bo the Wind Claimer <Flight Master>
Elder Chi
Elder Hou
Elder Shu (Quest Giver) <Village Elder>
Koa
Li Hai (Quest Giver)
Liu Ze <Innkeeper>
Lorewalker Cho (Quest Giver)
Shomi (Quest Giver) <The Blacksmith's Daughter>
Steelbender Doshu (Quest Giver) <Blacksmith>
Toshi
Zasha <Trades Goods>

20 ZOUCHIN STRAND
Sage Liao (Quest Giver)

21 SHADO-PAN FALLBACK
Fixxit Redhammer <Repair Vendor>
Jin Warmkeg
Kite Master Ni <Flight Master>
Old Lady Fung
Shado-Master Chong (Quest Giver)
Stained Mug <Innkeeper>
Sya Zhong (Quest Giver)
Trader Hozenpaw <Grummlecakes & Luckydos>
Wu Kao Lee
Ya Firebough

22 TALLMUG'S CAMP
Cousin Littlebrew (Quest Giver) <Keenbean Kafa Co.>
Uncle Tallmug (Quest Giver) <Keenbean Kafa Co.>

23 WINTER'S BLOSSOM
Ban Bearheart (Quest Giver)
Kite Master Len <Flight Master>
Lao-Chin the Iron Belly (Quest Giver)
Lin Silentstrike (Quest Giver)
Suna Silentstrike

24 THE OX GATE/SHADO-LI BASIN
Ban Bearheart (Quest Giver)
Lao-Chin the Iron Belly (Quest Giver)
Suna Silentstrike (Quest Giver)

25 TEMPLE OF THE WHITE TIGER
Anduin Wrynn (Quest Giver) <Prince of Stormwind>
Big Greenfeather <Flight Master>
Black Arrow <Repair Vendor>
Clever Ashyo
Coach Rok Rok
Full Flask <Grummlegrog and Souvenirs>
Gurgthock (Quest Giver) <Fight Promoter>
Master Lao <Innkeeper>

Sunwalker Dezco (Quest Giver) <Dawnchaser Chieftain>
Sweaty Glove <Munchies and Crunchies>
Taran Zhu <Lord of the Shado-Pan>
Wodin the Troll-Servant
Zhi the Harmonious <Caretaker>

26 GATE OF THE AUGUST CELESTIALS
Anduin Wrynn <Prince of Stormwind>
Anji Autumnlight
Bartender Tomro <Innkeeper>
Cook Tope
He Softfoot
Kun Autumnlight
Leven Dawnblade
Merchant Tantan <Supplies>
Ren Firetongue
Rook Stonetoe
Sun Tenderheart
Sunwalker Dezco <Dawnchaser Chieftain>
Zhi the Harmonious <Caretaker>

27 SHADO-PAN MONASTERY
Ban Bearheart (Quest Giver)

28 PEAK OF SERENITY
Fearsome Jang <Monk Trainer – Master Tiger>
Initiate Chuang
Iron-Body Ponshu <Monk Trainer – Master Ox>
Master Bier <First Aid Trainer>
Master Cannon <Tanner>
Master Chang <Brewmaster>
Master Cheng
Master Chow
Master Hight (Quest Giver) (Daily Quest Giver) <Grandmaster>
Master Hsu
Master Hwang < Staff Vendor>
Master Kistane
Master Lo <Fisherman>
Master Marshall <Botanist>
Master Tan <Fist Weapon Vendor>
Master Tsang
Master Woo
Master Yeoh
Master Yoon
Number Nine Jia <Monk Trainer – Master Crane>
Trainer Ko <Tiger Style>
Trainer Lin <Tiger Style>
Wise Scholar Lianji <Monk Trainer – Master Serpent>

29 SERPENT'S SPINE
Acon Deathwielder <Glorious Conquest Quartermaster>
Doris Chiltonius <Conquest Quartermaster>
Lok'nor Bloodfist <Honor Quartermaster>
Morla Skyblade <Flight Master>

SHRINE OF SEVEN STARS

Located in the southeast corner of Vale of Eternal Blossoms, Shrine of Seven Stars serves as the central hub for the Alliance on the continent of Pandaria.

REPUTATION INFORMATION
The Anglers, The August Celestials, The Lorewalkers, The Tillers, Order of the Cloud Serpent, the Shado-Pan, The Golden Lotus

SHRINE OF SEVEN STARS

10 (Downstairs from 9)

SHRINE OF SEVEN STARS LEGEND

① THE CELESTIAL VAULT
Coincounter Cammi <Guide>
Vaultkeeper Fizznoggin <Banker>
Vaultkeeper Jiaku <Banker>
Vaultkeeper Melka <Banker>
Vaultkeeper Pieta <Banker>
Vaultkeeper Shan <Banker>
Vaultkeeper Silverpaw <Banker>
Vaultkeeper Xifa <Banker>
Vinnie Morrison

② CHAMBER OF ENLIGHTENMENT
Advisor Kosa
Aqualyte Shashin
Arenji
Hans Shuffleshoe
Historian Jenji
Historian Winterfur

Seeker Arusshi
Vamuu

③ CHAMBER OF REFLECTION
Meglette <Guide>
Poolwatcher Gui
Ranna <Guide>
Riverwarden Tuushuu
Vienh Stormbrew <Guide>
Watershaper Sharu

④ THE EMPEROR'S STEP
Andrea Toyas
Apo the Joyful Heart <Guide>
Armorer Kisha
David Guerrero
Donnelly Firecask <Guide>
Graceful Jessi
Healer Nan

Isaac Eppstein <Guide>
Jai Maguri
Jenessa Riverbreeze <Guide>
Keilan Hearthsong
Keri Reynolds <Guide>
Kiang Redwhisker
Lil' Canny
Master Zhang
Murphy Diremoor <Engineering Supplies>
Philip Luke
Pink Peony <Sweet Treats>
Priest Whitebrow
Serenka <First Aid Supplies>
Taijing the Cyclone <Brews>
Tina Nguyen

⑤ ETHEREAL CORRIDOR
Thaumaturge Faraket <Arcane Reforger>

Vaultkeeper Edouin <Void Storage>
Warpweaver Ramahesh <Transmogrifier>

(6) THE GOLDEN LANTERN
Ann Stockton <Guide>
Bonni Chang <General Goods>
Brad Rhodes
Brewmaster Tsu (Quest Giver)
Collin Gilbert
Collin Gooddreg <Exotic Brews>
Duinn Steelbrew <Guide>
Fitz Togglescrew
Jafu WIndsword
Kavanna Gooddreg <Guide>
Kergan Swiftbeard <Trade Goods>
Kressu
Marsha Stockton <Guide>
Matron Vi Vinh <Innkeeper>
Meng Chi the Fist <Brews>
Sarya Teaflower <Barmaid>
Sway Dish Chef <Food & Drink>

(7) PATH OF SERENITY
Frostflower <Guide>
Jonathan Le Karf
Kata Arina <Guide>
Ying Thunderspear
Zooey

(8) THE STAR'S BAZAAR
Apothecary Greenmoss <Alchemy Supplies>
Bero <Jewelcrafting Supplies>
Clara Henry <Enchanting Supplies>

Cullen Hammerbrow <Blacksmithing Supplies>
Hara Alebelly <Barmaid>
Jojo <Cooking Supplies>
Michael Bedernik <Meats>
Missy Pickwicker <Mining Supplies>
Raishen the Needle <Tailoring Supplies>
Shing Lightningpaw <Guide>
Tanner Pang <Leatherworking & Skinning Supplies>
Tommy Tinkerspade <Herbalism Supplies>
Veronica Faraday <Inscription Supplies>
Wilhem Ken <Bread Vendor>
Yanyra Moonfell <Reagents>
Yuma Ironkettle <Guide>

(9) THE SUMMER TERRACE - UPSTAIRS
Alynna Whisperblade
Anduin Wrynn <Prince of Stormwind>
Aster <Flowers>
Cloudrunner Leng <Flying Trainer>
Connor
Dao Ironplow <Guide>
Ian Gerdes <Guide>
Jasso Strongbow <Guide>
Jaul Hsu <Stable Master>
Krystel <Spirit of Harmony Vendor>
Kuru the Light-Hearted <Caretaker>
Lyalia <Sentinel Commander>
Magister Xintar <Inscription Merchant>
Maia
Merra Finklestorm <Guide>
Narei Summersky <Guide>
Omar Gonzalez
Pera Firestone <Fireworks Vendor>

Raoshan the Eagleclaw <Guide>
Sapling of Lore
Sara Finkleswitch <Battle Pet Trainer>
Scott Smith <Guide>
Sharinga Springrunner <Flight Master>
Soignera Strongbow <Guide>
Waina Steelpaw <Guide>
Whippie Jennson <Guide>
Zhen Zhen Wang

(10) THE SUMMER TERRACE – DOWNSTAIRS
Challenger Soong (Daily Quest Giver) <Challenge Dungeons>
Elder Lin (Quest Giver) <Charm Maker>
Heiran Stonebelly <Guide>
Instructor Windspear (Quest Giver) <Order of the Cloud Serpent>
Kichi of the Hundred Kegs <The Brewmasters>
Lao Lang (Quest Giver) <The Shado-Pan>
Master Angler Marina (Quest Giver) <The Anglers>
Mishi <Lorewalker Cho's Companion>
Riki the Shifting Shadow (Quest Giver) <The Shado-Pan>
Sage Whiteheart (Quest Giver) <The August Celestials Quartermaster>
Scrollmaker Resshi (Quest Giver) <The Lorewalkers>
Tang Ironhoe (Quest Giver) <The Tillers>
Tan Strongpole <Fishing Vendor>
Xari the Kind (Quest Giver) <The Golden Lotus>

(11) THE IMPERIAL EXCHANGE
Eric Thibeau

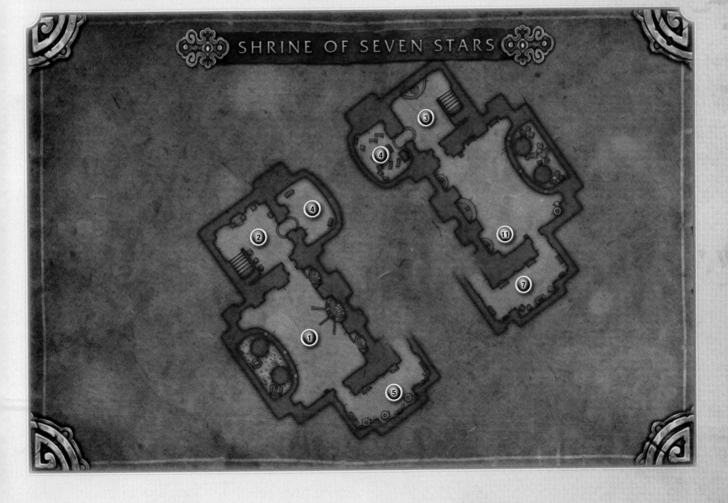

SHRINE OF SEVEN STARS

SHRINE OF TWO MOONS

The Shrine of Two Moons sits east of the entrance to Vale of Eternal Blossoms. This Shrine acts as the central hub for the Horde on the continent of Pandaria.

REPUTATION INFORMATION
The Anglers, The August Celestials, The Lorewalkers, The Tillers, Order of the Cloud Serpent, The Shado-Pan, The Golden Lotus

SHRINE OF TWO MOONS

3 4 4 (Downstairs from 3)

SHRINE OF TWO MOONS LEGEND

1 CHAMBER OF MASTERS
Ala'thinel <First Aid>
David Harrington <Guide>
Derenda Enkleshin <Enchanting Supplies>
Edward Hanes <Guide>
Esha the Loommaiden <Tailoring Supplies>
Fang Whitescroll <Inscription Supplies>
Frances Lin <Guide>
Gentle Dari <First Aid Supplies>
Hafuna Landwalker <Herbalism Supplies>
Jorunga Stonehoof <Blacksmithing Supplies>
Krogo Darkhide <Leatherworking & Skinning Supplies>
Moko Powderrun <Fireworks>
Mr. Creasey <Guide>
Razzie Coalwrench <Mining Supplies>
Sheena Sunweaver <Reagents>
Stephen Wong <Cooking Supplies>
Tixit Brightfuse <Engineering Supplies>
Vanaris Whitesong <Jewelcrafting Supplies>
Victor Pearce <Alchemy Supplies>

2 CHAMBER OF WISDOM
Dirki Tanboshi <Guide>
Erni Tanboshi <Guide>

3 THE GOLDEN TERRACE - UPSTAIRS
Andy <Guide>
Ba'kon <Meats>
Danky <Spirit of Harmony Vendor>
Eli
Evangelia <Guide>
Gentle San <Battle Pet Trainer>
Kat <Guide>
Mokimo the Strong <Caretaker>

Nala
Skydancer Shun <Flying Trainer>
Sunwalker Dezco <Dawnchaser Chieftain>
Tania Summerbreeze <Flight Master>
Tracker Lang <Stable Master>

4 THE GOLDEN TERRACE – DOWNSTAIRS
Bowmaster Ku <The Shado-Pan>
Brewmaster Linshi <The Brewmasters>
Challenger Wuli (Daily Quest Giver) <Challenge Dungeons>
Chan Hoi-San <Kun-Lai Refugee>
Clog Den <Kun-Lai Refugee>
Elder Liao (Quest Giver) <Charm Maker>
Farmhand Dooka (Quest Giver) <The Tillers>
Jong Jun-Keet
Jong Ming-Yiu <Kun-Lai Refugee>
Jong Wik-Wung
Lena Stonebrush (Quest Giver) <The Lorewalkers>
Master Angler Karu (Quest Giver) <Anglers>
Sang-Bo (Quest Giver) <The Shado-Pan>
Sage Lotusbloom (Quest Giver) <The August Celestials Quartermaster>
Wei Lakebreeze (Quest Giver) <Order of the Cloud Serpent>
Weng the Merciful (Quest Giver) <The Golden Lotus>

5 HALL OF THE CRESCENT MOON
Andrew Vestal <Guide>
Armorer Relna
Beige Sugar <Sweets>
Brewmaster Skye <Innkeeper>
D.E.N.T. <Mechanical Auctioneer>
Guyo Crystalgear <Explosive Expeditions>
Jinho the Wind Breaker

Joan Tremblay <Repairs>
Jontan Dum'okk <Guide>
Kurong Caskhead <Bartender>
Tivilix Bangalter <Explosive Expeditions>

6 HALL OF SECRETS
Thaumaturge Anjool <Arcane Reforger>
Vaultkeeper Meelad <Void Storage>
Warpweaver Shafiee <Transmogrifier>

7 HALL OF TRANQUILITY
Reeler Uko <Fishing Supplies>

8 THE JADE VAULTS
Vaultkeeper Goldpenny <Banker>
Vaultkeeper Kan <Banker>
Vaultkeeper Shifen <Banker>

9 THE KEGGARY
Barleyflower <Cooking Supplies>
Brewmaster Roland <Brews>
Brewmaster Vudia <Food & Drink>

10 SUMMER'S REST
Erin
Hoka Stonecrush <Trade Goods>
Madam Vee Luo <Innkeeper>
Marli Two-Toes <General Goods>
Mifan <Food and Drink>
Sadi
Tina Wang <Barmaid>
Uncle Gus

TOWNLONG STEPPES

Townlong Steppes is on the far west side of Pandaria and is separated from Kun-Lai Summit and Vale of Eternal Blossoms by the Pandaren Wall. Questing starts at Longying Outpost and takes you all the way around the zone to the islands on the west. After completing quests at Shado-Pan Garrison and Niuzao Temple, both areas offer daily quests. Look for world dungeons at The Gate of the Setting Sun atop the Serpent's Spine and Siege of Niuzao Temple.

REPUTATION INFORMATION
Shado-Pan

RESOURCE LEGEND

FISHING

FISH - FRESHWATER

Emperor Salmon

Flying Tiger Gourami (rare)

Redbelly Mandarin

Golden Carp

FISH - OCEAN

Giant Mantis Shrimp

Mimic Octopus (rare)

Reef Octopus

Golden Carp

FISH - SHA-TOUCHED WATER

Spinefish

Spinefish Alpha

MINING

METAL	MIN SKILL
Ghost Iron Deposit	500
Rich Ghost Iron Deposit	550
Kyparite Deposit	550
Rich Kyparite Deposit	575
Trillium Vein	600
Rich Trillium Vein	600

HERBALISM

HERB	MIN SKILL
Green Tea Leaf	500
Golden Lotus	550
Sha-Touched Herb	575
Fool's Cap	600

QUESTING IN TOWNLONG STEPPES

While in Kun-Lai Summit, speak to Elder Shiao in Eastwind Rest or Elder Tsulan at Westwind Rest. They give you a quest called "Beyond the Wall", which sends you to Longying Outpost. To get there, you must open The Ox Gate by completing the "Finish This" quest. It's the last step in a chain which begins with quests in Winter's Blossom and the Shado-Li Basin and includes a quest from Suna Silentstrike.

TOWNLONG STEPPES LEGEND

1 LONGYING OUTPOST
Alin the Finder <Adventuring Supplies>
Ban Bearheart
Kite Master Wong <Flight Master>
Saito the Sleeping Shadow <Innkeeper>
Supplier Xin <Gear Vendor>
Suna Silentstrike
Taoshi
Taran Zhu (Quest Giver) <Lord of the Shado-Pan>
Tigermaster Gai-Lin <Stable Master>
Xiao Tu
Yalia Sagewhisper

2 FIRE CAMP OSUL
Ban Bearheart (Quest Giver)
Katak the Defeated (Quest Giver)
Suna Silentstrike (Quest Giver)

3 HATRED'S VICE
Ban Bearheart (Quest Giver)
Xiao Tu (Quest Giver)
Yalia Sagewhisper (Quest Giver)

4 GAO-RAN BATTLEFRONT
Gao-Ran the Tempered
Ironshaper Peng <Mining Supplies>
Kim the Quiet <Innkeeper>
Kite Master Nenshi <Flight Master>
Lin the Brave <Supplies>
Septi the Herbalist (Quest Giver)
Tigermaster Liu-Do <Stable Master>
Taoshi (Quest Giver)
Taran Zhu (Quest Giver)

5 SHALLOWSTEP PASS
Mao the Lookout (Quest Giver)
Taoshi (Quest Giver)

6 LOWER SUMPRUSHES
Golgoss
Orbiss (Quest Giver)

7 AMBERMARSH
Initiate Chao (Quest Giver)
Initiate Feng (Quest Giver)

8 DUSKLIGHT HOLLOW
Initiate Pao-Me (Quest Giver)
Taoshi (Quest Giver)

9 DUSKLIGHT BRIDGE
Lao-Chin the Iron Belly (Quest Giver)
Taoshi
Taran Zhu (Quest Giver)

10 RENSAI'S WATCHPOST
Kite Master Li-Sen <Flight Master>
Lao-Chin the Iron Belly
Rensai Oakhide (Quest Giver)
Restless Leng
Supplier Qiao <Supplies>
Taoshi
Taran Zhu (Quest Giver)

11 FARWATCH OVERLOOK
Hawkmaster Nurong (Quest Giver)
Marksman Ye (Quest Giver)

12 THE WIDENING DEEP
Hawkmaster Nurong (Quest Giver)

13 SIK'VESS LAIR
Ban Bearheart
Hawkmaster Nurong
Lao-Chin the Iron Belly
Taoshi (Quest Giver)
Taran Zhu (Quest Giver)

14 SHADO-PAN GARRISON
Ban Bearheart (Quest Giver) (Daily Quest Giver)
Chao the Voice
Fei Li <"The Firecracker">
Hawkmaster Nurong
Kali the Night Watcher <Innkeeper>

Kite Master Yao-Li <Flight Master>
Lao-Chin the Iron Belly
Ling of the Six Pools (Quest Giver) (Daily Quest Giver)
Lorewalker Pao
Master Snowdrift (Quest Giver) (Daily Quest Giver)
Protector Yi
Provisioner Bamfu (Quest Giver)
Rushi the Fox <Shado-Pan Quartermaster>
Snow Blossom
Tai Ho (Quest Giver)
Taoshi
Tigermistress Min-To <Stable Master>
Yalia Sagewhisper

15 NIUZAO TEMPLE
Bluesaddle (Quest Giver)
Commander Lo Ping <Justice Quartermaster>
Commander Oxheart <Valor Quartermaster>
Ha-Cha
High Adept Paosha (Daily Quest Giver)
Ku-Mo
Ogo the Elder (Quest Giver) (Daily Quest Giver)
Ogo the Younger (Quest Giver) (Daily Quest Giver)
Niuzao <The Black Ox>
Sentinel Commander Qipan (Quest Giver)
Tai Ho
Yak-Keeper Kyana (Quest Giver) (Daily Quest Giver)

16 FIELDS OF NIUZAO
Bluesaddle (Quest Giver)
Cousin Bag-of-Rocks
Mooska <Good Yak>

VALE OF ETERNAL BLOSSOMS

Located in the heart of Pandaria, Vale of Eternal Blossoms holds two structures that act as central hubs for the Horde (Shrine of Two Moons) and the Alliance (Shrine of Seven Stars). Mogu'shan Palace and Gate of the Setting Sun, two world dungeons, are located here as well. You must complete Xuen's trials at The Temple of the White Tiger before accessing Vale of Eternal Blossoms. Look for daily quest hubs at The Golden Pagoda and Whitepetal Lake.

REPUTATION INFORMATION

The Anglers, The August Celestials, The Lorewalkers, The Tillers, Order of the Cloud Serpent

RESOURCE LEGEND

FISHING

FISH - FRESHWATER
Emperor Salmon
Flying Tiger Gourami (rare)
Jewel Danio
Redbelly Mandarin

MINING

METAL	MIN SKILL
Ghost Iron Deposit	500
Rich Ghost Iron Deposit	550
Trillium Vein	600
Rich Trillium Vein	600

HERBALISM

HERB	MIN SKILL
Green Tea Leaf	500
Rain Poppy	525
Golden Lotus	550

QUESTING IN VALE OF THE ETERNAL BLOSSOMS

After completing the Xuen's three trials at the Temple of the White Tiger, talk to Sunwalker Dezco or Anduin Wrynn at the Gate of the August Celestials. The gate is open and you are free to enter the new zone. Ahi the Harmonious waits for you inside to send you in the right direction.

VALE OF ETERNAL BLOSSOMS LEGEND

1 THE GOLDEN STAIR
Pako the Speaker (Quest Giver)

2 THE EMPEROR'S APPROACH
Bartender Tomro <Innkeeper>
Cook Tope
Mayor Shiyo

3 THE GOLDEN PAGODA
Anji Autumnlight (Daily Quest Giver)
Che Wildwalker (Daily Quest Giver)
Kun Autumnlight (Daily Quest Giver)
Leven Dawnblade (Quest Giver) (Daily Quest Giver)
Ren Firetongue
Rook Stonetoe
Sun Tenderheart (Quest Giver) (Daily Quest Giver)
Zhi the Harmonious <Caretaker>

4 MOGU'SHAN PALACE
Jaluu the Generous <The Golden Lotus Quartermaster>
Sinan the Dreamer

5 RUINS OF GUO-LAI
Anji Autumnlight (Quest Giver)
Kun Autumnlight (Quest Giver)

6 SERPENT'S SPINE
Bowmistress Li (Quest Giver) <Guard Captain>
Len at Arms <Adventuring Supplies>
Mai of the Wall <Flight Master>

7 WHITEPETAL LAKE
He Softfoot (Daily Quest Giver)
Merchant Tantan (Daily Quest Giver)
Ren Firetongue (Daily Quest Giver)

8 SEAT OF KNOWLEDGE
Brann Bronzebeard (Quest Giver) <Archaeology Trainer>
Kai Featherfall <Phoenix Egg Trader>
Lorewalker Cho (Quest Giver)
Lorewalker Huynh <Inscription Trainer>
Master Liu (Daily Quest Giver)
Mishi <Lorewalker Cho's Companion>
Ms. Thai (Daily Quest Giver)
Tan Shin Tiao <Lorewalkers Quartermaster>

VALLEY OF THE FOUR WINDS

The entrance from Jade Forest into the Valley of the Four Winds is located at Pang's Stead. This zone is mostly made up of farmland, with the jungle-like Krasarang Wilds to the south and mountains to the north. After helping out the farmers to the east, you must accompany Chen Stormstout and Li Li to Stormstout Brewery, the zone's lone world dungeon. Talk to the trainers at Halfhill Market to improve your Cooking skill and enjoy good hunting at Nesingwary's Safari in the far southwest.

REPUTATION INFORMATION
The Tillers

VALE OF ETERNAL BLOSSOMS

KRASARANG WILDS

PAOQUAN HOLLOW

THE HEARTLAND

HALFHILL

THUNDERFOOT

STONEPLOW

THE IMPERIAL GRANARY

SILKEN FIELDS

STORMSTOUT BREWERY

NESINGWARY'S SAFARI

RESOURCE LEGEND

FISHING

FISH - FRESHWATER
Emperor Salmon
Flying Tiger Gourami (rare)
Krasarang Paddlefish
Golden Carp

MINING

METAL	MIN SKILL
Ghost Iron Deposit	500
Rich Ghost Iron Deposit	550
Trillium Vein	600
Rich Trillium Vein	600

HERBALISM

HERB	MIN SKILL
Green Tea Leaf	500
Rain Poppy	525
Golden Lotus	550

QUESTING IN VALE OF THE ETERNAL BLOSSOMS

Once you have the "Moving On" quest, received from Fei at The Temple of the Jade Serpent, talk to her to move into the Valley of the Four Winds. Move up to Pang's Stead to get your questing started.

VALLEY OF THE FOUR WINDS LEGEND

1 PANG'S STEAD
Chen Stormstout (Quest Giver)
Claretta <Adventuring Supplies>
Clever Ashyo
Kang Bramblestaff
Ken-Ken
Li Li
Lin Tenderpaw
Little Tib <Stable Cub>
Muno the Farmhand (Quest Giver)
Nan Thunderfoot <Innkeeper>
Pang Thunderfoot (Quest Giver)
Princeton <Balloon Boy>
Xiao (Quest Giver)

2 THUNDERFOOT FARM
Ana Thunderfoot (Quest Giver)
Ang Thunderfoot (Quest Giver)

3 THUNDERFOOT RANCH
Cheng Stormstout
Liang Thunderfoot (Quest Giver)
Li Li

4 THUNDERFOOT FIELDS
Francis the Shepherd Boy (Quest Giver)
Shang Thunderfoot (Quest Giver)

5 GRASSY CLINE
Highroad Grummle
Kim of the Mountain Winds <Flight Master>
Messenger Grummle (Quest Giver)

6 SHANG'S STEAD
Chen Stormstout (Quest Giver)
Li Li
Shang Thunderfoot

7 MUDMUG'S PLACE
Chen Stormstout (Quest Giver)
Li Li (Quest Giver)
Mudmug (Quest Giver)

8 NEW CIFERA
Clever Ashyo (Quest Giver)
Gladecaster Lang (Quest Giver)
Lo Blackbrow
Mei Blackbrow

Rin Blackbrow
Sen the Optimist
Yan (Quest Giver)

9 POOLS OF PURITY
Clever Ashyo
Zhang Yue (Quest Giver)

10 SILKEN FIELDS
Journeyman Chu (Quest Giver)
Loommaster Jeng <Tailoring Supplies>
Master Goh (Quest Giver)
Masterweaver Li
Mothwrangler Min <Silk Vendor>
Silk Fist <Man of the Cloth>
Silkmaster Tsai (Quest Giver) <"The Tailor of Pandaria">
Silky
Sniff <Food Vendor>

11 HALFHILL
Boatbuilder Shu
Chen Stormstout (Quest Giver)
Danae
Den Den <Bartender>
Grainsorter Pei
Hopsmaster Chang (Quest Giver)
Innkeeper Lei Lan <Innkeeper>
Janae
Kim Won Gi <Fruit Dealer>
Kora Kang
Li Li
Lolo Lio (Quest Giver)
Mama Min
Mudmug
Nana Mudclaw
Old Man Whitewhiskers
Spicemaster Jin Jao
Stonecarver Mac (Quest Giver)
Su the Tamer <Stable Master>
Teng Firebrew (Quest Giver)
Trader Jambeezi <Adventuring Supplies>
Woodworker Laoren
Yun Applebarrel <Apples>

12 HALFHILL MARKET
Anthea Ironpaw (Quest Giver) (Daily Quest Giver) <Master of the Wok>

Bobo Ironpaw (Quest Giver) (Daily Quest Giver) <Master of the Brew>
Chian Chian
Ella (Daily Quest Giver)
Fish Fellreed (Daily Quest Giver)
Gina Mudclaw (Quest Giver) <Tillers Quartermaster>
Han Flowerbloom <Herbalism Trainer>
Jai Maguri
Jogu the Drunk (Quest Giver) (Daily Quest Giver)
Kol Ironpaw (Quest Giver) (Daily Quest Giver) <Master of the Grill>
Mei Mei Ironpaw (Quest Giver) (Daily Quest Giver) <Master of the Pot>
Merchant Cheng <Kitchen Storage Vendor>
Merchant Greenfield <Seed Vendor>
Nam Ironpaw (Daily Quest Giver) (Quest Giver) <Stockmaster>
Noodles <Cooking Supplies>
Old Hillpaw (Daily Quest Giver)
Sungshin Ironpaw (Quest Giver) (Daily Quest Giver) <Guide to the Ways>
Wing Nga <Flight Master>
Yan Ironpaw (Quest Giver) (Daily Quest Giver) <Master of the Steamer>

13 SUNSONG RANCH
Andi (Daily Quest Giver)
Farmer Fung
Farmer Yoon (Quest Giver) (Daily Quest Giver)
Fish Fellreed
Gai Lan (Quest Giver)

14 GILDED FAN
Mudmug (Quest Giver)

15 THE HEARTLAND
Chee Chee
Den Mudclaw (Quest Giver)
Ella
Farmer Hei Mung
Farmer Nishi <Grand Master Pet Tamer>
Gardener Fran (Quest Giver)

Haohan Mudclaw
Mina Mudclaw (Quest Giver)
Miss Rose
Mung-Mung (Quest Giver) <Farmhand>
Old Hillpaw
Stalwart Lo
Sturdy Po
Thunder
Tina Mudclaw
Wika-Wika <Farmhand>

16 CATTAIL LAKE

17 THE IMPERIAL GRANARY
Grainer Pan (Quest Giver)
Grainlord Kai (Quest Giver)
Li Li (Quest Giver)

18 WINDS' EDGE
Shai Cliffwatcher

19 STORMSTOUT BREWERY/ THIRSTY ALLEY
Chen Stormstout (Quest Giver)
Emmi (Quest Giver) <Stoneplow Emissary>
Ho Hai <Cooper>
Jon Greentill <Trader>
Li Li (Quest Giver
Mudmug (Quest Giver)
Tanya Thickfingers <Stillmaster>

20 STONEPLOW & STONEPLOW FIELDS
Bah Blacksoil
Chen Stormstout
"Dragonwing" Dan <Flight Master>
Feng Spadepaw
Fo Sho Knucklebump <Shado-Pan>
Guard Captain Oakenshield (Quest Giver)
Haiyun Greentill
Huizhong Greentill
Jooru Elderblade <Shado-Pan>
Ko-Yan Na <Shado-Pan>
Li Li
Lin Tenderpaw (Quest Giver)
Loon Mai (Quest Giver) <Shado-Pan Watch Commander>

Mah Blacksoil <Stew>
Master Bruised Paw (Quest Giver)
Mei Barrelbottom (Quest Giver)
Messenger Grummle (Quest Giver)
Mia Marlfur
Ming Marlfur
Miss Fanny
Mudmug (Quest Giver)
Nan the Mason Mug <Innkeeper>
Pang Thunderfoot
Ping Marlfur
Shu-Li Spadepaw
Spademender Yumba <Repairs>
Wei Blacksoil
Ying Greentill
Zhang Marlfur

21 PAOQUAN HOLLOW
Lin Tenderpaw (Quest Giver)
Master Bruised Paw (Quest Giver)

22 NESINGWARY'S SAFARI
Hemet Nesingwary (Quest Giver)
Hemet Nesingwary Jr. (Quest Giver)
Matt "Lucky" Gotcher (Quest Giver)
Mr. Pleeb <The Taxidermist>
Sally Fizzlefury <Engineering Trainer>
Steven Walker <Supplies>
Tani (Quest Giver)

23 THE TORJARI PIT
Hemet Nesingwary
Hemet Nesingwary Jr. (Quest Giver)

24 SERPENT'S SPINE
Ethan Natice <Glorious Conquest Quartermaster>
Hayden Christophen <Honor Quartermaster>
Lucan Malory <Conquest Quartermaster>
Tiper Windman <Flight Master>

25 SKYRANGE
Sho (Quest Giver)

THE VEILED STAIR

The Veiled Stair is a small zone that connects Valley of the Four Winds with Kun-Lai Summit. Tavern in the Mists gives you a place to rest and the nearby Black Market Auction House allows you to purchase goods from others. Terrace of Endless Spring is a raid located in the middle of the zone. At the end of The Spring Road, use The Spring Drifter to get through the Ancient Passage in peace.

REPUTATION INFORMATION
The Black Market

THE SECRET
AERIE

3

THE JADE FOREST

THE ANCIENT
PASSAGE

VALE OF ETERNAL
BLOSSOMS

2

TERRACE OF
ENDLESS SPRING

TAVERN IN THE
MISTS

1

RESOURCE LEGEND

FISHING
FISH - FRESHWATER
Flying Tiger Gourami (rare)
Tiger Gourami
Golden Carp

MINING	
METAL	MIN SKILL
Ghost Iron Deposit	500
Rich Ghost Iron Deposit	550

HERBALISM	
HERB	MIN SKILL
Golden Lotus	550

QUESTING IN THE VEILED STAIR

Lorewalker Cho gives you a quest to venture through The Veiled Stair to reach Kun-Lai Summit. Find Len the Whisperer along The Spring Road to get in some questing while you are here.

THE VEILED STAIR LEGEND

① TAVERN IN THE MISTS
Blacktalon Sentry <Servant of the Black Prince>
Kama the Beast Tamer <Stable Master>
Left <Blacktalon Bodyguard>
Makkie
Madam Goya <Leader of the Black Market>
Mister Chu <Madam Goya's Guardian>

Right <Blacktalon Bodyguard>
Shin the Weightless <Flight Master>
Tong the Fixer <Innkeeper>
Uigi
Wrathion (Quest Giver) <The Black Prince>

② THE SPRING ROAD
Brewmaster Boof (Quest Giver)

Egg Shell
Len the Whisperer (Quest Giver)

③ THE SECRET AERIE
Hawkmaster Liu <People of the Sky>

THE WANDERING ISLE

Separated from Pandaria for millennia, the Wandering Isle meanders the oceans of Azeroth. When the weather changes unexpectedly on the Isle and it begins erratically spiraling toward the Maelstrom, the elders at the Temple of Five Dawns request the aid of four elemental spirits to unravel the mystery. Heroes must figure out the cause of the land's illness before the entire island plunges into the abyss!

REPUTATION INFORMATION
Shang Xi's Academy

QUESTING IN THE WANDERING ISLE

Pandaren start their adventures on The Wandering Isle and continue to quest there until around Level 10.

THE WANDERING ISLE LEGEND

1 SHANG XI TRAINING GROUNDS
Instructor Mossthorn
Instructor Qun
Instructor Zhi
Ironfist Zhou
Master Shang Xi (Quest Giver)
Quiet Lam

2 TRANQUIL GROTTO
Jaomin Ro
Master Shang Xi (Quest Giver)

3 FU'S POND & CAVE OF MEDITATION
Merchant Lorvo (Quest Giver) <Training Supplies>
Aysa Cloudsinger (Quest Giver) <Master of Tushui>
Lamplighter Deng
Master Shang Xi (Quest Giver)

4 WU-SONG VILLAGE
Ji Firepaw (Quest Giver) <Master of Huojin>
Master Shang Xi (Quest Giver)
Lee Sunspark <Blacksmith>

5 THE DAWNING VALLEY & SHRINE OF INNER-LIGHT
Brewer Lin
Brewer Zhen
Chia-hui Autumnleaf
Master Li Fei (Quest Giver)
Huo (Quest Giver) <Ancient Spirit of Fire>

6 TEMPLE OF FIVE DAWNS
Aysa Cloudsinger <Master of Tushui>
Cai
Cheng Dawnscrive <Temple Scholar>
Dafeng <Ancient Spirit of Wind>
Delora Lionheart <Captain of the Skyseeker>
Deng
Elder Shaopai (Quest Giver)
Huo <Ancient Spirit of Fire>
Ji Firepaw <Master of Huojin>
Korga Strongmane
Master Shang Xi (Quest Giver)
Shu <Ancient Spirit of Water>
Wugou <Ancient Spirit of Earth>

7 THE SINGING POOLS
Aysa Cloudsinger (Quest Giver) <Master of Tushui>
Jojo Ironbrow (Quest Giver)
Old Man Liang (Quest Giver)
Teamaster Ren <Drink>
Whittler Dewei <Profession Trainer>

8 POOL OF REFLECTION
Aysa Cloudsinger (Quest Giver) <Master of Tushui>
Old Man Liang
Shu <Ancient Spirit of Water>

9 DAI-LO FARMSTEAD
Gao Summerdraft (Quest Giver) <Head of the Dai-Lo Farmstead>
Ji Firepaw (Quest Giver) <Master of Huojin>
Jojo Ironbrow (Quest Giver)
Jun Steelbreath <Blacksmith>
Lamplighter Sunny
Shu <Ancient Spirit of Water>
Wugou <Ancient Spirit of Earth>

10 MANDORI VILLAGE
Apothecary Jung
Bai Hua <Barmaid>
Chi Master Lim
Crimson Butterfly
Da Na
Elder Oakpaw <Profession Trainer>
Eng Dirtplow
Er <Drink>
Fan Slowplow
Foolish Chao
Gan Darkcask
Gao Longwagon
Gokan Sharphoe
Groundskeeper Amalia
Groundskeeper Shen
Hanshi One-Eye
Hyacinth
Jie
Jin
Jing Stoutgut
Kaydee Threesong
Ki-Ro the Contemplative
Kong
Lamplighter Mu
Lao Ma Liang <Innkeeper>
Lien-Hua Thunderhammer <Blacksmith>
Longbeard the Liar
Master Cranewing
Mei Chele
Naira Watergarden
Old Yang
San <Food>
Seeress Weng Wu
Shao-Li Ironbelly <Drinking Champion>
Shi <Drink>
Shun the Serene
Steepmaster Tira
Summer Lily
Trader Feng <General Goods>

Treeshaper Shu
Vu Blackbelly <Blacksmith>
Yi <Food>
Zach Chow

11 MORNING BREEZE VILLAGE
Aysa Cloudsinger (Quest Giver) <Master of Tushui>
Elder Shaopai (Quest Giver)
Ji Firepaw (Quest Giver) <Master of Huojin>
Jojo Ironbrow (Quest Giver)
Master Shang Xi
Shen Stonecarver <Blacksmith>

12 FE-FANG VILLAGE
Jade Tiger Pillar (Quest Giver)
Ji Firepaw (Quest Giver) <Master of Huojin>

13 RIDGE OF LAUGHING WINDS & CHAMBER OF WHISPERS
Aysa Cloudsinger (Quest Giver) <Master of Tushui>
Dafeng (Quest Giver) <Ancient Spirit of Wind>
Ji Firepaw <Master of Huojin>
Master Shang Xi (Quest Giver)

14 THE WOOD OF STAVES
Aysa Cloudsinger (Quest Giver) <Master of Tushui>
Ji Firepaw <Master of Huojin>
Master Shang Xi (Quest Giver)
Shu <Ancient Spirit of Water>
Wugou <Ancient Spirit of Earth>

15 FORLORN HUT
Korga Strongmane (Quest Giver)
Provisioner Drog <Supplies>
Wei Palerage (Quest Giver) <Hermit of the Forbidden Forest>

16 PEI-WU FOREST
Ji Firepaw (Quest Giver) <Master of Huojin>
Makael Bay (Quest Giver)

17 WRECK OF THE SKYSEEKER
Aysa Cloudsinger (Quest Giver) <Master of Tushui>
Delora Lionheart (Quest Giver) <Captain of the Skyseeker>
Ji Firepaw (Quest Giver) <Master of Huojin>
Jojo Ironbrow (Quest Giver)
Provisioner Phelps <Supplies>

18 DAWNING SPAN
Hao
Lorewalker Amai
Lorewalker Ruolin
Lorewalker Zan
Nan
Yin

DEATH KNIGHT

Death Knights are Azeroth's sole hero class, able to utilize powerful spells and melee strikes and manipulate the energies of shadow and frost to hinder and ultimately slaughter their foes.

Death Knights are the only class to start at a level other than 1 (in their case, 55). This means that, right away, they have an array of abilities already at their disposal, including the benefit of selecting some talents to help them overcome foes. Where other classes start their journey at a location determined by their race, Death Knights always start in Acherus, a gloomy section of Eastern Plaguelands where they train, eventually able to venture out into the world.

Being a hero class is not without its hindrances: in order to create a Death Knight, you must have already achieved level 55 on a different class. You wouldn't want a Death Knight to be the first class you experience Azeroth with anyways, as this class assumes you're already familiar with the basic mechanics of the game. Another restriction: you can only have one Death Knight per realm.

RACE AVAILABILITY

ALLIANCE

Draenei

Dwarf

Gnome

Human

Night Elf

Worgen

Pandaren

HORDE

Blood Elf

Goblin

Orc

Tauren

Troll

Undead

RACIAL ADVANTAGES

ALLIANCE

RACE	NOTES
Draenei	Heroic Presence grants Draenei +1% Hit chance. Gift of the Naaru heals the Draenei or any ally. Draenei take less damage from Shadow spells.
Dwarf	Stoneform is excellent for PvP and tanking, as it removes all bleeds, Poison and Disease effects and reduces damage taken. Mace Specialization provides increased Expertise with one and two hand maces. Dwarves take less damage from Frost spells.
Gnome	Escape Artist provides an extra ability for escaping slow or snare effects, making it great for PvP. Shortblade Specialization provides increased Expertise with daggers and one hand swords. Gnomes take less damage from Arcane spells.
Human	Every Man for Himself removes effects that cause loss of control. Sword and Mace Specialization provides Expertise with one and two hand swords and maces.
Night Elf	Night Elves are less likely to be hit by any physical attack (perhaps the best racial passive for tanking) and take less damage from Nature spells. Shadowmeld renders Night Elves invisible while motionless and cancels spells being cast by enemies on the Night Elf.
Worgen	Worgen get 1% increased Critical Strike from Viciousness. Darkflight increases movement speed temporarily. Worgen take less damage from Shadow and Nature spells.

HORDE

RACE	NOTES
Blood Elf	The signature Blood Elf racial, Arcane Torrent, provides Runic Power and an AoE silence. The former helps in tight situations, and the latter is great for PvP and certain PvE encounters. Blood Elves take less damage from Arcane spells.
Goblin	Rocket Jump is a great mobility tool. Additionally, Goblins get 1% increased Haste. Rocket Barrage is another source of damage for Goblins.
Orc	Blood Fury increases your attack power. Axe Specialization provides Expertise for axes. As a bonus, Orcs get increased pet damage, which benefits your ghouls. Hardiness reduces the duration of stun effects by 10%.
Tauren	Nature Resistance increases a Tauren's ability to stand up to harmful Nature effects. War Stomp provides an (AoE) stun in melee range, and Endurance boosts base health by 5%.
Troll	Berserking grants a temporary increase in attack speed. Da Voodoo Shuffle passively reduces the duration of movement impairing effects, which is important for Death Knights. Trolls regenerate Health faster than other races, and 10% of total Health regeneration may continue in combat.
Undead	Undead are more suited for PvP as they can break out of Charm, Fear, and Sleep effects with Will of the Forsaken. Their passive racial, Touch of the Grave, is a life leech and also provides a modest DPS increase in any situation. Undead take less damage from Shadow spells.

EQUIPMENT OPTIONS

ARMOR TYPE	SHIELD
Plate	No

USABLE WEAPONS

1 HAND WEAPON	2 HAND WEAPON
Axes	Axes
Maces	Maces
Swords	Polearms
	Swords

PROMINENT CLASS ABILITIES

RUNIC POWER

Death Knights use a unique resource called runic power, commonly recognized for its light blue tint.

This resource works similarly to a Warrior's Rage resource in that some abilities generate it, and some others spend it. The main difference between them is their volatility: runic power builds up at a slower, steadier pace, with many damaging abilities and melee strikes granting you a small amount, where rage builds and is spent faster. Think of runic power as a buffer that can be spent in the appropriate situation in order to deal more damage or increase your survivability.

RUNES

The other unique resource used by Death Knights is the rune system. Runes are a regularly replenishing resource spent by quite a few Death Knight abilities, providing a pacing mechanism that will require most of your attention in a fight.

The rune system is easy in its concept, but will likely require some practice in its execution if you wish to get the most out of it. There are three types of runes: blood, frost, and unholy (matching the names of the Death Knight specs, but not exclusive to them). You have two of each rune regardless of spec, gear, and abilities.

Instead of spending mana, energy, rage, or runic power, some of your abilities will simply spend, for example, "1 Blood."

This means one of your two blood runes will be activated in order to use that ability, triggering a 10-second cooldown on itself. Because you have two blood runes, you can use another ability that requires a single blood rune, but that will disable you from using any abilities that require blood runes until at least one of them is replenished. They replenish one at a time within their element, so you can be regenerating a blood and a frost rune at the same time, but two blood runes will recover one at a time.

This is fairly straightforward until you consider that some abilities consume two types of rune at once, and there's even a fourth type of rune—the death rune—that works as a wildcard. Arguably the most complex resource in the game, the rune system takes some time to get used to, but at some point, you'll keep track of everything without even noticing.

PRESENCES

Another concept shared between Death Knights and Warriors (called stances for Warriors) are the mutually exclusive Presences.

The three presences correspond to the three powers harnessed by Death Knights: Blood, Unholy, and Frost. Death Knights have access to any presence at any time if they meet the level requirement, but switching to a new presence will destroy any accrued runic power.

The three presences are described in the following table.

PRESENCE	DESCRIPTION
Frost Presence	Increases the generation rate of runic power, and reduces the duration of crowd control effects on you.
Blood Presence	Increases stamina, armor, and threat generation, and reduces the damage you take from all sources.
Unholy Presence	Increases Rune Regeneration by 10%, and also increases attack and movement speed.

SOUL REAPER

Death Knight's level 87 ability is Soul Reaper. This is available to any spec and uses a different rune depending on what type of Death Knight uses it.

This ability consumes a single rune, based on your spec, and is on a short 6-second cooldown, but requires you to be in melee range. It strikes an enemy for standard weapon damage and applies a debuff called Soul Reaper. After a short while, if the afflicted target is below 35% health, the debuff will deal a large amount of shadow damage. As a bonus, if the enemy dies before the debuff detonates, you'll gain a large amount of haste temporarily, alleviating the issue of using this ability at low percentages.

NAME	LEVEL		DESCRIPTION
Blood Plague	55		A disease dealing Shadow damage every 3 sec for 30 sec. Caused by Plague Strike and other abilities.
Blood Strike	55		Instantly strike the enemy, causing 40% weapon damage plus additional damage. Damage is increased by 12.5% for each of your diseases on the target.
Death Coil	55		Fire a blast of unholy energy, causing Shadow damage to an enemy target or healing damage on a friendly Undead target. Also refunds 20 Runic Power when used to heal.
Death Gate	55		Opens a gate which the Death Knight can use to return to Ebon Hold in Acherus.
Death Grip	55		Harness the unholy energy that surrounds and binds all matter, drawing the target toward the Death Knight and forcing the enemy to attack the Death Knight for 3 sec.
Frost Fever	55		A disease dealing Frost damage every 3 sec for 30 sec. Caused by Icy Touch and other spells.
Frost Presence	55		Strengthens you with the presence of Frost, increasing Runic Power generation by 20% and reducing the duration of effects that remove control of your character by 20%. Only one Presence may be active at a time, and assuming a new Presence will consume any stored Runic Power.
Icy Touch	55		Chills the target for Frost damage and infects them with Frost Fever, a disease that deals periodic frost damage for 30 sec.
Plague Strike	55		A vicious strike that deals 100% weapon damage plus additional damage and infects the target with Blood Plague, a disease dealing Shadow damage over time.
Runeforging	55		Allows the Death Knight to emblazon their weapon with runes.
Blood Boil	56		Boils the blood of all enemies within 10 yards, dealing Shadow damage. Deals 50% additional damage to targets infected with Blood Plague or Frost Fever.
Death Strike	56		Focuses dark power into a strike that deals 235% weapon damage plus additional damage to an enemy and heals you for 20% of the damage you have sustained during the preceding 5 sec (minimum of at least 7% of your maximum health). This attack cannot be parried.
Pestilence	56		Spreads existing Blood Plague and Frost Fever infections from your target to all other enemies within 10 yards.
Raise Dead	56		Raises a ghoul to fight by your side. You can have a maximum of one ghoul at a time. Lasts 1 min.
Blood Presence	57		You assume the presence of Blood, increasing Stamina by 8% and base armor by 55%, and reducing damage taken by 10%. Threat generation is also significantly increased. Only one Presence may be active at a time, and assuming a new Presence will consume any stored Runic Power.
Mind Freeze	57		Smash the target's mind with cold, interrupting spellcasting and preventing any spell in that school from being cast for 4 sec.
Chains of Ice	58		Shackles the target with frozen chains, reducing movement speed by 60% for 8 sec. Also infects the target with Frost Fever.
Strangulate	58		Shadowy tendrils constrict an enemy's throat, silencing them for 5 sec. Non-player victim spellcasting is also interrupted for 3 sec.
Death and Decay	60		Corrupts the ground targeted by the Death Knight, causing Shadow damage every sec that targets remain in the area for 10 sec.
On a Pale Horse	61		You become as hard to stop as death itself. The duration of movement-slowing effects used against you is reduced by 30% and your mounted speed is increased by 20%. This does not stack with other movement speed increasing effects.
Icebound Fortitude	62		The Death Knight freezes his blood to become immune to Stun effects and reduce all damage taken by 20% for 12 sec.
Horn of Winter	65		The Death Knight blows the Horn of Winter, which generates 10 Runic Power and increases attack power of all party and raid members within 45 yards by 10%. Lasts 5 min.
Path of Frost	66		Your freezing aura creates ice beneath your feet, allowing party or raid members within 50 yards to walk on water for 10 min. Works while mounted, and allows you to fall from a greater distance without suffering damage, but being attacked or receiving damage will cancel the effect.
Anti-Magic Shell	68		Surrounds the Death Knight in an Anti-Magic Shell, absorbing 75% of damage dealt by harmful spells (up to a maximum of 50% of the Death Knight's health) and preventing application of harmful magical effects. Damage absorbed generates Runic Power. Lasts 5 sec.
Control Undead	69		Dominates the target Undead creature, forcing it to do your bidding. While controlled, the time between the Undead minion's attacks is increased by 30% and its casting speed is slowed by 20%. Lasts up to 5 min.
Unholy Presence	70		You are infused with unholy fury, increasing attack speed and rune regeneration by 10%, and movement speed by 15%. Only one Presence may be active at a time, and assuming a new Presence will consume any stored Runic Power.
Raise Ally	72		Pours dark energy into a dead target, reuniting spirit and body to allow the target to reenter battle with 60% health and 20% mana.
Empower Rune Weapon	76		Empower your rune weapon, immediately activating all your runes and generating 25 Runic Power.
Army of the Dead	80		Summons an entire legion of Ghouls to fight for the Death Knight. The Ghouls will swarm the area, taunting and fighting anything they can. While channeling Army of the Dead, the Death Knight takes less damage equal to his Dodge plus Parry chance.
Outbreak	81		Instantly applies Blood Plague and Frost Fever to the target enemy.
Necrotic Strike	83		A vicious strike that deals 150% weapon damage, absorbs the next healing received by the target, and clouds the target's mind, slowing their casting speed by 50% (25% on player targets). Lasts 10 sec.
Dark Simulacrum	85		Places a dark ward on an enemy that persists for 8 sec, triggering when the enemy next spends mana on a spell, and allowing the Death Knight to unleash an exact duplicate of that spell. Against nonplayers, only absorbs some harmful spells.

TALENTS

TALENT		DESCRIPTION	NOTES
LEVEL 56 TIER (DISEASE)			
Roiling Blood		Your Blood Boil ability now also triggers Pestilence if it strikes a diseased target.	Basically removes the need to use Pestilence, saving you a blood rune if you use Blood Boil. Great for quickly spreading diseases and making them active on multiple enemies at once.
Plague Leech		Draw forth the infection from an enemy, consuming your Blood Plague and Frost Fever diseases on the target to activate a random fully-depleted rune as a Death Rune.	Great for when you need to use an ability but don't have the necessary resources. Note this talent has respectable range, which is great for when you're immobilized and your target is out of melee range.
Unholy Blight		Surrounds the Death Knight with a vile swarm of unholy insects for 10 sec, stinging all enemies within 10 yards every 1 sec, infecting them with Blood Plague and Frost Fever.	A great alternative to Roiling Blood and Pestilence altogether, this will instantly apply your diseases to nearby enemies for free. Best used in PvE situations when you need to AoE numerous enemies, as diseases don't have an AoE cap (meaning their damage won't diminish if you hit more enemies).
LEVEL 57 TIER (SURVIVABILITY)			
Lichborne		Draws upon unholy energy to become undead for 10 sec. While undead, you are immune to Charm, Fear, and Sleep effects, and Death Coil will heal you.	Because you're considered an undead creature under the effects of this spell, you can use Death Coil to heal yourself, which is great in addition to its immunity effects. This ability is free and instant; do note the considerable cooldown, however.
Anti-Magic Zone		Places a large, stationary Anti-Magic Zone that reduces spell damage done to party or raid members inside it by 75%. The Anti-Magic Zone lasts for 10 sec or until it absorbs a certain amount of spell damage.	Commonly referred to as simply "AMZ," this ability is an old favorite, allowing you to reduce magical damage taken on several allies at once. The maximum absorb is dependent on your level.
Purgatory		An unholy pact grants you the ability to fight on through damage that would kill mere mortals. When you would sustain fatal damage, you instead are wrapped in a Shroud of Purgatory, absorbing incoming healing equal to the amount of damage prevented, lasting 3 sec. If any healing absorption remains when Shroud of Purgatory expires, you die. Otherwise, you survive. This effect may only occur every 3 min.	In practice, this ability is easier to understand than it seems: instead of dying, you survive for an extra 3 sec, during which you have to recover a certain amount of health in order to survive. Great if there's a healer at hand!
LEVEL 58 TIER (MOVEMENT)			
Death's Advance		You passively move 10% faster, and movement-impairing effects may not reduce you below 70% of normal movement speed. When activated, you gain 30% movement speed and may not be slowed below 100% of normal movement speed for 6 sec.	This ability is a great way to close the distance between you and your opponent when Death Grip is on cooldown. A sprint ability is incredibly valuable to have in both PvE and PvP regardless of spec.
Chilblains		Victims of your Frost Fever disease are Chilled, reducing movement speed by 50% for 10 sec, and your Chains of Ice immobilizes targets for 3 sec.	Note that Frost Fever lasts longer than the chill effect granted by this talent, so you might have to reapply it early if you want to keep an enemy slowed through this. The Chains of Ice part provides an instant root that is invaluable for PvP.
Asphyxiate		Lifts an enemy target off the ground and crushes their throat with dark energy, stunning them for 5 sec. Functions as a silence if the target is immune to stuns. Replaces Strangulate.	This improved version of Strangulate lifts an enemy in the air, stunning it for the duration (instead of the standard silence). This adds more control, considering it hinders melee classes as much as it does casters.
LEVEL 60 TIER (HEALING)			
Death Pact		Drain vitality from an undead minion, healing the Death Knight for 50% of his maximum health and causing the minion to suffer damage equal to 50% of its maximum health.	You must have an undead minion to use this ability, so don't accidentally kill your ghoul if they are lower than 50% health. A 50% heal can be worth it in dire circumstances, however you can hurt your DPS if you accidentally kill your pet, especially as Unholy spec.
Death Siphon		Deals Shadowfrost damage to an enemy, healing the Death Knight for 100% of damage dealt.	This is one of the few abilities that uses a Death rune, which can only be generated under specific conditions. As such, it's a great tool that acts like Death Strike, but with a much larger range.
Conversion		Continuously converts Runic Power to health, restoring 3% of maximum health every 1 sec. Only base Runic Power generation from spending runes may occur while Conversion is active. This effect lasts until canceled, or Runic Power is exhausted.	This ability lasts until cancelled or you run out of runic power, so use it wisely—every second, some of your runic power will be drained, restoring a small percentage of your health. Once your runic power is depleted, this ability deactivates, but you can still generate some runic power by using rune abilities.
LEVEL 75 TIER (RUNE GENERATION)			
Blood Tap		Each damaging Death Coil, Frost Strike, or Rune Strike generates 2 Blood Charges, up to a maximum of 12 charges. Blood Tap consumes 5 Blood Charges to activate a random fully-depleted rune as a Death Rune.	The passive effect generates Blood Charges, which are capped at 12. In order to use the ability itself (which has no cooldown), you need to have at least 5.
Runic Empowerment		When you land a damaging Death Coil, Frost Strike, or Rune Strike, you have a 45% chance to activate a random fully-depleted rune.	A passive version of Blood Tap that grants a rune of a random depleted element instead of a Death Rune.
Runic Corruption		When you land a damaging Death Coil, Frost Strike, or Rune Strike, you have a 45% chance to activate Runic Corruption, increasing your rune regeneration rate by 100% for a set time.	Runic Corruption provides the most reliable Rune Regeneration of the three talents. Because you are simply increasing the rate at which runes regenerate, there is no guessing as to which spell you're going to be using next in your rotation when this talent procs.
LEVEL 90 TIER (CONTROL)			
Gorefiend's Grasp		Shadowy tendrils coil around all enemies within 20 yards of a target (hostile or friendly), pulling them to the target's location.	The range on this is pretty large, allowing you to cast it on virtually any target. Great for grouping numerous monsters up and then using AoE abilities on them; another great use is to allow a tank to gather all enemies by targeting him or her first and then using this ability.
Remorseless Winter		Surrounds the Death Knight with a swirling tempest of frigid air for 8 sec, chilling enemies within 8 yards every 1 sec. Each pulse reduces targets' movement speed by 15% for 3 sec, stacking up to 5 times. Upon receiving a fifth application, an enemy will be stunned for 6 sec.	The stun provided by this ability is one of the longest a player can use (6 sec), but requires an enemy to stay around you for at least 5 sec while you use this.
Desecrated Ground		Corrupts the ground in an 8 yard radius beneath the Death Knight for 10 sec. While standing in this corruption, the Death Knight is immune to effects that cause loss of control. This ability instantly removes such effects when activated.	Great for PvP and certain PvE encounters, providing another way to get out of crowd control instantly (the other being a PvP trinket). The immunity part requires you to stand in the relatively small patch of corruption, but you can always use Death Grip to get an enemy within reach.

BLOOD

Blood Death Knights manipulate the power of blood to sustain themselves in the face of an enemy attack, protecting allies with their durable plate armor and health-regenerating abilities. They are the only plate-wearing tank without a shield, usually tanking with a two-handed weapon. But that doesn't mean they're any less effective at any tank-related job, as several mechanics provide the defenses necessary to compensate.

MASTERY: BLOOD SHIELD

Grants you a shield that absorbs damage when you use Death Strike while in Blood Presence. The amount absorbed is based on your Mastery.

SPECIALIZATION ABILITIES

ABILITY	LEVEL		DESCRIPTION
Blood Rites	55		Whenever you hit with Death Strike, the Frost and Unholy Runes will become Death Runes when they activate. Death Runes count as a Blood, Frost, or Unholy Rune.
Vengeance	55		Each time you take damage, you gain 2% of the unmitigated damage taken as attack power for 20 seconds.
Veteran of the Third War	55		Increases your total Stamina by 9% and your chance to dodge by 2%.
Dark Command	58		Commands the target to attack you, but has no effect if the target is already attacking you.
Heart Strike	60		Instantly strike the target and up to two additional nearby enemies, causing 170% weapon damage plus additional damage on the primary target, with each additional enemy struck taking 25% less damage than the previous target. Damage dealt to each target is increased by an additional 15% for each of your diseases present.
Scent of Blood	62		Your successful main-hand autoattacks have a chance to increase the healing and minimum healing done by your next Death Strike within 20 sec by 20%, and to generate 10 Runic Power. This effect stacks up to 5 times.
Improved Blood Presence	64		Increases your rune regeneration by 20% and reduces the chance that you will be critically hit by melee attacks while in Blood Presence by 6%.
Rune Tap	64		Converts a Blood Rune into 10% of your maximum health.
Rune Strike	65		Strike the target for 175% weapon damage. This attack cannot be dodged, blocked, or parried.
Blood Parasite	66		Your melee attacks have a 10% chance to spawn a Bloodworm. The Bloodworm attacks your enemies, gorging itself with blood until it bursts to heal nearby allies. Lasts up to 20 sec.
Scarlet Fever	68		Cause your Blood Boil to refresh your diseases on targets it damages, and your Blood Plague to also afflict enemies with Weakened Blows.
Will of the Necropolis	70		When a damaging attack brings you below 30% of your maximum health, the cooldown on your Rune Tap ability is refreshed and your next Rune Tap has no cost, and all damage taken is reduced by 25% for 8 sec. This effect cannot occur more than once every 45 sec.
Sanguine Fortitude	72		Your Icebound Fortitude reduces damage taken by an additional 30% and costs no Runic Power to activate.
Dancing Rune Weapon	74		Summons a second rune weapon that fights on its own for 12 sec, mirroring the Death Knight's attacks. The rune weapon also assists in defense of its master, granting an additional 20% parry chance while active.
Vampiric Blood	76		Temporarily grants the Death Knight 15% of maximum health and increases the amount of health received from healing spells and effects by 25% for 10 sec. After the effect expires, the health is lost.
Bone Shield	78		Surrounds you with a barrier of whirling bones. The shield begins with 6 charges, and each damaging attack consumes a charge. While at least 1 charge remains, you take 20% less damage from all sources. Lasts 5 min.
Soul Reaper	87		Strikes an enemy for 100% weapon damage and afflicts the target with Soul Reaper. After 5 sec, if the target is below 35% health, this effect will deal additional Shadow damage. If the enemy dies before this effect triggers, the Death Knight gains 50% haste for 10 sec.

GETTING TO LEVEL 90

Blood is actually a respectable spec when it comes to leveling, even being a tank. Opt for a more damage-oriented rotation, using your runes to deal the most damage.

Like other Death Knight specs, choosing the right talents is key for leveling speed. Consider passive talents or talents on short cooldowns, such as Plague Leech, Death's Advance, and Death Siphon. At higher levels you can learn Runic Corruption, which provides a much needed boost to rune regeneration rate, allowing you to use abilities much more freely.

Death Knights have a slight advantage over other melee classes when it comes to survivability in the battlefield, with many cooldowns that can be used to prevent damage, restore health, or remove debuffs. Don't save these for a rainy day when leveling, as they will reduce your downtime from enemy to enemy.

PLAYING IN A GROUP

Being a tank is a big responsibility in groups, so make sure your gear is up to par for the content you're attempting to do. That said, Blood is all about managing your runes, especially the blood types. Note that Death Strike is not on a cooldown, but costs two runes of different types. It is ideal to use this Death Strike immediately after a large attack as you'll gain maximum benefit from the self heal, however all is not lost if you use this ability at max health because you can prepare for the next large incoming attack by building up your Blood Shield by using Death Strike on cooldown. As a side note, for bigger packs, you might want to consider using Pestilence, Blood Boil, and Death and Decay, as Heart Strike can only hit three targets at once.

For emergency situations, use your large cooldowns to hopefully survive a heavy siege. Because Death Knights have many defensive cooldowns, you should use these liberally.

BASIC ROTATION

Blood depends largely on the ability Death Strike as both an offensive and defensive mechanism. However, this doesn't mean you should ignore other abilities—try to save Death Strike for when you actually need it, otherwise opt for its single-rune counterparts. You have an outstanding number of defensive cooldowns, so remember to use them—Vampiric Blood, Dancing Rune Weapon, Rune Tap, and Bone Shield fall into this category, along with more situational ones like Anti-Magic Shell.

- Use Plague Strike if you have an unholy rune and you need to apply Blood Plague
- Use Icy Touch if you have a frost rune and you need to apply Frost Fever
- Use Heart Strike if you have a blood rune and don't need immediate healing, otherwise use Rune Tap
- Use Death Strike if you're in need of healing (note that it consumes a frost and unholy rune)
- Use Rune Strike whenever you have enough runic power

GROUP BUFFS AND DEBUFFS

All Death Knights provide the Attack Power buff with Horn of Winter.

Necrotic Strike imparts the Cast Speed Slow debuff, and Blood Death Knights afflict enemies with Weakened Blows from the ability Scarlet Fever.

GETTING READY FOR HIGH-END CONTENT

BLOOD

Being a tank, your gear levels will usually be more crucial to surviving an encounter than the rest of your group or raid. The good news is that tank gear is plentiful, and there are only one or two tanks per group or raid, and you won't need to compete for a shield. Upgrading your weapon provides the most threat, and indirectly, survivability. After that, prioritize your helm (because of the meta gem), legs, and chest. Don't be afraid to take up DPS-oriented gear if nobody needs it and then reforge undesirable stats (like Hit when over the Hit cap of 7.5%) to more survivability-oriented ones. Mastery is a great secondary stat—you can rarely go wrong with stacking lots of it, but it's most beneficial to obtain all the worthwhile gem bonuses by using gems of the right color. For red sockets, use an orange Parry and Mastery or Expertise and Mastery gem depending on whether you want more survivability or threat. For the rest, use Stamina or Mastery, depending on your playstyle—Mastery provides more controlled survivability while Stamina provides more raw health (perhaps best for encounters with magical damage).

FROST

Frost Death Knights specialize in dual wielding deadly weapons in order to defeat their foes. Making the most use of runic power, these icy harbingers have an array of frost-based abilities that can hinder and wound enemies while pummeling them with a flurry of lightning-quick attacks.

MASTERY: FROZEN HEART

Increases all frost damage done by a percentage determined by your Mastery.

SPECIALIZATION ABILITIES

ABILITY	LEVEL		DESCRIPTION
Blood of the North	55		Permanently transforms your Blood Runes into Death Runes. Death Runes count as a Blood, Frost, or Unholy Rune.
Frost Strike	55		Instantly strike the enemy causing 110% weapon damage as Frost damage.
Howling Blast	55		Blast the target with a frigid wind, dealing Frost damage to that foe, and additional Frost damage to all other enemies within 10 yards, infecting all targets with Frost Fever.
Icy Talons	55		Your melee attack speed is increased by 35%.
Obliterate	58		A brutal instant attack that deals 240% weapon damage. Total damage is increased by 12.5% for each of your diseases on the target.
Unholy Aura	60		Increases the melee and ranged attack speed of all party and raid members within 100 yards by 10%.
Killing Machine	63		Your autoattacks have a chance to grant a 100% critical strike bonus to your next Obliterate or Frost Strike.
Improved Frost Presence	65		While in Frost Presence, your Frost Strike ability costs 15 less Runic Power.
Brittle Bones	66		Your Frost Fever also applies the Physical Vulnerability effect.
Pillar of Frost	68		Calls upon the power of Frost to increase the Death Knight's Strength by 20%. Icy crystals hang heavy upon the Death Knight's body, providing immunity against external movement such as knockbacks. Lasts 20 sec.
Rime	70		Your Obliterate has a 45% chance to cause your next Howling Blast or Icy Touch to consume no runes.
Might of the Frozen Wastes	74		When wielding a two-handed weapon, your Obliterate deals 40% more damage, and all melee attacks deal an additional 10% damage.
Threat of Thassarian	74		When dual-wielding, your Death Strikes, Obliterates, Plague Strikes, and Frost Strikes also deal damage with your off-hand weapon, and your Frost Strike damage is increased by 50%.
Soul Reaper	87		Strikes an enemy for 100% weapon damage and afflicts the target with Soul Reaper. After 5 sec, if the target is below 35% health, this effect will deal additional Shadow damage. If the enemy dies before this effect triggers, the Death Knight gains 50% haste for 10 sec.

GETTING TO LEVEL 90

Frost is great for leveling with its quick attacks and AoE-friendly abilities. Note that, while it might be tempting to go to Unholy Presence for the added speed, you will benefit more from remaining in Frost Presence, as several passive abilities interact with your core spells to deal more damage.

Like other Death Knight specs, choosing the right talents is key for leveling speed. Consider passive talents or talents on short cooldowns, such as Plague Leech, Death's Advance, and Death Siphon. At higher levels you can learn Runic Corruption, which provides a much needed boost to rune regeneration rate, allowing you to use abilities much more freely, especially considering Frost has two permanent death runes instead of blood runes.

Death Knights have a slight advantage over other melee classes when it comes to survivability in the battlefield, with many cooldowns that can be used to prevent damage, restore health, or remove debuffs. Don't save these for a rainy day when leveling, as they will reduce your downtime from enemy to enemy.

PLAYING IN A GROUP

Execute your standard rotation for single enemies, using DPS-increasing cooldowns as desired, and making sure not to pull threat (this is especially important for Death Knights, as they are a melee class that has no threat reduction moves). When fighting multiple enemies, you can AoE them by using your AoE-friendly talents and Howling Blast.

If you pull aggro, or your tank happens to die, you can still save the day by quickly switching to Blood Presence. This will make you very durable, hopefully giving your group enough time to recover from a possible wipe. If you switched to Blood Presence because you pulled aggro, however, don't use any abilities until your tank has the monster's attention again, as they will generate a lot of threat.

BASIC ROTATION

An added feat of Frost Death Knights is their Blood of the North passive, which converts blood runes into death runes (thus providing two wildcards). This helps tremendously with your rotation, which uses mostly unholy and frost runes. While in Frost Presence, Frost Death Knights also have cheaper runic power abilities, making them a primary source of damage.

- Use Plague Strike to apply Blood Plague
- Use Howling Blast to apply Frost Fever, or to AoE enemies
- Use Obliterate when both of your diseases are up on the target
- Use Frost Strike when you have enough runic power

GROUP BUFFS AND DEBUFFS

All Death Knights provide the Attack Power buff with Horn of Winter. Groups get the Attack Speed buff from the Unholy Aura provided by Frost Death Knights.

Necrotic Strike imparts the Cast Speed Slow debuff, and Frost Death Knights use Brittle Bones to apply the Physical Vulnerability debuff.

GETTING READY FOR HIGH-END CONTENT

FROST

Like other melee-based classes, your priority should be increasing your Hit until you're no longer at risk of missing attacks on boss-level monsters (in this case, 93). This will increase your overall damage and runic power generation. If you hover over your Hit stat in the character screen, you can see how you're doing in that regard. This isn't as important for 5-man heroics, but it's best to reach the Hit cap before attempting raids. After that, go for Expertise until you're not getting dodged often (if at all). Note that you need to get 8% Hit, which eliminates special attack misses (non-autoattack strikes). You need to reach 17% Hit before you stop benefitting from Hit, as Frost Death Knights dual wield.

For sheer damage output, always prioritize Strength (even over Hit) in places that allow so, such as gems. At times, skipping gem bonuses in favor of more Strength gems is favorable—just don't pass up great bonuses (generally Strength bonuses, or any helm bonuses).

UNHOLY

Unholy Death Knights excel at defiling the ground with Death and Decay and then spreading powerful diseases amongst all their foes. They are also masters of undead control, being proficient at commanding ghouls and other undead minions, and making them powerful through dark abilities.

MASTERY: DREADBLADE

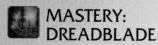

Increases all shadow damage done by a percentage determined by your mastery stat.

SPECIALIZATION ABILITIES

ABILITY	LEVEL		DESCRIPTION
Master of Ghouls	55		The Ghoul summoned by your Raise Dead spell is considered a pet under your control. Unlike normal Death Knight Ghouls, your pet does not have a limited duration.
Reaping	55		Whenever you hit with Blood Strike, Pestilence, Festering Strike, or Blood Boil, the Runes spent will become Death Runes when they activate. Death Runes count as a Blood, Frost, or Unholy Rune.
Unholy Might	55		Dark power courses through your limbs, increasing your Strength by 15%.
Scourge Strike	58		An unholy strike that deals 130% of weapon damage as Physical damage plus additional damage. In addition, for each of your diseases on your target, you deal an additional 25% of the Physical damage done as Shadow damage.
Shadow Infusion	60		Your successful Death Coils empower your active Ghoul, increasing its damage dealt by 10% for 30 sec. Stacks up to 5 times.
Unholy Aura	60		Increases the melee and ranged attack speed of all party and raid members within 100 yards by 10%.
Festering Strike	62		An instant attack that deals 200% weapon damage plus additional damage and increases the duration of your Blood Plague, Frost Fever, and Chains of Ice effects on the target by up to 6 sec.
Sudden Doom	64		Reduces the cost of Death Coil by 20%, and grants your main-hand autoattacks a chance to make your next Death Coil cost no Runic Power.
Unholy Frenzy	66		Incites a friendly party or raid member into a killing frenzy for 30 sec, increasing the target's melee and ranged haste by 20%, but causing them to lose health equal to 2% of their maximum health every 3 sec.
Ebon Plaguebringer	68		Increases the damage your diseases deal by 60%, and causes your Blood Plague to also apply the Physical Vulnerability effect.
Dark Transformation	70		Consume 5 charges of Shadow Infusion on your Ghoul to transform it into a powerful undead monstrosity for 30 sec. The Ghoul's abilities are empowered and take on new functions while the transformation is active.
Summon Gargoyle	74		A Gargoyle flies into the area and bombards the target with Nature damage modified by the Death Knight's attack power. Persists for 30 sec.
Improved Unholy Presence	75		While in Unholy Presence, your attack speed and rune regeneration are increased by an additional 10%.
Soul Reaper	87		Strikes an enemy for 100% weapon damage and afflicts the target with Soul Reaper. After 5 sec, if the target is below 35% health, this effect will deal additional Shadow damage. If the enemy dies before this effect triggers, the Death Knight gains 50% haste for 10 sec.

GETTING TO LEVEL 90

Unholy is arguably the fastest Death Knight leveling spec, considering you take full advantage of Unholy Presence, have a permanent pet, and can dispatch multiple enemies at once by using powerful diseases and Death and Decay.

Like other Death Knight specs, choosing the right talents is key for leveling speed. Consider passive talents or talents on short cooldowns, such as Plague Leech, Death's Advance, and Death Siphon. At higher levels you can learn Runic Corruption, which provides a much needed boost to rune regeneration rate, allowing you to use abilities much more freely.

Death Knights have a slight advantage over other melee classes when it comes to survivability in the battlefield, with many cooldowns that can be used to prevent damage, restore health, or remove debuffs. Don't save these for a rainy day when leveling, as they will reduce your downtime from enemy to enemy.

PLAYING IN A GROUP

Execute your standard rotation for single enemies, using DPS-increasing cooldowns as desired, and making sure not to pull threat. This is especially important for Death Knights, as they are a melee class that has no threat reduction moves, but less so for Unholy, as a portion of the damage comes from your pet. When fighting multiple enemies, you can AoE them by using your AoE-friendly talents and diseases.

If you pull aggro, or your tank happens to die, you can still save the day by quickly switching to Blood Presence. This will make you very durable, hopefully giving your group enough time to recover from a possible wipe. If you switched to Blood Presence because you pulled aggro, however, make sure not to use any abilities until your tank has the monster's attention again, as they will generate a lot of threat.

BASIC ROTATION

As an Unholy Death Knight, you want to be in Unholy Presence due to your Improved Unholy Presence. Unlike the other two specs, you actually have to manage your pet to some extent (which is permanent for Unholy), as a large portion of your damage will come from its swings, especially under the effects of Dark Transformation. To accomplish this, you can empower your ghoul by casting Death Coil on your enemies.

- Use Plague Strike to apply Blood Plague
- Use Icy Touch to apply Frost Fever
- Use Scourge Strike if you don't need to refresh your diseases yet
- Use Festering Strike if you do (note that it costs a blood and a frost rune)
- Use Dark Transformation upon reaching five stacks of Shadow Infusion, which is generated by Death Coiling your pet
- Use Death Coil whenever you have runic power

GROUP BUFFS AND DEBUFFS

All Death Knights provide the Attack Power buff with Horn of Winter. Groups get the Attack Speed buff from the Unholy Aura provided by Unholy Death Knights.

Necrotic Strike imparts the Cast Speed Slow debuff, and Unholy Death Knights use Ebon Plaguebringer to apply the Physical Vulnerability debuff.

GETTING READY FOR HIGH-END CONTENT

UNHOLY

Like other melee-based classes, your priority should be increasing your Hit until you're no longer at risk of missing attacks on boss-level monsters (in this case, 93). This will increase your overall damage and runic power generation. If you hover over your Hit stat in the character screen, you can see how you're doing in that regard. This isn't as important for 5-man heroics, but it's best to reach the Hit cap before attempting raids. After that, go for Haste as it will increase both your attack speed and Rune Regeneration. Note that you need to get 8% Hit, which eliminates special attack misses (non-autoattack strikes). At that point, Unholy stops benefitting from Hit.

For sheer damage output, always prioritize Strength (even over Hit) in places that allow so, such as gems. At times, skipping gem bonuses in favor of more Strength gems is favorable—just don't pass up great bonuses (generally Strength bonuses, or any helm bonuses).

DRUID

Druids are true hybrids and masters of shapeshifting. They are the class closest to nature, and the only one able to master four different specialization trees.

Each form adoptable by Druids grants unique abilities or bonuses and has a purpose either in combat or outside of it. Unlike other classes, Druids are able to play every role archetype proficiently: they can be melee DPS, tanks, casters, and healers. They truly are Jacks of all Trades. This makes them a perfect fit for those who wish to experience every aspect of combat in a single class. Though Druids are not without their own niches—for instance, they are the masters of heals over time (HoT) among healers. Because of their affinity to nature, Druids possess a great arsenal of nature-based spells, but they can also blast their enemies with arcane spells (chiefly Balance Druids), further increasing their spell variety.

RACE AVAILABILITY

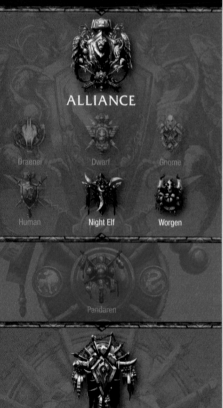

ALLIANCE

Draenei   Dwarf   Gnome

Human   Night Elf   Worgen

Pandaren

HORDE

Blood Elf   Goblin   Orc

Tauren   Troll   Undead

RACIAL ADVANTAGES

ALLIANCE

RACE	NOTES
Night Elf	Night Elves are less likely to be hit by any physical attack (perhaps the best racial passive for tanking) and take less damage from Nature spells. Shadowmeld cancels spells being cast by enemies on the Night Elf.
Worgen	Worgen get 1% increased Critical Strike from Viciousness. Darkflight increases movement speed temporarily. Worgen take less damage from Nature and Shadow spells.

HORDE

RACE	NOTES
Tauren	Nature Resistance increases a Tauren's ability to stand up to harmful Nature effects. War Stomp provides an (AoE) stun in melee range, and Endurance boosts base health by 5%.
Troll	Berserking grants a temporary increase in attack speed. Da Voodoo Shuffle passively reduces the duration of movement impairing effects, which is important for Druids. Trolls regenerate Health faster than other races, and 10% of total Health regeneration may continue in combat.

EQUIPMENT OPTIONS

ARMOR TYPE	SHIELD
Leather	No

USABLE WEAPONS

1 HAND WEAPON	2 HAND WEAPON
Daggers	Maces
Fist Weapons	Polearms
Maces	Staves

PROMINENT CLASS ABILITIES

FORMS

Shapeshifting is the bread and butter of Druid combat and travel.

At certain levels (starting at level 6) Druids are granted the ability to change their form into several different animals. Each animal has a specific function. The talent Incarnation also allows you to temporarily shift into an improved version of the forms.

While shapeshifted, you are immune to Polymorph effects, and the act of shapeshifting frees you from movement impairing effects. This makes Druids incredibly mobile, without even taking into account the abilities that grant speed boosts. Forms are very flexible; Druids can shift from one form to another without having to go back to their original form first.

FORM	TREE OF PROFICIENCY	FUNCTION
Cat / King of the Jungle	Feral	Melee DPS
Bear / Son of Ursoc	Guardian	Tanking
Travel	None	Ground traveling
Aquatic	None	Water traveling
Moonkin / Chosen of Elune	Balance	Caster DPS
Tree of Life	Restoration	Healing, Caster DPS (Cooldown)
Flight	None	Air traveling
Swift Flight	None	Air traveling

Mana is conserved across forms and continues to regenerate even while shapeshifted. This also applies to Cat Form's energy resource, allowing for more hybrid-like play. Forms that don't have a special resource such as energy or rage will show the standard mana bar instead.

RAGE, ENERGY, AND COMBO POINTS

While in Bear Form, Druids will have a combat resource shared by Warriors, called Rage. Rage is generated by dealing damage with auto-attacks, but is no longer generated by taking damage in battle. Most abilities consume rage instead of generating it, with a few exceptions like Mangle. The signature "excess rage" ability is still Maul, which deals additional damage against bleeding targets. The Enrage ability will allow Druids to instantly gain some rage, and then an additional amount over time. Many previously exclusive Feral talents are now available to all trees, encouraging hybrid play once again.

While in Cat Form, Druids will have a combat resource shared by Rogues and Monks, called Energy. This resource is constantly replenishing itself as time passes, usually in a speedier fashion than other resources (it's a matter of seconds for an Energy bar to go from empty to full). The highest amount of Energy is 100 by default. Unlike previously, this resource keeps regenerating in other forms.

Because this resource regenerates so quickly, abilities based on it often use a great amount at once, serving as a pacing mechanism for Cat DPS. Certain abilities also generate Combo Points, which can be seen around your target's character portrait. These points are required for other abilities—the more points, the stronger or more efficient these abilities will be. Some abilities, like Faerie Fire, don't generate or spend Combo Points.

SYMBIOSIS

Druid's level 87 ability is Symbiosis, a fun and useful unique spell that grants you and an ally a significant buff or ability based on both of your classes and specialization trees. This ability will single-handedly make groups desire the Druid class entirely, as the abilities granted (although usually weaker versions of the original) can greatly aid the group in combat. Conversely, the abilities obtained by the Druid are very useful, so you'll find yourself gauging what player is best to cast Symbiosis on so that both of you benefit the most. At times, however, you might have to take one for the team—most notably, giving tanks an extra cooldown through Symbiosis might prove useful for certain encounters.

When you cast Symbiosis on another class, you get:

ALLY'S CLASS	GUARDIAN	FERAL	RESTORATION	BALANCE
Death Knight	Bone Shield	Death Coil	Icebound Fortitude	Anti-Magic Shell
Hunter	Ice Trap	Play Dead	Deterrence	Misdirection
Mage	Frost Armor	Frost Nova	Ice Block	Mirror Image
Monk	Elusive Brew	Clash	Fortifying Brew	Grapple Weapon
Paladin	Consecration	Divine Shield	Cleanse	Hammer of Justice
Priest	Fear Ward	Dispersion	Leap of Faith	Mass Dispel
Rogue	Feint	Redirect	Evasion	Cloak of Shadows
Shaman	Lightning Shield	Feral Spirit	Spiritwalker's Grace	Purge
Warlock	Life Tap	Soul Swap	Demonic Circle	Unending Resolve
Warrior	Spell Reflection	Shattering Blow	Intimidating Roar	Intervene

And they get:

ALLY'S CLASS	SPECIALIZATION	SPECIALIZATION	SPECIALIZATION
Death Knight	Might of Ursoc (Blood)	Wild Mushroom: Plague (Frost)	Wild Mushroom: Plague (Unholy)
Hunter	Dash	Dash	Dash
Mage	Healing Touch	Healing Touch	Healing Touch
Monk	Survival Instincts (Brewmaster)	Bear Hug (Windwalker)	Entangling Roots (Mistweaver)
Paladin	Rebirth (Holy)	Retribution: Wrath	Protection: Barkskin
Priest	Cyclone (Discipline)	Cyclone (Holy)	Tranquility (Shadow)
Rogue	Growl	Growl	Growl
Shaman	Solar Beam (Elemental)	Solar Beam (Enhancement)	Prowl (Restoration)
Warlock	Rejuvenation	Rejuvenation	Rejuvenation
Warrior	Stampeding Shout (Arms)	Stampeding Shout (Fury)	Savage Defense (Protection)

NAME	LEVEL		DESCRIPTION
Wrath	1		Deals nature damage to an enemy.
Moonfire	3		Burns the enemy for Arcane damage and then an additional Arcane damage over 14 sec.
Rejuvenation	4		Heals the target and an additional amount every 3 sec for 12 sec.
Cat Form	6		Shapeshift into Cat form, causing Agility to increase attack power, increasing autoattack damage by 100%, and increasing movement speed by 25%. Also protects the caster from Polymorph effects and allows the use of various cat abilities. Energy regeneration continues while not in Cat form. The act of shapeshifting frees the caster of movement impairing effects.
Ferocious Bite (Cat)	6		Finishing move that causes damage per combo point and consumes additional Energy to increase damage by up to 100%. When used on targets below 25% health, Ferocious Bite will also refresh the duration of your Rip on your target. Critical strike chance increases by 25% against bleeding targets.
Mangle (Cat and Bear)	6		Mangle the target for physical damage. Damage varies by shapeshift form. Generates 5 Rage when used in Bear Form and awards 1 combo point when used in Cat Form.
Prowl	6		Allows the Druid to prowl around, but reduces movement speed by 30%. Lasts until cancelled. Using this ability activates Cat Form.
Rake (Cat)	6		Rake the target for Bleed damage and an additional Bleed damage over 15 sec. Awards 1 combo point.
Feline Grace	6		Reduces damage from falling while in Cat Form.
Bear Form	8		Shapeshift into Bear Form, increasing armor contribution from cloth and leather items by 120% and Stamina by 20%. Significantly increases threat generation, causes Agility to increase attack power, increases haste and critical strike from items by 50%, and also protects the caster from Polymorph effects and allows the use of various bear abilities. Rage is set to 10 upon shifting into Bear Form.
Growl	8		Taunts an enemy to attack you, but has no effect if the target is already attacking you. Using this ability activates Bear Form.
Maul (Bear)	8		Mauls the target for 110% weapon damage. Deals 20% additional damage against bleeding targets. Use when you have more Rage than you can spend.
Entangling Roots	10		Roots the target in place for 30 sec. Damage caused may interrupt the effect.
Revive	12		Returns the spirit to the body, restoring a dead target to life with 35% of maximum health and mana. Cannot be cast when in combat.
Teleport: Moonglade	14		Teleports you to Moonglade, the druid haven.
Travel Form	16		Shapeshift into travel form, increasing movement speed by 40%. Also protects the caster from Polymorph effects. Only useable outdoors.
Aquatic Form	18		Shapeshift into aquatic form, increasing swim speed by 50% and allowing the Druid to breathe underwater. Also protects the caster from Polymorph effects.
Swipe (Cat and Bear)	22		Swipe nearby enemies, inflicting physical damage. Damage dealt varies by shapeshift form. Deals 20% additional damage against bleeding targets.
Dash	24		Removes all roots and snares, and increases movement speed by 70% while in Cat Form for 15 sec. Does not break prowling. Using this ability activates Cat Form.
Healing Touch	26		Heals an ally for a moderate amount.
Faerie Fire	28		Faeries surround the target, preventing it from stealthing or turning invisible, and causing 3 applications of the Weakened Armor debuff. Deals damage and has a 25% chance to reset the cooldown on Mangle when cast from Bear Form.

NAME	LEVEL		DESCRIPTION
Primal Fury (Cat and Bear)	30		Gain an additional Rage every time you deal a critical strike with autoattack or Mangle and gain an additional combo point every time one of your single-target combo moves deals a critical strike.
Pounce (Cat)	32		Pounce, stunning the target for 4 sec and causing Bleed damage over 18 sec. Must be prowling. Awards 1 combo point.
Track Humanoids (Cat)	36		Allows you to see humanoids on your minimap.
Lacerate (Bear)	38		Lacerates the enemy target, dealing bleed damage and an additional amount over 15 sec. Stacks up to 3 times. Each time Lacerate hits, it has a 25% chance to reset the cooldown on Mangle.
Hurricane	42		Creates a storm at a target area causing Nature damage to enemies every 1 sec. Lasts 10 sec. Druid must channel to maintain the spell.
Barkskin	44		The Druid's skin becomes as tough as bark. All damage taken is reduced by 20% While protected, damaging attacks will not cause spellcasting delays. This spell is usable while stunned, frozen, incapacitated, feared, or asleep. Usable in all forms. Lasts 12 sec.
Nature's Grasp	52		While active, any time an enemy strikes the caster they will become afflicted by Entangling Roots. 1 charge. Lasts 45 sec.
Innervate	54		Causes the target to regenerate 10% of the caster's maximum mana over 10 sec. If cast on self, the caster will regenerate an additional 10% of maximum mana over 10 sec.
Rebirth	56		Returns the spirit to the body, restoring a dead taret to life with 60% health and 20% mana.
Flight Form	58		Shapeshift into flight form, increasing movement speed by 150% and allowing you to fly. Cannot use in combat.
Soothe	60		Removes all enrage effects from an enemy.
Mark of the Wild	62		Increases the friendly target's Strength, Agility, and Intellect by 5% for 1 hour. If target is in your party or raid, all party and raid members will be affected.
Hibernate	66		Forces the enemy target to sleep for up to 40 sec. Any damage will awaken the target. Only one target can be forced to hibernate at a time. Only works on Beasts and Dragonkin.
Frenzied Regeneration (Bear)	68		Instantly converts Rage into health.
Swift Flight Form	70		Shapeshift into swift flight form, increasing movement speed by 280% and allowing you to fly. Cannot use in combat. Replaces Flight Form.
Might of Ursoc	72		Increases current and maximum health by 30% for 20 sec. Activates Bear Form.
Tranquility	74		Heals 5 nearby lowest health party or raid targets within 40 yards with Tranquility every 2 sec for 8 sec. Stacks up to 3 times. The Druid must channel to maintain the spell.
Cyclone	78		Tosses the enemy target into the air, preventing all action but making them invulnerable for up to 6 sec. Only one target can be affected by your Cyclone at a time.
Maim (Cat)	82		Finishing move that causes damage and stuns the target. Causes more bonus damage and lasts 1 sec longer per combo points.
Stampeding Roar	84		The Druid roars, increasing the movement speed of all friendly players within 10 yards by 60% for 8 sec and removing all roots and snares on those targets. Does not break prowling. Using this ability outside of Bear Form or Cat Form activates Bear Form.
Symbiosis	87		Creates a symbiotic link which grants the Druid one ability belonging to the target's class, varying by the Druid's specialization. Also grants the target one Druid ability based on their class and combat role. Lasts 1 hour and persists through death. Effect cancelled if Druid and target become too far apart. (See Symbiosis entry.)

TALENTS

TALENT		DESCRIPTION	NOTES
LEVEL 15 TIER (MOBILITY)			
Feline Swiftness		Increases your movement speed by 15%.	Previously a Feral talent that only worked in Cat Form, this is a great way to get to and away from enemies—great for both PvE and PvP.
Displacer Beast		Teleports you forward and activates Prowl (and therefore Cat Form).	Works much like a mage's Blink ability in that it instantly teleports you in the direction you're facing. As a bonus, it makes you invisible, making this one of the best ways to avoid a PvP conflict or simply get away from an enemy.
Wild Charge		Grants a movement ability depending on your current form: None: Fly to an ally's position. Bear: Charge an enemy, immobilizing them for 4 sec. Cat: Leaps behind an enemy, dazing them for 3 sec. Moonkin: Jumps backward, away from an enemy. Travel: Leaps forward a short distance. Aquatic: Increases swim speed by an additional 150% for 5 sec.	Previously Feral Charge, this talent now affects all forms, not just Feral ones. Ideal for players who want to take advantage of a druid's hybrid capabilities, as this talent adds incredible flexibility for a large number of situations.
LEVEL 30 TIER (HEALING)			
Nature's Swiftness		Makes your next Cyclone, Entangling Roots, Healing Touch, Hibernate, Nourish, Rebirth or Regrowth instant, free and castable in all forms. The healing and duration of the spell is increased by 50%.	Very versatile ability, especially when you're at risk of getting interrupted, or just need to cast a heal immediately. Note that spells affected by this are castable in any form, which is a nice bonus.
Renewal		Instantly heals you for 30% of your maximum health. Useable in all shapeshift forms.	A straightforward self-heal similar to a priest's desperate prayer. Great emergency button, but note the relatively long cooldown.
Cenarion Ward		Protects a friendly target, causing any damage taken to heal the target every 2 sec for 6 sec. Gaining the healing effect consumes the Cenarion Ward. Useable in all shapeshift forms. Lasts 30 sec.	A steadier version of Renewal, this probably won't save your life under heavy siege, but can be used much more often (and on other players).
LEVEL 45 TIER (SNARING)			
Faerie Swarm		Grants an improved version of Faerie Fire that also reduces the target's movement speed by 50% for 15 sec. This talent replaces Faerie Fire.	Spells that inflict two debuffs at a time are a tremendous boon. You hurt the target in two ways and save yourself a global cooldown.
Mass Entanglement		Roots your target in place for 20 sec and spreads to additional nearby enemies. Affects 5 total targets. Damage caused may interrupt the effect. Useable in all shapeshift forms.	An instant AoE version of Entangling Roots that also breaks on damage. It affects up to five enemies, which is more than is usually necessary, making it a great escape tool for you or your allies. Great in battlegrounds!
Typhoon		Summons a violent Typhoon that strikes targets in front of the caster within 30 yards, knocking them back and dazing them for 6 sec. Useable in all shapeshift forms.	An old favorite that might be familiar to veteran moonkins, Typhoon is largely unchanged—a great way to get some space between you and various enemies, particularly melee types.
LEVEL 60 TIER (SPEC IMPROVEMENT)			
Soul of the Forest		Aessina's blessing grants a benefit which varies by your combat specialization. Balance: When a Lunar Eclipse ends you gain Solar Energy and when a Solar Eclipse ends you gain Lunar Energy. Feral: Your finishing moves grant 4 Energy per combo point. Guardian: Mangle now generates an additional 2 Rage. Restoration: You gain 50% haste for your next spell when you cast Swiftmend.	Note this is a passive talent, which provides sizable bonuses to all specs and requires little effort on your part. The Guardian version of this talent is particularly useful if rage is an issue.
Incarnation		Grants a superior shapeshifting form appropriate to your specialization for 30 sec. You may freely shapeshift in and out of this form for the duration of Incarnation. Balance (Chosen of Elune): Improved Moonkin Form that gains 25% increased Arcane and Nature damage while Eclipse is active. Feral (King of the Jungle): Improved Cat Form that allows the use of all abilities which normally require stealth, allows the use of Prowl while in combat, and removes the positional requirement of Ravage. Guardian (Son of Ursoc): Improved Bear Form that reduces the cooldown on melee damage abilities and Growl to 1.5 sec. Restoration (Tree of Life): Tree of Life Form that increases healing done by 15%, increases armor by 120%, and enhances Lifebloom, Wild Growth, Regrowth, and Entangling Roots spellcasts.	A more controlled set of spec-specific buffs that act as a major cooldown. Some of these abilities are a straight damage increase, like Balance, while others allow for more flexibility, like Feral and Restoration. Do note the long cooldown, however!
Force of Nature		Summons 3 treants to assist in the Druid's current combat role for 15 sec. Treant capabilities vary by specialization. Useable in all shapeshift forms.	An instant, free ability that resembles an Enhancement shaman's wolves. The treants act differently based on your spec, and, where previously they only attacked your current target, they are now controllable like most other pets. For example, Balance treants can cast Wrath and Entangling Roots.
LEVEL 75 TIER (CONTROL)			
Disorienting Roar		Invokes the spirit of Ursol to roar, disorienting all enemies within 10 yards for 3 sec. Any damage caused will remove the effect. Useable in all shapeshift forms.	An instant AoE crowd control on a short cooldown that especially shines in PvP encounters. Resembles a Tauren's War Stomp racial ability, but will break on damage.
Ursol's Vortex		Conjures a vortex of wind at the destination location that reduces the movement speed of all enemies within 8 yards by 50%. The first time an enemy attempts to leave the vortex, winds will pull that enemy back to its center. Lasts 10 sec. Useable in all shapeshift forms.	Especially useful against melee-based players in PvP, as it can save you or an ally. Note the pull aspect of the talent can only occur once per enemy.
Mighty Bash		Invokes the spirit of Ursoc to stun the target for 5 sec. Useable in all shapeshift forms.	An improved version of what used to be Bash, but usable in all forms. Only usable in melee range.
LEVEL 90 TIER (HYBRIDISM)			
Heart of the Wild		Passively increases Stamina, Agility and Intellect by 6% at all times. When activated, dramatically improves the Druid's ability to perform roles outside of their normal specialization for 45 sec. Grants the following benefits based on current specialization: Non-Guardian: While in Bear Form, Agility, Expertise, Hit Chance, and armor bonuses increased. Vengeance granted, chance to be hit by melee critical strikes reduced. Non-Feral: While in Cat Form, Agility, Hit Chance, and Expertise increased. Non-Restoration: Healing increased and mana cost of all healing spells reduced by 100%. Guardian Druids may also cast Rejuvenation while shapeshifted. Non-Balance: Spell Damage and Hit Chance increased. Mana cost of all damage spells reduced by 100%.	Heart of the Wild is the ultimate hybrid talent. It allows you to temporarily become proficient at a different specialization's primary form. The practical uses of this talents are endless, and just limited by your imagination—consider, for example, emergency tanking, temporarily nuking a melee-immune boss or healing an ally in PvP. It lasts 45 seconds, giving you enough time to enjoy the boosts, but note the considerable cooldown.
Dream of Cenarius		Wrath, Starfire, Starsurge and melee strikes increase the healing of your next spell by 30%. Tranquility is not affected. Nourish, Healing Touch, and Regrowth increase the damage done by your next 2 Moonfire or Sunfire casts by 50% or by your next 2 melee abilities by 50%. Each of these bonuses lasts 30 sec.	Another hybrid talent—this one passively grants you buffs to abilities that are not normally used by your spec. Great for healers that want to dish out some damage (perhaps to get a kill in PvP), casters that want to throw a heal, and so on.
Nature's Vigil		Increases all damage and healing done by 20% for 30 sec. While active, all single-target healing spells also damage a nearby enemy target for 25% of the healing done, and all single-target damage spells and abilities also heal a nearby friendly target for 25% of the damage done.	The third of the hybrid abilities, Nature's Vigil is on a much shorter cooldown than Heart of the Wild, but the bonuses to secondary roles are not as complete/significant.

BALANCE

Balance is a caster DPS tree focused on abilities that excel at dealing ranged, magical damage. Druids who specialize in Balance are able to stay at range and dish some serious damage through spells such as Wrath, Starfire, and Moonfire. In addition to a mana bar, Balance Druids have a unique Eclipse bar that indicates your Solar or Lunar energy.

MASTERY: TOTAL ECLIPSE

Increases the bonus damage granted by Eclipse by a percentage determined by your Mastery.

SPECIALIZATION ABILITIES

ABILITY	LEVEL		DESCRIPTION
Eclipse	10		Your Wrath now generates Lunar Energy and your Starfire now generates Solar energy. Solar Eclipse: When you reach 100 Solar Energy you will trigger a Solar Eclipse, increasing all Nature damage done by 15%. Lunar Eclipse: When you reach 100 Lunar Energy you will trigger a Lunar Eclipse, increasing all Arcane damage done by 15% and transforming your Hurricane spell into Astral Storm. When triggered, both Lunar and Solar Eclipse grant 15% spell haste for 15 sec and energize you for 35% of your maximum mana.
Natural Insight	10		Increases your mana pool by 400%.
Starfire	10		Deals Arcane damage to an enemy. Generates 20 Solar Energy.
Starsurge	12		You fuse the power of the moon and sun, launching a devastating blast of energy at the target. Causes Spellstorm damage to the target and generates 20 Lunar or Solar Energy, whichever is more beneficial to you.
Celestial Focus	14		Reduces the pushback suffered from damaging attacks while casting Wrath, Starfire, Entangling Roots, Hurricane, Astral Storm, Hibernate, Cyclone, and Starsurge by 70%.
Moonkin Form	16		Shapeshift into Moonkin Form, increasing Arcane and Nature damage you deal by 10% and reducing all damage you take by 15%. The Druid cannot cast healing spells while shapeshifted. While in this form, you increase the spell haste of all party and raid members within 100 yards by 5%.
Sunfire	18		Burns the enemy for Nature damage and then an additional Nature damage over 18 sec. Your Wrath and Starsurge critical strikes on the target will extend your Sunfire's duration by 2 sec.
Astral Communion	20		Commune with the sun and moon, gaining 25 Lunar or Solar Energy every 1 sec for 4 sec. Generates the power type most beneficial to you.
Remove Corruption	22		Nullifies corrupting effects on the friendly target, removing all Curse and Poison effects.
Shooting Stars	26		You have a 30% chance when you deal critical periodic damage with your Moonfire or Sunfire to instantly reset the cooldown of your Starsurge and cause its next cast within 12 sec to be instant.
Solar Beam	28		You summon a beam of solar light over an enemy target's location, interrupting the target and silencing all enemies under the beam while it is active. Solar Beam lasts for 15 sec.
Killer Instinct	34		Grants 100% of your Intellect as Agility when you shapeshift into Bear Form or Cat Form.
Euphoria	38		While not in an Eclipse state, your Wrath, Starfire, and Starsurge spells generate double the normal amount of Solar or Lunar Energy.
Owlkin Frenzy	48		Attacks done to you while in Moonkin Form have a 15% chance to cause you to go into a Frenzy, increasing your damage by 10% and causing you to be immune to pushback while casting Balance spells. Lasts 10 sec.
Balance of Power	64		Grants Hit equal to any Spirit gained from items or effects.
Celestial Alignment	68		Grants you the simultaneous damage benefit of both your Lunar Eclipse and Solar Eclipse, increasing damage done by your Nature and Arcane spells by 30%. In addition, casting Moonfire also applies the periodic damage effect of Sunfire to your target. Activating this ability consumes all Lunar and Solar Energy and prevents gaining more during its duration. Lasts 15 sec.
Starfall	76		You summon a flurry of stars from the sky on all targets within 40 yards of the caster that you're in combat with, each dealing Arcane damage. Maximum 20 stars. Lasts 10 sec. Triggering a Lunar Eclipse resets the cooldown of this spell. Shapeshifting into an animal form or mounting cancels the effect. Any effect which causes you to lose control of your character will suppress the Starfall effect.
Lunar Shower	82		When you cast Moonfire or Sunfire, you gain Lunar Shower. Lunar Shower increases the direct damage done by your Moonfire and Sunfire spells by 45%, and reduces the mana cost by 30%. This effect stacks up to 3 times and lasts 3 sec.
Wild Mushroom	84		Grow magical mushrooms with 5 health at the target location. After 6 sec, the mushrooms will become invisible. Other Wild Mushroom abilities can target these mushrooms for additional effects. Only 3 mushrooms can be placed one time.
Wild Mushroom: Detonate	84		Detonates all of your Wild Mushrooms, dealing Nature damage to all nearby targets within 8 yards, and creating a Fungal Growth in each mushroom's wake covering an area within 8 yards, slowing all enemy targets by 50% and lasting 20 sec.

GETTING TO LEVEL 90

Being the caster version of a Druid, you will benefit most from rooting abilities such as Entangling Roots and Nature's Grasp when leveling. Eclipse procs aren't as important as they would be in, say, a dungeon, but they will provide a nice boost in speed when leveling.

Consider Feline Swiftness and some healing (or hybrid) talents for maximum leveling speed.

PLAYING IN A GROUP

Execute your base rotation while making sure to use talents and other damage-increasing cooldowns when in Eclipse. Your Solar Beam ability is one of the few AoE silences available to players, so it is usually appreciated, especially against numerous caster enemies. Keep Faerie Fire in mind if nobody else can apply the Weakened Armor debuff.

BASE ROTATION

Balance rotation is about, well, balance. Your goal is to go into Eclipse mode by generating Solar or Lunar energy. Once you're in that mode, you will cast spells associated with the opposite energy (as they will deal more damage), allowing you to alternate. Either Eclipse will grant a significant spell haste and mana boost.

- Apply/refresh Moonfire if working toward Solar Eclipse
- Apply/refresh Sunfire if working toward Lunar Eclipse
- Cast Starsurge when available when you're working toward either Eclipse effect
- Cast Wrath if working toward Lunar Eclipse
- Cast Starfire if working toward Solar Eclipse

GROUP BUFFS AND DEBUFFS

Balance Druids apply the Stats buff with Mark of the Wild, and impart the Spell Haste buff when they're in Moonkin Form. Faerie Fire inflicts the Weakened Armor debuff.

GETTING READY FOR HIGH-END CONTENT

BALANCE

Like other casters, Balance Druids should always try to maximize their damage output for heroic dungeons and raids.

For raids, your priority should be reaching the Hit cap (15%, or 14% for Draenei). Like Elemental Shamans and Shadow Priests, Balance Druids have an advantage in this regard, as they can benefit from Spirit just as they would from Hit. Always prioritize Intellect when gemming, but don't pass up good socket bonuses. Note that all the secondary stats (Critical Stike, Haste, and Mastery) are roughly equally useful, with Haste slightly pulling ahead.

FERAL

Feral Druids now exclusively refer to the melee DPS version of Druids. Tanks have their own spec called Guardian, allowing Feral to make the most out of Cat Form and its abilities. Many abilities are still shared between Guardians and Feral Druids, making synergy between these two specs possible.

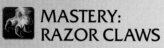

MASTERY: RAZOR CLAWS

Increases the damage done by your bleed abilities by a percentage determined by your Mastery.

SPECIALIZATION ABILITIES

ABILITY	LEVEL		DESCRIPTION
Tiger's Fury	10		Increases physical damage done by 15% for 6 sec and instantly restores 60 Energy. Cannot be activated while Berserk (Cat) is active. Only useable in Cat Form.
Feral Instinct (Cat)	14		Reduces the chance enemies have to detect you while Prowl is active.
Shred (Cat)	16		Shred the target, causing damage to the target. Must be behind the target. Awards 1 combo point. Deal 20% additional damage against bleeding targets.
Savage Roar	18		Finishing move that increases physical damage done by 30%. Lasts longer per combo point.
Rip (Cat)	20		Finishing move that causes Bleed damage over time. Damage increases per combo point. Each time you Shred, Ravage, or Mangle the target while in Cat Form the duration of your Rip on that target is extended by 2 sec, up to a maximum of 6 sec.
Remove Corruption	22		Nullifies corrupting effects on the friendly target, removing all Curse and Poison effects.
Predatory Swiftness	26		Your finishing moves have a 20% chance per combo point to make your next Cyclone, Entangling Roots, Healing Touch, Hibernate, or Rebirth become instant, free, and castable in all forms.
Thrash (Cat and Bear)	28		Thrash all nearby enemies, dealing immediate physical damage and periodic bleed damage, and also causes the Weakened Blows effect. Damage varies by shapeshift form.
Nurturing Instinct	34		Increases your nature spell power by 100% of your Agility.
Omen of Clarity	38		Your autoattacks have a small chance to cause you to enter a Clearcasting state. The Clearcasting state reduces the Mana, Rage, or Energy cost of your next cast-time damaging or healing spell or offensive feral ability by 100%.
Infected Wounds	40		Your Shred, Ravage, Maul, and Mangle attacks cause an Infected Wound in the target. The Infected Wound reduces the movement speed of the target by 50%. Lasts 12 sec.
Leader of the Pack (Cat and Bear)	46		While in Bear Form or Cat Form, increases critical strike chance of all party and raid members within 100 yards by 5%. Also causes your melee critical strikes to heal you for 4% of your health and energize you for 8% of your mana. This effect cannot occur more than once every 6 sec.
Berserk (Cat and Bear)	48		When used in Bear Form, removes the cooldown from Mangle and causes it to hit up to 3 targets and lasts 10 sec. When used in Cat Form, reduces the cost of all Cat Form abilities by 50% and lasts 15 sec.
Ravage (Cat)	54		Ravage the target, causing 750% damage plus additional damage to the target. Must be prowling and behind the target. Awards 1 combo point. Ravage has a 50% increased chance to critically strike targets with over 80% health.
Skull Bash (Cat and Bear)	64		You charge and skull bash the target, interrupting spellcasting and preventing any spell in that school from being cast for 4 sec. Increases the mana cost of the victim's spells by 25% for 10 sec.

GETTING TO LEVEL 90

Cats are very versatile levelers, especially because they can so easily turn stealth. Though this won't always be necessary—most of the time, you'll simply want to pull an enemy with Faerie Fire and then apply your bleeds as soon as possible. Don't wait for 5 combo points to use Rip on weaker enemies, as it's rarely worth it. Consider whether Savage Roar is necessary or not—at 5 combo points, it can last long enough to defeat several enemies.

For tougher enemies, consider using Prowl before a fight and opening with Pounce or Ravage. The latter can actually be a very good all-purpose opener, as its critical chance is greatly increased for targets with high health.

PLAYING IN A GROUP

Being melee-based, you must watch your threat near the start of a fight, particularly if the tank is less geared than you are. If you opted for hybrid talents, remember to use them to aid your group—particularly those that allow you to tank temporarily or heal allies while remaining in Cat Form. Use Faerie Fire often, as it will benefit you and other melee classes in your group.

BASE ROTATION

Cat DPS is all about maintaining bleed effects on targets that will live long enough for them to fully tick. Because of Shred, you will usually want to be behind your enemies.

- Apply/refresh the Rake bleed

- If you have 5 combo points and the effect isn't already active, use Savage Roar

- Use Rip when you have 5 combo points

- Use Ferocious Bite when you have 5 combo points and Rip is already active, or your target is below 25% health

- Use Shred if positioning allows it

- Use Mangle otherwise

GROUP BUFFS AND DEBUFFS

Druids grant the Stats buff with Mark of the Wild. Feral Druids provide the Critical Strike buff via Leader of the Pack.

Faerie Fire stacks impart the Weakened Armor debuff, while Thrash causes Weakened Blows on its target.

GETTING READY FOR HIGH-END CONTENT

FERAL

Like other melee classes, your goal is to avoid getting misses on raid bosses. This is fairly easy for Druids, as they don't dual wield, making the Hit cap much lower. It's not necessary to completely eliminate misses right away—get some Expertise where possible, too—but it will increase your damage significantly. After Hit is no longer a concern, Critical Strike, Mastery, and Haste all provide roughly the same benefit.

As your primary stat, gem for Agility wherever you can, while matching gem colors for good gem bonuses.

GUARDIAN

Previously part of the Feral Combat spec, tank Druids are now called Guardians. With many passive and active abilities that benefit Bear Form, Guardians can sustain the brunt of enemy attacks while still providing some utility to a group, mainly through hybrid talents.

MASTERY: NATURE'S GUARDIAN

Increases your armor by a percentage determined by your Mastery.

SPECIALIZATION ABILITIES

ABILITY	LEVEL		DESCRIPTION
Savage Defense (Bear)	10		Increases chance to dodge by 45% for 6 sec.
Vengeance (Bear)	10		Each time you take damage while in Bear Form, you gain 2% of the unmitigated damage taken as attack power. Entering Cat Form will cancel this effect.
Thick Hide	14		Increases the armor bonus of Bear Form to 330%, reduces all magical damage taken by 25%, and reduces the chance you'll be critically hit by melee attacks by 6%.
Bear Hug	18		Melee attack that stuns the target for 3 sec and each 1 sec deals 10% of the Druid's health in damage. The Druid is immobilized for 3 sec. Using this ability activates Bear Form.
Rip (Cat)	20		Finishing move that causes Bleed damage over time. Damage increases per combo point. Each time you Shred, Ravage, or Mangle the target while in Cat Form the duration of your Rip on that target is extended by 2 sec, up to a maximum of 6 sec.
Remove Corruption	22		Nullifies corrupting effects on the friendly target, removing all Curse and Poison effects.
Thrash (Cat and Bear)	28		Thrash all nearby enemies, dealing immediate physical damage and periodic bleed damage, and also causes the Weakened Blows effect. Damage varies by shapeshift form.
Nurturing Instinct	34		Increases your nature spell power by 100% of your Agility.
Infected Wounds	40		Your Shred, Ravage, Maul, and Mangle attacks cause an Infected Wound in the target. The Infected Wound reduces the movement speed of the target by 50%. Lasts 12 sec.
Leader of the Pack (Cat and Bear)	46		While in Bear Form or Cat Form, increases critical strike chance of all party and raid members within 100 yards by 5%. Also causes your melee critical strikes to heal you for 4% of your health and energize you for 8% of your mana. This effect cannot occur more than once every 6 sec.
Berserk (Cat and Bear)	48		When used in Bear Form, removes the cooldown from Mangle and causes it to hit up to 3 targets and lasts 10 sec. When used in Cat Form, reduces the cost of all Cat Form abilities by 50% and lasts 15 sec.
Ravage (Cat)	54		Ravage the target, causing 750% damage plus additional damage to the target. Must be prowling and behind the target. Awards 1 combo point. Ravage has a 50% increased chance to critically strike targets with over 80% health.
Survival Instincts (Bear)	56		Reduces all damage taken by 50% for 12 sec.
Skull Bash (Cat and Bear)	64		You charge and skull bash the target, interrupting spellcasting and preventing any spell in that school from being cast for 4 sec. Increases the mana cost of the victim's spells by 25% for 10 sec.
Enrage	76		Generates 20 Rage instantly, then additional 10 Rage over 10 sec.

GETTING TO LEVEL 90

Because Guardian Druids and Feral Druids share many abilities (most notably Ravage, Rip, Rake, and Mangle), you're better off leveling in Cat Form than as a bear. If you can spare the gold, however, dual specialization gives you a chance to have a proper leveling spec and still be able to tank dungeons as you level.

PLAYING IN A GROUP

As a tank, your role is to keep all enemies off your party members. To accomplish this, Bear Form grants you a large bonus to threat, making enemies much more likely to attack you. Thrash is a key ability when facing multiple enemies, as it weakens their attacks and deals damage to them, hopefully keeping them off more fragile party members. Naturally, use your taunting ability, Growl, if you can't seem to get a single enemy's attention.

Watch your health closely at all times, particularly when you predict large incoming damage. Try to save some Rage for these occasions in order to use your defensive abilities.

BASE ROTATION

As with other tanks, Guardians can benefit greatly from proper resource management. In this case, the Savage Defense ability will be your primary defensive rage consuming skill.

- Apply/refresh Lacerate up to 3 stacks (depending on how long your target will live)
- Apply/refresh Thrash, especially for multiple enemies
- Use Mangle
- If you have enough rage, consider Savage Defense or Frenzied Regeneration to increase your survivability

GROUP BUFFS AND DEBUFFS

Druids grant the Stats buff with Mark of the Wild. Guardian Druids provide the Critical Strike buff via Leader of the Pack.

Faerie Fire stacks impart the Weakened Armor debuff, while Thrash causes Weakened Blows on its target.

GETTING READY FOR HIGH-END CONTENT

GUARDIAN

Due to passive abilities, Guardian Druids greatly benefit from secondary, DPS-oriented stats, so they're able to use similar gear to Feral Druids. Hit-capping is not nearly as important, however—prioritize survivability instead, gemming for Agility, Stamina, and Mastery.

RESTORATION

Restoration is a Druid's healing specialization, mostly employing nature-based recovery spells in order to serve as a group's healer. Restoration Druids are masters of heal-over-time spells, but less so than before—instead, they can now provide extra utility with many hybrid abilities and talents.

MASTERY: HARMONY

Your direct healing is increased by an additional percentage and casting your direct healing spells grants you an additional percentage bonus to periodic healing for 20 sec.

SPECIALIZATION ABILITIES

ABILITY	LEVEL		DESCRIPTION
Natural Insight	10		Increases your mana pool by 400%.
Swiftmend	10		Instantly heals a friendly target that has an active Rejuvenation or Regrowth effect. In addition, restores health to the three most injured allies within 8 yards of the initial target every 1 sec for 7 sec.
Nourish	12		Heals a friendly target. Heals an additional 20% if you have a Rejuvenation, Regrowth, Lifebloom, or Wild Growth effect active on the target.
Meditation	14		Allows 50% of your mana regeneration from Spirit to continue while in combat.
Nature's Focus	16		Increases your chance to hit with Moonfire and Wrath by 15%. Reduces the pushback suffered from damaging attacks by 70% while casting Healing Touch, Regrowth, Tranquility, Rebirth, Entangling Roots, Cyclone, and Nourish.
Regrowth	18		Heals a friendly target plus additional amount over 6 sec. Regrowth has a 60% increased chance for a critical effect. Duration automatically refreshes to 6 sec each time Regrowth heals targets at or below 50% health.
Nature's Cure	22		Cures harmful effects on the friendly target, removing all Magic, Curse, and Poison effects.
Living Seed	28		When you critically heal a target with the direct healing portion of Swiftmend, Regrowth, Nourish, or Healing Touch you plant a Living Seed on the target. When the target is next attacked, the Living Seed will bloom and heal for 30% of the initial amount healed. Lasts 15 sec.
Killer Instinct	34		Grants 100% of your Intellect as Agility when you shapeshift into Bear Form or Cat Form.
Lifebloom	36		Heals the target over 15 sec. When Lifebloom expires or is dispelled, the target is instantly healed. This effect can stack up to 3 times on the same target. Duration refreshed each time you cast Healing Touch, Nourish, or Regrowth on the target. Lifebloom can be active only on one target at a time.
Omen of Clarity	38		Your periodic healing from Lifebloom has a 4% chance to cause you to enter a Clearcasting state. The Clearcasting state reduces the Mana, Rage or Energy cost of your next cast-time damaging or healing spell or offensive feral ability by 100%. Does not affect Nourish.
Swift Rejuvenation	46		Reduces the global cooldown of your Rejuvenation by 0.5 sec.
Ironbark	64		The target's skin becomes as tough as Ironwood, reducing all damage taken by 20%. Lasts 12 sec.
Wild Growth	76		Heals up to 5 friendly party or raid members within 30 yards of the target over 7 sec. Prioritizes healing most injured party members. The amount healed is applied quickly at first, and slows down as the Wild Growth reaches its full duration.
Malfurion's Gift	82		The cooldown of your Tranquility spell is reduced to 3 minutes and the cooldown of your Barkskin ability is reduced by 15 sec.
Wild Mushroom	84		Grow magical mushrooms with 5 health at the target location. After 6 sec, the mushrooms will become invisible. Other Wild Mushroom abilities can target these mushrooms for additional effects. Only 3 mushrooms can be placed one time.
Wild Mushroom: Bloom	84		Causes all of your Wild Mushrooms to bloom, healing all allies within 8 yards.

GETTING TO LEVEL 90

Restoration is not optimal for leveling, but keep in mind Druids have talents and abilities that allow them to use different forms efficiently. Chief among these is Killer Instinct, a Restoration passive that increases your Agility by an amount determined by your Intellect when you turn into a bear or a cat. This allows you to be relatively efficient at leveling, but never like a Feral Druid. Consider dual specialization if you want to be a healer in dungeons but level at maximum speed.

PLAYING IN A GROUP

Use your healing priority to conserve as much mana as possible, as you never know when you'll need it. Innervate also helps you accomplish this. Note that Restoration Druids can still use the crowd control abilities Hibernate and Cyclone, so don't be afraid to if you predict a large pack will make quick work of your tank. If someone dies but you think the fight is still doable, be quick to use Rebirth—note that other classes can use similar spells, however, if you're struggling to keep the group alive.

HEALING

Healer Druids, along with Discipline Priests, have the least standard of healing spells. They do have the three main types of heal, but the way they interact with passives and other abilities provides bonuses that might be less straightforward to a newcomer. You can stick to the following guidelines, however.

SITUATION(S)	USE...
An ally is in need of immediate healing	Swiftmend if the target has one of your main HoT spells, otherwise Regrowth
Healing a single target that's not in immediate danger	Keep Lifebloom up, especially if the target is a tank; it is now refreshed by other heals, making this task easier. Otherwise, Healing Touch or Nourish, depending on how much health is missing
Everyone is healthy, but you know there's going to be incoming damage	Cast Rejuvenation on all the targets you think will take damage. For Restoration Druids, this spell has a shorter cooldown, allowing you to accomplish this more easily
Heavy AoE damage from enemies	Get Wild Growth up on as many targets as possible. If this isn't enough, use Tranquility

GROUP BUFFS AND DEBUFFS

Restoration Druids provide only the baseline Druid buff (Stats) with Mark of the Wild and the Weakened Armor debuff with Faerie Fire.

GETTING READY FOR HIGH-END CONTENT

RESTORATION

Without having a Hit cap to worry about (most of your damage-based abilities and talents get hit chance boosts from passives), you should go straight for throughput (from Intellect, Haste, Critical Strike, and Mastery) and mana regeneration (from Spirit). How you balance these stats will be based on how often you feel like you need more mana. For instance, Haste will allow you to cast faster, thus healing more, but using more mana. Consider reforging some secondary stats to Spirit if you think you're holding back too much due to lack of mana.

HUNTER

Hunters are masters of archery and marksmanship, relying on their ranged weapons to eliminate their foes from afar, without the need to get close and personal. Hunters are close to nature, allowing them to tame and summon wild beasts to do their bidding. Azeroth has an immense variety of animal species, and Hunters are able to charm their way into getting aid in battle from most of them. Pets are an integral part of playing a Hunter, and there are a few pages devoted to them at the end of this section.

Hunters are the only ranged class that primarily deals physical damage, mainly using bows, crossbows, or guns. Because they're best at range, Hunters can master many slowing, snaring, and immobilizing mechanics to keep their enemies at bay. Among these are traps, which can slow enemies down, prevent them from acting altogether, or even help the Hunter deal more damage. Lastly, Hunters can take on the aspects of several different beasts, modifying their abilities in various interesting ways.

RACE AVAILABILITY

ALLIANCE

Draenei   Dwarf   Gnome

Human   Night Elf   Worgen

Pandaren

HORDE

Blood Elf   Goblin   Orc

Tauren   Troll   Undead

RACIAL ADVANTAGES

ALLIANCE

RACE	NOTES
Draenei	Heroic Presence grants Draenei +1% Hit chance. Gift of the Naaru heals the Draenei or any ally. Draenei take less damage from Shadow spells.
Dwarf	Stoneform is excellent for PvP, as it removes all poison, disease, and bleed effects and reduces damage taken. Crack Shot increases Expertise with ranged weapons by 1%. Dwarves take less damage from Frost spells.
Human	Every Man for Himself removes effects that cause loss of control of your character. Sword Specialization increases Expertise for swords by 1%.
Night Elf	Night Elves are less likely to be hit by any physical attack and take less damage from Nature spells. Shadowmeld renders the Night Elf invisible while motionless and cancels spells being cast by enemies on the Night Elf.
Worgen	Worgen get 1% increased Critical Strike from Viciousness. Darkflight increases movement speed temporarily.

PANDAREN

RACE	NOTES
Pandaren	Epicurean doubles the statistical bonuses from being Well Fed. Quaking Palm acts as a form of brief crowd control.

HORDE

RACE	NOTES
Blood Elf	The signature Blood Elf racial, Arcane Torrent, provides mana and an AoE silence. The former helps in tight Focus situations, and the latter is great for PvP and certain PvE encounters. Blood Elves take less damage from Arcane spells.
Goblin	Rocket Jump is a great mobility tool, allowing Hunters to stay at range; it can also be used as a second Disengage. Goblins get 1% increased Haste from Time is Money. Rocket Barrage is another source of damage for Goblins.
Orc	Orcs are great for maximizing damage. Blood Fury increases your attack power. Command increases your pet's damage output. Axe Specialization increases Expertise for axes by 1%. Hardiness reduces the duration of stun effects by 15%.
Tauren	Nature Resistance increases a Tauren's ability to stand up to harmful Nature effects. War Stomp provides an (AoE) stun in melee range, and Endurance boosts base health by 5%, making Tauren a good choice for PvP.
Troll	Berserking grants a temporary increase in attack speed. Da Voodoo Shuffle passively reduces the duration of movement impairing effects, which is important for Hunters. Dead Eye increases Expertise with ranged weapons by 1%. Trolls regenerate Health faster than other races, and 10% of total Health regeneration may continue in combat.
Undead	Undead are more suited for PvP as they can break out of Charm, Fear, and Sleep effects with Will of the Forsaken. Their passive racial, Touch of the Grave, is a life leech and also provides a modest DPS increase in any situation. Undead take less damage from Shadow spells.

EQUIPMENT OPTIONS

ARMOR TYPE	SHIELD
Leather until Level 40, then Mail	No

USABLE WEAPONS

1 HAND WEAPON	2 HAND WEAPON	RANGED
Axes	Axes	Bows
Daggers	Polearms	Crossbows
Fist Weapons	Staves	Guns
Swords	Swords	

PROMINENT CLASS ABILITIES

FOCUS

Focus is the resource that both Hunters and their pets use to activate their abilities. All Hunters and Hunter pets have a maximum Focus value of 100. Focus regenerates by itself over time, at a rate of 6 per second for the Hunter, and 5 per second for pets. There are a few different methods to increase the rate at which you regenerate Focus. Casting Steady or Cobra Shot instantly restores 9 Focus. Several talents also cause you or your pet to generate Focus instantly when specific conditions are met.

Focus is a resource to be used! Don't ever let yourself get to 100 Focus after the start of a fight. You should be doing something at all times, whether it is using Steady Shot to regenerate Focus that you've used, or using an ability that costs Focus. Most of your hardest-hitting abilities have cooldowns, so always try to have enough Focus to cast them as soon as they're ready.

TRAPS

An important aspect of playing Hunters is the ability to drop traps to hinder your enemies. They are valuable in a variety of situations, ranging from increasing your damage, long-term crowd-control, or creating a patch of ice that slows all enemies that approach it. The latter is one of the best ways to keep several enemies slowed at once.

Traps can be placed in one of two ways: right under your character, or shot at a target location. The latter is possible due to Trap Launcher, which is now a toggled ability. Until Mists of Pandaria, Hunters needed to keep using Trap Launcher before placing every trap. Now you can simply toggle Trap Launcher and throw every trap you use, or you can toggle it off and place a trap to fend off an enemy that's too close for comfort.

Note that traps trigger a cooldown based on their type. For example, you can place either Freezing Trap or Ice Trap. If you place either, the other becomes disabled for the duration of the cooldown. Additionally, only one target can be frozen by Freezing Trap at once, so pick your target wisely!

ASPECTS

Hunters can take on the aspect of several beasts, providing a buff to themselves or their allies. The aspects are instant and unlimited, but only one of them may be active at a time. Hunter Aspects require the use of a Global Cooldown in and out of Combat, so be sure to think carefully about the situation you are in, and if changing Aspects will be a net gain for you at that time.

STAMPEDE

The Hunter's level 87 ability is Stampede. This ability summons all your current pets (the ones not in the stable) to your aid for 20 seconds. Pets summoned via Stampede only deal 25% of their normal damage for the duration that they are active. During this time, they can be controlled much like a normal Hunter pet, and may be commanded to attack, follow, or Move To as the Hunter sees fit. This makes Stampede a pretty significant DPS burst for Hunters. It has a 5 minute cooldown, so don't use it frivolously.

NON-SPECIALIZATION ABILITIES

NAME	LEVEL		DESCRIPTION
Arcane Shot	1		An instant shot that causes 100% weapon damage plus additional Arcane damage.
Auto Shot	1		Automatically shoots the target until cancelled.
Revive Pet	1		Revive your pet, returning it to life with 100% of its base health.
Call Pet	1		Call an active Pet to your side.
Steady Shot	3		A steady shot that causes 70% weapon damage plus more. Generates Focus.
Tracking	4		Shows the location of all nearby Beasts, Demons, Dragonkin, Elementals, Giants, Hidden, Humanoids and Undead on the minimap. Activate through tracking interface..
Concussive Shot	8		Dazes the target, slowing movement speed by 50% for 6 sec.
Beast Lore	10		Gather information about the target beast. The tooltip will display damage, health, armor, any special resistances, and diet. In addition, Beast Lore will reveal whether or not the creature is tameable and what abilities the tamed creature has.
Serpent Sting	10		Causes Nature damage over 15 sec.
Tame Beast	10		Begins taming a beast to be your companion. If you lose the beast's attention for any reason, the taming process will fail.
Dismiss Pet	10		Temporarily sends this pet away. You can call it back later.
Feed Pet	11		Feed your pet the selected item, instantly restoring 50% of its total health. Cannot be used while in combat.
Aspect of the Hawk	12		The Hunter takes on the aspects of a hawk, increasing ranged attack power by 10%. Only one Aspect can be active at a time.
Disengage	14		You attempt to disengage from combat, leaping backwards. Can only be used while in combat.
Hunter's Mark	14		Places the Hunter's Mark on the target, increasing the ranged damage of all attackers against that target by 5%. In addition, the target of this ability can always be seen by the Hunter whether it stealths or turns invisible. The target also appears on the mini-map. Lasts for 5 min.
Scatter Shot	15		A short-range shot that deals 50% weapon damage and disorients the target for 4 sec. Any damage caused will remove the effect. Turns off your attack when used.
Eagle Eye	16		Zooms in the Hunter's vision. Only usable outdoors. Lasts 1 min.
Mend Pet	16		Heals your pet for 25% of its total health over 10 sec.
Call Pet 2	18		Summons your second pet to you.
Aspect of the Cheetah	24		The Hunter takes on the aspects of a cheetah, increasing movement speed by 30%. If the Hunter is struck, he will be dazed for 4 sec.
Multi-Shot	24		Fires several missiles, hitting your current target and all enemies within 8 yards of that target for 60% of weapon damage.
Freezing Trap	28		Place a frost trap that freezes the first enemy that approaches, preventing all action for up to 1 min. Any damage caused will break the ice. Only one target can be Freezing Trapped at a time. Trap will exist for 1 min.
Feign Death	32		Feign death, tricking enemies into ignoring you. Lasts up to 6 min.
Kill Shot	35		You attempt to finish the wounded target off, firing a long range attack dealing 420% weapon damage. Kill Shot can only be used on enemies that have 20% or less health. If Kill Shot fails to kill the target, the cooldown is instantly reset, but cannot be reset more often than once every 6 sec.

NAME	LEVEL		DESCRIPTION
Tranquilizing Shot	35		Attempts to remove 1 Enrage and 1 Magic effect from an enemy target.
Scare Beast	36		Scares a beast, causing it to run in fear for up to 20 sec. Damage caused may interrupt the effect. Only one beast can be feared at a time.
Explosive Trap	38		Place a fire trap that explodes when an enemy approaches, causing Fire damage and burning all enemies within 10 yards for additional Fire damage over 20 sec. Trap will exist for 1 min.
Flare	38		Exposes all hidden and invisible enemies within 10 yards of the targeted area for 20 sec.
Trueshot Aura	39		Grants 10% increased melee and ranged attack power to all party and raid members within 100 yards.
Widow Venom	40		A venomous shot that reduces the effectiveness of any healing taken by the enemy for 30 sec.
Call Pet 3	42		Summons your third pet to you.
Ice Trap	46		Place a frost trap that creates an ice slick around itself for 30 sec when the first enemy approaches it. All enemies within 10 yards will be slowed by 50% while in the area of effect. Trap will exist for 1 min.
Trap Launcher	48		While active, your Traps are launched to a target location within 40 yards. Lasts until cancelled.
Distracting Shot	52		Distracts the target to attack you, but has no effect if the target is already attacking you. Lasts 6 sec.
Rapid Fire	54		Increases ranged attack speed by 40% for 15 sec.
Aspect of the Pack	56		Party and raid members within 40 yards take on the aspects of a pack of cheetahs, increasing movement speed by 30%. If you are struck under the effect of this aspect, you will be dazed for 4 sec. Only one Aspect can be active at a time.
Readiness	60		When activated, this ability immediately finishes the cooldown on all Hunter abilities with a base cooldown less than 5 minutes.
Call Pet 4	62		Summons your fourth pet to you.
Snake Trap	66		Place a nature trap that will release several venomous snakes to attack the first enemy to approach. The snakes will die after 15 sec. Trap will exist for 1 min.
Master's Call	74		Your pet attempts to remove all root and movement impairing effects from itself and its target, and causes your pet and its target to be immune to all such effects for 4 sec.
Misdirection	76		The current party or raid member targeted will receive the threat caused by your next damaging attack and all actions taken for 4 sec afterwards. Transferred threat is not permanent, and will fade after 30 sec.
Deterrence	78		When activated, causes you to deflect melee attacks, ranged attacks, and spells, and reduces all damage taken by 30%. While Deterrence is active, you cannot attack. Lasts 5 sec.
Call Pet 5	82		Summons your fifth pet to you.
Aspect of the Fox	83		The Hunter takes on the aspects of a fox, allowing him to shoot Steady Shot, Cobra Shot, and Barrage while moving and causing him to gain 2 Focus whenever he receives a melee attack. Only one Aspect can be active at a time.
Camouflage	85		You blend into your surroundings, causing you and your pet to be untargetable by ranged attacks. Also reduces the range at which enemy creatures can detect you, and provides stealth while stationary. You can lay traps while camouflaged, but any damage done by you or your pet will cancel the effect. If cast while in combat, lasts for 6 sec. Otherwise, lasts for 1 min.
Stampede	87		Summons all of your pets to fight your current target for 20 sec. Your pets deal 25% of their normal damage while summoned this way.

Talents

TALENT	DESCRIPTION	NOTES
LEVEL 15 TIER (MOBILITY)		
Posthaste	Your Disengage frees you from all movement impairing effects and increases your movement speed by 60% for 8 sec.	The movement bit is very useful against melee-based PvP enemies, allowing you to get away more easily.
Narrow Escape	When you Disengage, you also activate a web trap which encases all targets within 8 yards in sticky webs, preventing movement for 8 sec.	As with Posthaste, great for getting away from melee enemies. It's like having an improved Ice Trap that you can drop at your current location.
Crouching Tiger, Hidden Chimera	Reduces the cooldown of Disengage by 10 sec, and the cooldown of Deterrence by 60 sec.	The cooldown reduction is significant, making it great for PvE encounters with lots of movement, or where you need to use Deterrence often. More importantly, this ability grants the Great Pun buff. No, not really.
LEVEL 30 TIER (CONTROL)		
Silencing Shot	A shot that silences the target and interrupts spellcasting for 3 sec.	Very useful when trying to prevent heals or damaging spells from being cast by other players or enemy mobs, including bosses.
Wyvern Sting	A stinging shot that puts the target to sleep for 30 sec. Any damage will cancel the effect. Only one Sting per Hunter can be active on the target at a time.	Adds another crowd-control ability to your repertoire, allowing you to disable a target for 30 seconds. Works similar to Freezing Trap in that any damage will break the effect.
Binding Shot	You fire a magical projectile, tethering the enemy and any other enemies within 5 yards of the landing arrow for 10 sec. If targets move 5 yards from the arrow they are stunned for 5 sec (3 sec PvP) and will be immune to the effects of Binding Shot for 10 sec.	Yet another AoE crowd control; this one is actually preventable by wise players, but enemy monsters will most likely get stunned by it. Stuns are great because you can keep dealing damage to affected targets without breaking them.
LEVEL 45 TIER (SURVIVABILITY)		
Exhilaration	Instantly heals you for 30% and your pet for 100% of total health.	An instant heal for yourself and your pet on a modest cooldown. It can save your life, especially during solo play.
Aspect of the Iron Hawk	Replaces Aspect of the Hawk. The Hunter takes on the aspects of an iron hawk, increasing ranged attack power by 10%, and reducing all damage taken by 15%. Only one aspect can be active at a time.	This talent is useful in every situation that the Hunter would have Aspect of the Hawk active, as it makes the Hunter more resilient, which is powerful in both PVP and PvE.
Spirit Bond	While your pet is active, you and your pet will regenerate 2% of total health every 2 sec.	Similar to Aspect of the Iron Hawk, this will passively make you live longer. Instead of preventing the damage, it heals it, however.
LEVEL 60 TIER (FOCUS)		
Fervor	Instantly restores 50 Focus to you and your pet and an additional 50 Focus over 10 sec.	On such a short cooldown, this ability is great for DPS output, especially when stacked with other damage-increasing cooldowns.
Dire Beast	Summons a powerful wild beast to attack your target for 15 sec. Each time the beast deals damage, you will gain 5 Focus.	Its short cooldown makes it an appealing choice for keeping Focus levels up. The summoned beast's damage isn't too significant, but ultimately, this is a DPS cooldown that will increase your overall damage.
Thrill of the Hunt	You have a 30% chance when you fire a ranged attack that costs Focus or Kill Command to reduce the Focus cost of your next 3 Arcane Shots or Multi-Shots by 20.	This ability is similar to Fervor in that it increases your DPS output. It's not controllable, however, but if you're lucky and get reduced cost during DPS-increasing cooldown, it's more added damage.
LEVEL 75 TIER (DAMAGE)		
A Murder of Crows	Summons a flock of crows to attack your target over the next 30 sec. If used on a target below 20% health, the cooldown is reduced to 60 seconds.	Works best in PvE encounters where the target has a very large amount of health, allowing you to use this several times below 20%. Otherwise, it's a cooldown that provides damage over time.
Blink Strike	Causes your pet to instantly teleport behind an enemy target up to 40 yards away from your pet and inflict 600% normal damage.	A powerful attack that can be devastating in PvP, particularly when you're facing spellcasters or other Hunters.
Lynx Rush	Your pet rapidly charges from target to target, attacking 9 times over 4 sec, dealing 200% of its normal attack damage to each target. The pet must be within 10 yards of the target to Lynx Rush.	This is best used as an AoE cooldown to complement your baseline AoE abilities. Because it's your pet dealing the damage, this can be used alongside Multi-Shot, Barrage, and Explosive Trap for maximum AoE.
LEVEL 90 TIER (VERSATILITY)		
Glaive Toss	You hurl two glaives toward a target, each dealing damage to each enemy struck and reducing movement speed by 30% for 3 sec. The primary target will take 4 times as much damage from each strike. The glaives will return back to you, damaging and snaring targets again as they return.	The short cooldown makes this a reliable tool to use when enemies are chasing you, it also provides an AOE DPS gain when used effectively.
Powershot	You wind up a powerful shot, which deals 800% weapon damage to the target and 400% weapon damage to all enemies in between you and the target. Enemies hit by Powershot are also knocked back.	Part DPS cooldown and part survivability tool, this shot is very satisfying to use when enemies line up between you and your target.
Barrage	Rapidly fire a spray of shots forward for 3 sec, dealing a total of 640% weapon damage to the enemy target and an average of 320% weapon damage to each other enemy target in front of you.	This ability deals respectable damage to your target and other enemies in front of you (whether they're lined up or not). Unlike Powershot, it will not affect your enemies' movement.

BEAST MASTERY

Hunters increase their affinity with beasts through Beast Mastery specialization, which also allows them to tame a wider variety of beasts and boost the damage caused by their pets. Exotic Beasts, which can be tamed starting at level 69, are a great way to fill gaps in your group's buffs due to class composition.

Intimidation is exclusive to Beast Mastery Hunters and it's an ability that comes in handy in every type of situation. Use Intimidation to stop casts, lock a target in place, or keep an enemy from fleeing an encounter with you.

MASTERY: MASTER OF BEASTS

Increases the damage done by your pets. Each point of Mastery increases pet damage by an additional amount.

SPECIALIZATION ABILITIES

ABILITY	LEVEL		DESCRIPTION
Kill Command	10		Give the command to kill, causing your pet to instantly inflict damage to its target. The pet must be within 25 yards of the target to Kill Command.
Go for the Throat	20		Your ranged auto-shot critical hits cause your pet to generate 15 Focus.
Intimidation	20		Command your pet to intimidate the target, stunning it for 3 sec.
Beast Cleave	24		After you Multi-Shot, your pet's melee attacks also strike all other nearby enemy targets for 30% as much for the next 4 sec.
Frenzy	30		Your pet has a 40% chance to gain 8% increased attack speed after attacking with a Basic Attack, lasting for 30 sec and stacking up to 5 times.
Focus Fire	32		Consumes your pet's Frenzy stack, restoring 6 Focus to your pet and increasing your ranged haste by 6% for each Frenzy stack consumed. Lasts for 20 sec.
Bestial Wrath	40		Send your pet into a rage causing 20% additional damage for 10 sec. The beast does not feel pity or remorse or fear and it cannot be stopped unless killed.
Cobra Strikes	43		You have a 15% chance when you hit with Arcane Shot to cause your pet's next 2 Basic Attacks to critically hit. This effect can stack up to 6 times.
The Beast Within	50		While your pet is under the effects of Bestial Wrath, you also go into a rage causing 10% additional damage and reducing the Focus cost of all shots and abilities by 50% for 10 sec.
Kindred Spirits	58		Increases your maximum Focus and your pet's maximum Focus by 20.
Invigoration	63		When your pet deals damage with a Basic Attack, you have a 15% chance to instantly regenerate 20 Focus.

GETTING TO LEVEL 90

Beast Masters are adept at leveling, considering pets will do much of the work. Do note that if your pet kills an enemy all by itself, you won't get any experience points or loot off it, so you must damage all enemies at least once. That said, the most important thing is getting an awesome pet to accompany you through your adventures. As soon as you can tame Exotic Pets, tame one. It is important to keep pets with you that provide the specific pet special abilities that you enjoy playing with. Keep in mind that all of your pets can be specced into Tank, DPS, or PVP/Defensive-oriented pets via the Pet Specialization trees. Your goal when fighting such enemies is primarily to keep the enemy off you by using Misdirection and Feign Death, and secondarily to keep your pet alive through Mend Pet and talents. Don't be afraid to fight several enemies at once—you can also use Misdirection to direct them to attack your pet instead of you. Remember to use your cooldowns often as well, especially Bestial Wrath.

For talents, consider taking up Spirit Bond, Thrill of the Hunt, and Lynx Rush, which is great for several enemies at once.

PLAYING IN A GROUP

When grouping, make sure your pet isn't accidentally tanking, unless this is the intent. Use your rotation against single targets, and use AoE abilities on groups of enemies that are not crowd-controlled. If you pull aggro (which is rare with Beast Mastery), use Feign Death. Since enemies usually won't be in melee range, focus on using your DPS abilities and talents as opposed to the ones geaered for survivability.

Another important aspect of grouping: keep your pet alive! It takes significantly less AoE damage than players, but that doesn't mean it's immortal. Let your healer(s) know if your pet is dying often.

ROTATION

As Beast Mastery, your pet becomes significantly brawnier and an important part of your damage output. Many passives grant your pet buffs based on your attacks, and vice versa. Beast Mastery's big cooldown, Bestial Wrath, will also increase your damage done and reduce the Focus cost of your abilities.

- Apply/refresh Serpent Sting
- If you know you won't be moving shortly, use your damage cooldowns once your pet reaches 5 Frenzy stacks: Bestial Wrath, Rapid Fire, and Focus Fire; they won't always line up, but try to use them simultaneously
- Use Kill Command when off cooldown
- Use Arcane Shot if you have enough Focus
- Use Cobra Shot to generate Focus
- Use Kill Shot if your target is under 20% health

GROUP BUFFS AND DEBUFFS

Hunters provide the Attack Power buff with Trueshot Aura and apply the Mortal Wounds debuff with Widow Venom.

Hunter pets provide a variety of buffs and debuffs, which are covered later in this chapter. Only Beast Mastery Hunters can use the Exotic Pets and their various buffs.

GETTING READY FOR HIGH-END CONTENT

ALL SPECS

All three Hunter specialization trees benefit roughly equally from stats that boost their ranged physical damage. Those are: Agility, Haste, Critical Strike, Hit, Mastery, and Expertise. Like other physical damage-dealers, Hunters benefit greatly from weapon DPS (ranged, in their case), so prioritize it over the other stats if possible.

When preparing for raids, your first priority should be to reach both the Hit and Expertise caps (7.5% each). Hunters must ensure they will not miss Boss level mobs, or be Dodged by Boss level mobs with their attacks. Meeting these criteria ensures you will not lose any DPS as a result of missing or dodging your attacks.

MARKSMANSHIP

Marksmanship Hunters excel at dealing damage from afar while relying less on their pets and more on their weapons and skills. Particularly adept at dealing burst damage, the Marksmanship tree excels in situations where survivability is not a concern.

Beast Mastery Hunters have an edge over other Hunter specs for providing Burst AOE DPS, due to the combination of Bestial Wrath and Beast Cleave. Concussive Barrage and Bombardment offer improvements to dealing damage to groups and controlling their movements. This doesn't turn the class into a gifted AoE selection, but they contribute well during AoE encounters or while attacking groups in PvP.

MASTERY: WILD QUIVER

Grants a chance for your ranged attacks to also instantly fire an additional ranged shot. Each point of Mastery increases the chance.

SPECIALIZATION ABILITIES

ABILITY	LEVEL		DESCRIPTION
Aimed Shot	10		A powerful aimed shot that deals 280% ranged weapon damage plus additional damage.
Careful Aim	20		Increases the critical strike chance of your Steady Shot and Aimed Shot by 75% on targets who are above 90% health.
Concussive Barrage	30		Your successful Chimera Shot and Multi-Shot attacks daze the target for 4 sec.
Bombardment	45		Your critical hits with Multi-Shot cause your Multi-Shot to cost 20 less Focus and cause 30% additional damage for 5 sec.
Rapid Recuperation	46		You gain 12 Focus every 3 sec while under the effect of Rapid Fire.
Master Marksman	58		You have a 60% chance when you Steady Shot to gain the Master Marksman effect, lasting 30 sec. After reaching 3 stacks, your next Aimed Shot's cast time and Focus cost are reduced by 100% for 10 sec.
Chimera Shot	60		An instant shot that causes 210% ranged weapon Nature damage plus additional damage, refreshing the duration of your Serpent Sting and healing you for 3% of your total health.
Steady Focus	63		When you Steady Shot twice in a row, your ranged attack speed will be increased by 15% and your Steady Shot will generate 3 additional Focus for 10 sec.
Piercing Shots	72		Your critical Aimed, Steady and Chimera Shots cause the target to bleed for 30% of the damage dealt over 8 sec.

GETTING TO LEVEL 90

Because Marksmanship is the tree that is most reliant on gear, its leveling effectiveness will vary. If you're well-geared (perhaps due to heirlooms), you can even kill monsters your level in one Aimed Shot critical hit (which happens often due to Careful Aim).

Normally, however, you apply Serpent Sting if the target will live long enough for it to run its full duration. Otherwise, open with Aimed Shot and follow with Chimera Shot. If the target ends up being under 20% health, finish it off with Kill Shot. For stronger targets, go the Beast Mastery route—use Misdirection to direct all threat to your pet temporarily, and then Feign Death if you pull aggro. After this happens, however, you must be careful not to pull aggro again (though Deterrence or kiting can still save your life). Generally, you will be kiting more than the other specs, so use Concussive Shot and frost-based traps liberally.

For talents, consider Exhilaration (as ideally monsters won't be alive for long enough to kill you or your pet) and Dire Beast. Marksman is best at quickly killing one enemy at a time.

PLAYING IN A GROUP

Execute your standard rotation against single targets. For AoE, Bombardment provides a great way to use Multi-Shot repeatedly. This also makes Marksmanship one of the best trees (out of any class) for dealing burst AoE damage. Sustained AoE damage is best left to Survival, however.

As usual, use Feign Death if you pull aggro, and help your tank out by using Misdirection often. Although your pet isn't as vital to your DPS as to Beast Mastery, it's still a significant source of damage, so try to keep it alive. Should it die, consider how long the current fight will last before reviving it.

ROTATION

Marksmanship damage is about watching out for Careful Aim vulnerable targets (targets at 90% HP or above), keeping Serpent Sting on the target, and Steady Focus active on the Hunter, and using Chimera Shot as often as possible.

- Apply/refresh Serpent Sting (Chimera Shot can refresh it too)
- If Master Marksman is stacked to 3, use Aimed Shot
- Use Chimera Shot as soon as it's off cooldown
- Use Arcane Shot to consume your Focus
- Use Steady Shot to generate Focus
- Use Kill Shot as often as possible if your target is under 20% health

GROUP BUFFS AND DEBUFFS

Hunters provide the Attack Power buff with Trueshot Aura and apply the Mortal Wounds debuff with Widow Venom.

Hunter pets provide a variety of buffs and debuffs, which are covered later in this chapter.

GETTING READY FOR HIGH-END CONTENT

ALL SPECS

All three Hunter specialization trees benefit roughly equally from stats that boost their ranged physical damage. Those are: Agility, Haste, Critical Strike, Hit, Mastery, and Expertise. Like other physical damage-dealers, Hunters benefit greatly from weapon DPS (ranged, in their case), so prioritize it over the other stats if possible.

When preparing for raids, your first priority should be to reach both the Hit and Expertise caps (7.5% each). Hunters must ensure they will not miss Boss level mobs, or be Dodged by Boss level mobs with their attacks. Meeting these criteria ensures you will not lose any DPS as a result of missing or dodging your attacks.

SURVIVAL

Survival Hunters have traded some of their damage potential for a bag of tricks that is a constant frustration to their enemies. In small groups, they shine their brightest. Survival Hunters are best at avoiding damage and dealing it while on the move. Many of a Survival Hunter's attacks are also magic-based and are boosted through their mastery.

Survivalists Hunter traps have stronger effects than those from other Hunter specializations. Entrapment locks down enemies, giving groups a few precious seconds to fight major enemies without worrying about peripheral targets.

MASTERY: ESSENCE OF THE VIPER

Increases all magical damage you deal. Each point of Mastery increases magical damage by an additional amount.

SPECIALIZATION ABILITIES

ABILITY	LEVEL		DESCRIPTION
Explosive Shot	10		You fire an explosive charge into the enemy target, dealing Fire damage initially and every second for 2 sec.
Lock and Load	43		You have a 100% chance when you trap a target with Freezing Trap or Ice Trap, and a 20% chance when your Black Arrow or Explosive Trap deals damage to cause your next two Explosive Shots to cost no Focus and trigger no cooldown. Effect lasts for 12 sec and cannot occur more often than once every 10 sec.
Black Arrow	50		Fires a Black Arrow at the target, dealing damage over 20 sec. Black Arrow shares a cooldown with other Fire Trap spells.
Entrapment	55		When your Ice Trap or Snake Trap are triggered you entrap all afflicted targets, preventing them from moving for 4 sec.
Viper Venom	63		You gain 3 Focus each time your Serpent Sting deals damage. This effect can only occur every 3 sec.
Trap Mastery	64		Reduces the cooldown of all traps and Black Arrow by 6 sec, and provides additional benefits on each Trap. Ice Trap and Freezing Trap: Increases duration by 30%. Explosive Trap and Black Arrow: Increases periodic damage done by 30%. Snake Trap: Increases number of snakes summoned by 4.
Serpent Spread	68		Targets hit by your Multi-Shot are also afflicted by your Serpent Sting.
Cobra Shot	81		Deals 70% weapon damage in the form of Nature damage and increases the duration of your Serpent Sting on the target by 6 sec. Generates 14 Focus.

GETTING TO LEVEL 90

Survival leveling is mobile and safe, but slightly slower than the other trees. The increased effectiveness of traps allows you to get away from enemies more easily, and your Focus-based abilities can be used on the move. As with Marksmanship, use Misdirection on your pet liberally in order to keep enemies off you. Because of Lock and Load procs, you still want to use Black Arrow, even if the enemy won't be alive for its full duration. For numerous weak enemies, use Ice Trap and proceed to AoE them down with Multi-Shot/Serpent Spread.

Notable talents are Crouching Tiger, Hidden Chimera (allows for the use of Disengage more often), Binding Shot (for safer AoE), and Lynx Rush.

PLAYING IN A GROUP

For single targets, execute your normal rotation. Make sure your pet is alive before starting a fight, and use Misdirection on the tank to help out with threat. Generally, you want to pick a target with a large health pool so Black Arrow will have time to deal its full damage. Survival really shines for AoE packs, especially ones that stay alive for a long time: with Serpent Spread, Multi-Shot applies the Serpent Sting DoT on all the enemies it hits. Depending on the situation, you can use all your Focus on Multi-Shots (generally for a large amount of enemies), or you can Multi-Shot once to apply the DoT on everything, and then continue your single-target rotation on a target with a large health pool. Naturally, use Feign Death if you pull aggro, and Deterrence as a last resort to stay alive.

ROTATION

Survival's rotation is similar to Marksmanship, but much more mobile. The most important difference in your DPS output is how often you can use Lock and Load procs, as Explosive Shot tends to be your top-damage ability. Note that Survival has great sustained AoE due to Serpent Spread, so Multi-Shot becomes a DPS increase with as few as 3 enemies in range.

- Apply/refresh Serpent Sting (Cobra Shot can refresh it too)
- Use Rapid Fire when available (preferably when you know you will stand still for its duration)
- Use Black Arrow when available
- Use Explosive Shot when available
- Use Arcane Shot to consume your Focus
- Use Cobra Shot to generate Focus
- Use Kill Shot on enemies under 20% health

GROUP BUFFS AND DEBUFFS

Hunters provide the Attack Power buff with Trueshot Aura and apply the Mortal Wounds debuff with Widow Venom.

Hunter pets provide a variety of buffs and debuffs, which are covered later in this chapter.

GETTING READY FOR HIGH-END CONTENT

ALL SPECS

All three Hunter specialization trees benefit roughly equally from stats that boost their ranged physical damage. Those are: Agility, Haste, Critical Strike, Hit, Mastery, and Expertise. Like other physical damage-dealers, Hunters benefit greatly from weapon DPS (ranged, in their case), so prioritize it over the other stats if possible.

When preparing for raids, your first priority should be to reach both the Hit and Expertise caps (7.5% each). Hunters must ensure they will not miss Boss level mobs, or be Dodged by Boss level mobs with their attacks. Meeting these criteria ensures you will not lose any DPS as a result of missing or dodging your attacks.

PETS

Hunters have the ability to tame nearly any wild beast they encounter, turning it into their sidekick. Whenever you tame a pet, you may give it a name and use its abilities as you wish. The Beast Mastery specialization is dedicated to improving pet performance, and even allows you to tame exotic beasts.

You are limited to five (depending on your Hunter's level) beasts with you at a time. You can store up to 20 more with the stable masters found throughout World of Warcraft.

Hunter pets bring a variety of buffs and debuffs to groups. While Hunters can have a single pet active at a time, they can change between a handful of pets between fights. Plan ahead and take the pets that fill in any missing buffs or debuffs provided by the rest of your group or raid.

PET SPECIALIZATIONS

Any pet can be assigned to one of the three specializations. Ferocity and Cunning pets are more damage-focused, while Tenacity pets act as tanks. Selecting a specialization for your pet gives it new abilities.

CUNNING

ABILITY		DESCRIPTION
Boar's Speed		Increases your pet's movement speed by 30%.
Bullheaded		Removes all movement impairing effects and all effects which cause loss of control of your pet, and reduces damage done to your pet by 20% for 12 sec.
Cornered		When at less than 35% health, your pet does 50% more damage and has a 60% reduced chance to be critically hit.
Dash		Increases your pet's movement speed by 80% for 16 sec.
Roar of Sacrifice		Protects a friendly target from critical strikes, making attacks against that target unable to be critical strikes, but 20% of all damage taken by that target is also taken by the pet. Lasts 12 sec.

FEROCITY

ABILITY		DESCRIPTION
Dash		Increases your pet's movement speed by 80% for 16 sec.
Heart of the Phoenix		When used, your pet will miraculously return to life with full health.
Rabid		Increases your pet's attack power by 50% for 20 sec.
Spiked Collar		Increases the damage done by your pet's Basic Attacks by 10%, increases your pet's haste by 10%, and increases your pet's critical strike chance by 10%.

TENACITY

ABILITY		DESCRIPTION
Blood of the Rhino		Increases all healing effects on your pet by 40%, increasing your pet's armor by 20%, and reduces your pet's chance to be critically hit by melee attacks by 6%.
Charge		Your pet charges an enemy, immobilizing the target for 1 sec, and increasing the pet's melee attack power by 25% for its next attack.
Great Stamina		Increases your pet's total health by 12%.
Last Stand		Your pet temporarily gains 30% of its maximum health for 20 sec. After the effect expires, the health is lost.
Thunderstomp		Shakes the ground with thundering force, doing Nature damage to all enemies within 8 yards. This ability causes a moderate amount of additional threat.

EXOTIC PETS

The following pets are all considered Exotics, which only Beast Mastery Hunters can tame.

EXOTIC PET ABILITIES

PET		ABILITY	DESCRIPTION
Chimaera		Frost Breath	Your pet simultaneously breathes frost and lightning at an enemy target, slowing the target for 5 sec.
		Froststorm Breath	The Chimaera channels a frozen breath attack, causing Froststorm damage every 2 sec for 8 sec to all enemies within 12 yards.
Core Hound		Ancient Hysteria	Increases melee, ranged, and spell casting speed by 30% for all party and raid members. Lasts 40 sec. Allies receiving this effect will become Sated and be unable to benefit from Bloodlust or Time Warp again for 10 min.
		Lava Breath	Your pet breathes a double gout of molten lava at the target, reducing the target's casting speed by 50% (25% on player targets) for 10 sec.
Devilsaur		Terrifying Roar	The devilsaur lets out a terrifying roar, increasing the critical strike chance of all party and raid members by 5%.
		Monstrous Bite	Your devilsaur ferociously bites the enemy, reducing the effectiveness of any healing received for 10 sec.
Quilen		Fearless Roar	The quilen lets out a fearless roar, increasing the critical strike chance of all party and raid members by 5% for 2 min.
		Eternal Guardian	Returns the spirit to the body, restoring a dead target to life with 60% health and 20% mana.
Rhino		Stampede	Your rhino slams into a nearby enemy, causing it to take 4% increased physical damage for 30 sec.
		Horn Toss	The rhino punts the enemy with its mighty horn, knocking them back a great distance.
Shale Spider		Embrace of the Shale Spider	Fills all friendly party and raid members with the Shale Spider's embrace, increasing Strength, Agility, and Intellect by 5%.
		Web Wrap	Encases the target in sticky webs, stunning them for 3 sec.
Silithid		Qiraji Fortitude	Increases party and raid members' Stamina by 10%.
		Venom Web Spray	Sprays toxic webs at the target, preventing movement for 5 sec.
Spirit Beast		Spirit Mend	The Spirit Beast heals the currently friendly target over 10 sec, with additional healing based on your attack power.
		Spirit Beast Blessing	The Spirit Beast blesses your allies, increasing the Mastery of all party and raid members by 3000 within 100 yards. Lasts 1 min.
		Spirit Walk	Puts your pet in stealth mode, but slows its movement speed by 50%. The first attack from stealth receives a 20% bonus to damage. Lasts until cancelled.
Water Striders		Surface Trot	Allows the Hunter and the Water Strider to walk across water for 10 min. Any damage will cancel the effect.
		Still Water	Infuses all party and raid members within vision with still water, increasing their spell power by 10% and their critical strike chance by 5%.
Worm		Acid Spit	Your worm spits acid, causing the enemy target to take an increased 4% physical damage for 25 sec.
		Burrow Attack	The worm burrows into the earth, shaking the ground above dealing Nature damage over 8 sec.

PETS AVAILABLE TO ALL HUNTER SPECS

Most of these pets debuff enemies, leaving only Furious Howl from the Wolf as a true party buff.

PET ABILITIES

PET		ABILITY	DESCRIPTION
Basilisks		Petrifying Gaze	Turns the target into stone for 3 sec, causing them to be invulnerable.
Bat		Sonic Blast	Emits a piercing shriek, stunning the target for 2 sec.
Bear		Demoralizing Roar	The bear roars, reducing the physical damage caused by all enemies within 8 yards by 10% for 15 sec.
Beetle		Harden Carapace	Hardens up, reducing damage taken by 50% for 12 sec.
Bird of Prey		Snatch	The bird of prey grabs the enemy's weapon with its talons, disarming them for 10 sec.
Boar		Gore	Your boar gores the enemy, causing it to take 30% additional damage from bleed effects for 15 sec.
Carrion Bird		Demoralizing Screech	The Carrion Bird screeches, reducing the physical damage caused by all enemies within 8 yards by 10% for 10 sec.
Cat		Prowl	Puts your pet in stealth mode, but slows its movement speed by 50%. The first attack from stealth receives a 20% bonus to damage. Lasts until cancelled.
Crab		Pin	Pins the target in place for 4 sec.
Cranes		Lullaby	Puts the target to sleep for 4 sec.
Crocolisk		Ankle Crack	Snap at the target's feet, reducing movement speed by 50% for 6 sec.
Dog		Lock Jaw	Dog locks its jaws on the target, holding it in place for 4 sec.
Dragonhawk		Fire Breath	Breathes Fire on the target, increasing magic damage taken by 8% for 45 sec.
Fox		Tailspin	Your fox twirls its tail around, kicking up an obscuring cloud of dust, causing all enemies within 10 yards to have their spell cast speed increased by 50% (25% on player targets) for 30 sec.
Goat		Trample	Your goat tramples the enemy, kicking up an obscuring cloud of dust, causing all enemies within 10 yards to have their spell cast speed increased by 50% (25% on player targets) for 30 sec.
Gorilla		Pummel	Pummel the target, interrupting spellcasting and preventing any spell in that school from being cast for 2 sec.

PET		ABILITY	DESCRIPTION
Hyena		Cackling Howl	The Hyena lets out a cackling howl, increasing the melee and ranged attack speed of all party and raid members within 100 yards by 10% for 2 min.
Monkey		Bad Manner	Hurls a handful of something special at the target, blinding them for 4 sec. Rude.
Moth		Serenity Dust	The moth's wings produce a cloud of dust that interrupts the enemy's spellcasting and prevents any spell in that school from being cast for 4 sec.
Nether Ray		Nether Shock	Instantly lashes an enemy, interrupting spellcasting and prevents any spell in that school from being cast for 2 sec.
Raptor		Tear Armor	Tears at the enemy's armor with the raptor's talons, causing Weakened Armor.
Ravager		Ravage	Violently attacks an enemy, causing the enemy target to take 4% increased physical damage for 25 sec.
Scorpid		Clench	The scorpid clenches the enemy's weapons with its claws, disarming their weapons and shield for 10 sec.
Serpent		Serpent's Swiftness	Increases the melee and ranged attack speed of all party and raid members within 100 yards by 10% for 2 min.
Spider		Web	Encases the target in sticky webs, preventing movement for 5 sec.
Sporebat		Spore Cloud	Dusts nearby enemies with spores, reducing casting speed of all enemy targets within 6 yards by 50% for 10 sec.
Tallstrider		Dust Cloud	Your tallstrider kicks up a cloud of dust, causing all enemies within 10 yards to be afflicted by Weakened Armor.
Turtle		Shell Shield	The turtle partially withdraws into its shell, reducing damage taken by 50% for 12 sec.
Warp Stalker		Time Warp	Slows time around the enemy, reducing their movement speed by 50% for 6 sec.
Wasp		Sting	Your wasp stings the target, stunning them for 2 sec.
Wind Serpent		Lightning Breath	Breathes lightning, increasing magic damage taken by 5% for 45 sec.
Wolf		Furious Howl	The wolf lets out a furious howl, increasing the critical strike chance of all party and raid members by 5%.

 # MAGE

The Mage is a powerful damage-oriented caster class that excels at harnessing the powers of Fire, Frost, and Arcane.

Mages are known to deal great amounts of direct and over-time damage from a distance, while also being capable of damaging multiple enemies at once with their numerous area of effect (AoE) spells. Mages are not without their share of utility, however, which includes teleportation spells (for the Mage and group members), reliable crowd control, and conjury of temporary items that replenish health and mana. Depending on the situation and the specialization chosen, Mages can be fragile but powerful wizards (often referred to as "glass cannons") or durable masters of snares and crowd control. Although all three of a Mage's specialization trees are involved in dealing damage, they're vastly different in their purpose and the way they're played.

RACE AVAILABILITY

ALLIANCE

Draenei
Dwarf
Gnome

Human
Night Elf
Worgen

Pandaren

HORDE

Blood Elf
Goblin
Orc

Tauren
Troll
Undead

RACIAL ADVANTAGES

ALLIANCE

RACE	NOTES
Draenei	Heroic Presence grants Draenei +1% Hit chance. Gift of the Naaru heals the Draenei or any ally. Draenei also take less damage from Shadow spells.
Dwarf	Stoneform is excellent for PvP, as it removes all bleeds and reduces damage taken. Dwarves take less damage from Frost spells.
Gnome	Escape Artist provides an extra ability for escaping slow or snare effects; great for PvP. Expansive Mind increases your mana pool by 5%. Gnomes take less damage from Arcane spells.
Human	Every Man for Himself removes effects that cause loss of control of your character. The Human Spirit increases your Spirit by 3%.
Night Elf	Night Elves are less likely to be hit by any physical attack and take less damage from Nature spells. Shadowmeld renders Night Elves invisible while motionless and cancels spells being cast by enemies on the Night Elf.
Worgen	Worgen get 1% increased Critical Strike from Viciousness. Darkflight increases movement speed temporarily. Worgen take less damage from Nature and Shadow spells.

HORDE

RACE	NOTES
Blood Elf	The signature Blood Elf racial, Arcane Torrent, provides mana and an AoE silence. The former helps in tight mana situations, and the latter is great for PvP and certain PvE encounters. Blood Elves take less damage from Arcane spells.
Goblin	Goblins get 1% increased Haste from Time is Money. Rocket Jump is a great mobility tool, allowing Mages to stay at a comfortable range. Rocket Barrage is another source of damage for Goblins.
Orc	Orcs are great for maximizing damage. Blood Fury increases your spell power. Command increases your pet's damage output. Hardiness reduces the duration of stun effects by 15%.
Troll	Berserking grants a temporary increase in attack speed. Da Voodoo Shuffle passively reduces the duration of movement impairing effects. Trolls regenerate Health faster than other races, and 10% of total Health regeneration may continue in combat.
Undead	Undead are very suited for PvP as they can break out of Charm, Fear, and Sleep effects with Will of the Forsaken. Their passive racial, Touch of the Grave, is a life leech and also provides a modest DPS increase in any situation. Undead take less damage form Shadow spells.

PANDAREN

RACE	NOTES
Pandaren	Epicurean doubles the statistical bonuses from being Well Fed. Quaking Palm acts as a form of brief crowd control.

EQUIPMENT OPTIONS

ARMOR TYPE	SHIELD
Cloth	No

USABLE WEAPONS

1 HAND WEAPON	2 HAND WEAPON
Daggers	Staves
Swords	
Wands	

PROMINENT CLASS ABILITIES

DIRECT DAMAGE

Mages are known to cast large, repeatable direct single-target damaging spells, commonly referred to as "nukes." Nukes are a Mage's primary source of damage; many other spells (and talents) will boost or complement your spell damage. Although each specialization tree has a primary spell, they each have different properties and special effects.

Arcane gets Arcane Blast, a nuke that increases Arcane damage done by building Arcane Charges, and Arcane Missiles, which is free but can only be cast when another spell activates it (40% chance).

Fire uses Fireball, which is a sizable Fire spell, and Pyroblast, which is a more damaging version of Fireball (with a longer casting time).

Frost has Frostbolt, which is less damaging than Fireball but applies a snare, and Ice Lance, which is an instant cast spell that deals quadruple damage to frozen targets.

DIRECT TRAVEL SPELLS

Direct Travel spells fall into two categories: Teleports and Portals. Teleports work only for the Mage who casts the spell. At the end of the cast, the Mage instantly appears in another location within a friendly and neutral city. Portals are small magical gateways that can be used by anyone grouped with the Mage.

The cities available depend on your level; each Teleport and Portal spell is learned independently. Spells related to cities located in high-level continents such as Outland and Northrend are learned when the caster's level is high enough to explore those areas. The Teleport spell for your race's home city is automatically learned at level 17, and the portal spell to that city is learned at level 42. The Teleport and Portal spells to the rest of the cities located on Kalimdor and Eastern Kingdoms must be learned from a trainer located in any major city. Note that these spells no longer require reagents.

Any damage caused to the caster will interrupt Teleport or Portal spells, so don't try to use these spells to escape from hostile enemies.

ELEMENTAL ARMORS

Mages can imbue their armor with three different Armor spells, increasing their offense and defense in various ways.

Armor spells now have a cast time, so it's probably not a good idea to constantly switch between them in combat; rather, you should pick one before starting a fight, based on the situation. Armor spells are also exclusive, meaning you can only have one of them active at a time. The three Armor spells are detailed in the following table.

ARMOR	OFFENSIVE EFFECT	DEFENSIVE EFFECT
Frost Armor	Increases spell Haste by 5%.	If an enemy strikes the caster, their movement is slowed by 30% for 5 sec.
Mage Armor	Increases Mastery	The duration of all harmful Magic effects used against you is reduced by 35%.
Molten Armor	Increases spell Critical Strike by 5%.	Reduces all physical damage taken by 6%.

As you can imagine, the defensive effects will be very important for survivability, especially in PvP. In PvE, you will most likely look at the offensive portion of the effect, but you might still use different Armor spells for the defensive part in certain encounters (chiefly Mage Armor).

ALTER TIME

Mage's level 87 ability is Alter Time. This nifty new spell will alter the fabric of time, causing your health, mana, buffs, debuffs, and location to be saved for a short time. When you use the ability again, or the short time expires, you'll be returned to the location you used it at, with the stats that were saved when you used it. It's akin to traveling back in time, with one exception: if you die, the effect is cancelled.

Alter Time is on a considerable cooldown, making it a veritable "emergency button." The best time to use it is going to vary on the situation—consider, for example, an Arcane Mage using Alter Time and then spending all of his or her mana through Arcane Power and Arcane Blast. Another practical use is found in an encounter which requires you to move to a different place and then back to where you started. Lastly, of course, Alter Time is great at saving your life should you predict you will be near death; just make sure you don't die before being able to use it again.

NAME	LEVEL		DESCRIPTION
Frostfire Bolt	1		Launches a bolt of frostfire at the enemy, causing Frostfire damage and slowing the target by 40% for 8 sec.
Frost Nova	3		Blasts enemies within 12 yds of the caster for Frost damage and freezes them in place for up to 8 sec. Damage caused may interrupt the effect.
Fire Blast	5		Blasts the enemy for Fire damage.
Blink	7		Teleports the caster 20 yards forward, unless something is in the way. Also frees the caster from stuns and bonds.
Counterspell	8		Counters the enemy's spellcast, preventing any spell from that school of magic from being cast for 6 sec, and silencing the target for 4 sec.
Polymorph	14		Transforms the enemy into a sheep, forcing it to wander around for up to 50 sec. While wandering, the sheep cannot attack or cast spells but will regenerate very quickly. Any damage will transform the target back into its normal form. Only one target can be polymorphed at a time. Only works on Beasts, Humanoids and Critters.
Shatter	16		Doubles the critical strike chance of all your spells against frozen targets plus an additional 50%.
Teleport	17		Teleports the caster to a major city.
Arcane Explosion	18		Causes an explosion of arcane magic around the caster, causing Arcane damage to all targets within 10 yards.
Ice Lance	22		Deals Frost damage to an enemy target. Ice Lance damage is quadrupled against Frozen targets.
Ice Block	26		You become encased in a block of ice, protecting you from all physical attacks and spells for 10 sec, but during that time you cannot attack, move or cast spells. Causes Hypothermia, preventing you from recasting Ice Block for 30 sec.
Cone of Cold	28		Targets in a cone in front of the caster take Frost damage and are slowed by 60% for 6 sec.
Remove Curse	29		Removes all Curses from a friendly target.
Slow Fall	32		Slows friendly party or raid target's falling speed for 30 sec.
Molten Armor	34		Increases your spell critical strike chance by 5%. Reduces all physical damage taken by 6%.
Conjure Refreshment	38		Conjures mana food providing the Mage and his allies with something to eat. Conjured items disappear if logged out for more than 15 minutes.
Evocation	40		Gain 15% of your mana instantly and another 45% of your total mana over 6 sec.
Portal	42		Creates a portal, teleporting group members who use it to a major city.
Flamestrike	44		Calls down a pillar of fire, burning all enemies within the area for Fire damage and additional Fire damage over 8 sec.
Conjure Mana Gem	47		Conjures a Mana Gem that can be used to instantly restore mana, and holds up to 3 charges. Conjured items disappear if logged out for more than 15 minutes.
Mirror Image	49		Creates 3 copies of the caster nearby, which cast spells and attack the Mage's enemies. Lasts 30 sec.
Blizzard	52		Ice shards pelt the target area doing Frost damage over 8 sec and slowing enemies by 50%.
Frost Armor	54		Increases your spell haste by 5%. If an enemy strikes the caster, their movement is slowed by 30% for 5 sec.
Invisibility	56		Turns the caster invisible over 3 sec, reducing threat each second. While invisible, you are untargetable by enemies. Lasts 20 sec. Invisibility is cancelled if you perform any actions.
Arcane Brilliance	58		Infuses the target with brilliance, increasing their spell power by 10% and their critical strike chance by 5% for 1 hour. If target is in your party or raid, all party and raid members will be affected.
Spellsteal	64		Steals a beneficial magic effect from the target. This effect lasts a maximum of 2 min.
Deep Freeze	66		Stuns the target for 5 sec. Only usable on Frozen targets.
Improved Counterspell	70		Your Counterspell also silences the target for 4 sec.
Conjure Refreshment Table	72		Conjures a refreshment table. Raid members can click the table to acquire Conjured mana food. The table lasts for 3 min or 50 charges.
Nether Attunement	74		Your spell haste also increases your mana regeneration, and the amount of mana gained from Mage spells.
Mage Bomb	75		Casts a powerful periodic damage effect based upon your talent choice.
Mage Armor	80		Increases your Mastery. The duration of all harmful Magic effects used against you is reduced by 35%.
Burning Soul	82		Reduces the casting time lost from taking damaging attacks by 70%.
Time Warp	84		Warp the flow of time, increasing melee, ranged, and spell casting speed by 30% for all party and raid members. Lasts 40 sec. Allies receiving this effect will become unstuck in time, and be unable to benefit from Bloodlust, Heroism, or Time Warp again for 10 min.
Alter Time	87		Alter the fabric of time, causing the caster to return to their current location, health, mana, buffs, and debuffs, when cast a second time, or after 6 sec. Effect negated if the caster dies within the 6 sec before the effect occurs or moves too far away.

TALENTS

TALENT		DESCRIPTION	NOTES
LEVEL 15 TIER (MOVEMENT)			
Presence of Mind		When activated, your next Mage spell with a casting time less than 10 sec becomes an instant cast spell. This spell is not on the global cooldown.	An old Mage favorite, Presence of Mind can be useful in a large number of situations, especially when combined with spells like Polymorph, or with spells with a long cast time, like Pyroblast.
Scorch		Scorch the enemy for Fire damage. Can be cast while moving.	Previously exclusive to Fire Mages, Scorch is now available to Mages that choose this talent. It's one of the few spells in the game that's usable on the go, and with no cooldown; this allows you to keep dealing damage when you're required to move. Scorch is also a very inexpensive spell, mana-wise.
Ice Flows		Allows you to move while casting and channeling the next 2 Mage spells that have a base cast or channel time less than 4 sec. This spell may be cast while a cast time spell is in progress and is not on the global cooldown.	Usable while casting (and off the global cooldown), this talent provides a way to cast your specialization tree's main spells while moving. Note that this can be used on channeled spells as well.
LEVEL 30 TIER (SURVIVABILITY)			
Temporal Shield		Envelops you in a temporal shield for 4 sec. Damage taken while shielded will be healed back over 6 sec. This spell is usable while stunned, frozen, incapacitated, feared or asleep, and is not on the global cooldown.	Similar to your level 87 ability (but on a much shorter CD), this talent allows you to keep your health pool at safe levels when predictable damage is about to happen. Great for PvP and certain PvE encounters where healer mana must be conserved.
Blazing Speed		Suppresses movement slowing effects and increases your movement speed by 150% for 1.50 sec. May only be activated after taking a melee or spell hit greater than 2% of your total health, or after you kill an enemy that yields experience or honor. This spell may be cast while a cast time spell is in progress and is not on the global cooldown.	Blazing Speed now provides a more controllable way to quickly escape enemies. Like other survivability talents in this tier, the cooldown is fairly short, allowing you to use it liberally.
Ice Barrier		Instantly shields you, absorbing damage. Lasts 1 min. While the shield holds, spellcasting will not be delayed by damage.	Now available to all kinds of Mages, Ice Barrier provides a straightforward but significant way to deter damage on demand. Ice Barrier's greatest advantage is that it can be used proactively, while the other two Level 30 Talents are more reactive. The downside to Ice Barrier is that it incurs a global cooldown when cast.
LEVEL 45 TIER (BURST)			
Ring of Frost		Summons a Ring of Frost at the target location. Enemies entering the ring will become frozen for 10 sec. Lasts 10 sec. 10 yd radius.	A great way to CC multiple enemies at once, like Frost Nova, with the added benefit that you can target the area where the spell will take effect. Do note the cast time, however.
Ice Ward		Places an Ice Ward on a friendly target. When an enemy strikes the target, all enemies within 10 yds will become frozen in place for 5 sec. 1 charge. Lasts 30 sec.	Now grantable to an ally, this talent is great for controlling multiple melee-based enemies. It can also act as a second Frost Nova—one that originates on an ally.
Frostjaw		Silences and freezes the target in place for 8 sec. Lasts half as long versus Player targets.	Note that the range is shorter than most other single-target abilities. Otherwise, a great way to reduce incoming damage from both enemy melee and casters.
LEVEL 60 TIER (SURVIVABILITY II)			
Greater Invisibility		Replaces Invisibility. Instantly makes the caster invisible, reducing all threat, and removing two damage over time effects. While invisible, you are untargetable by enemies. Lasts 20 sec. Invisibility is cancelled if you perform any actions. Damage taken is reduced by 90% while invisible and for 3 sec after coming out of invisibility.	This utility talent makes Invisibility much better, removing the delay before you go invisible, and removing some DoT effects so it doesn't break instantly. The damage reduction part is very significant, so this can be used as an emergency cooldown as well. It also has half of the cooldown of Invisibility (2.5 minutes compared to 5 minutes). Being able to become invisible more often is a powerful advantage.
Cauterize		An attack which would otherwise kill you will instead bring you to 50% of your maximum health, and you will burn for 40% of your maximum health over the next 6 sec. Cauterize cannot occur more than once every 2 min.	Previously only available to Fire Mages, this talent prevents you from dying. Best chosen when a healer is available, as you will take damage after the effect ends, potentially killing you if you take any more damage after being saved by this.
Cold Snap		When activated, this spell finishes the cooldown of your Ice Block, Frost Nova, and Cone of Cold spells. Instantly restores 30% of your health. This spell is usable while stunned, frozen, incapacitated, feared or asleep, and is not on the global cooldown.	Usable while stunned, incapacitated, frozen, asleep, and feared, this talent can save your life by healing you and allowing you to use frost-based survivability spells. Do note that using Ice Block twice in a row might sound enticing, but it isn't possible, as it places a debuff preventing you from doing so.
LEVEL 75 TIER (MAGE BOMBS)			
Nether Tempest		Places a Nether Tempest on the target which deals Arcane damage over 12 sec. Each time Nether Tempest deals damage, an additional 50% of that damage is also dealt to a random target within 10 yards.	Ideally used when there are two enemies that need to die near each other. Deals the same amount of damage regardless of the number of enemies greater than two. This is also the only spell in this tier that has no limit on the number of targets.
Living Bomb		The target becomes a Living Bomb, taking Fire damage over 12 sec. When this effect ends, or the target dies, it explodes to deal additional Fire damage to up to 3 enemies within 10 yards. Limit 3 targets. This spell has a 1.0 sec global cooldown.	The ideal situation for Living Bomb is three targets near each other, as they will all damage each other upon exploding. Note this spell has a shorter global cooldown, which is ideal for use on several enemies at a time (up to three, which is the limit).
Frost Bomb		Places a Frost Bomb on the target. After 5 sec, the bomb explodes, dealing Frost damage to the primary target, and Frost damage to all other targets within 10 yards. All affected targets are slowed by 70% for 2 sec. Frost Bomb's countdown and cooldown are reduced by haste.	This spell is unique in that haste will affect its cooldown, cast time, and the time before it detonates. Thus, it becomes much better with more haste. Note the damage dealt to the primary target is roughly double the AoE damage. The best situation for Frost Bomb is numerous nearby enemies that will be alive long enough for the explosion to take place.
LEVEL 90 TIER (MANA)			
Invocation		Reduces the cooldown of Evocation to 10 sec, but you passively regenerate 50% less mana. Completing an Evocation causes you to deal 25% increased spell damage for 40 sec.	The damage buff is significant and lasts a long time in comparison to similar buffs, making this a considerable DPS increase. However, the reduced mana regeneration means that you will be spending a good amount of time casting Evocation to avoid running out of mana.
Rune of Power		Replaces Evocation. Places a Rune of Power on the ground, which lasts for 1 min. While standing in your own Rune of Power, your mana regeneration is increased by 100% and your spell damage is increased by 15%. Only 2 Runes of Power can be placed at one time.	Note this removes your ability to use Evocation, so it's best chosen when the increased mana regeneration is sufficient to keep you from going out of mana. The spell damage increase is comparable to Invocation, but only applies when you're standing in a rune (you can summon up to two, preferably before a fight).
Incanter's Ward		Places a magical ward on you, absorbing damage for 8 sec. Absorbed damage will restore up to 18% of your maximum mana. When this effect ends, you gain up to 30% increased spell damage for 15 sec, based on the absorption used. Passive: Increases spell damage by 6% and increases mana regeneration by 65%. This effect is deactivated while Incanter's Ward is on cooldown.	The most situational of the three in this tier, this talent can potentially provide the best DPS increase. Best used in fights where you can absorb damage every time the cooldown is up.

ARCANE

Arcane Mages specialize in mana manipulation, utility, and burst damage (with an emphasis on the latter). Along with some Fire builds, and vastly depending on talent choices, Arcane Mages have a reputation for being "glass cannons." Mages who spec into this have some mobility options, primarily from Arcane Barrage.

MASTERY: MANA ADEPT
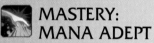

Increases all spell damage done by a percentage based on the amount of mana the Mage has unspent.

SPECIALIZATION ABILITIES

ABILITY	LEVEL		DESCRIPTION
Arcane Blast	10		Blasts the target with energy, dealing Arcane damage. Generates an Arcane Charge. Arcane Blast's damage is increased by 22% per Arcane Charge, and its mana cost is increased by 125% per Arcane Charge.
Arcane Charge	10		An arcane charge, generated by Arcane Blast, Arcane Missiles, and Arcane Explosion, and consumed by Arcane Barrage: Arcane Blast: Generates a charge. Arcane Blast's damage is increased by 22% per charge, and its mana cost increased by 125% per charge. Arcane Missiles: Generates a charge. Arcane Missiles' damage is increased by 22% per charge. Arcane Explosion: Refreshes charges and has a 30% chance to generate a charge if at least one target is hit. Arcane Barrage: Consumes all charges. Arcane Barrage's damage is increased by 22% per charge, and it hits 1 additional nearby target per charge for 50% damage. Stacks up to 6 times and lasts 10 sec.
Arcane Barrage	12		Launches bolts of arcane energy at the enemy target, causing Arcane damage. Consumes all Arcane Charges. Arcane Barrage's damage is increased by 22% per Arcane Charge, and it hits 1 additional nearby target per Arcane Charge for 50% damage.
Arcane Missiles	24		Launches five waves of Arcane Missiles at the enemy over 2 sec, causing Arcane damage per wave. Generates an Arcane Charge. Arcane Missiles' damage is increased by 22% per Arcane Charge. Arcane Missiles has a chance to be activated after each of your damaging spell casts. Limit 2 charges.
Slow	36		Reduces target's movement speed by 50%, and increases casting time by 50% (25% on player targets) for 15 sec. Slow can only affect one target at a time.
Arcane Power	62		When activated, you deal 20% more spell damage and damaging spells cost 10% more mana to cast. This effect lasts 15 sec.

GETTING TO LEVEL 90

Leveling as an Arcane Mage is fairly straightforward, but still requires you to manage your mana. In this scenario, you want to use your damage-increasing cooldowns frequently, and be as mana-conservative as possible (you will most likely still need to use Evocation often, however). Dispatch enemies with Arcane Blast, using Arcane Barrage at three or four arcane charges, and Arcane Missiles as often as possible. You can also use your damage-increasing cooldowns in order to dispatch several enemies in a short time by repeatedly using Arcane Blast, but you will likely have to use refreshments to replenish your mana afterward.

For talents, Ice Barrier provides the easiest survivability tool, and at higher levels, Nether Tempest allows you to deal with several enemies at once with ease.

PLAYING IN A GROUP

Due to the volatile and explosive nature of Arcane damage, threat is likely to be an issue on fights where you use all your damage-increasing cooldowns right away. Fortunately, Invisibility (and its improved version, Greater Invisibility) can alleviate the issue by providing a temporary threat drop. For AoE, you might want to take up the Living Bomb talent, which, although a fire spell, provides a large amount of damage, especially when paired with Arcane Power.

BASE ROTATION

Arcane's DPS rotation might seem straightforward, but rest assured—there's a fair deal of strategy involved, especially regarding mana usage. The talents you choose will affect Arcane DPS the most out of the three trees, so choose wisely.

- If you have more than three Arcane Charges and enough mana, cast all of your damage-increasing cooldowns

- Cast Arcane Missiles, if available

- Cast Arcane Barrage to clear Arcane Charges to avoid running out of mana (use less frequently when damage-increasing effects are active)

- Cast Arcane Blast

GROUP BUFFS AND DEBUFFS

Mages apply both the Spell Power and Critical Strike buffs with Arcane Brilliance.

Arcane Mages inflict the Cast Speed Slow debuff with Slow.

GETTING READY FOR HIGH-END CONTENT

ALL SPECS

Like other casters, Mages should always be trying to maximize their damage output for heroic dungeons. With two entire tiers of talents dedicated to survivability, Mages can safely prioritize raw damage over survival in their gear. It's very important that you learn how to manage your threat, especially as Arcane, or if you group with tanks that are less geared than you are. Mages are the most mana-dependent DPS casters, so keep an eye on that blue bar.

For raids, your priority should be reaching the hit cap (15%, or 14% for Draenei). Mages, unlike hybrid casters, cannot convert Spirit to hit rating, meaning all of your Hit must come from the hit rating stat found in gear. After you're hit-capped for raids, you will get the most benefit out of upgrading your weapon, pants, chest, and helm (due to the meta socket). Always prioritize Intellect when gemming, but don't pass up good socket bonuses. Note that all the secondary stats (Critical Strike, Haste, and Mastery) are useful for Mages, but certain spells benefit greatly from a single stat. For example, the Pyroblast mechanic used by the Fire tree benefits most from Critical Strike, and the Frost Bomb talent scales rapidly with your Haste.

FIRE

Fire Mages use an array of fire-based spells to burn their enemies. They are masters of AoE damage, a feat primarily attributed to the new Inferno Blast ability, which can spread hefty damage-over-time spells to numerous enemies. Fire Mages benefit a great deal from the critical strike stat, as their spells and passive abilities interact with and are dependent on critical strikes.

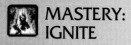 MASTERY: IGNITE

Your target burns for an additional 10% over 4 sec of the total damage caused by your Fireball, Frostfire Bolt, Inferno Blast, Scorch, and Pyroblast. If this effect is reapplied, any remaining damage will be added to the new Ignite.

SPECIALIZATION ABILITIES

ABILITY	LEVEL		DESCRIPTION
Pyroblast	10		Hurls an immense fiery boulder that causes Fire damage and additional Fire damage over 18 sec. Getting two single-target direct-damage Fire critical strikes in a row will make your next Pyroblast instant cast, cost no mana, and deal 25% additional damage.
Fireball	12		Hurls a fiery ball that causes Fire damage.
Inferno Blast	24		Replaces Fire Blast. Blasts the enemy for Fire damage, and is guaranteed to critical strike. Upon impact, it spreads any Pyroblast, Ignite, and Combustion effects to up to 2 nearby enemy targets within 10 yards.
Critical Mass	36		Multiplies the critical strike chance of your Fireball, Frostfire Bolt, Pyroblast, and Scorch by 1.5.
Dragon's Breath	62		Targets in a cone in front of the caster take Fire damage and are disoriented for 4 sec. Any direct damaging attack will revive targets.
Combustion	77		Instantly deals Fire damage and stuns the target for 3 sec. Burns the target for additional damage over 10 sec based on the Pyroblast and Ignite effects already on the target. When cast, resets the cooldown of your Inferno Blast ability.

GETTING TO LEVEL 90

Leveling as Fire is optimal when you have a large percentage of Critical Strike, as it will allow you to use instant Pyroblasts more often. Fire scales well with gear, so it can potentially be the fastest leveling tree depending on the talents chosen. Worthy of note is that Inferno Blast is your cheapest baseline spell and should be used often, especially considering it has no cast time and it always provides a critical hit toward your instant Pyroblast. If you get in trouble, Dragon's Breath provides some room for you to escape harm.

For talents, consider Scorch, which allows you to cast while moving (and counts toward Pyroblast, being a Fire spell). For tougher enemies, Frostjaw can be invaluable, as it keeps creatures in place for long enough to allow you to deal a large amount of damage.

PLAYING IN A GROUP

Fire provides, at its simplest, the steadiest damage output out of the Mage trees, meaning threat should be less of an issue for single targets. For AoE, naturally, Fire can deal a lot of damage, potentially attracting unwanted attention from enemies. Be quick with your threat-dropping abilities should this happen, as dungeon and raid enemies will likely make quick work of you.

BASE ROTATION

Because of Pyroblast, Fire Mages depend on critical strikes much more than the other trees. Luckily, Inferno Blast alleviates the luck factor, providing a guaranteed critical hit at your command. That said, the basic idea is to use as many instant Pyroblasts as possible, and fill the rest of your rotation with weaker spells.

- If your target is affected by Pyroblast and Ignite, use Combustion

- If AoE is required, use Inferno Blast to spread fire-based DoT spells

- If there's a single enemy, use Inferno Blast when you need an extra critical strike to get an instant Pyroblast

- Use Pyroblast when the buff is available

- Use Fireball as a filler

GROUP BUFFS AND DEBUFFS

Mages apply both the Spell Power and Critical Strike buffs with Arcane Brilliance.

GETTING READY FOR HIGH-END CONTENT

ALL SPECS

Like other casters, Mages should always be trying to maximize their damage output for heroic dungeons. With two entire tiers of talents dedicated to survivability, Mages can safely prioritize raw damage over survival in their gear. It's very important that you learn how to manage your threat, especially as Arcane, or if you group with tanks that are less geared than you are. Mages are the most mana-dependent DPS casters, so keep an eye on that blue bar.

For raids, your priority should be reaching the hit cap (15%, or 14% for Draenei). Mages, unlike hybrid casters, cannot convert Spirit to hit rating, meaning all of your Hit must come from the hit rating stat found in gear. After you're hit-capped for raids, you will get the most benefit out of upgrading your weapon, pants, chest, and helm (due to the meta socket). Always prioritize Intellect when gemming, but don't pass up good socket bonuses. Note that all the secondary stats (Critical Strike, Haste, and Mastery) are useful for Mages, but certain spells benefit greatly from a single stat. For example, the Pyroblast mechanic used by the Fire tree benefits most from Critical Strike, and the Frost Bomb talent scales rapidly with your Haste.

FROST

Frost Mages are powerful casters that employ ice and water spells to snare and deal damage to their enemies. They are the only Mages able to control a pet—the Water Elemental—to aid them in battle. Frost was previously considered a survivability tree, with many survivability tools in comparison to Arcane and Fire. These abilities are now talents available to every tree, evening the playing field for all Mage trees.

MASTERY: FROSTBURN

All your spells deal increased damage against Frozen targets. Increases the damage done by your Water Elemental.

SPECIALIZATION ABILITIES

ABILITY	LEVEL		DESCRIPTION
Summon Water Elemental	10		Summon a Water Elemental to fight for the caster. Casting Frostbolt on your Water Elemental will heal it.
Frostbolt	12		Launches a bolt of frost at the enemy, causing Frost damage and slowing movement speed by 50% for 15 sec. Also causes the target to take an additional 8% damage from your Frostbolt and Ice Lance.
Fingers of Frost	24		Your successful Frostbolts, Frostfire Bolts and Frozen Orb hits have a 12% chance, your Blizzard ticks have a 4% chance, and your successful Scorches have a 9% chance to grant you the Fingers of Frost effect. The Fingers of Frost effect causes your next Ice Lance or Deep Freeze to act as if your target were frozen, and increases Ice Lance damage by 25% for 15 sec. Limit 2 charges.
Icy Veins	36		Accelerates your spellcasting, granting 20% spell haste and reducing the pushback suffered from damaging attacks while casting by 100%. Lasts 20 sec.
Frozen Orb	62		Launches a Frozen Orb forward from the Mage's position, releasing Frostbolts that deal Frost damage to all nearby enemy targets for 10 sec. Grants the Mage 1 charge of Fingers of Frost when it first reaches a target. Targets damaged by the Frost Orb are slowed by 30% for 2 sec.
Brain Freeze	77		Your most recently applied Nether Tempest, Living Bomb, or Frost Bomb spell has a chance when it deals damage to grant you the Brain Freeze effect. The Brain Freeze effect causes your next Frostfire Bolt to be instant cast, cost no mana, and act as if your target were frozen for 15 sec.

GETTING TO LEVEL 90

As the only pet-enabled Mage tree, Frost holds its own on the leveling front. Note, however, that the previously cheap Frost-based spells are now up to par with the other schools when it comes to mana cost. This means you're likely to have some downtime if you're not careful with mana usage. Dispatch enemies by using the same rotation you would use in groups, but use Icy Veins liberally to get the most out of it.

The Ice Ward and Frostjaw talents interact with Ice Lance and Deep Freeze, becoming very useful for Frost Mages. Ice Floes is likely a better choice than Scorch for Frost Mages, allowing you to Frostbolt on the move every once in a while. Lastly, Cold Snap provides an extra Frost Nova, which gives you more opportunities to use Ice Lance for a high amount of damage.

PLAYING IN A GROUP

Threat should not be an issue unless your gear is significantly better than your tank's, as some of your damage will come from your pet. If you notice having to resummon your pet often, let your healer know that your Water Elemental could use some healing. Because your damage output is dependent on the Mage Bomb spells (level 75 line of talents), make sure to pick the most appropriate one based on the situation.

BASE ROTATION

Frost damage is largely dependent on the level 75 line of talents that affect Mage Bomb, as their ticks grant the Brain Freeze buff, allowing you to instantly use Frostfire Bolt. Make sure your pet is alive when you start a fight, and keep it alive through Frostbolt healing if necessary.

- Use Frost Orb and Icy Veins when available
- Make sure one of the three level 75 DoT abilities is active on at least one target
- Use Frostfire Bolt when you gain Brain Freeze
- Use Ice Lance when your target is frozen or you have stacks of the Fingers of Frost buff
- Use Frostbolt as a filler, or to heal your pet

GROUP BUFFS AND DEBUFFS

Mages apply both the Spell Power and Critical Strike buffs with Arcane Brilliance.

GETTING READY FOR HIGH-END CONTENT

ALL SPECS

Like other casters, Mages should always be trying to maximize their damage output for heroic dungeons. With two entire tiers of talents dedicated to survivability, Mages can safely prioritize raw damage over survival in their gear. It's very important that you learn how to manage your threat, especially as Arcane, or if you group with tanks that are less geared than you are. Mages are the most mana-dependent DPS casters, so keep an eye on that blue bar.

For raids, your priority should be reaching the hit cap (15%, or 14% for Draenei). Mages, unlike hybrid casters, cannot convert Spirit to hit rating, meaning all of your Hit must come from the hit rating stat found in gear. After you're hit-capped for raids, you will get the most benefit out of upgrading your weapon, pants, chest, and helm (due to the meta socket). Always prioritize Intellect when gemming, but don't pass up good socket bonuses. Note that all the secondary stats (Critical Strike, Haste, and Mastery) are useful for Mages, but certain spells benefit greatly from a single stat. For example, the Pyroblast mechanic used by the Fire tree benefits most from Critical Strike, and the Frost Bomb talent scales rapidly with your Haste.

MONK

Originally advocated by the Pandaren, the way of the Monk employs discipline and martial arts as combat proficiencies. Relying on their feet and fists as much as their weapons, Monks are quick and serene and can channel their inner energies to boost their efficiency in the battlefield.

Monks are newcomers to Azeroth with Mists of Pandaria, adding to the list of hybrid classes; this means they can fulfill all three roles: tanking, healing, and damage dealing. Like Rogues and Druids, Monks rely on their abilities more than their leather armor to survive enemy attacks. In order to perform their fighting skills, Monks of all types channel their Chi as a primary resource. Additionally, different stances provide a second resource—energy or mana—further adding depth to the class.

RACE AVAILABILITY

ALLIANCE

Draenei   Dwarf   Gnome

Human   Night Elf   Worgen

Pandaren

HORDE

Blood Elf   Goblin   Orc

Tauren   Troll   Undead

RACIAL ADVANTAGES

ALLIANCE

RACE	NOTES
Draenei	Heroic Presence grants Draenei +1% Hit chance. Gift of the Naaru heals the Draenei or any ally. Draenei take less damage from Shadow spells.
Dwarf	Stoneform is excellent for PvP and tanking, as it removes all bleeds and reduces damage taken. Mace Specialization provides increased Expertise with one and two hand maces.
Gnome	Escape Artist provides an extra ability for escaping slow or snare effects; great for PvP. Shortblade Specialization provides increased Expertise with daggers and one hand swords.
Human	Every Man for Himself removes effects that cause loss of control. Sword and Mace Specialization provides Expertise with one and two hand swords and maces.
Night Elf	Night Elves are less likely to be hit by any physical attack (perhaps the best racial passive for tanking) and take less damage from Nature spells. Shadowmeld renders the Night Elf invisible while motionless and cancels spells being cast by enemies on the Night Elf.
Worgen	Worgen get 1% increased Critical Strike from Viciousness. Darkflight increases movement speed temporarily.

PANDAREN

RACE	NOTES
Pandaren	Epicurean doubles the statistical bonuses from being Well Fed. Quaking Palm acts as a form of brief crowd control.

HORDE

RACE	NOTES
Blood Elf	The signature Blood Elf racial, Arcane Torrent, provides 1 Chi and an AoE silence. The former helps in tight mana situations, and the latter is great for PvP and certain PvE encounters.
Goblin	Rocket Jump is a great mobility tool, allowing Monk to stay at range. Goblins get 1% increased Haste, making them great for PvE. Rocket Barrage is another source of damage for Goblins.
Orc	Blood Fury is an activated ability that increases your attack or spell power. Axe Specialization provides Expertise for axes and fist weapons. Hardiness reduces the duration of stun effects by 15%.
Tauren	Nature Resistance increases a Tauren's ability to stand up to harmful Nature effects. War Stomp provides an (AoE) stun in melee range, and Endurance boosts base health by 5%.
Troll	Berserking grants a temporary increase in attack speed. Da Voodoo Shuffle passively reduces the duration of movement impairing effects. Trolls regenerate Health faster than other races, and 10% of total Health regeneration may continue in combat.
Undead	Undead are more suited for PvP as they can break out of Charm, Fear, and Sleep effects with Will of the Forsaken. Their passive racial, Touch of the Grave, is a life leech and also provides a modest DPS increase in any situation. Undead take less damage from Shadow spells.

EQUIPMENT OPTIONS

ARMOR TYPE	SHIELD
Leather	No

USABLE WEAPONS

1 HAND WEAPON	2 HAND WEAPON
Axes	Polearm
Fist Weapons	Staves
Maces	
Swords	

PROMINENT CLASS ABILITIES

WEAPON ATTUNEMENT

Way of the Monk attunes Monks to the weapons they have equipped, something no other class does. What that means is a Monk dual-wielding one-hand weapons will deal 40% more autoattack damage than another character with similar stats. A Monk wielding a staff or polearm swings 40% faster than another character with similar stats.

STANCES

Depending on their specialization, Monks can adopt one of three animal stances, granting them various significant boosts to their abilities.

Like other hybrids, these stances are best used in conjunction with their respective specialization trees.

STANCE	TYPE	DESCRIPTION
Stance of the Fierce Tiger	Damage	The only stance available to all three specialization trees, fighting like a fierce tiger increases damage output and Chi generation significantly. Though mainly advocated by Windwalker Monks, Brewmasters and Mistweavers can benefit from it when soloing or fighting weaker monsters.
Stance of the Sturdy Ox	Tanking	Exclusive to Brewmaster Monks, taking on this stance reduces damage taken, increases energy regeneration and health, and reduces the chance you'll be critically hit. Additionally, it adds an interesting new mechanic, Stagger, which allows you to take a portion of the incoming physical damage over time, rather than instantly.
Stance of the Wise Serpent	Healing	This stance is favored by (and exclusive to) Mistweaver Monks. It increases healing done significantly, replaces your energy resource for mana, and grants hit and expertise based on spirit. Additionally, it grants attack power based on your spell power. Yes, this means Mistweavers can get close and personal to enemies and dish some damage in certain situations!

CHI

Chi is a new resource introduced in Mists of Pandaria, and it's exclusive to Monks of all kinds. Along with energy or mana, it's used as a resource to execute most of the Monk's staple abilities.

Similar to a Rogue's combo points, Chi is generated by using certain abilities—most notably the melee attack Jab—and can be then used to perform more powerful moves. Chi can be accrued up to five times before capping, so make sure you use it before that happens.

TRANSCENDENCE

The Monk's level 87 ability is Transcendence. It splits your body and spirit, leaving your spirit behind for as long as the spell lasts and you stay in range. By using its complementary ability, Transcendence: Transfer, you can return to the spirit you left behind. This makes it very similar to a Warlock's Demonic Portal ability, with a few exceptions: your spirit lasts a long time in place, and both placing and using this ability have short cast times. Regardless, it's invaluable for PvE encounters where you know you will have to be somewhere quick or PvP encounters where you just need to get away from a melee siege.

NAME	LEVEL		DESCRIPTION
Stance of the Fierce Tiger	1		Increases damage done by 20% and increases the amount of Chi generated by your Jab and Expel Harm abilities by 1.
Jab	1		Deals damage and generates 1 Chi, or 2 Chi while in Stance of the Fierce Tiger.
Tiger Palm	3		Attack with the palm of your hand, dealing damage. Also grants you Tiger Power, causing your attacks to ignore 10% of enemies' armor for 20 sec. (Stacks up to 3 times.)
Roll	5		Roll a short distance.
Blackout Kick	7		Kick with a blast of Chi energy, dealing Physical damage.
Provoke	14		You mock the target, causing them to rush towards you with a 50% increased movement speed.
Resuscitate	18		Returns the spirit to the body, restoring a dead target to life with 35% of maximum health and mana. Cannot be cast when in combat.
Detox	20		Eliminates ailments from the friendly target, removing all harmful Poison and Disease effects.
Zen Pilgrimage	20		Your spirit travels to the Peak of Serenity in Pandaria, leaving your body behind. Use Zen Pilgrimage again to return near to where you were.
Legacy of the Emperor	22		You extol the words of the last emperor, increasing Strength, Agility, and Intellect by 5%. If target is in your party or raid, all party and raid members will be affected.
Touch of Death	22		You exploit the enemy target's weakest point, instantly killing them. Only usable on non-player targets who have equal or less health than you.
Swift Reflexes	23		Increases your chance to parry by 5%. Whenever you parry an attack, you reflexively strike back at the enemy. This effect has a 1 sec cooldown.
Fortifying Brew	24		Turns your skin to stone, increasing your health by 20%, and reducing damage taken by 20%. Lasts 20 sec.
Expel Harm	26		Instantly heals yourself and causes 50% of the amount healed to instantly be dealt to a nearby enemy as damage within 10 yards. Generates 1 Chi, or 2 Chi while in Stance of the Fierce Tiger.
Disable	28		You disable the target's movement, reducing their movement speed by 50%. The duration of Disable will be refreshed if the target remains within 10 yards of the Monk. Using Disable on a target already snared will cause them to be rooted for 8 sec instead.
Spear Hand Strike	32		You jab the target in the throat, interrupting their spell cast and preventing any spell in that school from being cast for 5 sec. If the enemy is facing you when cast, they are also silenced out of all schools for 4 sec.
Paralysis	44		You cause the target's muscles to contract, incapacitating them for 30 sec. If done from behind the target, the duration is doubled. Only one target can be victim to Paralysis at any given time. Any damage taken will cancel the effect.
Spinning Crane Kick	46		You spin while kicking in the air, dealing damage to all nearby enemies every 1 sec, within 8 yards. Movement speed is reduced by 30%. Generates 1 Chi, if it hits at least 3 targets. Lasts 3 sec. During Spinning Crane Kick, you can continue to dodge and parry.
Crackling Jade Lightning	54		Channels Jade lightning at the target, causing Nature damage over 6 sec. When dealing damage, you have a 25% chance to generate 1 Chi. If the enemy attacks you within melee range while victim to Crackling Jade Lightning, they are knocked back a short distance. This effect has an 8 sec cooldown.
Healing Sphere	64		You form a Healing Sphere out of healing mists at the target location for 2 min. If allies walk through it, they consume the sphere, healing themselves. Maximum of 3 Healing Spheres can be active by the Monk at any given time.
Path of Blossoms	64		You create a Fire Blossom at your feet every 1 sec for 3 sec. The blossom will last for 10 sec and deal Fire damage to the first enemy that walks over it. Fire Blossoms cannot be created within 3 yards of an existing blossom.
Grapple Weapon	68		You fire off a rope spear, grappling the target's weapons and shield, returning them to you for 10 sec. If you steal a better main-hand weapon, your damage or healing will be increased by 5% or damage taken reduced by 5%.
Zen Meditation	82		Reduces all damage taken by 90% and redirects to you up to 5 harmful spells cast against party and raid members within 30 yards. Lasts 8 sec. Being the victim of a melee attack will break your meditation, cancelling the effect.
Transcendence	87		You split your body and spirit, leaving your spirit behind for 15 min. Use Transcendence: Transfer to swap locations with your spirit.
Transcendence: Transfer	87		Your body and spirit swap locations.

TALENTS

TALENT	DESCRIPTION	NOTES
LEVEL 15 TIER (MOVEMENT)		
Celerity	Allows you to Roll and Chi Torpedo more often, increases their maximum number of charges by 1, and reduces their cooldown by 5 sec.	A great mobility tool in its own regard, it competes with Momentum in terms of sheer speed increase, though Celerity is likely better for certain situations where burst movement is needed.
Tiger's Lust	Instantly clears the target of all immobilizing and movement impairing effects, and increases their movement speed by 70% for 6 sec.	Note that, unlike Celerity and Momentum, allies can be targeted by this, making it a superb PvP tool that will make you invaluable in the battlefield.
Momentum	Every time you Roll or Chi Torpedo, your movement speed is increased by 25% for 10 sec. Stacks up to 2 times.	Similar to Celerity, Momentum will make you more mobile by increasing your run speed. Great for leveling—consider timing your Roll(s) so that the buff refreshes before running out, making you blaze from enemy to enemy.
LEVEL 30 TIER (VERSATILITY)		
Chi Wave	You cause a wave of Chi energy to flow through friend and foe, dealing damage or healing. Bounces up to 7 times to the nearest targets within 20 yards. When bouncing to allies, Chi Wave will prefer those injured over full health.	Great for nearly any group situation, this will alleviate the need for healing (especially for melee Mistweavers) and provide a decent AoE should everyone be healthy.
Zen Sphere	Forms a Zen Sphere above the target, healing the target and dealing damage to the nearest enemy within 10 yards of the target every 2 sec for 16 sec. Only one Zen Sphere can be summoned at any one time. If Zen Sphere is cast again while active, the Zen Sphere will detonate, dealing damage and healing to all targets within 10 yards.	This versatile ability allows you to cast a DoT and a HoT at the same time, and then detonate them for burst damage and healing. Note that it can be cast on yourself or allies with no cooldown, but at a relatively steep Chi cost. Great for using in moments of excess Chi.
Chi Burst	You summon a torrent of Chi energy and hurl it at the target, dealing damage to all enemies, and healing all allies in its path. Chi Burst will always heal the Monk. While casting Chi Burst, you continue to dodge, parry, and auto-attack.	Although this can't be used on the move (due to having a cast time), it's great for encounters where allies or enemies line up. Note that the healing bit will always target the Monk before going onto other targets.
LEVEL 45 TIER (CHI GENERATION)		
Power Strikes	Your Jab generates an additional Chi when used. This effect has a 20 sec cooldown. If you are already at maximum Chi, a Chi Sphere will be summoned near you.	This talent is a great "pick and forget" choice for increasing Chi generation passively for Brewmasters, Windwalkers, and melee Mistweavers. Ranged Mistweavers do not benefit from this talent.
Ascension	Increases the amount of maximum Chi by 1.	Ideal for fights that require you to pool some Chi, or players who would like to have a reserve of Chi rather than spending it as it comes.
Chi Brew	Instantly restores all of your Chi.	Provides more control over when the extra Chi is generated; great for proactive use while other cooldowns are active, or reactive use when Chi is needed immediately.
LEVEL 60 TIER (CONTROL)		
Deadly Reach	Your Paralysis ability is now usable from 20 yards away.	Extremely versatile in PvP (and certain PvE situations), this allows you to crowd control from a distance. Consider using it as an extra interrupt on a pesky healer when you're about to kill a player!
Charging Ox Wave	A mighty Ox effigy rushes forward 30 yards in front of you, stunning all enemies within its path for 3 sec.	Provides a directional AoE stun. The good thing about this talent is its large reach—Leg Sweep's stun is longer (and on a shorter cooldown), but Ox Wave can stun enemies out of melee range with ease.
Leg Sweep	You knock down all enemies within 5 yards, effectively stunning them for 5 sec.	On a short cooldown, this AoE stun is great as a survivability tool or an extra interrupt. It has no facing requirement (unlike the Ox Wave), but the radius of effect is pretty small.
LEVEL 75 TIER (SURVIVABILITY)		
Healing Elixirs	Anytime you drink from a Brew or Tea, you gain 10% of your total health. This effect cannot occur more than once every 15 sec.	Another "pick and forget" talent that will provide you with quite a bit of healing over the course of a fight.
Dampen Harm	You dampen the damage from the most harmful attacks done to you. The next 3 attacks within 45 sec that deal damage equal to 10% or more of your total health are reduced in half.	A great addition to a tank or PvP player's repertoire of defensive cooldowns, this talent will ignore the small hits and dampen the big ones. Very useful for predictable burst damage!
Diffuse Magic	Reduces all spell damage taken by 90% and clears all magical effects on you, reversing them back to their original caster if within 40 yards if possible. Lasts for 6 sec.	This is an unrivaled survivability tool against casters (especially PvP teams with multiple casters). The former half of the effect, particularly, is fun to experiment with.
LEVEL 90 TIER (DAMAGE)		
Rushing Jade Wind	You summon a whirling tornado that travels in front of you, dealing Nature damage to all targets in its path and increasing damage taken by your Spinning Crane Kick by 30% for 15 sec. Also triggers Shuffle for Brewmaster Monks and increases the healing done by your Spinning Crane Kick by 50% for 12 sec if you are a Mistweaver Monk.	Great for sheer AoE damage output, especially when followed by Spinning Crane Kick. The cooldown is short enough to use several times in an encounter where burst AoE is required.
Invoke Xuen, the White Tiger	Invokes the White Tiger Celestial, summoning an effigy at the command of the caster. The effigy will assist you, attacking your primary target and also inflicting tiger lightning every 6 sec to 3 nearby enemies within 10 yards dealing damage over 5 sec. Lasts for 45 sec. Xuen will also taunt the target for Brewmaster Monks.	Note that Xuen deals AoE lightning damage passively in addition to attacking your primary target, making him useful in either situation. This cooldown, reminiscent of an enhancement shaman's wolves, is particularly good for soloing numerous mobs.
Chi Torpedo	Torpedo a distance in front of you, dealing damage to all enemies and healing all allies in your path. Chi Torpedo replaces Roll.	Great for when numerous allies or enemies are bunched up together. Note that this talent benefits from Celerity, which adds an extra charge.

BREWMASTER

The sturdy Brewmaster Monks specialize in deflecting damage and protecting their allies. Like Windwalker Monks, Brewmasters use energy as a complementary resource to Chi. Unhindered by their inability to use shields, they rely on damage redirection and self-healing more than the rest of the tanking classes. Their signature battle pose, Stance of the Sturdy Ox, increases health, reduces damage, and causes physical damage taken by the Monk to deal its damage over time instead of instantly, making them unique amongst tanks.

MASTERY: ELUSIVE BRAWLER

Increases your Stagger amount by an additional percentage based on your mastery.

SPECIALIZATION ABILITIES

NAME	LEVEL		DESCRIPTION
Dizzying Haze	10		You hurl a keg of your finest brew, reducing the movement speed of all enemies within 8 yards by 50% for 15 sec. Deals a high amount of threat. Affected targets have a 3% chance to have their melee attacks misfire and strike themselves.
Stance of the Sturdy Ox	10		Reduces damage taken by 25%, increases Energy regeneration by 30%, reduces the chance to be critically hit by 6%, increases your Stamina by 20% and allows you to Stagger damage. Stagger: You shrug off attacks, causing 70% of the damage to happen instantly and the remaining 30% to be divided over 10 sec.
Vengeance	10		Each time you take damage, you gain 2% of the unmitigated damage taken as attack power for 20 sec.
Keg Smash	11		You swing a keg of brew, dealing damage to up to 3 nearby enemies within 8 yards. Also drenches the target in your Dizzying Haze and applies the Weakened Blows effect. Generates 2 Chi.
Breath of Fire	18		Breathes fire causing damage to all targets in front of you. If Dizzying Haze is on the target, they will burn for additional damage over 8 sec.
Clash	18		You and the target charge each other, meeting halfway then stunning all targets within 6 yards.
Guard	26		You Guard against future attacks, absorbing some damage for 30 sec. Any heals you apply to yourself while Guarding are increased by 30%.
Brewmaster Training	34		Spear Hand Strike no longer costs Energy. Fortifying Brew also increases your Stagger amount by 20% while active. Tiger Palm no longer costs Chi, and when you deal damage with Tiger Palm the amount of your next Guard is increased by 5%. Lasts 30 sec. Stacks up to 3 times. After you Blackout Kick, you gain Shuffle, increasing your parry chance by 20% and your Stagger amount by an additional 20% for 6 sec.
Brewing: Elusive Brew	36		Your autoattack critical strikes grant up to 2 charges of Elusive Brew, based on weapon speed. Use Elusive Brew to consume the charges. Elusive Brew can stack up to 15 times.
Elusive Brew	36		Increases your chance to dodge melee and ranged attacks by 30% for 1 sec per stack of Elusive Brew active, consuming your Elusive Brew charges.
Desperate Measures	45		While at or below 35% health, your Expel Harm has no cooldown.
Avert Harm	48		You reduce the damage taken by all nearby party and raid members within 10 yards by 20%, and cause half of all remaining damage they take to be re-directed to you. Lasts for 6 sec. Avert Harm is cancelled if you reach 10% or lower health.
Gift of the Ox	56		You have a chance when you deal melee damage to summon a Healing Sphere at the side of you that only you can see. When you move through your Healing Sphere summoned through Gift of the Ox, you heal yourself
Summon Black Ox Statue	70		Summons a Black Ox Statue at the target location. Lasts for 15 min. Only one Black Ox Statue can be summoned at any one time. The Black Ox Statue interacts with your Provoke and Leer of the Ox abilities. Sanctuary of the Ox (Passive) Everytime the Monk deals a specific amount of damage, the Black Ox statue will cast Guard on an injured party or raid member within 40 yards absorbing damage lasting 30 sec. This effect cannot be cast onto the Monk.
Purifying Brew	75		Instantly purifies all of your staggered damage.

GETTING TO LEVEL 90

Brewmasters are best suited in group play, but soloing to 90 is not completely inefficient. Because you're much more durable, you can fight several enemies at once. When doing so, make sure to Keg Smash to apply Dizzying Haze and follow this up with Breath of Fire. Use Spinning Crane Kick to use your energy and gain more Chi in order to keep using Breath of Fire. Naturally, use your tanking cooldowns for larger pulls (or even elites and group quests).

For weaker enemies, consider switching to Stance of the Fierce Tiger, which will greatly increase your Chi generation, allowing you to use Blackout Kick more often. Touch of Death might very well be one of the most satisfying abilities in the entire game, so be sure to use it often (it lights up on your bar by default).

For talents, consider any movement-boosting ones such as Momentum. The rest depend on your playstyle and the kind of enemies you'll be fighting.

PLAYING IN A GROUP

Grouping is where Brewmasters really shine, especially considering tanks are usually in high demand. As you might expect, your first priority is to get all of the enemies' attention, and your second priority is to survive their attacks. For the former, Brewmasters have several abilities, predominantly Keg Smash and Dizzying Haze. Keep in mind that Spinning Crane Kick will still let you mitigate damage, so use it for numerous enemies.

For survivability, first and foremost make sure to clear your staggered damage by using Purifying Brew. The Shuffle buff is great for increasing your overall avoidance so use Blackout Kick as often as possible. Don't be afraid to use Guard either as it provides you with a powerful shield and self heals like Expel Harm will be more effective during its duration. Being the tank (and having a cost-free interrupt), it's usually a good idea to stop enemy casts, whether they're damaging or healing spells. Additionally, Brewmasters can help mitigate party damage through Summon Black Ox Statue, which is particularly useful for boss fights with AoE damage.

ROTATION

More focused on survivability than damage, Brewmasters spend their Chi on abilities that boost absorbs, parry, and stagger. Because these abilities cost Chi, generated by either Jab, Keg Smash, Expel Harm and Spinning Crane Kick, it's often often a good idea to deal with heavy damage by conserving some Chi and using it in critical situations.

- Use Clash, Provoke, or Roll to quickly get into an enemy's melee range or pull safely from a distance with Dizzying Haze

- Use Keg Smash or Expel Harm, or Jab if both are on cooldown, to generate Chi

- Use Blackout Kick to gain Shuffle

- Use Guard to consume extra Chi if Shuffle is already applied

- Use Keg Smash on cooldown to apply the Weakened Blows debuff further reducing damage

- Follow with Breath of Fire in AoE situations

- If you predict heavy damage incoming, use Fortifying Brew or Elusive Brew (or both)

- Be diligent about using Purifying Brew to get rid of staggered damage. This becomes high priority if you have a Moderate or Heavy Stagger debuff

- If your Health is below 35% and you're about to die use Expel Harm on cooldown to quickly heal yourself back up

GROUP BUFFS AND DEBUFFS

Monks grant the Stats bonus with Legacy of the Emperor.

Brewmaster Monks inflict the Weakened Blows debuff with Keg Smash.

GETTING READY FOR HIGH-END CONTENT

BREWMASTER

Being a tank, your gear levels will usually be more crucial to surviving an encounter than the rest of your group or raid. The good news is that tank gear is plentiful, and there are only one or two tanks per group or raid. Because you have no shield, your biggest survivability upgrades will be your helm (because of the meta gem), legs, chest, and weapon. Don't be afraid to take up DPS-oriented gear if nobody needs it and then reforge undesirable stats (like Hit when over the cap of 7.5%) to more survivability-oriented ones. Note that, like Druids, you will benefit from Haste and Critical Strike when tanking, so you might have to compete with Rogues for some pieces.

MISTWEAVER

Mistweaver is the healing specialization for Monks. Unique to this specialization is the ability to go into melee range and dish some damage while still providing health replenishment to your party. This is accomplished through several abilities and the Stance of the Wise Serpent, which increases your hit and expertise based on your spirit.

MASTERY: GIFT OF THE SERPENT

You have a chance when you heal to summon a Healing Sphere nearby an injured ally. Allies who walk through the sphere will be healed based on your Mastery.

SPECIALIZATION ABILITIES

NAME	LEVEL		DESCRIPTION
Mana Meditation	10		Allows 50% of your mana regeneration from Spirit to continue while you are in combat.
Soothing Mist	10		Heals the target over 8 sec. When you heal with Soothing Mist, you have a 25% chance to generate 1 Chi.
Stance of the Wise Serpent	10		Increases healing done by 20%, replaces your Energy resource with Mana, grants hit and expertise equal to 50% Spirit gained from items or effects. Your attack power is equal to 200% of your spell power, and you no longer benefit from other sources of attack power. In addition, you also gain Eminence, causing you to heal the lowest health nearby target within 20 yards for an amount equal to 50% of non-autoattack damage you deal.
Internal Medicine	20		Your Detox spell now also clears all Magical effects when used.
Surging Mist	32		Heals the target. Generates 1 Chi. If cast while channeling Soothing Mist, Surging Mist will be instant cast and heal that target over all others.
Enveloping Mist	34		Heals the target over 6 sec, and increases the healing the target receives from your Soothing Mist by 30%. If cast while channeling Soothing Mist, Enveloping Mist will be instant cast.
Teachings of the Monastery	34		You become adept in the ways of the Mistweaver, amplifying three of your abilities. When you Blackout Kick, you gain Serpent's Zeal causing you to heal nearby injured targets equal to 25% of your auto-attack damage. Stacks up to 2 times. When you Tiger Palm, you gain Vital Mists reducing the cast time and mana cost of your next Surging Mist by 20%. Stacks up to 5 times. Lasts 30 sec. While channeling Spinning Crane Kick, you also heal up to 5 nearby injured allies every 1 sec for 3 sec. Healing yourself does not count for Chi generation.
Renewing Mist	42		You surround the target with healing mists, restoring health every 3 sec for 18 sec. Generates 1 Chi. Renewing Mist travels to closest nearby injured party and raid members within 20 yards, up to 3 times. Maximum 10 targets can have your Renewing Mist at any one time.
Dematerialize	45		When you are stunned, you phase out of existence temporarily causing all melee, ranged and spell attacks to miss you for 2.50 sec. This effect has a 10 sec cooldown.
Life Cocoon	50		Encases the target in a cocoon of Chi energy, absorbing damage and increasing all periodic healing taken by 50%. Lasts for 12 sec.
Brewing: Mana Tea	56		For each 4 Chi you consume through use of spells and abilities, you gain a charge of Mana Tea. Use Mana Tea to consume the charges. Mana Tea can stack up to 20 times.
Mana Tea	56		Restores 4% of your maximum mana per stack of Mana Tea active. Mana Tea must be channeled, lasting 1 sec per stack. Cancelling the channel will not waste stacks.
Uplift	62		Heals all targets with your Renewing Mist active.
Thunder Focus Tea	66		You receive a jolt of energy, doubling the healing done by your next Surging Mist or causing your next Uplift to refresh the duration of your Renewing Mists on all targets. Lasts for 30 sec.
Summon Jade Serpent Statue	70		Summons a Jade Serpent Statue at the target location. Lasts for 15 min. Only one statue can be active at a time. Eminence (Passive): When the Monk deals non-autoattack damage, the summoned Jade Serpent Statue will heal the lowest health nearby target within 20 yards equal to 50% of the damage done. Serpent's Accord (Passive): When you cast Soothing Mist, the Jade Serpent Statue will also cast Soothing Mist on an injured ally within 40 yards.
Revival	78		Instantly heals all party and raid members within vision, and clears them of any harmful Magical, Poison and Disease effects.

GETTING TO LEVEL 90

Mistweavers, being healers, are not ideal for those who want to opt for leveling speed. This doesn't necessarily mean they can't hold their own—especially when paired with a damage-dealing class. The dual-specialization feature also lets you choose another tree for leveling, should you want to try out Mistweavers in dungeons.

PLAYING IN A GROUP

As with other healers, your job is to keep your group alive. To accomplish this, the Mistweaver tree is capable of using several heals for different situations. Surging Mist is the staple quick (but mana inefficient) heal that you can use in emergency situations. If you're channeling Soothing Mist and you use Surging Mist, it will be instant, adding some extra relief for emergencies. Be wary not to spend all your mana using it, though!

As with Druids, Monk healers also depend largely on heals over time, the primary of which is Renewing Mist. Your job, then, is to keep it applied on targets that are likely to take damage (or have taken damage already), and then spend your Chi using Uplift in order to further heal them and refresh the heal-over-time effect. The other main heal, Soothing Mist, is slower and more mana efficient, making it ideal to use as a filler when not a lot of damage is being dealt to your allies. Lastly, Healing Sphere provides healing to allies that walk through it. Note that your mastery also produces these, so encourage your party and raid members to approach them should they need healing.

GROUP BUFFS AND DEBUFFS

Monks grant the Stats bonus with Legacy of the Emperor.

Mistweaver Monks use Rising Sun Kick to inflict the Mortal Wounds debuff.

GETTING READY FOR HIGH-END CONTENT

MISTWEAVER

Begin by trying to obtain a high-item-level weapon. Like tanks, meta gems are important to healers, so opt for a helm with a meta socket, even if slightly worse than one without. If you want to be a melee Mistweaver, consider the encounter's mechanics before doing so—it's generally fine for 5-man dungeons, however. Because of your passives, you don't need Hit or Expertise to go into the fray; you get that from Spirit.

WINDWALKER

Windwalker Monks excel at dealing melee damage, making great use of the Stance of the Fierce Tiger (the only one they can adopt). Being hybrids, they can still use some healing and tanking abilities to stay alive, especially considering their frail leather armor. Windwalkers, as their name suggests, are extremely mobile and versatile; getting away from one is by no means an easy task.

MASTERY: COMBO BREAKER

Combo Breaker grants a chance, based on your mastery, for Jab to cause your next Tiger Palm or Blackout Kick to cost no Chi.

SPECIALIZATION ABILITIES

NAME	LEVEL		DESCRIPTION
Fists of Fury	10		Pummel all targets in front of you with rapid hand strikes, stunning them and dealing damage immediately and every 1 sec for 4 sec. Damage is spread evenly over all targets.
Flying Serpent Kick	18		Soar through the air forwards at an increased speed. While traveling, use Flying Serpent Kick again to land yourself, dealing damage to all enemies within 8 yards, and slowing them by 70% for 4 sec.
Combat Conditioning	20		Your Blackout Kick now also deals an additional 20% damage over 4 sec if behind the target or heals you for 20% of the damage done if in front of the target.
Touch of Karma	22		All damage you take is redirected to the enemy target over 6 sec instead of you. Damage cannot exceed your total health. Lasts for 10 sec.
Afterlife	26		When you kill an enemy while gaining experience or honor, you have a 50% chance to summon a Healing Sphere. Enemies who die from Blackout Kick have a 50% chance to summon a Chi Sphere. Healing Sphere: Forms a healing sphere. If you walk through it, you are healed for 15% of your total health. Lasts for 30 sec. Chi Sphere: A sphere of energy forms from the wake of the fallen enemy. Walking through your Chi Sphere will restore 1 Chi. Lasts for 2 min.
Energizing Brew	34		Regenerates 60 Energy over 6 sec. Can only be used while in combat.
Sparring	42		When you are attacked by a melee enemy in front of you, you begin to spar their attacks, increasing your chance to parry by 5% for 10 sec. This effect has a 30 sec cooldown. When you attack them back, Sparring is amplified by an additional 5%. Stacks up to 3 times.
Adaptation	45		When you are disarmed, your chance to dodge is increased by 25% for 5 sec.
Spinning Fire Blossoms	48		Deals Fire damage to the first enemy target in front of you within 50 yards. If Spinning Fire Blossom travels further than 10 yards, the damage is increased by 50% and you root the target for 2 sec.
Brewing: Tigereye Brew	56		For each 4 Chi you consume through use of abilities and attacks, you gain a charge of Tigereye Brew. Use Tigereye Brew to consume the charges. Tigereye Brew can stack up to 10 times.
Rising Sun Kick	56		You kick upwards, dealing damage and applying Mortal Wounds to the target. Also causes all targets within 8 yards to take an increased 10% damage from your abilities for 15 sec.
Tigereye Brew	56		Increases damage done by 2% per stack of Tigereye Brew active, consuming your Tigereye Brew stacks. Lasts 15 sec.
Legacy of the White Tiger	81		You honor the White Tiger's legacy, increasing critical strike chance by 5%. If target is in your party or raid, all party and raid members will be affected.

GETTING TO LEVEL 90

Windwalker is the fastest leveling tree for Monks, with high burst damage and incredible mobility. Going back to basics, the gist of Windwalker DPS is to use Jab to generate Chi, and then, depending on the situation, use one of several abilities to spend it. Which skill you use will largely depend on the foe's health—sometimes you can even skip a fight altogether by instantly using Touch of Death (which you should use as often as possible when leveling).

Many PvP-oriented skills will have little use for leveling, but you might want to keep your interrupt (Spear Hand Strike) bound to a key for caster enemies. When pulling multiple mobs, use Spinning Crane Kick and Fists of Fury (which is also a great survivability tool). Remember to use Fortifying Brew often and proactively, or you might find yourself saving it for a rainy day that is not likely to come. Expel Harm is a great way to get your health up, but like Fortifying Brew, you should use it early and often considering the cooldown.

Lastly, use your mobility tools as much as possible! Flying Serpent Kick and Roll, namely, will make traveling to close objectives and monsters a breeze. For this purpose, the talents Celerity and Momentum both provide extra mobility, which is great for faster leveling.

PLAYING IN A GROUP

Your group rotation will be largely the same as playing solo, with the difference that monsters are much more likely to last longer (especially in raids), giving you a chance to stack Tiger Palm fully. Remember to use your cooldowns on bosses or tough packs, as they increase your damage significantly. If you're under heavy siege, help your healer out by using Expel Harm and your defensive buffs. As with all melee classes, you can interrupt enemy casts, which is handy for preventing extra incoming damage (or dealing with those pesky enemy healers). Also worthy of mention is your disarming ability, Grapple Weapon, which can help your tank survive heavy damage.

Because you're relatively frail, you will want to watch your threat, especially on the first few seconds of a fight. Windwalkers have no way to instantly shed their threat, and your healer might not be able to keep you alive should an angry dragon start attacking you. Being a hybrid, you can also resurrect dead players and cure negative poison and disease effects. Your healer will be thankful should you do so.

ROTATION

Windwalker's rotation will depend on what kind of enemy you're fighting. For groups of weak enemies, using your energy on Spinning Crane Kick and your Chi on Fists of Fury will be most beneficial. For single weak enemies, you can opt out of stacking Tiger Palm (sans Mastery procs), and go straight for Rising Sun Kick and Blackout Kick. If your enemy will live for long enough, however, consider the following:

- Use Jab and Expel Harm to generate Chi

- Use Tiger Palm to spend the Chi, up until you have a full stack of the armor penetration buff. Use again when you need to refresh it

- If you have the full stack, use your cooldowns, such as Tigereye Brew (if stacked high enough)

- Use Rising Sun Kick when available

- Use Touch of Death if available (e.g., enemy has less health than your total)

- Otherwise, use Blackout Kick to spend your Chi

- If under heavy siege, use Fortifying Brew, Expel Harm, or Touch of Karma to survive

GROUP BUFFS AND DEBUFFS

Monks grant the Stats bonus with Legacy of the Emperor. Windwalker Monks impart the Critical Strike buff with Legacy of the White Tiger.

Windwalker Monks apply Mortal Wounds with Rising Sun Kick.

GETTING READY FOR HIGH-END CONTENT

WINDWALKER

Like other melee-based classes, your priority should be increasing your hit rating until you're no longer at risk of missing attacks on boss-level monsters (in this case, 93). If you hover over your Hit stat in the character screen, you can see how you're doing in that regard. This isn't as important for 5-man heroics, but it's best to hit-cap before attempting raids. After that, go for Expertise until you're not getting dodged often (if at all).

For sheer damage output, always prioritize Agility in places that allow so, such as gems. At times, skipping gem bonuses in favor of more Agility gems is favorable—just make sure not to pass up great bonuses (generally Agility bonuses, or any helm bonuses).

# PALADIN

Paladins are protectors of the Light, sworn to vanquish evil from Azeroth. Always available to the Alliance, and relatively new to the Horde, Paladins have played a key role throughout history, protecting and healing allies, or using the power of the Light to destroy foes.

These heavily-armored warriors are one of the true hybrid classes available to players, having the ability to fill all three combat roles efficiently. For their DPS tree, Retribution, they prefer going into the fray and using their holy skills in melee range. They don't have a specialization tree entirely dedicated to casting spells, but they do have some offensive abilities they can use from range.

Only a few races have the necessary affinity to the Light that allows them to become Paladins.

RACE AVAILABILITY

ALLIANCE

Draenei · Dwarf · Gnome

Human · Night Elf · Worgen

Pandaren

HORDE

Blood Elf · Goblin · Orc

Tauren · Troll · Undead

RACIAL ADVANTAGES

ALLIANCE

RACE	NOTES
Draenei	Heroic Presence grants Draenei +1% Hit chance, which is powerful for Retribution and Protection in all situations. Gift of the Naaru heals the Draenei or any ally. Draenei take less damage from Shadow spells.
Dwarf	Stoneform is excellent for PvP, as it removes all poison, disease, and bleed effects and reduces damage taken. Mace Specialization provides increased Expertise with one and two hand maces. Dwarves take less damage from Frost spells.
Human	Every Man for Himself removes effects that cause loss of control of your character and movement impairing effects, which is very powerful in PvP. Sword and Mace Specialization provides Expertise with one and two hand swords and maces. The Human Spirit increases your Spirit by 3%.

HORDE

RACE	NOTES
Blood Elf	The signature Blood Elf racial, Arcane Torrent, provides mana and an AoE silence. The former helps in tight mana situations, and the latter is great for PvP and certain PvE encounters. Blood Elves take less damage from Arcane spells.
Tauren	Nature Resistance increases a Tauren's ability to stand up to harmful Nature effects. War Stomp provides an (AoE) stun in melee range, and Endurance boosts base health by 5%.

EQUIPMENT OPTIONS

ARMOR TYPE	SHIELD
Mail until Level 40, then Plate	Yes

USABLE WEAPONS

1 HAND WEAPON	2 HAND WEAPON
Axes	Axes
Maces	Maces
Swords	Polearms
	Swords

PROMINENT CLASS ABILITIES

HOLY POWER

Aside from mana, all Paladins now have a resource called Holy Power, which is generated by some abilities and spent by others.

The abilities that generate this resource (for example, Crusader Strike) only generate one at a time in their basic form—some other Paladin abilities boost this so you can get more than one at a time.

The abilities that spend Holy Power can spend up to three charges at a time, which is the maximum as a baseline. The passive ability Boundless Conviction, available to all Paladins and learned at higher levels, allows you to store up to five charges at a time. Even with this passive, however, abilities will only consume up to three charges at once. An ability's effectiveness is determined by the amount of Holy Power spent.

Looking at the big picture, this is one of the easiest secondary resources to keep track of, but don't neglect it, as the abilities that consume it are vital to all three specs.

SEALS

Previously, Paladins had several different perennial abilities called Auras. These have other uses now, and have been replaced with Seals in the hotbar.

Seals are powerful holy-based self buffs that grant a major benefit to all specs depending on the situation.

You learn your first seal as early as level 3, but it is later replaced with a more powerful version. At the highest level, you will have a total of three seals, or four if you're a Retribution Paladin.

SEAL	PREFERRED SPEC	BEST FOR...
Seal of Truth	Retribution and Protection	Tanking or dealing damage to a single enemy that will live long enough to stack the effect up to 5 times
Seal of Righteousness	Retribution and Protection	Dealing damage to several enemies that are bunched up together
Seal of Insight	Holy	Healing and recovering mana by using basic melee attacks on enemies when possible
Seal of Justice (Retribution)	Retribution	Slowing enemies down, allowing you to stay in melee range of them

BLINDING LIGHT

On a modest two-minute cooldown, this instant-cast spell emits a dazzling light that causes nearby enemies to wander disoriented for a short while, granting you (or your allies) some breathing room in situations where multiple enemies are involved. Note that the mana cost involved is trivial for Holy Paladins, but might dent a Retribution or Protection Paladin's reserves.

Being a considerable survivability tool, Blinding Light can prove useful in both PvE and PvP—especially the latter, and particularly in battleground matches, where all-out brawls between numerous allies and enemies are commonplace. Just make sure your teammates are not using AoE spells freely, as they will instantly break the effects of Blinding Light.

NAME	LEVEL		DESCRIPTION
Crusader Strike	1		An instant strike that causes 125% weapon damage plus additional damage.
Parry	1		Gives a chance to parry enemy attacks.
Seal of Command	3		Fills you with Holy Light, causing melee attacks to deal 10% additional Holy damage.
Judgment	5		A magic attack that unleashes the energy of a Seal to cause Holy damage.
Hammer of Justice	7		Stuns an enemy for 6 sec.
Word of Glory	9		Consumes up to 3 holy power to heal a friendly target.
Righteous Fury	12		Increases your threat generation while active, making you a more effective tank.
Redemption	13		Brings a dead ally back to life with 35% of maximum health and mana. Cannot be cast when in combat.
Flash of Light	14		A quick and mana expensive spell that heals an ally.
Reckoning	15		Taunts the target to attack you, but has no effect if the target is already attacking you.
Lay on Hands	16		Heals a friendly target for an amount equal to your maximum health. Cannot be used on a target with Forbearance. Causes Forbearance for 1 min.
Divine Shield	18		Protects you from all damage and spells for 8 sec, but reduces all damage you deal by 50%. Cannot be used on a target with Forbearance. Causes Forbearance for 1 min.
Cleanse	20		Removes all Poison and Disease effects from an ally.
Seal of Truth	24		Fills you with Holy Light, causing melee attacks to deal 12% additional Holy damage and apply Censure to the target. Censure: Deals additional Holy damage over 15 sec. Stacks up to 5 times.
Divine Protection	26		Reduces magical damage taken by 40% for 10 sec.
Blessing of Kings	30		Places a Blessing on the friendly target, increasing Strength, Agility, and Intellect by 5%.
Seal of Insight	32		Fills you with Holy Light, increasing your casting speed by 10%, improving healing spells by 5%, and giving melee attacks a chance to heal you and restore mana.
Supplication	34		For 8 sec after you kill an enemy that yields experience or honor, your next Flash of Light will be a critical.
Rebuke	36		Interrupts spellcasting and prevents any spell in that school from being cast for 4 sec.
Hammer of Wrath	38		Hurls a magical hammer that strikes an enemy for Holy damage. Only useable on enemies that have 20% or less health.
Seal of Righteousness	42		Fills you with Holy Light, causing melee attacks to deal 6% weapon damage to all targets within 8 yards.
Heart of the Crusader	44		Increases your mounted speed by 20%. This does not stack with other movement speed increasing effects.
Turn Evil	46		The power of the Light compels an Undead or Demon target to flee for up to 40 sec. Only one target can be turned at a time.
Hand of Protection	48		Places a Hand on a party or raid member, protecting them from all physical attacks for 10 sec, but during that time they cannot attack or use physical abilities. Players may only have one Hand on them per Paladin at any one time. Cannot be used on a target with Forbearance. Causes Forbearance for 1 min.
Hand of Freedom	52		Places a Hand on the friendly target, granting immunity to movement impairing effects for 6 sec. Players may only have one Hand on them per Paladin at any one time.
Sanctity of Battle	58		Melee haste effects lower the cooldown and global cooldown of your Judgment, Crusader Strike, and Hammer of Wrath.
Devotion Aura	60		Inspire all party and raid members within 40 yards, granting them immunity to Silence and Interrupt effects and reducing all magic damage taken by 20%. Lasts 6 sec.
Hand of Salvation	66		Places a Hand on the party or raid member, reducing their total threat by 2% every 1 sec for 10 sec. Players may only have one Hand on them per Paladin at any one time.
Avenging Wrath	72		Increases all of your damage and healing by 20% for 20 sec.
Hand of Sacrifice	80		Places a Hand on a party or raid member, transferring 30% damage taken to the Paladin. Lasts 12 sec or until the Paladin has transferred 100% of their maximum health. Players may only have one Hand on them per Paladin at any one time.
Blessing of Might	81		Places a Blessing on the friendly target, increasing Mastery. If the target is in your party or raid, all party and raid members will be affected. Players may only have one Blessing on them per Paladin at any one time.
Boundless Conviction	85		You may store an additional 2 Holy Power beyond the maximum of 3. No ability ever consumes more than 3 Holy Power.
Blinding Light	87		Emits a dazzling light in all directions, blinding enemies within 10 yards, causing them to wander disoriented for 6 sec.

TALENTS

TALENT		DESCRIPTION	NOTES
LEVEL 15 TIER (MOVEMENT)			
Speed of Light		Increases your movement speed by 70% for 8 sec.	The movement speed portion nearly doubles the speed at which you move. This talent is most useful for PvE situations that require infrequent movement.
Long Arm of the Law		A successful Judgment increases your movement speed by 45% for 3 sec.	The movement speed increase and duration are both much shorter than the ones granted by Speed of Light, however, this talent is ideal for closing the gap on enemies. Because Judgment is on such a short cooldown, however, this talent is ideal for closing the gap on enemies.
Pursuit of Justice		You gain 15% movement speed at all times, plus additional 5% movement speed for each current charge of Holy Power up to 3.	The movement speed increase is modest, naturally, as it is active at all times. The holy power portion only affects your movement speed to a maximum of three. This talent is best suited for situations where you would prefer a constant movement speed increase, rather than the bursty gains from Long Arm of the Law or Speed of Light.
LEVEL 30 TIER (CONTROL)			
Fist of Justice		Stuns your target for 6 sec. Replaces Hammer of Justice.	This improved version of the Paladin's signature stun has a much shorter cooldown, allowing you to use it more often, and increased range. A great choice if you find yourself relying on Hammer of Justice often.
Repentance		Puts the enemy target in a state of meditation, incapacitating them for up to 1 min. Any damage from sources other than Censure will awaken the target. Usable against Demons, Dragonkin, Giants, Humanoids, and Undead.	An old Paladin favorite, Repentance has had a few changes: it now has a cast time, so it cannot be used on the run; it has a much shorter cooldown, and its mana cost isn't trivial anymore. The effect lasts a long time in PvE, but is much shorter in PvP.
Burden of Guilt		Your Judgment hits fill your target with doubt and remorse, reducing movement speed by 50% for 12 sec.	Similar to Seal of Justice, this talent will make it relatively easy to stay atop most targets, which is great to avoid getting kited as a melee, or to help your teammates catch up to an enemy in PvP.
LEVEL 45 TIER (HEALING)			
Selfless Healer		Your successful Judgments reduce the cast time and mana cost of your next Flash of Light by 35% per stack and improves its effectiveness by 35% per stack when used to heal others. Stacks up to 3 times.	As its name suggests, this provides very good synergy when playing in a team, allowing you to use Flash of Light instantly, for free, and for a larger amount on a teammate.
Eternal Flame		Consumes up to 3 Holy Power to place a protective Holy flame on a friendly target, which heals them plus an additional amount every 3 sec for 30 sec. Healing increased per charge of Holy Power. Replaces Word of Glory.	This ability, like Word of Glory, uses your holy power to heal an ally. The improved version provided by Eternal Flame also places a hefty HoT that heals proportionally to the holy power spent.
Sacred Shield		Protects the target with a shield of Holy Light for 30 sec. The shield absorbs damage every 6 sec. Can be active only on one target at a time.	The shield can only be on a single ally at a time, and refreshes a shield on the target every six seconds for its duration. This means you only need to cast it once and it'll absorb damage several times over its duration.
LEVEL 60 TIER (VERSATILITY)			
Hand of Purity		Places a Hand on the friendly target, reducing the damage of harmful periodic effects by 70% for 6 sec. Players may only have one Hand on them per Paladin at any one time.	One of the best ways to counter a heavy siege of DoT effects in the game, this talent is strongly recommended in PvP against teams whose tactics consist of using many DoT spells to wear off your party. Works in PvE too, if an encounter has such effects.
Unbreakable Spirit		When your Divine Shield, Divine Protection, or Lay on Hands are on cooldown, spending Holy Power will reduce the remaining cooldown a percentage per Holy Power spent, up to a maximum of 50% reduction.	The cooldown reduction is based on how many holy power you use—you reduce 1% per charge (so up to 3% at a time), up to a maximum of 50%, effectively halving the cooldown on all these effects if you use enough holy power in that timeframe.
Clemency		You can use Hand of Freedom, Hand of Protection, Hand of Sacrifice, and Hand of Salvation twice each before incurring their cooldowns.	A great tool for mobility and survivability, this talent allows you to use Hand spells much more freely, and enables the use of certain tactics in PvP.
LEVEL 75 TIER (HOLY POWER)			
Holy Avenger		Abilities that generate Holy Power will deal 30% additional damage and healing, and generate 3 charges of Holy Power for the next 18 sec.	This is a great way to generate a lot of holy power in a short time. Consider pairing this up with the Unbreakable Spirit talent in the previous tier for maximum cooldown reduction. The duration of this effect is modest, but the spell itself is free and instant.
Sanctified Wrath		Avenging Wrath lasts 50% longer and grants more frequent access to one of your abilities while it lasts. Holy: Reduces the cooldown of your Holy Shock spell by 50%. Protection: Reduces the cooldown of your Judgment spell by 50%. Retribution: Reduces the cooldown of your Hammer of Wrath spell by 50%.	This allows you to use key abilities twice as often. The Avenging Wrath improvement is great for all specs, as it increases both healing and damage output.
Divine Purpose		Abilities that cost Holy Power have a 25% chance to cause the Divine Purpose effect. Divine Purpose: Your next Holy Power ability will consume no Holy Power and cast as if 3 Holy Power were consumed. Lasts 8 sec.	With a 25% chance to proc, this talent allows you to sometimes use holy power consuming abilities back to back at their maximum potency.
LEVEL 90 TIER (DAMAGE AND HEALING)			
Holy Prism		Sends a beam of light toward a target, turning them into a prism for Holy energy. If an enemy is the prism, they take Holy damage and radiate healing to 5 nearby allies within 15 yards. If an ally is the prism, they are healed and radiate Holy damage to 5 nearby enemies within 15 yards.	Its usefulness is twofold, but generally speaking, you want to use this when there are numerous targets around each other. Tactically, you can set this up by sending an ally into the midst of numerous enemies. The opposite is harder to set up, but might happen naturally on boss encounters where players surround an enemy.
Light's Hammer		Hurl a Light-infused hammer into the ground, where it will blast a 10 yard area with Arcing Light for 16 sec. Arcing Light: Deals Holy damage to enemies within the area and healing to allies within the area every 2 sec.	Another twofold ability that allows you to simultaneously deal damage to enemies in an area and heal allies in that same area. Great for when numerous targets are bunched up together.
Execution Sentence		A hammer slowly falls from the sky, causing Holy damage over 10 sec. This damage is dealt slowly at first and increases over time, culminating in a final burst of damage. Stay of Execution: If used on friendly targets, the falling hammer heals the target over 10 sec. This healing is dealt slowly at first and increases over time, culminating in a final burst of healing.	A single-target version of the previous abilities, Execution Sentence is technically the most powerful in terms of raw numbers, but the effect is the slowest and most predictable.

HOLY

Holy Paladins are the masters of healing spells that use the Light to provide relief to the wounds suffered by allies. Previously, Holy Paladins leaned toward single-target spells, mainly using heals that required a cast time. This has changed, as Paladins are now great AoE healers and can use Holy Shock and Word of Glory on the move.

MASTERY: ILLUMINATED HEALING

Allows your direct healing spells to also place an absorb shield on your target for a percentage based on your Mastery and lasts 15 sec.

SPECIALIZATION ABILITIES

ABILITY	LEVEL		DESCRIPTION
Holy Insight	10		Increases the effectiveness of your healing by 25%. Increases your mana pool by 400%. Allows 50% of your mana regeneration from Spirit to continue while in combat. Increases your chance to hit with Holy Shock, Judgment, and Denounce by 15%.
Holy Shock	10		Blasts the target with Holy energy, causing Holy damage to an enemy or healing to an ally, and granting a charge of Holy Power. Holy Shock has an additional 25% chance to be a critical strike.
Denounce	20		Casts down the enemy with a bolt of Holy Light, causing Holy damage and preventing the target from causing critical effects for the next 4 sec.
Sacred Cleansing	20		Your Cleanse spell now also dispels Magic effects.
Holy Radiance	28		Imbues a friendly target with radiant energy, healing that target and all allies within 10 yards for 50% of the target's healing amount. Grants a charge of Holy Power. Healing effectiveness diminishes for each player target beyond 6.
Holy Light	34		A mana-efficient, slow-casting heal that restores a modest amount of health.
Beacon of Light	39		The target becomes a Beacon of Light to all party and raid members within 60 yards. Only one target can be the Beacon of Light at a time. Beacon of Light: Your Holy Light will also heal the Beacon for 100% of the amount healed. Your Holy Radiance and Light of Dawn will heal for 15% of the amount healed. All other heals will heal for 50% of the amount healed.
Divine Plea	46		You gain 12% of your total mana over 9 sec, but the amount healed by your healing spells is reduced by 50%.
Infusion of Light	50		Your Holy Shock critical effects reduce the cast time of your next Holy Light, Divine Light, or Holy Radiance by 1.5 sec.
Divine Light	54		A large heal that heals a friendly target and is good for periods of heavy damage.
Daybreak	56		After casting Holy Radiance, your next Holy Shock will also heal other allies within 10 yards of the target for an amount equal to the original healing done, divided evenly among all targets.
Divine Favor	62		Increases spell casting haste by 20% and spell critical chance by 20% for 20 sec.
Tower of Radiance	64		Healing the target of your Beacon of Light with Flash of Light or Divine Light has a 100% chance to generate a charge of Holy Power.
Light of Dawn	70		Consumes up to 3 Holy Power to emanate a wave of healing energy, healing up to 6 of the most injured targets in your party or raid within 30 yards for an amount per charge of Holy Power.
Guardian of Ancient Kings	75		Summons a Guardian of Ancient Kings to help you heal for 30 sec. The Guardian of Ancient Kings will heal the target of your next 5 single-target heals, and nearby friendly targets for 10% of the amount healed. Every time the Guardian heals, it increases your haste by 10%.

GETTING TO LEVEL 90

Holy Paladins are arguably the slowest levelers in the game, so consider switching to Retribution in order to dispatch enemies quickly—the dual specialization feature allows you to keep Holy as a secondary spec if you want to use it in dungeons.

PLAYING IN A GROUP

As with any healer, your goal is to keep your group alive. To accomplish this, you must conserve mana and use the appropriate heals at the right time. You can technically just use Flash of Light over and over, but you'll learn that this will consume all of your mana quickly, leaving you with no resources for the rest of the fight. If this happens, keep using Holy Light as often as mana permits.

Using Divine Plea is a sort of art that you will master after you've played Holy for a long time. There's never necessarily a perfect moment to use it, considering it halves your healing output; you have to assess the risk and how badly you need the mana. Generally speaking, you benefit from it the most during a lull in incoming damage, where you can keep using Holy Light and keep everyone healthy.

HEALING

Paladin healing can be very effective in all sorts of situations. Like other specs, using your holy power efficiently can make the difference between going out of mana or keeping your group alive. For Holy, the two holy power-consuming spells are Word of Glory and Light of Dawn, providing hefty single target and AoE heals (respectively) free of mana cost.

SITUATION(S)	USE...
An ally is in need of immediate healing	Depending on the amount of healing needed, use Holy Shock or Flash of Light. For emergencies, use LoH, but consider the long cooldown
Healing a single target that's not in immediate danger	Ideally, you'll want to use Holy Light as often as possible. If the target is taking too much damage, switch to Divine Light
Everyone is healthy, but you know there's going to be incoming damage	Keep using Holy Shock to save some holy power, which can later be spent in Light of Dawn or Word of Glory. If you have time, melee an enemy to regenerate some mana via your seal
Heavy AoE damage from enemies	Use Holy Radiance to heal your allies and grant you holy power. When you have three, use Light of Dawn

GROUP BUFFS AND DEBUFFS

Paladins can provide either the Stats buff with Blessing of Kings or the Mastery buff with Blessing of Might.

GETTING READY FOR HIGH-END CONTENT

HOLY

Without having a Hit cap to worry about you should go straight for throughput (from Intellect, Haste, Critical Strike, and Mastery) and mana regeneration (from Spirit). How you balance these stats will be based on how often you feel like you need more mana. For instance, Haste will allow you to cast faster, thus healing more, but using more mana. Consider reforging some secondary stats to Spirit if you think you're holding back too much due to lack of mana.

Your Mastery is very subtle, and at times, it might seem like it's not doing much, but rest assured—the shields granted by your healing spells through Mastery add up to a great amount over time.

PROTECTION

Protection is a tanking spec that shares its name with the Warrior tanking tree (not to be confused!). Like Warriors, Protection Paladins are plate-clad juggernauts able to use shields to defend themselves and allies from enemy attacks. As with other Paladin specs, tanking Paladins use both mana and holy power in order to increase their effectiveness.

MASTERY: DIVINE BULWARK

Increases the damage reduction of your Shield of the Righteous, improves your Bastion of Glory, and increases your chance to block by a percentage determined by your Mastery.

SPECIALIZATION ABILITIES

ABILITY	LEVEL		DESCRIPTION
Avenger's Shield	10		Hurls your shield at an enemy target, dealing Holy damage, silencing and interrupting spellcasting for 3 sec, and then jumping to additional nearby enemies. Affects 3 total targets.
Guarded by the Light	10		Increases your total Stamina by 15% and your block chance by 10%. Reduces the chance you will be critically hit by melee attacks by 6%. Word of Glory is no longer on the global cooldown. Your spell power is now equal to 50% of your attack power, and you no longer benefit from other sources of spell power. Grants 6% of your maximum mana every 2 sec.
Vengeance	10		Each time you take damage, you gain 2% of the unmitigated damage taken as attack power for 20 sec.
Hammer of the Righteous	20		Hammer the current target for 20% weapon damage, causing a wave of light that hits all targets within 8 yards for 35% Holy damage and applying the Weakened Blows effect. Grants a charge of Holy Power. Weakened Blows: Demoralizes the target, reducing their physical damage dealt by 10% for 30 sec.
Holy Wrath	20		Sends bolts of power in all directions, causing Holy damage divided among all enemies within 10 yards, stunning Demons and Undead for 3 sec.
Judgments of the Wise	28		Your Judgment hits grant one charge of Holy Power.
Consecration	34		Consecrates the land beneath you, causing Holy damage over 9 sec to enemies who enter the area.
Shield of the Righteous	40		Instantly slam the target with your shield, causing Holy damage, reducing the physical damage you take by 30% for 3 sec, and causing Bastion of Glory. Bastion of Glory: Increases the strength of your Word of Glory when used to heal yourself by 10%. Stacks up to 5 times.
Grand Crusader	50		Your Crusader Strike and Hammer of the Righteous hits have a 20% chance of refreshing the cooldown on your next Avenger's Shield and causing it to generate a charge of Holy Power if used within 6 sec.
Sanctuary	64		Decreases damage taken by 15%, increases armor value from items by 10%, and increases your chance to dodge by 2%.
Ardent Defender	70		Reduce damage taken by 20% for 10 sec. While Ardent Defender is active, the next attack that would otherwise kill you will instead cause you to be healed for 15% of your maximum health.
Guardian of Ancient Kings	75		Summons a Guardian of Ancient Kings to protect you for 12 sec. The Guardian of Ancient Kings reduces damage taken by 50%.

GETTING TO LEVEL 90

Protection Paladins are relatively fast levelers among tanks, but never as fast as a Retribution Paladin would be. Execute your standard rotation and make sure to use your cooldowns (especially damage-increasing ones) often.

For talents, Long Arm of the Law provides the best benefit for leveling if you're using Judgment often, especially as an opening move. Sacred Shield is also great for leveling, as it will nullify some of the steady, weak damage dealt by standard enemy monsters. Lastly, Sanctified Wrath is great when paired with Long Arm of the Law, allowing you to use your short sprint much more often as protection.

PLAYING IN A GROUP

Being a tank is a big responsibility in groups, so make sure your gear is up to par for the content you're attempting.

As with other tanks, your number one job is simple: keep enemies attacking you instead of your teammates, and make sure you survive in the process. That said, Protection is all about managing your holy power, mana, and using defensive cooldowns in critical situations. Note your Shield of the Righteous ability is unlike most other holy power consuming skills, in that it doesn't scale with the amount of holy power you have. Instead, it flatly uses three of the resource, providing a sizable damage mitigation cooldown.

For emergency situations, use your large cooldowns to hopefully survive a heavy siege. Don't hesitate to use Lay on Hands on yourself should the situation get dangerous.

BASIC ROTATION

Protection Paladins are like other tanks when it comes to resources: their key defensive abilities are not on a long cooldown, but consume holy power, which is vital for survivability. Try to time these abilities with large amounts of damage in order to help your healers out.

- Use Avenger's Shield as an opening move, and then again whenever it's available

- Use Judgment whenever available

- Use Crusader Strike if Judgment is on cooldown

- Use Consecration whenever available

- Use Word of Glory when you have 3 Holy Power if Bastion of Glory is at five stacks, you are at low health, or the incoming damage is magical.

- Use Holy Wrath when everything else is on cooldown

- Use Shield of the Righteous when you have 3 holy power, depending on the amount of incoming damage

GROUP BUFFS AND DEBUFFS

Paladins can provide either the Stats buff with Blessing of Kings or the Mastery buff with Blessing of Might. Protection Paladins also apply the Weakened Blows debuffs with Hammer of the Righteous.

GETTING READY FOR HIGH-END CONTENT

PROTECTION

Being a tank, your gear levels will usually be more crucial to surviving an encounter than the rest of your group or raid. The good news is that tank gear is plentiful, and there are only one or two tanks per group or raid. Your biggest upgrade, survivability-wise, will likely be your shield. Don't be afraid to take up DPS-oriented gear if nobody needs it and then reforge undesirable stats to more survivability-oriented ones. Mastery is a great secondary stat—you can rarely go wrong with stacking it, but it's most beneficial to obtain all the worthwhile gem bonuses by using gems of the right color. For red gems, use Dodge or Parry (try to keep the two percentages close to each other due to diminishing returns). For the rest, use Stamina or Mastery, depending on your playstyle—Mastery provides more survivability against physical attacks while Stamina provides more raw health (perhaps best for encounters with magical damage).

RETRIBUTION

As their name suggests, Retribution Paladins use the power of the Light to unleash vengeance upon their foes. It is the only DPS-oriented spec available to Paladins, specializing in the use of two-handed weapons in melee range. It shares numerous abilities with Protection Paladins, but several passive skills make them completely different in how they're played.

MASTERY: HAND OF LIGHT

Allows your Crusader Strike, Hammer of the Righteous, Hammer of Wrath, Templar's Verdict, and Divine Storm abilities to deal extra Holy damage based on your Mastery.

SPECIALIZATION ABILITIES

ABILITY	LEVEL		DESCRIPTION
Sword of Light	10		Increase the damage you deal with two-handed melee weapons by 10%. Your spell power is now equal to 50% of your attack power, and you no longer benefit from other sources of spell power. Grants 6% of your maximum mana every 2 sec. Increases the healing done by Word of Glory and Flash of Light by 30%.
Templar's Verdict	10		A powerful weapon strike that consumes 3 charges of Holy Power to deal 275% weapon damage plus additional damage.
Hammer of the Righteous	20		Hammer the current target for 20% weapon damage, causing a wave of light that hits all targets within 8 yards for Holy damage and applying the Weakened Blows effect. Grants a charge of Holy Power. Weakened Blows: Demoralizes the target, reducing their physical damage dealt by 10% for 30 sec.
Judgments of the Bold	28		Your Judgment hits grant one charge of Holy Power and cause the Physical Vulnerability effect. Physical Vulnerability: Weakens the constitution of an enemy target, increasing their physical damage taken by 4% for 30 sec.
Divine Storm	34		An area attack that consumes 3 charges of Holy Power to cause 135% weapon damage as Holy damage to all enemies within 8 yards.
Exorcism	46		Forcefully attempt to expel the evil from the target with a blast of Holy Light. Causes Holy damage and generates a charge of Holy Power.
The Art of War	50		Your autoattacks have a 20% chance of resetting the cooldown of your Exorcism.
Emancipate	54		Unshackles your spirit, freeing you from one movement impairing effect.
Seal of Justice	70		Fills you with Holy Light, causing melee attacks to deal 16% additional Holy damage and reduce the target's movement speed by 50% for 8 sec.
Guardian of Ancient Kings	75		Summons a Guardian of Ancient Kings to help you deal damage for 30 sec. The Guardian of Ancient Kings will attack your current enemy. Both your attacks and the attacks of the Guardian will infuse you with Ancient Power that is unleashed as Ancient Fury when the Guardian departs.
Inquisition	81		Consumes up to 3 Holy Power to increase your Holy Damage by 30% and critical strike chance by 10%. Lasts 10 sec per charge of Holy Power consumed.

GETTING TO LEVEL 90

Retribution is the fastest leveler out of the three Paladin trees, dealing the most damage and converting holy power into speedier kills. Your basic rotation is sufficient for most enemies; remember to use cooldowns often, as they will increase your effectiveness (chiefly Avenging Wrath or its improved version).

For talents, Long Arm of the Law provides the best benefit for leveling if you're using Judgment often, especially as an opening move. Sacred Shield is also great for leveling, as it will nullify some of the steady, weak damage dealt by standard enemy monsters. Lastly, Sanctified Wrath is great when paired with Long Arm of the Law, allowing you to use your short sprint much more often as protection.

PLAYING IN A GROUP

Execute your standard rotation for single enemies, using DPS-increasing cooldowns as desired, and making sure not to pull threat (this is especially important for all melee classes, as they pull aggro off the tank more easily due to distance). When there are several enemies close together, you should use Divine Storm, but make sure Inquisition is always up. Switch your seals around based on the situation—most of the time, however, you'll be using Seal of Truth in groups. If you pull aggro, or your tank happens to die, you can still survive by using Divine Shield, or save party members through the use of Hand spells, coupled with the Reckoning taunt. Being a plate user, you're likely more durable than the rest of your group. Remember to keep your Blessing spells active on party members if nobody else in the group can provide the buffs they grant.

BASIC ROTATION

The most important thing to keep track of as Retribution is Inquisition, which provides a drastic damage increase as long as the buff is present. You usually want to save up the 3 holy power to get the longest duration, but consider using less if you predict a fight is going to end soon, or you need the healing from Word of Glory.

- Use Judgment when available

- Use Crusader Strike when available

- Use Exorcism when the Art of War passive procs

- Use Inquisition if you have 3 holy power and the buff is about to expire

- Use Templar's Verdict if you have 3 holy power and Inquisition is active

- Use Hammer of Wrath if your target is below 20% health

GROUP BUFFS AND DEBUFFS

Paladins can provide either the Stats buff with Blessing of Kings or the Mastery buff with Blessing of Might. Retribution Paladins use Hammer of the Righteous to inflict the Weakened Blows debuff on targets, while Judgments of the Bold apply the Physical Vulnerability debuff.

GETTING READY FOR HIGH-END CONTENT

RETRIBUTION

Like other melee classes, your goal is to avoid getting misses on raid bosses. This is fairly easy for Retribution Paladins, as they don't dual wield, making the Hit cap much lower for normal melee attacks. It's not necessary to completely eliminate misses right away—make sure you have some Expertise where possible, too—but it will increase your damage significantly. After Hit is no longer a concern, Critical Strike, Mastery, and Haste all provide roughly the same benefit.

As your primary stat, gem for Strength wherever you can, while matching gem colors for good gem bonuses.

PRIEST

Priests harness the power of Holy and Shadow magic. Priests are versatile healers with many instant spells that can save group members from certain death. They're also the only class with two different healing specializations, both with very different playstyles, each excelling at restoring or preventing different kinds of damage.

While the Priest might initially sound like a healing-exclusive class, they're also able to use many spells that deal damage directly or over time. Beyond healing and dealing damage, Priests possess many other utility spells, such as Mass Dispel, Leap of Faith, Hymn of Hope, Shackle Undead, Levitate, and Mind Vision.

RACE AVAILABILITY

ALLIANCE

Draenei | Dwarf | Gnome

Human | Night Elf | Worgen

Pandaren

HORDE

Blood Elf | Goblin | Orc

Tauren | Troll | Undead

RACIAL ADVANTAGES

ALLIANCE

RACE	NOTES
Draenei	Heroic Presence grants Draenei +1% Hit chance. Gift of the Naaru heals the Draenei or any ally. Draenei take 1% less damage from Shadow spells.
Dwarf	Stoneform is excellent for PvP and PVE as it removes all poisons, diseases, and bleed effects as well as reduces damage taken by 10%. Dwarves take 1% less damage from Frost spells.
Gnome	Escape Artist provides an extra ability for escaping slow or snare effects; great for PvP. Expansive Mind increases your mana pool by 5%. Gnomes take 1% less damage from Arcane spells.
Human	Every Man for Himself removes effects that impair movement and cause loss of control of your character which is great for PvP and PvE. The Human Spirit increases your Spirit by 3%.
Night Elf	Night Elves are 2% less likely to be hit by any physical attack and take 1% less damage from Nature spells. Shadowmeld renders the Night Elf invisible while motionless and cancels spells being cast by enemies on the Night Elf.
Worgen	Worgen get 1% increased Critical Strike from Viciousness. Darkflight increases movement speed temporarily. Worgen take 1% less damage from Shadow and Nature spells.

HORDE

RACE	NOTES
Blood Elf	The signature Blood Elf racial, Arcane Torrent, provides mana and an AoE silence. The former helps in tight mana situations, and the latter is great for PvP and certain PvE encounters. Blood Elves take 1% less damage from Arcane spells.
Goblin	Rocket Jump is a great mobility tool, allowing Priests to stay at range. Goblins get 1% increased Haste from Time is Money. Rocket Barrage is another source of damage for Goblins.
Tauren	Nature Resistance increases a Tauren's ability to stand up to harmful Nature effects. War Stomp provides an (AoE) stun in melee range, and Endurance boosts base health by 5%, making Tauren a good choice for PvP.
Troll	Berserking grants a temporary increase in attack speed. Da Voodoo Shuffle passively reduces the duration of movement impairing effects. Trolls regenerate Health faster than other races, and 10% of total Health regeneration may continue in combat.
Undead	Undead are more suited for PvP as they can break out of Charm, Fear, and Sleep effects with Will of the Forsaken. Their passive racial, Touch of the Grave, is a life leech and also provides a modest DPS increase in any situation. Undead take 1% less damage from Shadow spells.

PANDAREN

RACE	NOTES
Pandaren	Epicurean doubles the statistical bonuses from being Well Fed. Quaking Palm acts as a form of brief crowd control.

EQUIPMENT OPTIONS

ARMOR TYPE	SHIELD
Cloth	No

USABLE WEAPONS

1 HAND WEAPON	2 HAND WEAPON
Daggers	Staves
Maces	
Wands	

PROMINENT CLASS ABILITIES

HEALING VARIETY

Priests are extremely versatile healers, as they possess a large arsenal of heals. Priest healing boils down to three primary heals: Flash Heal, Heal, and Greater Heal. You must choose the right heal for a particular scenario; for example, a situation where a party member is quickly taking damage might not give you enough time to cast Greater Heal, meaning you must use Flash Heal. When possible, however, opt for the slower heals, as they conserve mana in the long run.

Other situational heals include Prayer of Mending and Renew, which alleviate the need for small heals in group situations and are relatively mana-efficient for their cost.

More specific heals are based on which healing specialization you select. For example, Discipline has Penance, which is great for quickly healing a single target, while Holy has Circle of Healing, which is great for instantly healing an entire group. Ultimately, the spells you choose for healing determine how quickly you spend your mana.

DAMAGE PREVENTION

Think of damage prevention as proactive healing. You put a buffer on your target that helps reduce the amount of health you need to restore later. The main tool for this is Power Word: Shield, which absorbs a certain amount of damage based on the Priest's level and Spell Power; moreover, it prevents spell pushback for as long as the shield is active. Discipline Priests in particular excel at Power Word: Shield, with passive abilities like Mastery: Shield Discipline to increase the amount of damage absorbed. Power Word: Shield is an invaluable tool for any Priest. It can be used both proactively and reactively, and it will often save your life when things go awry. Because Power Word: Shield is not a Holy spell, it's available while in Shadowform.

Another great tool is Leap of Faith, a spell (on a considerable cooldown) that instantly pulls a party member toward the casting Priest. Leap of Faith can be a priceless tool in encounters where a party member needs to be at a certain spot (or away from one) immediately. In boss encounters, this spell has proven very useful where a player (often the tank) is targeted by a boss ability and must quickly get away from it. In PVP, any ability that allows for quick movement out of danger is an invaluable tool.

DOMINATE MIND

One of the most interesting spells available to a Priest is Dominate Mind. This Level 15 Talent puts a target humanoid (player or NPC) under the Priest's command for a short period of time. While controlling a humanoid, the priest cannot use his own abilities; instead, the priest's action bar changes and includes some of the key abilities that the target humanoid can use. Dominate Mind can be broken at any time by cancelling the buff, or by using a Priest ability located somewhere other than the target's action bar (such as one of the sidebars).

The uses of Dominate Mind are up to the casting player; traditionally, this spell is used most for PvP situations where the Priest doesn't need to immediately heal his or her teammates. In dungeons, Dominate Mind can be used to reduce the number of mobs in a large pack of humanoids—simply Dominate Mind the closest enemy and the others will attack it as if it were your minion. Another use for Dominate Mind is to cast buffs on your group that only enemy mobs can cast. These usually have a short duration, however, so they're best used within the same area the mob was found. There are also other fun possibilities for this spell, such as healing or buffing the opposite faction (Alliance or Horde).

VOID SHIFT

Priest's level 87 ability is Void Shift. It swaps your current health (based on percentage) with an ally's, and then increases the health of whoever ends up with the lowest percentage to 25% (if the resulting percentage is under that amount). This ability is every bit as useful as it sounds, likely saving an ally from death as effectively as the holy tree's Guardian Spirit ability. Note, however, that Void Shift is on a six minute cooldown, which means that most of the time you'll only be able to use it once per encounter. Because swapped health is based on percentages, there is no downside to using it on a tank if your health percentage is greater than theirs.

NAME	LEVEL		DESCRIPTION
Smite	1		Smite an enemy for Holy damage.
Shadow Word: Pain	3		A word of darkness that causes Shadow damage instantly, and additional Shadow damage over 18 sec.
Power Word: Shield	5		Draws on the soul of the friendly target to shield them, absorbing damage. Lasts 15 sec. While the shield holds, spellcasting will not be interrupted by damage. Once shielded, the target cannot be shielded again for 15 sec.
Flash Heal	7		Heals a friendly target.
Inner Fire	9		A burst of Holy energy fills the caster, increasing the armor value from items by 60% and spell power by 10%. You can only have Inner Will or Inner Fire active at one time.
Divine Focus	10		Reduces the pushback suffered from damaging attacks while casting any Priest spell by 70%.
Psychic Scream	12		The caster lets out a psychic scream, causing 5 enemies within 8 yards to flee for 8 sec. Damage caused may interrupt the effect.
Resurrection	18		Brings a dead ally back to life with 35% health and mana. Cannot be cast when in combat.
Power Word: Fortitude	22		Infuses the target with vitality, increasing Stamina by 10% for 1 hour. If the target is in your party or raid, all party and raid members will be affected.
Fade	24		Fade out, temporarily removing all your threat for 10 sec.
Dispel Magic	26		Dispels Magic on the enemy target, removing 1 beneficial Magic effect.
Renew	26		Heals the target every 3 sec for 12 sec.
Shackle Undead	32		Shackles the target undead enemy for up to 50 sec. The shackled unit is unable to move, attack, or cast spells. Any damage caused will release the target. Only one target can be shackled at a time.
Levitate	34		Allows the friendly party or raid target to levitate, floating a few feet above the ground. While levitating, the target will fall at a reduced speed and travel over water. Any damage will cancel the effect. Lasts 10 min.
Mind Vision	42		Allows the caster to see through the target's eyes for 1 min. Will not work if the target is in another instance or on another continent.
Shadowfiend	42		Creates a shadowy fiend to attack the target. Caster receives 3% mana when the Shadowfiend attacks. Lasts 12 sec.
Shadow Word: Death	46		A word of dark binding that inflicts Shadow damage to the target. Only usable on enemies that have less than 20% health.
Binding Heal	48		Heals a friendly target and the caster. Low threat.
Mysticism	50		Increases your Intellect by 5%.
Fear Ward	54		Wards the friendly target against Fear. The next Fear effect used against the target will fail, using up the ward. Lasts 3 min.
Hymn of Hope	66		Restores 2% mana to 3 nearby low mana friendly party or raid targets every 2 sec for 8 sec, and increases their total maximum mana by 15% for 8 sec. Maximum of 12 mana restores. The Priest must channel to maintain the spell.
Prayer of Mending	68		Places a spell on the target that heals them the next time they take damage. When the heal occurs, Prayer of Mending jumps to a party or raid member within 20 yards. Jumps up to 5 times and lasts 30 sec after each jump. This spell can only be placed on one target at a time.
Mass Dispel	72		Dispels magic in a 15 yard radius, removing all harmful spells from each friendly target and 1 beneficial spell from each enemy target. Affects a maximum of 10 friendly targets and 10 enemy targets. This dispel is potent enough to remove Magic effects that are normally undispellable.
Mind Sear	76		Causes an explosion of shadow magic around the target, causing Shadow damage every 1 sec for 5 sec to all enemies within 10 yards around the target.
Inner Will	80		A burst of Holy energy fills the caster, reducing the mana cost of instant cast spells by 15% and increasing your movement speed by 10%. You can only have Inner Will or Inner Fire active at a time.
Leap of Faith	84		You pull the spirit of the friendly party or raid target to you, instantly moving them directly in front of you.
Void Shift	87		You and the currently targeted party or raid member swap health percentages. Increases the lower health percentage of the two to 25% if below that amount.

TALENTS

TALENT	DESCRIPTION	NOTES
LEVEL 15 TIER (UTILITY)		
Void Tendrils	Summons Shadowy tendrils out of the ground, rooting up to 5 enemy targets within 8 yards for 20 sec. Killing the tendril will cancel the effect.	Great for getting away from a melee onslaught. Do note, however, that the effect will end if the tendrils are killed.
Psyfiend	Summons a Psyfiend that stands in place for 10 sec. The Psyfiend casts a Psychic Terror on a nearby enemy within 20 yards every 1.5 sec., preferring anything attacking the Priest. Psychic Terror causes enemies to flee for 30 sec. Damage caused may interrupt the effect.	The Psyfiend cannot move, but this is a great tool for escaping or just reducing damage. You can't directly control who the Psyfiend fears, but it will prefer the last target that attacked you.
Dominate Mind	Controls a mind for 30 sec. Does not work versus Mechanical beings.	Puts a target humanoid (player or NPC) under the Priest's command for a short period of time.
LEVEL 30 TIER (MOVEMENT)		
Body and Soul	When you cast Power Word: Shield or Leap of Faith, you increase the target's movement speed by 60% for 4 sec.	Very popular in Cataclysm, this talent is invaluable for raid encounters where a player needs to move quickly. Needless to say, it's also great for escaping in PvP.
Angelic Feather	Place a feather at the target location. If allies walk through it, they gain 60% increased movement speed for 4 sec. Only 3 feathers can be placed at one time. Accumulates an additional charge once every 10 sec.	Only 3 feathers can be placed at once; a charge of this spell is created every 10 sec. Walking through a feather consumes it. Consider using this before a PvE encounter to give yourself time to accumulate more charges. This talent is best used in planned situations, but a well-placed feather can save someone's life.
Phantasm	When you Fade, you remove all movement impairing effects from yourself, you become untargetable by ranged attacks, and your movement speed is unhindered for 3 sec.	A great tool for PvP situations where you're stuck in one place and must get to your teammates to heal them, or your enemies to damage them. Also great for surviving heavy ranged damage, or just escaping from a melee onslaught.
LEVEL 45 TIER (BURST)		
From Darkness, Comes Light	Surge of Light: You have a 15% chance when you Smite, Heal, Spirit Shell, Flash Heal, Binding Heal or Greater Heal to cause your next Flash Heal to be instant cast and have no mana cost. Limit 2 charges. Surge of Darkness: Periodic damage from your Vampiric Touch has a 15% chance to cause your next Mind Spike to not consume your damage-over-time effects, become instant cast, cost no mana, and deal 50% additional damage. Limit 2 charges.	A versatile tool for damage and healing, this talent will let you have up to 2 charges of either buff at a time. In either case, it's great for instant burst healing or damage.
Mindbender	Grants an improved version of Shadowfiend that is substantially more effective at dealing damage and generating mana.	Makes your Shadowfiend better, which allows you to use mana more liberally as a healer, and provides some burst as a damage-dealer.
Power Word: Solace	Strike an enemy with the power of the heavens, dealing Holy damage and restoring .7% maximum mana.	Best used as a healer for recovering mana when nobody is in need of immediate healing. Also great to use if there is a natural break during an encounter. When in Shadowform, this talent changes to Shadow Word: Insanity (below).
Shadow Word: Insanity	Consumes your Shadow Word: Pain to deal Shadow damage to the target. Only usable while Shadow Word: Pain has less then 6 sec remaining.	Provides more burst and overall damage to the shadow tree. The downside is that when this ability is used, your Shadow Word: Pain is removed.
LEVEL 60 TIER (SURVIVABILITY)		
Desperate Prayer	Instantly heals the caster for 30% of their total health.	Fairly straightforward: provides an instant, free self-heal. Needless to say, it's the ultimate emergency ability when it comes to keeping yourself alive.
Spectral Guise	Your shadow blurs into the darkness, leaving your true form behind. As a shadow you are stealthed, but remain in combat. Lasts 6 sec or until your true form is hit by 3 direct attacks.	A very useful ability for escaping in PvP. Note that your decoy won't move, unlike a Mage's mirror images. Not as effective in PvE because it does not affect many abilities.
Angelic Bulwark	Anytime a damaging attack brings you below 30% health, you gain an absorption shield equal to 20% of your total health lasting for 20 sec. This effect cannot occur more than once every 90 sec.	A passive ability that provides survivability for dire situations. It can only occur every 90 sec, but the shield granted is pretty hefty.
LEVEL 75 TIER (SYNERGY)		
Twist of Fate	After damaging or healing a target below 20% health, you deal 15% increased damage and healing for 10 sec.	The healing bit is often uncontrollable, making this best for damage-dealing, where it acts as a straight damage increase on mobs below 20% health. This talent is also great for leveling where targets are constantly dying providing substantial uptime on the buff.
Power Infusion	Infuses the Priest with power, increasing casting speed by 20% and reducing the mana cost of all spells by 20%. Lasts 20 sec.	Provides a great burst tool for yourself. Best used along with other damage or healing cooldowns.
Divine Insight	Discipline: When you cast Penance, there is a 40% chance your next Power Word: Shield will both ignore and not cause the Weakened Soul effect. Holy: When you cast Greater Heal or Prayer of Healing, there is a 40% chance your next Prayer of Mending will not trigger its cooldown, and will jump to each target instantly. Shadow: Periodic damage from your Shadow Word: Pain has a 5% chance to reset the cooldown on Mind Blast and cause your next Mind Blast within 12 sec to be instant cast and cost no mana.	This talent grants different buffs based on your tree, but they're all proc chances. Determine how often you will be using the spell that triggers the buff to assess the effectiveness of this talent in comparison to the other two.
LEVEL 90 TIER (VERSATILITY)		
Cascade	Launches a Holy bolt at the target that grows in power as it travels, which causes damage to an enemy, or healing to an ally. This effect can bounce from allies to other allies, or from enemies to other enemies. Each time it bounces it will split into 2 bolts, preferring farther away targets, and never hitting the same target twice. Cascade can bounce up to 3 times. Deals Shadow damage or healing while in Shadowform.	A very versatile talent that allows you to AoE heal or damage. The effect cannot bounce to the same target twice, so make sure there are enough targets in range for it to be most effective.
Divine Star	Fires a Divine Star in front of you, traveling 24 yds, causing Divine damage to all enemies and healing to all allies within 6 yds of its path. After reaching its destination it will return to you, also dealing damage and healing to all targets in its path. Deals Shadow damage and healing while in Shadowform.	A more controllable version of Cascade (on a shorter cooldown). Because its effect happens in front of you, it's best used when allies or enemies line up.
Halo	Creates a ring of Holy energy around you that quickly expands and grows in power, up to 30 yds away. Deals Holy damage to enemies, and heals allies, with the greatest effect at 25 yds. Deals Shadow damage and healing while in Shadowform.	Like Divine Star, but effective around you. Note that the effect is strongest the farther away the targets are (within the ability's range), so position yourself accordingly.

DISCIPLINE

Discipline is one of the Priest's healing specializations. It excels at mobile restoration, agile casting, defensive abilities and, perhaps most importantly, damage prevention. Discipline is all about instant or quick casts, which allow the Priest to be constantly on the move. Discipline Priests are no deadlier than Holy Priests, but are slower killers than Shadow Priests, so it's an okay leveling specialization as long as you're patient.

Discipline Priests lack the raw aggression of a Shadow Priest. Penance is a long-range spell that damages enemies or heals allies. Discipline Priests, and only Discipline Priests, get Power Word: Barrier, an ability that protects an entire area.

MASTERY: SHIELD DISCIPLINE

Increases the potency of all your damage absorption spells. Each point of Mastery increases the potency of absorbs.

SPECIALIZATION ABILITIES

NAME	LEVEL		DESCRIPTION
Rapture	10		Removes the cooldown on Power Word: Shield When your Power Word: Shield is completely absorbed or dispelled you are instantly energized with mana qual to 150% of your Spirit. This effect can only occur once every 12 sec.
Penance	10		Launches a volley of holy light at the target, causing Holy damage to an enemy, or healing to an ally instantly and every 1 sec for 2 sec.
Meditation	10		Allows 50% of your mana regeneration from Spirit to continue while in combat.
Divine Fury	16		Increases your chance to hit with Penance, Smite, Power Word: Solace, Cascade, Divine Star, Halo, and Holy Fire by 15%
Holy Fire	18		Consumes the enemy in Holy flames that cause Holy damage and additional Holy damage over 7 sec.
Purify	22		Dispels harmful effects on the target, removing all Magic and Disease effects.
Divine Aegis	24		Critical heals and all heals from Prayer of Healing create a protective shield on the target, absorbing a percentage of the amount healed. Lasts 15 sec.
Heal	28		Heal your target.
Spirit Shell	28		For the next 15 sec, your Heal, Flash Heal, Greater Heal, and Prayer of Healing no longer heal but instead create absorption shields that last 15 sec.
Greater Heal	34		A slow casting spell that heals a single target.
Inner Focus	36		Reduces the mana cost of your next Flash Heal, Greater Heal or Prayer of Healing by 25% and increases its critical effect chance by 100%.
Evangelism	44		When you deal direct damage with Penance, Smite, or Holy Fire you gain Evangelism. Stacks up to 5 times. Lasts for 20 sec. Evangelism Increases the damage done by your Penance, Smite, and Holy Fire spells by 4% and reduces the mana cost of those spells by 6%.
Grace	45		Your Flash Heal, Greater Heal, Heal and Penance spells bless the target with Grace, increasing all healing received from the Priest by 10%. This effect will stack up to 3 times. Effect lasts 15 sec.
Prayer of Healing	46		A powerful prayer heals the friendly target's party members within 30 yards.
Archangel	50		Consumes your Evangelism, increasing your healing done for each Evangelism consumed for 18 sec.
Strength of Soul	52		When you heal a target with your Heal, Greater Heal or Flash Heal spell, the duration of the weakened soul debuff on the target is reduced by 2 sec.
Pain Suppression	58		Instantly reduces a friendly target's threat by 5%, and reduces all damage they take by 40% for 8 sec.
Atonement	60		When you deal damage with Smite, Holy Fire, and Penance, you instantly heal a nearby low health friendly target within 15 yards from the enemy target for 100% of the damage dealt. If the Priest is healed through Atonement, the effect is reduced by 50%.
Borrowed Time	62		Grants 15% spell haste for your next spell after casting Power Word: Shield. Lasts for 6 sec.
Power Word: Barrier	70		Summons a holy barrier on the target location that reduces all damage done to friendly targets by 25%. While within the barrier, spellcasting will not be interrupted by damage. The barrier lasts for 10 sec.
Train of Thought	78		When you heal with Greater Heal, the cooldown of your Inner Focus is reduced by 5 sec. When you Smite, the cooldown of your Penance is reduced by 0.5 sec.

GETTING TO LEVEL 90

Discipline isn't the fastest choice for Priest leveling, but it's decent when compared to other classes' healing specializations. Needless to say, Discipline Priests are durable; with all the boosts granted to Power Word: Shield, this might be the only healing (or damage prevention in this case) needed while leveling.

At lower levels, Smite and Shadow Word: Pain will be your bread and butter. Later, you can use Penance and Holy Fire for some added damage. Keep Power Word: Shield on you, if necessary, to avoid interruption or pushback, especially for channeled spells. At level 60, Discipline Priests learn Atonement which is significant in keeping your health up while also doing damage.

For talents, consider taking Void Tendrils, Body and Soul (for the increased speed), and Power Word: Solace if you have any mana problems.

PLAYING IN A GROUP

The Discipline healing style is a little less straightforward than other classes, but it's plenty of fun. Instead of simply healing through damage, the idea is to prevent it as much as possible, and then heal through what couldn't be prevented. The prime tool for this, naturally, is Power Word: Shield. If you take a quick look at the Discipline passives, note that some of them boost the effects of Power Word: Shield. Being a successful Discipline healer involves predicting which party members will take damage, and then using Power Word: Shield on them. The tank of your group will often require additional healing, for which Penance is a great tool. Flash Heal is also a great asset if Penance is still on cooldown and one of your group members needs quick healing. Pain Suppression serves as a sizable damage dampener on a friendly target. Lastly, Power Word: Barrier is a great spell to use in situations where the group is taking heavy AoE damage.

HEALING

Discipline is one of the most unique healing trees out of any class, providing incredible damage prevention (primarily through Power Word: Shield) and single-target healing.

SITUATION(S)	USE...
An ally is in need of immediate healing	Power Word: Shield; Flash Heal if not available
Healing a single target that's not in immediate danger	Penance when off cooldown, Heal or Greater Heal depending on the incoming damage
Everyone is healthy, but you know there's going to be incoming damage	Power Word: Shield and Prayer of Mending
Heavy AoE damage from enemies	Power Word: Barrier and Prayer of Healing

GROUP BUFFS AND DEBUFFS

Discipline Priests provide the Stamina buff with Power Word: Fortitude.

GETTING READY FOR HIGH-END CONTENT

DISCIPLINE

Discipline Priests benefit most from stats and ratings that help them cast faster and stronger spells while keeping their mana pool healthy. It's hard to simply stack a single stat for Discipline. The first thing to keep in mind when gearing a Discipline priest is mana regeneration. Since Meditation is one of Discipline's core abilities, Spirit becomes valuable and should be considered before everything else until mana regeneration is no longer an issue. Remember: instant spells are expensive. Following Spirit, other stats and ratings are similarly beneficial: Intellect increases the potency of your spells (along with mana and Critical Strike), Critical Strike occasionally makes your direct heals bigger and triggers effects like Divine Aegis, and Mastery contributes to your absorption effects, but you should choose Mastery and Haste over Critical Strike.

HOLY

Holy excels at sheer healing output, Area of Effect (AoE) heals, and heals over time (HoT). Because the Holy tree boosts AoE heals and introduces a new one (Circle of Healing), it is a useful addition to encounters with high amounts of AoE damage. Holy Priests can be dedicated tank healers as well, as their single-target heals can be formidable and mana efficient.

Holy Priests can create Lightwells to let people heal themselves even in the middle of a fight. As a pivotal healer in a group or raid, it's nice that Spirit of Redemtion allows Holy Priests to continue to heal for a little while after dying. Guardian Spirit is a protective buff unique to Holy Priests that increases healing received by the person and then saves them from a killing blow if necessary.

MASTERY: ECHO OF LIGHT

Your direct healing spells heal for an additional 10% over 6 sec. Each point of Mastery provides additional healing over 6 sec.

SPECIALIZATION ABILITIES

NAME	LEVEL		DESCRIPTION
Holy Word: Chastise	10		Chastise the target for Holy damage, and disorients them for 3 sec.
Meditation	10		Allows 50% of your mana regeneration from Spirit to continue while in combat.
Divine Fury	16		Increases your chance to hit with Penance, Smite, Power Word: Solace, Cascade, Divine Star, Halo, and Holy Fire by 15%
Holy Fire	18		Consumes the enemy in Holy flames that cause Holy damage and additional Holy damage over 7 sec.
Purify	22		Dispels harmful effects on the target, removing all Magic and Disease effects.
Heal	28		Heals your target.
Spirit of Redemption	30		Upon death, the Priest becomes the Spirit of Redemption for 15 sec. The Spirit of Redemption cannot move, attack, be attacked or targeted by any spells or effects. While in this form the Priest can cast any healing spell free of cost. When the effect ends, the Priest dies.
Greater Heal	34		A slow casting spell that heals a single target.
Serendipity	34		When you heal with Binding Heal or Flash Heal, the cast time of your next Greater Heal or Prayer of Healing spell is reduced by 20% and mana cost reduced by 10%. Stacks up to 2 times. Lasts 20 sec.
Lightwell	36		Creates a Holy Lightwell. Friendly players can click the Lightwell to restore some health over 6 sec. Attacks done to you equal to 30% of your total health will cancel the effect. Lightwell lasts for 3 min or 15 charges.
Evangelism	44		When you deal direct damage with Smite or Holy Fire you gain Evangelism. Stacks up to 5 times. Lasts for 20 sec. Evangelism: Increases the damage done by your Smite and Holy Fire spells by 4% and reduces the mana cost of those spells by 6%.
Prayer of Healing	46		A powerful prayer heals the friendly target's party members within 30 yards.
Circle of Healing	50		Heals up to 5 friendly party or raid members within 30 yards of the target. Prioritizes healing the most injured party members.
Chakra	56		See Chakra table on following page.
Rapid Renewal	64		Your Renew heals for an additional 15%, instantly heals the target for 15% of the total periodic effect, and has a 0.5 sec reduced global cooldown.
Guardian Spirit	70		Calls upon a guardian spirit to watch over the friendly target. The spirit increases the healing received by the target by 60%, and also prevents the target from dying by sacrificing itself. This sacrifice terminates the effect but heals the target of 50% of their maximum health. Lasts 10 sec.
Divine Hymn	78		Heals 5 nearby lowest health friendly party or raid targets within 40 yards every 2 sec for 8 sec, and increases healing done to them by 10% for 8 sec. The Priest must channel to maintain the spell.

CHAKRA

Holy Priest healing has perhaps the most tools out of any healing class, making them incredibly versatile. The three different Chakra spells work similarly to stances, granting significant buffs to different playstyles. Each spell is best used to adapt to certain situations.

NAME	DESCRIPTION	BEST FOR...
Chakra: Chastise	Increases the damage done by your Shadow and Holy spells by 15%, grants 10% chance for Smite to reset the cooldown of Holy Word: Chastise, reduces the mana cost of Smite and Holy Fire by 75% and transforms your Holy Word spell back into Holy Word: Chastise Holy Word: Chastise Chastise the target for Holy damage, and disorients them for 3 sec. 30 sec cooldown.	Increasing damage output
Chakra: Sanctuary	Increases the healing done by your area of effect healing spells by 15%, reduces the cooldown of your Circle of Healing spell by 2 sec, and transforms your Holy Word: Chastise spell into Holy Word: Sanctuary. Holy Word: Sanctuary Blesses the ground with Divine light, healing all within it every 2 sec for 30 sec. Only one Sanctuary can be active at any one time. 40 sec cooldown.	AoE healing
Chakra: Serenity	Increases the healing done by your single-target healing spells by 15%, causes them to refresh the duration on your Renew on the target, and transforms your Holy Word: Chastise spell into Holy Word: Serenity. Holy Word: Serenity Instantly heals the target and increases the critical effect chance of your healing spells on the target by 25% for 6 sec. 15 sec cooldown.	Single-target healing

Chakras have a 30-sec cooldown, so you cannot constantly switch back and forth between single-target and AoE healing, for instance. The cooldown is short enough, however, that you can adapt to the type of incoming damage several times in a fight.

GETTING TO LEVEL 90

Holy is now viable as a solo leveling spec. With Evangelism and the changes to Chakra: Chastise, Holy Priests are capable of outputting a lot of damage for very little mana. Coupled with talents such as Surge of Light (for free Flash Heals) and Power Infusion (for more burst), Holy Priests are comparable to Discipline in leveling speed, though Shadow remains faster than both.

PLAYING IN A GROUP

Being one of the most versatile healers, Holy Priests can be played in vastly different ways when grouping. It's all about striking a balance and adjusting to different encounters. Newcomers might find it easier to use the three main heals (Flash Heal, Heal, and Greater Heal) directly, but for maximum mana efficiency, take advantage of the Holy Priest's full repertoire of spells and abilities.

HEALING

SITUATION(S)	USE...
An ally is in need of immediate healing	Holy Word: Serenity if available, Flash Heal otherwise. If the target is very likely to die, use Guardian Spirit
Healing a single target that's not in immediate danger	Heal or Greater Heal depending on the incoming damage. Binding Heal if you need healing as well
Everyone is healthy, but you know there's going to be incoming damage	Prayer of Mending and Renew
Heavy AoE damage from enemies	Circle of Healing and Prayer of Healing

GROUP BUFFS AND DEBUFFS

Holy Priests provide the Stamina buff with Power Word: Fortitude.

GETTING READY FOR HIGH-END CONTENT

HOLY

You always want Intellect and Spirit on your gear but you must balance mana regeneration and healing output. Mana regeneration is indispensable, as a Priest without mana becomes problematic to any group. Healing output refers to all the stats that help make heals faster or more powerful. Stats such as Intellect, Critical Strike, Haste and Mastery all contribute to increasing healing output, or even damage output when healing isn't needed. Good Priests keep everyone healthy, and use most of their mana by the end of a tough fight.

SHADOW

Shadow is the primary damage-oriented Priest specialization tree. Like other spellcasters, Shadow Priests prefer to stay at range, especially considering Mind Flay, one of the primary Shadow spells, is channeled and suffers from spell pushback. Shadow Priests enjoy increased damage output and survivability, as well as decreased downtime due to mana regeneration. Because some healing spells can still be cast, Shadow Priests are reasonably durable when soloing.

Shadow Priest drawbacks depend on the situation. When soloing, mana might be a problem, and you might be forced to use your shadow fiend to finish off enemies. In groups, it is important to keep watch on your threat levels, especially if your gear is greater than the tank's in level and quality.

MASTERY: SHADOWY RECALL

Gives your periodic Shadow damage spells a chance to deal damage twice, each time they deal damage.

SPECIALIZATION ABILITIES

NAME	LEVEL		DESCRIPTION
Mind Flay	10		Assault the target's mind with Shadow energy, causing Shadow damage over 3 sec and slowing their movement speed by 50%.
Spiritual Precision	20		Grants hit equal to any Spirit gained from items or effects.
Mind Blast	21		Blasts the target for Shadow damage and generates 1 Shadow Orb.
Shadow Orbs	21		Generated by Mind Blast and Shadow Word: Death. Used to cast Devouring Plague and empower Psychic Horror.
Devouring Plague	21		Consumes all of the caster's Shadow Orbs to deal Shadow damage and additional Shadow damage every 1 sec for 6 sec. Also heals the caster for 1% of their maximum health when it deals periodic damage. Damage and healing increased based on the number of Shadow Orbs consumed.
Shadowform	24		Assume a Shadowform, increasing your Shadow damage by 20%, reducing all damage done to you by 15%, and increasing all party and raid members spell haste by 5%. However, you may not cast Holy spells while in this form.
Vampiric Touch	28		Causes Shadow damage over 15 sec. Each time Vampiric Touch deals damage the caster gains 2% of maximum mana.
Shadowy Apparition	42		When you deal critical periodic damage with your Shadow Word: Pain, you have a 100% chance to summon a shadow version of yourself which will slowly move towards a target which is afflicted by your Shadow Word: Pain. Once reaching the target, it will instantly deal Shadow damage. You can have up to 3 Shadowy Apparitions active at a time.
Mind Spike	44		Blasts the target for Shadowfrost damage, but extinguishes your Shadow damage-over-time effects from the target in the process.
Silence	52		Silences the target, preventing them from casting spells for 5 sec. Non-player victim spellcasting is also interrupted for 3 sec.
Dispersion	60		You disperse into pure Shadow energy, reducing all damage taken by 90%. You are unable to attack or cast spells, but you regenerate 6% mana every 1 sec for 6 sec. Dispersion can be cast while stunned, feared or silenced. Clears all snare and movement impairing effects when cast, and makes you immune to them while dispersed.
Psychic Horror	74		Consumes all Shadow Orbs to terrify the target, causing them to tremble in horror for 1 sec plus 1 sec per Shadow Orb consumed and to drop their weapons and shield for 10 sec.
Vampiric Embrace	78		Fills you with the embrace of Shadow energy, causing you and your allies to be healed for 50% of any single-target Shadow spell damage you deal, split evenly between them. Lasts 15 sec.

GETTING TO LEVEL 90

Shadow is the fastest Priest specialization for leveling. Keep in mind, however, that some higher-level abilities and passives significantly boost a Shadow Priest's solo ability. This means you might have some downtime at early levels, and accidental pulls with numerous enemies could make quick work of you.

That said, killing monsters in a solo setting is relatively straightforward: apply your DoT spells (you can skip Shadow Word: Pain if you feel the mob won't live long enough for it to be worth casting, but you usually want to cast Vampiric Touch anyway), then use Mind Blast and Mind Flay. If you get 3 Shadow Orbs while fighting an enemy (and you often will), hold off on using Devouring Plague until the next enemy, as the DoT portion is pretty significant and heals you. Remember you also have some survivability and healing tools at your command, like Dispersion, Flash Heal, and Power Word: Shield. The latter is best used over holy-based heals, as they will drop you out of Shadowform.

Because DoT spells continue to tick when an enemy is feared, consider taking up the Psyfiend talent, and use Psychic Scream for multiple enemies.

PLAYING IN A GROUP

Execute your base rotation against single targets, and remember to use other abilities as necessary. If the group is in need of heavy healing and the healer seems to be falling behind, use Vampiric Embrace. If a target is low on health, use Mind Spike to (hopefully) finish them off. Likewise, if you need burst damage, Mind Spike can provide it (especially when paired with some of the burst talents).

Against multiple enemies, you need to consider how long they will live. If there's a swarm of small enemies with low health, simply use Mind Sear for best results. If there are several enemies that are likely to live more than 15 seconds, it's worth it to cast your DoT spells on them, and then either Mind Sear or continue your normal rotation on a single enemy. The last tier of talents also provides some AoE abilities, but these are often based on positioning.

ROTATION

In its simplest form, the Shadow tree's rotation consists of keeping DoT spells active, and then using other abilities based on certain scenarios:

- Apply/refresh Shadow Word: Pain
- Apply/refresh Vampiric Touch
- If available, use Mind Blast
- If you have 3 Shadow Orbs, use Devouring Plague
- If the target is below 20% health, use Shadow Word: Death
- Use Mind Flay

GROUP BUFFS AND DEBUFFS

Shadow Priests provide the Stamina buff with Power Word: Fortitude and the Spell Haste buff when Shadowform is active.

GETTING READY FOR HIGH-END CONTENT

SHADOW

Like other casters, Shadow Priests should always maximize their damage output. Because Power Word: Shield can still be cast in Shadowform, Shadow Priests can prioritize raw damage over survival. It's important that you learn how to manage your threat, especially if you group with tanks that are less geared than you are. Mana shouldn't be a problem for Shadow Priests, so just gear for damage and use damage-based consumables.

For raids, your priority should be reaching the Hit cap (15%, or 14% for Draenei and Dwarves with maces) and piling on Intellect. Spiritual Precision is a tremendous boon for Shadow Priests as Spirit also provides Hit, making it significantly easier to reach the Hit cap. Because DoT spells can crit and are affected by Haste, Haste and Critical Strike are your next two best stats.

ROGUE

Rogues are known for their outstanding agility and skills that cloak them from enemies. They are exclusively melee damage dealers. All three of their specialization trees provide a different set of skills through which they deal melee damage.

Garbed in leather equipment, Rogues sport the weakest armor out of any melee-based class; that's not to say they're the frailest, however, as their abilities provide numerous ways to survive dangerous situations. A Rogue caught off-guard, however, is likely to perish quickly—Rogues are all about ambushing enemies, a technique they've long perfected.

RACE AVAILABILITY

ALLIANCE

Braenel   Dwarf   Gnome

Human   Night Elf   Worgen

Pandaren

HORDE

Blood Elf   Goblin   Orc

Tauren   Troll   Undead

RACIAL ADVANTAGES

ALLIANCE

RACE	NOTES
Dwarf	Stoneform is excellent for PvP, as it removes all poison, disease, and bleed effects and reduces damage taken. Mace Specialization provides increased Expertise with maces. Dwarves take less damage from Frost spells.
Gnome	Escape Artist provides an extra ability for escaping slow or snare effects; great for PvP. Shortblade Specialization provides increased Expertise with daggers and one hand swords. Gnomes take less damage from Arcane spells.
Human	Every Man for Himself removes effects that cause loss of control of your character. Sword Specialization increases Expertise for swords by 1%.
Night Elf	Quickness means Night Elves are less likely to be hit by any physical attack. Night Elves take less damage from Nature spells. Shadowmeld renders the Night Elf invisible while motionless and cancels spells being cast by enemies on the Night Elf. Elusiveness increases the Night Elf's movement speed while stealthed by 5%.
Worgen	Worgen get 1% increased Critical Strike from Viciousness. Darkflight increases movement speed temporarily. Worgen take less damage from Nature and Shadow spells.

PANDAREN

RACE	NOTES
Pandaren	Epicurean doubles the statistical bonuses from being Well Fed. Quaking Palm acts as a form of brief crowd control.

HORDE

RACE	NOTES
Blood Elf	The signature Blood Elf racial, Arcane Torrent, provides Energy and an AoE silence. The former helps in tight Energy situations, and the latter is great for PvP and certain PvE encounters. Blood Elves take less damage from Arcane spells.
Goblin	Rocket Jump is a great mobility tool. Goblins get 1% increased Haste from Time is Money, making them great for PVP and PVE. Rocket Barrage is another source of damage for Goblins.
Orc	Orcs are great for maximizing damage. Blood Fury increases your attack power for a short period of time. Axe Specialization increases Expertise with axes by 1%. Hardiness reduces the duration of stun effects by 15%.
Troll	Berserking grants a temporary increase in attack speed. Da Voodoo Shuffle passively reduces the duration of movement impairing effects, which is important for Rogues. Trolls regenerate Health faster than other races, and 10% of total Health regeneration may continue in combat.
Undead	Undead are more suited for PvP as they can break out of Charm, Fear, and Sleep effects with Will of the Forsaken. Their passive racial, Touch of the Grave, is a life leech and also provides a modest DPS increase in any situation. Undead take less damage from Shadow spells.

EQUIPMENT OPTIONS

ARMOR TYPE	SHIELD
Leather	No

USABLE WEAPONS

1 HAND WEAPON	2 HAND WEAPON
Daggers	(None)
Fist Weapons	
Axes	
Maces	
Swords	

PROMINENT CLASS ABILITIES

STEALTH

One of the signature Rogue abilities, Stealth, allows you to move throughout the world while remaining unseen to most enemies.

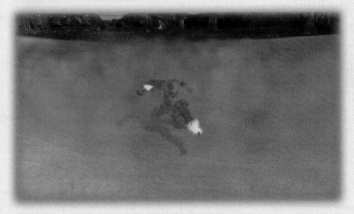

This ability single-handedly changes the way Rogues play, as catching an enemy off guard is extremely advantageous in a fight. While under the effects of Stealth, you can also use several abilities exclusive to this mode, such as Sap, Ambush, and Cheap Shot. Most of these abilities will end the Stealth effect, thus engaging you in combat; others, however, will not, allowing you to let the enemy know you're around without giving your location away.

In PvE, you can slide past enemies with Stealth, but they will spot you if you get too close, at which point they'll turn toward you. If you keep getting closer, they will open fire if they're aggressive. Both players and monsters alike can spot an invisible Rogue much more easily if they are higher level, so take this into consideration before trying to sneak past monsters ten levels higher than you!

COMBO POINTS

Another feature exclusive to the Rogue archetype (of which Cat Druids are also a part of) is combo points.

These points provide the Rogue with an additional resource that is generated through usage of several abilities, usually known as "combo point generators." Certain other abilities, known as "finishers," use this currency and have their effectiveness affected by the number of points you have.

Combo points are target-specific, meaning that, when you use a combo point generator, you gain combo points on your current target. When you switch targets, you cannot use the points you have accrued on the new target. Some Rogue abilities help alleviate this, allowing you to switch targets more efficiently.

Combo points can be seen around your character's portrait, up to their maximum of five—look for the red or gray dots that represent active or empty combo points, respectively.

ENERGY

Rogues' primary combat resource, shared by Cat Form Druids and Monks, is called Energy.

This resource is constantly replenishing itself as time passes, usually in a speedier fashion than other resources (it's a matter of seconds for an Energy bar to go from empty to full). The highest amount of Energy is 100 by default, but can be increased through equipment, set bonuses, and some abilities.

Because this resource regenerates so quickly, abilities based on it often use a great amount at once, serving as a pacing mechanism for Rogue DPS.

In some situations such as PvP combat, pooling energy is a common tactic that allows you to use crucial abilities in a pinch.

SHADOW BLADES

Rogues' level 87 ability is Shadow Blades. This fairly straightforward skill is on a 3-minute cooldown, and provides a large DPS boost to all specialization trees by making your combo point generator abilities produce an extra combo point for the duration.

As an added effect, your melee swings deal shadow damage (instead of physical) for the duration, which is useful when an enemy is temporarily immune to physical attacks (or vulnerable to shadow). Because of its considerable cooldown, this ability is best used in conjunction with other DPS-increasing cooldowns, and while Slice and Dice is active, especially in PvE.

NAME	LEVEL		DESCRIPTION
Sinister Strike	1		An instant strike that causes damage in addition to 155% of your normal weapon damage.
Throw	1		Hurls a dagger at an enemy from range.
Eviscerate	3		Finishing move that causes damage proportional to your combo points.
Stealth	5		Conceals you in the shadows, allowing you to stalk enemies without being seen. Lasts until canceled.
Ambush	6		Ambush the target, causing 325% weapon damage (470% plus additional damage if a dagger is equipped). Must be stealthed and behind the target. Awards 2 combo points.
Evasion	8		Increases your dodge chance by 50% for 15 sec.
Deadly Poison	10		Coats your weapons with a Lethal Poison that lasts for 1 hour. Each strike has a 30% chance of poisoning the enemy for Nature damage over 12 sec. Subsequent poison applications will instantly deal additional Nature damage.
Sap	12		Incapacitates the target for up to 1 min. Must be stealthed. Only works on Humanoids, Beasts, Demons, and Dragonkin that are not in combat. Any damage caused will revive the target. Only 1 target may be sapped at a time.
Slice and Dice	14		Finishing move that consumes combo points on any nearby target to increase melee attack speed by 40%. Lasts longer per combo point.
Pick Pocket	15		Attempts to steal an item from a target enemy. Requires Stealth.
Recuperate	16		Finishing move that consumes combo points on any nearby targets to restore 3% of maximum health every 3 sec. Lasts longer per combo point.
Kick	18		A quick kick that interrupts spellcasting and prevents any spell in that school from being cast for 5 sec.
Crippling Poison	20		Coats your weapons with a Non-Lethal Poison that lasts for 1 hour. Each strike has a 50% chance of poisoning the enemy, slowing their movement speed by 50% for 12 sec.
Gouge	22		Gouges the eyes of an enemy target, incapacitating the opponent for 4 sec. Target must be facing you. Any subsequent damage will cause the target to recover immediately.
Pick Lock	24		Allows you to open locked chests and doors within your skill range.
Sprint	26		Increases your movement speed by 70% for 8 sec. Does not break stealth.
Distract	28		Throws a distraction, attracting the attention of all nearby monsters for 10 sec. Does not break stealth.
Mind-Numbing Poison	28		Coats your weapons with a Non-Lethal Poison that lasts for 1 hour. Each strike has a 50% chance of poisoning the enemy, clouding their mind and slowing their casting speed by 50% (25% on player targets) for 10 sec. Shiv Effect: Increases the casting time of an enemy's next spellcast within 8 sec by 100%.
Cheap Shot	30		Stuns an enemy for 4 sec. You must be in Stealth mode. Awards 2 combo points.
Wound Poison	30		Coats your weapons with a poison that lasts for 1 hour. Each strike has a 30% chance of poisoning the enemy, which instantly inflicts Nature damage and reduces all healing effects on them for 15 sec.
Swiftblade's Cunning	30		Increases the melee and ranged attack speed of all party and raid members within 100 yards by 10%.
Vanish	34		Allows you to vanish from sight, entering an improved stealth mode for 3 sec. For the first 3 sec after vanishing, damage and harmful effects received will not break stealth. Also breaks movement impairing effects.
Expose Armor	36		Weaken the target's defenses, applying the Weakened Armor debuff. Awards 1 combo point. Weaken Armor: Weakens the armor of the target by 4% for 30 sec. Stacks up to 3 times.

NAME	LEVEL		DESCRIPTION
Blind	38		Blinds the target, causing it to wander disoriented for up to 1 min. Any damage caused will remove the effect. Does not break stealth.
Kidney Shot	40		Finishing move that stuns an enemy. The duration is based on your combo points.
Detect Traps	42		Greatly increased chance to detect traps.
Feint	44		Performs an evasive maneuver, reducing damage taken from area-of-effect attacks by 50% for 5 sec.
Rupture	46		Finishing move that causes damage over time, increased by your attack power. Lasts longer per combo point.
Garrote	48		Garrote the enemy, silencing them for 3 sec and causing damage over 18 sec, increased by your attack power. Must be stealthed. Awards 1 combo point.
Safe Fall	48		Reduces damage from falling.
Dismantle	52		Disarms an enemy, preventing them from using weapons or shields for 10 sec.
Relentless Strikes	54		Your finishing moves have a 20% chance per combo point to restore Energy.
Disarm Trap	56		Disarms a hostile trap. Requires Stealth.
Cloak of Shadows	58		Instantly removes all existing harmful spell effects, provides a brief moment of immunity against magical damage and harmful effects, and then causes you to resist all spells for 5 sec. Does not remove effects that prevent you from using Cloak of Shadows.
Fleet Footed	62		Your movement speed is increased by 15%. This does not stack with most other movement speed increasing effects.
Master Poisoner	64		Increases the spell damage taken by any target you have poisoned by 5%.
Fan of Knives	66		Instantly whirl around, releasing a spray of knives at all targets within 10 yards, dealing Physical damage. This attack has a chance of applying your active poisons at their normal rate. Awards 1 combo point if it strikes your current combo target.
Shadow Walk	72		Increases the effectiveness of Stealth for 6 sec.
Shiv	74		Strikes an enemy's pressure point with your off-hand weapon, dealing 25% weapon damage, dispelling an Enrage effect from the target, and applying a concentrated form of your active Non-Lethal poison.
Shroud of Concealment	76		Extends a cloak that wraps party and raid members within 20 yards in shadows, concealing them from sight for up to 15 sec. Requires Stealth.
Tricks of the Trade	78		The threat caused by your next damaging attack and all actions taken for 6 sec afterwards will be transferred to the target party or raid member, and all damage caused by the target is increased by 15% during this time. Transferred threat is not permanent and will fade after 30 sec.
Redirect	81		Transfers any existing combo points to the current enemy target. Requires active combo points.
Crimson Tempest	83		Finishing move that consumes combo points on any nearby target to slash at the flesh of all enemies within 8 yards, dealing Physical damage and causing victims to bleed and suffer an additional 30% of the initial damage over 12 sec.
Smoke Bomb	85		Creates a cloud of thick smoke in an 8 yard radius around the Rogue for 5 sec. Enemies are unable to target into or out of the smoke cloud.
Shadow Blades	87		Draw upon the surrounding shadows to empower your weapons, causing your autoattacks to deal pure Shadow damage and your combo-point-generating abilities to generate an additional combo point when used. Lasts 12 sec.

TALENTS

TALENT		DESCRIPTION	NOTES
LEVEL 15 TIER (STEALTH)			
Nightstalker		Increases movement speed while stealthed by 20%. Increases damage dealt while stealthed by 25%.	With the movement speed increase, you're likely to move as fast as you would normally. The added bonus is great, especially if you're ambushing enemies often.
Subterfuge		Your Stealth breaks 3 sec after dealing or receiving hostile actions, rather than doing so immediately.	This allows you to execute openers and still be in Stealth mode, further increasing the element of surprise, especially in PvP.
Shadow Focus		Abilities no longer cost Energy in Stealth mode.	This improves your opening sequence dramatically by allowing you to use more energy on an unsuspecting enemy—great for PvP, especially when opening with Cheap Shot.
LEVEL 30 TIER (REDUCTION)			
Deadly Throw		Finishing move that reduces the movement speed of the target by 50% for 6 sec. If performed with 5 combo points, also interrupts spellcasting and prevents any spell in that school from being cast for 6 sec. Damage dealt is based on number of combo points.	When you perform this ability at 5 combo points, it will also interrupt spellcasting, just as Kick would. You cannot use this in melee range (as it's meant to be used from range), and its damage is determined by your combo points.
Nerve Strike		A successful Kidney Shot or Cheap Shot also reduces the damage dealt by the target by 50% for 6 sec after the effect fades.	The effect starts after the stun portion wears off, allowing you to more effectively open on strong PvP opponents without risking a quick death. Consider choosing this before trying to kill, say, a geared Warrior!
Combat Readiness		Enter into a state of heightened awareness, deflecting enemy weapon strikes with increasing effectiveness. Successive attacks will deal 10% less damage per application, stacking 5 times. Lasts for 20 sec, but if 10 sec elapse without any incoming weapon strikes, this state will end.	The effect starts off weak, and becomes stronger as you take more attacks, up to 5 stacks of the buff. If you take no attacks for a while, the effect will end early. This is another great skill to use when under heavy melee siege, making up for the lack of defense provided by your leather armor.
LEVEL 45 TIER (SURVIVABILITY)			
Cheat Death		An attack that would otherwise be fatal will instead reduce you no lower than 10% of your maximum health, and damage taken will be reduced by 80% for 3 sec. This effect cannot occur more than once per 90 sec.	An old Subtlety Rogue favorite, and now available to all specs, Cheat Death definitely lives up to its name, allowing you to survive an attack that would've otherwise killed you. Note the health you survive with is humble, and you still take damage afterward (which although minimal, can still kill you).
Leeching Poison		Coats your weapons with a Non-Lethal Poison that lasts for 1 hour. Your melee attacks have a 50% chance to poison the target, and all your subsequent weapon strikes against the poisoned target will heal you for 10% of damage dealt.	The way this works: the poison has a chance to proc, and after it does, subsequent attacks will heal you for a small portion of the damage dealt (which definitely adds up). If you use Shiv, the poison will restore a portion of your health independent of the damage dealt.
Elusiveness		Your Feint ability also reduces all damage taken by 30% for 5 sec.	This makes Feint an ability that helps in all situations, not just AoE ones. Great survivability tool, but note that the percentage of damage reduction is smaller than the normal AoE reduction from Feint.
LEVEL 60 TIER (MOVEMENT)			
Preparation		When activated, this ability immediately finishes the cooldown on your Sprint, Vanish, Cloak of Shadows, Evasion, and Dismantle abilities.	Another Rogue favorite, Preparation (oft referred to as simply "prep") gives Rogues incredible flexibility by basically adding many more usable cooldowns in a fight. Especially good for PvP survivability.
Shadowstep		Step through the shadows and appear behind a target. Movement speed is increased by 70% for 2 sec afterwards.	This is a great ability to gap the distance between you and an enemy (or simply use another target to get away from another melee class). Note that this ability will also increase your movement speed briefly after you appear behind your target.
Burst of Speed		Increases movement speed by 70% for 4 sec. If you are afflicted by any movement-impairing effects, activating this ability will instead remove any such effects and grant immunity to their re-application for 4 sec.	One thing to note about Burst of Speed is that it has no cooldown, but costs 60 energy. This makes you basically unstoppable, as it adds a short immunity to movement impairments, but note that you will have significantly less energy to execute other abilities after this.
LEVEL 75 TIER (CONTROL)			
Prey on the Weak		When you disable an enemy with Kidney Shot, Cheap Shot, Gouge, Sap, or Blind, they suffer 10% increased damage from all sources for the duration of the effect.	This really shines in team PvP, as the damage increase is from all sources, not just yours. The ideal situation here, then, is to open with Cheap Shot and follow with Kidney Shot while your teammates blast the target.
Paralytic Poison		Coats your weapons with a Non-Lethal Poison that lasts for 1 hour. Each strike has a 20% chance of poisoning the enemy for 15 sec. Stacks up to 5 times on a single target, and upon a fifth application the enemy will be stunned for 4 sec.	A less controllable stun effect that will proc after five applications. The applications occur a fraction of the time, but you can estimate when the enemy will be stunned by looking at their debuffs. If you Shiv this poison, the enemy will be rooted temporarily, which is really useful against running enemies (especially when coupled with abilities like Shadowstep).
Dirty Tricks		Your Gouge and Blind no longer have an Energy cost, and no longer break from damage dealt by your Poison and Bleed effects.	The latter part of this effect is perhaps the most useful, as it allows you to Gouge enemies without having to worry about your DoT effects ticking, ending the effect early. Note that normal attacks will still end these temporary crowd controls, however. A bonus provided by this talent: because you're not bound by energy, you can use it freely and still interrupt a cast by using Gouge or Blind. This prevents those moments where you see an enemy casting a spell you want to interrupt, but you don't have enough energy for Kick.
LEVEL 90 TIER (VERSATILITY)			
Shuriken Toss		An improved ranged attack that deals Physical damage to an enemy target. Awards 1 combo point. Replaces Throw.	This version of Throw deals far more damage and removes the range restriction and cast time. In addition, it grants a combo point, allowing you to continue generating them should you be out of range of an enemy. This is a good choice when you find yourself constantly out of range of enemies.
Versatility		Removes the cooldown of your Redirect ability.	This ability greatly aids with the act of switching targets, and is especially useful on encounters where you have to DPS different enemies constantly, or PvP tactics that involve constant target switches.
Anticipation		When one of your attacks generates a combo point on a target that already has 5 combo points, you gain an Anticipation charge, up to a maximum of 5. When you perform an offensive finishing move on an enemy, any Anticipation charges are consumed to grant you an equal number of combo points on that target.	This talent is great when coupled with your level 87 ability, allowing you to produce a large amount of combo points. The Anticipation charges are capped at 5, like combo points, and are consumed to grant you combo points after using a finisher. This lets you pool combo points, potentially allowing you to use finishers back to back.

ASSASSINATION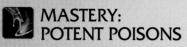

Assassination Rogues are the masters of poison effects, largely depending on their weapon poisons to deal damage and hinder enemies. Primarily using sharp and deadly daggers, Rogues that opt for this specialization prefer to use underhanded tactics to their advantage in order to defeat their opponents.

MASTERY: POTENT POISONS

Increases the damage done by your poisons by a percentage determined by your Mastery.

SPECIALIZATION ABILITIES

ABILITY	LEVEL		DESCRIPTION
Assassin's Resolve	10		While wielding daggers, your maximum Energy is increased and your damage is increased by 20%.
Improved Poisons	10		Increases the application chance of Deadly Poison and Wound Poison by 20%.
Mutilate	10		Instantly attacks with both weapons for 200% weapon damage plus an additional damage with each weapon. Awards 2 combo points. Requires Daggers.
Envenom	20		Finishing move that deals instant poison damage proportional to the number of combo points on the target. Following the Envenom attack, your poison application chance is increased by 15% for 1 sec plus an additional 1 sec per combo point. Replaces Eviscerate.
Seal Fate	30		When you critically strike with a single-target attack that generates combo points, you gain an additional combo point on your target.
Dispatch	40		A vicious strike that exploits the vulnerability of foes with less than 35% health remaining, causing 450% weapon damage plus an additional damage to the target. Awards 1 combo point. Replaces Sinister Strike. Requires Daggers.
Venomous Wounds	50		Each time your Rupture or Garrote deals damage to an enemy that you have poisoned, you have a 75% chance to deal additional Nature damage and to regain Energy. Garrote will not trigger this effect if the enemy is also afflicted by your Rupture. If an enemy dies while afflicted by your Rupture, you regain energy proportional to the remaining Rupture duration.
Cut to the Chase	60		Your Eviscerate refreshes your Slice and Dice duration to its 5 combo point maximum.
Blindside	70		Performing a successful Mutilate has a 30% chance of leaving you in an advantageous position, enabling a single use of Dispatch with no energy cost, regardless of the enemy target's health.
Vendetta	80		Marks an enemy for death, increasing all damage you deal to the target by 30% and granting you unerring vision of your target, regardless of concealments such as stealth and invisibility. Lasts 20 sec.

GETTING TO LEVEL 90

Like other Rogue specs, Assassination can level fast by choosing the right talents. Rogues have numerous survivability cooldowns, so make sure to use them should you accidentally pull several enemies at once. Note that Rupture and Slice and Dice are not always worth it, or sometimes you're better off using them at 1 or 2 combo points. Rupture, however, has an added bonus for Assassination: it restores energy proportional to the time left on it. It's still better to use it early in a short fight, however.

Talents are of great importance to Rogue leveling: consider Nightstalker if you decide to open fights with Ambush or Nerve Strike if you want the safer route of opening with Kidney Shot. Shadowstep provides a quick gap closer between you and enemies, and is usable in stealth, further improving stealth openers. Talents whose efficiency is largely affected by a large amount of damage (like Cheat Death) are best skipped for leveling.

PLAYING IN A GROUP

Rogues have one role in groups: dealing damage. With no abilities to heal other players, and being largely independent when it comes to surviving, you will be focusing on quickly dispatching enemies most of the time. Do note you have many interrupts and stuns for enemies that can be shunned from such effects.

Being a melee, naturally, you'll want to stand behind enemies to avoid parries and those nasty cleave effects that make quick work of Rogues. The buffs you provide for your group are passive, so you don't have to worry about casting them. Another benefit of being a melee: you bring a lot of useful debuffs you can apply on enemies!

Lastly, if your group needs long-term crowd control, your Sap ability will provide just that. Blind can also be used, even in combat, for a shorter crowd control that's usable from range.

BASIC ROTATION

Assassination Rogues have to keep track of two timers that greatly increase DPS output: Rupture and Slice and Dice. The duration of these effects is based on your combo points, but generally speaking, they last long enough that you don't have to constantly worry about generating enough points to use them. Because Mutilate consumes so much energy, you'll want to use Dispatch as often as possible—the Blindside passive lets you use it occasionally regardless of the enemy's health.

- **If you have 5 combo points (or less, depending on the monster's health), use Rupture**

- **If Rupture is active and you have 5 combo points, use Slice and Dice**

- **If both Rupture and Slice and Dice are up, use Envenom to consume your combo points**

- **Use Dispatch when available through Blindside, or when the enemy is below 35% health**

- **Use Mutilate to generate combo points**

GROUP BUFFS AND DEBUFFS

Rogues provide the Attack Speed buff with Swiftblade's Cunning. Rogues bring a host of debuffs to groups. Since the job of a Rogue is to deal damage without drawing attention, always let tanks apply any debuffs they have in common with you. Expose Armor applies the Weakened Armor debuff, Master Poisoner applies Magic Vulnerability, Wound Poison applies Mortal Strike, and Mind-Numbing Poison applies Slow Cast.

GETTING READY FOR HIGH-END CONTENT

ALL SPECS

Like other melee-based classes, your priority should be increasing your Hit until your Special Attacks (and Poisons) are no longer at risk of missing attacks on boss-level monsters (for raids, bosses are level 93). This will increase your overall damage, scaling with your other stats. If you hover over your Hit and Expertise stat in the character screen, you can see how you're doing in that regard. This isn't as important for 5-man heroics, whose bosses are a level lower than those found in raids, but don't hesitate to reforge some secondary stats into Hit or Expertise, and then you will benefit almost equally from the rest of the secondary stats.

For sheer damage output, always prioritize Agility in places that allow so, such as gems. At times, skipping gem bonuses in favor of more Agility gems is favorable—just don't pass up great bonuses (generally Agility-based bonuses).

COMBAT

Combat Rogues prefer to stand toe-to-toe against enemies, using their skills and knowledge to circumvent subtlety in favor of slaughter. Combat Rogues are not limited to dagger use, as their key abilities simply require any melee weapon to be equipped, making them proficient at the use of axes, fist weapons, and swords (all one-handed, of course).

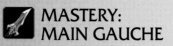

MASTERY: MAIN GAUCHE

Gives your main-hand attacks a chance, based on your Mastery, to execute an extra attack that's slightly stronger than the original.

SPECIALIZATION ABILITIES

ABILITY	LEVEL		DESCRIPTION
Ambidexterity	10		Increases the damage you deal with your off-hand weapon by 75%.
Blade Flurry	10		While active, your attacks strike an additional nearby opponent, but Energy regeneration is reduced by 30%. Lasts until canceled.
Vitality	10		Increases your Energy regeneration rate by 20% and your Attack Power by 25%.
Revealing Strike	20		An instant strike that deals 150% weapon damage and exposes the target's vulnerabilities, increasing the effectiveness of your offensive finishing moves on that target by 35%, and giving your Sinister Strikes a 20% chance to generate an extra combo point, for 18 sec. Awards 1 combo point.
Combat Potency	30		Gives your successful off-hand melee attacks and Main Gauche attacks a chance to generate Energy. Slower off-hand weapons have a proportionally higher chance to trigger Combat Potency.
Adrenaline Rush	40		Increases your Energy regeneration rate by 100% and your melee attack speed by 20% for 15 sec.
Restless Blades	50		Your damaging finishing moves reduce the remaining cooldown of your Adrenaline Rush, Killing Spree, Redirect, Shadow Blades, and Sprint abilities by 2 sec per combo point.
Bandit's Guile	60		Your training allows you to recognize and take advantage of the natural ebb and flow of combat. Your Sinister Strike and Revealing Strike abilities increase your damage dealt by up to 30%. After reaching this maximum, the effect will fade after 15 sec and the cycle will begin anew.
Killing Spree	80		Step through the shadows from enemy to enemy within 10 yards, attacking an enemy every 0.5 sec with both weapons until 7 assaults are made, and increasing all damage done by 20% for the duration. Can hit the same target multiple times. Cannot hit invisible or stealthed targets.

GETTING TO LEVEL 90

Like other Rogue specs, Combat can level fast by choosing the right talents. Combat is much more direct in its damage than Assassination or Subtlety, allowing you to simply go up to an enemy and start dealing damage. Rogues have numerous survivability cooldowns, so make sure to use them should you accidentally pull several enemies at once. Note that Slice and Dice is not always worth it, or sometimes you're better off using it at 1 or 2 combo points.

Talents are of great importance to Rogue leveling: consider Nightstalker if you decide to open fights with Ambush or Nerve Strike if you want the safer route of opening with Kidney Shot. Shadowstep provides a quick gap closer between you and enemies, and is usable in stealth, further improving stealth openers. Talents whose efficiency is largely affected by a large amount of damage (like Cheat Death) are best skipped for leveling.

PLAYING IN A GROUP

Rogues have one role in groups: dealing damage. With no abilities to heal other players, and being largely independent when it comes to surviving, you will be focusing on quickly dispatching enemies most of the time. Do note you have many interrupts and stuns for enemies that can be shunned from such effects.

Being a melee, naturally, you'll want to stand behind enemies to avoid parries and those nasty cleave effects that make quick work of Rogues. If you can't stand behind an enemy, it's not as big a deal as it would be for other Rogue specs (chiefly Subtlety), making you more versatile. The buffs you provide for your group are passive, so you don't have to worry about casting them. Another benefit of being a melee: you bring a lot of useful debuffs you can apply on enemies!

Lastly, if your group needs long-term crowd control, your Sap ability will provide just that. Blind can also be used, even in combat, for a shorter crowd control that's usable from range.

BASIC ROTATION

Because of its large DPS increase, you still want to keep Slice and Dice on yourself. Because Combat is all about finishing moves, they get several bonuses passively, including the ability to reduce the cooldown on damage-increasing abilities.

- Open with Revealing Strike, and keep it up. One great benefit of it is that it can proc an extra Combo Point, allowing you to reach 5 combo points faster

- If you have 5 combo points (or less, depending on the monster's health), use Slice and Dice

- If you have 5 combo points and Slice and Dice is up, use Eviscerate

- Use Sinister Strike to generate combo points

GROUP BUFFS AND DEBUFFS

Rogues provide the Attack Speed buff with Swiftblade's Cunning. Rogues bring a host of debuffs to groups. Since the job of a Rogue is to deal damage without drawing attention, always let tanks apply any debuffs they have in common with you. Expose Armor applies the Weakened Armor debuff, Master Poisoner applies Magic Vulnerability, Wound Poison applies Mortal Strike, and Mind-Numbing Poison applies Slow Cast.

GETTING READY FOR HIGH-END CONTENT

ALL SPECS

Like other melee-based classes, your priority should be increasing your Hit until your Special Attacks (and Poisons) are no longer at risk of missing attacks on boss-level monsters (for raids, bosses are level 93). This will increase your overall damage, scaling with your other stats. If you hover over your Hit and Expertise stat in the character screen, you can see how you're doing in that regard. This isn't as important for 5-man heroics, whose bosses are a level lower than those found in raids, but don't hesitate to reforge some secondary stats into Hit or Expertise, and then you will benefit almost equally from the rest of the secondary stats.

For sheer damage output, always prioritize Agility in places that allow so, such as gems. At times, skipping gem bonuses in favor of more Agility gems is favorable—just don't pass up great bonuses (generally Agility-based bonuses).

SUBTLETY

Subtlety Rogues live up to their name by using abilities that exploit the enemy's weak spots, and making use of the Stealth mechanic to its full extent. Rogues that opt to go the Subtlety route benefit greatly from being behind enemies, largely due to the Backstab ability, which deals a large amount of damage but can only be used if the enemy isn't facing you.

MASTERY: EXECUTIONER

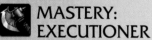

Increases the effectiveness of your finishing moves, and the effectiveness of your Slice and Dice, by a percentage determined by your mastery.

SPECIALIZATION ABILITIES

ABILITY	LEVEL		DESCRIPTION
Hemorrhage	10		An instant strike that deals 140% weapon damage (more if a dagger is equipped), causing profuse bleeding that deals an additional 50% of the direct strike's damage over 24 sec. Awards 1 combo point. Replaces Sinister Strike.
Master of Subtlety	10		Attacks made while stealthed and for 6 sec after breaking stealth cause an additional 10% damage.
Sinister Calling	10		Increases your total Agility by 30%.
Find Weakness	20		Your Ambush, Garrote, and Cheap Shot abilities reveal a flaw in your target's defenses, causing all your attacks to bypass 70% of that enemy's armor for 10 sec.
Premeditation	30		When used, adds 2 combo points to your target. You must add to or use those combo points within 20 sec or the combo points are lost.
Backstab	40		Backstab the target, causing 275% weapon damage plus additional damage to the target. Must be behind the target. Requires a dagger in the main hand. Awards 1 combo point.
Honor Among Thieves	50		When any player in your party or raid critically hits with a spell or ability, you gain a combo point on your current target. This effect cannot occur more than once every 2 sec, and can only occur while you are in combat.
Sanguinary Vein	60		Increases the damage of your Rupture ability by 50% and causes you to deal 25% additional damage to targets afflicted by your Rupture, Garrote, or Crimson Tempest.
Energetic Recovery	70		While your Slice and Dice ability is active, you regain Energy every 2 sec.
Shadow Dance	80		Enter the Shadow Dance for 8 sec, allowing the use of abilities that ordinarily require Stealth. The Energy cost of Ambush is reduced by 20 while Shadow Dance is active.

GETTING TO LEVEL 90

Like other Rogue specs, Subtlety can level fast by choosing the right talents. Being the spec that benefits the most from Stealth openers (primarily due to the Master of Subtlety passive, which increases your damage after Stealth breaks), you will likely want to dispatch enemies by starting a fight from Stealth mode. Rogues have numerous survivability cooldowns, so make sure to use them should you accidentally pull several enemies at once. Slice and Dice gives Energy, which can make leveling slightly faster (it can be automatically refreshed with the Deadly Momentum glyph). Rupture deals more damage as Subtlety due to the Sanguinary Vein passive, so keep that in mind.

Talents are of great importance to Rogue leveling: consider Nightstalker if you decide to open fights with Ambush or Nerve Strike if you want the safer route of opening with Kidney Shot. Shadowstep provides a quick gap closer between you and enemies, and is usable in stealth, further improving stealth openers. Talents whose efficiency is largely affected by a large amount of damage (like Cheat Death) are best skipped for leveling.

PLAYING IN A GROUP

Rogues have one role in groups: dealing damage. With no abilities to heal other players, and being largely independent when it comes to surviving, you will be focusing on quickly dispatching enemies most of the time. Do note you have many interrupts and stuns for enemies that can be shunned from such effects.

Being a melee (and especially as Subtlety), naturally, you'll want to stand behind enemies to avoid parries and those nasty cleave effects that make quick work of Rogues. If you can't stand behind an enemy, you can still use Hemorrhage as a combo point generator, but your overall DPS will be lower. The buffs you provide for your group are passive, so you don't have to worry about casting them. Another benefit of being a melee: you bring a lot of useful debuffs you can apply on enemies!

Lastly, if your group needs long-term crowd control, your Sap ability will provide just that. Blind can also be used, even in combat, for a shorter crowd control that's usable from range.

BASIC ROTATION

As previously stated, the unique aspect of Subtlety DPS is that you greatly benefit from being behind an enemy. You can still execute your rotation if you can't meet the positioning requirement, but this won't let you use Backstab, which is a hefty DPS increase. That aside, the rotation is similar to Assassination in that you have to keep track of Rupture and Slice and Dice.

- If available, use Premeditation to get 2 combo points on the target and activate Slice and Dice (if you're concerned about the loss of damage from Sanguinary Vein, open with a Garrotte)

- If you have 5 combo points (or less, depending on the target's health), use Rupture

- If both Rupture and Slice and Dice are up, use Eviscerate to consume your combo points

- Use Hemorrhage if you can't get behind an enemy

- Use Backstab to generate combo points

GROUP BUFFS AND DEBUFFS

Rogues provide the Attack Speed buff with Swiftblade's Cunning. Rogues bring a host of debuffs to groups. Since the job of a Rogue is to deal damage without drawing attention, always let tanks apply any debuffs they have in common with you. Expose Armor applies the Weakened Armor debuff, Master Poisoner applies Magic Vulnerability, Wound Poison applies Mortal Strike, and Mind-Numbing Poison applies Slow Cast.

GETTING READY FOR HIGH-END CONTENT

ALL SPECS

Like other melee-based classes, your priority should be increasing your Hit until your Special Attacks (and Poisons) are no longer at risk of missing attacks on boss-level monsters (for raids, bosses are level 93). This will increase your overall damage, scaling with your other stats. If you hover over your Hit and Expertise stat in the character screen, you can see how you're doing in that regard. This isn't as important for 5-man heroics, whose bosses are a level lower than those found in raids, but don't hesitate to reforge some secondary stats into Hit or Expertise, and then you will benefit almost equally from the rest of the secondary stats.

For sheer damage output, always prioritize Agility in places that allow so, such as gems. At times, skipping gem bonuses in favor of more Agility gems is favorable—just don't pass up great bonuses (generally Agility-based bonuses).

SHAMAN

Shamans are masters of nature and elemental magic. They are a hybrid class that can perform multiple roles with vastly different playstyles.

While Shamans are primarily spellcasters, they can excel at melee combat if the proper specialization tree is chosen. Shamans are also capable of deploying totems, which will grant significant temporary benefits to the Shaman and his or her allies. Totems are invaluable for grouping, and other Shaman buffs add to the desirability to group with a Shaman. Because of their ability to heal, coupled with their hefty armor and shield, Shamans are a great class for solo play as well. There are several totems across the four elements; choosing the right one for every situation is part of the fun of playing a Shaman.

RACE AVAILABILITY

ALLIANCE

Draenei
Dwarf
Gnome

Human
Night Elf
Worgen

Pandaren

HORDE

Blood Elf
Goblin
Orc

Tauren
Troll
Undead

RACIAL ADVANTAGES

ALLIANCE

RACE	NOTES
Draenei	Heroic Presence grants Draenei +1% Hit chance. Gift of the Naaru heals the Draenei or any ally. Draenei take less damage from Shadow spells.
Dwarf	Stoneform is excellent for PvP, as it removes all poison, disease, and bleed effects and reduces damage taken. Mace Specialization increases Expertise with maces, which are common Shaman weapons. Dwarves take less damage from Frost spells.

PANDAREN

RACE	NOTES
Pandaren	Epicurean doubles the statistical bonuses from being Well Fed. Quaking Palm acts as a form of brief crowd control.

HORDE

RACE	NOTES
Goblin	Rocket Jump is a great mobility tool, allowing Shaman to stay at range. Goblins get 1% increased Haste from Time is Money. Rocket Barrage is another source of damage for Goblins.
Orc	Blood Fury increases your attack and spell power. Axe Specialization increases Expertise for axes. Hardiness reduces the duration of stun effects by 15%.
Tauren	Nature Resistance increases a Tauren's ability to stand up to harmful Nature effects. War Stomp provides an (AoE) stun in melee range, and Endurance boosts base health by 5%.
Troll	Berserking grants a temporary increase in attack speed. Da Voodoo Shuffle passively reduces the duration of movement impairing effects. Trolls regenerate Health faster than other races, and 10% of total Health regeneration may continue in combat.

EQUIPMENT OPTIONS

ARMOR TYPE	SHIELD
Leather until 40, then Mail	Yes

USABLE WEAPONS

1 HAND WEAPON	2 HAND WEAPON
Axes	Axes
Daggers	Maces
Fist Weapons	Staves
Maces	

PROMINENT CLASS ABILITIES

TOTEMS

Placing totems is a Shaman's signature ability. As you level, you can learn to cast numerous different totem spells, each of which has a specific function for solo or group play. Totems are small friendly units that usually grant you (and your group) a buff, or inflict negative effects on hostile targets. They are very fragile and can usually be killed with one swing of an enemy's weapon. However, because they are unaffected by AoE, enemies must manually target your totems if they wish to destroy them.

Totems are grouped into four categories, each corresponding to one of the elements of nature: Fire, Wind, Earth, and Water. Their classification is relevant, because you can only drop one totem per element at a time. For example, if you have an earth-based totem on the ground and you drop a different earth-based totem, the first one will instantly perish. Totems are considered spells, and as such, cost mana and trigger the global cooldown (do note they are all instant, however). At times, you might want to purposefully destroy all your totems (perhaps to avoid an enemy from spotting them). Totemic Recall does just that—it instantly recalls all your totems, granting you a fraction of the mana spent to summon them. It is good practice to recall your totems whenever you move to a new spot, as wandering enemies might run toward you after spotting and killing your abandoned totems.

In the days of yore, totems were used to grant party members long-term buffs, most of which are passive now. To eliminate this redundancy, totems are now useful cooldown-like abilities with a very specific use. Naturally, their number has been greatly reduced, and the ability to drop numerous totems at once has been removed.

ELEMENTAL SHIELDS

As a Shaman, you can learn several different elemental shields that grant diverse bonuses passively or when struck in battle.

Lightning Shield is the simplest form of this spell category. It creates several lightning orbs that surround you and deal damage to any enemy that attacks you. The orbs only detonate every few seconds, so fast attackers will not deplete all your lightning orbs instantly. Certain passive abilities in the Enhancement and Elemental trees increase the usefulness of this skill.

Water Shield is very useful if you're aiming to be a healer-type Shaman. It creates three water globes that surround you and passively grant you mana regeneration through Resurgence. Resurgence is a passive Restoration ability, which makes it so that direct healing spell Critical Strikes also grant mana as long as Water Shield is active. Upon being struck, like Lightning Shield, one of the globes will detonate and grant you a small burst of mana.

Lastly, Earth Shield, exclusive to Restoration Shamans, is an outstanding skill for survivability. It surrounds the target with numerous earthen orbs, each providing a small heal upon detonation (when the target is struck). Earth Shield also increases healing taken by the target in question, which only applies to Shaman heals.

You can only have one shield on yourself, but as a rule of thumb, Enhancement and Elemental Shamans might prefer Lightning Shield (unless mana is a problem), and Restoration Shamans always prefer Water Shield. Earth Shield can be cast on others, but it is also useful if cast on yourself when survivability is an issue (such as PvP encounters).

WEAPON IMBUES

Like the elemental shields, weapon enchantments are self-cast buffs that enhance your abilities or hinder enemies. The main difference is that these enchantments are cast on your weapon, and remain active until they expire or they're cancelled.

As a bonus, the imbues have a special ability triggered by the Unleash Elements ability, which is a baseline Shaman spell with a short cooldown. The special ability is based on the type of imbue.

These imbues remain largely unchanged, but can now be selected through the Weapon Imbues ability, which groups them neatly. The imbues are detailed in the following table.

IMBUE	BUFFS	UNLEASH ABILITY
Flametongue Weapon	Increases magical damage done, and melee swings deal a small amount of fire damage.	Deals fire damage and greatly increases the damage of your next fire spell.
Frostbrand Weapon	Melee swings deal frost damage and apply a slowing debuff.	Deals frost damage and applies a slowing debuff, which is more effective if another frost slowing debuff is already active.
Rockbiter Weapon	Increases threat generation and slightly reduces damage taken.	Taunts an enemy to attack you.
Earthliving Weapon (Restoration only)	Increases healing and gives your heals a chance to place a HoT on their target.	Heals your target and greatly increases the effectiveness of your next healing spell.
Windfury Weapon (Enhancement only)	Gives your attacks a chance to trigger three extra attacks with bonus attack power.	Deals damage and increases your attack speed briefly.

ASCENDANCE

Shaman's level 87 ability is Ascendance. This ability allows you to surrender your physical form temporarily in order to harness the power of the elements, granting you a new form based on your specialization tree.

SPECIALIZATION TREE	NEW FORM	ABILITY
Elemental	Flame Ascendant	Removes the cooldown on Lava Burst, and Chain Lightning becomes a beam of flame.
Enhancement	Air Ascendant	Melee attacks and Stormstrike deal pure nature damage and can be used at range.
Restoration	Water Ascendant	Healing is duplicated and distributed among allies.

Ascendance is on a considerable cooldown, but can be invaluable for certain situations. One of the main reasons to use this ability is for damage throughput. The Shaman ignores the opponent's armor when this ability is active, as he is now dealing nature damage instead of physical. The Elemental version is a fairly straightforward DPS increase, while the Restoration version is one of the best abilities to employ in heavy AoE damage scenarios.

NAME	LEVEL		DESCRIPTION
Lightning Bolt	1		Casts a bolt of lightning at the target for Nature damage.
Primal Strike	3		An instant weapon strike that causes additional damage.
Earth Shock	6		Instantly shocks the target with concussive force, causing Nature damage and applying the Weakened Blows effect.
Healing Surge	7		Heals an ally for a moderate amount.
Lightning Shield	8		The caster is surrounded by a reactive lightning barrier. When a spell, melee, or ranged attack hits the caster, the attacker will be struck for Nature damage. This effect may only occur once every few seconds. Lasts 1 hour. Only one of your Elemental Shields can be active on you at once.
Flametongue Weapon	10		Imbue the Shaman's weapon with fire, increasing magical damage done. Each hit causes additional Fire damage, based on the speed of the weapon. Slower weapons cause more fire damage per swing. Lasts 60 minutes.
Flame Shock	12		Instantly sears the target with fire, causing Fire damage immediately and additional Fire damage over 24 sec.
Purge	12		Purges the enemy target, removing 1 beneficial Magic effect.
Ancestral Spirit	14		Returns the spirit to the body, restoring a dead target to life with 35% of maximum health and mana. Cannot be cast when in combat.
Ghost Wolf	15		Turns the Shaman into a Ghost Wolf, increasing speed by 30%.
Searing Totem	16		Summons a Fire Totem with 5 health at your feet for 1 min that repeatedly attacks an enemy within 20 yards for Fire damage.
Wind Shear	16		Disrupts the target's concentration with a burst of wind, interrupting spellcasting and preventing any spell in that school from being cast for 3 sec. Also lowers your threat, making the enemy less likely to attack you.
Cleanse Spirit	18		Removes all Curse effects from an ally.
Water Shield	20		The caster is surrounded by globes of water, granting mana per 5 sec. When a spell, melee, or ranged attack hits the caster, the reactive shield generates mana. This effect can only occur once every 3 seconds. Lasts 1 hour. Only one of your Elemental Shields can be active on you at once.
Frost Shock	22		Instantly shocks an enemy with frost, dealing Frost damage and reducing the target's movement speed by 50%. Lasts 8 sec. Causes a high amount of threat.
Water Walking	24		Allows the friendly target to walk across water for 10 min. Any damage will cancel the effect.
Earthbind Totem	26		Summons an Earth Totem with 5 health at the feet of the caster for 20 sec that slows the movement speed of enemies within 10 yards.
Chain Lightning	28		Hurls a lightning bolt at the enemy, dealing Nature damage and then jumping to additional nearby enemies. Each jump reduces the damage by 30%. Affects 3 total targets.
Healing Stream Totem	30		Summons a Water Totem with 5 health at the feet of the caster for 15 sec that heals the most injured party or raid member within 40 yards every 2 sec.
Totemic Recall	30		Returns your totems to the earth, giving you 25% of the mana required to cast each totem destroyed by Totemic Recall.
Reincarnation	32		Allows you to resurrect yourself upon death with 20% health and mana.
Astral Recall	34		Yanks the caster through the twisting nether back to your home location. Speak to an Innkeeper in a different place to change that home location.
Far Sight	36		Change the caster's viewpoint to the targeted location. Lasts 1 min. Only useable outdoors.
Magma Totem	36		Summons a Fire Totem with 5 health at the feet of the caster for 1 min that causes Fire damage to creatures within 8 yards every 2 seconds.
Grounding Totem	38		Summons an Air Totem with 5 health at the feet of the caster that will redirect one harmful spell cast on a nearby party member to itself, destroying the totem. Will not redirect area of effect spells. Lasts 15 sec.

NAME	LEVEL		DESCRIPTION
Burning Wrath	40		Fiery elemental energy emanates from the Shaman, empowering all nearby party and raid members and increasing their spell power by 10%.
Chain Heal	44		Heals the friendly target then jumps to heal the most injured nearby targets. If cast on a party or raid member, the heal will only jump to other members. Each jump reduces the effectiveness of the heal by 30%. Heals 4 total targets.
Frostbrand Weapon	46		Imbue the Shaman's weapon with frost. Each hit has a chance of causing additional Frost damage and slowing the target's movement speed by 50% for 8 sec. Lasts 60 minutes.
Tremor Totem	54		Summons an Earth Totem with 5 health at the feet of the caster that shakes the ground around it for 6 sec, removing Fear, Charm, and Sleep effects from party and raid members within 30 yards. This totem may be dropped even while the caster is afflicted with such effects.
Earth Elemental Totem	58		Summons an Earth Totem at the feet of the caster, calling forth a Greater Earth Elemental to protect the caster and his allies. Lasts 1 min.
Healing Rain	60		Calls forth healing rains to blanket the area targeted by the Shaman, restoring health to allies in the area every 2 sec for 10 sec. Healing effectiveness diminishes for each player beyond 6 within the area.
Capacitor Totem	63		Summons an Air totem with 5 health at the feet of the caster that gathers electrical energy from the surrounding air and then explodes after 5 sec to stun all enemies within 8 yards for 5 sec.
Fire Elemental Totem	66		Summons a Fire Totem at the feet of the caster, calling forth a Greater Fire Elemental to rain destruction on the caster's enemies. Lasts 1 min.
Bloodlust	70		Significantly increases your allies' melee, ranged and casting speed temporarily.
Heroism	70		Significantly increases your allies' melee, ranged and casting speed temporarily.
Bind Elemental	72		Binds the target hostile elemental for up to 50 sec. The bound unit is unable to move, attack, or cast spells. Any damage caused will release the target. Only one target can be bound at a time.
Hex	75		Transforms the enemy into a frog. While hexed, the target cannot attack or cast spells. Damage caused may interrupt the effect. Lasts 1 min. Only one target can be hexed at a time. Only works on Humanoids and Beasts.
Rockbiter Weapon	75		Imbue the Shaman's weapon with the fury of the earth, increasing all threat generation by 30% and reducing damage taken by 5%. Lasts 60 minutes.
Stormlash Totem	78		Summons an Air Totem with 5 health at the feet of the caster, empowering allies within 30 yards with lightning. While empowered, allies' spells and attacks will trigger bursts of electricity, dealing additional Nature damage to their target. Lasts 10 sec.
Grace of Air	80		Empowering winds swirl around the Shaman, granting all nearby party and raid members Mastery.
Unleash Elements	81		Focuses the elemental force imbued in the Shaman's weaponry, with the concentrated effects depending on the enchantment unleashed.
Spiritwalker's Grace	85		Calls upon spiritual guidance, permitting movement while casting non-instant Shaman spells. This spell may be cast while casting other spells. Lasts 15 sec.
Ascendance	87		The Shaman surrenders his physical form to the power of the elements, gaining the ability to transform into a being of raw elemental energy for 15 sec. Elemental: While in the form of a Flame Ascendant, Lava Burst has no cooldown and Chain Lightning is empowered to become Lava Beam. Enhancement: While in the form of an Air Ascendant, autoattacks and Stormstrike deal pure Nature damage and have a 30-yard range. Restoration: While in the form of a Water Ascendant, all healing done is duplicated and distributed evenly among nearby allies.

TALENTS

TALENT		DESCRIPTION	NOTES
LEVEL 15 TIER (SURVIVABILITY)			
Nature's Guardian		Whenever a damaging attack brings you below 30% health, your maximum health is increased by 25% for 10 sec, and your threat level towards the attacker is reduced. This effect cannot occur more often than once every 30 sec.	Powerful in both PvE and PvP, potentially saving you from death by shedding aggro and increasing your max health. An old shaman favorite.
Stone Bulwark Totem		Summons an Earth Totem with 5 health at the feet of the caster for 30 sec that grants the caster a shield absorbing damage for 10 sec, and an additional amount every 5 sec thereafter.	The effect lasts 30 seconds, and the ticks of the smaller shields occur every 5 sec. This makes it great for predictable periodic damage.
Astral Shift		Seek haven by shifting partially into the elemental planes, reducing damage taken by 40% for 6 sec.	The most straightforward in the tier, this talent is a very powerful emergency button that works like a tank's defensive cooldown. Keep in mind you can use this much less often than the other two in the tier, however.
LEVEL 30 TIER (CONTROL)			
Frozen Power		Your Frost Shock now also roots the target in ice for 5 sec.	Because Frost Shock is in such a short cooldown, this is one of the best ways to keep a single target at bay or from getting away. Diminishing returns prevent this ability from completely immobilizing a target perpetually, however.
Earthgrab Totem		Summons an Earth Totem at the feet of the caster for 20 sec. The totem pulses every 2 sec, causing roots to ensnare the legs of all enemies within 10 yards for 5 sec, preventing movement. Enemies that have already been rooted once by the totem will instead have their movement speed reduced by 50%. Replaces Earthbind Totem.	This is an improved version of Earthbind Totem, rooting enemies as well as slowing them if they were previously rooted. It ticks periodically throughout its 20-second duration.
Windwalk Totem		Summons an Air Totem with 5 health at the feet of the caster for 6 sec, granting raid members within 40 yards immunity to movement-impairing effects.	With a shorter duration than most totems, this talent will allow your allies to move unhindered for 6 seconds. Great for certain PvE encounters, and team PvP.
LEVEL 45 TIER (TOTEM IMPROVEMENT)			
Call of the Elements		When activated, immediately finishes the cooldown on all totems with a base cooldown shorter than 3 minutes.	The usefulness of this ability largely depends on the usefulness of your totems in a situation. Note that only totems with a 3-minute cooldown or less can be reset, which excludes the two Greater Elemental totems, as well as Spirit Link Totem, Mana Tide Totem, Healing Tide Totem, and Stormlash Totem.
Totemic Restoration		When a totem is replaced or destroyed before its duration expires naturally, its cooldown is reduced in proportion to the lost duration, up to a maximum of 50% of the full cooldown.	The maximum cooldown reduction is 50%, and the amount is determined by how early the totem is destroyed (the earlier, the bigger the reduction). Note that this applies to both totems that are replaced by you or destroyed by enemies.
Totemic Projection		Relocates your active totems to a target location.	On such a short cooldown, this ability is great when you know you will be moving great distances and you need your totems to remain in range of your allies, or when you want to place totems in melee range while staying at range.
LEVEL 60 TIER (SPELL EFFECTIVENESS)			
Elemental Mastery		Call upon elemental forces, empowering you with 30% Haste for 20 sec.	Previously exclusive to the Elemental tree, this ability is a major throughput-increasing cooldown that benefits all types of shaman.
Ancestral Swiftness		Your next Nature spell with a base casting time less than 10 sec, becomes an instant cast spell. Passive: Increases spell and melee haste by 5%.	This is a new version of Nature's Swiftness that passively increases your spell and melee haste. Note that only spells with a cast time shorter than 10 seconds can be affected (thus, no instant resurrect or hearthstone)!
Echo of the Elements		When one of your spells causes direct damage or healing, you have a chance to gain Echo of the Elements, duplicating that spell's effect.	Affects both damage and healing spells, but not basic melee attacks. This is a straightforward, passive effectiveness increase that does not require a cooldown to be used.
LEVEL 75 TIER (HEALING)			
Healing Tide Totem		Summons a Water Totem with 10% of the caster's health at the feet of the caster for 10 sec. The Healing Tide Totem pulses every 2 sec, healing the 5 most injured party or raid members within 40 yards.	This totem lasts 10 seconds and heals the 5 most injured party members for a large amount, as long as they're in range. Do note the hefty cooldown!
Ancestral Guidance		When you deal damage or healing for the next 10 sec, 40% of that amount is copied as healing to up to 3 nearby injured party or raid members.	The amount healed is based on the damage dealt or healing done by the spells you cast during its 10-sec duration. Great spell for helping other healers out, regardless of specialization tree!
Conductivity		When you cast Healing Wave, Greater Healing Wave, or Healing Surge on a target located within your Healing Rain, allies within the Healing Rain share healing equal to 20% of the initial healing done. If your Lightning Bolt, Chain Lightning, Earth Shock, or Stormstrike damages an enemy standing in your Healing Rain, allies within the Healing Rain share healing equal to 50% of the initial damage done.	The percentage is smaller for healing spells, but it's still a great healing cooldown, particularly if numerous allies stand in your Healing Rain. Likewise, damage specs can help healers out with this.
LEVEL 90 TIER (ELEMENTAL PROWESS)			
Unleashed Fury		Your elemental weapon imbues are empowered, granting additional effects when triggered with Unleash Weapon: Flametongue: Increases the enemy target's damage taken from your Lightning Bolt by 30% for 10 sec. Windfury: For 8 sec, your melee autoattacks can trigger Static Shock. Earthliving: Further increases the effectiveness of your next single-target heal on the targeted ally by 50%. Frostbrand: You leech heat from the enemy target, gaining 50% movement speed for 4 sec. Rockbiter: You take 40% reduced damage from the enemy target for 5 sec.	Makes Unleash Weapon much better, especially considering its short cooldown and the usefulness of the buffs/debuffs granted.
Primal Elementalist		Your Earth and Fire Elemental Totems draw forth powerful primal elementals directly from the elemental planes. These servitors are 50% more powerful than regular elementals, act as pets directly under your control, and gain additional abilities.	Makes you a pet class, but not permanently! With this, you can actually control what your elementals do, allowing you to damage or tank specific enemies. It also makes your elementals much more effective.
Elemental Blast		Harness and direct the raw power of the elements towards an enemy target, dealing Elemental damage and increasing the caster's Critical Strike, Haste, or Mastery for 8 sec.	The amount of damage dealt and the bonus to a secondary stat (Haste, Mastery or Critical Strike) are both hefty, making this something you'll want to use often as a DPS spec. Healers can benefit from it as well if they can afford the two-second cast (there's no mana cost, however).

ELEMENTAL

Elemental Shamans are the most durable damaging caster class when it comes to armor, as they can wear mail gear and a shield. The spells boosted by the Elemental tree are primarily nature-based. Lightning Bolt and Chain Lightning are the main sources of damage, but Shock spells of different elements, along with Lava Burst (one of the major sources of damage from an Elemental Shaman), benefit as well. If you're looking to stay at range and deal magical damage, Elemental is the specialization tree for you.

MASTERY: ELEMENTAL OVERLOAD

Gives your spells a chance to overload, dealing a portion of their damage again for free. The chance is based on your Mastery.

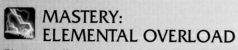

SPECIALIZATION ABILITIES

ABILITY	LEVEL		DESCRIPTION
Elemental Fury	10		Increases your spells' critical strike damage bonus by 50%.
Elemental Precision	10		Grants Hit equal to any Spirit gained from items or effects.
Elemental Reach	10		Increases the range of your Lightning Bolt, Chain Lightning, and Lava Burst spells by 10 yards, and increases the range of your Shock spells and Searing Totem by 15 yards.
Shamanism	10		Increases the damage of Lightning Bolt by 50% and Chain Lightning by 70% reduces the casting time of both spells by .5 seconds, and removes the cooldown from Chain Lightning.
Spiritual Insight	10		Increases your mana pool by 400%. Reduces the cooldown of your Earth Shock and Flame Shock spells by 1 second.
Thunderstorm	10		You can call down a bolt of lightning, energizing you and damaging nearby enemies within 10 yards. Restores 15% mana to you and deals Nature damage to all nearby enemies, reducing their movement speed by 40% for 5 sec and knocking them back 20 yards. This spell is usable while stunned.
Rolling Thunder	20		When you deal damage with Lightning Bolt or Chain Lightning while your Lightning Shield ability is active, you have a 60% chance to recover 2% of your mana and to generate an additional Lightning Shield charge, up to a maximum of 7 charges.
Fulmination	30		When you have more than 1 Lightning Shield charge active, your Earth Shock spell will consume any surplus charges, instantly dealing their total damage to the enemy target.
Lava Burst	34		You hurl molten lava at the target dealing Fire damage. If your Flame Shock is on the target, Lava Burst will deal a critical strike.
Elemental Focus	40		When you land a non-periodic critical strike with a Fire, Frost, or Nature damage spell, you enter a Clearcasting state. The Clearcasting state reduces the mana cost of your next 2 damage or healing spells by 25%, increases spell damage done by 10%, and increases single-target healing done by 50%
Lava Surge	50		Your Flame Shock periodic damage ticks have a chance to reset the cooldown of your Lava Burst spell and cause your next Lava Burst spell to be instant.
Elemental Oath	55		Grants 5% spell haste to all party and raid members within 100 yards.
Earthquake	60		You cause the earth at the target location to tremble and break, dealing Physical damage every 1 sec to enemies in an 8 yard radius, with a 10% chance of knocking down affected targets. Lasts 10 sec.

GETTING TO LEVEL 90

With outstanding armor, a shield, and healing spells, keeping your distance from mobs isn't as important as it is for other caster classes. As an Elemental Shaman, you will be very durable and capable of withstanding blows from several enemies at once. Remember to keep your weapon imbued at all times! Flametongue Weapon is the ideal choice for Elemental Shamans, as it will increase your spell damage. Keep your Lightning Shield up at all times. Flame Shock is always a good idea, even if the enemy won't last its full duration, as it guarantees Lava Burst will be a critical strike. Finish enemies with Lightning Bolt or Chain Lightning, and keep an eye on your mana pool.

Talents aren't as relevant to Shaman leveling as they would be for other classes, but consider Echo of the Elements and other passive talents.

PLAYING IN A GROUP

Shamans are incredibly versatile in groups and can greatly aid a struggling healer, potentially saving the party. Naturally, this is very dependent on your talents, especially the level 75 line. Because your totems act more like cooldowns than they did before, you only need to drop them in specific situations, such as an AoE fear effect on the party (for which you'd use Tremor Totem).

Make sure you watch your threat—overall, however, it shouldn't be much of a problem (and you can still take a hit if necessary).

ROTATION

Elemental has several passive abilities that interact with your core Shaman spells. Most notable among these is Rolling Thunder, which gives you a charge of Lightning Shield when using certain damage spells.

- Apply/refresh Lightning Shield on yourself

- Apply/refresh Flame Shock on an enemy

- If you have 7 charges of Lightning Shield, use Earth Shock to proc Fulmination

- Use Lava Burst whenever available

- Use Lightning Bolt as a filler

GROUP BUFFS AND DEBUFFS

All Shaman provide the Spell Power buff with Burning Wrath and the Mastery buff with Grace of Air. Elemental Shaman get the Elemental Oath ability, which provides the Spell Haste buff. Use Earth Shock to inflict the Weakened Blows debuff on your enemies.

GETTING READY FOR HIGH-END CONTENT

ELEMENTAL

Like other casters, Elemental Shamans should always try to maximize their damage output for heroic dungeons and raids.

For raids, your priority should be reaching the Hit cap (15%, or 14% for Draenei, a mace-wielding Dwarf, and an Orc using axes or fist weapons). Elemental Shamans have an advantage in this regard, as they can benefit from Spirit just as they would from Hit. Always prioritize Intellect when gemming, but don't pass up good socket bonuses. Note that all the secondary stats (Critical Strike, Haste, and Mastery) are useful, but note that Lava Burst (a large portion of your damage) is guaranteed to critically hit if Flame Shock is on a target, making Critical Strike significantly less appealing.

ENHANCEMENT

As an Enhancement Shaman, you can get up close with enemies and damage them using your weapons and other melee abilities. Enhancement is a specialization tree primarily dedicated to boosting your melee prowess, while using your mana pool to increase your damage through various spells. Enhancement is one of the few specializations that delves into the art of wielding two one-handed weapons at once. Enhancement Shamans are very durable, as they are still able to wear mail armor and heal themselves in a pinch.

MASTERY: ENHANCED ELEMENTS

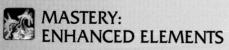

Increases damage done by your elemental (fire, frost, and nature) spells by a percentage determined by your Mastery.

SPECIALIZATION ABILITIES

ABILITY	LEVEL		DESCRIPTION
Dual Wield	10		You may equip one-handed weapons in your off-hand, and you have a chance to parry incoming frontal melee attacks.
Lava Lash	10		You charge your off-hand weapon with lava, instantly dealing 200% of that weapon's damage to an enemy target and spreading your Flame Shock from the target to up to four enemies within 12 yards. Damage is increased by 40% if your off-hand weapon is enchanted with Flametongue. Requires Melee Weapon.
Mental Quickness	10		Your spell power is now equal to 55% of your attack power, and you no longer benefit from other sources of spell power. Your instant beneficial, damaging, and totem spells cost 75% less mana. Your melee attacks have a 40% chance to immediately restore 5% of your mana.
Windfury Weapon	10		Imbue the Shaman's weapon with wind. Each hit has a 20% chance of triggering three extra attacks with bonus attack power. Lasts 60 minutes.
Flurry	20		After dealing a melee critical strike, your attack speed increases by 15% and you gain 50% additional benefit from Haste granted by items. Lasts 15 sec, or until 5 melee attacks have occurred.
Stormstrike	26		Instantly strike an enemy with both weapons, dealing 300% weapon damage and granting you an additional 25% chance to critically strike that enemy with your Lightning Bolt, Chain Lightning, Lightning Shield, and Earth Shock spells for 15 sec. Requires Melee Weapon.
Searing Flames	34		When your Searing Totem deals damage or your Fire Elemental lands a melee attack, the damage dealt by your Flametongue Weapon is increased by 8% for 15 sec. Stacks up to 5 times. Your Lava Lash ability will consume this effect, dealing 20% increased damage for each application present.
Static Shock	40		When you use your Stormstrike or Lava Lash abilities while having Lightning Shield active, you have a 45% chance to deal damage equal to a Lightning Shield orb.
Fire Nova	44		Ignites your Flame Shock spell on any nearby enemies, causing each of them to emit a wave of flames that deals Fire damage to every other enemy within 10 yards.
Maelstrom Weapon	50		When you deal damage with a melee weapon, you have a chance to reduce the cast time and mana cost of your next Nature spell with a base cast time shorter than 10 seconds by 20%. Stacks up to 5 times. Lasts 30 sec.
Unleashed Rage	55		Increases the melee and ranged attack speed of all party and raid members within 100 yards by 10%.
Feral Spirit	60		Summons two Spirit Wolves that aid the Shaman in battle, lasting 30 sec. Spirit Wolves' attacks heal them and their master for 150% of damage done.
Spirit Walk	60		Removes all movement-impairing effects and increases your movement speed by 60% for 15 sec.
Shamanistic Rage	65		Reduces all damage taken by 30% and causes your skills, totems, and offensive spells to consume no mana for 15 sec. This spell is usable while stunned.

GETTING TO LEVEL 90

Enhancement is perhaps the fastest of the three specialization trees when it comes to leveling solo. As Enhancement, you will be killing enemies quickly while keeping your health and mana pools healthy through healing spells and mana-regenerating abilities. Weapon enchants are particularly useful for Enhancement Shamans, as they will provide a sizable damage boost just by being active on a weapon.

Use your shock spells depending on the situation; generally, Flame Shock will deal the most damage if used early in a battle (and the battle lasts long enough for it to complete its duration). Use instant strikes, such as Primal Strike at low levels (replace it with Stormstrike as soon as Stormstrike becomes available) and Lava Lash whenever possible. Also keep your Lightning Shield up, unless mana is an issue, in which case switch to Water Shield. Remember to use your Enhancement-specific cooldowns (Shamanistic Rage and Feral Spirit) often in order to minimize your downtime.

PLAYING IN A GROUP

Being melee-based, you will often have to watch your threat near the start of a fight, particularly if the tank is less geared than you are. Use Wind Shear to interrupt caster enemies, as it can significantly reduce damage taken by the group, or the healing enemies do to each other. Like other Shaman specializations, you can greatly help a struggling healer with your healing abilities, chiefly Healing Stream Totem and the entire level 75 line of talents. This makes you much more versatile and desirable in a group (not to mention Shamans bring numerous group buffs as well).

ROTATION

Note that Enhancement Shamans use quite a few damage spells, making them one of the least physical-based melee classes. The passive Mental Quickness makes this possible, greatly reducing the mana cost of spells and increasing your spell power based on your attack. Another passive, Maelstrom Weapon, stacks and makes your next damage spell instant, so keep an eye on it.

- Place/refresh Searing or Fire Elemental Totem

- Apply/refresh Flame Shock

- Use Stormstrike whenever available

- Use Lava Lash whenever available

- If you have five stacks of Maelstrom Weapon, use Lightning Bolt (preferably after Stormstrike), or a healing spell if necessary

- Use Unleash Elements on cooldown

GROUP BUFFS AND DEBUFFS

All Shaman provide the Spell Power buff with Burning Wrath and the Mastery buff with Grace of Air. Exclusive to Enhancement Shaman is Unleashed Rage, which grants the Melee and Ranged Haste buff. Use Earth Shock to inflict the Weakened Blows debuff on enemies.

GETTING READY FOR HIGH-END CONTENT

ENHANCEMENT

Like other melee classes, your goal is to avoid getting misses on bosses. Because Enhancement Shamans dual wield, you must attain a higher percentage of Hit to reach this goal. It's not necessary to completely eliminate misses right away—make sure you have some Expertise where possible, too—but it will increase your damage significantly. After Hit is no longer a concern, stack Mastery over Critical Strike and Haste.

Remember that your attack power is converted to spell damage, so avoid using caster gear as Enhancement, as you will benefit significantly less from it. As your primary stat, gem for Agility wherever you can, while matching gem colors for good gem bonuses.

RESTORATION

Restoration is the healing-oriented specialization tree available to Shamans. It specializes in boosting Shaman abilities that restore health to the caster or other friendly units. Restoration Shamans, like Druids, use nature-based heals. They are one of the most resilient healer classes due to the ability to use mail armor and a shield. Like other specialization trees, Restoration is able to provide noticeable buffs through totems, which makes it a good healer choice for small and large groups alike.

MASTERY: DEEP HEALING

Increases the efficiency of your healing spells by a percentage based on your Mastery. The percentage is also proportional to the targets' current health—lower health targets are healed for more.

SPECIALIZATION ABILITIES

ABILITY	LEVEL		DESCRIPTION
Meditation	10		You retain 50% of your mana regeneration from Spirit while in combat.
Purification	10		Increases the effectiveness of your healing spells by 25%, and the healing done by your Water totems by an additional 50%. In addition, heals you cast increase allies' maximum health by 10% of the amount healed, up to a maximum of 10% of their health.
Riptide	10		Heals a friendly target plus an additional amount over 18 sec. Your Chain Heal spells are 25% more effective when their primary target is affected by your Riptide.
Spiritual Insight	10		Increases your mana pool by 400% and increases your chance to hit with Lightning Bolt, Lava Burst, Hex, and Flame Shock by 15%.
Purify Spirit	18		Removes all Curse and Magic effects from a friendly target.
Healing Wave	20		Slow-casting, cheap heal that heals a target.
Earth Shield	26		Protects the target with an earthen shield, increasing the effectiveness of Shaman healing spells on that target by 20%, and causing attacks to heal the shielded target. 9 charges. Lasts 10 min. This effect can only occur once every few seconds. Earth Shield can only be placed on one target at a time, only one Earth Shield may be on a target at a time, and only one of your Elemental Shields can be active on you at once.
Earthliving Weapon	30		Imbue the Shaman's weapon with earthen life. Increases spell healing and gives each heal a 20% chance to trigger the Earthliving effect on the target, healing an additional amount over 12 sec. Single-target direct heals on targets below 35% of maximum health will always trigger this effect. Lasts 60 minutes.
Ancestral Awakening	34		When you critically heal with a single-target direct heal, you summon an ancestral spirit to aid you, instantly healing the most injured party or raid target within 40 yards for 30% of the amount healed.
Lava Burst	34		You hurl molten lava at the target dealing Fire damage. If your Flame Shock is on the target, Lava Burst will deal a critical strike.
Resurgence	40		While Water Shield is active, you recover mana when your direct healing spells have a critical effect. You regain mana from a Healing Wave or Greater Healing Wave critical, and less so from a Healing Surge, Riptide, or Unleash Life critical, and even less from a Chain Heal critical
Tidal Waves	50		When you cast Chain Heal or Riptide, you gain the Tidal Waves effect, which reduces the cast time of your Healing Wave and Greater Healing Wave spells by 30% and increases the critical effect chance of your Healing Surge spell by 30%. 2 charges.
Mana Tide Totem	56		Summons a Water Totem with 10% of the caster's health at the feet of the caster for 16 sec. Party and raid members within 40 yards of the totem gain 200% of the caster's Spirit (excluding short-duration Spirit bonuses).
Greater Healing Wave	60		Heals a friendly target.
Spirit Link Totem	70		Summons an Air Totem with 5 health at the feet of the caster. The totem reduces damage taken by all party and raid members within 10 yards by 10%. Every 1 sec, the health of all affected players is redistributed, such that each player ends up with the same percentage of their maximum health. Lasts 6 sec.

GETTING TO LEVEL 90

Restoration is not the optimal choice for Shaman leveling, as it lacks the offensive capability of Enhancement or Elemental. If you want to be a viable dungeon healer while leveling, you can choose Elemental as your primary leveling specialization, as it will usually be proficient enough at healing. Note that, because Elemental benefits from Spirit, the gear between these two specs will often be identical, further encouraging Restoration Shamans to have the Elemental dual-specialization when leveling.

PLAYING IN A GROUP

Restoration is one of the most straightforward specialization trees when it comes to healing, while still being extremely versatile. In groups, your primary heals will be direct ones, along with your trusty Earth Shield and Riptide. Your totems will complement your ability to keep your group alive nicely, as they provide defenses or healing for several situations. Remember to use Totemic Recall whenever your group is relocating and you have totems active, so you can regain some of the mana spent.

Your main heals will be Healing Surge, Healing Wave, and Greater Healing Wave. Healing Surge and Greater Healing Wave both interact differently with Tidal Waves (and thus mana and HPS throughput). Generally, Healing Surge does the most healing per second but has the worst mana efficiency, and Greater Healing Wave is somewhere in between. Gauge the danger of the situation and react accordingly, while keeping Earth Shield on a target that takes constant damage (usually the tank). At times, there will be heavy incoming area of effect damage, which can be countered by using Chain Heal, Healing Stream Totem, Healing Rain, and talents. Remember to keep Earthliving Weapon active! Since Riptide is no longer consumed by Chain Heal, always have a Riptide active and Chain Heal through that target when needed, as it boosts your healing done significantly.

HEALING

Shaman healing is largely dependent on mana. Luckily, the passive Resurgence restores some mana from your critical heals, if Water Shield is active (and it should always be!). Other passives benefit from Critical Strike as well, making it a very attractive secondary stat for Restoration Shamans. As with all healing classes, the best way to improve your efficiency is to use different spells based on the situation.

SITUATION(S)	USE...
An ally is in need of immediate healing	Healing Surge
Healing a single target that's not in immediate danger	Healing Wave or Greater Healing Wave, depending on the frequency and amount of damage taken by the target
Everyone is healthy, but you know there's going to be incoming damage	Earth Shield on a target you know will take steady damage, such as a tank
Heavy AoE damage from enemies	Healing Rain if you have time and there are allies grouped together, then Chain Heal, preferably a target you used Riptide on

GROUP BUFFS AND DEBUFFS

All Shaman provide the Spell Power buff with Burning Wrath and the Mastery buff with Grace of Air. Use Earth Shock to inflict the Weakened Blows debuff.

GETTING READY FOR HIGH-END CONTENT

RESTORATION

Without a Hit cap to worry about (most of your damage-based abilities and talents get hit chance boosts from passives), you should go straight for throughput (from Intellect, Haste, Critical Strike, and Mastery) and mana regeneration (from Spirit). How you balance these stats will be based on how often you feel like you need more mana. For instance, Haste allows you to cast faster, thus healing more, but using more mana. Consider reforging some secondary stats to Spirit if you think you're holding back too much due to lack of mana.

# WARLOCK

Warlocks are powerful casters who delve into dark magic and the demonic arts. They are damage-oriented magic users with the ability to summon powerful pets to aid them. Warlocks possess hefty damage-over-time spells, and are good at summoning and controlling demons, applying various curses, and instilling fear into their enemies.

Like Mages, Warlocks lack physical defense, but they make up for this lack through skillful use of crowd control spells and defensive abilities like Unending Resolve, which reduces damage and prevents spell interruption for several seconds. Warlock specializations range from pure burst damage-dealing to slow and steady damage-over-time and proficiency in summoning demons. Though a Warlock's signature spell kit consists of Shadow spells, they can make effective use of the Fire school, particularly when specialized as Destruction. Among the utility repertoire of a Warlock lies the ability to summon other players, or even create portals through which they can travel in order to quickly change locations.

RACE AVAILABILITY

ALLIANCE

Draenei   Dwarf   Gnome

Human   Night Elf   Worgen

Pandaren

HORDE

Blood Elf   Goblin   Orc

Tauren   Troll   Undead

RACIAL ADVANTAGES

ALLIANCE

RACE	NOTES
Dwarf	Stoneform is excellent for PvP and PVE as it removes all poisons, diseases, and bleed effects as well as reduces damage taken by 10%. Dwarves take less damage from Frost spells.
Gnome	Escape Artist provides an extra ability for escaping slow or snare effects; great for PvP. Expansive Mind increases your mana pool by 5%. Gnomes take less damage from Arcane spells.
Human	Every Man for Himself removes effects that cause loss of control of your character. The Human Spirit increases Spirit by 3%.
Worgen	Worgen get 1% increased Critical Strike from Viciousness. Darkflight increases movement speed temporarily. Worgen take less damage from Nature and Shadow spells.

HORDE

RACE	NOTES
Blood Elf	Arcane Torrent provides mana and an AoE silence. The former helps in tight mana situations, and the latter is great for interrupting enemy spells mid-cast. Blood Elves take less damage from Arcane spells.
Goblin	Goblins get 1% increased Haste from Time is Money. Rocket Jump is a great mobility tool, allowing Warlocks to stay at a comfortable range. Rocket Barrage is another source of damage for Goblins.
Orc	Orcs are great for maximizing damage. Blood Fury increases your spell power. Command increases your pet's damage output. Hardiness reduces the duration of stun effects by 15%.
Troll	Berserking grants a temporary increase in attack speed. Da Voodoo Shuffle passively reduces the duration of movement impairing effects. Trolls regenerate Health faster than other races, and 10% of total Health regeneration may continue in combat.
Undead	Undead are more suited for PvP as they can break out of Charm, Fear, and Sleep effects with Will of the Forsaken. Their passive racial, Touch of the Grave, is a life leech and also provides a modest DPS increase in any situation. Undead take 1% less damage from Shadow spells.

EQUIPMENT OPTIONS

ARMOR TYPE	SHIELD
Cloth	No

USABLE WEAPONS

1 HAND WEAPON	2 HAND WEAPON
Daggers	Staves
Swords	
Wands	

PROMINENT CLASS ABILITIES

DEMONIC PETS

One of the most important aspects of playing a Warlock is the ability to summon minions. Although the Demonology tree is capable of summoning the powerful Felguard and Wild Imps, every specialization tree benefits from using summoned demons. The level 75 line of talents directly alters how demons are used in battle—you may even sacrifice your demon in order to boost your damage, if the correct talent is chosen.

The process of summoning is usually lengthy compared to other spells. But some abilities, such as Destruction's Flames of Xoroth, will allow you to instantly revive your pet. There are numerous demons that can be summoned, each useful depending on the scenario. It will often boil down to personal taste, however. Look for more details about Warlock pets later in this section.

DEALING DAMAGE OVER TIME

Regardless of what talent tree is chosen, a Warlock's offensive spell arsenal includes damage-over-time (DoT) spells. Such spells don't deal burst damage; instead, they place a debuff on an enemy target, slowly chipping away at their health. Don't be fooled by the relatively small numbers, however—DoT spells are among the most powerful damage dealing abilities in the game!

To get the most out of DoTs, apply them early in the fight so that they last for their entire duration. When in combat with more durable targets, recast your DoT spell shortly before the effect wears off in order to prolong duration of the DoT. One big advantage DoT spells have over direct damage is that they're usually fast casts (and are often instant), granting the Warlock some freedom to move around while still dealing damage.

SECONDARY RESOURCES

Although Warlocks use mana as their primary resource to cast spells, each of their specialization trees is capable of generating and spending a secondary resource.

The key to maximizing DPS and survivability is learning to manage these resources efficiently.

RESOURCE	DESCRIPTION
Soul Shards	Usable by Affliction Warlocks, Soul Shards are mostly unchanged from Cataclysm—they boost several abilities through Soulburn.
Demonic Fury	Demonology's special resource, Demonic Fury, is generated by casting offensive spells, and spent while in Demon Form.
Burning Embers	Burning Embers (exclusive to Destruction Warlocks) are generated by casting certain spells and consumed by either Chaos Bolt or Fire and Brimstone for a burst of big damage, or in order to do more damage, or Ember Tap in order to self-heal.

DEMONIC GATEWAY

The Warlock's level 87 ability is Demonic Gateway, which allows you to place a gateway at a target location. Actually, this spells places two portals: a purple one at your current location, and a green one at the target location. These portals allow players to quickly fly from one to the other, providing a fast way to get to a location specified by the Warlock who cast the spell. Because this is advanced magic, there are some restrictions. The gateways need "charges" in order to transport a player. They start with zero charges, and build one charge periodically, up to the maximum of five. A Gateway places a debuff on characters that use them, meaning it can be used by the same player only every so often. Note that this ability's range is immense—larger than the 40-yard standard—but the portals must usually be placed on level surfaces vertically close to one another.

NAME	LEVEL		DESCRIPTION
Shadow Bolt	1		Sends a shadowy bolt at the enemy, causing Shadow damage.
Summon Imp	1		Summons an Imp under the command of the Warlock. Imps cast ranged Firebolts and provide a health boost to nearby allies.
Corruption	3		Corrupts the target, causing Shadow damage over 18 sec.
Drain Life	7		Drains the life from the target, causing Shadow damage and restoring 2% of the caster's total health every 1 sec. Lasts 6 sec.
Summon Voidwalker	8		Summons a Voidwalker under the command of the Warlock. Voidwalkers can withstand heavy punishment.
Create Healthstone	9		Creates a Healthstone that can be used to instantly restore 20% of your maximum health.
Control Demon	10		Allows you to give commands to control your demon.
Health Funnel	11		Sacrifices 6% of your maximum health to restore 6% of your summoned Demon's maximum health every 1 sec. Lasts for 6 sec.
Fear	14		Strikes fear in the enemy, causing it to flee for up to 20 sec. Damage caused may cancel fear. Limit 1 target.
Life Tap	16		Restores mana at the cost of 15% health.
Curse of Enfeeblement	17		Binds the target in demonic energy, reducing physical damage by 20% and increasing the casting time of all spells by 50% (25% on player targets) for 30 sec. Less effective on dungeon and raid bosses. A Warlock can only have one Curse active per target.
Soulstone	18		When cast on living party or raid members, the soul of the target is stored and they will be able to resurrect upon death. If cast on a dead target, they are instantly resurrected. Targets resurrect with 60% health and 20% mana.
Summon Succubus	20		Summons a Succubus under the command of the Warlock. Succubi are dangerous, close-range spellcasters. They seduce Humanoid creatures, preventing them from attacking.
Eye of Kilrogg	22		Summons an Eye of Kilrogg and binds your vision to it. The eye is stealthed and moves quickly but is very fragile.
Unending Breath	24		Allows the target to breathe underwater for 10 min.
Soul Harvest	27		You and your demon absorb nearby wandering souls, regenerating 2% health every second while out of combat. This effect is disabled in arenas.
Enslave Demon	31		Enslaves the target demon, forcing it to do your bidding. Lasts up to 5 min. While enslaved, the time between the demon's attacks is increased by 30% and its casting speed is slowed by 20%.
Summon Felhunter	29		Summons a Felhunter under the command of the Warlock. Felhunters are drawn to magic and heal themselves by consuming beneficial magic effects from enemies.
Banish	32		Banishes an enemy Demon or Elemental for up to 30 sec. The target cannot act but is invulnerable. Limit 1 target. Casting Banish again will cancel the spell.
Twilight Ward	34		Absorbs a limited amount of Shadow or Holy damage. Lasts 30 sec.
Fel Armor	38		Increases your armor, total Stamina by 10% and the amount of health generated through spells and effects by 10%.
Ritual of Summoning	42		Begins a ritual that creates a summoning portal. The summoning portal can be used by allies to summon a targeted party or raid member. Requires the caster and 2 additional allies to complete.
Summon Infernal	49		Summons a meteor from the Twisting Nether, causing Fire damage and stunning all enemy targets in the area for 2 sec. An Infernal rises from the crater, under the command of the caster for 1 min. The Infernal deals strong area of effect damage, and will be drawn to attack targets near the impact point.
Nethermancy	50		Increases your intellect by 5%.
Curse of the Elements	51		Curses the target, increasing magic damage taken by 5% for 5 min. A Warlock can only have one Curse active per target.
Command Demon	56		Commands your demon to perform its most powerful ability. This spell will transform based on your active pet. Imp: Cauterize Master Voidwalker: Disarm Succubus: Whiplash Felhunter: Spell Lock Felguard: Felstorm

NAME	LEVEL		DESCRIPTION
Summon Doomguard	58		Summons a Doomguard to attack the target for 1 min. Doomguard will cast Doom Bolt until it departs. Doom Bolt – Sends a shadowy bolt at the enemy, causing Shadow damage. Deals 20% additional damage to targets below 20% health.
Unending Resolve	64		The Warlock hardens their skin, reducing all damage taken by 40% and preventing their spells from being interrupted or silenced for 8 sec.
Soulshatter	66		Reduces threat by 90% for all enemies within 50 yards.
Create Soulwell	68		Creates a Soulwell. Raid members can click the Soulwell to acquire a Healthstone. The Soulwell lasts for 2 min or 25 charges.
Demonic Circle	76		Summon: Summons a demonic circle at your feet, lasting 6 min. You can only have one Demonic Circle active at a time. Teleport: Teleports you to your Demonic Circle and removes all snare effects.
Fel Flame	77		Deals Shadowflame damage to an enemy and increases the duration of Corruption by 6 sec.
Dark Intent	82		Infuses all party and raid members with shadow, increasing their spell power by 10% for 1 hour. If the target is in your party or raid, all party and raid members will be affected.
Dark Soul	84		Grants a powerful effect based upon on your specialization. Instability (Destruction): Infuses your soul with unstable power, increasing your critical strike chance by 30% for 20 sec. Knowledge (Demonology): Your soul is infused with demonic knowledge, increasing your Mastery for 20 sec. Misery (Affliction): Infuses your soul with the misery of fallen foes, increasing spell haste by 30% for 20 sec.
Demonic Gateway	87		Create a demonic gateway between two locations. Stepping into the gateway causes any party member to be instantly transported to the other gateway. Limit 5 charges. The portal generates one charge every 15 seconds and lasts 10 min.
Pandemic	90		When refreshing your periodic damage effects, duration remaining on the previous effect is added to the new one, up to a maximum of 50% the base duration.

TALENTS

TALENT		DESCRIPTION	NOTES
LEVEL 15 TIER (HEALING)			
Dark Regeneration		Restores 30% of you and your pet's maximum health and increases all healing received by 25% over 12 sec.	On a 2-min cooldown, this ability is great in a pinch—think of it as a very powerful Healthstone.
Soul Leech		Your Shadow Bolt, Soul Fire, Chaos Bolt, Touch of Chaos, Incinerate, Haunt, Drain Soul and Malefic Grasp spells heal you and your pet for a percentage of the damage dealt.	Great for replenishing your health passively while casting spells in combat. Best for combat situations where a Warlock can attack a target without frequent interruption.
Harvest Life		Drains the life from all enemies within 15 yards of the target, causing Shadow damage and restoring 3-4.5% of the caster's total health every 1 sec. Lasts 6 sec. Replaces Drain Life.	Works like Drain Life, only AoE. Great for PvE encounters with adds.
LEVEL 30 TIER (CONTROL)			
Howl of Terror		Howl, causing 5 enemies within 10 yds to flee in fear for 20 sec. Damage caused may cancel Howl of Terror. When hit by a damaging attack, the cooldown on Howl of Terror is reduced by 1 sec.	An incredibly powerful crowd-control tool that can save your life, especially in PvP. Note that damage done can still break the fear effect early.
Mortal Coil		Causes the enemy target to run in horror for 3 sec. The caster restores 15% of their maximum health.	Works like Death Coil from Cataclysm and earlier. Great way to get away from a single enemy (especially melee users) while restoring your health.
Shadowfury		Shadowfury is unleashed, stunning all enemies within 8 yds for 3 sec.	This AoE stun remains largely unchanged from Cataclysm. You can choose the area to be affected, making it a great ranged CC tool on a short cooldown.
LEVEL 45 TIER (SURVIVABILITY)			
Soul Link		When active, all damage and healing you and your demon take is shared, but your demon's health is reduced by 50%. Recasting this spell cancels the effect. Replaces Health Funnel.	This greatly reduces the spike damage you take, but do note that, unlike Cataclysm, this works both ways, making you take damage if your demon is under siege.
Sacrificial Pact		Your demon sacrifices half its current health to shield its master for 200% of the sacrificed health. Lasts 10 sec. If you have no demon, your health is sacrificed instead.	The shield provided is surprisingly hefty (double the health sacrificed), making this a great survivability tool. It doesn't reduce spike damage as much as Soul Link would, but it's a life saver if you can predict you're about to die.
Dark Bargain		Prevents all damage for 8 seconds. When the shield fades, 50% of the damage prevented is dealt over 8 sec.	Contrary to popular belief, this talent does not instantly turn you into a Paladin. That said, this is a great tool for surviving heavy damage in both PvE and PvP. Be wary of its long cooldown and aftermath damage, however!
LEVEL 60 TIER (MOVEMENT)			
Blood Fear		Sacrifice 10% of maximum health to instantly strike fear in the enemy, causing it to flee for up to 20 sec.	An aggressive ability that makes Fear instant at the expense of 10% of your (max) health. Mostly PvP-oriented, its usefulness will be based largely on your playstyle—high risk, high reward. Do note the added 5-sec cooldown.
Burning Rush		Drains 4% of your maximum health per second to increase your movement speed by 50%. Lasts until cancelled.	This causes you to move significantly faster, but also deals a significant amount of damage per second. Great for leveling, or emergencies where you need to move fast. Not so great when trying to get away from enemies at low health.
Unbound Will		Sacrifices 20% of maximum health to purge all Magic effects, movement impairing effects and all effects which cause loss of control of your character.	The health requirement is pretty steep, which makes this ability pretty risky to use in PvP when under siege. Great for getting out of crowd controls when not directly under attack.
LEVEL 75 TIER (DEMON INSPIRATION)			
Grimoire of Supremacy		You Command Stronger Demons, Replacing Your Normal Minions. These Demons Deal 20% Additional Damage And Have More Powerful Abilities. Spells Learned: Summon Fel Imp Summon Voidlord Summon Shivarra Summon Observer Summon Abyssal Summon Terrorguard	Note that all your demons' utility is similar—they just deal more damage and undergo some cosmetic changes. If trying out this talent, it is strongly recommended you bask in the glory of the Shivarra's Mesmerize ability.
Grimoire of Service		Instantly summon a second demon, who fights for 20 sec.	Summons a second pet from the list of those currently available to the Warlock. The summoned pet will attack the Warlock's initial target for 20 seconds, making this an effective DPS-increasing cooldown.
Grimoire of Sacrifice		You sacrifice your demon to gain one of its abilities, increase the power of many of your single target spells by 25% to 50% and regenerate 2% of maximum health every 5 seconds. Lasts for 20 minutes. Summoning another demon cancels the effect.	This ability allows you to forgo pet management during combat in favor of an increase to the damage of some your spells. This is a strong talent but offers a risk-reward scenario to the Warlock, not least because only one of the active pet's utility abilities remains usable after the Sacrifice.
LEVEL 90 TIER (VERSATILITY)			
Archimonde's Vengeance		Causes an enemy to suffer 25% of all damage you take. Lasts 8 sec. Passive: Enemies who attack you suffer 5% of all damage they deal to you. This effect is disabled while on cooldown.	Great for PvE fights where you're constantly taking damage. The active ability should be used when a predictable damage spike is incoming. This ability is also particularly good for duels or other 1v1 PvP encounters.
Kil'Jaeden's Cunning		You can cast and channel while moving for 6 sec. Passive: You can cast and channel while moving, but doing so increases the cast time or channel period of the spell by 50%. Each cast reduces your movement speed by 10%, stacking up to 2 times. This effect is disabled while on cooldown.	Key ability for fights with lots of movement, especially as Destruction. In PvP, it makes for a great kiting tool.
Mannoroth's Fury		Increases the area of your area of effect spells by 500%.	The increase in radius is very, very large. This talent is great for fights where adds need to be killed through AoE, but they're spread out just out of range of your AoE spells.

AFFLICTION

Masters of damage-over-time spells, Affliction Warlocks employ an array of shadow-based debuffs and drains in order to deal damage. Affliction Warlocks are great at dealing with multiple enemies at once, but can also hold their own against single targets—thanks to Malefic Grasp and Haunt.

The three angular shapes that appear under your Affliction Warlock's health and mana bars are Soul Shards, which turn purple as they are filled. Use Soul Shards to activate Soulburn, which grants various bonuses to certain spells. The Soulburn effect lasts 30 seconds and consumes a single Soul Shard. Soulburn is a critical ability for Affliction Warlocks, improving the effects of Drain Life, Health Funnel, Curses, Seed of Corruption, Unending Breath, Demonic Circle: Teleport and Soul Swap.

Maintaining your Soul Shard supply is tremendously important. There are two ways to renew this resource, dependant on whether your Warlock is in combat or not. Out of combat, Soul Harvest (a passive ability) adds Soul Shards automatically over time; you should gain back all three within a minute. In combat, Warlocks must rely on Drain Soul, a channeled attack spell with a twelve second duration. It hits every 2 seconds and every second hit restores one Soul Shard. The Affliction passive ability Nightfall also grants a rare chance to generate a Soul Shard when Corruption deals damage to a target.

MASTERY: POTENT AFFLICTIONS

Increases the damage of Agony, Corruption and Unstable Affliction by 24%.

SPECIALIZATION ABILITIES

NAME	LEVEL		DESCRIPTION
Corruption	3		Corrupts the target, causing Shadow damage over 18 sec.
Unstable Affliction	10		Shadow energy slowly destroys the target, causing damage over 14 sec. If the Unstable Affliction is dispelled it will cause damage to the dispeller and silence them for 4 sec.
Drain Soul	19		Drains the soul of the target, causing Shadow damage every 2 sec and energizing one Soul Shard after it deals damage twice. If the target dies, three Soul Shards are energized. Lasts 12 sec. If the target is at or below 20% health when Drain Soul deals damage, it causes all of your other periodic Affliction damage effects to instantly deal 100% of their normal periodic damage.
Soulburn	19		Consumes a Soul Shard, unlocking the hidden power of your spells. Soulburn: Summon Demon has a 60 sec cooldown. (For Affected Spells, see table.)
Rain of Fire	21		Calls down a fiery rain to burn enemies in the area of effect for Fire damage over 6 sec.
Curse of Exhaustion	32		Reduces the target's movement speed by 30% for 30 sec. A Warlock can only have one Curse active per target.
Agony	36		Inflicts increasing agony on the target, causing Shadow damage over 24 sec. This damage is dealt slowly at first and builds up each time it deals damage.
Malefic Grasp	42		Binds the target in twilight, causing Shadow damage over 4 sec. Every 1 sec, when Malefic Grasp deals damage, it causes all of your other periodic Affliction damage effects to instantly deal 50% of their normal periodic damage.
Nightfall	54		Gives your Corruption spell a 5% chance to cause you to regain a Soul Shard.
Seed of Corruption	60		Embeds a demon seed in the enemy target, causing Shadow damage over 18 sec. When the target takes damage from the caster or dies, the seed will inflict additional Shadow damage to all enemies within 15 yards of the target.
Haunt	62		You send a ghostly soul into the target, dealing Shadow damage and increasing all damage done by your spells on the target by 25% for 8 sec.
Improved Fear	69		Causes your Fear spell to inflict a Nightmare on the target when the fear effect ends. Nightmare: The target's movement speed is reduced by 30% for 5 sec.
Soul Swap	79		You instantly deal damage, and remove your Shadow damage-over-time effects from the target. For 20 sec afterwards, the next target you cast Soul Swap: Exhale on will be afflicted by the Shadow damage-over-time effects and suffer damage. You cannot Soul Swap to the same target.

SPELLS AFFECTED BY SOULBURN	
SPELL	SOULBURN EFFECT
Summon Demon	Instant Cast
Drain Life	Healing increased by 50%.
Health Funnel	Your Health Funnel will instantly restore 36% health and reduce damage taken by 30% for 10 sec.
Soul Swap	Instantly applies Corruption, Unstable Affliction, and Agony.
Seed of Corruption	Your Seed of Corruption detonation effect will afflict Corruption on all enemy targets.
Unending Breath	Allows you to walk on water.
Demonic Circle	Your Demonic Circle: Teleport spell also increases your movement speed by 50% and makes you immune to snares and roots for 8 sec.
Curse (all)	Your Curses will afflict all enemies in a 10 or 15 yard radius around your target. Soulburn: Curse does not inflict a cooldown.

GETTING TO LEVEL 90

Leveling as Affliction is efficient and fun. You can DoT enemies as you run around to gather more targets. The best way to level is to pull enemies with Agony from as far away as possible, then apply Corruption while moving onto the next target. Finally, apply Unstable Affliction, which requires a brief pause to cast. While your DoT'ed up enemy is running towards you, find another one and repeat the cycle. More often than not, a single set of DoT spells will be enough to kill enemies. For extra efficiency, you can time Soul Swap (with or without the glyph) on low-health enemies in order to fully debuff another mob.

For talents, take Howl of Terror (use when enemies catch up to you after debuffing), Burning Rush, Grimoire of Supremacy, or Sacrifice, and Kil'Jaeden's Cunning.

PLAYING IN A GROUP

Similar to leveling, playing in a group is all about keeping damage debuffs up on enemies. Use your normal rotation on single enemies, and DoT multiple enemies if necessary. Keep a pet out unless you selected Grimoire of Sacrifice. Since your spells damage constantly (and often uncontrollably once applied), keep an eye on threat and use Soulshatter if you pull aggro.

ROTATION

The intent behind Affliction's rotation is to keep reapplying the damage-over-time debuffs as close to their expiration time as possible. Strongly consider downloading a debuff-tracking add-on to best see when debuffs are about to expire on enemies.

- Apply/refresh Corruption

- Apply/refresh Agony

- Apply/refresh Unstable Affliction

- Repeat for any adds that will live long enough for Corruption to fully tick

- Use Haunt if you have Soul Shards

- Channel Malefic Grasp if target is over 20% health

- Channel Drain Soul if target is under 20% health

GROUP BUFFS AND DEBUFFS

Affliction Warlocks convey the Spell Power buff with Dark Intent. Imp pets provide the Stamina buff with Blood Pact.

Warlocks can apply either the Magic Vulnerability debuff with Curse of the Elements, or apply the Slow Cast and Weakened Blows debuffs with Curse of Enfeeblement.

GETTING READY FOR HIGH-END CONTENT

ALL SPECS

All three Warlock specializations benefit roughly equally from stats that boost spells. Those stats are: Intellect, Spell Damage, Haste, Critical Strike, Hit, and Mastery.

When getting ready for raids, your priority should be to reach the Hit cap (15%). Because raid bosses are three levels higher than you, not having the 15% hit would result in a pretty sharp DPS loss. The only stat you should not sacrifice for Hit (up to the 15%) is Intellect, as it is far more valuable even below the hit cap. That leaves reforging and blue sockets (where you should put purple gems with Hit and Intellect) in order to reach the Hit cap.

DEMONOLOGY

Adept at demonic magic, Demonology Warlocks' favored party trick consists of turning into a demon to increase damage dealt. They're able to summon the powerful Felguard to do their bidding, as well as the small but helpful Wild Imps. Many damaging spells and familiar abilities generate Demonic Fury.

Demonic Fury is the resource used exclusively by Demonology Warlocks, while employing their Metamorphosis ability. When in Demon form, Warlocks consume 6 Demonic Fury per second and all spells have a Demonic Fury cost instead of a Mana cost. If Demonic Fury reaches zero, Warlocks revert to their normal selves. Demonic Fury will passively increase or decrease to a value of 200 when a Warlock remains in caster form and out of combat for a while. The maximum amount is 1000 Demonic Fury, so whenever you hit that, don't hesitate to use Metamorphosis to wreak havoc upon your foes.

MASTERY: MASTER DEMONOLOGIST

Increases the damage done by your demon servants by 8%. Increases the damage you deal in caster form by 8%. The damage done while using Metamorphasis is increased by 24%.

SPECIALIZATION ABILITIES

NAME	LEVEL		DESCRIPTION
Metamorphosis	10		Temporarily transform into a demon, increasing damage dealt by 24%. Metamorphosis prevents the use of Corruption and Hand of Gul'dan.
Demonic Fury	10		Demonic Fury is spent while using Metamorphosis. Your damaging spells and your demon's special attacks generate Demonic Fury.
Soul Fire	13		Burn the enemy's soul, causing fire damage. Soul Fire always critically strikes, and its damage is further increased based on your critical strike chance.
Hand of Gul'dan	19		Summons a falling meteor to strike the target and all enemies within 6 yards for Shadow damage and inflicting them with Shadowflame. Shadowflame reduces movement speed by 30% and deals Shadowflame damage over 6 sec. Generates 2 Demonic Fury every time it deals damage.
Hellfire	22		Ignites the area surrounding the caster, causing Fire damage to himself and all nearby enemies every 1 sec. Lasts 14 sec. Generates 3 Demonic Fury per target.
Wild Imps	32		Your Shadow Bolt, Soul Fire, and Touch of Chaos hits summon a Wild Imp from the Twisting Nether. This effect can occur every 20 sec. Each Wild Imp will cast 10 Firebolts before departing. Each Firebolt generates 5 Demonic Fury.
Summon Felguard	42		Summons a Felguard under the command of the Warlock. Felguard are powerful melee fighters who excel against multiple targets and reduce healing received by their target.
Molten Core	69		When Shadowflame or a Wild Imp deals damage you have an 8% chance to trigger Molten Core. Molten Core: Reduces the cast time and mana cost of your next Soul Fire spell by 50%.

ABILITIES GRANTED BY METAMORPHOSIS

NAME	LEVEL		DESCRIPTION
Demonic Leap	12		Leap into the air upon demonic wings, moving a short distance. Using this ability activates Metamorphosis.
Metamorphosis: Touch of Chaos	25		While using Metamorphosis, your Shadow Bolt spell transforms into Touch of Chaos. Touch of Chaos: Unleashes energy at the enemy, causing Chaos damage and extending the duration of Corruption.
Nether Plating	27		While using a Demon Form, your armor contribution from items increases by 250% and the duration of stun and snare effects is reduced by 35%.
Carrion Swarm	47		Flaps your wings, unleashing a wave of shadow which deals Shadow damage, knocking back enemies and interrupting spell casting.
Immolation Aura	62		While using Metamorphosis, your Hellfire spell no longer deals damage to you and does not need to be channeled.
Cursed Auras	67		While using Metamorphosis, your Curse of the Elements and Curse of Enfeeblement become auras. Aura of the Elements: Curses all targets within 20 yards, increasing magic damage taken by 5%. Aura of Enfeeblement: Binds all enemies within 20 yards in demonic energy, reducing physical damasge by 20% and increasing the casting time of all spells by 50%
Chaos Wave	79		While using Metamorphosis, your Hand of Gul'dan spell transforms into Chaos Wave. Chaos Wave: Hurls a wave of chaos to strike the target and all enemies within 6 yards, dealing Chaos damage and reducing movement speed by 30% for 6 sec.
Void Ray	85		While using Metamorphosis, your Fel Flame spell transforms into Void Ray. Void Ray: Deals Shadowflame damage to all enemies in a 20 yard line and increases the duration of Corruption by 6 sec.

GETTING TO LEVEL 90

As Demonology, it's best to keep your Felguard out. For weaker enemies, you can opt for the Affliction approach and use Corruption and Hand of Gul'dan on everything you encounter. Then turn into a demon and use Hellfire (to activate Immolation Aura), Chaos Wave, and Felstorm. In demon form, your curses become an aura which emanates from the Warlock, so it might be worthwhile to use Curse of the Elements while engaging bigger packs. Do note that Hand of Gul'dan makes enemies slower, allowing you to outrun them in a pinch.

For talents, take Grimoire of Supremacy (since you will be using your Felguard), then Burning Rush and Kil'Jaeden's Cunning to help you stay mobile while casting spells. Howl of Terror and Shadowfury should both be roughly equal in terms of usefulness when leveling as Demonology.

PLAYING IN A GROUP

Your standard rotation should be best against most enemies. Demonology Warlocks really shine when there are numerous enemies bunched up in a cluster—should this be the case, use your AoE abilities as described in the Rotation section for maximum damage. You need to be in melee range for some of the abilities to work, so make sure you're ready to Soulshatter to shed some aggro if necessary. Luckily, Metamorphosis form is quite resilient.

A quick note about Glyph of Demon Hunting: it allows you to taunt (through Soulshatter), makes you more resilient, and all-around transforms you into a pseudo-tank. The key here is "pseudo," as it will not transform you into a full-fledged tank. It might be sufficient for lower-level instances, or just for fun, but you might be visiting your friend Spirit Healer if you attempt to tank higher-level content with it.

ROTATION

Dealing damage as Demonology is all about proper use of Metamorphosis. Timing it with other damage-boosting abilities such as trinkets and Grimoire of Sacrifice is optimal.

- Use Metamorphosis if close to 1000 Demonic Fury (or judge how long the enemy is going to live)
- Apply/refresh Corruption (Doom in demon form)
- Apply/refresh Hand of Gul'dan
- If moving, use Fel Flame (Void Ray in demon form)

- Cast Soul Fire if Molten Core is active
- Cast Shadow Bolt
- If you need to AoE, go into demon form and use Hellfire and Chaos Wave. Remember to use your pet's Felstorm ability as well

GROUP BUFFS AND DEBUFFS

Demonology Warlocks convey the Spell Power buff with Dark Intent. Imp pets provide the Stamina buff with Blood Pact.

Warlocks can apply either the Magic Vulnerability debuff with Curse of the Elements, or apply the Slow Cast and Weakened Blows debuffs with Curse of Enfeeblement. The Felguard pet can apply the Mortal Strike debuff with Mortal Cleave.

GETTING READY FOR HIGH-END CONTENT

ALL SPECS

All three Warlock specializations benefit roughly equally from stats that boost spells. Those stats are: Intellect, Spell Damage, Haste, Critical Strike, Hit, and Mastery.

When getting ready for raids, your priority should be to reach the Hit cap (15%). Because raid bosses are three levels higher than you, not having the 15% hit would result in a pretty sharp DPS loss. The only stat you should not sacrifice for Hit (up to the 15%) is Intellect, as it is far more valuable even below the hit cap. That leaves reforging and blue sockets (where you should put purple gems with Hit and Intellect) in order to reach the Hit cap.

DESTRUCTION

Destruction Warlocks are fire-based spellcasters who rain down havoc upon their foes. This explosive specialization tree is especially fun for those who like fast damage, big critical hits, and ample self-healing. Burning Embers are the resource of the Destruction specialization. These appear below your health and mana bars, and you can hold a maximum of three at a time. If you choose the Glyph of Burning Embers, you get an extra for a total of four.

Chaos Bolt, Shadowburn, Ember Tap and Flames of Xoroth all consume one Burning Ember, and have great results, such as huge damage, an instantly revived Demon, or Health restoration. To gain Burning Embers, cast damaging Fire spells. Attacks such as Rain of Fire and Immolate have a chance to generate part of an Ember on critical hits, and Incinerate always generates some of an Ember, making it your primary path to replenishing your store of them. While it may take a little while to fill up one or two, the power of the spells that use them is vast. Since Burning Embers fade soon after combat ends, don't hesitate to use them to your advantage.

MASTERY: EMBERSTORM

Increases the damage of Immolate, Incinerate, Fel Flame and Conflagrate by 9%. Increases the effectiveness of Burning Ember consuming spells by 24%.

SPECIALIZATION ABILITIES

NAME	LEVEL		DESCRIPTION
Chaotic Energy	10		You drain energy directly from the twisting nether. Your mana regenerates faster and your spell haste also increases your mana regeneration. Replaces Life Tap.
Conflagrate	10		Target enemy instantly explodes, dealing Fire damage. If the target is afflicted by Immolate their movement speed is reduced by 50% for 5 sec.
Incinerate	10		Deals Fire damage to an enemy. Generates Burning Embers. Critical strikes double this effect.
Immolate	12		Burns the enemy for Fire damage and then an additional Fire damage over 6 sec. Replaces Corruption.
Rain of Fire	21		Calls down a fiery rain to burn enemies in the area of effect for Fire damage over 6 sec.
Backlash	32		Gives you a 25% chance when hit by a physical attack to reduce the cast time of your next Incinerate spell by 100%. This effect lasts 8 sec and will not occur more than once every 8 seconds.
Havoc	36		Causes the next Chaos Bolt or three other single target spells cast by the Warlock to also strike this target.
Burning Embers	42		Burning Embers are generated by primarily casting Incinerate and are consumed by Chaos Bolt to deal damage or Ember Tap to heal you.
Chaos Bolt	42		Consumes one Burning Ember to unleash a blast of chaos, causing Shadow damage. Chaos Bolt always critically strikes. In addition, the damage is increased by your critical strike chance. Replaces Soul Fire.
Ember Tap	42		Consumes one Burning Ember to restore some of your health.
Shadowburn	47		Instantly blasts the target for Shadow damage. Only useable on enemies that have less than 20% health. Restores 15% of your total mana after 5 sec. If the target dies within 5 sec, and yields experience or honor, the caster gains a Burning Ember instead.
Fire and Brimstone	54		Your next Immolate, Incenerate, Conflagrate, or Curse will hit all targets within 15 yards of the target and deal a percentage of their normal damage.
Aftermath	54		Your Rain of Fire does not need to be channeled and will Stun all enemies struck three times for 2 sec.
Backdraft	69		When you cast Conflagrate, the cast time and mana cost of your next three Incinerates or one Chaos Bolt is reduced by 30%.
Flames of Xoroth	79		The flames of Xoroth instantly revive your last demon.
Pyroclasm	86		Chaos Bolt will be affected by Backdraft, but consumes three charges.

GETTING TO LEVEL 90

Destruction leveling is smoother than it once was, thanks to the added effect of Conflagrate, which slows down enemies. Although you probably shouldn't chain-pull everything in sight like an Affliction Warlock would, you can quickly dispatch enemies one at a time. Cast Immolate and then immediately Conflagrate in order to slow the enemy down. Follow with Incinerate until the enemy dies, or is low enough on health for Immolate to kill it. Burning Embers can be used to open up on an enemy with Chaos Bolt (usually killing it instantly), or Ember Tap can be used, which should keep your health from ever dropping too low.

For talents, take Soul Leech, Shadowfury (another way to slow enemies from getting to you too quickly), Burning Rush, and Kil'Jaeden's Cunning. Grimoire of Sacrifice, along with Soul Leech and Ember Tap, will let you use Burning Rush pretty often.

PLAYING IN A GROUP

As Destruction, it's usually best to focus on a single enemy and then use Havoc on secondary targets. Using Immolate on secondary targets is worth it, but only for a marginal DPS increase, so only do it if it's easy for you to switch back and forth. As usual, keep an eye on threat (especially when using Chaos Bolt early) and Soulshatter as necessary. AoEing as Destruction is tricky, as you have to judge whether to Immolate the targets or not. If most of the enemies will be alive for more than 20 seconds, it's best to Immolate (preferably with Fire and Brimstone) and then Rain of Fire. If you don't have a Burning Ember banked and there are too many enemies to keep Immolate up on all of them, you can cast Rain of Fire, then use single-target spells until you generate an Ember. If you have Embers banked, you can use Fire and Brimstone to spread Immolate, cast Rain of Fire, then cast Incinerate (with or without Fire and Brimstone) to continue generating Embers.

ROTATION

Destruction damage consists of applying the Immolate DoT, using Conflagrate as often as possible, and timing Chaos Bolt with other damage increases.

- Apply/refresh Immolate
- Use Conflagrate if it's off cooldown (this will give you Backdraft, speeding Incinerate up)
- If moving, use Fel Flame
- Cast Chaos Bolt if you have a whole Burning Ember
- Cast Shadowburn if you have a whole Burning Ember, the target is below 20% health and you're moving, or the target is about to die
- Cast Incinerate
- If you need to AoE, just use Rain of Fire for numerous low-health enemies. For heftier enemies, Immolate everything and then Rain of Fire

GROUP BUFFS AND DEBUFFS

Destruction Warlocks convey the Spell Power buff with Dark Intent. Imp pets provide the Stamina buff with Blood Pact.

Warlocks can apply either the Magic Vulnerability debuff with Curse of the Elements, or apply the Slow Cast and Weakened Blows debuffs with Curse of Enfeeblement.

GETTING READY FOR HIGH-END CONTENT

ALL SPECS

All three Warlock specializations benefit roughly equally from stats that boost spells. Those stats are: Intellect, Spell Damage, Haste, Critical Strike, Hit, and Mastery.

When getting ready for raids, your priority should be to reach the Hit cap (15%). Because raid bosses are three levels higher than you, not having the 15% hit would result in a pretty sharp DPS loss. The only stat you should not sacrifice for Hit (up to the 15%) is Intellect, as it is far more valuable even below the hit cap. That leaves reforging and blue sockets (where you should put purple gems with Hit and Intellect) in order to reach the Hit cap.

WARLOCK PETS

All pets come with the abilities Fel Energy and Avoidance. Avoidance is a Passive ability that reduces the damage a summoned demon takes from non-player area of effect attacks by an additional 90%.

SHORT DURATION DEMON PETS

At level 50, Warlocks learn how to summon an Infernal. After being summoned, Infernals remain active for one minute and use powerful AoE attacks. Summon Doomguard, learned at level 56, works in a fashion similar to the Infernal. The difference being that Doomguards cast Doom Bolts at a single target while they are active.

Grimoire of Supremacy renames two demonic pets and boosts their damage output. An Abyssal is an upgraded Infernal, while the improved Doomguard is called a Terrorguard.

IMP

Imps are fragile casters with the ability to heal you over time and dispel magical debuffs. Imps augment the damage output of the Warlock with fire spells.

ABILITY	LVL		DESCRIPTION
Fire Bolt	1		Deals Fire damage to a target.
Blood Pact	4		Increases party and raid members' Stamina by 10%.
Flee	33		Escapes to the Master. Flee removes all stuns and roots.
Cauterize Master	68		Burns the Master's wounds, dealing a small amount of damage, then restoring 12% health over 12 seconds.
Singe Magic	71		Burns harmful magic off the target, removing 1 harmful Magic effect from a friend. Auto-Cast: Cast upon Master when he is stunned, silenced, polymorphed or feared by a magic effect.

FEL IMP

Fel Imps replace Imps when a Warlock selects the level 75 talent, Grimoire of Supremacy. Except where noted in the following table, Fel Imps have the same abilities as Imps.

ABILITY	LVL		DESCRIPTION
Felbolt (replaces Fire Bolt)	75		Deals Fire damage to a target.
Sear Magic (replaces Singe Magic)	75		Burns harmful magic off the target, removing 1 harmful Magic effect from up to 3 friends within 15 yards of the target. Cast upon master when he is stunned, silenced, polymorphed or feared by a magic effect.

VOIDWALKER

Voidwalkers are durable demons with the ability to disarm or taunt enemies to keep them away from you and your allies.

ABILITY	LVL		DESCRIPTION
Torment	10		Torments the target's soul dealing Shadowstrike damage.
Threatening Presence	10		Intimidates any target you attack, increasing your threat generation.
Void Reflexes	10		Increases the Void Walker's chance to dodge and parry by 10%.
Suffering	15		The Voidwalker taunts the target to attack it, but has no effect if the target is already attacking the Voidwalker. Auto-Cast: Taunts the current target if it is not attacking the Voidwalker and taunts any target who attacks its master.
Disarm	20		The Voidwalker strikes at the target's hand, disarming their weapons and shield for 10 seconds.
Shadow Shield	28		Encases the Voidwalker in shadow energy, reducing physical damage taken by 60% for 30 sec. Each time the Voidwalker is struck, a blast of Shadow damage is released, dealing Shadow damage and reducing the power of Shadow Shield by 20%.
Shadow Bulwark	54		Temporarily grants the Voidwalker 30% of their maximum health for 20 seconds. Auto-Cast: Use this ability when below 20% health.

VOIDLORD

Voidlords replace Voidwalkers when a Warlock selects the level 75 talent, Grimoire of Supremacy. Except where noted in the following table, Voidlords have the same abilities as Voidwalkers.

ABILITY	LVL		DESCRIPTION
Void Shield (replaces Shadow Shield)	75		Encases the Voidlord in shadow energy, reducing damage taken by 60% for 30 sec. Each time the Voidlord is struck, a blast of Shadow damage is released, dealing Shadow damage and reducing the power of Void Shield by 20%.

SUCCUBUS

Succubi are fragile seductresses with the ability to deal melee damage, knockback, and crowd control enemies. A Succubus is best used in situations where a foe must be kept at bay, such as PvP.

ABILITY	LVL		DESCRIPTION
Lash of Pain	20		An instant attack that lashes the target, causing Shadow damage.
Seduction	26		Seduces the target, preventing all actions for up to 30 seconds. Any damage will remove the effect. Only works against Humanoids. Auto-Cast: Cast upon targets who stun, silence, or fear their master.
Lesser Invisibility	33		Gives the Succubus Lesser Invisibility for up to 5 minutes. This spell can only be used out of combat.
Whiplash	56		Deals Shadow damage and instantly knocks back all enemies within 5 yards.

SHIVARRA

Shivarra replace Succubi when a Warlock selects the level 75 talent, Grimoire of Supremacy. Except where noted in the following table, Shivarra have the same abilities as Succubi.

ABILITY	LVL		DESCRIPTION
Bladedance (replaces Lash of Pain)	75		An instant attack that lashes the target, causing Shadow damage.
Fellash (replaces Whiplash)	75		Deals Shadow damage and instantly knocks back all enemies within 5 yards.
Mesmerize (replaces Seduction)	75		Mesmerizes the target, preventing all actions for up to 30 sec. Any damage caused will remove the effect. Works against Humanoids, Beasts, Dragonkin, Giants, Mechanical and Undead targets.

FELHUNTER

Felhunters are melee-range demons adept at silencing and stealing buffs from enemies. Because Warlocks don't have an offensive dispel or silence, Felhunters serve as a nice complement to their abilities, especially in PvP.

ABILITY	LVL		DESCRIPTION
Devour Magic	30		Purges 1 beneficial magic effect from an enemy. If an effect is devoured, the Felhunter will be healed and gain energy.
Shadow Bite	29		Bite the enemy, causing Shadow damage.
Spell Lock	50		Silences the enemy for 3 seconds. If used on a casting target, it will counter the enemy's spellcast, preventing any spell from that school of magic being cast for 6 seconds.

OBSERVER

Observers replace Felhunters when a Warlock selects the level 75 talent, Grimoire of Supremacy. Except where noted in the following table, Observers have the same abilities as Felhunters.

ABILITY	LVL		DESCRIPTION
Clone Magic (replaces Devour Magic)	75		Steals 1 beneficial magic effect from an enemy. If an effect is devoured, the Observer will be healed and gain energy.
Tongue Lash (replaces Shadow Bite)	75		Lick the enemy, causing Shadow damage.
Optical Blast (replaces Spell Lock)	75		Blasts the enemy with lasers, dealing damage and silencing the enemy for 3 seconds. If used on a casting target, it will counter the enemy's spellcast, preventing any spell from that school of magic being cast for 6 seconds.

DEMONOLOGY-ONLY PET

FELGUARD

The Felguard are powerful and well-rounded melee demons exclusive to the Demonology tree. Felguard are powerful melee fighters who excel against multiple targets and reduce healing received by their target.

ABILITY	LVL		DESCRIPTION
Legion Strike	10		A sweeping attack that does 130% of the Felguard's weapon damage divided among all targets within 6 yards. The Felguard's current target is also wounded, reducing the effectiveness of any healing received by 10% for 5 sec. Master gains 12 Demonic Fury.
Threatening Presence	10		Intimidates any target you attack, increasing your threat generation.
Void Reflexes	10		Life in the twisting nether has made this demon particularly agile, increasing their chance to dodge and parry by 10%.
Pursuit	43		Charge an enemy, instantly causing weapon damage and increasing the Felguard's movement speed by 30% for 6 seconds.
Felstorm	48		The Felguard recklessly swings its weapon, striking all nearby targets within 8 yards for 150% weapon damage every 1 second for 6 seconds. The Felguard cannot perform any other abilities during Felstorm.

WRATHGUARD

Wrathguards replace Felguards when a Warlock selects the level 75 talent, Grimoire of Supremacy. Except where noted in the following table, Wrathguards have the same abilities as Felguards.

ABILITY	LVL		DESCRIPTION
Axe Toss	75		The Wrathguard hurls his axe, stunning the target for 4 seconds.
Mortal Cleave (replaces Legion Strike)	75		A sweeping attack that does 195% of the Wrathguard's weapon damage divided among all targets within 6 yards. The Wrathguard's current target is also wounded, reducing the effectiveness of any healing received by 25% for 5 sec.

WARRIOR

Warriors are the juggernauts of Azeroth. They combine immense strength and building rage to destroy enemies or protect allies from harm. Warriors specialize in effectively using a variety of weapons in combat; they are able to choose between different combat styles, including dual wielding massive weapons that would normally encumber other classes.

The Warrior is an incredibly mobile melee class, able to charge and leap to quickly get to, or get away from, enemies. Because they're lacking in the ranged damage department, Warriors must keep enemies close with slowing abilities like Hamstring. Warriors depend on equipment quality more than other classes, as they use the full extent of their armor and weapons to both deal damage and prevent it.

RACE AVAILABILITY

ALLIANCE

Draenei
Dwarf
Gnome

Human
Night Elf
Worgen

Pandaren

HORDE

Blood Elf
Goblin
Orc

Tauren
Troll
Undead

RACIAL ADVANTAGES

ALLIANCE

RACE	NOTES
Draenei	Heroic Presence grants Draenei +1% Hit chance. Gift of the Naaru heals the Draenei or any ally. Draenei take less damage from Shadow spells.
Dwarf	Stoneform is excellent for PvP, as it removes all poison, disease, and bleed effects and reduces damage taken. Mace Specialization provides increased Expertise with maces. Dwarves take less damage from Frost spells.
Gnome	Escape Artist provides an extra ability for escaping slow or snare effects; great for PvP. Shortblade Specialization provides increased Expertise with daggers and one hand swords. Gnomes take less damage from Arcane spells.
Human	Every Man for Himself removes effects that cause loss of control of your character, which is great for PvP. Mace and Sword Specialization increases Expertise with swords and maces.
Night Elf	Quickness means Night Elves are less likely to be hit by any physical attack. Night Elves take less damage from Nature spells. Shadowmeld renders the Night Elf invisible while motionless and cancels spells being cast by enemies on the Night Elf.
Worgen	Worgen get 1% increased Critical Strike from Viciousness. Darkflight increases movement speed temporarily. Worgen take less damage from Nature and Shadow spells.

PANDAREN

RACE	NOTES
Pandaren	Epicurean doubles the statistical bonuses from being Well Fed. Quaking Palm acts as a form of brief crowd control.

HORDE

RACE	NOTES
Blood Elf	The signature Blood Elf racial, Arcane Torrent, provides Rage and an AoE silence. The former helps in tight Rage situations, and the latter is great for PvP and certain PvE encounters. Blood Elves take less damage from Arcane spells.
Goblin	Rocket Jump is a great mobility tool. Goblins get 1% increased Haste from Time is Money, making them great for PVP and PVE. Rocket Barrage is another source of damage for Goblins.
Orc	Orcs are great for maximizing damage. Blood Fury increases your attack power for a short period of time. Axe Specialization increases Expertise with axes. Hardiness reduces the duration of stun effects by 15%.
Tauren	Nature Resistance increases a Tauren's ability to stand up to harmful Nature effects. War Stomp provides an (AoE) stun in melee range, and Endurance boosts base health by 5%.
Troll	Berserking grants a temporary increase in attack speed. Da Voodoo Shuffle passively reduces the duration of movement impairing effects, which is important for Warriors. Trolls regenerate Health faster than other races, and 10% of total Health regeneration may continue in combat.
Undead	Undead are more suited for PvP as they can break out of Charm, Fear, and Sleep effects with Will of the Forsaken. Their passive racial, Touch of the Grave, is a life leech and also provides a modest DPS increase in any situation. Undead take less damage from Shadow spells.

EQUIPMENT OPTIONS

ARMOR TYPE	SHIELD
Mail until level 40, then Plate	Yes

USABLE WEAPONS

1 HAND WEAPON	2 HAND WEAPON
Axes	Axes
Daggers	Maces
Fist Weapons	Polearms
Maces	Staves
Swords	Swords

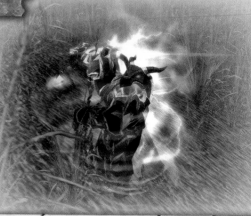

PROMINENT CLASS ABILITIES

STANCES

Warriors can adopt one of three stances, based on the situation and spec, in order to become more efficient at their role. Note that stances are now on the global cooldown, meaning you should not try to constantly switch between them. Instead, assess what the situation calls for in terms of rage, and switch accordingly. Protection Warriors will likely remain in Defensive Stance most of the time, as some of their key abilities require this in order to generate Rage (and it's difficult to tank without the increased threat generation). Arms and Fury Warriors will find themselves using all three stances at some point. For most fights, Battle Stance provides the most Rage. For fights with a steady stream of damage taken (and PvP encounters), Berserker Stance grants more rage. Shields are not recommended for standard DPS use, but they're a requirement for Shield Wall, which can definitely save your life—just remember to switch to a shield/one-hander setup first!

SHOUTS

Warriors use various Shouts to inspire groups or demoralize enemies. Some shouts are available only as talents, and some available only to certain specializations, but every Warrior has a few to choose from.

Commanding Shout and Battle Shout are used to provide benefits for your party or raid, and to generate initial Rage before a fight. These shouts share a 1 minute cooldown. Also, a Warrior's own shouts will over-write each other, therefore in raid groups Warriors must split the shouts between them to enjoy the benefits of both shouts.

The remaining shouts can cause an enemy to flee, reduce the damage they can inflict, do AoE damage, and snare or root enemies within the Warrior's shout radius. Learning how and when to best use these shouts can make the difference between winning or losing an encounter, so keep a level head during combat, and surprise your foe with a mighty roar!

QUICK MOVES

Warriors have always been one of the most mobile classes, which helps to offset their lack of ranged abilities. Though Intercept is gone, talents provide hefty buffs to Charge, which can now be used in combat. Juggernaut allows you to use Charge nearly twice as often, while Double Time lets you use it twice before it incurs its cooldown (and it looks similar to using Charge and then Intercept in previous expansions). Additionally, Heroic Leap allows you to jump a great distance, and there's a glyph to reduce its cooldown. Lastly, Intervene allows you to charge towards an ally and intercept the next single attack made toward them. These abilities, along with Hamstring, should allow you to stay on top of fleeing enemies.

WAR BANNER

Warriors have three level 87 abilities which are mutually exclusive due to cooldowns. You can only use one War Banner at a time, but the buffs (or debuffs) granted by them are significant, and you can also use them as targets for the Intervene ability. The cooldown is on the long side, so expect to be able to use them only once or twice per fight. You choose the location the banners land at, which is great considering their effects are position-sensitive.

NAME	LEVEL		DESCRIPTION
Throw	1		Hurl a dagger at an enemy target. Unlimited ammo used for pulling.
Battle Stance	1		An aggressive combat stance. Generates high Rage from normal melee attacks.
Heroic Strike	1		An attack that instantly deals 100% weapon damage plus extra damage if a one-handed weapon is equipped.
Charge	3		Charge to an enemy, stunning it for 1.50 sec. Generates 20 Rage.
Victory Rush	5		Instantly attack the target, causing damage and healing you for 20% of your maximum health. Can only be used within 20 sec after you kill an enemy that yields experience or honor.
Execute	7		Attempt to finish off a wounded foe, causing physical damage. Only usable on enemies that have less than 20% health.
Defensive Stance	9		Decreases damage taken by 15%. Significantly increases threat generation. Generates 1 Rage every 3 sec while in combat.
Taunt	12		Taunts the target to attack you, but has no effect if the target is already attacking you.
Enrage	14		Mortal Strike, Bloodthirst and Colossus Smash critical strikes and critical blocks Enrage you, generating 10 Rage and increasing physical damage done by 10% for 6 sec.
Sunder Armor	16		Sunders the target, causing Weakened Armor. Weakened Armor: Weakens the armor of the target, increasing melee damage.
Thunder Clap	20		Blasts enemies within 8 yards for damage and applies the Weakened Blows effect. Weakened Blows: Demoralizes the target, reducing their physical damage dealt.
Heroic Throw	22		Throw your weapon at the enemy, causing 50% weapon damage.
Pummel	24		Pummel the target, interrupting spellcasting and preventing any spell in that school from being cast for 4 sec.
Disarm	28		Disarm the enemy's weapons and shield for 10 sec. Disarmed creatures deal significantly reduced damage.
Deep Wounds	32		Your Mortal Strike, Bloodthirst, and Devastate cause the target to bleed for Physical damage over 15 sec.
Berserker Stance	34		A reckless combat stance. Generates some Rage from normal melee attacks and some Rage from damage taken.
Hamstring	36		Maims the enemy, reducing movement speed by 50% for 15 sec.
Battle Shout	42		Increases the attack power of all raid and party members within 100 yards by 10%. Lasts 5 min. Generates 20 Rage.
Cleave	44		A sweeping attack that strikes the target and an additional nearby target, dealing 82% weapon damage.
Shield Wall	48		Reduces all damage taken by 40% for 12 sec.
Intimidating Shout	52		Causes the targeted enemy to cower in fear, and up to 5 additional enemies within 8 yards to flee. Lasts 8 sec.
Berserker Rage	54		You become Enraged, generating 10 Rage and increasing physical damage done by 10% for 6 sec. Also removes and grants immunity to Fear, Sap and Incapacitate effects for the duration of Berserker Rage.
Recklessness	62		Grants your special attacks an additional 50% chance to critically hit. Lasts 12 sec.
Deadly Calm	64		You enter a battle trance, reducing the cost of your next 3 Heroic Strike or Cleave attacks by 10 Rage.
Spell Reflection	66		Raise your shield, reflecting the next spell cast on you. Lasts 5 sec.
Commanding Shout	68		Increases the Stamina of all party and raid members within 100 yards by 10%. Lasts 5 min. Generates 20 Rage.
Intervene	72		Run at high speed towards a party or raid member, intercepting the next melee or ranged attack while the target remains within 10 yards.
Shattering Throw	74		Throws your weapon at the enemy causing damage, reducing the armor on the target by 20% for 10 sec or removing any invulnerabilities.
Rallying Cry	83		Temporarily grants you and all party or raid members within 30 yards 20% of maximum health for 10 sec. After the effect expires, the health is lost.
Heroic Leap	85		Leap through the air towards a targeted location, slamming down with destructive force to deal Physical damage to all enemies within 8 yards.
Demoralizing Banner	87		Throw down a war banner within 30 yards that decreases the damage dealt by all enemies within 30 yards of the banner by 10%. Lasts 15 sec. You can Intervene to your war banner.
Mocking Banner	87		Throw down a war banner within 30 yards that forces all enemies within 15 yards of the banner to focus attacks on the Warrior for 6 sec. Lasts 30 sec. You can Intervene to your war banner.
Skull Banner	87		Throw down a war banner at your feet that increases the critical damage of party or raid members within 30 yards of the banner by 20%. Lasts 10 sec. You can Intervene to your war banner.

TALENTS

TALENT	DESCRIPTION	NOTES
LEVEL 15 TIER (MOVEMENT)		
Juggernaut	You can Charge every 12 sec instead of every 20 sec.	A great mobility tool that allows you to use Charge much more often.
Double Time	You can use charge twice in a row. Each use has a 20 sec recharge time. Charge can only grant Rage once every 12 sec.	A more burst-like version of Juggernaut, this also lets you use Charge more often. Note that you can only gain rage from Charge every 12 seconds.
Warbringer	Your Charge also knocks a target to the ground and stuns it for 3 sec.	This talent won't make you any more mobile; instead, it extends Charge's stun by knocking the target to the ground. Good for keeping a target still, preferably during other cooldowns.
LEVEL 30 TIER (HEALING)		
Enraged Regeneration	Instantly heals you for 10% of your total health, and an additional 10% over 5 sec. Can be used while stunned. Costs no Rage if used while Enraged.	Of the three in this tier, this one will most likely save your life in an emergency, but it has the longest cooldown. As a bonus, it can be used while stunned and costs no rage if you're enraged.
Second Wind	Whenever you are below 35% health, you regenerate 3% health per second. Whenever you are struck by a Stun or Immobilize effect, you generate 20 Rage over 10 sec.	This talent is best used to survive attrition battles where you know you'll be constantly below 35% health. The stun or immobilize part happens quite often in PvP, so it's also good should you be short on rage in that situation.
Impending Victory	Replaces Victory Rush. Instantly attack the target causing damage and healing you for 10% of your maximum health. Killing an enemy that yields experience or honor resets the cooldown of Impending Victory and causes your next Impending Victory to heal for 20% of your maximum health.	This is an improved version of Victory Rush that allows you to use it at any time with a penalty to efficiency (and a cooldown). Note that if you kill an enemy, the cooldown resets, allowing you to use its boosted version. This talent is the staple of solo leveling, and holds its own in several other situations.
LEVEL 45 TIER (CONTROL)		
Staggering Shout	Causes all enemies within 20 yards that are snared to become rooted for 5 sec.	Fairly straightforward AoE root that allows you to leap out of sticky situations, or maybe even save a dying teammate in PvP.
Piercing Howl	Snares all enemies within 15 yards, reducing their movement speed by 50% for 15 sec.	An old Warrior favorite, this ability is great for kiting several enemies, or just slowing one that's just out of range of Hamstring.
Disrupting Shout	Interrupts all spellcasting within 10 yards and prevents any spell in that school from being cast for 4 sec.	This situational talent really excels when there are numerous casters that must be interrupted. It can also be used in conjunction with Pummel to interrupt more often in PvP (and Charge, and Intimidating Shout, and Shockwave).
LEVEL 60 TIER (CONTROL)		
Bladestorm	You become a whirling storm of destructive force, striking all targets within 8 yards for 120% weapon damage every 1 sec for 6 sec. During a Bladestorm, you can continue to dodge, block, and parry, and are immune to movement impairing and loss of control effects. However, you can be disarmed and you can only perform shout abilities.	Bladestorm provides the best AoE burst for Warriors, which is best used in situations where there are numerous weak enemies around you (e.g., leveling or certain boss fights).
Shockwave	Sends a wave of force in a frontal cone before you, causing damage and stunning all enemy targets within 10 yards for 4 sec.	The short cooldown makes this an excellent control tool, especially for tanks. As with other stuns, it provides an extra interrupt in PvP, should you need one.
Dragon Roar	Roar ferociously, causing damage to all enemies within 8 yards, knocking them back and knocking them down for 3 sec. Dragon Roar is always a critical strike and ignores all armor on the target.	Dragon Roar is like a mix of Shockwave and Bladestorm, having a moderate cooldown, stunning enemies shortly and also dealing the best on-demand burst damage that a Warrior can get. When combined with other cooldowns, such as Skull Banner and Avatar, it can be extremely powerful.
LEVEL 75 TIER (AID)		
Mass Spell Reflection	Reflects the next spell cast on you and on all party and raid members within 20 yards for 5 sec.	Great for situations where allies are in danger of dying to single-target spells. Protection Warriors can use this on the pull for enemy packs that have a lot of casters.
Safeguard	Replaces Intervene. Run at high speed towards a party or raid member, removing all movement-impairing effects upon you, intercepting the next melee or ranged attack made against them and reducing their damage taken by 20% for 6 sec.	Transforms Intervene into a very useful damage-reducing cooldown on an ally (cannot be used on yourself, however). Additionally, it removes movement-impairing effects, which is very important for warriors in PvP.
Vigilance	Focus your protective gaze on a party or raid member, transferring 30% of damage taken to you for 12 sec. During the duration of Vigilance, your Taunt has no cooldown.	Like Safeguard, this is a potential life-saver on an ally. The Taunt cooldown removal is great for when there are numerous enemies that must be attacking you.
LEVEL 90 TIER (DAMAGE)		
Avatar	You transform into an unstoppable colossus for 20 sec, increasing your damage dealt by 20% and causing your attacks to generate 30% extra Rage. While transformed you are immune to movement impairing effects.	This makes you pretty much unstoppable for a short time, working as both a damage-increasing and movement cooldown. Great for both PvE and PvP, but do notice the considerable cooldown.
Bloodbath	For the next 12 sec, causes your melee special attacks to deal an additional 30% damage as a bleed over 6 sec. While bleeding, the target moves at 50% reduced speed.	While active, this cooldown applies a very large DoT based on how much damage your skills deal. The movement speed part is great for PvP, as you won't have to worry about using Hamstring when this is active. The DoT is a bleed, which cannot be cleansed by normal means.
Storm Bolt	Hurl your weapon at an enemy, causing 100% weapon damage and stunning the target for 3 sec. Deals an additional 300% weapon damage to targets that are permanently immune to stuns.	The shortest cooldown on this tier, Storm Bolt is also useful in both PvE and PvP. Do note, however, that this ability is ranged, similarly to Weapon Throw, providing an extra ranged stun in PvP on a modest cooldown.

ARMS

Arms Warriors, as their name suggests, excel in the mastery of weapons. Being able to use nearly all weapons available in the game, these battle-hardened juggernauts use mobility and finesse to defeat their opponents. Because of passive skills like Seasoned Soldier, Arms Warriors prefer the use of two-handed weapons to dish out their damage. In contrast with the Fury specialization, Arms damage is more controlled and has on-demand burst, including skills that can greatly aid in damaging multiple enemies at once.

Arms Warriors benefit from having multiple targets to attack. Their use of Sweeping Strikes allows for far more damage output when there are more targets to hit.

MASTERY: STRIKES OF OPPORTUNITY

Grants a chance for your melee attacks to instantly trigger an additional melee attack for 55% normal damage.

SPECIALIZATION ABILITIES

ABILITY	LEVEL		DESCRIPTION
Mortal Strike	10		A vicious strike that deals 195% weapon damage plus more and causes Mortal Wounds on the target. Generates 10 Rage.
Seasoned Soldier	10		While wielding a two-handed melee weapon, your Physical damage dealt is increased by 20%.
Slam	18		Slams the opponent, causing 215% weapon damage plus more.
Whirlwind	26		In a whirlwind of steel you attack all enemies within 8 yards, causing 85% weapon damage to each enemy.
Overpower	30		Only usable after the target dodges. Instantly overpower the enemy causing 130% weapon damage. Cannot be blocked, dodged or parried. Overpower has a 60% increased chance to be a critical strike.
Blood and Thunder	46		Your Thunder Clap now also applies Deep Wounds.
Taste for Blood	50		Your Mortal Strike also enables the use of Overpower. In addition, Overpower hits have a 30% chance to enable the use of an additional Overpower and increase the damage of your next Heroic Strike or Cleave within 9 sec by 100%. This effect stacks up to 5 times.
Die by the Sword	56		Increases your parry chance by 100% and reduces damage taken by 20% for 8 sec.
Sweeping Strikes	60		Your melee attacks strike an additional nearby opponent. Lasts 10 sec.
Colossus Smash	81		Smashes a target for 175% weapon damage plus more and weakens their defenses, allowing your attacks to entirely bypass 100% of their armor for 6 sec, and causes the Physical Vulnerability effect on the target. Bypasses less armor on players.
Sudden Death	81		Your melee hits have a 20% chance of resetting the cooldown on your Colossus Smash.

GETTING TO LEVEL 90

Arms Warriors are one of the most efficient leveling machines in the game. The way it works is fairly straightforward: Charge in order to get to your enemy and generate rage, then use Colossus Smash on cooldown and Mortal Strike. This allows you to use Overpower (which has a 60% increased critical chance), which sometimes allows for an extra Overpower (this can keep going on forever if you're lucky). If Overpower didn't let you use another Overpower use Slam and Mortal Strike as soon as it's back up, and then repeat the process. Below 20%, use Execute.

For talents, Juggernaut lets you use Charge much more often, Impending Victory lets you instantly gain health in emergency situations (Second Wind is a solid alternative), and Bladestorm allows you to defeat several enemies at once. Instead of the latter, Dragon Roar is also a good choice.

PLAYING IN A GROUP

Use your standard rotation for single enemies, using DPS-increasing cooldowns as desired while avoiding stealing the tank's threat (this is especially important for Warriors, as they are a melee class that has no threat reduction moves). When there are two enemies close together, you should use Sweeping Strikes, as this results in an incredible DPS increase and is one of the most efficient ways to dispatch two enemies at once. For a greater number of enemies, still use Sweeping Strikes, but use your excess rage on Cleave (instead of Heroic Strike) and Whirlwind.

If you pull aggro, or your tank happens to die, you can still save the day by using Die by the Sword, which provides 100% parry chance and will keep you from taking damage for 8 seconds. If that doesn't work, equip a shield and a one-handed weapon (this can be done through a macro as well) and use Shield Wall, which will hopefully give your group enough time to recover.

BASIC ROTATION

Arms Warriors deal damage primarily through instant melee-based abilities, while taking advantage of the Colossus Smash debuff. In PvE, during what's called "execute range" (an enemy is below 20% health), Arms and Fury warriors shine due to their damage output from Execute, which can be devastating when paired with other damage-increasing cooldowns.

- Use Charge to quickly close the distance to your enemy and generate some initial rage

- If available, use Colossus Smash so your subsequent attacks bypass the enemy's armor

- If the enemy is below 20% health, use Execute

- If available, use Mortal Strike

- If available, use Overpower

- Versus single targets, dump rage with Slam; against more than one target, dump rage with Whirlwind

GROUP BUFFS AND DEBUFFS

Warriors provide the Attack Power buff with Battle Shout and the Stamina buff with Commanding Shout. They inflict the Weakened Armor debuff with Sunder Armor and Weakened Blows with Thunderclap.

Arms Warriors add to the debuffs provided by other Warriors by applying Mortal Wound with Mortal Strike and Physical Vulnerability via Colossus Smash.

GETTING READY FOR HIGH-END CONTENT

ARMS

Like other melee-based classes, your priority should be increasing your Hit until you're no longer at risk of missing attacks on boss-level monsters. After that, go for Expertise until boss enemies have a low chance of dodging your attacks.

For sheer damage output, always prioritize Strength (even over Hit) in places that allow it, such as gems. At times, skipping gem bonuses in favor of more strength gems is favorable—just don't pass up worthwhile bonuses (meaning those that include Strength, generally). Critical Strike and Mastery are important to have, but not as important as Strength, Hit, and Expertise.

FURY

Fury Warriors are designed to deal massive, constant melee damage with either two one-handed weapons, or (starting at level 38) two two-handed weapons. Crazed Berserker increases autoattack damage by 10%, and off-hand damage by 25%. While other classes, like Rogues, can dual wield one-handed weapons, the ability to dual wield the heavier set of weapons is exclusive to Fury Warriors. This makes them quick-attacking berserkers that deal an immense amount of steady damage.

Additionally, the Fury-exclusive passive Single-Minded Fury increases your damage output while dual wielding one-handed weapons, making them roughly similar to two-handers in terms of damage.

Fury Warriors often trade their safety for increased damage output. This puts them at risk of dying in groups. However, when played well, you can learn to avoid stealing threat and let the tanks do their job. Avoid grabbing the attention of the monster, kill your targets, and know how to get out of trouble.

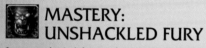 MASTERY: UNSHACKLED FURY

Increases physical damage done while Enraged.

SPECIALIZATION ABILITIES

ABILITY	LEVEL		DESCRIPTION
Bloodthirst	10		Generates 10 Rage. Instantly attack the target, dealing 100% weapon damage plus more with your main hand weapon and restoring 1% of your health. Bloodthirst has double the normal chance to be a critical strike.
Crazed Berserker	10		You are a master of dual-wield combat, and can equip one-hand and off-hand weapons in your off-hand. Increases autoattack damage by 10% and off-hand damage by 25%.
Wild Strike	18		A quick strike with your off-hand weapon that deals 220% weapon damage plus more and causes Mortal Wounds on the target.
Whirlwind	20		In a whirlwind of steel you attack all enemies within 8 yards, causing 85% weapon damage to each enemy.
Raging Blow	30		A mighty blow that deals 200% weapon damage from both melee weapons. Becoming Enraged enables one use of Raging Blow. Limit 2 charges.
Single-Minded Fury	38		When you dual-wield one-handed weapons, all damage is increased by 35%, and your off-hand weapon will deal an additional 35% damage.
Titan's Grip	38		Allows you to dual-wield a pair of two-handed weapons.
Bloodsurge	50		Your Bloodthirst hits have a 20% chance of lowering the global cooldown to 1 sec and reducing the Rage cost by 20 of your next 3 Wild Strikes.
Die by the Sword	56		Increases your parry chance by 100% and reduces damage taken by 20% for 8 sec.
Meat Cleaver	58		Dealing damage with Whirlwind increases the number of targets that your Raging Blow hits by 1. This effect stacks up to 3 times. Using Raging Blow will consume this effect.
Flurry	60		Your melee hits have a 9% chance to increase your attack speed by 25% for your next 3 swings.
Colossus Smash	81		Smashes a target for 175% weapon damage plus more and weakens their defenses, allowing your attacks to entirely bypass 100% of their armor for 6 sec, and causes the Physical Vulnerability effect on the target. Bypasses less armor on players.

GETTING TO LEVEL 90

Fury Warriors level at a respectable pace thanks to Bloodthirst and Victory Rush. Note that Fury is more gear-dependent than Arms when it comes to leveling, so its efficiency will be based on your weapons and how much Hit and Expertise you have through your gear. That said, the leveling process itself is fairly simple: Charge, use Bloodthirst (to generate Rage and get the Bloodsurge buff to reduce Wild Strike rage requirements), then continue your normal rotation. There are several factors that can increase how quickly an enemy is dispatched, most important of which is how many times you proc Enrage.

For talents, Juggernaut lets you use Charge much more often, Impending Victory allows you to gain health in emergency situations (Second Wind is a viable alternative), and Bladestorm allows you to defeat several enemies at once, though Dragon Roar (same level as Bladestorm) is a good choice as well.

PLAYING IN A GROUP

Execute your standard rotation for single enemies, using DPS-increasing cooldowns but do not to pull threat (this is especially important for Warriors, a class that has no threat reducing moves). When fighting multiple enemies, it's important to take advantage of Meat Cleaver, which increases the number of targets hit by your Raging Blow every time you use Whirlwind (stacking up to 3 times). Because Raging Blow deals a large amount of damage, this passive makes Fury Warriors with sufficient Rage a great AoE specialization.

If you pull aggro, or your tank happens to die, you can still save the day by using Die by the Sword, which provides 100% parry chance and will keep you from taking damage for 8 seconds. If that doesn't work, equip a shield and a one-handed weapon (this can be done through a macro as well) and use Shield Wall, which will hopefully give your group enough time to recover.

BASIC ROTATION

Fury Warriors deal damage primarily through instant melee-based abilities. Colossus Smash should be used consistently, almost every time it is available, in order to maintain the Physical Vulnerability debuff. In PvE, during what's called "execute range" (the enemy is below 20% health), Fury Warriors shine due to Execute, which can be devastating when paired with other damage-increasing cooldowns.

- Use Charge to quickly close the distance to your enemy and generate some initial rage

- If available, use Bloodthirst to generate Rage and deal damage

- If the enemy is below 20% health, use Execute

- If you have any charges, use Raging Blow

- Use Wild Strike

GROUP BUFFS AND DEBUFFS

Warriors provide the Attack Power buff with Battle Shout and the Stamina buff with Commanding Shout. They also inflict the Weakened Armor debuff with Sunder Armor and Weakened Blows with Thunderclap.

Fury Warriors add to the debuffs provided by other Warriors with Wild Strike inflicting Mortal Wound and Colossus Smash imparting Physical Vulnerability.

GETTING READY FOR HIGH-END CONTENT

FURY

Your goal is stack Strength while still being able to hit boss-level enemies. Your next stat priority is Expertise. After Hit and Expertise are no longer concerns, the stat to prioritize next depends on whether you're running out of Rage frequently or not. If so, Haste provides more Rage but less damage than Mastery or Critical Strike.

PROTECTION

Protection Warriors are shield-bearing tanks that protect allies from harm by holding the attention of enemies. One of the best tools Protection Warriors have for keeping attention on them is Devastate. Devastate replaces Sunder Armor and applies the Weakened Armor debuff but has the added benefit of inflicting a good bit of damage at the same time. At higher levels, Protection Warriors get more tools that enhance their survivability (Last Stand, Bastion of Defense, Shield Barrier) and ability to tank multiple targets at the same time (Revenge, Blood and Thunder).

What sets Protection Warriors apart from other tanks is their superior mobility. Between Charge, Intervene and Heroic Leap, Protection Warriors can move almost instantaneously to a hostile target (and stun it at the same time), a friendly target (and save it from an incoming attack at the same time), or to a specific location (and damage nearby enemies at the same time).

MASTERY: CRITICAL BLOCK

Increases your chance to block and your chance to critically block.

SPECIALIZATION ABILITIES

ABILITY	LEVEL		DESCRIPTION
Shield Slam	10		Slam the target with your shield, causing damage. Generates 15 Rage in Defensive Stance.
Unwavering Sentinel	10		Increases your total Stamina by 15%. Reduces the chance you will be critically hit by melee attacks by 6%. Increases your armor value from items by 10%. Reduces the Rage cost of Thunder Clap by 100%.
Vengeance	10		Each time you take damage in Defensive Stance, you gain 5% of the damage taken as attack power, up to a maximum of 10% of your health.
Shield Block	18		Raise your shield, blocking every melee attack against you for 6 sec. These blocks can be critical blocks.
Devastate	26		Replaces Sunder Armor. Deals 220% weapon damage plus more and sunders the target, causing Weakened Armor.
Revenge	30		Instantly attack an enemy and two additional enemies. A successful dodge or parry will reset the cooldown on Revenge. Generates 10 Rage in Defensive Stance.
Last Stand	38		Increases current and maximum health by 30% for 20 sec.
Blood and Thunder	46		Your Thunder Clap now also applies Deep Wounds.
Sword and Board	50		Your Devastate has a 30% chance of resetting the cooldown of your Shield Slam and increasing the Rage it generates by 5. Lasts 5 sec.
Demoralizing Shout	56		Demoralizes all enemies within 10 yards, reducing the damage they do to you by 20% for 10 sec.
Ultimatum	56		Your Shield Slam has a 30% chance to make your next Heroic Strike or Cleave cost no Rage.
Bastion of Defense	60		Increases your block chance by 10% and your dodge chance by 2%. Reduces the cooldown of your Shield Wall by 3 min.
Shield Barrier	81		Raise your shield, absorbing damage for the next 6 sec. Consumes up to 60 Rage to increase the amount absorbed. Absorption amount increases with attack power.

GETTING TO LEVEL 90

Protection is the slowest leveler of the three Warrior specializations, but Victory Rush makes Protection Warriors close to indestructible when facing same-level monsters with a shield. When you tackle multiple enemies at once, Shield Slam has a good chance to make Cleave Rage-free, while Blood and Thunder makes Thunder Clap apply Deep Wounds on all nearby enemies. Revenge strikes three targets at once, so try to pull groups of three enemies at a time once you feel comfortable with your rotation. Stay in Defensive Stance through these fights since Vengeance is the source of a good deal of your damage output, and there are abilities that will only generate Rage in Defensive Stance.

For talents, Juggernaut lets you use Charge much more often, and Impending Victory lets you instantly gain health in emergency situations (Second Wind is a viable alternative to Impending Victory). Dragon Roar is a good choice since it's another source of AoE damage and also knocks down nearby enemies. Bladestorm deals bonus damage for Protection Warriors, so it is a viable alternative to Dragon Roar, especially for leveling.

PLAYING IN A GROUP

Playing a Protection Warrior is all about managing Rage and using defensive cooldowns in critical situations. You can use Shield Block twice every 9 seconds, but it costs 60 Rage, which means you should save it for the times you know it will mitigate damage and save healer mana. Skilled Protection Warriors know when to use Shield Block and Shield Barrier, and when it's best to spend the Rage generating more threat by using damage-inflicting skills.

In emergency situations, use long cooldown abilities—Last Stand and Shield Wall—to survive a heavy siege. Don't hesitate to use Disarm on enemies that have weapons, as it doesn't cost any rage now.

BASIC ROTATION

Your number one job as a tank is to generate threat as quickly as possible and maintain it throughout the fight. When you're confronted with a pack of enemies, consider using Heroic Leap instead of Charge to open the fight. Heroic Leap deals damage to all enemies near the landing location, giving you a head start on threat. Otherwise, use Charge and then Thunder Clap to get their attention.

- Use Charge to quickly close the distance to your enemy and generate some initial rage
- Use Shield Slam to deal damage and generate rage
- Use Thunderclap to apply the Weakened Blows debuff
- To increase your defenses, use Shield Block or Shield Barrier if you have sufficient rage
- If available, use Revenge
- Use Devastate

GROUP BUFFS AND DEBUFFS

Protection Warriors provide the Attack Power buff with Battle Shout and the Stamina buff with Commanding Shout. They also inflict the Weakened Armor debuff with Devastate and Weakened Blows with Thunderclap.

GETTING READY FOR HIGH-END CONTENT

PROTECTION

Being a tank, your gear levels are more crucial to surviving an encounter than the rest of your group or raid. Your biggest upgrade, survivability-wise, will likely be your shield. Don't be afraid to take up DPS-oriented gear of higher item level than your current gear if nobody needs it. Reforge undesirable stats (like Hit when over the Hit cap) to more survivability-oriented ones. Mastery is a great secondary stat—you can rarely go wrong with stacking it, but it's most beneficial to obtain all the worthwhile gem bonuses by using gems of the right color. For red gems, use Dodge or Parry (try to keep the two percentages close to each other due to diminishing returns). For the rest, use Stamina or Mastery, depending on your playstyle. Mastery provides more survivability against physical attacks while Stamina provides more raw health and is perhaps better for encounters with magical damage.

PLAYER VERSUS PLAYER COMBAT

PvP Combat comes in many flavors, and there's bound to be at least one type you'll enjoy. Some players like to test their skills in one-on-one duels. Battlegrounds provide opportunities for larger teams to work toward objectives while stopping the other side from accomplishing those same objectives. World PvP is often a chaotic affair with no guarantee of meeting foes of the same level or in the same numbers. There are also two types of PvP where you could find yourself facing off against your own faction: Arenas and Rated Battlegrounds. Arenas offer deathmatch-style battles where small teams face off. Rated Battlegrounds use a limited selection of Battleground maps and require full groups of 10 to queue for them.

DUELING

Dueling another player is one way to practice your PvP skills. You can duel on any kind of server, and you can duel players from either faction.

To start a duel, right-click on a player's portrait and click "Duel." A duel flag appears, and your opponent can choose to accept or decline. If they accept, a countdown begins, indicating when the duel will start. A duel ends when one player's health is reduced to 1. Anyone who runs too far away from the duel flag loses by default, so that is another way that the match can end.

Outside of an achievement, there are no tangible rewards to dueling other players. You cannot gain Honor in this way, nor can you loot anything from your opponents. The person who loses the duel doesn't actually die, so they won't have to deal with durability loss or reclaiming their body.

WORLD PvP: PvP SERVERS

On PvP servers, Horde and Alliance players are actively at war. Anytime you enter neutral, contested, or enemy territory, you can be attacked by players of the opposite faction. This completely changes the nature of the game; while you are completing quests, you must also look for and defend against the enemy. Many players on PvP servers game with regular groups for protection.

PvP kills of the opposite faction yield Honor. But you never know what's ahead. Even if you find a solo character and kill them, there could be all kinds of trouble heading your way as a result!

PvP deaths that don't involve damage from monsters or falling won't cost you money. There isn't a durability loss as a result of these fights. You must still run back and claim your body or resurrect at a graveyard, though.

WORLD PvP: PvE SERVERS

If you are on a PvE server, you can choose to engage in PvP combat. Right-click your own character portrait and click PvP-Enable. You can now engage in PvP with other players who have turned on their PvP flags. When you click Disable, your PvP flag remains on for another 5 minutes.

You can tell that another player is flagged for PvP because their colors change. Someone flagged (when you are not) will look like a neutral target. As soon as you flag, they become red, signaling that combat can initiate at any time. Honor rewards and combat dynamics are exactly the same on PvE and PvP servers. Needing to flag for combat is the only difference between them.

If you get in over your head, enemies might kill you and corpse camp your character. That means that they wait for you to resurrect near your body, hoping to kill you again. Wait for 5 minutes, if necessary, and let your PvP flag fall. Doing so allows you to come back to life safely.

As an alternative, call for help from buddies or from people in the region. Use /general chat to let other players know that flagged targets are in a certain area. Someone might show up for a free fight!

BATTLEGROUNDS

Battlegrounds are instanced PvP combat areas for players above level 10. Players fight Horde versus Alliance in a structured game setting. You can enter a battleground alone or with a group of comrades. To get the most out of your time in Battlegrounds, try random Battlegrounds and spend time in the Battleground Call to Arms during the weekends. The Battleground Call to Arms changes every week, and the schedule appears on the in-game calendar. There are 10 total battlegrounds, including two new maps for Mists of Pandaria: Silvershard Mine and Temple of Kotmogu.

PVP CURRENCY

You earn Honor Points by killing players from the opposing faction or by participating in Battlegrounds. If you accumulate enough points, you can use them to purchase items, such as PvP gear. Honor Points are listed in the Currency tab of your Character window. While there's no limit on how many Honor Points you earn each week, there is a limit on how many you can store at any given time. If you hit the cap, you must spend some Honor Points and you can start earning additional points immediately.

Conquest Points work similarly to Honor Points, but are a bit harder to obtain. Conquest Points come from participating in Arenas, Rated Battlegrounds, taking part in random Battlegrounds or the cyclical Battleground Call to Arms. There is a weekly cap on how many Conquest Points you can earn, and how many you can store at any given time.

When each new Arena season begins, all your Conquest Points are converted to Honor Points, and some of the Conquest Rewards from the previous season are made available for purchase with Honor Points.

RATED BATTLEGROUNDS

Rated Battlegrounds offer a way for players who enjoy PvP, but not Arena matches, to obtain the best gear possible. Rated Battlegrounds are 10 vs. 10 and use the following maps: Warsong Gulch, Arathi Basin, Eye of the Storm, Silvershard Mines, Temple of Kotmogu, Battle for Gilneas, and Twin Peaks.

Only fully premade groups can take part in Rated Battlegrounds. Just as with Arenas, your group will be matched up with teams of similar ranking, and level of gear. Good Premades aren't just going to know each other. They're going to use voice chat extensively, tactics that they've played before, and use every trick in the book. They're almost undefeatable if your team isn't similarly prepared.

Other than improved equipment, rewards from participation in Rated Battlegrounds include mounts, titles for your character, and Achievements.

RATINGS

You are given two different ratings if you take part in Arena fights or Rated Battlegrounds. There is a Personal Rating that reflects your win/loss performance in Rated Battlegrounds and Arenas. There is also a Team Rating that reflects the win/loss performance of a given Arena or Rated Battleground Team.

Team Ratings are used to match up teams in Arenas and Rated Battlegrounds. You must have a minimum Personal Rating in order to purchase the best PvP equipment available in each current season.

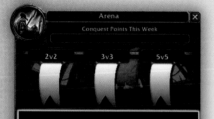

ARENA

Arena combat offers unstructured, highly competitive PvP. Teams of 2, 3, or 5 compete against each other in a ranked series of tournaments. There are seasons for this, and the rewards that come from Arena are on par with what you can get from Ranked Battleground matches.

There is no forum more competitive than the Arena. People must specialize their characters extremely well. They really must know all the ins and outs of their class and be able to use them at just the right moment. They must also find partners who complement their playstyle and skill as well as possible. Tactics and strategies for the Arena change constantly, and the best way to stay on top of things is to read forums and visit websites dedicated to Arena tactics.

WAR GAMES

War Games allows you to challenge a specific guild, or group of friends, and face them in a Battleground or Arena. There are no rewards from War Games, other than practice in a controlled environment and bragging rights. War Games ignores faction ties, which means you can challenge any other similarly-sized group, even if that group is comprised of other people from your guild! The groups can agree on a Battleground, or they can let the game pick one for them.

NEW BATTLEGROUND MAPS

Silvershard Mine

Style of Play	Escort
Level Brackets	90

This battleground takes place underneath Stranglethorn Vale in a Venture Co. goblin mine. Silvershard Mines is a 10 vs. 10 escort battleground, where each side attempts to control diamond carts until they reach the mine depot.

Mine carts continually spawn in the center mine depot and head out in one of three directions on mine tracks. These tracks head out to different depots and some tracks have track switch locations to redirect the mine cart. These switches require you to stand near them for a few seconds to switch the current track of the cart.

Mine carts have a circle of control around them, and once a faction has more teammates than their enemy, control moves towards their end of the dominance bar. When the cart reaches the depot destination whoever is currently in control of the cart receives points towards total victory.

Temple of Kotmogu

Style of Play	Powerball
Level Brackets	90

The Horde and Alliance wage battle for the ancient Mogu artifact that is foretold to hold great powers.

Temple of Kotmogu is a 10 vs. 10 powerball battleground where each side attempts to control the Mogu Artifacts for as long as possible in different scoring zones. The longer you hold an Orb of Power the more damage your character receives from enemies and the less healing you receive from allies. There is also a very significant damage boost the longer you hold an Orb of Power.

Inside the Temple, players see four pillars of light where the Orbs of Power are located. These locations are set and the Orbs of Power always return to their respective location if a player is ever defeated while holding one. There are three different scoring areas in the Temple of Kotmogu while holding the Orbs of Power. The least valuable area is the outer courtyard and garden area giving you very little points over time. Next are the walkways where the Orbs spawn. This area is surrounded by Mogu statues and ancient Mogu archways which gives you an average amount of points while in the area if you are carrying an Orb. Finally, there is the lower courtyard in the middle of the map, which is the most vulnerable location of the three but the most rewarding for your team if you are carrying an Orb of Power. There are only two exits from this location making escape very hard without support from your team.

NEW ARENA

TOL'VIRON ARENA

The Tol'Viron Arena is a new map located in the desert area of Uldum. When players enter the arena they see a large open area surrounded by sandstone walls with hieroglyphics etched into their surface. Three large statues are also inside this arena, which are the only structures that can be used to break line of sight from your opponents. This map is fairly straightforward with no traps or environmental effects to hurt you or lure your opponents into.

PvP Tips by Class

PvP tactics change considerably depending on the situation, and the goals of the battleground or arena in which you find yourself. They also change constantly as new abilities and talents are introduced to the game, or existing abilities and talents are modified. If you want to remain at the top of the PvP heap, look for active discussion boards, find the other top PvP players on your server or battlegroup and stay current.

The following pages provide the tools available to each class and should serve only as a starting point for your journey to the top of the rankings. They are broken down into broad categories so you can easily find the tools you need for your character, or the abilities of other classes you may need to counter.

DEATH KNIGHT

Death Knights have an impressive array of tools available to them, so you must be proficient with their proper use. Additionally, you need to be incredibly familiar with your keybindings. Death Knight is predominantly a melee class with a handful of utility spells that work at range. Regardless, keep the fight up close and personal or you won't enjoy much success.

Immunities

Anti-magic Shell isn't a true immunity, but it does allow the Death Knight to absorb 75% of damage dealt by harmful spells (up to 50% of the Death Knight's total health) for 5 seconds. Additionally, it prevents the application of harmful magic debuffs for five seconds.

Icebound Fortitude grants immunity to stuns, and incoming damage is reduced by 20%. For Level 72 and higher Blood Death Knights that number is improved by an additional 30%.

Bone Shield is exclusive to Blood Death Knights. The shield has 6 charges, and so long as one charge remains, the Death Knight takes 20% less damage.

There are two Level 57 Talents that grant partial immunities. Anti-Magic Zone places a large, stationary sphere that reduces spell damage done to party or raid members inside it by 75%. Using Lichborne, a Death Knight becomes undead and therefore immune to Charm, Fear, and Sleep effects. As a bonus, Death Coil works as a heal.

A Death Knight who stays within the area affected by the Level 90 Talent Desecrated Ground is immune to effects that cause loss of control of your character and instantly removes such effects when activated.

Interrupts

Mind Freeze is an interrupt with limited range. Strangulate silences its target for five seconds.

Unholy Death Knight pets gain Shambling Rush with Dark Transformation. It replaces Leap and gives the pet the ability to charge enemies, root them in place, and interrupt spellcasting.

Quick Moves

Think of Death Grip as a quick move in reverse. Death Knights can target an enemy and pull the target into melee range. Death Grip is extremely powerful in PvP, as your entire team can, for example, hide behind a pillar or wall while the Death Knight peeks out and yanks someone from the opposing team into the area for a quick kill. Gorefiend's Grasp, a Level 90 Talent that acts like an AoE Death Grip, is great for pulling numerous targets into one spot and then using AoE abilities on them.

Slows/Snares

Chains of Ice is a feared and effective snare. It has a range of 30 yards, reduces movement speed by 60% for 8 seconds, and due to Death Knight rune mechanics can be active on multiple targets simultaneously.

Chillblains is a Level 58 Talent that causes Frost Fever to slow the target by 50% for 10 seconds and your Chains of Ice immobilizes targets for 3 seconds. With one application of Pestilence after hitting a target with Frost Fever, it's possible to snare an entire group at the same time.

The winds created by the Level 90 Talent Remorseless Winter pulse and chill nearby enemies. Each pulse reduces targets' movement speed by 15% for 3 seconds stacking up to 5 times. A fifth application stuns an enemy for 6 seconds.

Stuns

The Level 58 Talent Asphyxiate replaces Strangulate and stuns its target for 5 seconds. If the target is immune to stuns, then Asphyxiate acts as a silence.

The stuns from the Unholy tree are all tied to the Death Knight's ghoul pet. Gnaw is a 3 second stun available to a standard ghoul, while Dark Transformation grants ghouls the previously mentioned Shambling Rush, and Monstrous Blow.

DRUID

Due to their reputation as PvP healers, Druids are a favorite opening target for opposing teams. Note that the following paragraphs discuss the abilities native to Druids. For more information about the abilities granted via Symbiosis, refer to the appropriate class's page in this section of the guide.

Applied Debuffs

Faerie Fire prevents targets from stealthing or turning invisible, and applies Weakened Armor. The Level 45 Talent Faerie Swarm replaces Faerie Fire and adds a movement reduction to boot. Feral and Guardian Druids apply the Weakened Blows debuff with Thrash.

Buff Removal

Soothe removes all Enrage effects from an enemy. There aren't many classes that become Enraged, but Soothe will come in handy when you face the ones that do.

Debuff Removal

Balance, Feral and Guardian Druids can remove all Curse and Poison effects with Remove Corruption. Restoration Druids get Nature's Cure which removes all Magic, Curse, and Poison effects. Dash removes all roots and snares on the Druid and activates Cat Form.

Crowd Control

Cyclone is a short-term solution (6 seconds) for holding an enemy in place. Hibernate gets less use, but you can take out a Hunter's pet or another Druid in an animal form so don't completely discount it.

Immunities

Barkskin (and Ironbark for Restoration Druids) reduces incoming damage by 20%. Barkskin makes Druids immune to pushback on spellcasting due to damaging attacks. It is usable while stunned, frozen, incapacitated, feared, or asleep. Guardian Druids get Survival Instincts, which reduces damage taken by 50% for 12 seconds.

Interrupts

Skull Bash is limited to Feral and Guardian Druids, but it interrupts spellcasting and prevents any spell in that school from being cast for 4 seconds. As an added bonus, targets of Skull Bash must spend 25% more mana to cast spells for the next 10 seconds.

Balance Druids get Solar Beam which affects an area around its target. The target's spellcast is interrupted and all affected enemies are silenced over Solar Beam's 10 second duration.

Knockbacks

Typhoon, a Level 45 Talent, affects targets within 30 yards in front of the Druid. They are knocked back and dazed for 6 seconds.

Quick Moves

Dash increases movement speed by 70% while in Cat Form for 15 seconds. The Level 15 Talent Wild Charge has different effects. In your non-shapeshifted form, you fly to an ally's location. As a Bear, you charge an enemy. While a Cat, you leap behind an enemy. If you're a Moonkin, you jump backward like a Hunter using Disengage. In Travel Form you leap forward. Aquatic Form increases swim speed an additional 150%.

Slows/Snares

Entangling Roots is a root which can be applied on enemies in one of two ways. First, it's a targeted spell that can hold one target in place. Second, Druids can apply Nature's Grasp to themselves. Any enemy who strikes that Druid could be wrapped up by Entangling Roots.

When Balance and Restoration Druids detonate Wild Mushrooms, any affected target is slowed by 50%. Feral and Guardian Druids slow targets with the passive ability Infected Wounds. Certain attacks by these Druids (Shred, Ravage, Maul, and Mangle) can slow their target's movement by 50%. Druid Talents provide a few different slows and snares. Wild Charge (Level 15) immobilizes if you're in Bear form, or dazes if you're in Cat form. The Level 45 Talent Faerie Swarm replaces Faerie Fire, and reduces the target's movement speed by 50% while also applying Weakened Armor.

Mass Entanglement, another Level 45 Talent, roots your target in place for 20 seconds and spreads to additional nearby enemies, up to 5 total targets. At level 75, you can choose between Disorienting Roar (disorients all enemies within 10 yards for 3 seconds) or Ursol's Vortex (targets an area and reduces the movement speed of all enemies within 8 yards by 50% and pulls enemies back to the center the first time it tries to leave the area).

Stuns

Druids in Cat form get two abilities that stun a target. Pounce must be done while prowling, but provides a 4 second stun. Maim is a finishing move that stuns the target based on how many combo points have been applied. Guardian Druids learn Bear Hug, which stuns its target for 3 seconds. The downside to this ability is the Druid is unable to move over those 3 seconds. Mighty Bash, a Level 75 Talent, stuns an enemy for 5 seconds, but the target must be in melee range.

HUNTER

While all Hunters fight best at range, you must become familiar with aspects of melee combat since that's where your pet spends most of its PvP time. Pet choice is important but picking the right one depends on many factors. The more time spent learning your pets' abilities, the more rounded (and tougher) you'll become in PvP.

Please note that the abilities of Hunter pets are not covered here. For information about Hunter pet abilities, check out page 318.

Applied Debuffs

Widow Venom reduces the effectiveness of any healing taken by the enemy for 30 seconds.

Buff Removal

Tranquilizing Shot attempts to remove one Enrage effect from a target. Additionally, it dispels one Magic effect on the target, so this can be used to strip off buffs such as Bloodlust/Heroism or Power Word: Shield.

Crowd Control

Place Freezing Traps on the ground to capture the character who triggers it. Any damage breaks the effect, but these traps are a great way to keep the heat off you (or a healer) for a short time.

Debuff Removal

Master's Call orders a pet to remove most slow and snare effects from the pet and its target (friendly one), and causes your pet and its target to be immune to all such effects for 4 seconds.

Fears

Scare Beast allows the Hunter to fear a beast opponent, which in many cases is simply another Hunter's pet.

Immunities

While not a true immunity, Deterrence is the next best thing. When activated, you deflect melee attacks, ranged attacks, and spells. All damage taken is reduced by 30%. The trade-off is that you can't attack while Deterrence is active and it only lasts 5 seconds.

Interrupts

Scatter Shot isn't a traditional interrupt, but serves nearly the same purpose. Scatter Shot causes targets to become disoriented for 4 seconds, which stops any attacks or spells. Silencing Shot is a Level 30 Talent that silences its target for 3 seconds.

Quick Moves

Disengage is a quick escape move. Upon triggering it, the Hunter immediately leaps backwards many yards. This can be used in conjunction with jumping at the same time to travel farther, and even while leaping off of something. This can be used both as an escape tool or to close distance, if you face the other direction before using it.

Slows/Snares

Concussive Shot is a long-range snare, with a short duration; for 6 seconds, the target's movement suffers a 50% movement reduction and is considered dazed.

When an enemy triggers an Ice Trap, a 10 yard area becomes covered with a snow-like effect. Opponents caught or entering this area lose 50% of their movement speed.

Stuns

Beast Mastery Hunters can command their pet to stun their opponent using Intimidation. It only lasts for 3 seconds and has a minute cooldown, however, so avoid using it capriciously.

Mage

If you plan to PvP as a Mage, you must become familiar with all the ways to escape melee attackers at your disposal. You have a few tricks to combat other spellcasters, but your only defense against melee classes is range. Freeze them in place, Blink away, it doesn't matter. Just get away and take them down before they reach you again.

Applied Debuffs

When Arcane Mages learn Slow, they can reduce their target's movement speed and increase the target's casting time for 15 seconds. Slow can only affect one target at a time.

Buff Removal

Mages not only remove magical buffs from a target, but they actually take its benefits for themselves with Spellsteal. The downside is that any buff stolen in this way has its duration decreased to 2 minutes regardless of its normal duration.

Debuff Removal

Mages are the only class without a healing spell who have the capability to remove a debuff from others. The good news is that Remove Curse removes all curses from a friendly target.

Crowd Control

Polymorph comes in many flavors, but the end result is the same: your Humanoid or Beast target is transformed into a small animal. The affected character loses all control and remains in that form until the spell expires or becomes damaged in any way.

Immunities

Ice Block protects Mages from harm for up to 10 seconds, but leaves them unable to move or cast spells for the duration of the effect. Unless you have help in the area, or are simply waiting on a cooldown, Ice Block just delays the inevitable. Ice Barrier is a Level 30 Talent that absorbs some damage and also allows you to ignore pushback on spellcasting due to damage.

Temporal Shield, a Level 30 Talent, envelops Mages in a temporal shield for 4 seconds. Damage taken while shielded is healed over 6 seconds. Since the spell is usable while stunned, frozen, incapacitated, feared, or asleep, it's a nice panic button to fall back on.

Interrupts

Counterspell interrupts an enemy cast. If successful, it also prevents the enemy from casting a spell from the same school of magic for up to 6 seconds. Level 70 Mages get Improved Counterspell, which silences its target.

Quick Moves

Blink teleports you away a short distance, and also removes snare and stun effects. Keep it somewhere easy to remember as Blink should get quite a bit of use in PvP.

Slows/Snares

Various Frost-based spells such as Frostbolt and Cone of Cold have a chance to apply the Chill effect. Chill slows enemies movement speed significantly.

Frost Nova is a great way to escape multiple melee attackers. For 8 seconds (unless they take damage) anyone near the caster becomes snared in ice.

The Level 45 Talent Ring of Frost places a 10 yard wide ring on the ground. Enemies entering the ring become frozen for 10 seconds.

Stuns

Deep Freeze stuns an already frozen target for 5 seconds.

Fire Mages get one true stun from Combustion. This spell will stun the target for 3 seconds. Dragon's Breath isn't really a stun, but its disorienting effect works about the same. Targets in a cone in front of the Mage lose control of their character for up to 4 seconds.

MONK

Monks must fight in melee range to remain effective. Even the Mistweavers, the healing specialization of Monks, must stay in close combat to be fully effective at their job.

Applied Debuffs

Tiger Palm grants tiger power, causing the Monk's attacks to ignore 10% of the enemies' armor for 20 seconds and stacks up to 3 times, while Rising Sun Kick (exclusive to Windwalker Monk) puts the Mortal Wounds debuff on its target.

Use Grapple Weapon to Disarm a target's weapons and shield for 10 seconds. If you steal a better main-hand weapon, your damage or healing is increased or your damage taken is reduced.

Crowd Control

Paralysis is a short-term incapacitating effect for a single target. If you can apply it from behind, its duration is doubled.

Debuff Removal

All Monks learn Detox to remove all Poison and Disease effects. When Mistweaver Monks learn Internal Medicine, their Detox spells also remove all Magical effects.

Tiger's Lust, a Level 15 Talent, clears your target of all immobilizing and movement impairing effects, and increases their movement speed by 70% for 6 seconds.

The Level 75 Talent, Diffuse Magic, reduces all spell damage taken by 90%, clears all magical effects on the Monk, and even applies the effects to their original caster if he's within 40 yards.

Immunities

Fortifying Brew increases your health and reduces damage taken by 20% for 20 seconds. Dampen Harm, a Level 75 Talent, reduces the damage from the most harmful attacks done to you. Attacks that would otherwise deal in excess of 10% of your health have their damage cut in half.

Mistweaver Monk's Dematerialize when stunned, causing all melee, ranged and spell attacks to miss for 2.5 seconds.

Interrupts

Use Spear Hand Strike to interrupt spell casts and prevent any spell of the interrupted school from being cast for 5 seconds. Striking an enemy that is facing you turns it into a silencing effect.

Knockbacks

If an enemy attacks you within melee range while they are afflicted with Crackling Jade Lightning, they are knocked back a short distance.

Quick Moves

Roll is a quick move that is improved with two of the Level 15 Talents. Select Celerity to reduce the cooldown on Roll and increase its maximum number of charges by 1. Momentum briefly boosts your movement speed by 25% and stacks up to 2 times.

Transcendence splits a Monk's body and spirit, leaving the spirit behind for as long as the spell lasts and he stays in range. Use Transcendence: Transfer to return to the spirit's location.

Slows/Snares

Disable reduces a target's movement speed by 50%. Use Disable on a target a second time (so long as the first application remains) to root it for 8 seconds.

Brewmaster Monks get Dizzying Haze, which reduces the movement speed of all enemies within 8 yards of the target area by 50% for 15 seconds. As a bonus, affected targets have a 3% chance to have their melee attacks misfire and strike themselves instead!

Stuns

Charging Ox Wave, a Level 60 Talent stuns all enemies in front of the Monk for 3 seconds. The Level 60 Talent Leg Sweep knocks down all enemies within 5 yards. Brewmaster Monks learn Clash, which brings the Monk and target together and stuns all targets within 6 yards of the collision point.

PALADIN

Paladins can be a handful for other melee classes to take down due to their thick armor, shields, and frustrating bag of tricks. In many situations, Paladins are initially CC'ed while other softer targets are taken down. As a Paladin, you must become familiar with the effects of Hands and the best times to put them to use.

Applied Debuffs

Protection and Retribution Paladins both get Hammer of the Righteous, which applies the Weakened Blows debuff.

Debuff Removal

All Paladins get Cleanse, which removes all Poison and Disease effects from an ally, but when Holy Paladins learn Sacred Cleansing, their Cleanse spells also remove Magic effects.

Hand of Freedom grants immunity from movement impairing effects for 6 seconds and can be cast on an ally. Retribution Paladins learn Emancipate, which frees them from one movement impairing effect.

Crowd Control

An old Paladin favorite, Repentance, is now a Level 30 Talent and has had a few changes. It now has a cast time, but a much shorter cooldown.

Fears

Turn Evil is a niche spell, only working on demon or undead targets. However, two of the most irritating aspects of PvP are Warlock pets and Death Knight pets! Turn Evil causes these pets to run in fear for up to 40 seconds.

Immunities

Divine Shield protects Paladins from all damage and spells for 8 seconds, but reduces damage dealt. Save Divine Shield for absolute emergencies, such as when you are about to die, or when you absolutely need to cast a spell.

Divine Protection reduces magical damage taken by 40% for 10 seconds.

Hand of Protection prevents all physical attacks from reaching the targeted ally for 10 seconds. The downside is that the ally cannot attack or use physical abilities.

Devotion Aura grants immunity to Silence and Interrupt effects to allies within 40 yards and reduces magic damage taken by 20%.

Sacred Shield, a Level 45 Talent, absorbs damage every 6 seconds. It works largely how it did in the past—it procs, then absorbs a certain amount of damage, but stays active until it's off cooldown, at which point it can proc again. This means you only need to cast it once and it'll absorb damage several times over its duration.

The Level 60 Talent Hand of Purity reduces the damage of harmful periodic effects by 70% for 6 seconds. This is one of the best ways to counter a heavy load of DoT effects.

Protection Paladins can use Ardent Defender to Reduce damage taken by 20% for 10 seconds. Another perk of the ability is that with Ardent Defender active, one attack that would otherwise kill you will instead restore a small percentage of your health. The Protection Paladin version of Guardian of Ancient Kings reduces damage taken by 50% for 12 seconds.

Interrupts

Rebuke stops casting for 4 seconds. This is a melee range interrupt, and it deals no damage. Avenger's Shield, exclusive to Protection Paladins, silences and interrupts spellcasting for 3 seconds. It jumps to additional nearby enemies and can affect up to 3 total targets.

Slows/Snares

Blinding Light dazzles enemies within 10 yards, leaving them disoriented for 6 seconds. Seal of Justice, exclusive to Retribution Paladins, causes the Paladin's melee swings to limit the movement speed of the target. Burden of Guilt, a Level 30 Talent, reduces the movement speed of your target by 50% for 12 seconds.

Stuns

Hammer of Justice stuns a target for 6 seconds. Use Hammer of Justice to set up a target to be killed, as its duration ensures it can't escape. Alternatively use it on healers to stop casting for a while, or even on someone who's about to kill you, so you have time to heal.

The Level 30 Talent Fist of Justice acts like an improved version of Hammer of Justice, with a much shorter cooldown and increased range.

PRIEST

Priests are fragile, and Shadow Priests (even with extra defensive abilities) are not exempt. Coupled with the "healer dies first" mindset prevalent in PvP encounters, you need to keep your friends much, much closer than your enemies. When necessary, use Void Shift to keep yourself alive a bit longer when you're the primary target in a PvP encounter.

Applied Debuffs

Psychic Horror, available only to Shadow Priests, Disarms affected characters, causing them to drop their weapons and shield.

Buff Removal

Dispel Magic removes one magic buff from an enemy. Mass Dispel removes all harmful spells from allies (up to 10 allies), or one magic buff from enemies (up to 10 enemies) in a wide area. Mass Dispel is the only way to remove player invulnerabilities such as Ice Block and Divine Shield.

Crowd Control

With Dominate Mind, you possess a target humanoid, taking control of their actions. You also gain access to a limited number of their abilities, and can control their movement, such as running them off a cliff. Shackle Undead comes in handy against Death Knights. Their pets are considered Undead targets, so you can lock them into place.

Debuff Removal

In addition to Dispel Magic and Mass Dispel, Discipline and Holy Priests are also able to use Purify to remove all Magic and Disease effects.

Fears

Psychic Scream causes up to 5 enemies close to the Priest to flee in terror for up to 8 seconds. Use Psychic Scream to catch your breath when you're in trouble. Psyfiend, a Level 15 Talent, casts a Psychic Terror on a nearby enemy, preferring anything attacking the Priest.

Psychic Horror is a Shadow spell which fears one target for up to 4 seconds, and also Disarms them for 10 seconds. Melee characters are much easier to handle when they're down a weapon.

Immunities

Power Word: Shield blocks incoming damage, and Discipline Priests get abilities that make it even better. You can put it on any friendly character, including yourself. Power Word: Barrier, exclusive to Discipline Priests, reduces all damage done to friendly targets by 25%, and affects an area instead of a specific character.

Pain Suppression, also Discipline exclusive, reduces the damage taken by its target by 40%. Not a true immunity, but it does a passable job at keeping someone alive a bit longer.

Dispersion is a Shadow talent that reduces incoming damage by 90% for 6 seconds. Dispersion can be cast while you're stunned, feared, or silenced, and grants immunities to the same over its duration. You can't really do anything while Dispersed, but nothing can really harm you either.

The Level 30 Talent, Phantasm, empowers Fade. Fade removes all movement impairing effects, makes you untargetable by ranged attacks, and your movement speed is unhindered for 3 seconds.

Angelic Bulwark, a Level 60 Talent, is a passive ability that kicks in when you are knocked below 30% health. Once every 90 seconds, you gain an absorption shield equal to 20% of your total health.

It may be a stretch to call Spirit of Redemption an immunity, so think of it as a contingency plan for Holy Priests. Yes, you must die before this kicks in, but for 15 seconds you're free to continue healing and there's nothing anyone can do about it.

Interrupts

Shadow Priests can Silence targets for 5 seconds. It works whether your targets are in the middle of casting a spell or if they're simply standing around.

Quick Moves

Leap of Faith doesn't move the Priest who casts it, but it's a way to pull an ally in danger to your location quickly. The level 30 talent, Angelic Feather, briefly boosts movement speed by 60%.

Slows/Snares

Mind Flay is a core Shadow Priest ability learned at level 10. In addition to the damage it deals, Mind Flay slows its target's movement speed by 50% during its duration. The Level 15 Talent, Void Tendrils, roots up to 5 enemies within 8 yards for 20 seconds. The tendrils must be destroyed to cancel the effect.

ROGUE

Keep fights at melee range when you're playing as a Rogue. For group-based PvP, Rogues picked up a wonderful addition in the form of Shroud of Concealment. This ability extends their Stealth to party members within 20 yards for 15 seconds.

Applied Debuffs

Mind-Numbing Poison slows the casting speed of affected targets for 10 seconds. Expose Armor applies the Weakened Armor debuff. Master Poisoner increases the spell damage taken by any target suffering from any of your applied poisons. Dismantle disarms an enemy of both weapons and shields for 10 seconds.

Combat Rogues get Revealing Strike, which deals damage and increases the effectiveness of their offensive finishing moves on that target by 35%.

Buff Removal

Shiv dispels Enrage effects off targets only. There aren't many classes with Enrage effects, but it's a powerful buff for those classes that you can remove.

Crowd Control

Sap is a long-term Crowd Control ability (although in PvP its effect is diminished to 10 seconds) that essentially removes one character from the battle. The only catches are that the target can't be in combat already, and you must be stealthed to use Sap.

Debuff Removal

Use Vanish to escape being targeted, avoid magical spells, and more importantly, break out of movement impairing effects. Vanish automatically puts you into stealth.

Burst of Speed, a Level 60 Talent, removes any movement-impairing effects and grants immunity to their re-application for 4 seconds. The downside is its steep Energy cost.

Healing Reductions

Wound Poison inflicts damage and reduces all healing the target receives. It has a 30% chance to proc on any damaging swing, meaning this debuff is almost always up on the Rogue's target of choice.

Immunities

Cloak of Shadows is a short but powerful immunity from debuffs. It removes harmful effects from the Rogue and any magical spells cast for its brief (5 seconds) duration are similarly ineffective. The catch is that it does not remove the effects that prevent the use of Cloak of Shadows.

Evasion is not total immunity, but it does provide a 50% chance to dodge attacks. Save it for fights against classes who deal physical damage and who aren't Warriors. Feint now reduces the damage taken from area-of-effect attacks by 50% for 5 seconds.

Use Smoke Bomb to keep spellcasters and Hunters from hurting your allies or healing your targets within 8 yards of the spot where you popped Smoke Bomb. Enemies are unable to target into or out of the smoke cloud. Cheat Death, a Level 45 Talent, allows you to survive an attack that would've otherwise killed you. The health you survive with is minimal, and you still take some damage (reduced by 80% for 3 seconds) afterward.

Interrupts

Kick is an effective melee interrupt, which locks out spells from the interrupted school for 5 seconds.

Quick Moves

Sprint increases your movement speed for 8 seconds, allowing you to catch up to an escaping enemy, come to the aid of an ally, or to flee to fight another day. Shadowstep, a Level 60 Talent, puts you behind your target and increases your movement speed by 70% for 2 seconds. Use Shadowstep to close the distance between you and an enemy.

Slows/Snares

Crippling Poison is one of the most effective snares in the game. Each strike has a high chance of reducing a target's movement speed by 50% for 12 seconds.

Deadly Throw, a Level 30 Talent, is a finishing move that reduces the movement speed of the target by 50% for 6 seconds. If it's used with 5 combo points, it also interrupts spellcasting and locks out the interrupted spell type for 6 seconds.

Stuns

Kidney Shot is tied with Hammer of Justice for being the most effective stun in the game. The duration varies based on the number of combo points on the target.

Cheap Shot must be used from stealth, meaning you must decide if it's a better opener than something that deals damage. Blind disorients instead of stuns, but the effect is essentially the same for the target: loss of control for a short time.

Gouge incapacitates a target (which must be facing you) for 4 seconds. You also stop auto-attacking a Gouged target. When Paralytic Poison, a Level 75 Talent, reaches 5 stacks on a target, that target is stunned for 4 seconds. If you Shiv this poison, the target is rooted temporarily.

SHAMAN

While your approach to PvP as a Shaman changes considerably depending on your talent tree choice, there are many elements to PvP that are universal. You must become proficient at totem selection. Many of your situational abilities are tied to totems, so it's in your best interest to know when to drop a certain totem.

Applied Debuffs

All Shamans can use Earth Shock to apply the Weakened Blows debuff. The Level 90 Talent Unleashed Fury, combined with the Flametongue weapon imbue, increases a target's damage taken from your Lightning Bolt spell by 30% for 10 seconds. Combining Unleashed Fury with a Rockbiter weapon imbue reduces the damage dealt by the enemy afflicted by it by 40%.

Buff Removal

All Shamans have access to Purge, which removes one magic-based buff from an enemy target.

Debuff Removal

Cleanse Spirit is available to all Shamans and removes Curse debuffs that have been applied to you or an ally. Restoration Shamans learn Purify Spirit, which removes all Curse and Magic debuffs. Enhancement Shamans learn Spirit Walk, which removes all movement-impairing effects and increases your movement speed by 60% for 15 seconds.

There are two totems designed to keep you safe from debuffs. Use Tremor Totem reactively to remove Fear, Charm, and Sleep effects; it remains usable while you're afflicted with any of those effects. Place a Grounding Totem proactively to absorb a single, targeted (it's not effective against AoE spells) damage or debuff spell. It only works once, so you need to drop a new one to block additional spells.

Crowd Control

In PvP situations, the only applicable Crowd Control spell for Shamans is Hex. It turns its target into a frog, which is unable to attack or cast spells, although it does nothing to restrict movement.

Immunities

Two Level 15 Talents grant some form of immunity. Stone Bulwark Totem provides a shield that absorbs damage for 10 seconds, and an additional amount every 5 seconds thereafter (30 second total duration). Astral Shift reduces damage taken by 40% for 6 seconds.

Enhancement Shamans learn Shamanistic Rage, which reduces all incoming damage by 30% while it's active. Windwalk Totem, a Level 30 Talent makes everyone in your party or raid immune to movement-impairing effects for 6 seconds.

Interrupts

While Wind Shear's reduction in threat has no PVP value, its ability to interrupt an enemy's spellcasting and prevent that enemy from casting spells from the same school for 3 seconds is invaluable. Elemental Shamans learn Earthquake, which isn't exactly designed as an interrupt, but since it knocks down enemies it is as effective as anything else.

Knockbacks

Elemental Shamans retain Thunderstorm, which knocks back enemies within 10 yards and reduces their movement speed by 40% for 5 seconds and restores 15% of the Shaman's mana. As a bonus, Thunderstorm can be used while stunned.

Quick Moves

Shamans lack a true quick move ability, but their travel form, Ghost Wolf, is usable in combat. The Level 90 Talent Unleashed Fury combined with a Frostbrand weapon imbue grants a 50% movement speed boost for 4 seconds.

Slows/Snares

Shamans have multiple tools when it comes to slowing enemies. Frostbrand Weapon and Frost Shock both apply a magic debuff that slows your target.

Earthbind Totem has a 10 yard range but its effect can only be removed by destroying the totem or moving out of its range. The Level 30 Talent, Earthgrab Totem (which replaces Earthbind Totem), pulses every 2 seconds for 20 seconds, and roots every enemy within 10 yards. Any enemy who was rooted once already will be slowed by 50% by additional pulses of the totem.

Stuns

Capacitor Totem is an Air totem that explodes after 5 seconds, stunning all enemies within 8 yards for 5 seconds. Its weakness is a low health pool. Expect it to be targeted as soon as you drop it.

WARLOCK

With fears and pets and a variety of instant-cast spells, Warlocks are often near the top of most hated classes to fight against in PvP. Spend time with each pet and learn how to use it effectively based on different situations. You should also learn to effectively apply your enhanced abilities granted by each specialization's secondary resource.

Applied Debuffs

Curse of Elements makes its target vulnerable to Magic damage. Curse of Enfeeblement does double duty, slowing casting speed and reducing melee damage done by enemies. You can have only one Curse active on a target at a time, so choose wisely. Voidwalkers and Voidlords are both able to Disarm opponents.

Felguards and Wrathguards are exclusive to Demonology Warlocks, but each has an ability that applies the Mortal Strike debuff. The Felguard's Legion Strike ability causes a 10% reduction, while Mortal Cleave from a Wrathguard reduces healing by 25%.

Buff Removal

Felhunters use Devour Magic to consume one buff (at a time) from a target. The bonus is that each consumed buff also heals the Felhunter.

Crowd Control

A Succubus can Charm a Humanoid target, making it unable to move or act until the effect expires or it takes damage. Shivarra does the same with Mesmerize, but can apply it to Humanoids, Beasts, Dragonkin, Giants, Mechanical and Undead targets.

Warlocks can Banish demons and elementals, which comes into play when you're facing Mages, Shaman, or other Warlocks.

Debuff Removal

Imps use Singe Magic to remove one Magic effect from a friendly target. An Observer uses Clone Magic to steal 1 beneficial magic effect from an enemy. Unbound Will, a Level 60 Talent, removes Magic effects, movement impairing effects and all effects which cause loss of control of your character. The freedom comes at the cost of 20% of your health. Demonic Circle: Teleport removes snares, but if you apply Soulburn (exclusive to Affliction Warlocks) to Demonic Circle: Teleport, you become immune to snares and roots for 8 seconds.

Fears

Fear causes an enemy to flee in terror until the effect expires. Damage may interrupt the effect early, so let others know who you plan to target. The Level 30 Talent Howl of Terror causes up to five enemies to flee in terror until the effect expires. You don't need to target anyone for the effect to take hold. Damage may interrupt the effect early. Mortal Coil, another Level 30 Talent, causes one enemy to run in horror for 3 seconds. You are also healed 15% of your maximum health. Blood Fear, a Level 60 Talent, is a longer duration fear (20 seconds) but you sacrifice 10% of your maximum health when you use it.

Immunities

Use Unending Resolve to reduce all damage taken by 40%. Over the spell's 8 second duration, you're immune from spell interrupts and silence.

Use Sacrificial Pact, a Level 45 Talent, to trade half of your demon's health for a damage shield around your Warlock.

The Level 45 Talent, Dark Bargain, prevents all damage for 8 seconds, but half of the damage taken over that time is dealt over the following 8 seconds.

Interrupts

Felhunters can Spell Lock targets, which silences them for 3 seconds, and if a spell was being cast, locks out that school of magic for 6 seconds. Observer's use Optical Blast to silence enemies for 3 seconds and counter an enemy's active spellcast, preventing any spell from that school of magic being cast for 6 seconds.

Knockbacks

Whiplash from Succubus and Fellash from Shivarra both knock back all enemies within 5 yards of their location.

Quick Moves

Demonic Circle: Teleport requires some set up, but is an invaluable escape from potentially hazardous situations. Set up your circle (with Demonic Circle Summon) in a safe spot, then go out and fight. When things look bad, use the Teleport to escape to the location of the circle. If you use Soulburn with Demonic Circle: Teleport, your movement speed is increased by 50%.

Burning Rush, a Level 60 Talent, drains 4% of your maximum health per second to increase your movement speed by 50% (lasts until cancelled).

Slows/Snares

Curse of Exhaustion reduces an enemy's movement speed by 30%. Unfortunately, only one Curse can be active on an enemy at a time, so you must decide if it's worth the loss of another Curse's effects to apply this.

Stuns

Felguards are Demonology only pets, but their Axe Toss ability acts as a 4 second stun. Shadowfury, a Level 30 Talent, stuns enemies for 3 seconds. Summoning an Infernal stuns enemies caught within its landing area for 2 seconds.

WARRIOR

Where Rogues control range with stuns and other disorienting effects, Warriors use a number of quick move abilities and snares to keep enemies within the range of their weapons. Switching between your Warrior stances has become trickier in this expansion.

Applied Debuffs

Warriors can Disarm an enemy, removing both weapons and shields. Warriors also inflict Weakened Blows with Thunderclap. Depending on your specialization, you can also apply Physical Vulnerability with Colossus Smash, and reduce opponent's armor with Sunder Armor, Shattering Throw, or Devastate.

Buff Removal

Shattering Throw removes any invulnerabilities on a target and reduces the opponent's armor.

Fears

Intimidating Shout is a unique fear in that it's not considered a magical effect. However, it does have a lengthy cooldown and works against a maximum of only five nearby enemies.

Healing Reductions

Arms Warriors apply Mortal Wounds with Mortal Strike. Fury Warriors use Wild Strike to do the same.

Immunities

Shield Wall reduces all damage taken by 40%, but you must have a shield equipped for it to work. The Protection Warrior ability Shield Barrier absorbs damage for 6 seconds. The amount absorbed increases with attack power.

Berserker Rage removes and grants immunity to Fear, Sap, and Incapacitate effects over its duration. Bladestorm, a Level 60 Talent, makes Warriors immune to abilities that impair movement and loss of control. Avatar, a Level 90 Talent, makes Warriors immune to movement impairing effects.

Interrupts

Pummel interrupts a spell being cast and also locks out that school of spells for 4 seconds. The Level 45 Talent, Disrupting Shout, Interrupts all spellcasting within 10 yards and prevents any spell from the interrupted school from being cast for 4 seconds.

Knockbacks

Dragon Roar, a Level 60 Talent, damages all enemies within 8 yards, knocks them back, and knocks them to the ground for 3 seconds.

Quick Moves

Charge is learned early and is an integral part of Warrior play. You get extra Rage and briefly stun your target, so what's not to love about Charge? Heroic Leap is a quick, 40 yard move where you target an area instead of another character. Use it to escape or to deal damage to the enemies in the targeted area.

Intervene works a bit differently, since you actually target an ally. You rush to your target and absorb the next melee or ranged attack intended for that target.

Slows/Snares

Hamstring has no cooldown and a low Rage cost, meaning you can apply it to nearly any enemy you encounter. Snaring your opponents ensures both that they cannot escape you if you are focusing on them, and that they will not be able to chase you or your allies if you need to escape.

Piercing Howl, a Level 45 Talent, is one of the most powerful snares in the game. It has no cooldown, and affects unlimited targets within its effective range. Any enemy within 15 yards is instantly slowed by 50% for 15 seconds.

The Level 45 Talent Staggering Shout roots any slowed enemy within its range. Bloodbath, a Level 90 Talent, causes enemies to bleed when struck by your special attacks. While bleeding, the target moves at 50% reduced speed.

Stuns

Outside of Charge's one second stun on a single target, Warrior stuns all come from choices made with your Talents. Warbringer, a Level 15 Talent, adds a knockdown to Charge and extends the stun effect to a 3 second duration.

The Level 60 Talent Shockwave affects all enemies in a cone-shaped area of effect up to 10 yards in front of your Warrior. Storm Bolt, a Level 90 Talent, stuns one enemy for 3 seconds. Another Level 60 Talent, Dragon Roar, knocks down enemies for 3 seconds.

PROFESSIONS

Each character can learn two major Professions and as many secondary Professions as are available in the game. These modes of character progression are optional; you can avoid them entirely if you want. However, there are advantages to having these skills.

Many Professions let you craft items for yourself and others. Making your own gear can be kind of fun. Mastering various tiers of a Profession also grants various bonuses, so even heavy combat characters have something to gain.

LEARNING A PROFESSION

To learn a Profession, you must follow a process:

1. Learn the Apprentice level from a Profession Trainer.

2. Learn specific recipes from the trainer.

3. Acquire any necessary tools or ingredients in the recipes.

4. Create items from the recipes, which also increases your skill level in your chosen profession.

5. Return to #2. Repeat.

6. Every 75 points, you need to find a trainer so that your character can advance to a new grade of that profession. Not all trainers teach every recipe, so you may need to search out various factions and vendors in the world as you reach higher levels.

BECOMING AN APPRENTICE

You can receive Apprentice training from any Profession trainer in the beginning regions of the game. Some of them are found near or in starting villages, but trainers for every Profession are found in each capital city (and if you don't know where to find one, ask a guard). For most Professions, you need to learn a variety of recipes. When you train to be an Apprentice, you automatically learn several initial recipes, patterns, or schematics. Each Profession has its own term for a new type of item, so you know what to search for in the Auction House or when researching things online.

To learn a new Profession, right-click on the trainer that is teaching the skill you want to learn. This is identified by the tag under the Trainer's name. It might say "Journeyman Cook" or something to that effect. Train with that person and pay the cost associated with it. In the very beginning of the game these expenses are moderate, but entirely affordable if you put in some effort.

Your General Chat Log records everything that you learn from your trainer. These abilities are added to your Profession menu. Like other spells and abilities, you can add shortcuts to one of your Action Bars. You should add the Profession and any associated Abilities in this way. The recipes themselves can be chosen from the Profession menu when you are creating items. If you need basic tools as an Apprentice, look for a trade vendor near the trainer.

CHANGING PROFESSIONS

The game limits you to two Primary Professions, but you aren't locked into the first two you select. You can drop a Profession and learn a new one.
The bad news is that you lose everything from your old Profession, so this is useful only if you find that you don't like the way a Profession progresses. When that happens, don't lament. Drop the Profession you dislike and try something new; it's better than having a slot taken up by something that you never plan on using again!

To drop a Profession, open the Spellbook (with "p") and click on the Professions Tab. Look for small red symbols that look like Do Not Enter signs. These are the unlearn buttons for each Profession. Don't click on them unless you are absolutely sure that you know what you're doing. You lose everything as soon as you say "Unlearn" to the final query.

INCREASING YOUR SKILL LEVEL

The Apprentice level of a Profession covers your skill from 1 to 75. Using your profession advances it until it hits each cap (every 75 points). Whether you're gathering materials or creating them, the color of the activity is your guide to its difficulty.

Green recipes are easy, yellow are moderate, and orange are harder. The harder the recipe, the more likely it is to boost your level. The following colors apply to both gathering and non-gathering Profession recipes.

Red	Your character isn't high enough in the profession to make an attempt to gather an item or learn a crafting recipe
Orange	Success increases your skill points every single time you complete this activity (with the exception of Skinning)
Yellow	There is a high chance of increasing your skill points
Green	This activity is too easy; you aren't likely to gain points from completing it
Grey	There isn't a chance of gaining any skill points whether you complete this activity or not

As a crafter, you'll always have limited resources; you can only carry so much metal or leather or herbs. To get access to the next recipe, you must raise your Profession level. If you need to raise your level, it's important to decide what you make. Look for pieces that require the least amount of material components but are almost certain to give you a point (orange recipes or those that have just turned yellow). That way, you get the most out of your materials.

Once you reach 75, you cannot increase your points until you train again as a Journeyman. Each proficiency level also has a character level requirement.

As your points increase, you can train in more recipes. Returning to your Profession trainer tells you when you can get more recipes or when you can train a higher proficiency. There are also many recipes hidden throughout the world, as a reward from certain quests, or as random drops. Check the Auction House for any new finds!

SPIRIT OF HARMONY

Many crafted items in Mists of Pandaria require the use of Spirits of Harmony. Motes of Harmony bind when picked-up, and are acquired as random drops from enemies on the continent of Pandaria. You need to combine 10 Motes of Harmony to make one Spirit of Harmony.

You might notice that the skill points for professional tiers don't add up evenly. Apprentices go from 1-75, but Journeyman can start as low as 50 This is because you can train a new tier in a Profession a bit early. That's a good idea because you don't want to hit the cap and waste any skill points. Train early as long as you have the money; there are no downsides in completing your training ahead of schedule.

COMPLEMENTARY PROFESSIONS

Following is a list of Professions and classes that complement each other:

Profession	Good Additional Professions To Take
Alchemy	Herbalism, Fishing
Blacksmithing	Mining
Enchanting	Tailoring
Engineering	Mining
Herbalism	Alchemy or Inscription
Inscription	Herbalism
Jewelcrafting	Mining
Leatherworking	Skinning
Mining	Blacksmithing, Engineering, or Jewelcrafting
Skinning	Leatherworking
Tailoring	Any gathering or Enchanting

FISHING AND ALCHEMY

Fishing is a great Profession to pick up if you plan on being an Alchemist. Some ingredients for Alchemy are obtained through Fishing. What's even better is that Fishing is a Secondary Profession, so you're still able to take Herbalism as your second Primary Profession.

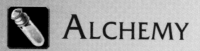 # ALCHEMY

Alchemy is one of the easier crafting professions to pick up and learn. If you want to be self-sufficient, pair Alchemy with Herbalism so that you can gather your own materials. The main components to Alchemy are herbs and vials. Other items are required for specific creations, but for the most part it's herbs and vials.

Alchemists also learn how to transmute certain items into other items. This ability often involves changing element-based items (such as Primals and Eternals) but also covers meta gems and certain ores. A Philosopher's Stone (a trinket created through Alchemy) is required for transmuting items. Transmuting an item sometimes leads to the discovery of a new recipe.

Proficiency Level Name	Character Level Minimum	Skill Level Minimum	Skill Level Maximum
Apprentice	5	0	75
Journeyman	10	50	150
Expert	20	125	225
Artisan	35	200	300
Master	50	275	375
Grand Master	65	350	450
Illustrious Grand Master	75	425	525
Zen Master	80	500	600

PRACTICING ALCHEMY

Alchemists don't need to be in a special place or to have a specific item in their inventory to do most of their work; they just need their herbs and purchasable vials. Good Alchemists carry spare vials around if they plan on making any new potions out in the field. More extensive creations (like elixirs and flasks) are better to do in town, where you can be certain to have what you need.

When you reach the new recipes for Mists of Pandaria, the trainer has only two to teach you (Alchemist's Rejuvenation and Master Healing Potion). You must discover the rest as you create Alchemy items.

ALCHEMY BONUSES

Upon reaching skill level 50, Alchemists gain a bonus known as Mixology. With Mixology, you receive an increased effect and duration when you drink any elixir or flask you are able to make. For example, when you consume an elixir or flask with a 1 hour duration, you gain the benefit for 2 hours.

Additionally, you are able to create special trinkets at various levels. There are trinkets that apply to every role, so there's a solid choice for everyone.

ALCHEMY SPECIALTIES

When you reach level 68 and have an Alchemy skill of at least 325, you are given the opportunity to complete a quest that allows you to select an Alchemy specializion. Your choices are Potion Mastery, Elixir Mastery, and Transmutation Mastery.

Potion Mastery and Elixir Mastery work the same way. When you create a potion or an elixir (depending on your specialty), there is a chance you will create additional potions or elixirs of the same type with the same number of reagents. Transmutation Mastery does the same for materials that are created by any recipe tagged as a Transmute. When you transmute any item, there is a chance you will create an additional item at no additional reagent cost.

If you wish to change your specialization at any time, speak with the NPC who granted you the ability, then speak with one of the other specialists. Keep in mind that there is a cost associated with dropping a specialization.

GOBLIN BONUS

Goblins have a racial ability—Better Living Through Chemistry— which increases their Alchemy skill by 15.

MAKING MONEY AS AN ALCHEMIST

Healing and mana potions are constant points of sales because people go through them at a considerable pace. Later on, you start to see an expanding market for elixirs and their longer-term buffs. In the late game, flasks become important as well. These products are very expensive, but their effects are the strongest and they last through death (making them essential tools for raiders focusing on new content or very difficult dungeon runs).

Herbs from Pandaria's Zones

Green Tea Leaf	Silkweed	Fool's Cap
Rain Poppy	Snow Lily	Golden Lotus

NEW RECIPES FOR MISTS OF PANDARIA

Item	Skill Level	Reagents
Alchemist's Rejuvenation	500	Crystal Vial, Green Tea Leaf
Master Healing Potion	500	Crystal Vial, Green Tea Leaf
Elixir of Weaponry	N/A	Crystal Vial, Silkweed (x2)
Mad Hozen Elixir	N/A	Crystal Vial, Rain Poppy (x2)
Mantid Elixir	N/A	Crystal Vial, Green Tea Leaf (x2)
Monk's Elixir	N/A	Crystal Vial, Rain Poppy, Silkweed
Potion of the Jade Serpent	N/A	Crystal Vial, Green Tea Leaf, Silkweed
Potion of the Mountains	N/A	Crystal Vial, Green Tea Leaf, Rain Poppy
Desecrated Oil	N/A	Spinefish (x3)
Elixir of Mirrors	N/A	Crystal Vial, Silkweed, Fool's Cap
Elixir of Peace	N/A	Crystal Vial, Rain Poppy, Fool's Cap
Elixir of Perfection	N/A	Crystal Vial, Silkweed, Snow Lily
Elixir of the Rapids	N/A	Crystal Vial, Rain Poppy, Snow Lily
Flask of Falling Leaves	N/A	Crystal Vial, Green Tea Leaf (x4), Golden Lotus
Flask of Spring Blossoms	N/A	Crystal Vial, Snow Lily (x4), Golden Lotus
Flask of the Earth	N/A	Crystal Vial, Rain Poppy (x4), Golden Lotus
Flask of the Warm Sun	N/A	Crystal Vial, Silkweed (x4), Golden Lotus
Flask of Winter's Bite	N/A	Crystal Vial, Fool's Cap (x4), Golden Lotus
Potion of Mogu Power	N/A	Crystal Vial, Green Tea Leaf, Fool's Cap
Transmute: River's Heart	N/A	Lapis Lazuli, Golden Lotus
Transmute: Wild Jade	N/A	Alexandrite, Golden Lotus
Virmen's Bite	N/A	Crystal Vial, Green Tea Leaf, Snow Lily
Darkwater Potion	N/A	Crystal Vial, Desecrated Oil (x3)
Master Mana Potion	N/A	Crystal Vial, Golden Lotus
Transmute: Imperial Amethyst	N/A	Roguestone, Golden Lotus
Transmute: Sun's Radiance	N/A	Sunstone, Golden Lotus
Transmute: Vermilion Onyx	N/A	Tiger Opal, Golden Lotus
Potion of Focus	N/A	Crystal Vial, Snow Lily (x2)
Potion of Luck	N/A	Crystal Vial, Golden Lotus (x3)
Transmute: Living Steel	N/A	Trillium Bar (x6)
Transmute: Primal Diamond	N/A	Wild Jade (x2), Vermilion Onyx (x2), Imperial Amethyst (x2)
Transmute: Primordial Ruby	N/A	Pandarian Garnet, Golden Lotus
Transmute: Trillium Bar	N/A	Ghost Iron Bar (x10)
Riddle of Steel	N/A	Trillium Bar (x3), Spirit of Harmony (x3)

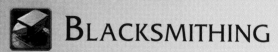

BLACKSMITHING

Blacksmithing is the shaping of bars, gems, stones and trade goods into armor and melee weapons. At low levels, Blacksmiths also turns stones uncovered by miners into temporary weapon enhancements. Many unique weapons and armor pieces can be created only by player Blacksmiths for their own use. To be a self-sufficient Blacksmith, take Mining as a second Profession.

Proficiency Level Name	Character Level Minimum	Skill Level Minimum	Skill Level Maximum
Apprentice	5	0	75
Journeyman	10	50	150
Expert	20	125	225
Artisan	35	200	300
Master	50	275	375
Grand Master	65	350	450
Illustrious Grand Master	75	425	525
Zen Master	80	500	600

PRACTICING BLACKSMITHING

Most Blacksmithing items require a Blacksmithing Hammer to be in your inventory. In addition, work must be completed near an anvil. Anvils are found in any town or city, most often near the Blacksmithing trainers. Some recipes call for items available only from a trade vendor as well, so don't head for the anvil until you're sure you have everything you need for your creation.

BLACKSMITHING BONUSES

At higher levels, Blacksmiths learn how to add extra gem sockets to their bracers and gloves. Enchantments can be applied to these pieces in addition to the gem sockets placed on the gloves and bracers.

Making Money as a Blacksmith

Blacksmithing is a brutal profession on your in-game gold. It's hard to find a market for your created items as most of these items are only on par with green quest rewards. Only specific Blacksmithing gear at high levels warrants the higher investment in time and materials.

To cut down on the price, take Mining and gather your own ore. Even here you should be careful. Someone joining a guild is likely to have access to their own Blacksmith. Only take this Profession if you know what you're getting into.

Metals from Pandaria

Ghost Iron Bars	Trillium Bars
Kyparite Bars	Living Steel

NEW GENERAL RECIPES FOR MISTS OF PANDARIA

Item	Skill Level	Reagents
Ghostly Skeleton Key	500	Ghost Iron Bar (x4)
Ghost Iron Shield Spike	540	Ghost Iron Bar (x12)

Item	Skill Level	Reagents
Living Steel Weapon Chain	540	Living Steel
Living Steel Buckle	600	Living Steel

NEW PLATE ARMOR & SHIELD RECIPES FOR MISTS OF PANDARIA

Item	Skill Level	Reagents
Ghost-Forged Bracers	500	Ghost Iron Bar (x5)
Ghost-Forged Belt	525	Ghost Iron Bar (x7)
Ghost-Forged Gauntlets	525	Ghost Iron Bar (x7)
Ghost-Forged Boots	530	Ghost Iron Bar (x7)
Ghost-Forged Legplates	530	Ghost Iron Bar (x12)
Lightsteel Shield	535	Ghost Iron Bar (x9)
Ghost-Forged Shoulders	540	Ghost Iron Bar (x7)
Spiritguard Shield	545	Ghost Iron Bar (x9)
Ghost-Forged Breastplate	550	Ghost Iron Bar (x12)
Ghost-Forged Helm	550	Ghost Iron Bar (x12)
Contender's Revenant Belt	575	Ghost Iron Bar (x7)
Contender's Revenant Boots	575	Ghost Iron Bar (x7)
Contender's Revenant Bracers	575	Ghost Iron Bar (x5)
Contender's Revenant Breastplate	575	Ghost Iron Bar (x12)
Contender's Revenant Gauntlets	575	Ghost Iron Bar (x7)
Contender's Revenant Helm	575	Ghost Iron Bar (x12)
Contender's Revenant Legplates	575	Ghost Iron Bar (x12)
Contender's Revenant Shoulders	575	Ghost Iron Bar (x7)
Contender's Spirit Belt	575	Ghost Iron Bar (x7)
Contender's Spirit Boots	575	Ghost Iron Bar (x7)
Contender's Spirit Bracers	575	Ghost Iron Bar (x5)
Contender's Spirit Breastplate	575	Ghost Iron Bar (x12)
Contender's Spirit Gauntlets	575	Ghost Iron Bar (x7)
Contender's Spirit Helm	575	Ghost Iron Bar (x12)
Contender's Spirit Legplates	575	Ghost Iron Bar (x12)
Contender's Spirit Shoulders	575	Ghost Iron Bar (x7)
Masterwork Lightsteel Shield	575	Ghost Iron Bar (x12)
Masterwork Spiritguard Belt	575	Ghost Iron Bar (x7)
Masterwork Spiritguard Boots	575	Ghost Iron Bar (x7)
Masterwork Spiritguard Bracers	575	Ghost Iron Bar (x5)
Masterwork Spiritguard Breastplate	575	Ghost Iron Bar (x12)
Masterwork Spiritguard Gauntlets	575	Ghost Iron Bar (x7)
Masterwork Spiritguard Helm	575	Ghost Iron Bar (x12)
Masterwork Spiritguard Legplates	575	Ghost Iron Bar (x12)
Masterwork Spiritguard Shield	575	Ghost Iron Bar (x12)
Masterwork Spiritguard Shoulders	575	Ghost Iron Bar (x7)
Breastplate of Ancient Steel	600	Living Steel (x8), Spirit of Harmony (x8)
Gauntlets of Ancient Steel	600	Living Steel (x5), Spirit of Harmony (x8)
Ghost Reaver's Breastplate	600	Living Steel (x8), Spirit of Harmony (x8)
Ghost Reaver's Gauntlets	600	Living Steel (x5), Spirit of Harmony (x8)
Living Steel Breastplate	600	Living Steel (x8), Spirit of Harmony (x8)
Living Steel Gauntlets	600	Living Steel (x5), Spirit of Harmony (x8)

NEW WEAPON RECIPES FOR MISTS OF PANDARIA

Item	Skill Level	Reagents
Forgewire Axe	545	Ghost Iron Bar (x4), Ghost Iron Bolts (x2), High Explosive Gunpowder (x2), Spirit of Harmony
Ghost-Forged Blade	545	Ghost Iron Bar (x7), Spirit of Harmony (x2)
Phantasmal Hammer	560	Ghost Iron Bar (x8), Spirit of Harmony (x2)
Ghost Shard	565	Ghost Iron Bar (x7), Spirit of Harmony (x2)
Spiritblade Decimator	565	Ghost Iron Bar (x10), Spirit of Harmony (x2)
Masterwork Forgewire Axe	575	Ghost Iron Bar (x12), Spirit of Harmony (x2)
Masterwork Ghost Shard	575	Ghost Iron Bar (x15), Spirit of Harmony (x2)
Masterwork Ghost-Forged Blade	575	Ghost Iron Bar (x12), Spirit of Harmony (x5)
Masterwork Phantasmal Hammer	575	Ghost Iron Bar (x12), Spirit of Harmony (x2)
Masterwork Spiritblade Decimator	575	Ghost Iron Bar (x15), Spirit of Harmony (x2)

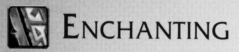

ENCHANTING

Enchanting recipes add various buffs to your weapons and armor, such as improved statistics for your character or procs with random effects to your weapons. They also create low-level wands, and oils (which are short term buffs to weapons).

Enchanters learn a second ability, known as Disenchanting, which they use to create their own materials. That sounds like a great deal, right? You get to make the materials that you need to advance your craft. There's a catch. You can't gather Enchanting materials without destroying magical items. Green, blue, and purple items each have their own types of Enchanting reagents stored inside them. Beyond that, you need to destroy higher level equipment of these quality levels to complete higher level enchantments.

Proficiency Level Name	Character Level Minimum	Skill Level Minimum	Skill Level Maximum
Apprentice	5	0	75
Journeyman	10	50	150
Expert	20	125	225
Artisan	35	200	300
Master	50	275	375
Grand Master	65	350	450
Illustrious Grand Master	75	425	525
Zen Master	80	500	600

PRACTICING ENCHANTING

Clicking the Enchanting icon opens a menu of all the magic recipes you know. Clicking the Disenchant icon enables you to extract magical elements from targeted items by destroying them forever. To enchant any item, you must have the proper Enchanting Rod in your inventory.

Up until skill level 60 or so, you can get points from destroying magical items. That trails off fairly soon, and then you need to use Enchanting to get skill points. Some Enchanting suppliers sell components necessary for lowest level enchanting recipes. As long as you have the materials, you can enchant the same item multiple times, but an item can only retain one Enchantment at a given time (you "overwrite" the Enchantment). There are also vellums created via Inscription which can hold enchants for later use.

ENCHANTING BONUSES

Enchanters are able to improve their own rings with a number of enchantments. You can improve your Agility, Intellect, Stamina, or Strength.

BLOOD ELF BONUS

Blood Elves have a racial ability—Arcane Affinity—which increases their Enchanting skill by 10.

MAKING MONEY AS AN ENCHANTER

Enchanting is in high demand as many players are always striving to collect better and better gear. Buying cheap greens off of the Auction House is one way to stockpile materials, but it's still not the best way to get everything you need. Enchanters frequently run dungeons to scoop up lower level blue and green items. You might even find an Enchanter running lower level dungeons by themselves for this exact purpose.

The other option is to take another Profession that creates destructable items. The best one for this is Tailoring; because it doesn't have its own gathering Profession (anyone can get cloth). You can make any number of simple green cloth armor pieces and then Disenchant them to make your Enchanting ingredients. It's expensive, time consuming, you need to level up two Professions at the same time, and sometimes you won't be able to easily (or cheaply) make the items you need, but it's an option for a self-sufficient Enchanter.

Enchanters, through the use of vellums, have the ability to distribute their enchantments on the Auction House. You no longer need to wait around for other players to buy your Enchantments, which means more time for you to do other activities.

ENCHANTING MATERIALS OBTAINED
THROUGH DISENCHANTING

There are four types of enchanting materials: Dust, Essences, Shards, and Crystals. The types of materials that come from Disenchanting items is based on the item level of the object.

Essences are more commonly obtained from weapons than armor of Uncommon quality. Dust is more commonly obtained from armor than weapons of Uncommon quality. Essences can be either Lesser or Greater. Three Lesser Essences can combine to become one Greater Essence, and one Greater Essence breaks down into three Lesser Essences.

Shards come from Superior quality items, or rarely from Uncommon quality items. You can get either Small or Large Shards when disenchanting an item. In most cases, three Small Shards can be combined into one Large Shard, and one Large Shard can be broken down into three Small Shards.

Crystals come from Epic quality items, and rarely from Superior quality items. At higher skill levels, you can learn how to convert these Crystals into other types of Enchanting materials.

Item Levels	Dust	Essence	Shard	Crystal
Items from Pandaria zones	Spirit	Mysterious	Ethereal	Sha

NEW RECIPES FOR MISTS OF PANDARIA

Enchant	Skill Level	Reagents
Enchant Bracer - Mastery	500	Spirit Dust (x4)
Enchant Cloak - Superior Critical Strike	500	Mysterious Essence
Mysterious Essence	500	Spirit Dust (x5)
Enchant Boots - Greater Precision	525	Spirit Dust (x2), Mysterious Essence
Enchant Bracer - Major Dodge	525	Spirit Dust (x3), Mysterious Essence (x2)
Enchant Chest - Mighty Spirit	525	Spirit Dust (x4)
Enchant Chest - Super Resilience	525	Spirit Dust (x3), Mysterious Essence
Enchant Cloak - Superior Intellect	525	Spirit Dust (x3), Mysterious Essence (x3)
Enchant Gloves - Greater Haste	525	Spirit Dust (x4)
Enchant Weapon - Elemental Force	525	Mysterious Essence (x3)
Mysterious Diffusion	535	Mysterious Essence
Enchant Boots - Blurred Speed	550	Ethereal Shard (x2)
Enchant Boots - Greater Haste	550	Spirit Dust (x2), Mysterious Essence
Enchant Chest - Superior Stamina	550	Mysterious Essence (x4), Mysterious Essence
Enchant Cloak - Accuracy	550	Spirit Dust (x7)
Enchant Gloves - Superior Expertise	550	Mysterious Essence (x2)
Enchant Weapon - Windsong	550	Spirit Dust (x12)
Ethereal Shard	550	Mysterious Essence (x5)
Enchant Boots - Pandaren's Step	575	Spirit Dust (x4), Mysterious Essence (x3)
Enchant Chest - Glorious Stats	575	Spirit Dust (x2), Mysterious Essence (x3)
Enchant Cloak - Greater Protection	575	Ethereal Shard (x2)
Enchant Gloves - Super Strength	575	Spirit Dust (x3), Mysterious Essence (x1)
Enchant Gloves - Superior Mastery	575	Mysterious Essence (x3)
Enchant Off-Hand - Major Intellect	575	Mysterious Essence (x3)
Enchant Shield - Greater Parry	575	Mysterious Essence (x3), Ethereal Shard
Enchant Weapon - Colossus	575	Ethereal Shard (x3)
Ethereal Shatter	585	Ethereal Shard
Enchant Weapon - Dancing Steel	600	Spirit Dust (x10), Sha Crystal (x10)
Enchant Weapon - River's Song	600	River's Heart, Mysterious Essence (x50)
Sha Crystal	600	Ethereal Shard (x5)
Sha Shatter	600	Sha Crystal

NOTE: ALL ENCHANTS LISTED IN THIS TABLE REQUIRE A LEVEL 372 OR HIGHER ITEM.

NEW ENCHANTER-ONLY RECIPES FOR MISTS OF PANDARIA

Enchant	Skill Level	Reagents
Enchant Ring - Greater Agility	550	Spirit Dust (x2)
Enchant Ring - Greater Intellect	550	Spirit Dust (x2)
Enchant Ring - Greater Stamina	550	Spirit Dust (x2)
Enchant Ring - Greater Strength	550	Spirit Dust (x2)

ENGINEERING

Engineering creates a variety of items such as goggles, explosives, ranged weapon scopes, bombs, and mechanical animals. Creating different items with Engineering requires a handful of tools, most of which are created by the Engineer. Many (but not all) of the items created by Engineers require the Engineering skill to use. One of the fun things about being an Engineer is that you never know when some of your creations will misfire, often leading to unexpected results.

Mining is a perfect way to make an Engineer self-sufficient. Pretty much everything an Engineer needs is found while you're out hunting for metal veins.

Proficiency Level Name	Character Level Minimum	Skill Level Minimum	Skill Level Maximum
Apprentice	5	0	75
Journeyman	10	50	150
Expert	20	125	225
Artisan	35	200	300
Master	50	275	375
Grand Master	65	350	450
Illustrious Grand Master	75	425	525
Zen Master	80	500	600

PRACTICING ENGINEERING

Clicking the Engineering icon opens a menu of all the schematics you know. Engineers have a few tools that are needed to make various items, so you might want to carry them around with you if you prefer crafting on the fly (or just get a Gnomish Army Knife!). Otherwise, it's better to work when you're back in town, near a Bank.

ENGINEERING BONUSES

Engineers are able to create specialized mounts. They aren't any faster than other mounts, but who cares when you're flying in a steam-powered helicopter!

Engineers also get a few Engineering-only trinkets, but the big boost for Engineers comes in the form of specialized enchantments for Gloves, Belts, Cloaks, and Boots. These enchantments range from Hand-Mounted Pyro Rockets to turning your cloak into a parachute.

GNOME BONUS

Gnomes have a racial ability—Engineering Specialization—which increases their Engineering skill by 15.

ENGINEERING SPECIALTIES

When you reach an Engineering skill of 200, you are given a choice to specialize in Gnomish Engineering or Goblin Engineering. For the most part, items created by one specialization are usable by any Engineer with a high enough skill level. The main difference is that Goblin Enginners are able to teleport to Everlook (in Winterspring) and Area 52 (in Netherstorm), while Gnomes can travel instantly to Gadgetzan (in Tanaris) or Toshley's Station (in Blade's Edge Mountains).

You can change your specialization if you like. There is a fee involved with dropping your specialization, so you may not want to do this too often.

MAKING MONEY AS AN ENGINEER

Engineering is not the best way to go when you're trying to make gold off your Profession. Because many items created with Engineering require Engineering to use them, your market is reduced. However, some of an Engineer's products are viable for selling. Selling various explosives and scopes is a decent way to make up for the expense of new schematics and materials. There are some big-ticket items (such as the Mechano-hog) that provide some nice income; you just can't depend on selling these items consistently.

NEW RECIPES FOR MISTS OF PANDARIA

Name	Skill Level	Reagents
Ghost Iron Bolts	500	Ghost Iron Bar (x3)
High-Explosive Gunpowder	500	Ghost Iron Bar
Locksmith's Powderkeg	500	Simple Wood, High-Explosive Gunpowder
Big Game Hunter	525	Ghost Iron Bolts (x12), Hair Trigger, Walnut Stock, Mirror Scope
G91 Landshark	525	Ghost Iron Bolts (x2), High-Explosive Gunpowder (x2)
Mirror Scope	525	Ghost Iron Bolts (x4), Lapis Lazuli (x2)
Mist-Piercing Goggles	525	Ghost Iron Bolts (x8), Spirit of Harmony (x2)
Flashing Tinker's Gear	550	Ghost Iron Bar (x2)
Fractured Tinker's Gear	550	Ghost Iron Bar (x2)
Ghost Iron Dragonling	550	Ghost Iron Bar (x4), Ghost Iron Bolts (x8), High-Explosive Gunpowder
Goblin Flame Thrower, Mark II	550	Ghost Iron Bar (x2), High-Explosive Gunpowder (x8)
Goblin Glider	550	Tinker's Kit
Incendiary Fireworks Launcher	550	Tinker's Kit
Phase Fingers	550	Tinker's Kit
Precise Tinker's Gear	550	Ghost Iron Bar (x2)
Quick Tinker's Gear	550	Ghost Iron Bar (x2)
Rigid Tinker's Gear	550	Ghost Iron Bar (x2)
Smooth Tinker's Gear	550	Ghost Iron Bar (x2)
Sparkling Tinker's Gear	550	Ghost Iron Bar (x2)
Subtle Tinker's Gear	550	Ghost Iron Bar (x2)
Synapse Springs	550	Tinker's Kit
Thermal Anvil	550	Ghost Iron Bar (x6), Ghost Iron Bolts (x6)
Tinker's Kit	550	Ghost Iron Bolts (x2), Windwool Cloth (x2), High-Explosive Gunpowder (x2)
Watergliding Jets	550	Tinker's Kit
Lord Blastington's Scope of Doom	560	Ghost Iron Bolts (x10), Primordial Ruby (x2), Trillium Bar (x1)
Long-Range Trillium Sniper	565	Trillium Bar (x12), Hair Trigger, Walnut Stock, Lord Blastington's Scope of Doom
Wormhole Generator: Pandaria	570	Trillium Bar (x12)
Mechanical Pandaren Dragonling	575	Ghost Iron Bar (x4), Trillium Bar (x6), Spirit of Harmony (x2)
Agile Retinal Armor	600	Living Steel (x6), Primal Diamond, Ghost Iron Bolts (x6)
Blingtron 4000	600	Living Steel (x6), Trillium Bar (x6), Ghost Iron Bar (x12), Pandaren Garnet (x10), Wild Jade (x2), Spirit of Harmony (x4)
Camouflage Retinal Armor	600	Living Steel (x6), River's Heart, Ghost Iron Bolts (x6)
Deadly Retinal Armor	600	Living Steel (x6), Wild Jade, Ghost Iron Bolts (x6)
Depleted-Kyparium Rocket	600	Living Steel (x6), Kyparite (x200), Orb of Mastery (x3), High-Explosive Gunpowder (x12), Spirit of Harmony (x12), Ghost Iron Bolts (x20)
Energized Retinal Armor	600	Living Steel (x6), River's Heart, Ghost Iron Bolts (x6)
Geosynchronous World Spinner	600	Living Steel (x12), Trillium Bar (x12), Spirit of Harmony (x12), Ghost Iron Bolts (x20), Orb of Mystery (x3)
Lightweight Retinal Armor	600	Living Steel (x6), River's Heart, Ghost Iron Bolts (x6)
Reinforced Retinal Armor	600	Living Steel (x6), Ghost Iron Bolts (x12)
Specialized Retinal Armor	600	Living Steel (x6), Sun's Radiance, Ghost Iron Bolts (x6)

INSCRIPTION

In addition to Staffs and Off-hand items, Scribes create Glyphs, scrolls, cards, and other paper and book items with paper purchased from Trade vendors, and inks. Scribes automatically learn Milling, which turns herbs into pigments, and other Inscription abilities turn the pigments into ink. While Inscription creates many items, it's best known for making Glyphs. Glyphs are class-specific recipes that enhance characters' abilities. There are two types of glyphs: Minor and Major.

Inscription is an expensive profession, unless you take Herbalism as well. Scribes need a Virtuoso Inking Set in their inventory to create many of their goods. The set isn't expensive, and it never wears out. Keep one in your inventory and your character will be able to Inscribe anywhere in the world.

Proficiency Level Name	Character Level Minimum	Skill Level Minimum	Skill Level Maximum
Apprentice	5	0	75
Journeyman	10	50	150
Expert	20	125	225
Artisan	35	200	300
Master	50	275	375
Grand Master	65	350	450
Illustrious Grand Master	75	425	525
Zen Master	80	500	600

PRACTICING INSCRIPTION

Clicking the Inscription icon opens a menu of all the Inscription patterns you know. Milling turns five similar herbs into one of two types of pigments (most herbs have a common pigment result and an uncommon pigment result). You must have five of the same herb in order to Mill them for pigments. The herbs are used up, but you get the pigments necessary to create inks. Creating ink is a good way to skill up Inscription each time you learn a new type of ink.

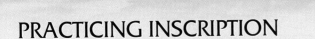

THE INKMASTERS

When you reach a certain proficiency with your Inscription skill, weekly quests become available at the Arboretum in The Jade Forest from Inkmasters Wei, Jo-Po, and Glenzu. These quests help you become a better Scribe.

Quest Givers	Quests
Inkmaster Wei	A Thing of Beauty
Inkmaster Jo Po	Staves for Tian Monastery
Inkmaster Glenzu	Set in Jade
	Incarnadine Ink
	Portrait of a Lady
	A Tribute to the Dead

INSCRIPTION BONUSES

One bonus for Inscription is the ability to create shoulder armor Inscriptions which are superior to what is available to anyone else in the game. There are shoulder armor Inscriptions for every role, meaning any class and spec benefit from them. There are also epic staffs that bind to your Battle. Net account that are eligible for upgrades over time.

MAKING MONEY AS A SCRIBE

When it comes time to switch Glyphs, players need a steady supply of Tome of the Clear Mind, which can be created with Inscription. Inscription is now the only source for Shoulder slot Enhancements. Scribes can create and sell Epic off-hand items. Finally, the sets of Darkmoon Cards draw quite a bit of interest. The downside to these cards is the random nature of its creation. You never know which card you'll create. Hit the right ones, though, and you could make a small fortune selling them to other players.

PIGMENT TYPE

Herb	Milled Into
Green Tea Leaf, Rain Poppy, Silkweed, Snow Lily, Fool's Cap	Shadow Pigment, Misty Pigment

INK TYPE

Pigment	Ink
Shadow Pigment	Ink of Dreams
Misty Pigment	Starlight Ink

NEW GENERAL RECIPES FOR MISTS OF PANDARIA

Item	Skill Level	Reagents
Ink of Dreams	500	Shadow Pigment (x2)
Starlight Ink	500	Misty Pigment (x2)
Tome of the Clear Mind	500	Light Parchment, Ink of Dreams
Scroll of Wisdom	545	Light Parchment, Ink of Dreams (x3)
Runescroll of Fortitude III	580	Light Parchment (x5), Ink of Dreams (x10)
Darkmoon Card of Mists	600	Light Parchment, Ink of Dreams (x10), Scroll of Wisdom
Chi-ji Kite	600	Light Parchment, Ink of Dreams (x4)
Origami Crane	600	Light Parchment, Ink of Dreams (x4)
Origami Frog	600	Light Parchment, Ink of Dreams (x4)
Yu'lon Kite	600	Light Parchment, Ink of Dreams (x4)

NEW OFF-HAND ITEMS FOR MISTS OF PANDARIA

Item	Skill Level	Reagents
Inscribed Fan	560	Light Parchment, Ink of Dreams (x5), Spirit of Harmony
Inscribed Jade Fan	560	Inscribed Fan, Starlight Ink (x3), Scroll of Wisdom (x5)
Inscribed Red Fan	560	Inscribed Fan, Starlight Ink (x3), Scroll of Wisdom (x5)

HIGH LEVEL STAFFS FOR MISTS OF PANDARIA

Item	Skill Level	Reagents
Ghost Iron Staff	560	Plain Wooden Staff, Ink of Dreams (x8), Spirit of Harmony (x2), Ghost Iron Bar (x3)
Inscribed Tiger Staff	560	Ghost Iron Staff, Starlight Ink (x20), Scroll of Wisdom (x20), Spirit of Harmony (x5)
Rain Poppy Staff	560	Plain Wooden Staff, Ink of Dreams (x8), Spirit of Harmony (x2), Rain Poppy (x3)
Inscribed Crane Staff	560	Rain Poppy Staff, Starlight Ink (x20), Scroll of Wisdom (x20), Spirit of Harmony (x5)
Inscribed Serpent Staff	560	Rain Poppy Staff, Starlight Ink (x20), Scroll of Wisdom (x20), Spirit of Harmony (x5)

NEW SHOULDER ENCHANTMENTS FOR MISTS OF PANDARIA

Item	Skill Level	Reagents
Tiger Fang Inscription	540	Light Parchment, Ink of Dreams (x3)
Tiger Claw Inscription	540	Light Parchment, Ink of Dreams (x3)
Crane Wing Inscription	540	Light Parchment, Ink of Dreams (x3)
Ox Horn Inscription	540	Light Parchment, Ink of Dreams (x3)
Greater Tiger Fang Inscription	570	Light Parchment, Starlight Ink (x3)
Greater Tiger Claw Inscription	570	Light Parchment, Starlight Ink (x3)
Greater Crane Wing Inscription	570	Light Parchment, Starlight Ink (x3)
Greater Ox Horn Inscription	570	Light Parchment, Starlight Ink (x3)
Tiger Fang Inscription	540	Light Parchment, Ink of Dreams (x3)

NEW INSCRIPTION-ONLY SHOULDER ENCHANTMENTS FOR MISTS OF PANDAIRA

Item	Skill Level	Reagents
Secret Tiger Fang Inscription	575	Light Parchment, Ink of Dreams (x3)
Secret Tiger Claw Inscription	575	Light Parchment, Ink of Dreams (x3)
Secret Crane Wing Inscription	575	Light Parchment, Ink of Dreams (x3)
Secret Ox Horn Inscription	575	Light Parchment, Ink of Dreams (x3)
Secret Tiger Fang Inscription	575	Light Parchment, Ink of Dreams (x3)

JEWELCRAFTING

Initially, Jewelcrafters create the wire and settings necessary to craft low level rings and necklaces, then start making rings, necklaces, and other random items. A Jeweler's Kit is required, but it is available at a trivial cost from a Trade vendor. At higher skill levels, Jewelcrafters learn how to cut gems that provide statistical bonuses to socketed equipment. Even at higher skill levels, Jewelcrafters continue to create rings and necklaces for anyone to use.

Jewelcrafting can be an expensive Profession to skill up, so strongly consider Mining as a second Profession, to gather your own ore. Jewelcrafters learn a second ability, called Prospecting, which allows them to break down raw ore and extract different minerals and gems that are otherwise available only through mining.

Proficiency Level Name	Character Level Minimum	Skill Level Minimum	Skill Level Maximum
Apprentice	5	0	75
Journeyman	10	50	150
Expert	20	125	225
Artisan	35	200	300
Master	50	275	375
Grand Master	65	350	450
Illustrious Grand Master	75	425	525
Zen Master	80	500	600

PRACTICING JEWELCRAFTING

Clicking Prospecting enables you to search five ore of the same type to find gems. Some types of ore of Uncommmon quality, such as Silver, cannot be Prospected. The ore is destroyed in the process, but you gain your shiny jewelcrafting ingredients.

For high-level Jewelcrafting, you need a base set of gems to work with. These are then turned into finished cut gems that provide bonuses when slotted into equipment. Note that you don't gain points in Jewelcrafting for slotting equipment, only for making the gems.

JEWELCRAFTING BONUSES

Jewelcrafters, at many skill levels, create bind on pick up trinkets that work for any role, making them useful to every class and spec. Jewelcrafters also have access to specialty gems that are superior to Epic quality gems available to other players. There is a limit to how many of these specialty gems can be socketed into the Jewelcrafter's gear.

DRAENEI BONUS

Draenei have a racial ability—Gemcutting—which increases their Jewelcrafting skill by 10.

MAKING MONEY AS A JEWELCRAFTER

After reaching high skill levels in this profession, Jewelcrafting turns from a major money sink into a considerable money maker. There's constant demand for high-end gems (Serpent's Eye in Pandaria) as many players are striving to collect better gear.

TWO SPECIAL CASES: PRISMATIC AND META GEMS

Prismatic gems are considered Unique (meaning you can have only one socketed in all your equipment at a time), provide a boost to all stats, and don't have a defined color. These gems count as every color when it comes to a socket bonus.

Meta gems are a special gem that provide bonuses beyond simple statistical boosts. These gems fit only into meta sockets, and no other gem can go into a meta socket; meta sockets appear only in hats or helmets. Before you choose a meta gem, carefully read what other gems are required for its effect to be active. Raw meta gems are created by Alchemists, then cut by Jewelcrafters.

PROSPECTING

The following tables list the possible gems that come from Prospecting (remember, you need five of the same ore type in order to Prospect). These results are identical to the types of gems that may be obtained from Mining the ore's vein or node.

PROSPECTING ORE FROM PANDARIA

Ore Type	Gems Prospected
Ghost Iron Ore	Lapis Lazuli, River's Heart, Tiger Opal, Primordial Ruby, Sunstone, Sun's Radiance, Roguestone, Wild Jade, Pandarian Garnet, Vermillion Onyx, Alexandrite, Imperial Amethyst
Kyparite Ore	Lapis Lazuli, River's Heart, Tiger Opal, Primordial Ruby, Sunstone, Sun's Radiance, Roguestone, Wild Jade, Pandarian Garnet, Vermillion Onyx, Alexandrite, Imperial Amethyst

GEMS BY COLOR

Gem Color	Pandaria Gems
Blue	Lapis Lazuli, River's Heart
Red	Tiger Opal, Primordial Ruby
Yellow	Sunstone, Sun's Radiance
Green	Roguestone, Wild Jade
Orange	Pandarian Garnet, Vermillion Onyx
Purple	Alexandrite, Imperial Amethyst
Meta	Primal Diamond

RING RECIPES FOR MISTS OF PANDARIA

Name	Skill Level	Reagents
Ornate Band	500	Lapis Lazuli (x4), Sunstone, Jeweler's Setting
Band of Blood	575	Vermillion Onyx (x2), Serpent's Eye (x6), Jeweler's Setting
Heart of the Earth	575	Wild Jade (x2), Serpent's Eye (x6), Jeweler's Setting
Lionsfall Ring	575	Sun's Radiance (x2), Serpent's Eye (x6), Jeweler's Setting
Lord's Signet	575	Primorial Ruby (x2) Serpent's Eye (x6), Jeweler's Setting
Roguestone Shadowband	575	Roguestone (x6) Serpent's Eye (x6), Jeweler's Setting

AMULET RECIPES FOR MISTS OF PANDARIA

Name	Skill Level	Reagents
Shadowfire Necklace	510	Roguestone, Alexandrite, Pandarian Garnet, Jeweler's Setting
Golembreaker Amulet	575	Pandarian Garnet (x6), Serpent's Eye (x6), Jeweler's Setting
Reflection of the Sea	575	River's Heart (x2) Serpent's Eye (x6), Jeweler's Setting
Skymage Circle	575	Imperial Amethyst (x2) Serpent's Eye (x6), Jeweler's Setting
Tiger Opal Pendant	575	Tiger Opal (x6) Serpent's Eye (x6), Jeweler's Setting
Widow Chain	575	Sunstone (x6) Serpent's Eye (x6), Jeweler's Setting

OTHER RECIPES FOR MISTS OF PANDARIA

Name	Skill Level	Reagents
Scrying Roguestone	525	Roguestone
Jade Owl	600	Wild Jade (x3), Spirit of Harmony (x3)
Jade Panther	600	Orb of Mystery, Wild Jade, Living Steel (x4), Serpent's Eye (x2)
Jeweled Onyx Panther	600	Sunstone Panther, Jade Panther, Ruby Panther, Sapphire Panther
Ruby Panther	600	Orb of Mystery, Primordial Ruby (x20), Living Steel (x4), Serpent's Eye (x2)
Sapphire Cub	600	River's Heart (x3), Spirit of Harmony (x3)
Sapphire Panther	600	Orb of Mystery, River's Heart (x20), Living Steel (x4), Serpent's Eye (x2)
Sunstone Panther	600	Orb of Mystery, Sun's Radiance (x20), Living Steel (x5), Serpent's Eye (x2)

WHAT CUT GEM NAMES MEAN

The following table provides the names for the cuts for each gem of a specific color. Sometimes when you create a gem of Uncommon quality, you will get a Perfect cut with slightly better stats.

Color	Cut Name	Stat(s) Provided
Blue	Rigid	Hit
	Solid	Stamina
	Sparkling	Spirit
	Stormy	PVP Power
Red	Bold	Strength
	Brilliant	Intellect
	Delicate	Agility
	Flashing	Parry
	Precise	Expertise
Yellow	Fractured	Mastery
	Mystic	PVP Resilience
	Quick	Haste
	Smooth	Critical Strike
	Subtle	Dodge
Green	Balanced	Hit and PVP Resilience
	Effulgent	PVP Power and Mastery
	Energized	Haste and Spirit
	Forceful	Haste and Stamina
	Jagged	Critical Strike and Stamina
	Lightning	Hit and Haste
	Misty	Critical Strike and Spirit
	Nimble	Hit and Dodge
	Puissant	Mastery and Stamina
	Radiant	Critical Strike and Spell Penetration
	Regal	Dodge and Stamina
	Sensei's	Hit and Mastery
	Shattered	Haste and PVP Power
	Steady	PVP Resilience and Stamina
	Turbid	PVP Resilience and Spirit
	Vivid	PVP Power and PVP Resilience
	Zen	Spirit and Mastery

Color	Cut Name	Stat(s) Provided
Orange	Adept	Agility and Mastery
	Artful	Intellect and Mastery
	Champion's	Strength and Dodge
	Crafty	Expertise and Critical Strike
	Deadly	Agility and Critical Strike
	Deft	Agility and Haste
	Fierce	Strength and Haste
	Fine	Parry and Mastery
	Inscribed	Strength and Critical Strike
	Keen	Expertise and Mastery
	Lucent	Agility and PVP Resilience
	Polished	Agility and Dodge
	Potent	Intellect and Critical Strike
	Reckless	Intellect and Haste
	Resolute	Expertise and Dodge
	Resplendent	Strength and PVP Resilience
	Stalwart	Parry and Dodge
	Tenuous	Expertise and PVP Resilience
	Wicked	Expertise and Haste
	Willful	Intellect and PVP Resilience
Purple	Accurate	Expertise and Hit
	Defender's	Parry and Stamina
	Etched	Strength and Hit
	Glinting	Agility and Hit
	Guardian's	Expertise and Stamina
	Mysterious	Intellect and Spell Penetration
	Purified	Intellect and Spirit
	Retaliating	Parry and Hit
	Shifting	Agility and Stamina
	Sovereign	Strength and Stamina
	Timeless	Intellect and Stamina
	Veiled	Intellect and Hit

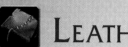 # LEATHERWORKING

Leatherworking uses leather and hides gathered from slain beasts to create different pieces of armor, and kits that boost armor in different ways. There are no special tools required for Leatherworking, save for the Salt Shaker needed to cure certain lower level hides. Some Leatherworking patterns require items purchased from trade vendors.

PRACTICING LEATHERWORKING

It's best to do your Leatherworking near a Bank, because you need to carry around a huge amount of leather as well as any products that you're creating.

Proficiency Level Name	Character Level Minimum	Skill Level Minimum	Skill Level Maximum
Apprentice	5	0	75
Journeyman	10	50	150
Expert	20	125	225
Artisan	35	200	300
Master	50	275	375
Grand Master	65	350	450
Illustrious Grand Master	75	425	525
Zen Master	80	500	600

LEATHERWORKING BONUSES

Leatherworkers get to apply Fur Lining to their wrist slot items. There are many types of Fur Lining, and there's at least one for each role. That means there's a solid choice regardless of your class or spec. In addition, Leatherworkers can create kits for their leg armor at a greatly reduced price and at a lower level than what is available for non-Leatherworkers.

MAKING MONEY AS A LEATHERWORKER

Leatherworkers don't have extensive sales, but they also don't need to invest as heavily in their Profession. Anyone with Leatherworking and Skinning should have an easy time, especially due to the nature of Skinning. It's easy to find creatures that are skinnable, so reagents are somewhat cheap and plentiful.

The problem is that Leatherworking is a poor money maker until you skill up to high-end armor kits, in the expansion areas. These are some of the few products in Leatherworking that have widespread appeal. Otherwise, this is more of a niche market.

Skins and Hides from Pandaria

Sha-Touched Leather	Prismatic Scale
Exotic Leather	Magnificent Hide

COMBINING SCRAPS AND LEATHER

Leatherworkers are able to take a number of lesser leather and combine it into a better quality of leather. That hasn't changed for Mists of Pandaria, where Leatherworkers can purify Sha-Touched Leather.

Start with	Turns Into	Skill Required
5 Sha-Touched Leather	1 Exotic Leather	500
50 Exotic Leather	1 Magnificent Hide	550

NEW ARMOR KIT RECIPES FOR MISTS OF PANDARIA

Name	Skill Level	Reagents
Sha Armor Kit	525	Exotic Leather (x4)
Brutal Leg Armor	535	Exotic Leather (x12)
Sha-Touched Leg Armor	545	Exotic Leather (x12)
Toughened Leg Armor	555	Exotic Leather (x12)
Angerhide Leg Armor	575	Magnificent Hide, Spirit of Harmony
Ironscale Leg Armor	575	Magnificent Hide (x50), Spirit of Harmony
Shadowleather Leg Armor	575	Magnificent Hide (x50), Spirit of Harmony

NEW LEATHER ARMOR RECIPES FOR MISTS OF PANDARIA

Name	Skill Level	Reagents
Misthide Boots	525	Exotic Leather (x8)
Misthide Bracers	530	Exotic Leather (x5)
Misthide Belt	535	Exotic Leather (x8)
Misthide Shoulders	540	Exotic Leather (x8)
Misthide Gloves	545	Exotic Leather (x8)
Misthide Leggings	550	Exotic Leather (x10)
Misthide Helm	555	Exotic Leather (x10)
Misthide Chestguard	560	Exotic Leather (x10)
Contender's Leather Belt	575	Exotic Leather (x15)
Contender's Leather Boots	575	Exotic Leather (x15)
Contender's Leather Bracers	575	Exotic Leather (x12)
Contender's Leather Chestguard	575	Exotic Leather (x20)
Contender's Leather Gloves	575	Exotic Leather (x15)
Contender's Leather Helm	575	Exotic Leather (x20)
Contender's Leather Leggings	575	Exotic Leather (x20)
Contender's Leather Shoulders	575	Exotic Leather (x15)
Contender's Wyrmhide Belt	575	Exotic Leather (x15)
Contender's Wyrmhide Boots	575	Exotic Leather (x15)
Contender's Wyrmhide Bracers	575	Exotic Leather (x12)
Contender's Wyrmhide Chestguard	575	Exotic Leather (x20)
Contender's Wyrmhide Gloves	575	Exotic Leather (x15)
Contender's Wyrmhide Helm	575	Exotic Leather (x20)
Contender's Wyrmhide Leggings	575	Exotic Leather (x20)
Contender's Wyrmhide Shoulders	575	Exotic Leather (x15)
Chestguard of Nemeses	600	Magnificent Hide (x3), Spirit of Harmony (x4), Blood Spirit (x8)
Greyshadow Chestguard	600	Magnificent Hide (x3), Spirit of Harmony (x8)
Greyshadow Gloves	600	Magnificent Hide (x2), Spirit of Harmony (x6)
Liferuned Leather Gloves	600	Magnificent Hide (x2), Spirit of Harmony (x3), Blood Spirit (x6)
Murderer's Gloves	600	Magnificent Hide (x2), Spirit of Harmony (x3), Blood Spirit (x6)
Nightfire Robe	600	Magnificent Hide (x3), Spirit of Harmony (x4), Blood Spirit (x8)
Wildblood Gloves	600	Magnificent Hide (x2), Spirit of Harmony (x6)
Wildblood Vest	600	Magnificent Hide (x3), Spirit of Harmony (x8)

NEW MAIL ARMOR RECIPES FOR MISTS OF PANDARIA

Name	Skill Level	Reagents
Stormscale Bracers	525	Prismatic Scale (x5)
Stormscale Belt	530	Prismatic Scale (x8)
Stormscale Boots	535	Prismatic Scale (x8)
Stormscale Gloves	540	Prismatic Scale (x8)
Stormscale Shoulders	545	Prismatic Scale (x8)
Stormscale Helm	550	Prismatic Scale (x10)
Stormscale Chestguard	555	Prismatic Scale (x10)
Stormscale Leggings	560	Prismatic Scale (x10)
Contender's Dragonscale Belt	575	Prismatic Scale (x15)
Contender's Dragonscale Boots	575	Prismatic Scale (x15)
Contender's Dragonscale Bracers	575	Prismatic Scale (x12)
Contender's Dragonscale Chestguard	575	Prismatic Scale (x20)
Contender's Dragonscale Gloves	575	Prismatic Scale (x15)
Contender's Dragonscale Helm	575	Prismatic Scale (x20)
Contender's Dragonscale Leggings	575	Prismatic Scale (x20)
Contender's Dragonscale Shoulders	575	Prismatic Scale (x15)
Contender's Scale Belt	575	Prismatic Scale (x15)
Contender's Scale Boots	575	Prismatic Scale (x15)
Contender's Scale Bracers	575	Prismatic Scale (x12)
Contender's Scale Chestguard	575	Prismatic Scale (x20)
Contender's Scale Gloves	575	Prismatic Scale (x15)
Contender's Scale Helm	575	Prismatic Scale (x20)
Contender's Scale Leggings	575	Prismatic Scale (x20)
Contender's Scale Shoulders	575	Prismatic Scale (x15)
Chestguard of Earthen Harmony	600	Magnificent Hide (x3), Spirit of Harmony (x8)
Fists of Lightning	600	Magnificent Hide (x2), Spirit of Harmony (x3), Blood Spirit (x6)
Gloves of Earthen Harmony	600	Magnificent Hide (x2), Spirit of Harmony (x6)
Lifekeeper's Gloves	600	Magnificent Hide (x2), Spirit of Harmony (x6)
Lifekeeper's Robe	600	Magnificent Hide (x3), Spirit of Harmony (x8)
Raiment of Blood and Bone	600	Magnificent Hide (x3), Spirit of Harmony (x4), Blood Spirit (x8)
Raven Lord's Gloves	600	Magnificent Hide (x2), Spirit of Harmony (x3), Blood Spirit (x6)
Stormbreaker Chestguard	600	Magnificent Hide (x3), Spirit of Harmony (x4), Blood Spirit (x8)

NEW CLOAK RECIPES FOR MISTS OF PANDARIA

Name	Skill Level	Reagents
Stormscale Drape	550	Prismatic Scale (x20), Spirit of Harmony
Cloak of the Mists	555	Exotic Leather (x5), Prismatic Scale (x5)
Quick Strike Cloak	560	Exotic Leather (x20), Spirit of Harmony

TAILORING

Tailoring creates cloth armor, shirts, bags, and other items out of different types of cloth. Cloth is available as drops from humanoid and many undead enemies, and the silks dropped by spiders are often required for some patterns as well. Tailors also learn how to improve various types of cloth. These improved pieces of cloth are then used to create more powerful equipment, including special types of Spellthreads that act as Enchantments for leg armor.

PRACTICING TAILORING

Click on the Tailoring icon to bring up your list of patterns. This can be done at many locations, but like Leatherworking it's best to do near a Bank or trade vendor because there might be additional reagents involved in the creation process.

Proficiency Level Name	Character Level Minimum	Skill Level Minimum	Skill Level Maximum
Apprentice	5	0	75
Journeyman	10	50	150
Expert	20	125	225
Artisan	35	200	300
Master	50	275	375
Grand Master	65	350	450
Illustrious Grand Master	70	425	525
Zen Master	80	500	600

TAILORING BONUSES

Tailors have the ability to enhance their own cloaks with specialized embroidery patterns. These embroidery patterns help out damage dealing and healing specs. In Northrend, Tailors eventually learn the Northrend Cloth Scavenging ability, which allows them to obtain additional Frostweave from defeated enemies. If you're a fan of flying carpets, Tailoring has what you want. There are three patterns for flying carpets that only Tailors can use to fly around the world.

MAKING MONEY WITH TAILORING

Bags are the most widespread product from this Profession. Tailors have a long-term market for these, especially once they start getting into bags from the later game. In addition, Tailors can create a variety of shirts and other specialized clothing for fun and role-playing purposes. The high level enchantment threads are also in high demand as players earn better and better leg armor pieces.

NEW CREATED CLOTH FOR MISTS OF PANDARIA

Name	Skill Level	Reagents
Bolt of Windwool Cloth	500	Windwool Cloth (x5)
Imperial Silk	550	Bolt of Windwool Cloth (x8)

NEW TAILORING RECIPES FOR MISTS OF PANDARIA

Name	Skill Level	Reagents
Windwool Bracers	525	Bolt of Windwool Cloth (x3)
Windwool Gloves	525	Bolt of Windwool Cloth (x4)
Windwool Belt	535	Bolt of Windwool Cloth (x4)
Windwool Shoulders	535	Bolt of Windwool Cloth (x4)
Windwool Boots	545	Bolt of Windwool Cloth (x4)
Windwool Pants	545	Bolt of Windwool Cloth (x5)
Windwool Hood	555	Bolt of Windwool Cloth (x5)
Windwool Tunic	555	Bolt of Windwool Cloth (x5)
Contender's Satin Amice	575	Bolt of Windwool Cloth (x4)
Contender's Satin Belt	575	Bolt of Windwool Cloth (x4)
Contender's Satin Cowl	575	Bolt of Windwool Cloth (x5)
Contender's Satin Cuffs	575	Bolt of Windwool Cloth (x3)
Contender's Satin Footwraps	575	Bolt of Windwool Cloth (x4)
Contender's Satin Handwraps	575	Bolt of Windwool Cloth (x4)
Contender's Satin Pants	575	Bolt of Windwool Cloth (x5)
Contender's Satin Rainment	575	Bolt of Windwool Cloth (x5)
Contender's Silk Amice	575	Bolt of Windwool Cloth (x4)
Contender's Silk Belt	575	Bolt of Windwool Cloth (x4)
Contender's Silk Cowl	575	Bolt of Windwool Cloth (x5)
Contender's Silk Cuffs	575	Bolt of Windwool Cloth (x3)
Contender's Silk Footwraps	575	Bolt of Windwool Cloth (x4)
Contender's Silk Handwraps	575	Bolt of Windwool Cloth (x4)
Contender's Silk Pants	575	Bolt of Windwool Cloth (x5)
Contender's Silk Rainment	575	Bolt of Windwool Cloth (x5)
Gloves of Creation	600	Imperial Silk (x4)
Imperial Silk Gloves	600	Imperial Silk (x4), Blood Spirit (x5)
Legacy of the Emperor	600	Imperial Silk (x6), Blood Spirit (x8)
Robe of Eternal Rule	600	Imperial Silk (x6), Blood Spirit (x8)
Robes of Creation	600	Imperial Silk (x6)
Royal Satchel	600	Imperial Silk (x12)
Spelltwister's Gloves	600	Imperial Silk (x4)
Spelltwister's Grand Robe	600	Imperial Silk (x6)
Touch of the Light	600	Imperial Silk (x4), Blood Spirit (x5)

NEW SPELLTHREAD FOR MISTS OF PANDARIA

Name	Skill Level	Reagents
Pearlescent Spellthread	530	Bolt of Windwool Cloth (x4)
Cerulean Spellthread	540	Bolt of Windwool Cloth (x4)
Greater Pearlescent Spellthread	575	Imperial Silk
Greater Cerulean Spellthread	575	Imperial Silk

HERBALISM

Herbalism is the harvesting of herbs from plant nodes, and from some enemies (usually Elemental enemies that look like walking vegetation) which have some affinity with nature. These herbs are primarily used by Alchemists and Scribes.

When you learn Herbalism, you gain the Find Herbs skill. When this skill is active, herb nodes appear on your mini-map. Watch for these icons while hunting and questing and you should see your skill increase rapidly.

When you find a node, the herb sparkles and your mouse cursor changes into a flower blossom. To gather, right-click on the herb in question. The same thing applies when you find harvestable enemies. When you mouse over a corpse, your mouse cursor changes to a flower blossom if you can harvest from it.

Proficiency Level Name	Character Level Minimum	Skill Level Minimum	Skill Level Maximum
Apprentice	1	0	75
Journeyman	1	50	150
Expert	10	125	225
Artisan	25	200	300
Master	40	275	375
Grand Master	55	350	450
Illustrious Grand Master	70	425	525
Zen Master	80	500	600

HERBALISM BONUSES

Herbalists gain an ability known as Lifeblood. Lifeblood restores health to the Herbalist over time and also provides a boost to Haste. Lifeblood has a two minute cooldown, and its effects scales with your skill in Herbalism.

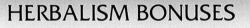

TAUREN BONUS

Taurens have a racial ability—Cultivation—which increases their Herbalism skill by 15 and allows them to harvest herbs faster than other races.

MAKING MONEY WITH HERBALISM

Herbalism is a good Profession for making money. People buy herbs at lucrative prices, even from the beginning levels forward. There is always a market for most of these herbs, and a new player stands to make plenty of cash if they sell herbs in the Auction House.

NEW HERB NODES IN PANDARIA

Node	Required Skill	Loot
Green Tea Leaf	500	Green Tea Leaf, Life Spirit, Water Spirit
Rain Poppy	525	Rain Poppy, Life Spirit, Water Spirit
Silkweed	545	Silkweed, Life Spirit, Water Spirit
Snow Lily	545	Snow Lily, Life Spirit, Water Spirit
Golden Lotus	550	Golden Lotus
Sha-Touched Herb	575	Random Pandaria Herb
Fool's Cap	600	Fool's Cap, Life Spirit, Water Spirit

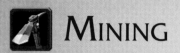 # MINING

With Mining, you extract ore, gems, and (in lower level zones) stones from raw metal veins, deposits, and from some enemies (usually rocky Elemental creatures). These materials are used primarily in Jewelcrafting, Blacksmithing, and Engineering. A Mining Pick (or any item that acts as a Mining Pick) is required to mine. You do not need to equip the Mining Pick; just keep it in your Backpack. Miners learn a second ability, Smelting, which turns the ore into metal bars.

Mining also imparts the ability to Find Minerals. When it is active, mineral nodes appear on your mini-map. When you find a node, it sparkles and the cursor changes into a pick axe. To mine, right-click on the node. The same thing applies when you find harvestable enemies. When you mouse over a corpse, your mouse cursor changes to a pick axe if you can harvest from it.

Proficiency Level Name	Character Level Minimum	Skill Level Minimum	Skill Level Maximum
Apprentice	1	0	75
Journeyman	1	50	150
Expert	10	125	225
Artisan	25	200	300
Master	40	275	375
Grand Master	55	350	450
Illustrious Grand Master	70	425	525
Zen Master	80	500	600

Another way to increase your Mining skill level is to Smelt ore. To Smelt, you need access to a forge and ore. Click on the Smelting icon to see you what you can currently Smelt. Gaining skill ups from Smelting varies wildly with each new ore you learn to Smelt. Any time you work with a new metal, Smelt as much of it as you can as soon as you can. The skill ups from Smelting dry up much faster than the skill ups you get from mining.

MINING BONUSES

Miners gain extra Stamina due to Toughness. The extra Stamina provided by Toughness increases as your skill level in Mining increases.

MAKING MONEY WITH MINING

Mining can be incredibly profitable. With three distinct Professions all requiring ore, you have a large potential market. Try selling your metal in both bar and ore form as some people want the refined bars, while others (particularly Jewelcrafters) want the raw ore.

NEW MINING NODES IN PANDARIA

Node	Required Skill	Loot
Ghost Iron Deposit	475	Ghost Iron Ore
Rich Ghost Iron Deposit	540	Ghost Iron Ore
Kyparite Deposit	550	Kyparite Ore
Rich Kyparite Depsoit	575	Kyparite Ore
Trillium Vein	600	Black Trillium Ore, White Trillium Ore
Rich Trillium Vein	600	Black Trillium Ore, White Trillium Ore

SKINNING

Skinners are able to harvest the leather and hides from slain beasts. After you slay a beast and loot it (assuming it's a skinnable creature) your mouse cursor changes into an animal hide when you mouse over it. A Skinning Knife (or another item that acts as a Skinning Knife) is required for Skinning; however, you don't need to equip the item, just keep it in your Backpack. To skin, right-click on a skinnable beast. You can also skin another player's looted corpses, but it's good form to ask for permission first unless the other player leaves the area.

Proficiency Level Name	Character Level Minimum	Skill Level Minimum	Skill Level Maximum
Apprentice	1	0	75
Journeyman	1	50	150
Expert	10	125	225
Artisan	25	200	300
Master	40	275	375
Grand Master	55	350	450
Illustrious Grand Master	70	425	525
Zen Master	80	500	600

Enemy Level	Skinning Needed
85	500
86	515
87	530
88	545
89	560
90	575

The leathers and hides are primarily used by Leatherworkers. Skinning is faster to advance than Herbalism or Mining, due to the prevalence of beasts in the game.

When you first learn Skinning, you can skin any creature level 10 or lower. For creatures from levels 11 through 20, your skinning must be [10 x (Creature's Level - 10)], meaning your Skinning skill must be 20 if you wish to skin a level 12 beast, while a level 20 beast calls for a skill of 100.

For creatures from levels 21 through 79, your Skinning skill must be equal to five times the creature's level to skin it successfully. That means your Skinning skill must be at 300 to skin level 60 beasts, and 350 for level 70 beasts. When you reach level 85 enemies, use the table above to determine what skill level you need to skin beasts.

SKINNING BONUSES

Skinners gain extra Critical Strike chance through Master of Anatomy. The extra Critical Strike chance provided by Master of Anatomy increases as you improve your Skinning skill level.

MAKING MONEY WITH SKINNING

Hides are always in demand at the Auction House, but they don't fetch as much as the materials from herbalism and mining. Skins are arguably easier to acquire than ore and herbs since those nodes often appear alone, and you can find packs of beasts for Skinning, which leads to a greater supply, and lower prices.

WORGEN BONUS

Worgen have a racial ability Flayer—which increases their Skinning skill by 15 and allows them to skin faster than other races. They also do not need a Skinning Knife.

NEW SKINS AND HIDES FROM PANDARIA

Leather	Source
Sha-Touched Leather	Skinnable Enemies, Level 85-86
Exotic Leather	Skinnable Enemies, Level 85-90
Magnificent Hide	Skinnable Enemies, Level 85-90
Prismatic Scale	Skinnable Enemies, Level 85-90

PLUMP INTESTINES

Sometimes when you skin, you'll get an item called Plump Intestines in your inventory. Plump Intestines hold bonus gold. Right-click on the item to claim what's inside.

ARCHAEOLOGY

Archaeology is all about exploration and uncovering the past. There are two steps in the Archaeological process. First, you visit digsites and use Surveying to locate and unearth artifact fragments of items from various cultures. After collecting enough pieces, you assemble them into a restored piece.

Unlike other gathering skills, digsites are player-specific. There is no competition for artifact fragments between players. Other players searching at the same digsite are uncovering their own fragments.

Proficiency Level Name	Character Level Minimum	Skill Level Minimum	Skill Level Maximum
Apprentice	20	0	75
Journeyman	20	50	150
Expert	20	125	225
Artisan	35	200	300
Master	50	275	375
Grand Master	65	350	450
Illustrious Grand Master	75	425	525
Zen Master	80	500	600

PRACTICING ARCHEOLOGY

Open your world map and look for the small shovel icons that appear around the world. There should be up to four zones appropriate to your character's level per continent (Eastern Kingoms, Kalimdor, Draenor, Northrend, and Pandaria) that include active digsites for you. When you zoom into a zone with an active digsite, the area shaded red on the map provides the exact location for you to visit. There's an option at the bottom of the map frame to toggle the red-shading at the dig sites.

DWARF BONUS

Dwarves have a racial ability—Explorer—which allows them to find additional fragments when looting archaeological finds and survey faster than other archaeologists.

When you reach the area, use the Survey ability to get directions to the exact location of the fragments. The survey instrument that appears indicates both the direction of, and distance to, the fragments. A red light means the fragments are far away, the yellow light indicates you are getting closer and the green light means you are very close to the fragments. When you are close enough to the fragments, a container of some sort appears instead of your survey tools. Right-click on the item to collect the fragments. You don't carry these items around in your Backpack. Instead, they're stored as currency.

Click on the appropriate Archaeology crest to watch your progress. After you collect enough fragments, click on the Solve button to create the listed item. The item goes into your backpack, you get a skill up, and you start on the next object. Any leftover fragments are applied to the new item, so you don't need to worry about wasted pieces.

Most of the items uncovered with Archaeology are not for combat purposes. There are a few special pieces here and there, but mostly this Profession leads to more peripheral elements, like fun pets and mounts.

ARCHAEOLOGY ON PANDARIA

While the process of uncovering and recreating artifacts remains the same when you start on the continent of Pandaria, there are a few new twists. The first is the Ancient Haunt, a creature that will attack you after you uncover a cache of fragments. When you defeat the Ancient Haunt, loot it for the extra fragments it drops.

Type/Fragments	Keystones	Minimum Skill To Get Digsites
Dwarf	Dwarf Rune Stone	1
Fossil	N/A	1
Night Elf	Highborne Scroll	1
Troll	Troll Tablet	1
Draenei	Draenei Tome	300
Nerubian	Nerubian Obelisk	300
Orc	Orc Blood Text	300
Vrykul	Vrykul Rune Stick	300
Tol'Vir	Tol'vir Hieroglphic	450
Mogu	Mogu Statue Piece	500
Pandaren	Pandaren Pottery Shard	500

The Seat of Knowledge

Visit the Seat of Knowledge, located above the Mogu'shan Palace in Vale of Eternal Blossoms, to further your Archaeology studies. Ms. Thai and Master Liu both offer daily quests. These quests send you on archaeological expeditions around Pandaria and reward you with Valor Points.

Brann Bronzebeard is also located at the library and gives you access to training, plus items in exchange for Restored Artifacts. The items he offers include different types of Archaeology fragments from Azeroth and Outland, and even items that reset your digsites!

Quest Givers	Quests
Master Liu	Research Project: The Mogu Dynasties
Ms. Thai	Research Project: The Pandaren Empire
	Uncovering the Past

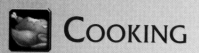

COOKING

Cooking turns various items (raw meat and fish, flour, and spider parts to name a few) into food that restores health and even conveys short-term buffs to various statistics. Cooking requires a heat source of some type, such as a stove or cooking fire. Fortunately, when you first train cooking you also gain the ability to create a fire anywhere with Basic Campfire. You don't need any tools to create a Basic Campfire.

At higher levels, Cooking buffs go beyond Stamina improvements and start to provide bonuses to different stats. These are very nice, especially considering the low cost involved in creating them. Food isn't hard to gather, and it takes only a few moments to start a fire.

Proficiency Level Name	Skill Level Minimum	Skill Level Maximum
Apprentice	0	75
Journeyman	50	150
Expert	125	225
Artisan	200	300
Master	275	375
Grand Master	350	450
Illustrious Grand Master	425	525
Zen Master	500	600

Any character benefits from Cooking. It's easiest to keep up with when you start as soon as possible and use the materials you get from looting enemies. If you are also working on Fishing, there are many recipes available that allow you to cook your catches.

PRACTICING COOKING

Put Cooking and Basic Campfire abilities on an Action Bar. Clicking Cooking opens a menu of all the recipes you know. Clicking Basic Campfire creates a fire should you need a heat source. Some recipes call for special spices or other items, but these are available from Cooking vendors, and most Trade vendors.

MORE FUN WITH COOKING

There are daily quests available only to characters with Cooking. Visit Shattrath City in Outland, Dalaran in Northrend, and any of the Horde and Alliance cities to obtain these quests. Until you learn Pandaren Cooking, these daily quests reward Epicurean's Awards. When you become proficient in Pandaren Cooking, the quests found in your faction's cities award Ironpaw Tokens instead. There are Achievements tied to these daily quests as well as unique recipes, which can't be obtained in any other way.

PANDAREN BONUSES

Pandarens have two racial abilities related to Cooking. Gourmand increases their Cooking skill by 15. Epicurean doubles the statistical benefit from food buffs.

On a final note, you can't go wrong learning Cooking if you plan on raiding or running heroic dungeons. Cooked meals provide a variety of statistical bonuses (although only one type of statistical boost from cooking can be active at a time), and there are even feasts you can set out for anyone in your party to eat and reap their benefits. While not everyone needs to be a cook, someone needs to create and distribute the food to your group and only you know what type of food buff is best for your character.

ZEN MASTER AND PANDAREN COOKING

The masters of Pandaren cooking are found at the Halfhill Market in Valley of the Four Winds. Speak with Sungshin Ironpaw to complete the quest "So You Want to be a Chef..." and its follow-up "Ready for Greatness". You must have a Cooking Skill of 525 to complete the second quest. If your skill isn't that high, Sungshin offers recipes to help get you there, and also sells most of the items you need to skill up (depending on where your Cooking level starts, you may need to obtain Golden Carp via Fishing or the Auction House). The reward for completing these quests is Zen Master Cooking and additional quests that introduce you to each of the Pandaren cooking masters.

Each cooking style levels up independently of the others, but your overall cooking skill will match your highest Pandaren Cooking skill level. Each Master offers a handful of recipes that provide different bonuses, ending with Banquets that feed 10 characters and Grand Banquets, which are intended for 25 characters.

PANDAREN COOKING - DAILY QUESTS

Each of the masters of Pandaren cooking offers daily quests when you become a proficient enough cook.

Quest Giver	Quest
Yan Ironpaw	The Thousand-Year Dumpling
Anthea Ironpaw	Cindergut Peppers
Jian Ironpaw	The Truffle Shuffle
Mei Mei Ironpaw	The Mile-High Grub
Kol Ironpaw	Fatty Goatsteak

NEW RECIPES FOR MISTS OF PANDARIA

Name	Skill Level	Ingredients
Sliced Peaches	1	Pandaren Peach
Perfectly Cooked Instant Noodles	30	Instant Noodles
Toasted Fish Jerky	60	Golden Carp
Dried Needle Mushrooms	90	Needle Mushrooms
Pounded Rice Cake	120	Rice
Yak Cheese Curds	150	Yak Milk
Dried Peaches	180	Pandaren Peach
Boiled Silkworm Pupa	210	Silkworm Pupa
Roasted Barley Tea	240	Barley
Golden Carp Consomme	270	Golden Carp (x2)
Fish Cake	300	Golden Carp (x2)
Blanched Needle Mushrooms	330	Needle Mushrooms (x2)
Red Bean Bun	360	Red Beans
Skewered Peanut Chicken	390	Farm Chicken
Green Curry Fish	420	Rice, Golden Carp (x2)
Peach Pie	450	Pandaren Peach (x2)
Tangy Yogurt	480	Yak Milk, Pandaren Peach
Pearl Milk Tea	495	Yak Milk (x2)
Spicy Salmon	500	Ginseng, Wildfoul Breast
Spicy Vegetable Chips	500	Viseclaw Meat
Wildfowl Ginseng Soup	510	Krasarang Paddlefish
Rice Pudding	520	Rice, Yak Milk
Krasarang Fritters	525	100 Year Soy Sauce, Jewel Danio (x10), Pink Turnip (x50)
Viseclaw Soup	525	100 Year Soy Sauce, Jewel Danio (x20), Pink Turnip (x100)
Banana Infused Rum	600	Emperor Salmon (x5), Witchberries (x25), Rice
Four Senses Brew	600	Jade Squash (x25), Pink Turnip (x25)
Great Pandaren Banquet	600	Tel'Abim Banana, Volatile Rum, Silkworm Pupa, Black Pepper
Pandaren Banquet	600	100 Year Soy Sauce, Rice Flour, Pandaren Peach, Red Blossom Leek

REPLENISHING THE PANTRY

Nam Ironpaw offers a repeatable quest called "Replenishing the Pantry" that allows you to exchange a cooking item for which you have a surplus for an Ironpaw Token. You must buy a specific Empty Green Container from Merchant Cheng to facilitate the exchange. There are no other rewards for completing this quest.

Way of the Brew

Bobo Ironpaw is the Master of the Brew. His non-Banquet recipes often have a kick to them, but do not provide statistical bonuses.

Item	Way Of the Brew Skill Level	Well-Fed Bonus
Ginseng Tea	525	N/A
Jade Witch Brew	550	N/A
Banquet of the Brew	575	+250 in one stat for 10 characters
Great Banquet of the Brew	575	+250 in one stat for 25 characters
Mad Brewer's Breakfast	600	N/A

Way of the Pot

Mei Mei Ironpaw is the Master of the Pot and offers recipes that improve Intellect.

Item	Way Of The Pot Skill Level	Well-Fed Bonus
Swirling Mist Soup	525	+250 Intellect
Braised Turtle	550	+275 Intellect
Banquet of the Pot	575	+250 in one stat for 10 characters
Great Banquet of the Pot	575	+250 in one stat for 25 characters
Mogu Fish Stew	600	+300 Intellect

Way of the Grill

Kol Ironpaw is the Master of the Grill and offers recipes that improve Strength.

Item	Way Of The Grill Skill Level	Well-Fed Bonus
Charbroiled Tiger Steak	525	+250 Strength
Eternal Blossom Fish	550	+275 Strength
Banquet of the Grill	575	+250 in one stat for 10 characters
Great Banquet of the Grill	575	+250 in one stat for 25 characters
Black Pepper Ribs and Shrimp	600	+300 Strength

Way of the Steamer

The Master of the Steamer is Yan Ironpaw who offers recipes that improve Spirit.

Item	Way Of The Steamer Skill Level	Well-Fed Bonus
Shrimp Dumplings	525	+250 Spirit
Fire Spirit Salmon	550	+275 Spirit
Banquet of the Steamer	575	+250 in one stat for 10 characters
Great Banquet of the Steamer	575	+250 in one stat for 25 characters
Steamed Crab Surprise	600	+300 Spirit

Way of the Oven

The Master of the Oven is Jian Ironpaw and she offers recipes that improve Stamina.

Item	Way Of The Oven Skill Level	Well-Fed Bonus
Wildfowl Roast	525	+375 Stamina
Twin Fish Platter	550	+415 Stamina
Banquet of the Oven	575	+250 in one stat for 10 characters
Great Banquet of the Oven	575	+250 in one stat for 25 characters
Chun Tian Spring Rolls	600	+450 Stamina

Way of the Wok

Anthea Ironpaw is the Master of the Wok and offers recipes that improve Agility.

Item	Way Of The Wok Skill Level	Well-Fed Bonus
Sauteed Carrots	525	+250 Agility
Valley Stir Fry	550	+275 Agility
Banquet of the Wok	575	+250 in one stat for 10 characters
Great Banquet of the Wok	575	+250 in one stat for 25 characters
Sea Mist Rice Noodles	600	+300 Agility

FIRST AID

First Aid enables you to create bandages which are used to restore health, and antidotes to remove poisons. Bandages are created from cloth drops in the game, and they can be used outside of combat or even while in the middle of it. Bandages can be used on yourself, other players, or pets.

Characters that are damage dealers should use First Aid even more aggressively than most. In really big team fights, the tanks and healers get the most attention when it comes to healing. Damage dealers are last on the list, and if there isn't enough mana to go around they are the ones that come up short. Being able to restore some health during these fights is a godsend.

Proficiency Level Name	Character Level Minimum	Skill Level Minimum	Skill Level Maximum
Apprentice	1	0	75
Journeyman	1	50	150
Expert	1	125	225
Artisan	35	200	300
Master	50	275	375
Grand Master	65	350	450
Illustrious Grand Master	75	425	525
Zen Master	80	500	600

You shouldn't try to use a bandage when an enemy is in the middle of attacking you. This disrupts the process, ending your health restoration. Bandages have a cooldown period, so you can't continually apply them. Stun an enemy or otherwise get away from them for a few moments and use your First Aid.

PRACTICING FIRST AID

Creating bandages can be done anywhere, and all you need are the cloth pieces required for the specific bandages, or spider venom glands to create anti-venoms.

Bandages come in two varieties per type of cloth: regular and heavy. Each regular bandage requires one piece of cloth. You need two pieces of a given type of cloth to create a heavy bandage. Heavy Windwool bandages initially require 3 pieces of Windwool Cloth, but when you reach skill level 600, Heavy Windwool goes from 3 to 2 material cost.

Bandage	Skill Level To Create	Skill Level To Use
Windwool Bandage	500	500
Heavy Windwool Bandage	550	550

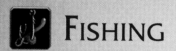 FISHING

Fishing allows you to cast your line into any body of water deep enough and see what you bring up. You can catch fish, of course, but you may also catch other marine life, junk, or treasure. A fishing pole is required but, unlike the other Professions, you must equip it (fishing poles are considered two-hand weapons) in order to do some fishing.

Fish have many uses, including Alchemy, but they are mainly used for food. Most types of fish can be eaten raw by your character or Hunter pets, but it's better to cook the fish first if you have the appropriate Cooking recipe.

The types of fish available from a body of water are not determined by your Fishing skill. Instead, the types of fish are determined by the area. However, if your skill isn't considered high enough for the area, you only catch random trash items.

Proficiency Level name	Character Level minimum	Skill Level minimum	Skill level maximum
Apprentice	5	0	75
Journeyman	5	50	150
Expert	5	125	225
Artisan	5	200	300
Master	5	275	375
Grand Master	5	350	450
Illustrious Grand Master	5	425	525
Zen Master	5	500	600

There are also schools of fish in the waters around the world. These schools enable you to catch specific fish, if your casting is accurate. When you gain the ability to track fish, these schools of fish appear on your mini-map making it easy to find them.

PRACTICING FISHING

Purchase a fishing pole (there's often a vendor near the fishing trainers) and put Fishing on one of your Action Bars. Click on Fishing and watch your character cast a line. A bobber appears on the water's surface; move your mouse cursor over the bobber until it turns into the fishhook icon. Watch that carefully until the bobber moves, and then quickly right-click the bobber. If successful, you receive a loot window that includes a fish or another item of some value.

There are many unique Fishing Poles in the game, some with improved Fishing skills or other buffs, such as underwater breathing. You can also use a variety of baits, lures and enchanted fishing lines to improve your odds of catching a fish.

COMBAT CAUTION

If you are attacked while fishing, your weapon is your Fishing Pole. Fishing Poles are not really designed to be combat weapons, so switch back to your normal weapon if something's pounding on your back.

MORE FUN WITH FISHING

There are daily quests available only to characters with Fishing. Visit your faction's capital, Shattrath City in Outland, and Dalaran in Northrend to obtain these quests. There are Achievements tied to these daily quests as well as unique pets that can't be obtained in any other way.

There are also weekly fishing contests on two continents. The goblins of Booty Bay host an event, and the Kalu'ak of Northrend host another in the city of Dalaran. There are some great rewards for the players who manage to win these contests.

THE ANGLERS

When you hit level 90, look for a quest called "The Anglers" given by Master Angler Karu in Shrine of the Two Moons or Master Angler Marina in Shrine of the Seven Stars. The Anglers are a new Fishing-themed faction in Mists of Pandaria and offer a number of fun rewards as you increase your reputation with them via daily quests. There is more information on Anglers in the New Factions section of this guide.

On a final note, Fishing is essentially a necessity if you want to create the best food available via the Cooking Profession. Cooked fish provide a variety of statistical boosts, and there are even fish feasts you can set out for anyone in your party to eat and reap the rewards.

MISTS OF PANDARIA BESTIARY

Exploring the new continent means encounters with never-before-seen creatures. As you work with the Pandaren on their home continent, expect to run into the following enemies.

The Champions listed with each new type of enemy are rare (and sometimes elite) spawns who drop nice rewards for those fortunate enough to find them and powerful enough to defeat them.

VIRMEN

The obnoxious and impulsive Virmen are rabbit-like pests prone to stealing any edibles and hoarding them underground or in caves. Though they lack the technology to shape metal weapons, they're often seen using stolen daggers.

JINYU

Jinyu flourish near bodies of water, which shouldn't be a surprise considering many revered Jinyu are Waterspeakers, able to speak and listen to the waters that flow throughout Pandaria. Jinyu society is built upon a rigid caste system, with workers, warriors and priests chosen at a young age.

Jinyu Champions

Name	Location	Level
Aethis	Jade Forest	85
Sele'na	Valley of the Four Winds	86
Cournith Waterstrider	Krasarang Wilds	87
Norlaxx the Outcast	Kun-Lai Summit	88
Eshelon	Townlong Steppes	89
Nalash Verdantis	Dread Wastes	90
Sahn Tidehunter	Vale of the Eternal Blossoms	91

SPRITES

Sprites are known for both their mischievous nature and their propensity to take on the characteristics of their surroundings. Physically, they blend in with their surroundings, which allows them to blend into their environment. Their activities also match their environment: forest Sprites play mostly harmless tricks, but the mountain Sprites are known to cause rockslides and knock the unwary off cliffs.

MOGU

Mogu are an ancient race who founded an empire thousands of years in the past. They use the slave labor of conquered races to build imposing structures. They made contact with an ancient ally and now seek to rebuild an empire.

Mogu Champions

Name	Location	Level
Kor'nas Nightsavage	Jade Forest	85
Sulik'shor	Valley of the Four Winds	86
Gaarn the Toxic	Krasarang Wilds	87
Borginn Darkfist	Kun-Lai Summit	88
Norlaxx	Townlong Steppes	89
Karr the Darkener	Dread Wastes	90
Kang the Soul Thief	Vale of the Eternal Blossoms	91
Morgrinn Crackfang	Jade Forest	85
Jonn-Dar	Valley of the Four Winds	86
Qu'nas	Krasarang Wilds	87
Havak	Kun-Lai Summit	88
Kah'tir	Townlong Steppes	89
Krol the Blade	Dread Wastes	90
Urgolax	Vale of the Eternal Blossoms	91

HOZEN

Hozen are a short-lived race with quick tempers whose lives are centered around hunting and gathering. Despite their primitive technology, these simian-like humanoids manage to work together and live in groups throughout Pandaria. Some Hozen possess more even temperments, and have been seen working alongside Pandarens.

Hozen Champions

Name	Location	Level
Mister Ferocious	Jade Forest	85
Bonobos	Valley of the Four Winds	86
Spriggin	Krasarang Wilds	87
Scritch	Kun-Lai Summit	88
The Yowler	Townlong Steppes	89
Ik-Ik the Nimble	Dread Wastes	90
Major Nanners	Vale of the Eternal Blossoms	91

MANTID

Mantid are an intelligent and highly evolved race of insect-like creatures who have menaced the people of Pandaria since prehistoric times. Though these insect-like humanoids consider the Dread Wastes their homeland, they were driven out and are now found throughout the continent of Pandaria.

Mantid Champions

Name	Location	Level
Krax'ik	Jade Forest	85
Nal'lak the Ripper	Valley of the Four Winds	86
Torik-Ethis	Krasarang Wilds	87
Ski'thik	Kun-Lai Summit	88
Lith'ik the Stalker	Townlong Steppes	89
Gar'lok	Dread Wastes	90
Kal'tik the Blight	Vale of the Eternal Blossoms	91

KUNCHONG

Kunchong are a powerful subset of the Mantid race. These four-legged monsters are protected by incredibly thick, natural armor and are known to act as battering rams.

SAUROK

Saurok are the lizard-like descendants of creatures flesh-shaped by Mogu to maintain order throughout their empire. The Saurok turned on their Mogu masters but paid a terrible price. Today, they are found throughout Pandaria and the Wandering Isle.

Saurok Champions

Name	Location	Level
Sarnak	Jade Forest	85
Salyin Warscout	Valley of the Four Winds	86
Arness the Scale	Krasarang Wilds	87
Nessos the Oracle	Kun-Lai Summit	88
Siltriss the Sharpener	Townlong Steppes	89
Omnis Grinlok	Dread Wastes	90
Moldo One-Eye	Vale of the Eternal Blossoms	91

YAUNGOL

Due to living on Pandaria since the Sundering, the history of the Yaungol is largely unknown. What is known is that they are fierce fighters who employ both magic and fire as weapons and Mushan as mounts. Don't expect to encounter one alone, these nomadic warriors are always found in groups.

Yaungol Champions

Name	Location	Level
Ferdinand	Jade Forest	85
Blackhoof	Valley of the Four Winds	86
Go-Kan	Krasarang Wilds	87
Korda Torros	Kun-Lai Summit	88
Lon the Bull	Townlong Steppes	89
Dak the Breaker	Dread Wastes	90

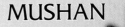

MUSHAN

Mushans are large, reptilian creatures found on the continent of Pandaria. Most Mushan are docile, content to serve as beasts of burden for the many races on Pandaria. Even the ones which remain in the wild won't attack unless provoked. However, herds of Mushan are often headed by aggressive protectors who strike out should anyone approach too closely.

SHA

Sha is a dark energy unique to Pandaria, a legacy left behind by the last Pandaren emperor. Two known Sha have come to embody Hate and Fear, and seek to dominate the minds of any creature who falls under their influence.

MISTLURKER

Mistlurkers are elemental beasts who, until recently, weren't known to be threats to the humanoid races of Pandaria. However, Yaungol Shaman have twisted these one-eyed creatures, who now attack intruders who wander into their territory.

OTHER RARE AND ELITE ENEMIES

Rare Enemies

Name	Location	Description	Level
Yorik Sharpeye	Vale of the Eternal Blossoms	Tauren	91
Urobi the Walker	Jade Forest	Pandaren	85
Nasra Spothide	Valley of the Four Winds	Pandaren	86
Ruun Ghostpaw	Krasarang Wilds	Pandaren	87
Ahone the Wanderer	Kun-Lai Summit	Pandaren	88
Yul Wildpaw	Townlong Steppes	Pandaren	89
Ai-Li Skymirror	Dread Wastes	Pandaren	90
Ai-Ran the Shifting Cloud	Vale of the Eternal Blossoms	Pandaren	91

Elite Enemies

Name	Location	Description	Level
Martar the Not-So-Smart	Jade Forest	Gnoll	86
Huggalon the Heart Watcher	Townlong Steppes	Northrend Giant	92
Scotty	Townlong Steppes	Wood Sprite	89
Sungraze Behemoth	Valley of the Four Winds	Mushan	86
Feverbite	Krasarang Wilds	Spider	87
Zhing	Kun-Lai Summit	Goat	88
Pengsong	Dread Wastes	Yak	90
Gokk'lok	Dread Wastes	Clam	91

QUILEN

Quilen are ancient guardians found in two varieties: organic and stone. They are rarely found in the wild, but are often encountered in ruins associated with the Mogu empire. Hunters who choose the Beast Mastery specialization are able to tame these magnificent creatures.

JIANG-SHI

Jiang-shi are tormented spirits who haunt the lands of Pandaria. Very little is known about these mysterious beings, but they are a threat to every living creature they encounter.

Elite Lobstrok Enemies

Name	Location	Level
Akkalou	The Jade Forest	90
Akkalar	The Jade Forest	90
Damlak	Krasarang Wilds	90
Clamstok	Dread Wastes	90
Odd'nirok	Townlong Steppes	90
Kishak	Kun-Lai Summit	90
Clawlord Kril'mander	Krasarang Wilds	90

Rare Elite Enemies

Name	Location	Description	Level
Dr. Theloen Krastinov	Scholomance (Heroic, LFD only, 3% chance to appear)	Forsaken	91
Alani the Stormborn	Vale of Eternal Blossoms	Red Lightning Serpent	92
Sha of Anger	Kun-Lai Summit	Sha Boss	93
Galleon (Salyis' Warband)	Valley of the Four Winds	Mushan + Saurok	93

ACHIEVEMENTS

Achievements are a different way to show what you have accomplished in World of Warcraft. To see a full list of Achievements, click on the icon in the interface bar, or press the "y" key. This area lists hundreds of in-game Achievements. You get them for almost anything you can imagine.

While Achievements won't lead to improved weapons or armor, they do provide special titles, companion pets, and mounts. Sometimes you get a reward for getting a certain Achievement, while others require you to unlock a set of Achievements that take an entire year to earn! Achievements are in the game purely for fun. Love them or leave them, but these Achievements are not supposed to make or break your day. They give you an awesome way to smell the roses while exploring the world.

TYPES OF ACHIEVEMENTS

Click on individual Achievements to learn more about them. Most of these are quite specific, so it isn't hard to understand what is required to earn them. Sometimes making the events happen is the trickier part.

Achievements are now account-wide, though some are still specific to each character. Account-wide Achievements have a blue header, while character-specific Achievements retain the brown look familiar to most players.

Achievements are broken down into different categories to make it easier to find which Achievements are available to you depending on where your interests lie. The Achievement categories are General, Quests, Exploration, Player vs. Player, Dungeons & Raids, Professions, Scenarios, Reputation, World Events, Pet Battles, and Feats of Strength. Guild Achievements has its own tab and includes the following categories: General, Quests, Player vs. Player, Dungeons & Raids, Professions, Reputation, and Guild Feats of Strength.

GENERAL

Some Achievements don't fall easily into other categories, so General is a catchall category. There are many extras available from these Achievements, including a tabard and a few bonus mounts for mount collectors.

QUESTS

There are two Achievements that award extras in the Quest category. When you complete enough quests, you earn the title "The Seeker." When you earn the Loremaster Achievement, you get the title "Loremaster" and a bonus tabard.

One change here is that for Pandaria zones, Quest Achievements are often tied to experiencing the game's storyline as opposed to getting through a given number of quests in a zone.

EXPLORATION

Almost every Exploration Achievement is tied to uncovering hidden nooks and discovering the out of the way places found in every zone. The other type of Exploration Achievement is tied to finding and killing one of the rare enemies which spawn in Outland, Northrend, and Pandaria (the Pandaren rare spawns are considered champions of their race).

Exploring the known world provides you with the title "Explorer" while Brann Bronzebeard awards the characters who explore all of Northrend with a special tabard.

Oot the Explorer

PLAYER VS. PLAYER

Player vs. Player Achievements are linked to battlegrounds and arenas. Many of these Achievements call for meeting incredibly specific conditions in a single battleground, or for long-term accomplishments such as being on the winning side in a battleground 100 times! Most of the rewards for Player vs. Player Achievements are titles.

DUNGEONS & RAIDS

Many Dungeons & Raids Achievements are given for defeating the bosses which appear in the world dungeons and raids of World of Warcraft. When you start running heroic versions of dungeons, there are additional Achievements tied to meeting specific conditions while facing the bosses in the dungeons. There are even more Achievements tied to the raid bosses, some requiring heroic attempts while others can be done during the regular version of the boss encounter. The rewards for Achievements in Dungeons & Raids include titles, bonus mounts, and transmogrifiable armor.

SCENARIOS

Scenario Achievements are similar to the ones found in Dungeons & Raids. Many of them are tied to simply completing each Scenario, but others call for meeting specific conditions while completing an encounter. Perhaps the oddest Achievement is Scenaterday, which requires the completion of scenarios on a Saturday.

PROFESSIONS

Profession Achievements are more focused on the Secondary Professions (Archaeology, Cooking, First Aid, and Fishing) since each character is limited to only two Primary Professions. The change to account-wide Achievements has opened the door to a few new Profession Achievements, but they're tied to reaching the maximum skill level in each Profession.

Archaeology Achievements include a few titles, and you can become a "Chef" and "Master of the Ways" with enough patience with Cooking. A Fishing-exclusive reward, a Titanium Seal of Dalaran, calls for a little luck and a great deal of patience, as does the "Salty" title.

REPUTATION

Improving your Reputation with the many factions found in World of Warcraft has become an increasingly important facet of the game to every type of player, and for many reasons. Many factions are the source of improved equipment, mounts, and companion pets. The Achievements tied to these improved Reputations are mainly new titles, but the Achievement for earning Exalted reputation with the Pandaren factions awards a kite mount.

WORLD EVENTS

World Events are special dates (typically marked on the in-game calendar) that include holidays and celebrations. There are Achievements tied to each date, and these Achievements take on many forms. While many are tied to completing quest lines, some holiday Achievements require trips to dungeons to face bosses that appear only during the holiday or visiting battlegrounds.

There are many titles to earn from World Event Achievements, but if you complete the Achievement "What A Long, Strange Trip It's Been" you earn a Violet Proto-Drake mount.

PET BATTLES

Pet Battles Achievements are a brand new set of Achievements for you to earn. To earn these Achievements, you must collect pets, use them in battle, and improve your pets to the maximum level. The rewards from this category of Achievements include titles, daily quests, and additional pets.

GUILD

Guild Achievements can be unlocked only while you are in a guild, and most of these Achievements require groups made up mainly of characters from the same guild to work together in various ways. Many of these Achievements mirror those found in other categories (mainly Dungeons & Raids and Player vs. Player) so you should earn an individual Achievement at the same time as the Guild Achievement.

FEATS OF STRENGTH

Feats of Strength Achievements are generally awarded from one-time occurrences, such as logging in during an Anniversary celebration, obtaining a Collector Edition pet, or being part of a leading Arena Team for a specific season. Other Feats of Strength are the result of changes to the game which remove the ability to earn some Achievements. Recent examples are the changes to the way characters obtain weapon skills. Before Cataclysm, there were Achievements for raising your Unarmed, or raising your skills in four different weapon types, to their maximum levels. However, the system changed in Cataclysm, and characters are no longer required to level up weapon skills.

READ ORIGINAL NOVELS BASED ON

WORLD OF WARCRAFT

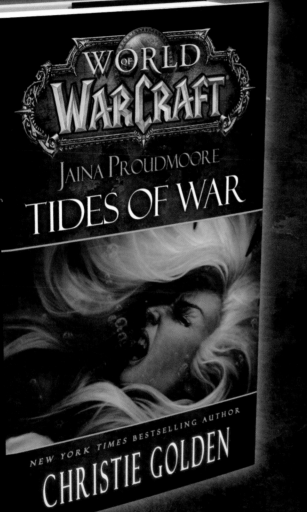

The ashes of the Cataclysm have settled across Azeroth's disparate kingdoms. As the broken world recovers from the disaster, the renowned sorceress Lady Jaina Proudmoore continues her long struggle to mend relations between the Horde and the Alliance. Yet of late, escalating tensions have pushed the two factions closer to open war...

ALSO AVAILABLE:

AVAILABLE IN PRINT, EBOOK, AND AUDIO DOWNLOAD EDITIONS.